HISTORY IN DISPUTE

ADVISORY BOARD

Robert Cowley
  Founding Editor, *Military History Quarterly*

John Lewis Gaddis
  Robert A. Lovett Professor of Military and
  Naval History, Yale University

James G. Hershberg
  Assistant Professor of History and International Affairs, George Washington University

Townsend Hoopes
  Undersecretary of the Air Force (1967–1969)

William Manchester
  Professor of History Emeritus, Wesleyan University

Michael Spirtas
  Center for National Policy and U.S.-CREST

Janice Gross Stein
  Professor of Political Science, University of Toronto

Marc Trachtenberg
  Professor of History, University of Pennsylvania

Fareed Zakaria
  Managing Editor, *Foreign Affairs*

HISTORY IN DISPUTE

Volume **13**

Slavery in the
Western Hemisphere,
circa 1500-1888

Edited by **Mark G. Malvasi**

A MANLY, INC. BOOK

GALE®

TM
GALE

Detroit • New York • San Diego • San Francisco • Cleveland • New Haven, Conn. • Waterville, Maine • London • Munich

THOMSON
GALE

History in Dispute
Volume 13: Slavery in the Western Hemisphere,
circa 1500–1888
Mark G. Malvasi

Editorial Directors
Matthew J. Bruccoli and Richard Layman

Series Editor
Anthony J. Scotti Jr.

ISBN 1-55862-471-6

Printed in the United States of America
10 9 8 7 6 5 4 3 2 1

CONTENTS

CONTENTS

CONTENTS

CONTENTS

CONTENTS

CONTENTS

CONTENTS

ABOUT THE SERIES

History in Dispute is an ongoing series designed to present, in an informative and lively pro-con format, different perspectives on major historical events drawn from all time periods and from all parts of the globe. The series was developed in response to requests from librarians and educators for a history-reference source that will help students hone essential critical-thinking skills while serving as a valuable research tool for class assignments.

Individual volumes in the series concentrate on specific themes, eras, or subjects intended to correspond to the way history is studied at the academic level. For example, early volumes cover such topics as the Cold War, American Social and Political Movements, and World War II. Volume subtitles make it easy for users to identify contents at a glance and facilitate searching for specific subjects in library catalogues.

Each volume of *History in Dispute* includes up to fifty entries, centered on the overall theme of that volume and chosen by an advisory board of historians for their relevance to the curriculum. Entries are arranged alphabetically by the name of the event or issue in its most common form. (Thus, in Volume 1, the issue "Was detente a success?" is presented under the chapter heading "Detente.")

Each entry begins with a brief statement of the opposing points of view on the topic, followed by a short essay summarizing the issue and outlining the controversy. At the heart of the entry, designed to engage students' interest while providing essential information, are the two or more lengthy essays, written specifically for this publication by experts in the field, each presenting one side of the dispute.

In addition to this substantial prose explication, entries also include excerpts from primary-source documents, other useful information typeset in easy-to-locate shaded boxes, detailed entry bibliographies, and photographs or illustrations appropriate to the issue.

Other features of *History in Dispute* volumes include: individual volume introductions by academic experts, tables of contents that identify both the issues and the controversies, chronologies of events, names and credentials of advisers, brief biographies of contributors, thorough volume bibliographies for more information on the topic, and a comprehensive subject index.

ACKNOWLEDGMENTS

James F. Tidd Jr., *Editorial associate.*

Philip B. Dematteis, *Production manager.*

Kathy Lawler Merlette, *Office manager.*

Ann M. Cheschi and Carol A. Cheschi, *Administrative support.*

Ann-Marie Holland, *Accounting.*

Sally R. Evans, *Copyediting supervisor.* Phyllis A. Avant, Caryl Brown, Melissa D. Hinton, Philip I. Jones, Rebecca Mayo, Nancy E. Smith, and Elizabeth Jo Ann Sumner, *Copyediting staff.*

Zoe R. Cook, *Series team leader layout and graphics.* Janet E. Hill, *Layout and graphics supervisor.* Sydney E. Hammock, *Graphics and prepress.*

Scott Nemzek and Paul Talbot, *Photography editors.*

Amber L. Coker, *Permissions editor and Database manager.*

Joseph M. Bruccoli, *Digital photographic copy work.*

Donald K. Starling, *Systems manager.*

Kathleen M. Flanagan, *Typesetting supervisor.* Patricia Marie Flanagan, Mark J. McEwan, and Pamela D. Norton, *Typesetting staff.*

Walter W. Ross, *Library researcher.*

The staff of the Thomas Cooper Library, University of South Carolina are unfailingly helpful: Tucker Taylor, *Circulation department head, Thomas Cooper Library, University of South Carolina.* John Brunswick, *Interlibrary-loan department head.* Virginia W. Weathers, *Reference department head.* Brette Barclay, Marilee Birchfield, Paul Cammarata, Gary Geer, Michael Macan, Tom Marcil, and Sharon Verba, *Reference librarians.*

PREFACE

Europeans had known slavery from antiquity. In one sense, therefore, the coming of slavery to the Americas was nothing new. Yet, by the Middle Ages, slavery had virtually disappeared from Europe, and thus the rise of slavery in the New World involved the reintroduction of a system of labor that had been dormant for five hundred years. During the fifteenth century the Portuguese and the Castilians established sugar plantations on the islands of the eastern Atlantic (the Madeira, Canary, Azores, and Cape Verde Islands) and worked them with slave labor. These island plantations became the prototypes of those that emerged in the New World during the sixteenth century.

Europeans entered the uncharted waters of the Atlantic Ocean during the thirteenth and fourteenth centuries, first exploring the Canary and Madeira Islands. Portuguese interest in the islands grew after 1417 because of competition from the Kingdom of Castile. King John I of Portugal (reigned 1385–1433) sent an expedition of some one hundred persons to Madeira and Porto Santo, the principal islands of the Madeiras, and charged them to establish permanent settlements there.

The Madeira Islands were uninhabited and fertile, but the soil required careful and extensive preparation before the settlers could cultivate sugar and other crops. They had to clear forests, construct irrigation canals, and terrace fields because rainfall was irregular and insufficient. By approximately 1450, Portuguese colonists in the Madeiras were at last beginning to profit from grain production, and by the mid 1450s they were using slaves brought from Morocco and the neighboring Canary Islands to work sugar plantations.

For the next fifty years the colonists prospered, but by the early sixteenth century Madeira had fallen into economic decline. A growing population and diminishing economic opportunities in Portugal had driven many free Portuguese workers to Madeira. Their presence reduced the demand for slaves, since the wages of free laborers fell and employers did not have to incur the expense of feeding, clothing, and housing them as they did the slaves. During the fifteenth century, Madeira had presaged the future of European colonies in the New World. In the sixteenth century, by contrast, its social and economic development transformed it into a replica of metropolitan Portugal.

Aided by the huge capital investment of the Welsers, a German banking family, the Castilians also began to cultivate sugar in the Canary Islands. By 1526 the Canaries had replaced Portuguese Madeira as the center of European sugar production. Of greater importance, relations between the Castilians and the native population foreshadowed the relations that predominated among Europeans, Indians, and Africans in the New World.

In the initial phase of their conquest, the Castilians needed to make quick profits to pay for the expedition, which they had financed mostly on credit. The sale of slaves offered an easy and attractive way to raise the capital needed to repay outstanding loans. Consequently, the Castilians enslaved the native peoples of the Canaries and sold them in Spain or Madeira. Those who remained found themselves put to work as domestic servants, which was at first the most common occupation of slaves in the Canary Islands.

The Canarians, though, never made a substantial or enduring addition to the international slave trade. The population of the islands was small and declined steadily as the result of disease once the Castilians arrived. Furthermore, Castilian law permitted the enslavement only of those Canarians who resisted the Spanish incursion, and slaves had many ways to attain their freedom. By the early decades of the sixteenth century, the Canarian slave trade had ceased, and the surviving natives increasingly intermarried with the colonists and assimilated to Iberian culture.

With the natives unable to satisfy the labor needs of the settlers, the Castilians began to recruit free workers from Portugal, Castile, and other parts of the Spanish Peninsula. At the same time, they welcomed Moors and Moriscos from Spain and North Africa and brought Native Americans from the New World until the Spanish Crown prohibited the trade. Enslaved Africans, however, came to constitute the most significant element in the workforce of the Canary Islands.

Portuguese traders acquired slaves in West Africa, while Castilian mariners raided the coasts of North Africa. Many of the Africans taken during these forays were Muslims. If they converted to Christianity their captors usually freed them, although the sincerity of their religious convictions remains in doubt. As often as not, Muslim captives were themselves slaveholders and negotiated for their freedom by offering in exchange some of their own slaves. These ransoms became one of the most common means by which enslaved Africans arrived in the Canary Islands.

By the sixteenth century the Castilians had imported ten thousand slaves into the Canaries, between 67 percent and 75 percent of them coming from Africa. Slaves constituted 10 to 12 percent of the population, and, as with the transatlantic slave trade, males vastly outnumbered females by a ratio of 62 percent to 38 percent. Although these slaves often worked side by side with free laborers, the connection between slavery and sugar had forever been confirmed. In the Atlantic islands, the Portuguese and Spanish laid the foundation for the expansion of the plantation system and the rise of slavery in the New World.

At the same time that the Portuguese and the Castilians were conquering the Atlantic islands, they were also reconnoitering the western coast of Africa. For a time the Spanish rivaled the Portuguese in Africa, but after Pope Sixtus IV conferred a monopoly on African exploration and commerce to Portugal with the Treaty of Alcaçovas in 1480, the Spanish had to strike out in another direction. In 1492 Christopher Columbus provided an opportunity to do so. Sailing under the flag of the newly unified Kingdom of Spain, Columbus set out to find a western route to Asia but ended up discovering lands the existence of which few Europeans ever imagined.

As these events unfolded in the western Mediterranean, an equally portentous series of changes took place in the eastern Mediterranean. The Ottoman Turks completed their conquest of the Byzantine Empire, capturing Constantinople in 1453. Thereafter, the Turks asserted their sway over the Muslim regions of the Mediterranean basin. This development had significant repercussions for the history of slavery. After the Ottoman conquests, the traditional sources of slaves in North and West Africa and along the Black Sea were no longer accessible to Europeans. At precisely the moment when the demand for labor increased in the European colonies of the New World, the supply of labor diminished. Europeans could not enslave other Christians, and the Castilian defeat of the Kingdom of Granada in 1492 removed the last Muslim enclave from Spanish soil, thereby eliminating a reservoir of potential slaves.

However, a rich source of slaves existed that Europeans had barely exploited: Africans who lived south of the Sahara Desert. The Spanish and the Portuguese were chronically short of money, and the Portuguese also suffered from shortages of food. To purchase grain necessitated additional revenue. Yet, the Muslims, not the Spanish or the Portuguese, controlled the caravan routes from Africa, which meant, in effect, that the Muslims also controlled the supply of gold that filtered into the Mediterranean basin. Expansion into sub-Saharan African could thus help to solve several pressing economic problems that the Spanish and Portuguese experienced, rectifying the shortages of grain, gold, and labor. Slaves soon became the most important and valuable commodity in the Iberian commerce with Africa, for slaves not only provided an abundant source of cheap labor, but they could also be traded or sold for grain or gold.

Since the Portuguese had secured a monopoly on African commerce, they led the way in expanding the African slave trade. Portuguese merchants brought horses, saddles, stirrups, cloth, lead, iron, copper, brass, wine, saffron, and salt from Europe and Morocco to exchange for gold and slaves. Most of the slaves initially went to the Spanish and Portuguese colonies on the Atlantic islands. After the Spanish reached the Americas and established colonies there, the Portuguese were prepared to supply them with all the African slaves they needed to work the mines and the sugar plantations and thus to take advantage of the boundless economic opportunities that the New World had to offer.

The Spanish conquest of the American mainland brought with it a massive importation of slaves from Africa. The Viceroyalty of New Granada, which comprised the present-day states of Panama, Colombia, Venezuela, and Ecuador, contained the highest concentration of blacks in continental Spanish America. Reliable statistics are not available before the nineteenth century, but the census of 1810 reports that in Panama there were approximately 210,000 blacks and mulattoes in a population of 1.4 million. The percentage in Venezuela was even greater, with blacks and mulattoes numbering 493,000 out of a total population of 900,000. Ecuador had 50,000 blacks and mulattoes in a population of 600,000. Panama, Caracas, and Cartagena were among the largest slave markets in the New World.

Throughout New Granada, slaves cultivated sugar, cacao, and tobacco and mined gold; in cities they performed domestic service. Their principal occupations, though, involved engagement with commerce itself. From the sixteenth to the eighteenth centuries the most traveled route between the Atlantic and Pacific Oceans crossed Central America at Panama. To make this commercial activity profitable required slave labor. Slaves performed an array of tasks, many of them involving specialized knowledge and skills. Slaves built and maintained warehouses and worked as stevedores, shipbuilders, and sailors. As muleteers they also drove and cared for the pack animals that transported goods from the interior to such coastal cities as Porto Bello to be shipped abroad.

In the Viceroyalty of Peru, which consisted of present-day Peru and Chile, the Spanish used African slaves to mine gold. Indians mined silver, but the location of gold deposits in the tropical lowlands far from the center of Indian population made the use of Indian labor in gold mining expensive and impractical. As early as the 1540s Africans in gangs of 10 to 15 worked the gold mines. As lucrative as mining was, Spanish colonists in Peru also found uses for African slaves in agriculture. Commercial farming in Peru was much more diverse than that practiced elsewhere in Latin America and the Caribbean. To supply Lima, the capital of the Viceroyalty of Peru, with fresh fruits and vegetables, families of slaves cultivated small gardens and orchards on the outskirts of the city. Larger and more ambitious agricultural enterprises developed both along the coast and in the interior, especially sugar plantations and vineyards. It was in Lima and other Peruvian cities that slaves played their most important economic roles. They predominated in the skilled trades such as metalworking; textile, clothing, shoe, and hat manufacturing; tanning; shipbuilding; carpentry; and construction. Slaves also worked as fishermen, porters, cooks, masons, and even as armed watchmen guarding warehouses, public buildings, and private homes.

In Lima and other Peruvian cities, slave rental was as common as slave ownership. Many owners hired out their slaves, particularly those with skills, to bring in additional income. Often those hired out absorbed their own expenses for housing and food by renting themselves out and providing their masters with a monthly sum earned from their labor. Renters also frequently paid both the wages and the mainte-

nance costs for the slaves whose labor they engaged. A complex network of ownership, rental, and self-employment thus developed in Peru, rendering Peruvian slaves more versatile, mobile, and independent than those of Brazil and the Caribbean.

At the center of New Spain, Mexico was the first Spanish mainland colony to receive a large influx of slaves from Africa. Between 1528 and 1620 Mexico served as the principal American market for slaves. An average of 1,000 slaves disembarked at Veracruz each year during this period, with the largest importations occurring between 1570 and 1610. More than 100,000 Africans came to New Spain before the end of the colonial period. Most worked in one of four important sectors of the Mexican economy: silver mining, commercial ranching, textile manufacturing, and sugar production. Yet, compared to New Granada and Peru, slavery was relatively unimportant in Mexico.

In 1570 there were an estimated 20,000 slaves in Mexico, and that number grew to 35,000 in 1646 but represented less than 2 percent of the population. During that same period in Peru, the slave population reached 100,000 and constituted 12.5 percent of the population. Although the growth of the slave population in Peru stagnated after 1650, it never experienced the precipitous decline of the Mexican slave population. By the 1790s, Peru still had close to 90,000 slaves; Mexico had only 6,000.

The history of slavery in Mexico demonstrates the impact that a large Indian population had on the labor market. Since the Mexican economy developed at a much slower rate than the Peruvian economy, the larger mass of propertyless Indian labor, displaced and dispossessed by the Spanish conquest, could simultaneously fill the labor needs of the mining, ranching, textile, and sugar industries. In both Peru and Mexico, the 1650s marked the end of massive slave importation. By then the Spanish colonists had brought approximately 300,000 slaves from Africa to the American mainland. After 1650 the demand for slaves shifted to Brazil and the islands of the Caribbean that Spanish and Portuguese colonists had previously neglected.

Slavery in Brazil lasted 350 years. The first shipment of Africans arrived in Bahia in 1538, and not until 1888 did Brazilian slaves achieve emancipation. Portugal claimed Brazil as its territory after a Portuguese merchant fleet accidentally discovered it in 1500. The Portuguese title initially rested on the Treaty of Tordesillas with Spain, negotiated in 1494, that granted to Portugal jurisdiction over all islands in the South Atlantic (the Portuguese initially believed Brazil to be an island). Even after they learned that Brazil was part of a new continent, the Portuguese treated it as an extension of the African territories granted them in 1480 by the Treaty of Alcaçovas. Fearing that their hold on Brazil was precarious and that another European power would attempt to seize it, the Portuguese undertook to colonize Brazil beginning in the 1530s.

The Portuguese Crown divided Brazil into fifteen huge districts, known as captaincies, and awarded control of them to twelve court favorites. These men financed the recruitment of colonists and the transportation of the supplies that they needed to survive. The grantees expected to make enough money from their holdings in Brazil to enrich themselves. Since sugar was the only product they knew that could yield such large returns, the Portuguese duplicated in Brazil the sugar plantations of the Atlantic islands and worked them with slave labor brought from Africa. The fateful marriage of sugar and slaves in the late fifteenth century eventually produced the sugar colonies of the Americas. Thus, for 350 years Brazil and parts of Africa were linked as Portuguese colonies. Brazil became the more profitable of the two, but Africa supplied the people who made it so.

By 1600 Brazil dominated sugar production in the Western world. There were approximately two hundred *engenhos* (sugar plantations) producing between eight thousand and nine thousand metric tons of sugar per annuum. Brazilian output had risen to fourteen thousand metric tons by 1625. For the next two decades Brazilian sugar commanded European markets. During these same years the slave population of Brazil topped 200,000, with approximately 6,000 slaves imported every year. Without these importations, the slave population of Brazil would have declined at an annual rate of approximately 5 percent.

Sugar prices and profits began to fall after 1650, and of necessity plantations became more self-sufficient. Planters, who could not afford to purchase all the food that they needed, permitted slaves to raise their own provisions. Some now honored the longstanding requirements of the Catholic Church that slaves rest on Sundays. Finally, planters reassigned slaves to household service when they no longer needed their labor in the fields. During this period of economic decline the manor house became the crucible of racial and cultural mixing in which modern Brazilian society was born.

The discovery of gold in the Brazilian highlands during the 1680s inaugurated the first gold rush in history. Tens of thousands of Portuguese flocked to Brazil to make their fortunes, and more than one million Africans followed as slaves to labor in the mines. The price of slaves increased dramatically after the turn of the eighteenth century as a consequence of the mining boom, and the importations from Africa more than doubled, rising to 15,000 per year. Miners preferred slaves from the Costa da Mina region along the slave coast, south of Sierra Leone and north of Angola, because they already knew mining techniques. Eventually, however, shipments of slaves from Angola, favored for their unsurpassed stamina, exceeded those from Costa da Mina. Despite rising prices, nearly 2 million slaves arrived in Brazil during the eighteenth century.

With the depletion of the rich ore veins, the mining industry in Brazil went into decline in the 1750s. As with the plantation economy, this change improved conditions for the slaves, lightening their workload and encouraging economic diversification. Many sons and grandsons of miners bought a slave or two and set out to farm or raise cattle. By the late eighteenth and early nineteenth centuries small farmers and ranchers had incorporated the slaves into their extended families and households. Nowhere else in Latin America or the Caribbean was slavery adapted to small-scale agricultural production, an arrangement that not only was profitable but also permitted the natural increase of the slave population for the first time in Brazilian history.

After 1770 the production and export of coffee once more stimulated the Brazilian economy and the slave trade, which peaked in the 1840s when imports reached about 38,000 slaves per year. In 1850, however, the Brazilian government abolished the international slave trade to Brazil with the Queiroz Law, creating something of a labor shortage in the coffee-growing regions. Planters solved this problem by initiating an interprovincial slave trade, with slave owners in the depressed sugar regions selling slaves to planters in the booming coffee regions. This internal slave trade resembled the one that developed in the United States in which planters in the declining tobacco- and older cotton-growing regions of the Chesapeake Bay and the Carolinas sold slaves to planters in the newer cotton- and sugar-producing regions of Georgia, Alabama, Mississippi, and Louisiana.

Nineteenth-century coffee barons tried to reproduce the seignorial life that had prevailed among the seventeenth-century sugar planters. They built huge manor houses, purchased noble titles, arranged financially advantageous marriages for their children, and spent luxuriously until the money ran out. In the end, however, the dream of a Brazilian coffee aristocracy faded. The erosion of the land, the aging of the Brazilian slave population after the closure of the slave trade, and the limits of the world demand for coffee combined to halt the expansion of Brazilian coffee production. Coffee, it turned out, ignited the last economic boom in Brazil to be based on slave labor.

The long arc of islands that extends from Cuba in the northwest Caribbean to Trinidad near the Venezuelan coast became home to several million Africans. Using slave labor, colonial European planters created some of the most profitable enterprises of the day in these islands.

European colonization of the Caribbean officially began in 1494, when Columbus established the first permanent European settlement in the New World on an island that he christened Hispaniola, or "Little Spain," which comprises modern Haiti and the Dominican Republic. Residents of the fledgling colony supported themselves at first by exploiting the indigenous peoples. As a result of war, mistreatment, and disease, the native population rapidly diminished, and a series of epidemics that struck Hispaniola, Cuba, and Jamaica in the sixteenth century nearly wiped them out. Particularly devastating were the outbreaks of smallpox in 1518 and 1519 and measles in 1529. By 1600 the original inhabitants of the Caribbean had all but perished. The disappearance of the native population and the absence of a servile class of Europeans led settlers to clamor for the importation of African slaves. The first slaves arrived in Hispaniola in 1502, and by 1530 slavery had spread to Cuba, Puerto Rico, and Jamaica.

Like the Portuguese, Spanish colonists began planting sugarcane soon after their arrival in the Caribbean, replicating their experience in the Canary Islands. They erected the first sugar mill in the Caribbean in 1516 and began to export sugar from Hispaniola as early as 1522. A little more than a century later, beginning in the 1630s, the English were cultivating sugar with slave labor first in Barbados and then in Jamaica, which they seized from the Spanish in 1655. The Dutch in Surinam and the Netherlands Antilles and the French in Saint Domingue, the former Spanish colony of Hispaniola, also grew sugar using slave labor. The Spanish stimulated the last great Caribbean sugar boom, which took place during the nineteenth century in Cuba and Puerto Rico.

English planters in Barbados recognized that sugarcane could most profitably be grown on large plantations. As a consequence they consolidated their farms into larger units and purchased slaves from Dutch traders. This process of land consolidation, in time, eliminated small landowners from the colony. By 1680 a mere 7 percent of the planters owned more than 50 percent of the arable land and 60 percent of the slaves. Throughout the Caribbean the alliance between sugar, slavery, and the plantation system was sealed.

The same pattern of land consolidation and slave ownership repeated itself on the other islands of the British West Indies. In Jamaica, for example, 467 persons owned more than 77 percent of the land in 1754. In addition to the dramatic change in patterns of land ownership, the sugar boom in the British West Indies, as elsewhere in the Caribbean, shifted the demographic structure of the islands. In 1645, before the sugar boom exploded, there were 5,680 blacks and 37,000 whites on Barbados. Within forty years, by 1685, the consolidation of land and the emigration of poor whites reduced the European population by more than half, to 17,187. Meanwhile, the black population rose to 46,602. By 1750 there were four blacks for every one white in Barbados.

Black demographic supremacy was most pronounced in the British, Dutch, Danish, and French colonies. As a general rule, wherever slaves were imported in large numbers, poor whites virtually disappeared. In the British colony of Antigua, for instance, the slaves accounted for 80 percent of the population in 1724 and 90 percent in 1745. The French colony of Montserrat had 8,853 slaves and 1,117 whites in 1745, and Guadeloupe, another French colony, had a population of 80,000 blacks and only 12,000 whites in 1770. In the Dutch colony of St. Thomas the black population reached 4,504 in 1720, while whites numbered only 524.

An additional reason for the high ratio of blacks to whites in the British, Dutch, Danish, and French colonies was absentee ownership. Many white planters did not wish to live on their plantations or to make their homes in the colonies. They saw their West Indian property, including their human property, as a source of income and investment, not as the basis for a way of life. For English plantation owners, and their French, Dutch, and Danish counterparts, the islands served to yield quick fortunes, which they could then use to establish their social status at home. The colonies, in short, were not where one lived but where one made money.

The consequences for the slaves were predictable. On West Indian plantations, owners and overseers considered laborers more as "work-units" than as human beings. Historical evidence indicates a mixture of kindliness and comfort, cruelty and hardship. Births and deaths were reckoned as profits and losses. Planters assessed the expense of rearing children to adulthood against the cost of purchasing new slaves from Africa. This approach to slavery characterized the institution in North America to some degree; in the West Indies it predominated.

The character and quality of slave life in the Caribbean does not lend itself to easy generalization. It is nearly impossible to imagine what it felt like, physically, emotionally, and spiritually, to be the property of another person. African-born slaves usually experienced the greatest difficulty adjusting to servitude. Creoles, or slaves born in the Caribbean, were subject to slavery from birth and, although they suffered, they knew no other life.

When the first English colonists settled in Jamestown in 1607, they did not have it in mind to establish a slave society. Yet, it is not surprising that those who came to British North America eventually turned to slavery; more surprising is how long they waited to do so.

The enormous transfer of men and women that took place as a result of the Atlantic slave trade brought a comparatively small portion of Africans to the British North American mainland. Of all those who crossed the sea, less than 5 percent came to the mainland colonies (this figure represents fewer slaves than entered Cuba). The most extensive trade to North America occurred between 1680 and 1808 and accounted for 7 percent of the slave traffic crossing the Atlantic during those years and 20 percent of the total English slave trade.

North America, though, was an integral part of an emerging Atlantic colonial system that produced staple crops for the European market. In the Atlantic world of the mid seventeenth century, African chattel slavery was a legally recognized and increasingly preferred form of labor. Throughout Latin America and the Caribbean, slavery was spreading, and thus the British colonists in North America were not experimenting with some radical innovation when, after 1680, they began to purchase Africans in large numbers. They were instead following what by then had become a conventional pattern in the Atlantic world.

The development of slavery in North America, however, differed markedly from its evolution elsewhere in the Western Hemisphere. Three distinct slave systems emerged in the mainland colonies of North America: the nonplantation system in New England and the Middle Colonies; the plantation system of the Chesapeake region; and the plantation system of the Carolina and Georgia low country (and later the cotton states of the Deep South). These areas had differing economies and societies and distinct demographic configurations, especially in the proportion of blacks to whites and African-born to Creole slaves. The interplay of these factors helped to determine the nature of the slave system that originated in each quarter.

The black population in New England and the Middle Colonies was small. Only 50,000 blacks lived north of the Chesapeake, constituting not quite 4.5 percent of the population. More than 400,000 blacks, by comparison, lived south of the Chesapeake, accounting for 40 percent of the population. Numbers alone dilute the presence of blacks and underestimate the importance of slave labor in the New England and Middle Colonies. In larger cities and productive agricultural regions, blacks composed a much greater share of the population, sometimes constituting 33 percent of the population and 50 percent of the workforce.

The vast majority of slaves in the North, as Ira Berlin has pointed out in his seminal essay "Time, Space, and the Evolution of Afro-American Society on British Mainland North America" (1980), lived and worked in the countryside. A minority of these toiled in rural industries. The iron furnaces of Pennsylvania and the leather tanneries of New York, for example, relied heavily on slave labor. Most slaves, however, were agricultural workers. According to Berlin, southern New England, Long Island, and northern New Jersey contained the densest black populations. Slaves in these regions worked primarily in what was then called the provisioning trade, raising livestock and crops for export to the sugar islands of the West Indies. This type of agriculture did not support the plantation system, and, as a consequence, most slaves lived on small farms. The typical slave in the Northern countryside lived alone, or perhaps in the company of one or two other slaves. Slaves might even have resided with the family of their owner and labored alongside them in the fields.

The origin of Northern slaves was also different from those in the South. Before 1740 it was rare for slaves to arrive in the North directly from Africa. Most came, instead, from the West Indies or the Southern colonies. Only between 1740 and 1770 was there direct importation of Africans into Northern slave markets, and even then the number of imports never approached those of the plantation colonies farther to the south.

In northern New England, the Hudson Valley, and Pennsylvania, cereal and grain farming undermined the viability of slave labor. In these areas, farmers relied on white indentured servants and wage laborers to supplement their workforce at the busiest times of the year. Slaves thus became something of a status symbol rather than useful, productive agricultural workers. Most slaves in these locales worked at least part of the year as household servants, stable keepers, or gardeners.

The ownership of slaves was nearly universal among the elite in Northern cities and quite common among the middle class as well. Urban slaves generally worked as household servants, although some worked in the shipyards of Rhode Island and Massachusetts. Few urban masters had the room or the means to support more than one or two slaves. Hence, they discouraged slaves from establishing families. To lower the costs of maintenance, masters sometimes granted slaves permission to live outside the household and hire themselves out to earn their own keep. These slaves ordinarily worked as teamsters, stevedores, and in the maritime trades as sailors or sail makers.

Urban blacks also lived and worked in close proximity to whites. As a result they learned at least the rudiments of the English language, the Christian faith, and the Anglo-American culture of their masters. In the North, the cosmopolitan life of the cities coupled with previous exposure to whites in the West Indies or the Southern colonies transformed Africans into African Americans in a matter of years rather than decades.

The increased importation of Africans between 1730 and 1770 reoriented Northern blacks away from complete assimilation to Anglo-American culture as Africans reacquainted African Americans with aspects of their African heritage. Northern blacks began consciously to incorporate African social customs and practices into a nascent African American culture. The greater autonomy that many Northern blacks enjoyed, especially in the cities, enabled them to sustain African customs even as they conformed to the white culture that surrounded them. Their smaller numbers also made it possible for them to do so without appearing to threaten whites.

As quickly as possible Northern slaves formed new ties of kinship and community. They established stable families, their masters' discouragement notwithstanding, and increased their numbers by natural means during the first generation of captivity. The ability of blacks to live and work on their own—in exchange for a stipulated amount of annual tribute—enlarged their opportunities, gave them a sense of autonomy, and permitted the development of a strong and cohesive African American community.

The indulgence of slaves in the North originated in, and was always tied to, the masters' feelings of security. White numerical superiority gave them the confidence to believe that their slaves could never successfully rise up against them. Assured of their dominance, whites could afford to be lenient. Yet, slave codes cast their shadow everywhere in the New England and Middle Colonies, always reminding slaves that they were a people apart, living on sufferance in a system amply geared for their oppression.

The first English settlers in the Chesapeake, noted Donald R. Wright in *African Americans in the Colonial Era* (1990), found a temperate climate and land that was abundant, fertile, and thinly populated. "The mildnesse of the aire, the fertilitie of the soile, and the situations of the riv-

ers," wrote John Smith in *A Map of Virginia* (1612), "are so propitious to the nature and use of man as no place is more convenient for pleasure, profit, and man's sustenance." This land seemed ideal for farming and, the Englishmen hoped, for making quick fortunes.

Within a decade of settlement, English colonists in Virginia were exporting tobacco. Although they died in alarming numbers until the 1630s, the colonists who survived made a good profit from the tobacco trade, and the colony prospered. A Dutch ship brought the first Africans to the British North American mainland in 1619. John Rolfe, a Jamestown planter, made a casual entry in his diary to record the event: "About the last of August came in a dutch man of warre that sold us twenty Negars."

To make the cultivation of tobacco profitable, Chesapeake planters extracted from their slaves, as well as their white indentured servants, all the labor they could. If the condition of the slaves in the Chesapeake was better than that of slaves on the sugar plantations of the Caribbean, it was not appreciably so. Still, the unsettled, frontier conditions that prevailed in the Chesapeake enabled many blacks to set the conditions of their labor, to establish a relatively stable family life, and on occasion even to barter for their freedom. Throughout the seventeenth century, black freedmen could be found throughout the Chesapeake owning land, holding servants, voting, and from time to time occupying minor political offices. They could sue and be sued and give testimony in court. If they did acquire property they could sell it or pass it on to their children. Until outlawed in 1691, interracial marriages between blacks and whites—marriages even between white women and black men—were accepted, if uncommon.

Blacks in the Chesapeake thus initially enjoyed many of the same rights as subjects of the English Crown or were at least not systematically denied them. As in the New England and Middle Colonies, however, there was a direct correlation between the growing numbers of blacks in the Chesapeake and the need to develop laws defining and regulating slavery. Berlin was careful to emphasize that the condition of the slaves deteriorated as their numbers increased. By the middle of the seventeenth cenury the trend was clear: when the black population rose, the rights of black men and women, slave and free, diminished. Some free blacks, of course, continued to be respected members of their communities. Yet, as Wright indicated, the dike holding back the deluge of legislation that condemned blacks to slavery broke when the importation of large numbers of Africans began after 1680. Blacks in the Chesapeake quickly lost the freedoms that remained to them and found themselves legally, socially, and culturally isolated from whites.

By the 1720s the English colonies in the Chesapeake were well on their way to becoming slave societies. During the next century the evolution of slavery altered nearly every facet of life in the Chesapeake. Gone were the days when the status of blacks approximated that of whites. Of the considerable number of blacks who lived in the Chesapeake, practically all were slaves.

English settlement in the Carolina and Georgia low country was different in several respects from that of the Chesapeake. Early immigrants to the region came from other English colonies, especially Barbados, rather than from the British Isles, and had left to escape overcrowding and the shortage of arable land. For the first thirty years of settlement they concentrated on providing livestock and timber for the Caribbean and deerskins for England. Only later did they turn to the production of rice.

The first immigrants to the Carolina colony (divided into North Carolina and South Carolina in 1712) arrived after 1670. Familiar with slavery in Barbados, they adopted it more quickly than other English colonists on the North American mainland. Slaves were present a year after the colony was founded. The proprietors of Carolina, in fact, rewarded settlers with grants of land for bringing slaves into the colony. As a result, between 25 percent and 33 percent of migrants to Carolina were slaves. So heavy was the importation of slaves that after a generation of settlement, blacks constituted a majority of the low-country population.

The subtropical climate of Carolina had more in common with the West Indies and Africa than it did with England or the other mainland colonies. Slaves who had acquired some immunity to malaria and yellow fever thus had advantages over their English masters. They also knew more about the local flora and fauna and understood better how to make the land productive. In the early years of settlement, therefore, English masters were more dependent upon their slaves than was usually the case. Africans' knowledge and expertise were essential to the economic development of the low country, particularly in devising methods to breed and raise the livestock and to cultivate the rice that gave planters commodities for the export market.

The Fulbe, who had lived along the Gambia River, were especially adept at breeding and raising cattle. Their skill helps to explain Carolinians' overwhelming preference for Gambian slaves. Other West African slaves facilitated the shift to a rice economy. The Jola, Papel, Baga, Temne, and Mende, who lived along the West African coast, had produced wet rice for centuries before their contact with Europeans. Inland peoples, such as the Bambara and the Mandinka, had also cultivated rice in Africa and now applied the same techniques to growing rice in the Carolina low country. They taught these methods to the English.

By 1710 Carolina planters exported 1.5 million pounds of rice; the figure swelled to 6 million by 1720 and 20 million in 1730. During the 1760s rice accounted for 60 percent of all exports from the Carolinas. "The only Commodity of Consequence produced in South Carolina is Rice," noted former royal governor James Glen in 1761, "and they reckon it as much their staple Commodity, as sugar is to Barbados and Jamaica, or Tobacco to Virginia and Maryland."

Geography limited the spread of rice culture. Rice grew only in the coastal regions where tidal rivers irrigated fields, restricting its cultivation to a narrow strip of land along the Atlantic seaboard seldom more than twenty miles wide. Southward along the Carolina coast, rice culture flourished, but it halted at the Savannah River.

Along those southerly coastal lands the English founded Georgia, which was designed as a penal colony to reform criminals through a regime of hard work, forced sobriety, and instruction in Christian morals. The trustees of Georgia banned slavery by statute in 1734, fearing that slavery would hinder development of the society of small landowners they sought to create. During the first twenty years of its existence, Georgia was more or less free of slaves.

Slavery might have come to Georgia eventually, but the utter failure of the colonists to produce any commodity of value hastened its appearance. Georgians initially acquired their slaves from the Carolinas. By 1773 Georgia had a black population of approximately 15,000, which was nearly equal to the number of whites. Most slaves in Georgia were concentrated along the coast, where they grew rice and vastly outnumbered whites.

The emergence of rice culture in the low country effected the rise of a plantation system previously unknown on the North American mainland. More than any other region, the low country resembled the sugar islands of the West Indies. Large plantations peopled by enormous numbers of slaves and few whites became the norm. To maintain the workforce, Carolinians and Georgians had also to import huge numbers of slaves. Between 1706 and 1776 94,000 slaves entered Charleston harbor for sale throughout the low country. By 1740 blacks made up 90 percent of the low-country population.

The difficult working and living conditions brought on by the turn to staple agriculture led to rising mortality rates among the slaves, just as they had in the West Indies and Brazil. Masters were not particularly mindful of the consequences. A decline in the price of slaves coincided with the rice boom, and so low-country planters could easily afford to purchase fresh slaves to replace those who had died. Not until the years immediately prior to the American War for Independence (1775–1783) did the low-country slave population begin to reproduce itself, and even then its numbers were bolstered by the regular influx of slaves from Africa.

As in other colonies, when the proportion of blacks to whites began to increase, white anxiety also escalated. In the Carolinas and Georgia the outcome was similar to developments elsewhere: the steady erosion of rights for blacks until they endured the strictest laws and the harshest treatment in any mainland colony. Punishment for a host of offenses was swift and severe and included castrations; nose splitting; chopping off of hands, ears, and toes; branding; hanging; shooting; and burning at the stake.

Yet, disguised social and cultural advantages emerged for blacks living on the isolated low-country rice plantations. First, rice cultivation, although labor intensive, lent itself to task work rather than to gang labor. When slaves had completed their assigned tasks, their time was their own. They could plant and tend gardens, hunt, fish, or spend time with their families (if they had one) and other slaves without interference from whites. Second, because of the unhealthy climate of the low country, most planters spent all or part of the year in Charleston or on other plantations. They left the daily operation of their low-country plantations and supervision of the slaves to overseers. Even if the overseer was uncommonly diligent, he was but one man. The influence of English and European culture was thus less felt on the low-country rice plantations than elsewhere throughout the mainland colonies. The effects of this isolation and limited freedom contributed to the emergence of a distinct culture among low-country slaves—a culture that preserved intact many more elements of their African heritage than that of other slaves who were less isolated from whites and who enjoyed less personal autonomy.

By the early nineteenth century the production of cotton had become the foundation of the Southern economy. The decline of the Chesapeake tobacco economy, which fell into a prolonged depression after the War of 1812 (1812–1815) and never recovered, along with the inherent limits of the low-country rice economy, might have compelled Southerners to engage in other, nonagricultural pursuits had it not been for the cultivation of short-staple cotton. A hardier strain than the more delicate long-staple, luxury cotton, which could be grown only in low-country coastal regions, the short-staple variety succeeded in many climates and an array of soils. The greatest problem associated with the cultivation of short-staple cotton was the tedious but essential process of removing the seeds from the cotton fiber. With its long fibers and smooth black seeds, long-staple cotton was easy to clean. The sticky green seeds of short-staple cotton, by contrast, were difficult to separate; a skilled worker could clean no more than a few pounds a day by hand. The inability to overcome this obstacle diminished the appeal of short-staple cotton, making it impossible for Southern planters to meet the soaring demand for cotton that came from textile manufacturers in Great Britain and New England.

In 1793 Eli Whitney invented a machine that quickly and efficiently performed the arduous task of dislodging seeds from cotton fiber. The cotton gin (engine) transformed life in the South. Using this device, a single operator could clean as much cotton in a few hours as a group of workers had formerly done in a day. Beginning in the 1820s the cotton economy spread deep into the Southern interior, encompassing South Carolina, Georgia, Alabama, Mississippi, Louisiana, Texas, and Arkansas. Southern planters had harvested five hundred thousand bales of cotton in 1820; by 1850 the yield was nearly three million bales a year; and by 1860 it stood at five million. Despite periodic fluctuations in the price of cotton, which sometimes brought on long and severe depressions, the cotton economy continued to expand. At the time the Civil War began in April 1861, cotton constituted 67 percent of the American export trade with an annual valuation of almost $200 million. Little wonder that Southerners proclaimed, "Cotton is King!"

The prospect of making a fortune drew settlers to the Deep South by the thousands. Some who came were already wealthy planters from the Chesapeake or the low country, seeking new opportunities in the Cotton South. Most were small slave owners or nonslaveholding farmers who aspired to ascend into the ranks of the planter class.

With the genesis of the Cotton Kingdom, slavery, which had for some time been in decline, regained its importance. In the forty years between 1820 and 1860 the number of slaves in Alabama increased from 41,000 to 435,000 and in Mississippi from 32,000 to 436,000. Estimates suggest that in the two decades before the Civil War, 410,000 slaves relocated from the upper South to the cotton states. While some accompanied their masters, the majority were sold to planters already living in the region, commodities in a lucrative domestic slave trade. In either event, the growth of the cotton economy so firmly entrenched slavery in the South that only a long and bloody war could eradicate it.

PREFACE

For more than three hundred years the Portuguese, Spanish, English, Dutch, Danish, and French competed with each other in the profitable trade in African slaves. Together, slave traders from these nations carried nearly 11 million Africans to the New World. As David Brion Davis showed in *The Problem of Slavery in the Age of Revolution, 1770–1823* (1975), slavery extended from the St. Lawrence River basin in Canada all the way to the Rio de la Plata in Brazil and was the chief system of labor in the colonies that Europeans valued most.

Slaves worked the mines; they cleared land for planting; they labored on the plantations that provided sugar, tobacco, rice, indigo, and cotton for the world market. Where the production of such staple crops did not develop, as in the Northern colonies of British North America, slavery did not become as important. The economies of the Northern colonies, however, also came indirectly to depend on slavery. Merchants and manufacturers in the North supplied the slave colonies with agricultural tools, cheap clothing and shoes, and food. The slave trade stimulated shipbuilding, the insurance industry, capital investment, and banking. It encouraged the expansion of seaport cities on both sides of the Atlantic.

Participation in the trade among Europe, Africa, and the New World often generated staggering profits. Money was to be made in exporting iron, textiles, guns, rum, and brandy to Africa, in selling slaves to planters in North and South America and the Caribbean, and in transporting sugar, tobacco, rice, and cotton to Europe. By the eighteenth century many wealthy European merchants were in some way connected to the African and West Indian trade. The capital accumulated from these ventures often helped to finance the construction of canals, railroads, and factories. In the nineteenth century the principal export of the United States, cotton grown with slave labor, was a fundamental component of the Industrial Revolution and sustained American economic growth and development. Without slavery, Europeans would neither have settled nor prospered in the New World.

Yet, in time, slavery entangled Europeans, and later Americans, in a predicament from which they could not easily free themselves. Requisite to the economic viability of the New World, slavery came to represent in Western culture the ultimate limit of dehumanization, the reduction of human beings to mere things. Despite significant variations between the slaveholding colonies that arose from different environments, economic conditions, and social, religious, and political institutions, to say nothing of the personalities of individual masters, slaves were everywhere defined as property. They were, according to the laws of slavery, a mobile and transferable possession whose labor power and, more important, whose persons another not only controlled but also owned.

At the same time, it was impossible to ignore the essential humanity of the slaves or to deny them, however contrary to the law, certain rights and privileges. More thoughtful and compassionate masters entertained cautious hopes of augmenting these rights and privileges until, through a process of social, cultural, and moral evolution, the obvious evils of slavery would wither away and grateful blacks would willingly render service without coercion. All such aspirations, however sincere and noble, ran counter to one simple and inescapable fact: slaves were not property or the subhuman instruments of another's will. They were men and women, human beings, held down by force.

–MARK G. MALVASI
RANDOLPH-MACON COLLEGE
ASHLAND, VIRGINIA

PREFACE

CHRONOLOGY

1300
The slave trade ends in Europe.

1344
Pope Clement VI awards the Canary Islands to the Kingdom of Castile despite Portuguese objections.

1348–1349
The bubonic plague ravages western Europe, killing between 25 and 40 percent of the population. The resulting labor shortage prompts the return to slavery, especially along the Italian Peninsula. (*See* **Peculiar Institution**)

1418–1419
The Portuguese begin to explore the Madeira Islands where, during the 1440s, they establish sugar plantations worked by slave labor. Because of competition from the Kingdom of Castile, King João (John) I of Portugal sends an expedition of one hundred persons to Madeira and Porto Santo, the principal islands in the Madeiras, to establish permanent settlements there.

1434
17 DECEMBER: Pope Eugenius IV issues *Creator Omnium* excommunicating anyone who enslaved those natives of the Canary Islands who had converted to Christianity.

1441
Portuguese explorer Antam Goncalves seizes Moors near Cape Blanc in West Africa and carries them back to his homeland, thereby reintroducing the slave trade into Europe.

1442
Prince Henry the Navigator orders that the Moors whom Goncalves captured be returned to Africa and exchanged for ten African slaves and gold. These slaves are sold in the slave markets of Lisbon. The Portuguese establish forts along the west coast of Africa and begin to engage in a thriving slave trade. (*See* **Complicity**)

19 DECEMBER: Pope Eugenius IV issues *Illius Qui,* according the act of enslaving Africans the status of a holy crusade and declaring that all who perish in the enterprise will receive full remission from sin. Eugenius thus renders the African slave trade a "just war" waged with the blessing of the Roman Catholic Church.

Circa 1445
The Portuguese introduce slavery into the Madeira islands. By 1501 there are 2,000 slaves working on sugar plantations in the Madeiras.

1445
An auction of African slaves takes place at Lagos, Portugal. (*See* **Peculiar Institution**)

1452
18 JUNE: In *Dum Diversas* Pope Nicholas V empowers King Alfonso of Portugal to attack pagans and to enslave the captives in a just war. (*See* **Peculiar Institution**)

1455
8 JANUARY: Pope Nicholas V issues *Romanus Pontifex,* in which he confers on Portugal a commercial monopoly in West Africa and grants the Portuguese the right to subdue and convert the Africans.

1456
Sugar cultivated in Madeira with slave labor reaches markets in Bristol, England.

Pope Calixtus III reconfirms *Dum Diversas* (1452) and *Romanus Pontifex* (1455).

1462

Pope Pius II, concerned primarily about the enslavement and sale of European prisoners of war, proclaims the opposition of the Roman Catholic Church to the slave trade.

1480

6 MARCH: The Treaty of Alcaçovas reconfirms the assignment of the Canary Islands to the Kingdom of Castile, and the monopoly on African (West Africa, Guinea, and the islands off the West African coast) exploration, conquest, settlement, and commerce to Portugal.

1490

Portuguese begin to cultivate sugar on the island of São Tomé using African slaves transported primarily from the kingdom of Benin.

1491

Castilians begin to cultivate sugar on the Canary Islands, at first using enslaved natives and later African slaves purchased from the Portuguese.

1492

3 AUGUST: Christopher Columbus sets sail from Palos, Spain, on an expedition to discover a shorter route to the Spice Islands and Cathay (China).

12 OCTOBER: Columbus makes landfall at Watlings Island in the Bahamas. Luis de Torres and Rodrigo de Jarez, members of Columbus's expedition, make first known reference to smoking tobacco, which will become one of the principal crops cultivated with slave labor.

18 OCTOBER: The Columbus expedition reaches Cuba.

6 DECEMBER: The expedition reaches modern Haiti, which Columbus christens "Hispaniola" (Little Spain).

1493

15 MARCH: Columbus returns to Spain.

4 MAY: Pope Alexander VI issues papal bull *Inter cetera divina,* in which he divides the world between Spain and Portugal. Portugal receives control of Africa, and Spain receives control of North and South America. Later, the Portuguese will claim Brazil as part of their African grant. Yet, with Spain barred from African commerce, Portuguese merchants are the first to bring African slaves to the New World.

25 SEPTEMBER: Columbus departs on a second voyage to the New World during which he discovers Puerto Rico, Dominica, and Jamaica.

1494

7 JUNE: Spain and Portugal agree to the Treaty of Tordesillas, which reconfigures the papal line of demarcation but reconfirms the Portuguese dominance of African commerce, including the slave trade.

DECEMBER: Columbus establishes first permanent European settlement in the New World on Hispaniola.

Columbus sends an unspecified number of Arawaks and 500 Carib Indians taken in wars with the Caciques to be sold as slaves in Seville, thus initiating the Atlantic slave trade, which initially brings slaves from the New World to the Old.

1495

Queen Isabella suspends the royal order authorizing the sale of Native Americans and requests an inquiry into the legitimacy and morality of the slave trade. Her theological advisers are uncertain about the legality of slavery. As a consequence the Spanish Crown eventually orders the captives to be returned to their homes. (*See* **New World Vision**)

1496

11 JUNE: Columbus returns from second voyage to the New World, after a journey of two years, eight months. Romano Pane, a monk who accompanied Columbus, provides the first description of a tobacco plant.

1498

The Spanish send between 200 and 600 Carib Indians, whom they believe practiced cannibalism, to Spain to be sold as slaves.

1500

21 APRIL: Portuguese explorer Pedro Alvarez Cabral discovers Brazil, which he calls *Tierra de Vera Cruz* (Land of the True Cross), and claims it in the name of Portugal under the terms of the Treaty of Alcaçovas (1480). Although questions remain, some historians now believe that the Portuguese already knew of the existence of Brazil at the time they signed the treaty and, therefore, doubt that Cabral's landing there was accidental.

1501

The Spanish Crown authorizes Nicolas de Ovando, the colonial governor of Hispaniola, to import African slaves. (*See* **Middle Passage** *and* **Transatlantic Slave Trade**)

1502

The first African slaves arrive in the New World and are set to work in Hispaniola. (*See* **Middle Passage** *and* **Transatlantic Slave Trade**)

1503

3 MAY: Pope Alexander VI issues two edicts: the first gives the Spanish the right to attack pagans and other enemies of the Church; and the second entitles the Spanish to enslave the captives in these wars and to enjoy a commercial monopoly in the areas they discover.

1505

Governor Ovando imports 17 African slaves from Seville to labor in the copper mines of Hispaniola. (*See* **Middle Passage** *and* **Transatlantic Slave Trade**)

1506

Using slave labor the Spanish begin to produce sugar throughout the Greater Antilles.

1507

The Portuguese capture Zafi in Morocco and begin to trade in captive Moors, Berbers, and Jews. Many of these slaves are female. The Portuguese refer to all of them as "white slaves" to distinguish them from slaves taken in sub-Saharan Africa.

1509

Dominican priest Bartolomé de Las Casas, who later denounced Spanish cruelty toward the Indians in *A Short Account of the Destruction of the Indies* (1542), proposes that each Spanish colonist to the New World bring African slaves with him. Originally a Spanish planter in Hispaniola, Las Casas is the first man ordained in the Western Hemisphere. He turns his attention to serving the oppressed natives and returns to Spain to plead their case to Carlos I. (*See* **New World Vision**)

1510

The Portuguese transport a consignment of African slaves to Brazil to labor on Portuguese sugar plantations. (*See* **Middle Passage** *and* **Transatlantic Slave Trade**)

King Ferdinand II of Spain orders fifty slaves to be sent to Hispaniola to mine gold.

1511

Spanish colonists in Cuba import African slaves as laborers because the native Carib population has died off in alarming numbers. (*See*

Middle Passage *and* Transatlantic Slave Trade)

1512

Spanish colonists import black slaves into the western settlement of Hispaniola to replace Indian slaves who have died in great numbers from disease and from overwork in the mines.

27 DECEMBER: The Spanish Crown enacts the Laws of Burgos in response to Dominican priests who complain that Spanish settlers mistreat the native peoples of the Americas. The laws protect the Indians but permit them to be enslaved.

1513

The slave trade thrives as evidenced by the tremendous profits that the sale of licenses to import slaves to the New World generates for the Spanish Crown. (*See* **Middle Passage** *and* **Transatlantic Slave Trade**)

The Spanish Crown authorizes the use of slave labor in Cuba.

Five hundred sixty-five African slaves from Guinea arrive in Portugal.

1514

The African population of Spain reaches 25 percent, prompting King Ferdinand II to prohibit the additional importation of enslaved Africans.

1515

An additional 1,423 Guinean slaves arrive in Portugal.

1516

The Spanish establish the first sugar mill in Hispaniola.

1518

King Charles I of Spain establishes an *asiento* (contract) legalizing the slave trade to Spanish colonies in the New World. (*See* **Middle Passage** *and* **Transatlantic Slave Trade**)

1521

25 DECEMBER: A revolt of African slaves takes place in Hispaniola, the first recorded incident of a slave uprising in the Western Hemisphere. (*See* **Means of Resistance, Outcome of Rebellions,** *and* **Slave Rebellion**)

1522

The first sugar cultivated in Hispaniola with slave labor is exported.

1526

The Spanish Crown issues *Réal Cedula* (Royal Decree) preventing the introduction of *Negros ladinos* (Africans who had lived for at least two years in the Iberian Peninsula) into the Spanish colonies of the New World.

1527

An uprising of African slaves and Arawak Indians takes place in Puerto Rico. (*See* **Means of Resistance, Outcome of Rebellions,** *and* **Slave Rebellion**)

1528

Estimates suggest that 10,000 slaves are present in the New World.

1531

The Spanish Crown declares illegal the enslavement of the indigenous peoples of the Americas.

1533

A slave insurrection takes place in Cuba. (*See* **Means of Resistance, Outcome of Rebellions,** *and* **Slave Rebellion**)

1537

In *Veritas Ipsa,* Pope Paul III declares Catholic opposition to the slave trade and maintains that the natives of the Americas are not to be enslaved. Among his primary concerns, however, as with Pius II in 1462, is to prevent European captives taken in war from being sold into slavery. (*See* **Middle Passage** *and* **Transatlantic Slave Trade**)

1538

The first African slaves arrive in Brazil.

10 JULY: The Spanish government decrees that any slave who marries a free person remains a slave. The children born of such a union are also slaves. (*See* **Legal Definition**)

1539

Spanish scholar Francisco de Vitoria argues in a series of lectures delivered in Spain that the native peoples of the Americas are freeborn and thus exempt from slavery. (*See* **New World Vision**)

1542

22 FEBRUARY: King Charles I of Spain (Holy Roman Emperor Charles V) issues the New Laws of the Indies, making it more difficult for Spanish colonists to enslave natives through the *encomienda,* a system for extracting labor and tribute from the Indians. Spaniards in the Americas routinely ignore or circumvent this legislation. (*See* **Peculiar Institution**)

1547

Spanish scholar Juan Ginés Sepúlveda publishes *Democrates alter,* in which he maintains that the Spanish have a legal and moral right to enslave the native peoples of the Americas.

1548

A slave uprising in Colombia leaves 20 Spanish settlers dead. (*See* **Means of Resistance, Outcome of Rebellions,** *and* **Slave Rebellion**)

1550

A slave revolt in Peru results in the burning of the Spanish settlement at Santa Marta. Colonial officials impose a strict curfew on all slaves in the region. (*See* **Means of Resistance, Outcome of Rebellions,** *and* **Slave Rebellion**)

1553

Eight hundred fugitive slaves establish a maroon community near Nombre de Dios in Panama. (*See* **Maroon Communities**)

1562

English explorers Sir John Hawkins brings 300 slaves from West Africa to Hispaniola. So lucrative is the voyage that it prompts the English government to pursue further involvement with the slave trade. With the permission of Queen Elizabeth I, Hawkins later includes an image of a bound African on his family crest. (*See* **Middle Passage, Profits,** *and* **Transatlantic Slave Trade**)

1571

King Charles IX of France ends slavery for all persons in France who convert to Christianity.

1573

Bartolomé de Albormoz, a law professor at the University of Mexico, writes an essay in which he questions the legal foundation of slavery. (*See* **Legal Definition**)

Circa 1580

Sugar planters in Brazil begin to shift to slave labor.

1605

Fugitive slaves in Brazil establish the maroon community of Palmares. (*See* **Maroon Communities**)

1607

King Henry IV of France reinforces the decree of 1571.

1609

Spanish troops in Mexico are unable to destroy a slave community led by Gaspar Yanga, and the colonial authorities grant the slaves their freedom. (*See* **Maroon Communities**)

1616

The Dutch import slaves into Guiana.

1618

King James I of England enhances British participation in the slave trade by granting a commercial monopoly on the newly established Company of Royal Adventurers of London to engage in the slave trade. James grants a similar monopoly to Sir Robert Rich to operate along the Guinean coast of West Africa.

1619

30 JULY: The Virginia House of Burgesses, meeting at Jamestown, enacts a measure legalizing white indentured servitude.

AUGUST: Blacks arrive in Jamestown, the first in British North America. John Rolfe, a settler at Jamestown, noted the event, writing: "About the latter end of August, a Dutch man of Warr . . . [arrived] at Point- Comfprt. . . . He brought not any thing but 20 and odd Negroes w[hich] the Covernor and Cape Merchant bought."

1621

A group of Dutch merchants headed by Willem Usselinx charter the Dutch West India Company to establish commercial colonies and to carry on the transatlantic slave trade in the New World.

1625

Dutch jurist Hugo Grotius publishes *De jure belli ac Pacis* (*Rights of War and Peace*) in which he catalogued 160 different types of slavery. Of "complete slavery" he wrote: "That is complete slavery which owes life-long service in return for nourishment and other necessaries of life; and if the condition is accepted within natural limits it contains no element of undue severity." (*See* **Legal Definition**)

1627

The French establish a colony in St. Kitts.

1629

The French begin to import slaves into St. Kitts.

1630

English settlers cultivate sugar in Barbados using slave labor. (*See* **English Colonies**)

1637

The Huguenot (Protestant) synod in France proclaims slavery is not contrary to the laws of God. (*See* **Christianity**)

1639

Pope Urban VIII issues a papal encyclical to the *Cámara de Apostólica de Portugal* (Apostolic Chamber of Portugal), in which he promises to excommunicate all Roman Catholics who continue to engage in the African slave trade, which he characterizes as a crime. As with earlier, similar papal decrees, Urban is concerned about preventing European prisoners of war from being sold into slavery.

1641

DECEMBER: Massachusetts becomes the first colony in British North America to give legal recognition to slavery. (*See* **English Colonies** *and* **Legal Definition**)

1642

The French colony of Martinique begins to import slaves.

1648

George Fox founds the Society of Friends (Quakers) in England. The Quakers are the first group to condemn the slave trade and slavery. They were instrumental in launching and sustaining the international antislavery movement. (*See* **Abolitionists** *and* **Christianity**)

1650

The French begin to cultivate sugar in Martinique using slave labor.

1651

In an attempt to limit the influence of the Dutch West India Company, the British Parliament passes the English Navigation Act that restricts the slave trade in English colonies to English merchants. (*See* **Middle Passage, Profits,** *and* **Transatlantic Slave Trade**)

1652

The government of the Netherlands grants the Dutch West India Company permission to import African slaves into the Dutch colony of New Netherlands (later New York). (*See* **Middle Passage** *and* **Transatlantic Slave Trade**)

1654

King Louis XIV of France charters the *Compagnie des Indies Occidentales* (The French West Indies Company). (*See* **Middle Passage** *and* **Transatlantic Slave Trade**)

1655

10 MAY: The British seize control of Jamaica from Spain.

1663

The English grant freedom to the Jamaican maroons whom they have been unable to defeat in war. (*See* **Maroon Communities**)

13 SEPTEMBER: First extensive slave conspiracy in colonial North America involves white indentured servants and black slaves in Gloucester County, Virginia. An indentured servant betrays the plot to authorities. (*See* **Means of Resistance, Outcome of Rebellions,** *and* **Slave Rebellion**)

1664

English Puritan George Baxter publishes the *Christian Directory,* in which he characterizes the slave trade as theft and the purchase of a slave as a sin.

20 SEPTEMBER: Maryland enacts the first "antiamalgamation law" to prohibit interracial marriages between whites and blacks, especially between white women and black men. Similar laws will be passed in Virginia (1691), Massachusetts (1705), North Carolina (1715), South Carolina (1717), Delaware (1721), and Pennsylvania (1725). (*See* **Legal Definition**)

1667

The English Parliament enacts *The Act to Regulate the Negroes on the British Plantations,* which proposes severe punishments for "unruly, barbarous, and savage" African slaves. (*See* **Legal Definition**)

1670

The French Crown authorizes French participation in the African slave trade to the French colonies in the Caribbean. (*See* **Middle Passage** *and* **Transatlantic Slave Trade**)

1671

The Danish West India Company is chartered to colonize St. Thomas.

1672

The English Parliament passes legislation to enable the charter of the Royal African Company (RAC) and confers upon it a monopoly over the English slave trade between Africa and the Americas. (*See* **Middle Passage** *and* **Transatlantic Slave Trade**)

1684

Pope Innocent XI attempts to mitigate the worst aspects of the African slave trade but to no avail. The Protestant Dutch and English, who now dominate the trade, ignore his decrees.

1685

The French Crown enacts the *Code Noir* (Black Code), applicable in all French colonies. It requires that slaves receive religious instruction, permits racial intermarriage, and outlaws labor on Sundays and holidays.

Fugitive slaves in the Dutch colony of Surinam establish a maroon community. (*See* **Maroon Communities**)

1688

18 FEBRUARY: The first organized protest against slavery and the slave trade in the British North American colonies takes place at the Quaker monthly meeting in Germantown, Pennsylvania. (*See* **Abolitionists** *and* **Christianity**)

1693

Gold is discovered in the Minas Gerais region of Brazil, prompting the importation of vast numbers of slaves to work the mines.

1694

Gold is discovered in Taubaté, Brazil, prompting the importation of vast numbers of slaves to work the mines.

1695

The Portuguese finally destroy the maroon settlement at Palmares. (*See* **Maroon Communities**)

1698

The Royal African Company loses its monopoly on the African slave trade, and participation is opened to all English subjects upon payment of a 10 percent duty to the RAC. Many New England merchants begin to earn handsome profits from commerce in slaves. (*See* **Middle Passage** *and* **Transatlantic Slave Trade**)

1700

AUGUST: *The Blessing* became the first vessel to sail from Liverpool, England, to West Africa to participate in the Atlantic slave trade. In time, Liverpool will become one of the European ports most fully and actively engaged in the slave trade. (*See* **Middle Passage, Profits,** *and* **Transatlantic Slave Trade**)

1701–1714

The French government establishes the French Royal Senegal Company to supply slaves to the Spanish colonies during the War of the Spanish Succession. The French Royal Senegal Company acquires the *asiento* that requires the annual delivery of 38,000 slaves to Spanish colonies in the Americas. (*See* **Middle Passage** *and* **Transatlantic Slave Trade**)

1708

28 FEBRUARY: A slave revolt in Newton, Long Island, New York, claims the lives of seven whites. Authorities execute two male slaves and their Indian accomplice and burn to death a black female slave. (*See* **Means of Resistance, Outcome of Rebellions,** *and* **Slave Rebellion**)

1711

The English South Sea Company receives the right to transport Africans to the Americas to be sold as slaves. (*See* **Middle Passage** *and* **Transatlantic Slave Trade**)

A mulatto named Audrestoe leads a slave uprising in Venezuela. (*See* **Means of Resistance, Outcome of Rebellions,** *and* **Slave Rebellion**)

The Spanish government grants an *asiento* to the French West Indies Company to bring slaves to Spanish colonies in the Americas for an unspecified number of years. (*See* **Middle Passage** *and* **Transatlantic Slave Trade**)

1712

7 APRIL: A slave revolt in New York City claims the lives of nine whites. Authorities execute twenty-one slaves. (*See* **Means of Resistance, Outcome of Rebellions,** *and* **Slave Rebellion**)

1713

26 MARCH: The English South Sea Company receives an *asiento* to bring 4,800 slaves per year for thirty years to the Spanish colonies in the Americas. (*See* **Middle Passage** *and* **Transatlantic Slave Trade**)

1715

The Spanish introduce slavery into Puerto Rico.

Ricardo O'Farrill establishes a slave market in Havana, Cuba, that operates for nearly 150 years and is the most notorious in the Western Hemisphere.

1716

16 SEPTEMBER: The Portuguese Crown decrees that any blacks who set foot in Portugal are free. The decree, however, does not apply to slaves in the Portuguese colony of Brazil.

1720

The Portuguese Crown issues an order prohibiting colonial officials from participating in the African slave trade.

The French begin to cultivate coffee in Martinique using slave labor.

1723

The coffee boom begins in Brazil and Saint Domingue (Haiti). (*See* **Saint Domingue**)

1725

The First Maroon War begins in Jamaica. (*See* **Maroon Communities**)

1726

A slave revolt breaks out in the Dutch colony of Suriname (formerly Surinam). (*See* **Means of Resistance, Outcome of Rebellions,** *and* **Slave Rebellion**)

1728

Diamonds are discovered in the Minas Gerais, prompting the importation of many slaves into Brazil to work the mines.

1729

Attorney General Sir Philip Yorke and Solicitor General Charles Talbot issue the Yorke-Talbot decision that declares neither entry into Great Britain nor conversion to Christianity confers emancipation from slavery.

1731

Slave revolts occur in Cuba and Guiana. (*See* **Means of Resistance, Outcome of Rebellions,** *and* **Slave Rebellion**)

1739

The English sign a treaty with the Jamaican maroons permitting them to maintain their autonomy. (*See* **Maroon Communities**)

9 SEPTEMBER: A slave revolt in Stono, South Carolina, led by a slave named Jemmy, results in the death of twenty-five whites.

(*See* **Means of Resistance, Outcome of Rebellions,** *and* **Slave Rebellion**)

1741

Pope Benedict XIV condemns the slave trade as practiced in Brazil.

MARCH–APRIL: A series of suspicious fires in New York City creates fear of a slave conspiracy. Authorities execute thirty-one slaves and five whites. (*See* **Means of Resistance, Outcome of Rebellions,** *and* **Slave Rebellion**)

1744

Fifty percent of the commerce conducted at Liverpool is connected with the African slave trade. (*See* **Profits** *and* **Transatlantic Slave Trade**)

1752

The British Parliament charters the Company of Merchants Trading to Africa. (*See* **Middle Passage** *and* **Transatlantic Slave Trade**)

1760

7 APRIL: Tacky's Rebellion begins in Jamaica. (*See* **Means of Resistance, Outcome of Rebellions,** *and* **Slave Rebellion**)

1761

The English introduce slavery in Dominica.

OCTOBER: British forces suppress Tacky's Rebellion. (*See* **Means of Resistance, Outcome of Rebellions,** *and* **Slave Rebellion**)

1763

The English introduce slavery into Grenada and St. Vincent.

23 FEBRUARY–MAY: Led by Cuffy and Accara, a slave rebellion breaks out in the Dutch colony of Berbice (part of modern Guyana) that involves half the slaves residing in the colony. The rebellion collapses within three months, although rebels are still being sought a year after the revolt. (*See* **Means of Resistance, Outcome of Rebellions,** *and* **Slave Rebellion**)

1768

The Spanish begin to cultivate coffee in Cuba using slave labor.

1770

Abbé Guillaume-Thomas François de Raynal publishes *Histoire philosophique et politique du commerce et des établishssements des Européens dans lex deux Indies* in which he predicts the rise of a black Spartacus to liberate and avenge the slaves. (*See* **New World Vision**)

1771

King Louis XV of France decrees that persons of African descent do not enjoy the same rights and privileges as whites in the French colonies. (*See* **Legal Definition**)

1772

JUNE: In the Somersett case, Chief Justice Lord Mansfield (William Murray, first Earl of Mansfield) abolishes slavery in England. In overturning the Yorke-Talbot decision (1729), Mansfield declares "the air of England has long been too pure for a slave, and every man is free who breathes it." (*See* **Legal Definition**)

Charles III of Spain condemns slavery and announces that any fugitive slave who seeks refuge in Spain will be freed, but that slavery will continue in the Spanish colonies.

A massive slave rebellion breaks out in Demerara (Guyana) against Dutch colonial rule. (*See* **Means of Resistance, Outcome of Rebellions,** *and* **Slave Rebellion**)

1773

6 JANUARY: Slaves in Massachusetts petition the legislature for their freedom.

16 JANUARY: Under the leadership of Sebastião José de Carvalho e Mello, the Marquis de Pombal, the Portuguese government abolishes slavery in Portugal but continues it in the Portuguese colonies.

1774

John Wesley, founder of Methodism, publishes *Thoughts on Slavery*, in which he condemns the biblical defense of slavery and declares slavery to be sinful. (*See* **Christianity**)

1775

14 APRIL: The first formal abolitionist society in the United States is organized in Philadelphia. (*See* **Abolitionists**)

7 NOVEMBER: Lord Dunmore, deposed royal governor of Virginia, promises freedom to all male slaves who enlist in the British Army. (*See* **American Revolution**)

1776

For the first time the British Parliament considers a measure to abolish the African slave trade. (*See* **Middle Passage** *and* **Transatlantic Slave Trade**)

1777

The French government prohibits the immigration of blacks and mulattoes, slave or free, to France.

CHRONOLOGY

2 JULY: After declaring itself an independent republic, Vermont becomes the first region in British North America to abolish slavery.

1778

The British Parliament establishes a special commission to investigate the conduct of the African slave trade.

FEBRUARY: In opposition to the Continental Congress and officers of the Continental Army, both of which had barred slaves from service, the General Assembly of Rhode Island authorizes the enlistment of slaves in the state militia. (*See* **American Revolution**)

1779

British abolitionist Granville Sharp appeals to the Anglican bishops to denounce the African slave trade. (*See* **Christianity**)

1781

29 NOVEMBER: Luke Collingwood, captain of the slave ship *Zong*, orders that 133 slaves be thrown overboard because they were ill and could not be sold. The insurance underwriter protects against the loss of slaves from drowning but not from illness. The shipowners eventually collect on the claim. (*See* **Middle Passage** *and* **Transatlantic Slave Trade**)

1783

The London Meeting for Sufferings, a special committee that the Quakers had established, publishes *The Case of Our Fellow Creatures, the Oppressed Africans, Recommended to the Serious Consideration of the Legislature of Great Britain, by the People called Quakers,* to urge Parliament to end the African slave trade. (*See* **Abolitionists** *and* **Christianity**)

1787

British abolitionists establish the Society for the Abolition of Slavery. (*See* **Abolitionists**)

13 JULY: The Continental Congress excludes slavery from the Northwest Territory.

17 SEPTEMBER: Adopted by the Philadelphia Convention, the Constitution of the United States protects slavery. (*See* **American Revolution** *and* **Legal Definition**)

1788

19 FEBRUARY: Opponents of slavery in France create the Société des Amis des Noirs (Society of the Friends of Blacks). (*See* **Abolitionists**)

British abolitionists organize a petition campaign to pressure Parliament to outlaw the African slave trade. Parliament responds by regulating the conditions under which the slave trade can be conducted, and the Privy Council Committee investigates British commercial relations in Africa. (*See* **Abolitionists**)

1789

The Society of the Friends of Blacks petitions the Estates General to abolish slavery in all French colonies and to end the African slave trade. (*See* **Abolitionists**)

Writing under the pseudonym Gustavus Vassa, Olaudah Equiano publishes *The Interesting Narrative of the Life of Olaudah Equiano Written by Himself,* which became extremely popular with, and influential to, British abolitionists.

The leading abolitionist in Parliament, William Wilberforce, introduces twelve resolutions in the House of Commons calling for the abolition of the African slave trade. Parliament does not act on Wilberforce's resolutions. (*See* **Abolitionists**)

1790

21 OCTOBER: Free mulattoes Vincent Ogé and Jean-Baptiste Chauvanne lead an abortive uprising of mulattoes in Saint Domingue. (*See* **Means of Resistance, Outcome of Rebellions, Saint Domingue,** *and* **Slave Rebellion**)

1791

A slave named Farcel leads a slave uprising in the English colony of Dominica. (*See* **Means of Resistance, Outcome of Rebellions,** *and* **Slave Rebellion**)

Parliament rejects Wilberforce's resolutions demanding the abolition of slavery and the African slave trade.

FEBRUARY: Ogé and Chauvanne are executed. (*See* **Means of Resistance, Outcome of Rebellions, Saint Domingue,** *and* **Slave Rebellion**)

15 MAY: The French National Assembly extends suffrage to all free colonists, regardless of skin color, who meet the property qualifications for voting. The National Assembly rescinds this measure when violence breaks outs in Saint Domingue. (*See* **Saint Domingue**)

22 AUGUST: A massive slave revolt breaks out in Saint Domingue, which lasts for more than a decade. Under the leadership of former slave Toussaint L'Ouverture, the rebels not only end slavery but also establish the first African American state. (*See* **Means**

of Resistance, Outcome of Rebellions, Saint Domingue, *and* Slave Rebellion)

22 SEPTEMBER: The French National Assembly abolishes slavery throughout the French Empire.

1792

The French Legislative Assembly decrees that free blacks and mulattoes in the colonies have equal rights with whites.

The British Parliament receives 499 abolitionist petitions. The House of Commons supports a resolution to end the African slave trade, but the House of Lords rejects it.

The Danish Crown decrees an end to the African slave trade to Danish colonies by 1803, thereby becoming the first state to ban the trade.

1793

12 FEBRUARY: Congress enacts the first fugitive slave law, which makes it a criminal offense to harbor a runaway or prevent his arrest.

1794

14 MARCH: Eli Whitney patents the cotton gin, which increases the demand for slave labor in the South. (*See* **Economic Impact**)

1795

The British Parliament rejects a bill that Wilberforce introduces to abolish the African slave trade.

The Second Maroon War begins on Jamaica. During the 2-year conflict British troops burn many villages and destroy crops. Colonial authorities deport six hundred maroons to Nova Scotia. (*See* **Maroon Communities, Means of Resistance, Outcome of Rebellions, *and* Slave Rebellion**)

17 AUGUST: A slave rebellion, led by Tula and Carpata, breaks out in the Dutch colony of Curaçao. (*See* **Means of Resistance, Outcome of Rebellions, *and* Slave Rebellion**)

1796

A slave rebellion breaks out in the British colony of St. Lucia. (*See* **Means of Resistance, Outcome of Rebellions, *and* Slave Rebellion**)

1800

2 JANUARY: The free blacks of Philadelphia present an abolitionist petition to Congress. (*See* **Abolitionists**)

30 AUGUST: Gabriel Prosser and an estimated one thousand slaves plan to attack Rich-

mond, Virginia, but severe thunderstorms force them to suspend the assault. Two slaves betray the conspiracy to authorities. (*See* **Means of Resistance, Outcome of Rebellions, *and* Slave Rebellion**)

7 OCTOBER: Authorities hang Prosser and fifteen of his followers. (*See* **Means of Resistance, Outcome of Rebellions, *and* Slave Rebellion**)

1801

Toussaint L'Ouverture becomes Governor-General for life of Saint Domingue. (*See* **Saint Domingue**)

1802

The French capture Toussaint L'Ouverture and imprison him in Fort de Joux in the Jura Mountains, where he dies in 1803.

12 MAY: First Consul Napoleon Bonaparte of France reinstates slavery and the slave trade throughout the French Empire.

1804

The House of Commons at last approves Wilberforce's bill to end the African slave trade, but Prime Minister William Pitt delays the vote on the measure in the House of Lords.

1 JANUARY: Jean Jacques Dessalines, one of Toussaint L'Ouverture's lieutenants, proclaims the independence of Haiti (fomerly Saint Domingue), the first African American republic. (*See* **Saint Domingue**)

1805

The House of Commons reverses course and rejects Wilberforce's bill to end the African slave trade. Pitt, however, issues an order-in-council reducing the volume of the trade, limiting slave imports to 3 percent annually of the slave population of a colony.

1806

JUNE: The British Parliament approves the resolution of abolitionist Charles James Fox to end the African slave trade but fails to enact it. (*See* **Abolitionists**)

17 OCTOBER: Political rivals assassinate Jean Jacques Dessalines. Civil war breaks out in Haiti between the forces of Henri Christophe and Alexandre Pétion. (*See* **Saint Domingue**)

1807

Parliament rejects a measure proposed by Earl Percy calling for the abolition of slavery in British colonial possessions.

2 MARCH: Congress bans the slave trade to the United States and its territories. The ban takes effect on 1 January 1808.

25 MARCH: Parliament enacts statutes abolishing the African slave trade, which become effective on 1 March 1808.

1808

1 MARCH: The General Abolition Act takes effect, ending the involvement of Great Britain in the African slave trade. (*See* **Transatlantic Slave Trade**)

1809

The first in a series of slave revolts breaks out in Brazil. The revolts continue until 1835. (*See* **Means of Resistance, Outcome of Rebellions,** *and* **Slave Rebellion**)

1810

The Supreme Junta of Caracas, Venezuela, orders an end to the African slave trade.

1811

8–10 JANUARY: A slave rebellion in Louisiana is the largest in the history of the United States but is easily suppressed by the local militia and the United States army. (*See* **Means of Resistance, Outcome of Rebellions,** *and* **Slave Rebellion**)

1812

A slave insurrection breaks out in Venezuela. (*See* **Means of Resistance, Outcome of Rebellions,** *and* **Slave Rebellion**)

1814

15 JANUARY: The government of the Netherlands officially ends Dutch involvement in the African slave trade. (*See* **Middle Passage** *and* **Transatlantic Slave Trade**)

1815

29 MARCH: Upon his return from exile in Elba, Napoleon declares the end of French involvement in the African slave trade.

30 JULY: After the final defeat of Bonaparte, King Louis XVIII ends French participation in the slave trade, but the French government does not effectively enforce the ban.

1816

South American revolutionary Simón Bolivar obtains military supplies from the government of Haiti and, in exchange, promises to free the slaves throughout South America.

South American revolutionary José de San Martin issues a proclamation freeing all the slaves who aid him during the invasion of Chile.

28 DECEMBER: The American Colonization Society, which advocates the emancipation of slaves and the colonization of freed blacks outside the United States, is formed in Washington, D.C. (*See* **Abolitionists**)

1817

23 SEPTEMBER: In exchange for £400,000, Spain agrees to end the African slave trade north of the equator.

19 DECEMBER: In a treaty signed with Great Britain, the government of Portugal agrees to end the slave trade north of the equator. (*See* **Transatlantic Slave Trade**)

1819

France officially ends its participation in the African slave trade. (*See* **Transatlantic Slave Trade**)

DECEMBER: Bolivar fails to secure ratification of a decree of emancipation at the Congress of Angostura.

1820

6 FEBRUARY: *Mayflower of Liberia* departs New York harbor with 86 free blacks aboard who plan to return to Africa.

3 MARCH: Congress enacts the Missouri Compromise, which prohibits slavery north of a line running 36° 30'. Although this line forms the southern boundary of Missouri, Missouri itself enters the Union as a slave state.

9 MARCH: *Mayflower of Liberia* reaches Sierra Leone.

20 MAY: The Spanish government abolishes the slave trade south of the equator.

1821

The Congress of Cúcuta adopts a program of gradual emancipation for the slaves in the Republic of Gran Colombia.

The British Parliament terminates the charter of the Royal Africa Company and confiscates all company assets.

French abolitionists found the Société de la Morale Chrétinne (Society of Christian Morals) to advocate the abolition of slavery. (*See* **Abolitionists**)

1822

30 MAY: A house servant betrays the conspiracy of Denmark Vesey to stage a slave uprising

in Charleston, South Carolina, and its environs. The Vesey plot, the existence of which some historians have recently questioned, allegedly involved thousands of slaves. (*See* **Means of Resistance, Outcome of Rebellions**, *and* **Slave Rebellion**)

2 JULY: South Carolina authorities hang Vesey and five of his lieutenants at Blake's Landing, near Charleston. (*See* **Means of Resistance, Outcome of Rebellions**, *and* **Slave Rebellion**)

7 SEPTEMBER: Brazil declares its independence from Portugal.

1823

Chile outlaws African slavery.

British abolitionists organize the Society for the Migration and General Abolition of Slavery, more popularly known as the British Anti-Slavery Society, and elect Wilberforce as the first president. (*See* **Abolitionists**)

1824

Parliament declares participation in the African slave trade an act of piracy.

24 MARCH: The British House of Commons supports the resolution of George Canning for the improvement of the condition of the slaves in the British Empire.

1825

Argentina, Bolivia, Chile, Paraguay, and Peru adopt programs of gradual emancipation.

José Bonifácio de Andrada e Silva, architect of Brazilian independence, denounces slavery and embraces free labor as the key to economic progress and prosperity.

1827

4 JULY: New York abolishes slavery.

1829

15 SEPTEMBER: Under the leadership of President Vincente Guerrero, Mexico abolishes slavery.

28 SEPTEMBER: David Walker publishes *Appeal to the Colored Citizens . . .*, in which he denounces slavery and calls for a violent slave revolt. (*See* **Abolitionists**)

1830

Great Britain, Portugal, and Brazil agree that Brazil will end the slave trade south of the equator and deem participation in the slave trade an act of piracy. The treaty is not consistently enforced.

1831

Mary Prince publishes *The History of Mary Prince, a West Indian Slave, Related by Herself,* the first slave narrative written by a female slave. (*See* **Abolitionists**)

The French government bans citizens from participating in the African slave trade. (*See* **Transatlantic Slave Trade**)

1 JANUARY: Abolitionist William Lloyd Garrison publishes the first issue of *The Liberator,* destined to become the leading abolitionist newspaper in the United States. (*See* **Abolitionists**)

21–23 AUGUST: The Nat Turner Rebellion in Southampton County, Virginia, leaves 60 whites dead. (*See* **Means of Resistance, Outcome of Rebellions**, *and* **Slave Rebellion**)

30 OCTOBER: Authorities capture Turner. (*See* **Means of Resistance, Outcome of Rebellions**, *and* **Slave Rebellion**)

7 NOVEMBER: The Brazilian government enacts a measure to end the African slave trade, but the legislation is ignored.

11 NOVEMBER: Turner is hanged in Jerusalem, Virginia. (*See* **Means of Resistance, Outcome of Rebellions**, *and* **Slave Rebellion**)

27 DECEMBER: The Christmas Rebellion breaks out in Jamaica. The uprising causes $3.5 million in damages, brings economic ruin to many planters, and hastens the passage of the Emancipation Act, which frees the slaves in the British Empire. (*See* **Means of Resistance, Outcome of Rebellions**, *and* **Slave Rebellion**)

1832

6 JANUARY: Delegates establish the New England Anti-Slavery Society in Boston. (*See* **Abolitionists**)

1833

1 AUGUST: The British Parliament passes the Emancipation Act, abolishing slavery throughout the British Empire. By 1838 all slaves in the British Empire are freed.

4 DECEMBER: Delegates organize the American Anti-Slavery Society in Philadelphia. (*See* **Abolitionists**)

1834

8 AUGUST: Italian Kingdom of Piedmont-Sardinia enters into a treaty with Great Britain and France outlawing the African slave trade.

1835

Slave revolts break out in Cuba. (*See* **Means of Resistance, Outcome of Rebellions,** *and* **Slave Rebellion**)

1836

JANUARY: James G. Birney launches the abolitionist newspaper *Philanthropist* in Cincinnati. (*See* **Abolitionists**)

26 MAY: The U.S. Congress imposes a "gag rule" to prevent the reading, circulation, and debate of antislavery petitions.

DECEMBER: The Portuguese Crown outlaws the export of slaves from any colonial possession. Notwithstanding this prohibition, Africans seized in Angola and Mozambique continue to be sent to Brazil.

1837

The U.S. House of Representatives declares that slaves do not enjoy the right to petition the federal government.

The government of Mexico enacts a second decree abolishing slavery in Mexico with compensation to the slave owners.

9 JUNE: The cities of the Germanic Hanseatic League enter into a treaty with Great Britain and France outlawing the African slave trade.

7 NOVEMBER: A mob in Alton, Illinois, murders abolitionist editor Elijah P. Lovejoy and destroys his press. (*See* **Abolitionists**)

24 NOVEMBER: The Italian Kingdom of Tuscany enters into a treaty with Great Britain and France outlawing the slave trade.

25 DECEMBER: A combined force of Seminole Indians and blacks defeat American troops at the Battle of Okeechobee in Florida during the Second Seminole War (1835–1842). John Horse, a black man, is one of the Seminole commanders.

1838

14 FEBRUARY: The Italian Kingdom of Naples enters into a treaty with Great Britain and France outlawing the African slave trade.

15 FEBRUARY: In defiance of the gag rule, Whig Congressman John Quincy Adams of Massachusetts introduces 350 antislavery petitions into the House of Representatives. (*See* **Abolitionists**)

3 SEPTEMBER: Future abolitionist Frederick Douglass escapes from slavery in Baltimore, Maryland. (*See* **Abolitionists**)

3 DECEMBER: Ohio Representative Joshua R. Giddings, the first abolitionist elected to Congress, takes his seat in the House of Representatives. (*See* **Abolitionists**)

1839

The British Parliament enacts the Palmerston Act, which empowers the British Royal Navy to search Portuguese vessels and ships of other countries suspected of carrying slaves to the Americas.

Abolitionist Theodore Dwight Weld and his future wife Angelina Grimké publish the influential antislavery polemic *Slavery As It Is: Testimony of a Thousand Witnesses*. (*See* **Abolitionists**)

25 FEBRUARY: Some Seminoles and their black allies depart Florida for Indian Territory west of the Mississippi River. That blacks could accompany the Seminoles and not be turned over to U.S. authorities is a major concession forced upon the American government.

JULY: Led by Joseph Cinquez (Cinqué), slave rebels kill Captain Ramón Ferrer and take over the slaver *Amistad*. (*See* **Means of Resistance, Middle Passage,** *and* **Transatlantic Slave Trade**)

26 AUGUST: American authorities capture the *Amistad* rebels off the coast of Long Island, New York.

13 NOVEMBER: The Liberty Party, the first American political party devoted to antislavery principles, is founded in Warsaw, New York. (*See* **Abolitionists**)

3 DECEMBER: In *In Supremo*, Pope Gregory XVI asserts Roman Catholic opposition to slavery and the slave trade.

1840

1 APRIL: Delegates to the Liberty Party convention nominate abolitionist James G. Birney for president.

1841

Virginia Baptist minister and proslavery theorist Thornton Stringfellow publishes *A Brief Examination of Scripture Testimony on the Institution of Slavery,* in which he argues that the Bible sanctions slavery, in the *Religious Herald*. (*See* **Christianity**)

MARCH: Free black Solomon Northup is kidnapped in Washington, D.C., and sold into slavery in Louisiana, where he spends the next dozen years as a slave.

9 MARCH: The U.S. Supreme Court acquits and frees the *Amistad* rebels. Former president and current congressman from Massachu-

setts, John Quincy Adams, argues the rebels' case.

7 NOVEMBER: A slave uprising aboard the *Creole,* en route to New Orleans from Hampton, Virginia, results in the slaves taking over the vessel and sailing for the Bahamas, where they receive their freedom and asylum. (*See* **Means of Resistance, Middle Passage, Outcome of Rebellions,** *and* **Slave Rebellion**)

25 NOVEMBER: Thirty-five survivors of the *Amistad* rebellion return to Africa.

20 DECEMBER: Austria, France, Great Britain, Prussia, and Russia outlaw the African slave trade.

1842

Cuban authorities enact the *Regiamento de Esclavos* (Rules for Slaves), a harsh slave code.

21–22 MARCH: Joshua R. Giddings introduces the "Giddings Resolutions," denouncing the federal sanction and the coastal slave trade.

23 MARCH: Censured by his colleagues in the House, many of whom believe that he has encouraged incidents such as that which took place aboard the *Creole,* Giddings resigns. Voters, however, reelect him in November.

1 AUGUST: At the National Convention of Colored Men in Buffalo, New York, black abolitionist Henry Highland Garnet calls for slaves in the South to revolt. (*See* **Abolitionists**)

9 AUGUST: The United States and Great Britain agree to the Webster-Ashburton Treaty, one provision of which creates the African Squadron to patrol the coast of West Africa to detain ships engaged in the slave trade. Freed slaves are repatriated either to Liberia or Sierra Leone.

20 AUGUST: Congress ratifies the Webster-Ashburton Treaty.

18 OCTOBER: The capture of runaway slave George Latimer in Boston leads to the first of the fugitive slave cases that poison relations between North and South. Boston abolitionists purchase Latimer's freedom.

1843

Slave revolts erupt in Cuba, Colombia, and Venezuela. (*See* **Means of Resistance, Outcome of Rebellions,** *and* **Slave Rebellion**)

MARCH: The Massachusetts state legislature decriminalizes miscegenation.

1844

Agitation over slavery divides the Methodist and Baptist churches into Northern and Southern conventions. (*See* **Christianity**)

3 DECEMBER: The U.S. House of Representatives rescinds the antislavery gag rule by a vote of 108 to 80.

1845

Former slave and leading black abolitionist Frederick Douglass publishes the first of his three autobiographies, *Narrative of the Life of Frederick Douglass.* (*See* **Abolitionists**)

The governments of Chile and Portugal declare the African slave trade to be an act of piracy.

The British Parliament enacts the Aberdeen Law, authorizing the Royal Navy to search Brazilian vessels suspected of participating in the slave trade.

1846

British abolitionists pay £150 ($711) to secure the freedom of Douglass. (*See* **Abolitionists**)

8 AUGUST: The U.S. House of Representatives approves Democratic Congressman David Wilmot's (Pennsylvania) Wilmot Proviso, by which he hopes to exclude slavery forever from any territory that the United States may acquire from Mexico. (*See* **U.S. Civil War**)

1847

30 JUNE: Slave Dred Scott files a lawsuit in the Circuit Court of St. Louis, Missouri, seeking his freedom. (*See* **Legal Definition**)

26 JULY: President Joseph Jenkins Roberts declares his country of Liberia an independent African republic.

3 DECEMBER: With black abolitionist Martin R. Delany, Douglass publishes the first issue of his abolitionist newspaper, the *North Star,* in Rochester, New York. (*See* **Abolitionists**)

1848

27 APRIL: The French government abolishes slavery in all French colonies.

9–10 AUGUST: The Free Soil Party, composed of members of the Liberty Party and dissident, antislavery Whigs and Democrats, is founded at a convention in Buffalo, New York. The delegates nominate former president Martin Van Buren of New York as their presidential candidate. (*See* **U.S. Civil War**)

1849

SUMMER: Harriet Tubman escapes from slavery in Maryland but returns to the South nineteen times to lead more than 300 other slaves to freedom. (*See* **Means of Resistance**)

1850

4 SEPTEMBER: The Brazilian government adopts the Queiróz Law, ending the African slave trade to Brazil.

18 SEPTEMBER: As one of the provisions of the Compromise of 1850, Congress passes the Fugitive Slave Act.

1851

Black abolitionist William C. Nell publishes *Services of Colored Americans in the Wars of 1776 and 1812,* the first study of African American history.

Black abolitionists storm a courtroom in Baltimore, Maryland, to rescue fugitive slave Rachel Parker. (*See* **Abolitionists**)

15 FEBRUARY: Black abolitionists storm a courtroom in Boston, Massachusetts, to rescue fugitive slave Shadrach Minkins. (*See* **Abolitionists**)

11 SEPTEMBER: In Christiana, Pennsylvania, free blacks, determined to resist the Fugitive Slave Act, confront slave hunters. The blacks kill one white and wound three others.

1 OCTOBER: Black and white abolitionists storm a courtroom in Syracuse, New York, to rescue a fugitive slave. (*See* **Abolitionists**)

1852

Martin R. Delany publishes *The Condition, Elevation, Emigration and Destiny of the Colored People of the United States,* the first major exposition of black nationalism.

A group of Southern thinkers publishes *The Pro-Slavery Argument,* in which they offer a variety of justifications for slavery. (*See* **Christianity** *and* **Free Society**)

The government of Ecuador emancipates all the slaves under its jurisdiction.

1 JANUARY: All slaves in Colombia are freed.

20 MARCH: Harriet Beecher Stowe publishes her abolitionist novel *Uncle Tom's Cabin, Or Life Among the Lowly.* Originally serialized in the abolitionist newspaper *National Era* in 1851, *Uncle Tom's Cabin* sells more than 1.2 million copies by December 1853. The novel offers an emotional account of the brutality of slavery that prompts many in the North finally to adopt an antislavery posture. (*See* **Abolitionists**)

1853

JANUARY: Northup is freed from slavery.

1854

Slavery apologist George Fitzhugh of Port Royal, Virginia, publishes *Sociology for the South; or, the Failure of Free Society,* in which he not only defends slavery but denounces free society. (*See* **Free Society**)

Poet William J. Grayson of South Carolina publishes the didactic poem "The Hireling and the Slave" to counter *Uncle Tom's Cabin*. Like Fitzhugh, Grayson emphasizes the benefits of chattel slavery in the South and the horrors of "wage slavery" in the North. (*See* **Free Society**)

Connecticut and Rhode Island enact personal liberty laws designed to circumvent the federal Fugitive Slave Act of 1850.

The program of gradual emancipation undertaken in Venezuela is complete.

All slaves in Paraguay are freed.

The Portuguese government emancipates all slaves on royal estates in the Portuguese Empire.

24 MAY: U.S. deputy marshals apprehend fugitive slave Antony Burns in Boston.

30 MAY: President Franklin Pierce signs the Kansas-Nebraska Act into law, thereby repealing the Missouri Compromise and opening Northern territory to slavery. (*See* **U.S. Civil War**)

3 JUNE: Two thousand federal troops escort Burns through the streets of Boston and return him to slavery in the South.

1855

Frederick Douglass publishes *My Bondage and My Freedom.* (*See* **Abolitionists**)

Maine, Massachusetts, and Michigan enact personal liberty laws.

1856

The Portuguese government frees all slaves who belong to town councils, religious brotherhoods, and churches.

22 FEBRUARY: Members of the newly formed Republican Party hold their first national convention in Pittsburgh, Pennsylvania.

17–19 JUNE: Delegates to the Republican nominating convention select John C. Frémont of California as their first presidential candidate.

1857

Proslavery advocate George Fitzhugh publishes *Cannibals All!: or Slaves Without Masters,* in which he argues that free workers ("wage slaves") of the North are in a worse condition than the slaves of the South. Fitzhugh concludes that capitalism is a more brutal and exploitive system than slavery. (*See* **Free Society**)

6 MARCH: The U.S. Supreme Court renders its decision in the case of *Dred Scott* v. *Sanford,* denying American citizenship to blacks and

reconfirming that Northern territory is open to slavery, even in those locales where the law prohibits slavery. (*See* **Legal Definition**)

1858

Kansas and Wisconsin enact personal liberty laws.

14 APRIL: Fugitive slave Archy Lee wins his freedom in court and moves to Victoria, British Columbia.

AUGUST–OCTOBER: Senatorial debates between incumbent Stephen A. Douglas and challenger Abraham Lincoln take place in Illinois; the questions of slavery and racial equality figure prominently.

SEPTEMBER: Several hundred students from Oberlin College, along with one of their professors and local abolitionists, rescue fugitive slave John Price in Wellington, Ohio, and help him escape to Canada. (*See* **Abolitionists**)

1859

The *Clothilde,* the last vessel to carry slaves to the United States, weighs anchor at Mobile Bay, Alabama. (*See* **Middle Passage** *and* **Transatlantic Slave Trade**)

16–17 OCTOBER: Abolitionist John Brown attacks the federal arsenal at Harpers Ferry, Virginia, in the company of thirteen white men and five blacks. (*See* **Abolitionists**)

2 DECEMBER: Virginia authorities hang Brown at Charlestown, Virginia.

16 DECEMBER: John Copeland and Shields Green, two black members of Brown's troops, are hanged at Charlestown. Two black members of Brown's force died in the original assault and another escaped.

1860

The government of the Netherlands abolishes slavery in all Dutch colonial possessions, though the act does not become effective until 1863.

6 NOVEMBER: Republican candidate Abraham Lincoln of Illinois is elected president of the United States. (*See* **U.S. Civil War**)

20 DECEMBER: South Carolina secedes from the Union. (*See* **U.S. Civil War**)

1861

Writing under the name Linda Brent, Harriet Jacobs publishes *Incidents in the Life of a Slave Girl, Written By Herself,* in which she presents a chilling account of the exploitation that female slaves face.

9 JANUARY: Mississippi secedes from the Union. (*See* **U.S. Civil War**)

10 JANUARY: Florida secedes from the Union. (*See* **U.S. Civil War**)

11 JANUARY: Alabama secedes from the Union. (*See* **U.S. Civil War**)

19 JANUARY: Georgia secedes from the Union. (*See* **U.S. Civil War**)

26 JANUARY: Louisiana secedes from the Union. (*See* **U.S. Civil War**)

1 FEBRUARY: Texas secedes from the Union. (*See* **U.S. Civil War**)

4–9 FEBRUARY: Southern delegates meet at Montgomery, Alabama, to form the Confederate States of America. (*See* **U.S. Civil War**)

9 FEBRUARY: Delegates to the Montgomery Convention elect former senator Jefferson Davis of Mississippi as provisional president of the Confederacy. (*See* **U.S. Civil War**)

4 MARCH: Lincoln is inaugurated as the sixteenth president of the United States. He declares his intentions to preserve the Union and not to interfere with slavery in the Southern states. (*See* **U.S. Civil War**)

21 MARCH: Vice President of the Confederacy, Alexander H. Stephens of Georgia, delivers his famous "Cornerstone Speech" in which he declares that the Confederacy "rests upon the great truth that the Negro is no equal to the white man, that slavery, subordination to the superior race, is a natural and normal condition." (*See* **U.S. Civil War**)

12 APRIL: Confederate forces bombard Fort Sumter in Charleston Harbor, South Carolina, beginning the Civil War.

15 APRIL: Lincoln calls for 75,000 volunteers to suppress what he characterizes the Southern "rebellion."

17 APRIL: Virginia secedes from the Union.

6 MAY: Arkansas and Tennessee secede from the Union.

20 MAY: North Carolina secedes from the Union.

6 AUGUST: The U.S. Congress passes the first Confiscation Act, authorizing the freeing of slaves formerly employed to aid the Confederate cause in areas under control of the Union Army.

30 AUGUST: General Frémont frees the slaves of Confederate supporters in Missouri. Lincoln revokes the order.

1862

The program of gradual emancipation undertaken in Peru in 1825 is complete.

22 FEBRUARY: Davis is inaugurated as president of the Confederacy.

13 MARCH: The U.S. Congress prohibits Union military commanders from capturing fugitive slaves and returning them to their masters.

MARCH: The National Freedman's Relief Association is formed in New York City to help former slaves make the transition to freedom. (*See* **Emancipation**)

16 APRIL: The U.S. Congress outlaws slavery in Washington, D.C., and appropriates $1 million to compensate slave owners and $100,000 to fund the resettlement of the freed blacks in Liberia, Haiti, or other locations.

9 MAY: General David Hunter frees slaves in South Carolina, Georgia, and Florida.

19 MAY: Lincoln rescinds Hunter's order and urges the Border States of Delaware, Kentucky, Maryland, and Missouri to adopt a program of gradual emancipation.

19 JUNE: The U.S. Congress prohibits slavery in all federal territories.

17 JULY: The U.S. Congress passes the second Confiscation Act, granting freedom to all slaves whose masters have supported the Confederacy.

22 JULY: Lincoln submits a preliminary draft of the Emancipation Proclamation to his cabinet but decides to wait for a major Union victory before making it public.

14 AUGUST: Lincoln meets with a group of black leaders at the White House and urges them to adopt a program of colonization to Central America or Africa for blacks.

22 SEPTEMBER: Lincoln issues a preliminary draft of the Emancipation Proclamation shortly after the Union victory at the Battle of Antietam in Maryland.

11 OCTOBER: To quell unrest among the slaves, the Confederate Congress issues the "Twenty-Slave Rule," exempting slave owners who own twenty or more slaves from military service. The rule prompts many Southerners to characterize the conflict "as a rich man's war but a poor man's fight."

23 DECEMBER: President Davis signs an executive order mandating that black Union troops and their white commanders when captured are not to be treated as prisoners of war but as criminals.

1863

1 JANUARY: The Emancipation Proclamation goes into effect, freeing all the slaves in states still in rebellion against the United States and not yet under the control of Federal troops. It does not apply to the Border States. (*See* **Emancipation**)

26 JANUARY: Secretary of War Edwin M. Stanton authorizes the governor of Massachusetts, John A. Andrew, to organize a company of black troops. The 54th Massachusetts Volunteers, under the command of Colonel Robert Gould Shaw, becomes the first black regiment raised in the North.

16 MARCH: Stanton establishes the American Freedman's Inquiry Commission to investigate conditions among the freed slaves and to recommend how best to look after their welfare. (*See* **Emancipation**)

1 MAY: The Confederate Congress identifies black Union troops and their white officers as criminals. Captured black solders will either be executed or enslaved; captured white officers will be executed.

1 JULY: The Netherlands abolishes slavery in the Dutch West Indies and Suriname, though the government requires freed slaves in Suriname to work as wage laborers on the plantations for an additional ten years. The Netherlands also abolishes the slave trade and prohibits Dutch citizens from participating in it.

13–17 JULY: Draft Riots take place in New York City. White mobs display virulent antiblack sentiments in one of the bloodiest race riots in the history of the United States. The riots result in 1,200 deaths, most of them blacks.

18 JULY: The 54th Massachusetts Volunteers make their famous assault on Fort Wagner in Charleston harbor, South Carolina. The event is later commemorated in the film *Glory* (1989).

1864

12 APRIL: During the Battle of Fort Pillow near Memphis, Tennessee, Confederates, under the command of General Nathan Bedford Forrest, massacre 300 black solders, many after they surrender.

8 NOVEMBER: Lincoln is elected to a second term.

1865

11 JANUARY: General Robert E. Lee, commander of the Army of Northern Virginia, recommends that the Confederacy begin to arm black troops.

16 JANUARY: U.S. General William T. Sherman issues Special Field Order No. 15, which grants forty-acre plots on the sea islands of South Carolina, Georgia, and Florida as well as abandoned rice fields thirty miles inland from the coast to be distributed to freed slaves. (*See* **Emancipation**)

3 MARCH: The U.S. Congress authorizes the creation of the Bureau of Refugees, Freedmen, and Abandoned Lands. The first public welfare agency in American history, the Freedmen's Bureau is empowered to aid the former slaves to make the transition to freedom. (*See* **Emancipation**)

13 MARCH: The Confederate government authorizes the use of male slaves between the ages of eighteen and forty-five to fill out the ranks of the army. The war ends before any slaves can be inducted into Confederate service.

9 APRIL: Lee surrenders to Grant at Appomattox Court House, Virginia, effectively ending the Civil War.

14 APRIL: Actor John Wilkes Booth shoots Lincoln while he is attending the play "Our American Cousin" at the Ford Theater in Washington, D. C.

15 APRIL: Lincoln dies. Vice President Andrew Johnson of Tennessee becomes the seventeenth president of the United States.

16 SEPTEMBER: Republican Congressman Thaddeus Stevens of Pennsylvania urges the confiscation of all the estates belonging to former Confederate leaders for redistribution to adult male freedmen. Stevens's proposal fails. (*See* **Emancipation**)

18 DECEMBER: The Thirteenth Amendment abolishing slavery is incorporated into the Constitution. (*See* **Emancipation**)

1867

The Middle Passage, in operation since 1502, ends when the last shipload of African slaves arrives in Cuba. (*See* **Middle Passage** *and* **Transatlantic Slave Trade**)

1869

The Legislative Assembly of Portugal frees all remaining slaves in the Portuguese colonies.

1870

23 JUNE: The Spanish government enacts the Moret Law, which begins the process of gradual emancipation in Cuba.

1871

28 SEPTEMBER: The Brazilian government enacts the Rio Buanco Law (Law of Free Birth), which begins the process of gradual emancipation in Brazil.

1873

The Spanish government abolishes slavery in Puerto Rico.

1880

The Spanish government enacts the Law of Patronato, which begins the process of gradual emancipation in the Spanish colonies to take place over a period of eight years.

7 SEPTEMBER: The Brazilian Anti-Slavery Society is founded in Rio de Janeiro. (*See* **Abolitionists**)

1883

Brazilian abolitionist Joaquin de Araujo publishes *O abolicionismo* (Abolitionism), which galvanizes public opinion in Brazil against slavery. Social and economic progress, Nabuco asserts, are possible only under a system of free labor.

AUGUST: Nabuco, along with other Brazilian abolitionists, including André Rebouças, José do Patrocinó, and Joaquin Serra, found the Abolitionist Confederation and call for an immediate end to slavery in Brazil. (*See* **Abolitionists**)

1885

The Brazilian government enacts the Sexagenarian Law, freeing all slaves more than sixty-five years of age.

1886

The Spanish government abolishes slavery in Cuba and all other colonial possessions where the institution remains.

1888

13 MAY: The Brazilian government ends slavery with the passage of the *Lei Aurea* (Golden Law). The act frees approximately 750,000 Brazilian slaves.

1891

13 MAY: The Brazilian government orders the destruction of all documents relating to slavery.

ABOLITIONISTS

Were abolitionists effective in their opposition to slavery?

Viewpoint: Yes. The sustained moral and political opposition to slavery that came from abolitionist groups was instrumental in ending slavery.

Viewpoint: No. The achievements of abolitionists in Britain notwithstanding, abolitionists in the Americas accomplished little because of the economic need for slavery, racism, and divisions within the movement.

Only toward the end of the eighteenth century did slavery become a serious moral, intellectual, social, and political problem for Europeans and Americans. Beginning in the 1750s, Quakers such as Anthony Benezet and John Woolman articulated a cogent and compelling religious critique of slavery. By encouraging absolute tyranny in the master and abject subservience in the slave, they declared, slavery corrupted the manners and morals of all connected with it. Simply put, slavery was incompatible with the gospel and could not be reconciled with the biblical injunction to "love thy neighbor as thyself." Although these ideas had little influence in the British North American colonies, the American quest for independence and liberty that began a few decades later also seemed incompatible with, and discredited by, the continued existence of slavery. Similarly, the emphasis of French revolutionaries on the rights of man and citizen prompted efforts to end slavery and the slave trade. As a result, the National Convention abolished slavery in the French Caribbean on 4 February 1794, though Napoleon Bonaparte reinstated it in 1802. Not until 1848 did the French government at last eliminate slavery in its Caribbean and African colonies.

The success of British abolitionists was more dramatic. British abolitionism received early inspiration and support from the decision of Lord Chief Justice Baron Mansfield (William Murray) in the celebrated *Somerset* case (1772). Mansfield ruled it illegal to return to bondage James Somerset, a slave from Virginia who had travelled with his owner to England and left his service, thereby demolishing the legitimacy of slavery under British law. By the late 1770s, Quakers had begun to expel members who participated in the slave trade and then banned those owners who refused to free their slaves. In 1787 Quaker abolitionists were instrumental in creating the Society for the Abolition of the Slave Trade and in launching a massive campaign to petition Parliament to abolish slavery throughout the British Empire. Not even the most ardent and optimistic abolitionists were prepared for the response. The initial effort generated one hundred petitions that contained approximately sixty thousand signatures. The outbreak of the French Revolution (1789) and war with France (1793) dampened public enthusiasm for abolition. Yet, despite these temporary setbacks, the abolitionist cause steadily gained momentum among the English people and in Parliament until passage of the Abolition of Slavery Act, or Emancipation Act, of 1833.

Abolitionism progressed more slowly in the Americas. Historians such as Frank Tannenbaum and Gilberto Freyre once attributed the death of slavery in Latin America and the Caribbean, except for Saint Domingue (Haiti), to old age, by which they meant that emancipation took place with little confrontation or conflict. A younger generation of historians challenged that conclusion, maintaining instead that a protracted and bitter struggle preceded abolition. The Enlightenment ideals of liberty, reason, and justice; the liberal politics that emerged during the Age of Revolution and the Napoleonic Wars (1789–1815); the efforts of Great Britain and subsequently the United States to outlaw and suppress the international slave trade; the decline of the export sector; the rise in the cost of slaves; and the eruption of several bloody slave rebellions all contributed to the demise of slavery throughout Latin America and the Caribbean. Although their ranks were small, abolitionists kept sustained pressure on various colonial, national, and metropolitan governments, denouncing the inefficiency and immorality of slavery. Under the leadership of Joaquim Aurelio Baretto Nabuco de Araujo, for example, militant abolitionists in Brazil during the 1880s encouraged slaves to run away, helped them to elude capture, and provided them with weapons. In time, economic and political pressure, combined with the growing threat of violent insurrection, convinced politicians and slaveholders alike that slavery had to end.

In the United States, opponents of slavery confronted an entrenched proslavery faction with enough authority in the federal government to protect its interests. Racial prejudice also inhibited the development of an antislavery movement, where the objective became not merely to end slavery but to return freed blacks to Africa. Yet, these impediments notwithstanding, antislavery sentiment took root and grew. By the early nineteenth century, in fact, most Americans living north of the Mason-Dixon Line could plausibly have described themselves as harboring such views. The majority certainly regarded slavery as morally wrong even if at the same time they saw it as ineradicable. The abolitionists were different. They sought the immediate elimination of slavery without compensation to the slaveholders and advocated the incorporation of blacks as equals into American society. For their efforts the abolitionists met with hostility and violence from their fellow citizens. Southern determination to justify and preserve slavery and the mounting concerns over its extension into the Western territories proved more effective than abolitionist argument and invective in focusing and mobilizing Northern resistance to "the Slave Power." When military exigencies transformed a war for Union into a war against slavery, federal troops, whether intentionally or not, completed the work the abolitionists had begun.

Viewpoint:
Yes. The sustained moral and political opposition to slavery that came from abolitionist groups was instrumental in ending slavery.

In the modern context the word *abolitionist* has entirely positive connotations. One impulsively associates the word with the antebellum reformers who fought against popular racism, apathy, and proslavery sentiments to destroy slavery within American society, to secure freedom for America's black population, and to guarantee for them the rights of citizenship. Contemporaries, however, rarely viewed abolitionists with charity. At best, they deemed them radical firebrands, and at worst, criminals intent upon the destruction of the Union. Northerners and Southerners alike regarded abolitionist rhetoric with dismay and alarm. During the 1830s and 1840s the expression of antislavery sentiments was a popular political expedient, but abolitionism was seen as the language of madmen. By the 1850s, however, abolitionists managed to find a secure niche in the national debate concerning slavery, tailoring their agenda to correspond to Northern concerns for "free labor, free soil, and free men." The exigencies of war and the political maneuvering of the Republican Party during the Civil War (1861–1865) and Reconstruction (1865–1877) ultimately advanced the abolitionists' primary objectives, which were to end slavery and to guarantee civil and political rights to freed blacks.

Abolitionists were a minority of the population and represented a small portion of popular sentiment. The origins of their movement derived from the fundamental philosophy of the early republic, most particularly the ideology of the rights of man, and from the millennialism and perfectionism associated with evangelical Christianity. Defense of the rights of man was at the core of eighteenth-century enlightened philosophy and social thought, and it subsequently became the keystone of the ideology of the American Revolution (1775–1783). The creation of a new nation predicated upon these principles seemed incompatible with slaveholding. Secular manumission societies appeared in America as early as 1775, and by the 1790s many state and local antislavery societies emerged in the middle and upper Atlantic states. By 1804, states from Pennsylvania northward had provisions in their constitutions for the abolition or eventual eradication of slavery. As early as 1807, however, it was clear that the South would not follow the same commitment to free labor.

By the 1830s many evangelical Protestants agreed that the reign of God on Earth, marked by one thousand years of peace and prosperity,

would be an actual event in history that occurred before the Second Coming of Christ and the Last Judgment. Belief in the millennium assured many Americans that a perfect world was possible, but that vision also contrasted starkly with the imperfections of antebellum society. Evangelical clergymen such as Charles Grandison Finney told Americans that they could, and indeed that they must, help God to usher in his earthly kingdom. Millennialism and perfectionism thus spurred reformers into action, convincing them that before God's rule on earth could be established, a terrible battle between good and evil had to ensue. No vice more than slavery, and the growing sectional turmoil and controversy that slavery was generating, represented the disorder and corruption that threatened to overwhelm American society. Slavery seemed a clear repudiation of both the enlightened commitment to the rights of man and the Christian principle of love. Having long asserted that America occupied a special place in God's design, antebellum reformers now intoned that slavery prevented America from realizing its providential mission. It was thus all the more urgent that America be purged of its sins. The fate and future of humanity depended upon such a plan of action.

Although Northern states were clearly on course by the early nineteenth century to eliminate slavery from within their borders, the concepts of antislavery, and especially abolitionism, troubled many people in the North as well as the South. The majority of persons who identified themselves as opposing slavery were not, in fact, abolitionists. The ideology of antislavery came to suggest the curtailment of the slave trade, the containment of slavery in areas where it already existed, and the prohibition of its expansion. Antislavery sentiments were based on the political and economic issues of the day and were more often than not concerned with the advancement of free white labor. Slaves were widely understood to be property, and inherent in the argument that men were entitled to the inalienable rights to life, liberty, and the pursuit of happiness was the implication that a man's property was sacrosanct; no enlightened government could deprive a citizen of his property, nor could it encourage insurrectionary activities that would culminate in that effect. Since eighteenth- and nineteenth-century property rights were much better defined and recognized than human rights—that is, since people then did not as readily separate human from property rights—most Americans were unwilling to ignore the huge capital investment that Southerners had in their slave property. Secular antislavery societies sought to contain slavery on the basis that it was unfair competition to free labor, not because it was morally offensive.

Abolitionists represented a radical derivative of the antislavery movement. Only 1 percent of the Northern population identified with the abolitionist cause, which insisted on making slavery illegal in the United States and demanded its immediate elimination. The basis of their argument was that slavery was cruel and immoral and that individuals who engaged in the practice were evil and sinned against both their fellowmen and God. The most controversial aspects of the abolitionists' stance were that slavery violated the human rights of the slave; that all slaves should be immediately freed without compensation for their former masters; and that as freed people, blacks should enjoy all the rights and privileges of American citizens, including the right to vote and to hold public office. Their most inflammatory speeches rejected the idea of repatriating freed slaves to colonies in Africa but instead encouraged the notion that blacks and whites could live in America as equals. These messages are especially remarkable within the context of social views held by the abolitionists themselves. The movement's leadership was white and middle class with a strong moral agenda. A few former slaves, such as Frederick Douglass, were permitted a voice within the platform of the group, but the abolitionist leadership was largely of the opinion that although slavery was morally wrong, black Americans were still incapable of ending their own enslavement.

Masthead of William Lloyd Garrison's abolitionist newspaper

(Boston Athenaeum)

ABOLITIONISTS

To succeed in their quest to abolish slavery, the abolitionists had to overcome the swell of popular contempt that usually greeted their message. The public's general disposition toward property rights, combined with prevailing racist attitudes toward blacks, made Americans a poor audience for the abolitionist gospel. In the 1830s abolitionists were regarded as such troublemakers that their meetings were raided, attacked, and in some cases, outlawed. Their arguments about the immorality of slavery did not resonate with most Americans, who could never countenance interfering with the property of others, even if that property consisted of human beings. In 1835 several abolitionist conventions were violently closed down in Northern cities, and several Northern states enacted gag orders prohibiting public abolitionist lectures and demonstrations. Even Congressional support for their plans was nonexistent. Massachusetts representative John Quincy Adams, Kentucky senator Henry Clay, and Massachusetts senator Daniel Webster all had strong words for the abolitionists, accusing them of conspiring to disrupt the Union by using incendiary propaganda, by not supporting the colonization of freed blacks, by fostering the idea that blacks and whites could live amicably together, and by plotting to deprive slave owners of millions of dollars worth of slave property.

The difficulties abolitionists faced throughout the 1830s were intensified by the extraordinary announcements made by their chief spokesman, William Lloyd Garrison, who was explicitly in favor of black enfranchisement. In the American Anti-Slavery Society's Declaration of Sentiments of 1833, he proposed immediate abolition, equal protection under the law for blacks, and equal opportunity in the workplace. Garrison's extremist views did not initially play on the nation's heartstrings and ultimately created a permanent rift within the antislavery movement that left the abolitionists isolated from a majority that favored a gradualist approach. During the next twenty years Garrison redefined the abolitionist position from a purely moral and self-serving argument to a compelling case against the antidemocratic swell of slave-based power that bloated the South and that allegedly advanced regional concerns at the expense of national interests. This transformation was bolstered by the territorial conflicts of the 1840s and 1850s, which conveniently forced the problem of slavery upon the national consciousness, shifting the slavery question from its traditional position as a purely moral issue into the highly charged forum of political and economic debate. Once entwined with the explosive issues of sectionalism, free soil, and free labor, abolition found the broad base of support it had always lacked.

How did these abolitionists, a minority, succeed in ending slavery, especially when abolitionism was widely regarded as an implausible and troublesome solution? Influential persons and groups had no interest in the cause, and many feared its consequences should it succeed. Immediate emancipation was too drastic for other antislavery groups to consider, and many Americans were astonished at, and disturbed by, the humanitarian and civil rights concessions for blacks that abolitionists were willing to entertain. Mainstream religious sects shared group culpability in avoiding the slavery issue or in not actively trying to eliminate it. Politicians who wanted to enjoy long careers in Washington did not take up the abolitionist banner. Though many Americans would have agreed that slavery was probably bad, most also believed that it was better for everyone that the mass of the nation's black population remained in the South.

Nevertheless, despite these impediments, abolitionists continued to press their message onto the American people with a persistence that in part accounts for their eventual success. During the 1850s they arrested national attention through highly dramatic literature and actions. Harriet Beecher Stowe's *Uncle Tom's Cabin* (1852) elicited tremendous sympathy for the slaves' plight and attracted a huge number of readers in Europe and the United States. For many, the novel marked their first acquaintance with the more distasteful aspects of slave life. The violence of John Brown's raid in Harpers Ferry (1859) also riveted the nation's attention to sensational acts committed in the name of abolition. Through Stowe's novel, a variety of abolitionist tracts and pamphlets, and the exploitation of Brown's raid and other violent events, abolitionists seized a highly visible position within the panoply of American reform movements to become at last *the* reform movement. Through their vigilance, the effort to reform American society came to mean reforming the slave South. Under Garrison's leadership, the abolitionists effectively portrayed slaveholders as indolent aristocrats whose moral and economic philosophy was at odds with the national interest. This strategy changed the abolitionists' image from highbrow moral handwringers to the defenders of republicanism and democracy. Their success hinged on linking their cause to the hot political issues of the day, free soil and free labor, and hitching their hopes on the rising Republican Party.

This connection was further strengthened when ordinary persons developed an appetite for the abolitionist position, which they had previously found distasteful. As the abolitionist cause was swept up into the agenda of the Republican Party, Northerners showed signs of shedding some of their hostility toward abolition, while Southerners felt more and more threatened by abolitionist gains. Stowe had portrayed Southerners as an unsavory mix of indifferent, self-absorbed, barbaric, and homicidal slave owners. Slaveholders worried that the increasing preeminence of the abolitionist message would encourage slaves to run away, or worse, to rise up against them. The enemies of slavery had already demonstrated, in Kansas and at Harpers Ferry, a willingness to use violence as a means to prevent the spread of slavery. Abolitionists shrewdly took advantage of the realities of the late 1850s; the platform of the Republican Party was incompatible with the South's agenda, and Abraham Lincoln's election to the presidency of the United States in 1860 made many Southerners feel politically isolated, alienated, and vulnerable. Agitated by an increasingly poor public image, and on the defensive, Southerners made hasty and ill-conceived policy decisions based on real and imagined attacks inflicted by the abolitionist camp.

Ultimately, it was through war that abolitionists fully realized their goals. Although many abolitionists were morally opposed to war, they quickly came to understand the enormous utility of the conflict. Abolitionists preached that the war was vital to breaking the slave power and that the Union's survival and salvation necessitated a suppression of the insurrection of arrogant Southerners who deliberately threatened free institutions by their willful indulgence in slavery. If the slave power was to be stopped, then slavery had to be eliminated. Northern sentiments toward emancipation were also reinforced with the Union defeat at the First Battle of Bull Run (1861), which led to much finger-pointing about the amount of damage that slave labor could inflict upon the Union. Even with this example, abolitionists recognized that Northern support for their agenda was never solid. As Northerners wavered in their tolerance for emancipation, abolitionists reinforced the concept that Confederate strength lay in the slave labor that supported it, and that labor pool consequently gave the Confederacy a decided advantage in the conflict.

It was ultimately beneficial for the federal government to adopt a policy of emancipation, which was a delicate undertaking. Lincoln risked alienating many people in the Border States as well as in his own party with his move toward emancipation, and he was careful to make the distinction between emancipation and equality. Whatever qualms Lincoln had about pursuing this program, it was good foreign policy. The Emancipation Proclamation (1863) placed the Union war effort on the moral high ground in the eyes of the British and other Europeans, as it

made the fight seem less about political and economic supremacy and more about humanitarian concerns. By the time Lincoln issued the preliminary Proclamation, the abolitionists and Radical Republicans had made common cause, although different motives and purposes impelled them to rally around abolition. Conferring full civil rights upon emancipated slaves served two divergent purposes. First, it represented a major step in the fulfillment of the abolitionist agenda. Second, it was also the weapon of choice for Radical Republicans in their quest to establish a firm grip on the politics of the South after the war.

In the aftermath of the Civil War the first measure of the abolitionists' success became apparent. The Thirteenth (1865), Fourteenth (1868), and Fifteenth (1870) Amendments and the Civil Rights Act (1866) offer a remarkable testimony to their altering the American consciousness and outlook. The Thirteenth Amendment articulates what abolitionists had asserted for more than thirty years: that slavery had no legal status in the United States and that anyone forced into bondage was deprived of their natural rights. Although this amendment did not concern the legal condition of freed people, the abolitionists and Radical Republicans intended to make African Americans citizens. Early implications of this intention appear in the Freedmen's Bureau Act (1865), which provided for abandoned lands in rebel states to be set aside for every male citizen, including blacks.

The Civil Rights Act and the Fourteenth Amendment were passed in response to the independent actions of Andrew Johnson, who became president after the assassination of Lincoln in 1865, and the enactment of Black Codes in the South. An attempt to protect the civil rights of all citizens, this legislation was explicitly concerned with the citizenship of the freedmen. The Fourteenth Amendment emphasizes the state's role in defining and ensuring the rights of citizenship, asserting that a state may not abridge the privileges or immunities of citizens and that Congressional representation would be proportionally reduced in any state that withheld suffrage to males twenty-one and older, but it did not state explicitly that blacks had the right to vote. The Fifteenth Amendment was subsequently required to assert that no citizen's right to vote would be denied or abridged "on account of race, color, or previous condition of servitude." By 1869 the abolitionists had succeeded beyond their wildest hopes.

In defining what was wrong about slavery, they had been instrumental in the destruction of the institution. Shrewdly changing the presentation of their message to fit evolving perceptions and circumstances, they managed to align themselves with the tide of popular opinion about

GALLING FETTERS OF TYRANNY

In December 1833 the American Anti-Slavery Society, representing several abolitionist groups, met in Philadelphia and issued a declaration written by William Lloyd Garrison. Portions of that document appear below:

But those, for whose emancipation we are striving,—constituting at the present time at least one-sixth part of our countrymen,—are recognised by the laws, and treated by their fellow beings, as marketable commodities—as goods and chattels—as brute beasts;—are plundered daily of the fruits of their toil without redress;—really enjoy no constitutional nor legal protection from licentious and murderous outrages upon their persons;—are ruthlessly torn asunder—the tender babe from the arms of its frantic mother—the heart-broken wife from her weeping husband—at the caprice or pleasure of irresponsible tyrants;—and, for the crime of having a dark complexion, suffer the pangs of hunger, the infliction of stripes, and the ignominy of brutal servitude. They are kept in heathenish darkness by laws expressly enacted to make their instruction a criminal offence.

These are the prominent circumstances in the condition of more than TWO MILLIONS of our people, the proof of which may be found in the thousands of indisputable facts, and in the laws of the slaveholding States.

Hence we maintain—

That no man has a right to enslave or imbrute his brother—to hold or acknowledge him, for one moment, as a piece of merchandise—to keep back his hire by fraud—or to brutalize his mind by denying him the means of intellectual, social and moral improvement.

The right to enjoy liberty is inalienable. . . . Every man has a right to his own body—to the products of his own labor—to the protection of law—and to the common advantages of society. It is piracy to buy or steal a native African, and subject him to servitude. Surely the sin is as great to enslave an AMERICAN as an AFRICAN.

Therefore we believe and affirm—

That there is no difference, *in principle,* between the African slave trade and American slavery;

That every American citizen, who retains a human being in involuntary bondage, is a MAN-STEALER;

That the slaves ought instantly to be set free, and brought under the protection of law; . . .

That all those laws which are now in force, admitting the right of slavery, are therefore before God utterly null and void; being an audacious usurpation of the Divine prerogative, a daring infringement on the law of nature, a base overthrow of the very foundations of the social compact, a complete extinction of all the relations, endearments and obligations of mankind, and a presumptuous transgression of all the holy commandments—and that therefore they ought to be instantly abrogated.

That all persons of color who possess the qualifications which are demanded of others, ought to be admitted forthwith to the enjoyment of the same privileges, and the exercise of the same prerogatives, as others; and that the paths of preferment, of wealth, and of intelligence, should be opened as widely to them as to persons of a white complexion.

We maintain that no compensation should be given to the planters emancipating their slaves—

Because it would be a surrender of the great fundamental principle that man cannot hold property in man;

Because SLAVERY IS A CRIME, AND THEREFORE IT IS NOT AN ARTICLE TO BE SOLD;

Because the holders of slaves are not the just proprietors of what they claim;—freeing the slaves is not depriving them of property, but restoring it to the right owner;—it is not wronging the master, but righting the slave—restoring him to himself; . . .

Because if compensation is given at all, it should be given to the outraged and guiltless slaves, and not to those who have plundered and abused them.

We regard, as delusive, cruel and dangerous, any scheme of expatriation which pretends to aid, either directly or indirectly, in the emancipation of the slaves, or to be a substitute for the immediate and total abolition of slavery.

We fully and unanimously recognise the sovereignty of each State, to legislate exclusively on the subject of the slavery which is tolerated within its limits. We concede that Congress, *under the present national compact,* has no right to interfere with any of the slave States, in relation to this momentous subject.

But we maintain that Congress has a right, and is solemnly bound, to suppress the domestic slave trade between the several States, and to abolish slavery in those portions of our territory which the Constitution has placed under its exclusive jurisdiction.

We also maintain that there are, at the present time, the highest obligations resting upon the people of the free States, to remove slavery by moral and political action, as prescribed in the Constitution of the United States. They are now living under a pledge of their tremendous physical force to fasten the galling fetters of tyranny upon the limbs of millions in the southern States;—they are liable to be called at any moment to suppress a general insurrection of the slaves;—they authorise the slave owner to vote for three-fifths of his slaves as property, and thus enable him to perpetuate his oppression;—they support a standing army at the south for its protection;—and they seize the slave who has escaped into their territories, and send him back to be tortured by an enraged master or a brutal driver.

Source: The Liberator, *14 December 1833.*

ABOLITIONISTS

free labor, which they used to their advantage to strike a blow against slavery. Connecting with a cause that was integral to the Republican Party, they subsequently took advantage of factionalism between radicals and moderates. The Radical Republicans, many of whom sympathized with abolition and who were determined to break the power of the aristocratic slaveholders, executed the extreme abolitionist platform as their most effective weapon in the battle for political control of the South. Through this process, the abolitionists helped guide national policy toward the implementation and acceptance of emancipation. They supported essential legislation guaranteeing that slavery would be illegal in the United States and that the rights of freedmen would be defined and protected by the Constitution.

Their own assessment of their work was mixed. Garrison believed that the abolitionists had fully accomplished their objective, which was to end slavery. Boston reformer Wendell Phillips, president of the Anti-Slavery Society from 1865 to 1870, and others argued their work was not complete. C. L. Redmond, a black abolitionist, advised that continued vigilance was essential, as their work had only begun. Redmond perhaps understood better than most of his comrades that the majority of whites, in the North as well as in the South, did not accept, and were even hostile to, the extraordinary changes that had taken place since the end of the war. Arguably, the abolitionists did not finish the mission they started, but they probably did the best they could. They advanced radical legislation in a highly divisive time and managed to do so without changing the hearts and minds of the majority of lawmakers who made their aspirations a reality.

—PAULA M. STATHAKIS,
CHARLOTTE, NORTH CAROLINA

Viewpoint:
No. The achievements of abolitionists in Britain notwithstanding, abolitionists in the Americas accomplished little because of the economic need for slavery, racism, and divisions within the movement.

Though inspired by the successes of their British counterparts, abolitionists in the Americas, particularly the United States, could not duplicate their accomplishments. Plagued either by weak central governments or decentralized federal political systems and powerful slaveholding elites, American abolitionists instead managed only to stir antislavery sentiment. By themselves, they did not have the influence to effect emancipation. Although their tireless efforts made people more aware of the injustice of slavery, abolitionists in the United States suffered from the same divisiveness that was troubling the rest of the nation in the decades before the Civil War (1861–1865).

The radical opponents of slavery found themselves hobbled by the U.S. Constitution (1787). As many historians have pointed out, the Founders studiously avoided the word *slavery* even as they accorded it legal status in the new country. With the inclusion of a fugitive slave clause, the acceptance of the Three-fifths Compromise, and the agreement to permit slave and free states equal representation in Congress, the Founders provided slaveholders with enough power to protect and sustain their interests. In fact, the only significant victory that the antislavery faction won was the agreement to end the international slave trade to the United States in 1808. For twenty years after the adoption of the Constitution, however, slaveholders could import as many slaves from Africa and the West Indies as they could afford. Whatever contradictions between liberty and slavery the American Revolution (1775–1783) exposed, in the years that followed, antislavery activity remained largely confined to Quaker communities, who kept up a continuous but ineffectual protest.

The situation in the United States was more complex than in Latin America and the Caribbean because slavery so glaringly violated the principles upon which the new nation had been created. In addition, slavery was essential to the economic, and hence the political and military, survival of the United States and was increasingly becoming the basis of social order in the South. Slavery gained new economic vitality and importance when cotton agriculture developed in the South during the early nineteenth century, spurred on by Eli Whitney's invention of the cotton gin (1793). The spread of cotton culture accelerated westward expansion into the Mississippi Delta region, which, in turn, prompted an increased demand for slaves. The importance of cotton to the health of the national economy strengthened the slaveholders' hand. Even if Americans denounced slavery, most were inclined to think it a necessary evil, indispensable to continued American economic growth and affluence. Such attitudes, combined with practical political and economic considerations that prevailed in the national government, inhibited the growth and influence of an abolitionist movement in the United States. Rather than wait for legislative and judicial victories to be won in Washington, the slaves instead carried out their own forms of limited protest in the guise of disobedience, escape, and on rare occasions, rebellion.

With the emergence of a militant abolitionist movement in the United States during the early 1830s, however, the opponents of slavery adopted a new, more aggressive, uncompromising, and combative approach, insisting, for example, on the immediate end of slavery without compensation to the slaveholders. The leading voice among the radical abolitionists was William Lloyd Garrison, a young man from Massachusetts who combined the brave heroism of a martyr with the blind zeal of a demagogue. Garrison could not have made his intentions and methods clearer than he did in an editorial that he wrote for the first issue of his abolitionist newspaper, *The Liberator,* which appeared in January 1831. Garrison announced: "I shall strenuously contend for the immediate enfranchisement of our slave population. . . . On this subject I do not wish to think, or speak, or write with moderation. . . . I am in earnest—I will not equivocate—I will not excuse—I will not retreat a single inch AND I WILL BE HEARD." Garrison's call to arms galvanized various antislavery groups throughout the country.

Even though Garrison's sensational methods and rhetoric awakened Northerners to the abuses of slavery (Southerners, of course, regarded Garrison as the most dangerous man in the United States and denounced his every word), they failed to convince many Americans that the slaveholders themselves were evil or that slavery could be done away with as easily as he seemed to think. Many in both in the North and the South were willing to admit that in principle slavery was wrong. Yet, at the same time, only a minority welcomed the prospect of granting social and political equality to free blacks. Before the Civil War and, indeed, for a long time afterward, most white Americans did not believe that blacks were, or could be, their equals. Even many who opposed slavery thought blacks incapable of the responsible exercise of liberty. If freed, these abolitionists believed, blacks ought therefore to be resettled in Africa or somewhere else outside the United States. They could never become American citizens and could never live in harmony with whites.

More than emancipation bothered many white Americans. Intricately bound to the debate over slavery were such troubling questions as states' rights, the jurisdiction of Congress and the courts, the threat of British influence in American domestic affairs, and the sanctity of property. If Garrison dismissed these questions with impatience and disdain, most of his contemporaries did not. The fate of the republic seemed at stake, and most thought it best to proceed with caution lest the cure for slavery become worse than the disease itself.

Thus, despite the repeated efforts of abolitionists to make slavery a question of conscience, most Northerners held themselves aloof from the antislavery movement or actively opposed it. Adding to the hostility toward the abolitionists and their cause was the evident refusal of Garrison and his followers to compromise, as the British abolitionists had done in order to achieve their goal. Many Americans found equally distasteful the religious fervor with which the abolitionists pursued and promoted their cause. They were, at the least, impolitic and impractical if not, as Southerners loudly proclaimed, disruptive and dangerous.

The growing conviction that abolitionism threatened the fragile unity of the country also troubled many Americans. Garrison did nothing to help his cause when he publicly burned a copy of the Constitution, which he denounced for its complicity with slavery, and declared that the North ought to secede from the South rather than remain any longer in a sinful union with slaveholders. As a consequence, Northern public opinion was at best suspicious of, and at worst antagonistic toward, abolitionist extremism.

The abolitionists soon faced mounting violence. Many abolitionist speakers were widely denounced and abused. Some, such as Elijah P. Lovejoy, editor of the *St. Louis Observer,* were killed. In Boston, Garrison himself narrowly escaped death when a mob put a rope around his neck and dragged him through the streets. Only the rope breaking spared his life. Mobs attacked abolitionists in other Northern communities, while Southerners burned antislavery pamphlets and made every effort to exclude them from the mails. Meanwhile, Congress adopted a gag rule (1836 to 1844) to avoid debating, or even acknowledging receipt of, antislavery petitions. These actions led many Americans to fear for their constitutional rights. Abolitionists exploited these fears, and antislavery sentiment began to spread. By 1838 more than 1,350 antislavery societies existed boasting almost 250,000 members, many of them women.

Still, these gains seemed incidental next to the divisions within the movement itself. Although abolitionists united in denouncing the efforts to colonize free blacks in Africa, they began to disagree among themselves as to how their goal of eliminating slavery might best be reached. Garrison initially believed that moral suasion was the only weapon. Abolitionists ought to persuade slaveholders of the error of their ways but not coerce them to give up their slaves. Garrison and his followers also argued that women should participate fully in all antislavery activities, but this breach of decorum and propriety disturbed more-conservative members. When in 1840 the Garrisonians passed a resolution permitting women full and equal participation in the American Anti-Slavery Society, a large faction led by the Tappan brothers withdrew from the organization and formed the American and Foreign Anti-Slavery Society. The abolitionists were never again united as a single movement.

Perhaps the most damaging conflict within the abolitionist movement took place not between radicals and conservatives but between white and black members. Besides having to deal with racial hostility and violence outside the movement, black abolitionists also faced racist condescension from their white colleagues. White abolitionists expected their black counterparts to follow, not to lead. When Frederick Douglass broke away from Garrison to start his own abolitionist newspaper, *The North Star*, Garrison vilified him for doing so, heightening the racial fault lines already weakening the movement.

In the United States it required a civil war for the abolitionists at last to achieve their goal. Politics and war, rather than a moral crusade, freed the slaves. Although the abolitionists at times were quite cognizant of the inherent paradox that existed between the reality of slavery and the principle of freedom, they also failed to notice the same tensions and contradictions at work in their own movement. Their impact on the history of American race relations continues to resonate, for good and ill. Although they spoke out against slavery, abolitionists, by according blacks a subordinate status, vitiated their claims to moral superiority in the short term and, in the long term, helped to maintain the second-class citizenship of African Americans for years to come.

–MEG GREENE,
MIDLOTHIAN, VIRGINIA

References

Herbert Aptheker, *Abolitionism: A Revolutionary Movement* (Boston: Twayne, 1989).

Gilbert Hobbs Barnes, *The Antislavery Impulse, 1830-1844* (New York & London: Appleton, 1933).

Robin Blackburn, *The Overthrow of Colonial Slavery, 1776-1848* (London & New York: Verso, 1988).

William E. Cain, ed., *William Lloyd Garrison and the Fight against Slavery: Selections from The Liberator* (Boston: Bedford Books of St. Martin's Press, 1995).

Robert Edgar Conrad, *The Destruction of Brazilian Slavery, 1856-1888* (Berkeley: University of California Press, 1972).

David Brion Davis, *The Problem of Slavery in the Age of Revolution, 1770-1823* (Ithaca, N.Y.: Cornell University Press, 1975).

Seymour Drescher, *Capitalism and Antislavery: British Mobilization in Comparative Perspective* (London: Macmillan, 1986).

Drescher, *Econocide: British Slavery in the Era of Abolition* (Pittsburgh: University of Pittsburgh Press, 1977).

Stanley Harrold, *The Abolitionists and the South, 1831-1861* (Lexington: University of Kentucky Press, 1995).

Albert Bushnell Hart, *Slavery and Abolition, 1831-1841* (New York & London: Harper, 1906).

Hugh Hawkins, ed., *The Abolitionists: Means, Ends, and Motivations* (Lexington, Mass.: Heath, 1972).

Aileen S. Kraditor, *Means and Ends in American Abolitionism: Garrison and His Critics on Strategy and Tactics, 1834-1850* (New York: Pantheon, 1969).

Richard S. Newman, *The Transformation of American Abolitionism: Fighting Slavery in the Early Republic* (Chapel Hill: University of North Carolina Press, 2002).

Benjamin Quarles, *Black Abolitionists* (New York: Oxford University Press, 1969).

C. Duncan Rice, *The Rise and Fall of Black Slavery* (New York: Harper & Row, 1975).

Rebecca J. Scott, *Slave Emancipation in Cuba: The Transition to Free Labor, 1860-1899* (Princeton: Princeton University Press, 1985).

Gerald Sorin, *Abolitionism: A New Perspective* (New York: Praeger, 1972).

James Brewer Stewart, *Holy Warriors: The Abolitionists and American Slavery* (New York: Hill & Wang, 1976).

Howard Temperley, *British Antislavery, 1833-1870* (London: Longman, 1972).

AFRICAN CULTURES

Did African slaves sustain their cultures in North America?

Viewpoint: Yes. Slaves in North America managed to retain important elements of their cultural lives and practices, such as kinship networks, family structures, and religious beliefs.

Viewpoint: No. The shock of capture and the horrors of the Middle Passage caused slaves to lose connection with their African past quickly.

Questions about the Americanization of African slaves have kindled a widespread and ongoing debate among scholars. In general, this debate has set those who believe that the slaves discarded their African past in the New World against those who believe that the slaves clung to their African culture and heritage. Sociologist E. Franklin Frazier, in *The Negro Family in the United States* (1939), was perhaps the first to argue that "probably never before in history has a people been so nearly completely stripped of its social heritage as the Negroes who were brought to America." The opposite view, that blacks had maintained their cultural inheritance, which anthropologist Melville J. Herskovits introduced during the 1940s, initially attracted few proponents. In the turbulent political climate of the 1960s, however, Herskovits's thesis received considerable support from Leftist and black nationalist historians eager to rediscover and commemorate African culture. The most extreme attempt to demonstrate the African character of slave life is that of Sterling Stuckey, who insists that slaves were almost untouched by Western influences and that their culture remained predominately African.

Although a disagreement inspired by such ideological passion is not likely soon to abate, the dichotomy between American adaptation and African survival is deceptive. According to historian Peter Kolchin, in *American Slavery, 1619–1877* (1993), "African identity among blacks was, ironically, a product of their presence in America." Africans came from different regions, spoke a variety of languages, and practiced an array of customs. Most did not think of themselves as Africans. In the New World, however, consciousness of a generalized African identity became more important as a means of uniting disparate peoples facing the same oppression and exploitation.

Viewpoint:
Yes. Slaves in North America managed to retain important elements of their cultural lives and practices, such as kinship networks, family structures, and religious beliefs.

Over the last several decades, historians have debated the question of how much African culture influenced African American slaves. To argue that Africans left behind their cultural beliefs and practices upon their arrival in America is, in effect, to say that they somehow created out of nothing a slave culture special to the United States. African slaves, in fact, brought with them many of their former cultures, rituals, and traditions and adapted these folkways as a means to survive their enslavement.

In *Slave Culture: Nationalist Theory and the Foundations of Black America* (1987), historian Sterling Stuckey argues that African American slaves were "basically African in culture," fundamentally untouched by European and American cultural influences. It is also important to remember that the African culture that came to the United States was not monolithic but was instead a diverse mosaic of different cultures, languages, religious beliefs, folkways, and even agricultural practices. Because of this variety a diverse assortment of African cultures took root, grew, and flourished in the soil of North America. Many tribal groups, however, shared some common geography, family and kinship patterns, moral values, and secular and sacred rituals.

The majority of African slaves brought to North America came from Central and West Africa, a vast area that included Senegambia, the Congo, Angola, Nigeria, Dahomey, Togo, the Gold Coast, and Sierra Leone. The geography of the region ranged from broad, open savannas to heavy forests and swamplands; most of the area had a subtropical climate. According to historian Daniel C. Littlefield, although many slaves had never encountered the cold and sometimes harsh winters that they would experience in North America, they were often better equipped than their masters to cope with the semitropical environment they found upon coming to Virginia, the Carolinas, and other Southern colonies. Slaves who hailed from Senegambia, for example, located at the western tip of Africa, found themselves living in a familiar climate when they arrived in South Carolina. Because of their ability to adapt, Senegambian slaves soon proved invaluable to Carolina rice planters struggling to establish farms and homesteads. These slaves also demonstrated their prowess at navigating

the inland waterways and swamps of coastal Carolina through the use of canoes and pirogues. Further, their knowledge of how to use nets and harpoons for fishing suggests that in important respects the slaves were capable of surviving in their new environment.

With the introduction of rice as a staple crop in the South Carolina and Georgia low country during the mid eighteenth century, plantation owners benefited from the knowledge of their slaves, many of whom came from rice-growing regions in Africa. With the help of the slaves, English colonists soon learned a variety of different agricultural practices including shifting hoe cultivation and, in some instances, crop rotation and fallowing.

Slaves from Senegambia also helped to develop the cattle industry in South Carolina. Again drawing on their experience in Africa, these slaves implemented the practices of free grazing, nighttime penning for protection, and seasonal burning to freshen pastures, all of which were routine practices in West Africa. Littlefield suggests that the word *cowboy*, which is usually associated with the Western plains during the late nineteenth century, might have originated in low country South Carolina and Georgia during the seventeenth century.

Some historians have argued that the African slaves in the Carolinas might have had an easier time psychologically in preserving their cultural identity and heritage because they were more likely to come into contact with large numbers of people from their own, and related, ethnic groups and because they had comparatively little contact with whites. This assertion was certainly true of the Senegambians, who were preferred slaves because of their skills, knowledge, and stamina. Being thrown together allowed slaves from different groups to establish a network of moral, spiritual, and cultural support. The greatest number of Africanisms, the cultural remnants from Africa in North America, persisted among slaves in the Carolina low country. The oldest surviving examples are found among the residents of the sea islands off the coast of South Carolina and Georgia, many of whom still speak Gullah and Geechee, which combine English words within an African grammatical structure.

The expression of African culture also united form and function in the tradition of basket weaving and in the "colono-ware" pottery that developed among low country slaves. The Akan-like drum and the banjo, which frequently accompanied black singing and dancing in the colonial South, were also of African origin. African folklore persisted as well, a practice that modern griots (storytellers) have revived.

Many African rituals found their way into the everyday lives of the slaves. Sleeping arrange-

SLAVE MAGIC

Henry Bibb, who escaped in 1837 from enslavement in the South, recalled the activities of conjurers:

There is much superstition among the slaves. Many of them believe in what they call "conjuration," tricking, and witchcraft; and some of them pretend to understand the art, and say that by it they can prevent their masters from exercising their will over their slaves. Such are often applied to by others, to give them power to prevent their masters from flogging them. The remedy is most generally some kind of bitter root; they are directed to chew it and spit towards their masters when they are angry with their slaves. At other times they prepare certain kinds of powders, to sprinkle about their masters dwellings. This is all done for the purpose of defending themselves in some peaceable manner, although I am satisfied that there is no virtue at all in it. I have tried it to perfection when I was a slave at the South. I was then a young man, full of life and vigor, and was very fond of visiting our neighbors slaves, but had no time to visit only Sundays, when I could get a permit to go, or after night, when I could slip off without being seen. If it was found out, the next morning I was called up to give an account of myself for going off without permission; and would very often get a flogging for it.

I got myself into a scrape at a certain time, by going off in this way, and I expected to be severely punished for it. I had a strong notion of running off, to escape being flogged, but was advised by a friend to go to one of those conjurers, who could prevent me from being flogged. I went and informed him of the difficulty. He said if I would pay him a small sum, he would prevent my being flogged. After I had paid him, he mixed up some alum, salt and other stuff into a powder, and said I must sprinkle it about my master, if he should offer to strike me; this would prevent him. He also gave me some kind of bitter root to chew, and spit towards him, which would certainly prevent my being flogged. According to order I used his remedy, and for some cause I was let pass without being flogged that time.

I had then great faith in conjuration and witchcraft. I was led to believe that I could do

almost as I pleased, without being flogged. So on the next Sabbath my conjuration was fully tested by my going off, and staying away until Monday morning, without permission. When I returned home, my master declared that he would punish me for going off; but I did not believe that he could do it while I had this root and dust; and as he approached me, I commenced talking saucy to him. But he soon convinced me that there was no virtue in them. He became so enraged at me for saucing him, that he grasped a handful of switches and punished me severely, in spite of all my roots and powders. . . .

But my attention was gradually turned in a measure from this subject, by being introduced into the society of young women. This for the time being took my attention from running away, as waiting on the girls appeared to be perfectly congenial to my nature. I wanted to be well thought of by them, and would go to great lengths to gain their affection. I had been taught by the old superstitious slaves, to believe in conjuration, and it was hard for me to give up the notion, for all I had been deceived by them. One of these conjurers, for a small sum agreed to teach me to make any girl love me that I wished. After I had paid him, he told me to get a bull frog, and take a certain bone out of the frog, dry it, and when I got a chance I must step up to any girl whom I wished to make love me, and scratch her somewhere on her naked skin with this bone, and she would be certain to love me, and would follow me in spite of herself; no matter who she might be engaged to, nor who she might be walking with.

So I got me a bone for a certain girl, whom I knew to be under the influence of another young man. I happened to meet her in the company of her lover, one Sunday evening, walking out; so when I got a chance, I fetched her a tremendous rasp across her neck with this bone, which made her jump. But in place of making her love me, it only made her angry with me. She felt more like running after me to retaliate on me for thus abusing her, than she felt like loving me.

Source: *Henry Bibb,* Narrative of the Life and Adventures of Henry Bibb, An American Slave *(New York: Published by author, 1849), pp. 25–27, 30–31.*

AFRICAN CULTURES

ments were serious matters determined by folk custom. Often slaves slept with blankets pulled over their heads, even if their feet froze, in an effort to ward off evil spirits that might be lurking in the dark. If slaves built bedsteads, they positioned them to face east to west (as in Africa), so they would not sleep in "the crossways of the world" but would instead be in harmony with its rhythms. When slaves became ill, they might let the master or mistress treat them, but those who were suspicious of white medical practices either concealed their illness or turned to their own "doctors" within the slave community. These so-called root doctors relied on mixing various herbs and potions to treat any number of aches, pains, and ailments. Variations of these treatments had been used in Africa as well as in the Caribbean and often combined medicine with magic. Masters and their families sometimes availed themselves of African folk medicine when their own remedies failed them.

Certain rituals concerned with death were extensions of West African burial traditions, which stressed a safe journey for the soul of the departed and also sought to prevent ghosts from bothering the living. Those rituals included digging graves aligned from east to west and burying food and personal effects with the deceased to sustain them on their journey. Slaves also exhibited their African heritage in the practice of decorating graves with objects that had belonged to the deceased such as seashells or artistically carved or sculpted grave markers.

Recent archaeological discoveries at such sites as Thomas Jefferson's Monticello support the notion that African influences were enduring among slave communities in North America. Archaeologists have uncovered many different artifacts that cast new light on how African folkways shaped everyday lives. Items such as cowrie shells, pierced coins, and finger rings made from animal horn all point to the survival of elements of African heritage. Until the late nineteenth century many West African cultures used shells as currency. In some cases, these shells also held a religious significance and were sewn onto ceremonial dress. Finger rings served as a mojo (magic charm), probably worn to ward off evil spirits. Pierced coins were a form of jewelry and were spiritually significant as well. The discovery of these and other artifacts is physical evidence of the persistence of African culture in African American slave life.

The slaves' religious practices also reveal deep spiritual roots in West African traditions. The ring shout, an African-influenced dance used in worship, evolved from West Africa. Despite attempts on the part of white masters to curtail or eliminate the independent religious lives of their slaves, which owners often found uncivi-

lized and frightening, slaves usually managed to retain bits and pieces of their traditional faiths. These beliefs included worshiping a multitude of gods and spirits, many of which were maternal in nature. Perhaps more important were the deep beliefs with regard to one's family and heritage. Ancestor worship played an important role in African American slave religion, as it had in the religions of West and Central Africa. Many slaves viewed their ancestors as "the living dead" who held immense power because they were close to the living as well as to the divine. Commemorating the lives of these ancestors marked many important religious occasions and ceremonies. One of the most fundamental beliefs that slaves shared was the idea that the value of the individual was defined by his or her connection to the community at large. Slave communities, often made up of individuals from different areas throughout Africa, formed bonds and created a strong sense of unity that provided them solace and comfort under the strenuous circumstances of slavery.

In time, much of this cultural inheritance would be incorporated, redefined, and reshaped into a vital African American culture, as slaves took on some of the beliefs and values of their white masters. Although the links to Africa diminished over time, they never completely disappeared. For many slaves and their descendants, the power of Africa remained strong.

–MEG GREENE,
MIDLOTHIAN, VIRGINIA

Viewpoint:
No. The shock of capture and the horrors of the Middle Passage caused slaves to lose connection with their African past quickly.

Traditionally, individuals who took a generous view of Africans congratulated them on the progress they had made ascending from savagery to civilization. Scholars routinely assumed the inferiority of Africans. Joseph Alexander Tillinghast, in *The Negro in Africa and America* (1902), warned that

the interval to be traversed . . . in passing from West African savagery to American civilization was so immense, that we must beware of losing true perspective in our view of the problem. . . . The question is: did American slavery develop in the negro his indolence, carelessness, brutality to animals, and aptness in deception, or did it merely fail to eradicate them as well as some better devised system might have done? Every characteristic just

Painting of slaves participating in a secular West African dance, circa 1800

(Colonial Williamsburg Foundation, Williamsburg, Va.)

named we know to have been an integral part of the West African's nature long before any slaver ever touched our shore.

In *The Negro from Africa to America* (1924), W. D. Weatherford echoed Tillinghast's presuppositions and conclusions. Weatherford begged indulgence for "the American Negro," insisting that he be judged "as to the distance he has traveled since he left his African home, rather than compared with the white man who had thousands of years the start." He added that "we believe that much of the present response of the Negro to social environment is influenced by the social heritage, not only from slavery but from the far African past. This is in no way an intimation that the Negro has not progressed far beyond that past. Indeed no one can read the story of his marvelous progress without great amazement." Tillinghast and Weatherford were typical not only in the views they expressed about black inferiority but also in their failure to take account of the trauma that Africans had suffered. The pertinent question ought to be not whether blacks were inferior but how the vital and dynamic cultures of Africa came to be so degraded in North America.

The obvious explanation, of course, is slavery. During the 1930s and 1940s anthropologist Melville J. Herskovits, whose conclusions scholars have since challenged, was among the first to dispose of the stereotype of African cultures as backward and primitive. Yet, the research and field studies that Herskovits and others conducted only heightened the need to explain the impact of slavery upon Africans. Herskovits argued that Africans retained many vestiges of their cultural life when transported to the Americas. In such books as *Dahomey: An Ancient West African Kingdom* (1938) and *The Myth of the Negro Past* (1941), Herskovits dignified the African cultural heritage and suggested that it was a benefit and a comfort to the slaves. However, even Herskovits did not consider the adverse effects of slavery on the retention of African culture. "Few ethnic groups," wrote historian Stanley M. Elkins in *Slavery: A Problem in American Institutional and Intellectual Life* (1959), "seem to have been so thoroughly and effectively detached from their prior cultural connections as was the case in the Negro's transit from Africa to North America."

Enslaved Africans endured a series of paralyzing psychological jolts long before their arrival in the New World. The first was the shock of capture. Most slaves were taken in war or in surprise raids on their villages. C. B. Wadström wrote in "Observations on the Slave Trade 1789" that

> The Wars which the inhabitants of the interior parts of the country, beyond Senegal, Gambia, and Sierra Leona [*sic*] carry on with each other, are chiefly of a predatory nature, and owe their origin to the yearly number of slaves, which the Mandingoes, or the inland traders suppose will be wanted by the vessels that will arrive on the coast.

Under these circumstances, no one was spared. Neither peasants nor warriors, priests nor kings, could protect themselves from abduction. "The most potent negroe," wrote Willem Bosman in *A New and Accurate Description of the Coast of Guinea, Divided into the Gold, the Slave, and the Ivory Coasts* (1705), "can't pretend to be insured from slavery; for if he ever ventures himself in the wars it may easily become his lot." European traders purchased few Africans who were already enslaved. Tribal chieftains ordinarily sold only prisoners of war or those whom they had seized in raids, and kept for themselves their native and ancestral slaves. Among many African peoples, tribal law proscribed the sale of domestic slaves, except if they had committed a crime, although it was apparently simple to fabricate charges against them. These strictures notwithstanding, "it is an effort to remember," as Elkins has cautioned, "that while enslavement occurred in Africa every day, to the individual it occurred just once."

The second shock was the long march from the interior of Africa to the sea. This difficult trek might take weeks. Those who survived the elements, hunger, and thirst experienced the third shock: sale to European slave traders. Herded en masse into holding pens, the slaves were stripped of their clothing, examined, classified as fit or unfit, branded, and driven onto the waiting ships. Bosman, who had participated in the slave trade, outlined the process at length:

> When the slaves come . . . they are put in prison all together, and when we treat concerning buying them, they are all brought out together in a large plain; where, by our Chirurgeons [surgeons], whose province it is, they are thoroughly examined, even to the smallest member, and that naked too both men and women, without the least distinction and modesty. Those which are approved as good are set on one side; and the lame or faulty are set by as *invalides,* which are here called *mackrons.* These are such as are above five and thirty years old, or are maimed in the arms, legs, hands or feet, have lost a tooth, are grey-haired, or have films over their eyes; as well as all those which are affected by any venereal distemper, or with several other diseases.

The fourth shock, the dreaded Middle Passage, followed. Even if the journey were not an unmitigated horror, it is impossible to imagine the terror that must have overwhelmed the Africans. Suffocating in the heat, enduring the filth, and suffering from diseases, many of the slaves died. Others took their own lives rather than accept enslavement. Olaudah Equiano, one of the few slaves to leave an account of the Middle Passage, gave a chilling description of conditions onboard the slave ships:

> I was soon put under the decks, and there I received such a salutation in my nostrils as I had never experienced in my life: so that, with the loathsomeness of the stench, and crying together, I became so sick and low that I was not able to eat, nor had I the least desire to taste anything. I now wished for the last friend, death, to relieve me; but soon, to my grief, two of the white men offered me eatables; and, on my refusing to eat, one of them held me fast by the hands, and laid me across, I think, the windlass, and tied my feet, while the other flogged me severely. I had never experienced anything of this kind before, and, . . . could I have got over the nettings, I would have jumped over the side.

Few slaves traveled directly from Africa to North or South America. Most underwent a period of "seasoning" in the West Indies. Arrival there constituted the fifth shock that enslavement administered. When slave ships anchored in the harbor at Kingston, according to Bryan Edwards, crowds rushed onboard, assailing the slaves and throwing them into panic. The legislature at last "corrected this enormity" by dictating that the sale of slaves be conducted on land. In his *History, Civil and Commercial, of the British Colonies in the West Indies* (1806), Edwards could not conceal his disgust and remorse at witnessing the Africans exposed naked in public and auctioned to the highest bidder.

By the time the African captives reached the West Indies, much of their past had already been lost and nearly every connection with their family, village, and homeland had been severed. They had not forgotten the past—the kinship networks, religions, rituals, taboos, languages, and the names by which they had once been known—but none of those aspects of their former lives seemed now to have much importance for surviving in North America. The harrowing experiences that the slaves had undergone drained the meaning from their former ways of life. Old references, standards, beliefs, and values seemed, at worst, empty abstractions, and, at best, distant memories. Did enslaved Africans carry elements of their cultures with them to North America? That they did is not in doubt or dispute. A better question might be to what extent those cultural traditions still operated in a new context and under agonizing circumstances. Could African cultures any longer provide solace, a guide to conduct, a foundation of identity, or a way to make sense of the world? The question, then, ought to be not whether African culture disappeared in North America but whether the fragments that remained continued to matter.

–MARTINA NICHOLAS,
YOUNGSTOWN STATE UNIVERSITY

References

John W. Blassingame, *The Slave Community: Plantation Life in the Antebellum South,* revised edition (New York: Oxford University Press, 1979).

Willem Bosman, *A New and Accurate Description of the Coast of Guinea, Divided into the Gold, the Slave, and the Ivory Coasts* (London: Knapton, 1705).

T. H. Breen and Stephen Innes, *"Myne Owne Ground:" Race and Freedom on Virginia's Eastern Shore, 1640–1676* (New York: Oxford University Press, 1980).

Orville Vernon Burton, *In My Father's House Are Many Mansions: Family and Community in Edgefield, South Carolina* (Chapel Hill: University of North Carolina Press, 1985).

Elizabeth Donnan, ed., *Documents Illustrative of the History of the Slave Trade to America,* 4 volumes (Washington, D.C.: Carnegie Institution of Washington, 1930–1935).

Bryan Edwards, *History, Civil and Commercial, of the British Colonies in the West Indies* (Philadelphia: James Humphreys, 1806).

Stanley M. Elkins, *Slavery: A Problem in American Institutional and Intellectual Life* (Chicago: University of Chicago Press, 1959).

Olaudah Equiano, *The Interesting Narrative of the Life of Olaudah Equiano,* edited by Robert J. Allison (Boston: Bedford Books of St. Martin's Press, 1995).

E. Franklin Frazier, *The Negro Family in the United States* (Chicago: University of Chicago Press, 1939).

Frazier, *Race and Culture Contacts in the Modern World* (New York: Knopf, 1957).

Eugene D. Genovese, *Roll, Jordan, Roll: The World the Slaves Made* (New York: Pantheon, 1974).

Melville J. Herskovits, *Dahomey: An Ancient West African Kingdom* (New York: Augustin, 1938).

Herskovits, *The Myth of the Negro Past* (New York & London: Harper, 1941).

Charles W. Joyner, *Down by the Riverside: A South Carolina Slave Community* (Urbana: University of Illinois Press, 1984).

Peter Kolchin, *American Slavery, 1619–1877* (New York: Hill & Wang, 1993).

Allan Kulikoff, *Tobacco and Slaves: The Development of Southern Cultures in the Chesapeake, 1680–1800* (Chapel Hill: University of North Carolina Press, 1986).

Lawrence W. Levine, *Black Culture and Black Consciousness: Afro-American Folk Thought from Slavery to Freedom* (New York: Oxford University Press, 1977).

Daniel C. Littlefield, "'Abundance of Negroes of that Nation': The Significance of African Ethnicity in Colonial South Carolina," in *The Meaning of South Carolina History: Essays in Honor of George C. Rogers, Jr.,* edited by David R. Chesnutt and Clyde N. Wilson (Columbia: University of South Carolina Press, 1991), pp. 19–38.

Littlefield, *Rice and Slaves: Ethnicity and the Slave Trade in Colonial South Carolina* (Baton Rouge: Louisiana State University Press, 1981).

Leslie Howard Owens, *This Species of Property: Slave Life and Culture in the Old South* (New York: Oxford University Press, 1976).

Albert J. Raboteau, *Slave Religion: The "Invisible Institution" in the Antebellum South* (New York: Oxford University Press, 1978).

Sterling Stuckey, *Slave Culture: Nationalist Theory and the Foundations of Black America* (New York: Oxford University Press, 1987).

John Thornton, *Africa and Africans in the Making of the Atlantic World, 1400–1680* (Cambridge & New York: Cambridge University Press, 1992).

Joseph Alexander Tillinghast, *The Negro in Africa and America* (New York: American Economic Association by Macmillan / London: Sonnenschein, 1902).

John Michael Vlach, *The Afro-American Tradition in Decorative Arts* (Cleveland: Cleveland Museum of Art, 1978).

W. D. Weatherford, *The Negro from Africa to America* (New York: Doran, 1924).

AMERICAN REVOLUTION

Did the American Revolution weaken slavery in the United States?

Viewpoint: Yes. Influenced by the Enlightenment, many Patriots maintained that the revolution could be justified only if Americans rid their country of slavery.

Viewpoint: No. The American Revolution protected slavery and ensured its continuation, enabling Southerners to fashion the most thoroughgoing slave society in the New World.

Not until the middle of the eighteenth century did Americans begin systematically to question the morality of slavery. Since antiquity, thinkers as diverse as fourth-century B.C.E. Greek philosopher Aristotle, thirteenth-century Italian philosopher Thomas Aquinas, and seventeenth-century British philosopher John Locke had agreed that slavery was compatible with human progress and happiness, and few challenged this unanimity of opinion. The issue was not so much that slavery received a vigorous defense in the Thirteen Colonies as that people merely took it for granted as an unexceptional and unobjectionable fact of life. This casual acceptance of slavery changed only with the approach of the American War for Independence (1775–1783).

Although relatively few Americans during the age of revolution demanded the immediate abolition of slavery, growing numbers, including some slaveholders, expressed misgivings about continuing to hold Africans in bondage. Influenced by Enlightenment ideas of justice, natural rights, and freedom, many thinkers in both North America and Western Europe criticized slavery as a violation of basic human dignity and decency. No longer did Africans appear to observers as innately and permanently savage, depraved, and uncivilized. During the 1750s an emerging consciousness of, and emphasis on, diversity and tolerance combined with a new interest in using environmental factors to explain human nature and conduct, which altered the view that blacks were fit only for slavery. Some observers began to wonder if the "slavishness" attributed to the enslaved did not, after all, arise from their nature but from their degraded condition.

Such convictions prevailed nowhere more strongly than among the Quakers, who initiated the first organized abolitionist movement. The Quakers concluded that slavery, rather than nature, had rendered blacks indolent and unreliable. In response to a Virginia planter who asserted that blacks were too lazy and shiftless to be free, Quaker abolitionist John Woolman replied "that free Men, whose Minds were properly on their Business, found a Satisfaction in improving, cultivating, and providing for their Families; but Negroes, labouring to support others who claim them as their Property, and expecting nothing but slavery during Life, had not the like Inducement to be industrious." The Quakers linked the new theories of environmentalism to an enlightened sense of justice and a capitalist belief in hard work to fashion a moral condemnation of slavery.

Yet, many of the Americans infused with the ideas of the Enlightenment and the spirit of revolution were also slaveholders. Virginia leaders George

17

Washington, Thomas Jefferson, James Madison, Patrick Henry, George Mason, and Edmund Randolph come immediately to mind. They might have opposed slavery in principle as a violation of "natural rights," even as they defended it in practice as a "necessary evil." American independence helped to effect the abolition of slavery in the North, the emancipation of growing numbers of slaves in the upper South, and ultimately the end of the transatlantic slave trade, which came in 1808. At the same time, however, independence freed Southerners from the interference of a metropolitan government in Great Britain that, in 1833, outlawed slavery in its realm. The U.S. Constitution (1787), by contrast, protected slave property and thus implicitly endorsed the legitimacy of slavery.

Viewpoint:
Yes. Influenced by the Enlightenment, many Patriots maintained that the revolution could be justified only if Americans rid their country of slavery.

During the course of his 1858 debates with Senator Stephen Douglas (D-Illinois), Republican senatorial candidate Abraham Lincoln insisted that the Founding Fathers had placed slavery "on the course of ultimate extinction." According to Lincoln's understanding of American history, the Founders proclaimed the equality of man in the Declaration of Independence (1776). They then proceeded to put their ideals into practice and placed a noose around the institution of slavery by prohibiting its extension into the Northwest Territory and providing in the Constitution of the United States (1787) for the abolition of the transatlantic slave trade after 1808.

Lincoln was a better rhetorician than historian, but he was correct to suggest that the American Revolution (1775–1783) placed slavery "on the course of ultimate extinction." Moreover, this event occurred despite the fact that the institution of slavery expanded into newly opened territory in the Southwest in the years following independence. Military necessities and economic disruptions of the War for Independence weakened slavery in the short term in the new United States. From a longer perspective, the social and political changes wrought by the Revolution doomed American chattel slavery.

Many slaves saw in the confusion of war an opportunity to run away. Fortunately for would-be runaways, the Revolution in the Southern colonies degenerated into a chaotic civil war that increased their chances of escape. Loyalists encouraged slaves to run away from Patriot masters. Either the British or their Loyalist allies liberated thousands more or stole them from their masters to be sold in the West Indies. Historian Benjamin Quarles estimates that the evacuating British carried off at least four thousand blacks from Savannah, six thousand from Charleston, and another four thousand from New York after the surrender at York Town (1781). To these figures must be added the unknown number who left with the French and the perhaps five thousand more carried off by the British prior to 1781. On the American side, according to scholar Randall M. Miller, about five thousand blacks joined the army and navy to fight for independence, "helping to reinforce blacks' claim to the revolutionary heritage." As a result of the war, slaves became an insecure form of property and consequently declined in value. In their groundbreaking cliometric study, *Time on the Cross: The Economics of American Negro Slavery* (1974), Robert W. Fogel and Stanley L. Engerman showed that although slave prices later rebounded, they were "acutely depressed during the last years of the Revolution." By thus temporarily rendering property in slaves insecure, the military and economic turmoil of the Revolution weakened the institution of slavery for the short term.

Slavery was further weakened, and eventually abolished, in the United States by the ideological thrust of the Revolution. Before independence, slavery thrived throughout British North America without serious challenge. Under British rule only Connecticut, Rhode Island, and the Quaker colony of Pennsylvania prohibited the importation of slaves. After independence, many people, even in the South, found it difficult to reconcile fighting for liberty and the ideals of the Revolution, as expressed in the Declaration, with the institution of chattel slavery. In the North, the Revolution sounded the death knell of slavery. Every state north of Delaware moved to outlaw slavery, making it a sectional, and truly peculiar, institution. In the words of historian Winthrop D. Jordan, "The 'real American Revolution' involved a newly intense scrutiny of colonial society, including the peculiarly un-English institution of Negro slavery. American thinking about the status of Negroes could never again be characterized by placid and unheeding acceptance." The Revolution therefore weakened slavery by placing its apologists in the uncomfortable position of defending bondage and inequality among a people who were increasingly coming to view such ideas as backward, immoral, and eventually un-American.

"It is important to realize that the Revolution suddenly and effectively ended the cultural climate that had allowed black slavery, as well as other forms of bondage and unfreedom, to exist

AMERICAN REVOLUTION

throughout the colonial period without serious challenge," historian Gordon S. Wood explains in *The Radicalism of the American Revolution* (1992). "With the revolutionary movement, black slavery became excruciatingly conspicuous in a way that it had not been in the older monarchical society with its many calibrations and degrees of unfreedom; and Americans in 1775–76 began attacking it with a vehemence that was inconceivable earlier." Not by accident, the world's first antislavery society was founded in 1775 in Philadelphia, a mere five days before the Battles of Lexington and Concord. Viewing liberty and slavery as incompatible, Northern states quickly moved to emancipate their slaves. Vermont's constitution of 1777 prohibited slavery. In 1780 Pennsylvania provided for the gradual emancipation of all children thereafter born to slave mothers when the children reached the age of twenty-eight. The Massachusetts constitution of 1780 did not explicitly prohibit slavery but in language reminiscent of the Declaration of Independence declared that "All men are born free and equal, and have certain natural, essential, and unalienable rights." In the Quock Walker case (1783), Massachusetts chief justice William Cushing held that the state constitution made all men free. New Hampshire abolished slavery in 1784. That same year, Rhode Island declared free all children thereafter born to slaves upon reaching age eighteen for females and age twenty-one for males. Connecticut similarly endorsed gradual emancipation in 1784. New York adopted a plan of gradual emancipation in 1799, followed by New Jersey in 1804.

Slavery also came under attack in the South. The Virginia legislature passed a law in 1778, proposed by Thomas Jefferson, that banned the further importation of slaves from Africa. This act was followed in 1782 by legislation that, for the first time, allowed for the manumission of slaves by their owners. This measure may sound insignificant but, as J. Franklin Jameson pointed out in *The American Revolution Considered as a Social Movement* (1926), it appears to have led to the manumission of more than ten thousand slaves within eight years. By contrast, only half that number were freed by the Massachusetts constitution. Jefferson's ambivalence toward slavery has been well documented. Though a slave owner himself, he denounced the institution as a violation of the "most sacred rights of life and liberty" in his draft of the Declaration of Independence (1776). In 1783 he privately suggested a plan for the gradual abolition of slavery in Virginia. The plan, never acted upon, would have forbidden the introduction of any more slaves into Virginia and declared free all persons born after 31 December 1800. Also in 1783, Jefferson proposed to Congress a scheme for prohibiting slavery in the Western territory after 1800. Though his proposal was rejected, a similar antislavery provision was later applied to the Western territory north of the Ohio River in the Northwest Ordinance (1787).

In fact, awareness of the seeming incompatibility between slavery and the ideals of the Revolution was far from unusual, even in the South. Before the early 1830s few white Southerners could be found to defend bondage. Noting "the incompatibility of a state of slavery with the principles of our government, and of that revolution upon which it is founded," the jurist St. George Tucker in 1796 proposed another plan for the gradual abolition of slavery in Virginia. Henry Laurens, George Washington, Patrick Henry, George Mason, James Madison, John Randolph, William H. Crawford, and Roger B. Taney all expressed misgivings about slavery. David Ramsay of Charleston, South Carolina, concluded *The History of the American Revolution* (1789) with an exhortation to his countrymen to extend the Revolutionary principle of universal justice to Africans and Indians both. Henry Clay later echoed Jefferson's ambivalence toward slavery. Clay, a Kentucky slave owner whom Lincoln looked to as a role model, denounced the abolitionists yet publicly endorsed gradual emancipation. He also served as president of the American Colonization Society, which sought to make emancipation more palatable to white Americans by colonizing free blacks in Africa.

However, beginning in the early 1830s, with slavery extinguished in their own section, Northerners increasingly began to attack Southern slave ownership. Viewing slavery as inconsistent with Revolutionary ideals and an embarrassment to the nation, Northern abolitionists began pressing for the immediate abolition of slavery in the South. From this point forward, Southerners actively took up the defense of their peculiar institution, and slavery entered the national political discourse as a divisive sectional issue that would only find resolution on the battlefield.

Scant evidence exists that the Founders actually intended to place slavery "on the course of ultimate extinction," as Lincoln had proposed. Nevertheless, the ultimate extinction of slavery was the inescapable, if unintended, consequence of the revolution they led. As historian William W. Freehling has noted, "the abolitionist process proceeded slowly but inexorably from 1776 to 1860: slowly in part because of what Jefferson and his contemporaries did not do, inexorably in part because of what they did." What Jefferson and his contemporaries in the founding generation did do was confine slavery to the South and place its advocates on the defensive. As slavery became an ever more divisive and sectional issue in American politics, it became increasingly difficult for national political parties to hold together. Northern politicians found running against the Southern slave power too rewarding to abstain

AN ACT FOR THE GRADUAL ABOLITION OF SLAVERY

In 1780 Pennsylvania passed a law that allowed for the gradual abolition of slavery; this statute was the first of its kind in the Western Hemisphere:

WHEN we contemplate our abhorrence of that condition to which the arms and tyranny of Great-Britain were exerted to reduce us; when we look back on the variety of dangers to which we have been exposed, and how miraculously our wants in many instances have been supplied, and our deliverances wrought, when even hope and human fortitude have become unequal to the conflict; we are unavoidably led to a serious and grateful sense of the manifold blessings which we have undeservedly received from the hand of that Being from whom every good and perfect gift cometh. Impressed with these ideas, we conceive that it is our duty, and we rejoice that it is in our power, to extend a portion of that freedom to others, which hath been extended to us; and a release from that state of thraldom, to which we ourselves were tyrannically doomed, and from which we have now every prospect of being delivered. It is not for us to inquire, why, in the creation of mankind, the inhabitants of the several parts of the earth were distinguished by a difference in feature or complexion. It is sufficient to know, that all are the work of an Almighty Hand. We find in the distribution of the human species, that the most fertile, as well as the most barren parts of the earth, are inhabited by men of complexions different from ours, and from each other, from whence we may reasonably, as well as religiously infer, that He, who placed them in their various situations, hath extended equally His care and protection to all, and that it becometh not us to counteract His mercies. We esteem it a peculiar blessing granted to us, that we are enabled this day, to add one more step to universal civilization, by removing as much as possible, the sorrows of those who have lived in undeserved bondage, and from which, by the assumed authority of the Kings of Britain, no effectual legal relief, could be obtained. Weaned by a long course of experience, from those narrow prejudices and partialities we had imbibed, we find our hearts enlarged with kindness and benevolence, towards men of all conditions and nations; and we conceive ourselves at this particular period extraordinarily called upon, by the blessings which we have received, to manifest the sincerity of our profession, and to give a substantial proof of our gratitude.

AND WHEREAS the condition of those persons who have heretofore been denominated Negroe and Mulatto slaves, has been attended with circumstances, which not only deprived them of the common blessings that they were by nature entitled to, but has cast them into the deepest afflictions, by an unnatural separation and sale of husband and wife from each other, and from their children; an injury the greatness of which, can only be conceived, by supposing, that we were in the same unhappy case. In justice therefore, to persons so unhappily circumstanced, and who, having no prospect before them, whereon they may rest their sorrows and their hopes, have no reasonable inducement, to render that service to society, which they otherwise might; and also, in grateful commemoration of our own happy deliverance, from that state of unconditional submission, to which we were doomed by the tyranny of Britain.

Be it enacted, and it is hereby enacted, by the Representatives of the Freemen of the Commonwealth of Pennsylvania, in General Assembly met, and by the authority of the same, that all persons, as well Negroes and Mulattos as others, who shall be born within this State, from and after the passing of this Act, shall not be deemed and considered as servants for life or slaves; and that all servitude for life, or slavery of children, in consequence of the slavery of their mothers, in the case of all children born within this State, from and after the passing of this Act as aforesaid, shall be, and hereby is utterly taken away, extinguished and for ever abolished.

Provided always, and be it further enacted by the authority aforesaid, that every Negroe and Mulatto child born within this State, after the passing of this Act as aforesaid, who would, in case this Act had not been made, have been born a servant for years, or life or a slave, shall be deemed to be and shall be by virtue of this Act, the servant of such person or his or her assigns, who would in such case have been intitled to the service of such child, until such child shall attain unto the age of twenty eight years, in the manner and on the conditions whereon servants bound by indenture for four years, are or may be retained and holden; and shall be liable to like correction and punishment, and intitled to like relief in case he or she be evily treated by his or her master or mistress, and to like freedom dues and other privileges as servants bound by indenture for four years, are or may be intitled, unless the person to whom the service of any such child shall belong, shall abandon his or her claim to the same, in which case the Overseers of the Poor of the city, township or district respectively, where such child shall be so abandoned, shall by indenture bind out every child so abandoned, as an apprentice for a time not exceeding the age herein before limited, for the service of such children.

Source: *Gary B. Nash,* Race and Revolution *(Madison, Wis.: Madison House, 1990), pp. 112–114.*

AMERICAN REVOLUTION

from even when it threatened party unity; Southern politicians discovered the same thing when confronting Northern abolitionism. Such political decisions further inflamed sectional animosity while working to erode party, and national, unity. Under such circumstances, national parties could not hold together over the long run.

To further complicate matters, demographics also worked against the South and national unity. In the years between the Revolution and Civil War (1861–1865), the North's population grew at a faster rate than the South's. It was only a matter of time before a truly sectional, antislavery party arose in the North intent upon dominating the Southern minority. By 1856 the Whig Party was dead. In the North, just such a sectional party, the Republicans, inherited most of the Whigs' strength. In 1860 the national Democratic Party split along sectional lines, opening the door to Republican triumph in the presidential election. The election of Lincoln, an overtly sectional candidate whose name did not even appear on the ballot in the Southern states, in turn, drove the South to secession. In the words of historian Michael F. Holt, in *The Rise and Fall of the American Whig Party: Jacksonian Politics and the Onset of the Civil War* (1999), the Civil War "resulted primarily from the fact that an exclusively northern and overtly antisouthern Republican party, not a bisectional Whig party, . . . defeated Democrats for the presidency in 1860."

The American Revolution did not bring about an immediate end to slavery, but it weakened the institution and placed it on the course of ultimate extinction. "The American Revolution," Freehling reminds us, "did not end in 1790. Over several generations, antislavery reforms inspired by the Revolution helped lead to Southern division, desperation, and defeat in war."

–SEAN R. BUSICK,
KENTUCKY WESLEYAN COLLEGE

Viewpoint:
No. The American Revolution protected slavery and ensured its continuation, enabling Southerners to fashion the most thoroughgoing slave society in the New World.

By the middle of the eighteenth century, slavery had become an integral component of the economy and society of the British North American colonies. For many Americans who were contemplating independence from Great Britain, however, slavery was also becoming a disturbing embarrassment. The apparent contradiction between Americans' quest for liberty and their defense of slavery did not escape the English man of letters Samuel Johnson. "How is it," Johnson wondered, "that we hear the loudest *yelps* for liberty among the drivers of negroes?"

Slavery had always been something of a problem for Englishmen who, by enslaving Africans, violated their own legal traditions, since the common law did not recognize slavery. The introduction of slavery into the English colonies was thus a radical innovation of the sort that usually left the English vexed and troubled. For generations they had made their peace with or ignored the contradiction between ancient custom and modern practice, even as they benefited from the labor of their slaves. As the call went out in the 1760s to throw off the yoke of British oppression and reassert their traditional rights as freeborn Englishmen, American colonists could disregard this incongruity no longer. To do so would have marked them as hypocrites in the eyes of the world.

Many of the men who pondered independence from Great Britain thought themselves products of the Enlightenment. For eighteenth-century thinkers, the Enlightenment had emancipated the mind from authority and superstition, unveiled the truths of nature, vindicated the rights of man, and pointed the way not only toward human improvement but human perfection. To these apostles of liberty, slavery was a criminal violation of the rights of man. Its continued existence rendered impossible social order, morality, and peace and confounded the essence of enlightened civilization.

The Americans' faith in human intelligence, reason, and benevolence encouraged them to believe that they could establish a more perfect union in which justice and liberty reigned. In the new order they were creating there would be no more oppression from despotic monarchs. All men thereafter would be free to use their God-given talents for their own benefit as well as for that of their fellow citizens. Life would become something more than an endless contest of greed and power. Slavery did not fit into this enlightened worldview. How could the American revolutionaries justify slavery while at the same time proclaiming the natural right of all men to freedom?

During the struggle for independence from Great Britain (1775–1783), many American leaders admitted that slavery was contrary to the principles for which they fought. Several reformers warned that the revolution could be justified only by a decision to rid the land of slavery. They argued that Americans could not secure their own freedom until they had emancipated their slaves. That result, of course, did not take place. Neither the revolution nor the creation of an

independent American republic ended slavery. On the contrary, independence from Great Britain freed the United States to develop in its midst the most thoroughgoing slave society in the Western Hemisphere. Had the revolution failed and the North American colonies remained subject to the Crown, the Americans would have been compelled to emancipate their slaves in 1833 when Parliament abolished slavery throughout the British Empire.

American slaveholders, like slave owners everywhere, refused to free their bondsmen in the name of a principle or an ideal, however much they professed to cherish it. Instead, they accepted emancipation only when coerced by a central government, a superior military force, or the slaves themselves. Despite their celebration of liberty, American slaveholders proved just as resistant to change.

In addition, if the American colonists fought for anything, it was above all for the right of self-determination. Slavery was of crucial importance to the national economy. Americans could not have sustained their economic viability, and hence their political independence, without it. Then, too, they believed that liberty rested on property, and, whatever else they might have been, slaves were property. Liberty required independence and independence required property. Property was thus the foundation of liberty. Eighteenth-century Americans did not simply value property rights over human rights. In their view of the matter, human rights were intimately connected with, and supported by, property rights. The two were so intimately intertwined that one could not survive without the other. Any scheme of emancipation, however gradual, would have destroyed a legitimate form of property and thereby imperiled not only economic prosperity but the foundations of republican liberty as well. Slavery, it seemed, was interwoven so tightly into the fabric of the American republic that it could not be eradicated without unraveling it. The American War for Independence might have exposed more starkly the contradiction between slavery and freedom, and might have fashioned a set of ideals to which the opponents of slavery could appeal, but the withdrawal of imperial authority also enabled slaveholders to gain sufficient power in the new national government to protect their interests. They fastened slavery on the United States to such an extent that only a long and bloody Civil War (1861–1865) could at last eradicate it.

The central paradox in the history of the British North American colonies was that the rise of liberty coincided with the introduction of slavery. As Edmund S. Morgan has argued, Englishmen in a sense purchased their liberty, and eventually their independence from the mother country, by enslaving Africans. This development was not a fortuitous inconsistency. After all, nothing novel exists about the freedom and independence of some men depending on the coercion and oppression of others. Even as the Americans rejoiced in their ideal of liberty, they were building a society in which slavery played an increasingly prominent role. When black slaves began to replace propertyless whites at the bottom of the social order, Americans, especially those from such slaveholding colonies as Virginia, could begin to entertain such radical ideas as "all men are created equal" and "are endowed by their Creator with certain unalienable rights; that among these are life, liberty, and the pursuit of happiness. . . ."

During the seventeenth century the colonial elite deemed all efforts of the propertyless to exert their rights as disruptive of social order and moved to crush them swiftly and efficiently. Governor William Berkeley of Virginia was obsessed with the danger of rebellion. The widespread introduction of slavery into the colony after 1680, however, enabled Virginians to nurture representative government in a plantation society. Slavery, according to Morgan, transformed the Virginia of Berkeley into the Virginia of Thomas Jefferson and permitted Virginians to

dare speak a political language that amplified and extended the rights of poor, white men. The freedom of Englishmen in America was thus from the outset dependent upon the enslavement of Africans.

Americans were not trapped in an unintentional contradiction between slavery and freedom. Like all people, in the past as well as the present, they had created their society by making a series of related choices to solve the immediate problems that confronted them. They did not deliberately set out to construct a slave society, but they ended up with one. Africans simply proved to be the most economical form of labor that the planters could acquire. Although slavery might have come to America gradually, it enabled the colonists, for a time, to resolve the age-old tension between individual liberty and social order that on some level troubles all but the most tyrannical societies. Yet, their solution, however alluring, was ultimately false, and Americans paid dearly for their temporary comfort.

In America, freedom and independence depended on the continuation of slavery. The American Revolution made the contradiction between principles and practices more glaring, the separation between rhetoric and reality more complete. Having once attained their independence and assured their liberty, however, American leaders for the most part tried to ignore the existence of slavery and did their best to keep it from contaminating political life.

No one embodied the dilemma of the revolutionary generation more fully or more painfully than Jefferson, the principal author of the Declaration of Independence (1776). For all his opposition to slavery (he once declared that one hour of slavery was worse than ages of British oppression) Jefferson built with slave labor a model plantation on his little mountain outside of Charlottesville, Virginia, and all his life actively participated in the world the slaveholders were making in the land whose freedom he had helped to win.

Jefferson owned approximately two hundred slaves. He engaged in the slave trade, hunted down runaways, wrote the slave code for Virginia, and opposed any limits on the expansion of slavery throughout the Southern states and the Western territories. During his lifetime he emancipated only two of his slaves, and one of these individuals bought his own freedom. Willingly or unwillingly, Jefferson was locked into the support of a slave system for pragmatic reasons. With ten thousand acres of land to cultivate, Jefferson could hardly have afforded to free his slaves; without their labor his property would have lost most of its value. For more than fifty years, therefore, Jefferson, the champion of liberty and enlightenment, devoted himself to defending slavery as a legitimate form of property.

Yet, in *Notes on the State of Virginia* (1785), the only book that Jefferson ever wrote, he condemned slavery as a perversion of civility so fundamental that it precluded even an education in virtue. Within both the family and the state, the existence of slavery provided instead for an irresistible invitation to indolence and an equally irresistible education in tyranny.

> There must doubtless be an unhappy influence on the manners of our people produced by the existence of slavery among us. The whole commerce between master and slave is a perpetual exercise of the most boisterous passions, the most unremitting despotism on the one part, and degrading submissions on the other. Our children see this, and learn to imitate it. . . . The parent storms, the child looks on, catches the lineaments of wrath, puts on the same airs in the circle of smaller slaves, gives loose to his worst of passions, and thus nursed, educated, and daily exercised in tyranny, cannot but be stamped by it with odious peculiarities. The man must be a prodigy who can retain his manners and morals undepraved by such circumstances. . . . With the morals of the people, their industry also is destroyed. For in a warm climate, no man will labour for himself who can make another labor for him.

This combination of vices was a sure invitation to disaster, for Jefferson had always placed his hopes for the future of America squarely on the virtue of its citizens. The degeneration into indolence and tyranny would destroy the virtues necessary to sustain an independent republic.

Jefferson admitted that slavery was an evil, but he also had to concede that it had become so entrenched in American society that only the most violent means could now dispose of it. The cure, he feared, would be worse than the disease. "We have a wolf by the ears," Jefferson wrote to John Holmes, the congressman from the district of Maine, in 1820, "and we can neither hold it nor safely let it go. Justice is in one scale, and self-preservation in the other."

–MARK G. MALVASI,
RANDOLPH-MACON COLLEGE

References

Bernard Bailyn, *The Ideological Origins of the American Revolution* (Cambridge, Mass.: Belknap Press of Harvard University Press, 1967).

Ira Berlin and Ronald Hoffman, eds., *Slavery and Freedom in the Age of Revolution* (Charlottesville: University Press of Virginia, 1983).

William Cohen, "Thomas Jefferson and the Problem of Slavery," *Journal of American History,* 56 (December 1969): 503–526.

David Brion Davis, *The Problem of Slavery in the Age of Revolution, 1770–1823* (Ithaca, N.Y.: Cornell University Press, 1975).

Davis, *The Problem of Slavery in Western Culture* (Ithaca, N.Y.: Cornell University Press, 1966).

Richard Beale Davis, *Intellectual Life in Jefferson's Virginia, 1790–1830* (Chapel Hill: University of North Carolina Press, 1964).

Davis, *Intellectual Life in the Colonial South, 1585–1763,* 3 volumes (Knoxville: University of Tennessee Press, 1978).

Stanley M. Elkins, *Slavery: A Problem in American Institutional and Intellectual Life* (Chicago: University of Chicago Press, 1959).

Paul Finkelman, *Slavery and the Founders: Race and Liberty in the Age of Jefferson,* second edition (Armonk, N.Y.: Sharpe, 2001).

Robert W. Fogel and Stanley L. Engerman, *Time on the Cross: The Economics of American Negro Slavery,* 2 volumes (Boston: Little, Brown, 1974).

William W. Freehling, "The Founding Fathers and Slavery," in *American Negro Slavery: A Modern Reader,* third edition, edited by Allen Weinstein, Frank Otto Gatell, and David Saransohn (New York: Oxford University Press, 1979), pp. 3–19.

Eugene D. Genovese, *The World the Slaveholders Made: Two Essays in Interpretation* (New York: Pantheon, 1969).

Michael F. Holt, *The Rise and Fall of the American Whig Party: Jacksonian Politics and the Onset of the Civil War* (New York: Oxford University Press, 1999).

J. Franklin Jameson, *The American Revolution Considered as a Social Movement* (Princeton: Princeton University Press, 1926).

Thomas Jefferson, *Notes on the State of Virginia,* edited by William Peden (Chapel Hill: University of North Carolina Press, 1954).

Jefferson, *The Portable Thomas Jefferson,* edited by Merrill D. Peterson (New York: Viking, 1975).

Winthrop D. Jordan, *The White Man's Burden: Historical Origins of Racism in the United States* (New York: Oxford University Press, 1974).

Abraham Lincoln, "Lincoln's Rejoinder: Quincy, October 13, 1858," in *Created Equal? The Complete Lincoln-Douglas Debates of 1858,* edited by Paul M. Angle (Chicago: University of Chicago Press, 1958), pp. 353–360.

John Chester Miller, *The Wolf by the Ears: Thomas Jefferson and Slavery* (New York: Free Press, 1977).

Randall M. Miller, "Slavery and the American Revolution," in *Dictionary of Afro-American Slavery,* revised edition, edited by Miller and John David Smith (Westport, Conn.: Praeger, 1997), pp. 47–54.

Edmund S. Morgan, *American Slavery, American Freedom: The Ordeal of Colonial Virginia* (New York: Norton, 1975).

Morgan, "Slavery and Freedom: The American Paradox," in *Colonial America: Essays in Politics and Social Development,* third edition, edited by Stanley N. Katz and John M.

Murrin (New York: Knopf, 1983), pp. 572–596.

Peter N. Onuf, ed., *Jeffersonian Legacies* (Charlottesville: University Press of Virginia, 1993).

Benjamin Quarles, "Evacuation with the British," in *Black History: A Reappraisal,* edited by Melvin Drimmer (Garden City, N.Y.: Doubleday, 1968), pp. 134–146.

David Ramsay, *The History of the American Revolution,* edited by Lester H. Cohen (Indianapolis: Liberty Classics, 1990).

St. George Tucker, "On the State of Slavery in Virginia," in *View of the Constitution of the United States, with Selected Writings,* edited by Clyde N. Wilson (Indianapolis: Liberty Fund, 1999), pp. 402–446.

Gordon S. Wood, *The Radicalism of the American Revolution* (New York: Knopf, 1992).

AMERICAN REVOLUTION

CHRISTIANITY

Did Christianity provide an effective defense of slavery?

Viewpoint: Yes. Proslavery theorists used the Bible to support their position that slavery was ordained by God, arguing that the Israelites, God's Chosen People, had owned slaves, that Jesus never denounced slavery, and that St. Paul admonished slaves to obey their masters.

Viewpoint: No. Slavery violated the spirit of Christianity; opponents of slavery believed that it was wrong because it prevented master and slave alike from living virtuous, moral, and Christian lives.

Antebellum Southerners had every confidence that both the Old and New Testaments sanctioned slavery. God himself, they reasoned, had instituted slavery as part of his plan to expose the heathen peoples of Africa to the blessings of Christian civilization. Those who mounted a scriptural defense of slavery regarded it as a "positive good" rather than a "necessary evil" for which there existed no practical alternative. Slavery, for example, compelled masters to live up to the doctrines of Christian ethics by nurturing their slaves. Proslavery theorists argued that slaves enjoyed better lives than did industrial wageworkers in the North and Europe, to say nothing of impoverished rural peasants, in whose welfare employers and landlords took no interest. Slavery was God's way of providing social, political, institutional, and familial structures in which morally frail human beings could live together in peace, each free to serve him according to his station.

Opponents of slavery, by contrast, increasingly viewed the institution as immoral for violating the fundamental law of Christ: love thy neighbor as thyself. The tortured and blasphemous efforts of apologists to justify slavery masked its inherent and ruthless exploitation. Moreover, argued the abolitionists, slavery imperiled the souls of both blacks and whites, preventing both from living Christian lives. Slavery made of the master a vicious tyrant and of the slave a helpless victim. The resulting degradation of manners and morals spread evil throughout society. For some, the existence of slavery portended divine retribution as atonement for the national sin of the United States.

**Viewpoint:
Yes. Proslavery theorists used the Bible to support their position that slavery was ordained by God, arguing that the Israelites, God's Chosen People, had owned slaves, that Jesus never denounced slavery, and that St. Paul admonished slaves to obey their masters.**

By the 1830s, Southern thinkers had come to depend on religion to justify their defense of slavery. Confronted with abolitionist pronouncements that slavery mocked and defiled the spirit of Christianity, Southerners introduced detailed evidence from both the Old and the New Testaments to demonstrate that God himself had sanctioned it. God's Chosen People, the Israelites, including Abraham and the other patriarchs, had owned slaves. Jesus and the Apostles, who denounced every imaginable sin, spoke no word against slavery, even as Christ drove the money changers from the temple. St. Paul admonished slaves to obey their masters.

Southerners also credited the Israelites with establishing a more benevolent and humane form of slavery. South Carolina planter and statesman James Henry Hammond emphasized that the Israelites, finding slavery in a barbarous state, had attempted to reform rather than to eradicate it. They understood slavery to be the *"inevitable condition of human society."* In "The Bible Argument: or Slavery in the Light of Divine Revelation" (1850), one of the most popular and influential proslavery tracts, Baptist minister Thornton Stringfellow of Virginia argued that slavery, "when engrafted on the Jewish constitution, was designed . . . to ameliorate the condition of the slaves in the neighboring nations." Similarly, Episcopalian cleric and editor of *Southern Review* Albert Taylor Bledsoe wrote in "Liberty and Slavery: or, Slavery in the Light of Moral and Political Philosophy" (1856) that

> the treatment of slaves among the heathen was far more severe and rigorous than it could lawfully be under the Mosaic law. The heathen master possessed the power of life and death, of scourging or imprisoning, or putting to excessive toil, even to any extent that he pleased. Not so among the Hebrews.

Moreover, Bledsoe hastened to add, the Jews had exposed their slaves to a knowledge of "the one living and true God."

Reverend Frederick A. Ross, a Presbyterian from Huntsville, Alabama, did not linger over the question of what God had permitted the Israelites. In *Slavery Ordained of God,* published in 1857 explicitly to refute abolitionist argu-

ments, Ross announced that God had commanded the Israelites to be slaveholders. "He *made* it the law of their social state. He *made* it one form of his ordained government among many." Ross, further, reminded abolitionists that those who called themselves Christian had to accept Scripture as the revealed word of God and had to concede that God, not man, defined sin and virtue. He thereupon proceeded to defend Southern slavery as an extension and continuation of Hebrew slavery, and attested that slavery furnished a model of social and political order:

> Every Southern planter is not more truly a slaveholder than Abraham. And the Southern master, by divine authority, may today, consider his slaves part of his social and religious family, just as Abraham did. . . . He is a slaveholder in no other sense than was Abraham. . . . So, then, Abraham lived in the midst of a system of slave-holding, exactly the same in nature with that in the South—a system ordained of God as really as the other forms of government round about him.

In his *Inquiry into the Law of Negro Slavery in the United States of America* (1858), the jurist Thomas R. R. Cobb of Georgia distinguished two classes of slaves among the Israelites. The first consisted of their Hebrew brethren, the second of strangers and heathens. "Hebrew slaves," Cobb explained, "were subject to six-year terms of service, and had the option of accepting perpetual servitude if they could not care for themselves as free men." He clarified the status of "Hebrew slaves," writing:

> A marked difference was made in the law as to the status of a Hebrew servant and one bought from the heathen. He was not to serve as a bond-servant, but as a hired servant and sojourner. He was not to be treated with rigor, but as a brother "waxen poor." He lost, in his bondage, only his liberty, none of his civil rights. He was still a citizen, and might acquire property of his own. . . . In case of war, the slaves "born in the house" were frequently armed and went forth to battle with the master.

Those whom Cobb described as "pure" or "foreign" slaves, bought "from stranger and heathen, or captives taken in war," were, by contrast, subjected to "rigorous treatment." Unlike "Hebrew slaves," they had no civil or legal rights, could not file a complaint against their master, could not give testimony in court, and could not own property. Foreign slaves were also bound in perpetuity, as were their children and their descendants.

Largely silent on the question of how Mosaic law applied to foreign as opposed to Hebrew slaves, Cobb nevertheless distinguished variations in the nature of slavery and the treatment of slaves that enabled him more clearly to define the practice in the South. Southern slavery, he declared, was not absolute slavery, which deprived the slaves of the rights that common law guaranteed to every citizen: the right to security, the right to liberty, and the right to property. In the South, Cobb wrote, the system of slavery had been so modified that "partly by natural law, partly by express enactment, and more effectively by the influence of civilization and Christian enlightenment," the rights of slaves received a measure of security and protection, the denial of which "would shock an enlightened public sense." Louisa S. McCord echoed these sentiments, pointing out that in the South "the Negro has in many cases an appeal from the judgments of his master who is responsible to the law for cruel oppression," while "perfect slavery implies authority without appeal, in the one individual, and subjection, without right of resistance, in the other."

Even when the Israelites had been brutal masters, as doubtless on occasion they were, the existence of such cruelty, proslavery advocates argued, did not provoke God to withdraw his approval of slavery itself. Proclaiming that God had ordained slavery among the Israelites, the eminent political economist, statistician, journalist, and editor J. D. B. De Bow wrote that although it was "not improbable, many of the Jews . . . abused the institution, as they did other laws. . . . we may well affirm that slavery presents no worse aspect in the civilized nations of the present day, than it did among the Hebrews." Reverend George D. Armstrong of Norfolk, Virginia, declared in *The Christian Doctrine of Slavery* (1857) that "the condition of slaves in Judea, in our Lord's Day, was no better than it is now in our Southern states, while in all other countries it was greatly worse." An anonymous writer in *De Bow's Review* avowed that the Israelites had, in fact, been far more vicious masters than were Southerners. "The [Hebrew] master could punish or chastise the slave, and even maim him, at his pleasure. He exercised rights which no Southern planter would dare to exercise, and which a Southern negro would not submit to." The laws regulating the Hebrew system of slavery were "worse for the slave than the laws of any Southern states."

However dubious this assertion, it evinced a tendency among Southern slaveholders and their spokesmen to regard slaves as members of an extended family who warranted the consideration of their masters. No passing sentimentality to quiet uneasy consciences and no mere rationalization for the exercise of despotic power, the expression "my family, black and white" offered the assurance that the South was a community of Christian households into which the slaves had been assimilated. In *Lecture Delivered before the Young Men's Library Association, of Augusta, April 10th, 1851, Showing African Slavery to be Consistent with the Moral and Physical Progress of a Nation* (1851), Christopher G. Memminger, the future Confederate secretary of the treasury, described the familial relations that theoretically prevailed among the slaveholders of the South:

> The Slave Institution at the South increases the tendency to dignify the family. Each planter in fact is a Patriarch—his position compels him to be a ruler in his household. From early youth, his children and servants look up to him as the head, and obedience and subordination become important elements of education. Where so many depend upon one will, society assumes the Hebrew form. Domestic relations become those which are most prized—each family recognizes its duty—and its members feel a responsibility for its discharge. The fifth commandment becomes the foundation of Society. The state is looked to only as the ultimate head in external relations while all internal duties, such as support, education, and the relative duties of individuals, are left to domestic regulation.

The duties of the masters included the responsible management of property, which Southerners deemed part of man's social nature. Yet, Southerners expressly denied the bourgeois concept of property that gave owners an absolute right to do with it as they pleased. Secular and religious law required that the masters of slaves protect, nurture, and govern all their household dependents, including their human chattel. Perhaps it had always been necessary that one class of men labor for the benefit of another, as proslavery theorists reasoned. A genuinely Christian slavery, however, organized and institutionalized inequality and exploitation to correspond to the ethical canons of the Bible, and thus alone made possible material progress without the terrible economic, social, political, and moral disturbances that plagued the North and Europe.

Reverend James Henley Thornwell, president of South Carolina College (later the University of South Carolina) and editor of the *Southern Presbyterian Review,* went so far as to proclaim that the South stood as the last bastion against a multitude of ideologies and heresies that threatened to undo Christian civilization. Slavery, preferably in a form compatible with the teachings of Scripture, would everywhere have to prevail over the social relations of free society if that civilization were now to survive. During the secession crisis of 1860–1861, Thornwell clarified the ideas upon which he had ruminated for more than a decade:

non-slaveholding states will eventually have to organize labour, and introduce something so like to slavery that it will be impossible to discriminate between them, or else to suffer from the most violent and disastrous insurrections.

The Christian view of slavery that Thornwell expounded implied that slaves, as children of God and as human beings with immortal souls, had rights that masters dare not abridge. Along with many other Southern social thinkers and theologians, Thornwell repudiated the conviction that masters had limitless authority over their slaves. "The idle declamation about degrading men to the condition of chattels and treating them as oxen or swine, the idea that they are regarded as tools and instruments and not as beings possessed of immortal souls," Thornwell wrote, "betray a gross ignorance of the real nature of the relation." Masters who violated the rights or neglected the welfare of their slaves ought to expect a rebuke from the church, but also punishment from the state. Thornwell minced no words: "In treating slavery as an existing institution, a fact involving most important moral relations, one of the prime duties of the State is to protect, by temporal legislation, the real rights of the slave." That, too, was the will of God.

Divine law, in Thornwell's judgment, superseded property rights. Masters held their slaves only in trust, to discharge the will and purpose of God on earth. The sinful abuse of that authority, therefore, invited his wrath. Thornwell argued repeatedly, and with unquestioned sincerity, that should the Christian people of the South ever become convinced that slavery was a sin, they would not waste a moment eradicating it. Slavery, in Thornwell's view, was not sinful, and his writing in its defense grew into an extraordinary critique of modernity.

In a sermon titled "The Christian Doctrine of Slavery," Thornwell launched a general denunciation of the radicalism of the age. He assailed the abolitionists not only for attacking slavery but also for threatening the foundations of social order. He traced abolitionists' errors to misconceptions about human nature. Like other species of radicals, Thornwell charged, abolitionists had forgotten that men, if left to their own devices, were neither good nor benevolent. They lived instead in a fallen world for which God had established relations of authority and subordination as the principle of order. It was, therefore, not slavery that was sinful, but the attempt to erase all distinctions between men and to impose absolute equality of condition upon them. In what must surely rank among Thornwell's most ardent polemics, he announced that the combatants in the present struggle were not merely the abolition-

ists and the slaveholders. The ranks also included "Atheists," "Socialists," "Communists," "Red republicans," and "Jacobins" on one side, and the friends of civilization on the other. The world, Thornwell professed, had become a battleground divided between Christianity and atheism, with the fate of mankind hanging in the balance.

Thornwell undertook to institute in the South a Christian polity that reconciled, as far as was possible in this world, social order with social justice and the duties of men with the dignity of man. For that purpose the complacent support and heartless celebration of the free market would not serve. Thornwell proposed instead the imposition of some form of personal servitude on all workers, white as well as black, which would spare them the anarchy of the market and afford them a sense of security and decency that current economic, social, and political regimes did not provide. Such arrangements, he knew, would impede economic growth and development. Yet, in his view there was no other option, for the costs of material progress had become too great to bear if men did not wish to rebel against God and imperil their souls.

–MARK G. MALVASI,
RANDOLPH-MACON COLLEGE

Viewpoint:
No. Slavery violated the spirit of Christianity; opponents of slavery believed that it was wrong because it prevented master and slave alike from living virtuous, moral, and Christian lives.

Proslavery theorists were fond of reminding their opponents of the many ways in which the Bible sanctioned slavery. They pointed out that the Israelites, including Abraham and the other patriarchs, had held slaves. Christ remained silent on slavery, except to advise the faithful "to render unto Caesar that which was Caesar's," and from the Southern perspective, slavery belonged unequivocally to Caesar. St. Paul, finally, instructed slaves to accept their fate and obey their masters. Nowhere in Scripture did Southerners find justification for the belief that slavery was a sin.

The abolitionists were dismayed at the biblical evidence arrayed in defense of slavery. Such antislavery spokesmen as Reverend William Ellery Channing, a noted evangelist, and Dr. Francis Wayland, president and professor of

CHRISTIANITY

THE CORRECT PLAN

Dr. Charles Hodge of Princeton, New Jersey, submitted for publication to E. N. Elliott an article that included the following passages:

It is on all hands acknowledged that, at the time of the advent of Jesus Christ, slavery in its worst forms prevailed over the whole world. The Saviour found it around him in Judea; the apostles met with it in Asia, Greece and Italy. How did they treat it? Not by the denunciation of slaveholding as necessarily and universally sinful. Not by declaring that all slaveholders were men-stealers and robbers, and consequently to be excluded from the church and the kingdom of heaven. Not by insisting on immediate emancipation. Not by appeals to the passions of men on the evils of slavery, or by the adoption of a system of universal agitation. On the contrary, it was by teaching the true nature, dignity, equality and destiny of men; by inculcating the principles of justice and love; and by leaving these principles to produce their legitimate effects in ameliorating the condition of all classes of society. We need not stop to prove that such was the course pursued by our Saviour and his apostles, because the fact is generally acknowledged, and various reasons are assigned, by the abolitionists and others, to account for it. The subject is hardly alluded to by Christ in any of his personal instructions. The apostles refer to it, not to pronounce upon it as a question of morals, but to prescribe the relative duties of masters and slaves. They caution those slaves who have believing or Christian masters, not to despise them because they were on a perfect religious equality with them, but to consider the fact that their masters were their brethren, as an additional reason for obedience. It is remarkable that there is not even an exhortation to masters to liberate their slaves, much less is it urged as an imperative and immediate duty. They are commanded to be kind, merciful and just; and to remember that they have a Master in heaven. Paul represents this relation as of comparatively little account; "Let every man abide in the same calling wherein he was called. Art thou called being a servant (or slave), care not for it; though, should the opportunity of freedom be presented, embrace it. These external relations, however, are of little importance, for every Christian is a freeman in the highest and best sense of the word, and at the same time is under the strongest bonds of Christ." 1 Cor. vii:20–22. It is not worth while to shut our eyes to these facts. They will remain, whether we refuse to see them and be instructed by them or not. If we are wiser, better, more courageous than Christ and his apostles, let us say so; but it will do no good, under a paroxysm of benevolence, to attempt to tear the Bible to pieces, or to exhort, by violent exegesis, a meaning foreign to its obvious sense. Whatever inferences may be fairly deducible from the fact, the fact itself cannot be denied that Christ and his inspired followers did treat the subject of slavery in the manner stated above. This being the case, we ought carefully to consider their conduct in this respect, and inquire what lessons that conduct should teach us.

We think no one will deny that the plan adopted by the Saviour and his immediate followers must be the correct plan, and therefore obligatory upon us, unless it can be shown that their circumstances were so different from ours, as to make the rule of duty different in the two cases. The obligation to point out and establish this difference, rests of course upon those who have adopted a course diametrically the reverse of that which Christ pursued. They have not acquitted themselves of this obligation. They do not seem to have felt it necessary to reconcile their conduct with his; nor does it appear to have occurred to them, that their violent denunciations of slaveholding and of slaveholders is an indirect reflection on his wisdom, virtue, or courage. If the present course of the abolitionists is right, then the course of Christ and the apostles were wrong. For the circumstances of the two cases are, as far as we can see, in all essential particulars, the same. They appeared as teachers of morality and religion, not as politicians. The same is the fact with our abolitionists. They found slavery authorized by the laws of the land. So do we. They were called upon to receive into the communion of the Christian Church, both slave owners and slaves. So are we. They instructed these different classes of persons as to their respective duties. So do we. Where then is the difference between the two cases? If we are right in insisting that slaveholding is one of the greatest of all sins; that it should be immediately and universally abandoned as a condition of church communion, or admission into heaven, how comes it that Christ and his apostles did not pursue the same course? We see no way of escape from the conclusion that the conduct of the modern abolitionists, being directly opposed to that of the authors of our religion, must be wrong and ought to be modified or abandoned.

Source: *Charles Hodge, "The Bible Argument on Slavery," in* Cotton is King and Pro-Slavery Arguments, *edited by E. N. Elliott (Augusta, Ga.: Pritchard, Abbott & Loomis, 1860), pp. 847–849.*

moral philosophy at Brown University, insisted that if anyone could show that the Bible vindicated slavery, then sincere Christians had an obligation to discard the Bible as an evil book. (The Brown family of Providence, Rhode Island, whose fortune derived from the slave trade, had endowed Brown University.) Whatever false lessons desperate men and women might deduce from Scripture, abolitionists insisted that slavery so completely and obviously violated the spirit of Christianity that all arguments to the contrary required no serious refutation.

For others, such as the Quakers, or Society of Friends, opposition to slavery became a crucial test of religious purity and faith. According to radical Philadelphia Quaker Benjamin Lay, for example, "*As God gave his only begotten Son, that whosoever believed in him might have everlasting Life;* so the Devil gives his only begotten Child, *the Merchandize of Slaves and Souls of Men,* that whosoever believes and trades in it might have everlasting Damnation.*" Slavery was, according to Lay, a "Hellish Practice," a "filthy sin," "the greatest Sin in the World, of the very Nature of Hell itself, and in the Belly of Hell." If, as historian David Brion Davis has suggested, Lay was not quite sane, "one should remember that the sanest minds found excuses for Negro slavery." In his impressive studies of the problem of slavery, Davis has shown that Lay's antislavery religion evolved from a long process of soul-searching that took place within the Society of Friends.

Initially, slavery presented few, if any, moral problems for the Quakers. The growth of the Society, in fact, coincided with the imperial expansion of Great Britain and the advent of the slave trade. "Indeed," writes Davis, "the destiny of the Society of Friends was intertwined with American slavery in an almost providential design." Quakers were slaveholders in Barbados and Jamaica, which William Penn's father, who was not himself a Quaker, had captured from Spain in 1655. Quaker merchants in Rhode Island, New Jersey, and Pennsylvania participated extensively in the slave trade, from which they made their fortunes. Although George Fox, the founder of the Society of Friends, encouraged slaveholders to practice Christian charity, brotherhood, and love in their relations with the slaves, Fox also acquiesced in slavery as one, albeit extreme, instance of the subjugation of man to God. The bondage to sin, St. Augustine had taught, was the only bondage that mattered; temporal bondage ought not concern the elect, who remained spiritually free.

Not until Christians changed their minds about the nature and meaning of sin could they question the justice of slavery. "Men could not fully perceive the moral contradictions of slavery," Davis insists, "until a major religious transformation had changed their ideas of sin and spiritual freedom; they would not feel it a duty to combat slavery as a positive evil until its existence seemed to threaten the moral security provided by a system of values that harmonized individual desires with socially defined goals and sanctions." As early as the 1670s, Quaker William Edmundson had pointed the way toward the Christian rejection of slavery.

Unlike Fox, Edmundson was not convinced that Christianity would inspire masters to conduct themselves with greater humanity toward their slaves, a belief that had traditionally formed the basis of the Christian defense of slavery. In 1676, Edmundson circulated a general letter to Quakers in the slaveholding colonies. He observed that although slaves in the Caribbean were free to act according to their own sinful natures, they were not free to be baptized and to devote their lives to loving and serving the Lord. Slavery thus prevented the slaves from becoming good Christians. Blacks, Edmundson declared, were slaves to sin because they were slaves to men. Slavery was incompatible with Christianity and was, therefore, sinful.

Christianity also motivated such early British and American abolitionists as Granville Sharp, James Ramsay, Thomas Clarkson, William Wilberforce, Samuel Hopkins, Samuel Sewall, and Benjamin Rush, to say nothing of their nineteenth-century counterparts William Lloyd Garrison, Wendell Phillips, and Theodore Dwight Weld. In some respects, the antislavery movement was an extension of the philanthropic tradition that had begun to take shape during the fifteenth and sixteenth centuries and was predicated on the teaching that morality required good Christians not only to behave well but also to love their neighbors. The growth of charity, however, had done nothing to prevent or mitigate the slave trade and had excited no general denunciations of slavery itself. Beneficence could not be permitted to interfere with the rights of property or the requirements of social order. The Christian impulse to oppose slavery thus moved in another direction.

For many mainstream Protestants, slavery facilitated the idolatrous worship of Mammon (material wealth or possessions). Always mistrustful of unlimited power, antislavery Protestants also feared that those masters who systematically denied their slaves religious instruction had substituted themselves for God. Such blasphemies could not be allowed to prevail. Slavery, sinful in itself, was the occasion for even greater sins: greed, lust, and impiety, to name only the most obvious and the most deadly.

Those who rejected Calvinism, particularly the belief in predestination and human depravity, also came to find slavery abhorrent. During

CHRISTIANITY

THE NEGRO IN HIS OWN COUNTRY.

THE NEGRO IN AMERICA.

the eighteenth and nineteenth centuries, the Latitudinarians, as they were known, increasingly turned to societies more primitive than England as models of virtue and probity. The heathen, they argued, although ignorant of the gospel, might carry within himself a truer spirit of Christianity than the urbane sophisticate who had committed the Articles of Faith to memory. It was not long before the righteous but downtrodden slaves and the lawful but heartless masters became religious and literary conventions, representing, on the one hand, compassion, solace, fellowship, and truth, and on the other, luxury, power, decadence, and sin. The slaves were innocents, undeserving of their fate. Their pleas for freedom and justice could not go unheeded among Christian men and women. The progress,

and perhaps the survival, of humanity depended upon their emancipation. The abolition of slavery gave proof through human agency of God's benevolence and love.

American abolitionist James Freeman Clarke, in *Slavery in the United States: A Sermon Delivered in Amory Hall, on Thanksgiving Day, November 24, 1842* (1843), asserted that it was "a mistake to speak of the African as an inferior race to the Caucasian." Similarly, essayist and poet Ralph Waldo Emerson declared: "Here is a man: and if you have a man, black or white is an insignificance. The intellect–that is miraculous! Who has it, has the talisman: his skin and bones, though they were of the color of night, are transparent, and everlasting stars shine through, with attractive beams." Only the depraved institution of slavery kept blacks from realizing their infinite potential as human beings. In 1841, Channing extended the implications of this argument to include a condemnation of slaveholders. He exclaimed that "a people, upholding or in any way giving countenance to slavery, contract guilt in proportion to the light which is thrown on the injustice and evils of this institution. . . . The weight of guilt on this nation is great and increasing." Channing called forth images of guilt in

> The wars, the sacked and burning villages, the kidnapping and murders of Africa, which begin this horrible history; the crowded hold, the chains, stench, suffocation, burning thirst, and agonies of the slave ship; the loathsome diseases and enormous waste of life in the middle passage; the wrongs and sufferings, of the plantation, with its reign of terror and force, its unbridled lust, its violation of domestic rights and charities—these all are revealed.

"To shut our eyes against all this," he concluded, "to shut our ears and hearts . . . this, surely, is a guilt which the justice of God cannot wink at, and one which insulted humanity, religion, and freedom call down fearful retribution." Slavery, it seems, was becoming the American national sin. Only its abolition could expiate the guilt and reconcile the nation to the Almighty; failure would incite his wrath

For Clarke there was an "'irrepressible conflict' between Freedom and Slavery. The opposition is radical and entire; there can be no peace nor permanent truce between them, till one has conquered the other." Unitarian clergyman Theodore Parker demanded repentance and atonement, implicating Northerners and Southerners alike, along with every current citizen of the United States, and all previous generations, in the sin of slavery. He agonized in "A Letter to the People of the United States Touching the Matter of Slavery" (22 December 1847):

> Think of the nation's deed, done continually and afresh. God shall hear the voice of your brother's blood, long crying from the ground; His justice asks you even now, "America, where is thy brother?" This is the answer which America must give: "Lo, he is there in the rice-swamps of the South, in the fields teeming with cotton and the luxuriant cane. He was weak and I seized him; naked and I bound him; ignorant, poor and savage, and I over-mastered him. I laid on his feebler shoulders my grievous yoke. I have chained him with my fetters; beat him with my whip. Other tyrants had dominion over him, but my finger was thicker than their loins. I have branded the mark of my power, with red-hot iron, upon his human flesh. I am fed with his toil; fat, voluptuous on his sweat, and tears, and blood. I stole the father, stole also the sons, and set them to toil; his wife and daughters are a pleasant spoil to me. Behold the children also of thy servant and his handmaidens—sons

swarthier than their sire. Askest Thou for the African? I found him a barbarian. I have made him a beast. Lo, there Thou hast what is Thine."

Nor in their zeal did abolitionists spare institutional religion, appealing to a more unspoiled and often private version of Christianity. They assailed the churches of both regions and all denominations as the "refuge and hiding-place" of slavery. Stephen Symonds Foster, in *The Brotherhood of Thieves* (1886), characterized the clergy who refused to condemn slavery as a "brotherhood of thieves." "If the Church must be cast down by the strugglings of Humanity to be free," wrote Garrison, "then let the Church fall, and its fragments be scattered to the four winds of heaven, never more to curse the earth." Most abolitionists, however, exhorted Christians not to abandon the faith but to abide fully by its precepts, which required the steadfast opposition to slavery. "Thus, we see, that the Christian religion not only forbids slavery," affirmed Wayland in *Elements of Moral Science* (1835), "but that it also provides the only method in which, after it has once been established, it may be abolished, and that with entire safety and benefits to both parties."

In the end, many who called themselves "Christian" believed they had to decide whether slavery was right or wrong. The question, if not the decision, was simple. That people could arrive at contradictory answers ought to be obvious. After all, most of the Protestant churches in the United States divided over the question of slavery years before political partisans set the nation asunder. Both sides appealed to God to justify their convictions and their cause. The advocates of slavery found much in Scripture to bolster their arguments, but in time events compelled them to admit that it was the enemies of slavery whom God had vindicated. Although he was president of the triumphant Union, Abraham Lincoln reflected not upon impending victory in his Second Inaugural Address (1865) but upon the searing tragedy that slavery had wrought in the United States. His words serve as a reminder that no matter how men and women may use religion, the Almighty has purposes of his own:

> If we shall suppose that American Slavery is one of those offences which, in the providence of God, must needs come, but which, having continued through His appointed time, He now wills to remove, and that He gives to both North and South, this terrible war, as the woe due to those by whom the offence came, shall we discern therein any departure from those divine attributes which the believers in a Living God always ascribe to Him? Fondly do we hope—fervently do we pray—that this mighty scourge of war may speedily pass away. Yet, if God wills that it continue, until all the wealth piled by the bond-man's two hundred and fifty years of unrequited toil

shall be sunk, and until every drop of blood drawn with the lash, shall be paid for by another drawn with the sword, as was said three thousand years ago, so still it must be said "the judgments of the Lord, are true and righteous altogether."

–S. D. BLACK,
RICHMOND, VIRGINIA

References

George D. Armstrong, *The Christian Doctrine of Slavery* (New York: Scribner, 1857).

William Ellery Channing, *Emancipation* (New York: American Anti-Slavery Society, 1841).

James Freeman Clarke, *Slavery in the United States: A Sermon Delivered in Amory Hall, on Thanksgiving Day, November 24, 1842* (Boston: Greene, 1843).

Thomas R. R. Cobb, *An Inquiry into the Law of Negro Slavery in the United States of America: To Which is Prefixed an Historical Sketch of Slavery* (Philadelphia: T. & J. W. Johnson / Savannah: W. T. Williams, 1858).

David Brion Davis, *The Problem of Slavery in the Age of Revolution, 1770–1823* (Ithaca, N.Y.: Cornell University Press, 1975).

Davis, *The Problem of Slavery in Western Culture* (Ithaca, N.Y.: Cornell University Press, 1966).

Clement Eaton, *The Mind of the Old South* (Baton Rouge: Louisiana State University Press, 1964).

Stanley M. Elkins, *Slavery: A Problem in American Intellectual and Institutional Life,* third edition (Chicago: University of Chicago Press, 1976).

E. N. Elliott, ed., *Cotton is King and Pro-Slavery Arguments* (Augusta, Ga.: Pritchard, Abbott & Loomis, 1860).

Drew Gilpin Faust, *Southern Stories: Slaveholders in Peace and War* (Columbia: University of Missouri Press, 1992).

Faust, ed., *The Ideology of Slavery: Proslavery Thought in the Antebellum South, 1830–1860* (Baton Rouge: Louisiana State University Press, 1981).

Eugene Genovese, *The Slaveholder's Dilemma: Freedom and Progress in Southern Conservative Thought, 1820–1860* (Columbia: University of South Carolina Press, 1992).

Genovese, *The World the Slaveholders Made: Two Essays in Interpretation* (Hanover, N.H.: Wesleyan University Press, 1988).

Genovese and Elizabeth Fox-Genovese, "The Divine Sanction of Social Order: Religious Foundations of the Southern Slaveholders' World View," *Journal of the American Academy of Religion,* 55 (1987): 211–233.

Genovese and Fox-Genovese, "The Religious Ideals of Southern Slave Society," *Georgia Historical Quarterly,* 70 (Spring 1986): 1–16.

William Sumner Jenkins, *Pro-Slavery Thought in the Old South* (Chapel Hill: University of North Carolina Press, 1935).

Arthur Young Lloyd, *The Slavery Controversy, 1831–1860* (Chapel Hill: University of North Carolina Press, 1939).

Anne C. Loveland, *Southern Evangelicals and the Social Order, 1800–1860* (Baton Rouge: Louisiana State University Press, 1980).

Jack P. Maddex Jr., "'The Southern Apostasy' Revisited: The Significance of Proslavery Christianity," *Marxist Perspectives,* 2 (Fall 1979): 132–141.

Theodore Parker, "The Slave Power," in *The Works of Theodore Parker,* volume 5, *Lessons from the World of Matter and the World of Man,* edited by Rufus Leighton (Boston: American Unitarian Association, 1908).

Frederick A. Ross, *Slavery Ordained of God* (Philadelphia: Lippincott, 1857).

William A. Smith, *Lectures on the Philosophy and Practice of Slavery, As Exhibited in the Institution of Domestic Slavery in the United States: With the Duties of Masters and Slaves,* edited by Thomas O. Summers (Nashville: Stevenson & Evans, 1856).

James Brewer Stewart, *Holy Warriors: The Abolitionists and American Slavery* (New York: Hill & Wang, 1976).

James Henley Thornwell, *The Collected Works of James Henley Thornwell,* 4 volumes, edited by John B. Adger (Richmond, Va.: Presbyterian Committee of Publication, 1871–1873).

Larry E. Tise, *Proslavery: A History of the Defense of Slavery in America, 1701–1840* (Athens: University of Georgia Press, 1987).

Francis Wayland, *Elements of Moral Science* (New York: Cooke, 1835).

COMPLICITY

Did Africans willingly collaborate in the transatlantic slave trade?

Viewpoint: Yes. The traffic in slaves had existed in Africa for centuries before the arrival of Europeans, and it took little adjustment to sell captives to European rather than African or Arab traders.

Viewpoint: No. Many African leaders resisted the transatlantic slave trade because of the destructive impact it had on their communities.

The nature and extent of African collaboration in the slave trade remains controversial. Why did some Africans enslave and sell others? Were they eager or reluctant participants in the slave trade? Did they control the commerce in slaves, or were they merely the pawns of Europeans? The evidence indicates no clear or certain answers to these questions. The willingness of Africans to take part in the domestic and later in the transatlantic slave trade admitted wide variations. The rulers of Benin, for instance, resisted and eventually dissociated themselves and their kingdom from the slave trade. In the Congo and Senegambia, by contrast, those who dominated the slave trade not only garnered huge profits but in time also rose to political power. The societies most active in the slave trade developed both the potent military apparatus and the complex economic mechanisms required to capture and transport large numbers of slaves for sale in distant markets. If nothing else, the emergence of such instruments demonstrates that African societies were neither backward nor isolated, long discredited stereotypes that nonetheless continue to find their way into scholarly and popular literature.

Moreover, the African market for slaves did not disappear with the expansion of the transatlantic slave trade. Yet, unlike Europeans who preferred male slaves, Africans wanted mainly females. Women worked as field hands and domestics or served as concubines. African slaveholders also thought female slaves less likely to run away or rebel, and they regarded them as generally easier to govern. By the seventeenth century the growth of the transatlantic slave trade in conjunction with the survival of the African slave trade had made the number of persons in bondage in Africa equivalent to the number of persons in bondage in the Americas. Throughout the eighteenth century, wars among states along the western coast of Africa, specifically in the Bight of Benin, yielded on average fifteen thousand slaves per year for export.

As the population of the Bight of Benin declined, the price of slaves rose considerably between 1690 and 1730. The quest for an alternate source of slaves forced other regions into the slave trade, including the Bight of Biafra (southern Nigeria), Sierra Leone, the Gold Coast (Ghana), Angola, and the Congo. To satisfy the demands of the market, Africans dispossessed these societies of their men. In West and Central Africa the ratio of women to men reached ten females for every seven males. Meanwhile, the ratio of women to men in Angola and the Bight of Biafra stood at two to one.

The gradual abolition of the transatlantic trade beginning in the late eighteenth century actually caused the expansion of slavery and the slave trade in Africa. As slave exports from West Africa to the Americas declined, those from Angola, the Congo, the Sahara, the Horn, and East Africa increased or held steady. By the 1850s, the British Royal Navy had nearly eliminated the transatlantic slave trade. For the next eighty years, however, slavery and the slave trade flourished in Africa. As a consequence, by the late nineteenth century, after the emancipation of the slaves in the United States (1865), Cuba (1866), and Brazil (1888), there were more slaves in Africa than at any other time in its history.

Viewpoint:
Yes. The traffic in slaves had existed in Africa for centuries before the arrival of Europeans, and it took little adjustment to sell captives to European rather than African or Arab traders.

Among the agrarian societies of western and Central Africa, slavery was long established as a social and economic institution. Although the practice of slavery in Africa varied considerably, it had continuing importance. The Scotsman Mungo Park, one of the first Europeans to make his way into the African interior, wrote that during the 1790s "the slaves . . . are nearly in the proportion of three to one to the freemen." In some regions of West Africa during the nineteenth century, slaves composed 75 percent of the population.

Slavery in Africa differed from slavery in the New World. Almost everywhere that slavery existed in Africa, it was tied to kinship networks and household production. The addition of slaves to a household enhanced the status and power of its head as well as increased its productive capacity. Kinship often distinguished a slave from a free person in Africa. Put simply, slaves and their descendants were always outsiders, thus making possible their economic, political, and social exploitation by insiders, the original members of the family and household. In *Travels in the Interior Districts of Africa: Performed in the Years 1795, 1796, and 1797* (1816), Park again provided a revealing description:

> The domestic slave, or such as are born in a man's own house, are treated with more lenity than those which are purchased with money. The authority of the master over the domestic slave . . . extends only to reasonable correction: for the master cannot sell his domestic, without first having brought him to a public trial, before the chief men of the place. But these restrictions on the power of the master extend not to the case of prisoners taken in war, nor to that of slaves purchased with money. All these unfortunate beings are considered as strangers and foreigners, who have no right to the protection of the law, and may be treated with severity, or sold to a stranger, according

to the pleasure of their owners. There are, indeed, regular markets, where slaves of this description are bought and sold; and the value of a slave in the eye of an African purchaser, increases in proportion to his distance from his native kingdom. . . . The slaves which are purchased by Europeans on the Coast, are chiefly of this description.

Over several generations, slaves could become recognized and even valued members of a household, but they never quite lost their status as "other than kin."

As in most places where slavery existed, Africans obtained slaves usually by violent means. War, banditry, and kidnapping were among the most common, but men and women were also enslaved for debt or such criminal offenses as stealing, adultery, and murder. Others found themselves sold into slavery by their relatives or their rulers. Prisoners of war were usually enslaved as an alternative to being put to death. Generally, as Park indicated, captives were not especially valuable near their homes. They knew the terrain too well and were more likely to try to escape. Hence, their masters usually sold them away as quickly as possible if there were no pressing need for their labor. Merchants eager to buy prisoners of war at bargain prices and to sell them in distant markets commonly followed African armies into battle and negotiated for captives on the field.

As the transatlantic trade grew, slavery probably became a more common punishment for a variety of crimes. In 1854, for example, a German missionary in Sierra Leone named S. W. Koelle collected biographical information on 179 former slaves. He found that many had been enslaved for violating the laws of their societies or defying the authorities who ruled them. Two typical examples gleaned from Koelle's interviews include:

> Asu, or Thomas Harry of Hastings . . . married two wives, the unfaithfulness of one of whom led him to slay a man, on which account he was sold [into slavery] by the king.

> Aboyade, or James Cole, . . . born in the town of Ogbomosho, where he lived till his first child was about three years old, when he was sold by a war-chief, because he refused to give him his wife.

COMPLICITY

African societies that regularly acquired slaves were also accustomed to selling them. The African slave trade that brought slaves across the Sahara to North Africa, in fact, extending from before 700 C.E. into the twentieth century, lasted far longer than the transatlantic slave trade. Central Africans sold slaves in India for almost as long. The onset of the transatlantic slave trade did not signal something new for Africans. By the time Europeans appeared, Africans already had social and economic institutions in place to provide slaves in exchange for the commodities that they preferred, including textiles, iron, copper, knives, swords, jewelry, alcohol, and guns.

Between 1796 and 1805 estimates suggest that English merchants alone imported 1,615,309 guns into West Africa, and their rivals from other nations brought at least as many. Although the principal use to which Africans put firearms remains unclear and controversial, the Nigerian-born historian Joseph E. Inikori maintains that there is substantial evidence of:

> The imported firearms being used primarily for raids and wars directed to the acquisition of captives for sale. . . . The strong preference of the slave sellers for guns indicates very strongly the connexion between firearms and the acquisition of slaves. It reinforces the slave-gun cycle theory according to which the states and individuals or groups of individual slave gatherers bought more firearms to capture more slaves to buy more firearms.

Others who acquired guns, Inikori explains, frequently did so to protect themselves from those Africans who sought to enslave them either through raids or wars.

The most arresting and novel aspect of the transatlantic slave trade was its scale. No other movement of slaves, before or since, approached the massive, involuntary transportation of people out of western and Central Africa to the New World during the four centuries between 1450 and 1850. Equally remarkable, this process went forward without a major war between Africans and Europeans. The decisive European conquests of Africa occurred years after the slave trade had come to an end. Furthermore, Europeans largely purchased rather than captured the slaves who flooded the Atlantic sea lanes and sustained the colonization of the New World. The Portuguese put this system into place between 1456 and 1462, and it continued to characterize relations between Africans and Europeans for centuries to come.

Africans thus played an active and important role in developing the transatlantic slave trade with Europeans and did so on their own initiative. After all, little difference existed between trading slaves with other Africans and trading them with Europeans. The impetus that induced African participation in the slave trade was not the effort to obtain essentials but

Slave Market on the West Coast of Africa, painting by François-Auguste Biard, 1840

(Wilberforce House, Hull City Museums Art Gallery and Archives, Kingston-upon-Hull, U.K.)

COMPLICITY

was rather the desire to satisfy caprice, to augment wealth, and to enhance prestige.

The slave trade, therefore, did not retard African economic growth and development. It did not disrupt industrial production or upset commercial activity. As a consequence, Africans found no compelling reasons to eradicate it. Instead, they sought to control and even to monopolize it, although ultimately they were no more successful in doing so than were the Europeans. Nevertheless, the authorities in various African kingdoms insisted that they benefit from the slave trade, either directly or through the payment of tribute, and were content to allow business to continue without interference once they had received their share.

Slavery was indigenous to African societies and was deeply rooted in African legal, social, political, and institutional structures. Europeans simply entered an existing slave market. Africans responded to the increased demand, and the economic opportunity it represented, by providing more slaves for sale and purchase. The transatlantic slave trade was thus an outgrowth of the internal African slave trade. Africans participated in the slave trade from the beginning, not only as individuals but also as organized societies and states. They also exercised significant, if incomplete, control over the traffic in slaves until those slaves boarded European ships bound for the New World.

In response to European demand, Africans began exporting slaves with astonishing speed. By the middle of the fifteenth century, annual exports totaled between 700 and 1,000 slaves and reached as many as 2,500 by 1500. Most of the early slave trading that took place in West Africa resulted from the diversion of internal commerce into European markets. The same statement is true for Central Africa. Early in the sixteenth century, slaves from Central Africa became so numerous that the Brazilian market could not absorb them all, hastening Portuguese merchants to locate buyers in the colonies of other European powers. The commerce in slaves could never have become so extensive in so short a period of time without a developed African system of slavery, marketing, and transport that predated European contact.

The transatlantic slave trade originated in Africa, where slavery was already firmly entrenched. The capture, ownership, purchase, transfer, and sale of slaves was ubiquitous and accepted. These preexisting conditions and arrangements were as responsible as any external interference or coercion for the evolution and conduct of the transatlantic slave trade.

–MEG GREENE,
MIDLOTHIAN, VIRGINIA

Viewpoint: No. Many African leaders resisted the transatlantic slave trade because of the destructive impact it had on their communities.

No dispute exists about whether Africans participated in the transatlantic slave trade. The more important questions are why they took part, under what conditions, and with what consequences. In the strictest sense of the term, the slave trade might have been a form of commerce, but it was commerce predicated on social violence. Unlike other commercial relations and transactions, the transatlantic slave trade was not mutually beneficial to all parties involved. Europeans prospered, but for Africans the trade brought economic underdevelopment, political upheaval, and social destruction. The slave trade became the major, though not the only, stimulus for violence within and between African communities. War, and more often raiding and kidnapping, increased as Africans sought captives in an effort to meet the growing demand for slaves, thereby taking advantage of the economic opportunities that European slave traders presented.

The expansion of the slave trade also stunted the development of other forms of commerce between Europeans and Africans. Traffic in slaves, for example, disrupted English efforts to foster the growth of an agricultural economy in West and Central Africa during the nineteenth century. Earlier, in the seventeenth century, the Portuguese and the Dutch had tried to discourage the trade in slaves along the Gold Coast because it inhibited the trade in gold. Slave raiding and kidnapping made it unsafe to mine for, or travel with, gold. In addition, the slave trade proved more immediately lucrative than gold mining. A European slave trader noted that "as one fortunate marauding makes a native rich in a day, they therefore exert themselves rather in war, robbery and plunder than in their old business of digging and collecting gold." The transformation from gold mining to slave trading occurred during a period of only ten years, between 1700 and 1710, when the Gold Coast came to supply approximately five thousand to six thousand slaves per annum.

Like other sectors of the African economy, agriculture also suffered with the advent of the transatlantic slave trade. In certain locales, food production increased to accommodate the needs of the slave ships, but in general the slave trade depressed agriculture throughout Africa. As with mining, the slave trade and associated activities drew labor away from agriculture with predictable results. Dahomey, for instance, which during the sixteenth century had produced enough of a surplus to export food, was by the nineteenth century suffering from famine. Unlike the African commerce in slaves, in which captives had been utilized in African communities, the transatlantic slave trade removed potential workers from Africa and thus inhibited or halted the growth of African manufacturing and agriculture. The drain on population and especially the loss of adult males, which began early in such areas as Angola, unbalanced the sex ratio, disrupted family and community life, and altered the sexual division of labor. Separate from considerations about the inhumanity of the slave trade, it was destructive to African economy and society. "The years of trial," wrote the eminent African historian Basil Davidson, "were years of isolation and paralysis wherever the trade with Europe, essentially a trade in slaves, could plant its sterilizing hand. . . . Viewed as a factor in African history, the precolonial connection with Europe . . . had powerfully degrading consequences for the structure of society."

If the slave trade was such harmful commerce, why did Africans participate in it? Were they so blinded by greed that they did not see the extent to which the slave trade was damaging to Africa? In one way or another, Europeans forced the slave trade upon unwilling Africans, either through the commercial inequities that emerged between Europe and Africa, the military pressure that Europeans brought to bear, or both. Europeans subjected the African continent to external forces that were beyond the ability of Africans to mitigate or control.

The rising demand for slaves after 1650 altered African demographics, society, and government. In the Bight of Benin and along the Gold Coast the volume of slave exports increased during the first three decades of the eighteenth century to the limits of population tolerance. Accompanying this decline in population came the disruption of established social patterns and practices. Inventories have shown that for the Bight of Benin, slaves came almost exclusively from the Aja-speaking peoples who lived in and around the kingdom of Dahomey, near the coast. This group experienced an estimated loss in population of more than 3 percent for forty consecutive years, a decline sufficient to reduce the Aja population in absolute terms as well as in relation to nearby ethnic groups such as the Yoruba.

By the late eighteenth century annual slave exports averaged one hundred thousand. A reduction in population occurred throughout the whole of Africa as regional populations, especially in West Africa, could not reproduce themselves to an extent sufficient to counteract slave exports. If not devastating, the losses incurred as a result of the slave trade were certainly severe. The western coast of Africa, with an estimated

MARKED ON THE BREAST

The Portuguese founded Elmina Castle on the Gold Coast in the late fifteenth century to protect their interests in the local gold trade. By 1705 it became the site of a flourishing slave market. William Bosman, a factor of the Dutch West India Company, left the following account of activities at the fort:

Not a few in our country fondly imagine that parents here sell their children, men their wives, and one brother the other: but those who think so deceive themselves; for this never happens on any other account but that of necessity, or some great crime. But most of the slaves that are offered to us are prisoners of war, which are sold by the victors as their booty.

When these slaves come to Fida, they are put in prison all together, and when we treat concerning buying them, they are all brought out together in a large plain; where, by our surgeons, whose province it is, they are thoroughly examined, even to the smallest member, and that naked too, both men and women without the least distinction or modesty. Those which are approved as good are set on one side; and the lame and faulty are set by as invalids. . . . These are such as are above five and thirty years old, or are maimed in the arms, legs, hands, or feet, have lost a tooth, are grey haired or have films over their eyes; as well as all those which are affected with any venereal distemper, or with several other diseases.

The invalids and the maimed being thrown out, as I have told you, the remainder are numbered, and it is entered who delivered them. In the meanwhile a burning iron, with the arms or name of the companies, lies in the fire; with which ours are marked on the breast.

This is done that we may distinguish them from the slaves of the English, French or others; (which are also marked with their mark) and to prevent the Negroes exchanging them for worse; at which they have a good hand.

I doubt not but this trade seems very barbarous to you, but since it is followed by mere necessity it must go on; but we yet take all possible care that they are not burned too hard, especially the women, who are more tender than the men.

We are seldom long detained in the buying of these slaves, because their price is established, the women being one fourth or fifth part cheaper than the men.

Source: William Bosman, A New and Accurate Description of the Coast of Guinea, Divided into the Gold, the Slave, and the Ivory Coasts (1705), in Steven Mintz, ed., African American Voices: The Life Cycle of Slavery (St. James, N.Y.: Brandywine, 1999), pp. 48–50.

population of twenty-five million in 1700, lost six million persons to slavery during the course of the eighteenth century. Projections suggest that the total number enslaved approached twelve million, with four million retained in domestic service and two million slave deaths. Under these circumstances, the population of West Africa substantially diminished.

The export of young adults from West Africa, with twice as many men as women taken, sometimes altered, but in some cases reinforced, the organization of African society. In many locations a surplus of women developed that enhanced the traditional African practice of polygyny, by which a man took more than one wife at the same time. Those men who remained also began to marry earlier; the surplus of women meant that men no longer had to postpone marriage until their late twenties or early thirties. Other changes had more far-reaching implications. No matter how deeply entrenched, the structure of the family and the division of labor could not withstand these demographic changes. Female workers replaced males to adapt to the shortage of men, and in such places as Zaire and Angola the existing practice of female agricultural labor expanded.

In the northern savanna and the Horn of Africa, where slave exports rarely exceeded twenty thousand per year, conditions were reversed, although the results were similar. Africans felt the losses more keenly than the numbers by themselves indicate. More women than men were enslaved, and the deprivation of female reproductive potential throughout the eighteenth and nineteenth centuries made it difficult, if not impossible, for the population to reproduce itself by natural means. Periodic famine and drought served at once to accelerate and depress the slave trade. In hard times the destitute sold themselves or their children into slavery, but the fall in population reduced the numbers available to be enslaved. Ecological recovery initiated economic growth, which again augmented slave exports.

The slave trade assuredly changed African politics, but its impact admitted wide variations. The history of the kingdoms of Asante and Oyo provide a case in point. During the late seventeenth century, Asante challenged Denkyira, the dominant power of the Gold Coast. In time, Asante incorporated most of the Twi-speaking peoples of the region. As a direct result of this conquest, the number of Asante exported as slaves declined after 1730, while the largest body of slaves exported from the Gold Coast came from among the Voltaic peoples. In the Oyo Empire, by comparison, a protracted constitutional crisis and a series of factional disputes that began in the 1770s brought political instability to the regime. The magnitude of slave exports increased as the power of the state declined.

Europeans did not themselves need to come to Africa to overwhelm the continent and dominate the slave trade. If the rulers of Benin, Ashanti, Congo, Dahomey, and Loango sold great numbers into slavery over many generations, the monarchs of Europe benefited most from those transactions. Ferdinand of Aragon granted the first license to carry slaves, who had been purchased in the slave markets of Seville, to the New World. King John III of Portugal was responsible for an even more dangerous innovation. He agreed in 1530 that slaves could be transported directly from Africa to the Americas. King Louis XIV of France permitted his ministers to pay a bounty for every slave delivered to the New World—a bounty that the French government was still disbursing in 1790.

As Hugh Thomas has pointed out, many others had unexpected connections to the slave trade from which they indirectly profited. The father of the French writer François-Auguste-René de Chateaubriand was a slave merchant. The leisure that the English historian Edward Gibbon enjoyed to write his masterpiece, *The History of the Decline and Fall of the Roman Empire* (1776–1788), derived from the fortune his grandfather had accumulated as director of the South Sea Company, the principal occupation of which was to carry African slaves in British ships to the Spanish Empire. John Locke, the philosopher of revolution, liberty, and property, was a shareholder in the Royal Africa Company, the initials of which, RAC, were branded upon many black chests during the last twenty-five years of the seventeenth century.

Those who trafficked in slaves, the merchants who bought and sold them, and the captains and crews of the slave ships that delivered them into bondage, were no worse than the planters who constituted the market. A few African leaders tried to escape participation in the slave trade. Mostly they failed, and Africa grew poorer and weaker as a result. Lamentably, the merchants, ship captains, planters, rulers, and, of course, the slaves themselves were all entangled in a vast commercial network from which few could escape and to which, at least until the 1780s, fewer still took exception.

–MARK G. MALVASI,
RANDOLPH-MACON COLLEGE

References

Basil Davidson, *The African Slave Trade,* revised edition (Boston: Little, Brown, 1980).

COMPLICITY

Davidson, *Black Mother: The Years of the African Slave Trade* (Boston: Little, Brown, 1961).

David Eltis, *The Rise of African Slavery in the Americas* (New York: Cambridge University Press, 2000).

Olaudah Equiano, *The Interesting Narrative of the Life of Olaudah Equiano,* edited by Robert J. Allison (Boston: Bedford Books of St. Martin's Press, 1995).

John D. Fage, "Slavery and the Slave Trade in the Context of West African History," *Journal of African History,* 10 (1969): 393–404.

P. E. H. Hair, "The Enslavement of Koelle's Informants," *Journal of African History,* 6 (1965): 193–201.

Joseph E. Inikori, "The Import of Firearms into West Africa, 1750–1807: A Quantitative Analysis," *Journal of African History,* 18 (1977): 339–368.

Patrick Manning, "Contours of Slavery and Social Change in Africa," *American Historical Review,* 88 (October 1983): 835–857.

Manning, *Slavery and African Life: Occidental, Oriental and African Slave Trades* (New York: Cambridge University Press, 1990).

Manning, "Slaves, Palm Oil, and Political Power on the West African Coast," *African Historical Studies,* 2 (1969): 279–288.

Joseph C. Miller, *The Way of Death: Merchant Capital and the Angolan Slave Trade* (Madison: University of Wisconsin Press, 1988).

David Northrup, ed., *The Atlantic Slave Trade,* second edition (Boston: Houghton Mifflin, 2002).

Mungo Park, *Travels in the Interior Districts of Africa: Performed in the Years 1795, 1796, and 1797* (London: Murray, 1816).

Walter Rodney, *How Europe Underdeveloped Africa,* revised edition (Washington, D.C.: Howard University Press, 1972).

Hugh Thomas, *The Slave Trade: The Story of the Atlantic Slave Trade, 1440–1870* (New York: Simon & Schuster, 1997).

John Thornton, *Africa and Africans in the Making of the Atlantic World, 1400–1800,* second edition (New York: Cambridge University Press, 1998).

COMPLICITY

ECONOMIC IMPACT

Did slavery stifle the economy of the American South?

Viewpoint: Yes. Slavery restricted economic diversification, industrial development, and technological innovation.

Viewpoint: No. Slavery was a viable economic institution that generated substantial rates of return for slaveholders.

Northern landscape architect Frederick Law Olmsted, who spent more than a year traveling in the South during the 1850s, was appalled at the ignorance and poverty he discovered there. Olmsted attributed Southern backwardness to slavery. In Virginia, Senator William Henry Seward (Whig/Republican–New York) found "exhausted soil, old and decaying towns, wretchedly-neglected roads, and, in every respect, an absence of enterprise and improvement. . . . Such has been the effect of slavery." Olmsted and Seward thought the South to be generally poorer and in a more wretched condition than the North. As critics of slavery, they were hardly objective in reaching such conclusions. Their biases notwithstanding, were Olmsted and Seward wrong?

Before the American Revolution (1775–1783), no one on either side of the Atlantic Ocean considered the South backward. During the first half of the eighteenth century, the British valued the Southern slaveholding colonies of North America above all other provinces in the New World. Profits from Southern cash crops, principally tobacco, made viable the North American imperial project. Economist Robert William Fogel not only concurred with this assessment but also extended Southern economic viability to 1860. In *Without Consent or Contract: The Rise and Fall of American Slavery* (1989), Fogel maintained that had the South attained its independence in 1860, it would have constituted the fourth most prosperous nation on earth.

Yet, by 1860, few Americans, Northern or Southern, denied that the South lagged behind Northern economic, social, and cultural development. Southern industrial output declined from 18 to 16 percent of the national total. At the same time, population, education, and urbanization did not keep pace with Northern (or Western) rates of growth. Slavery, by its nature, did not lend itself to economic modernization or social progress. The profits it generated obscured basic structural deficiencies in the Southern economy that virtually guaranteed backwardness. Nevertheless, in one sense Fogel was right: slavery did not impede Southern economic growth. It remains to determine the significance of that insight.

Viewpoint:
Yes. Slavery restricted economic diversification, industrial development, and technological innovation.

From the time of its introduction into the New World until the outbreak of the Civil War (1861–1865), slavery was closely linked to commercial agriculture. The products of slave labor, including tobacco, rice, indigo, sugar, and especially cotton, made up the bulk of exports that fueled American economic growth and prosperity. Slavery also helped to support an array of business enterprises from shipbuilding to textile manufacturing to insurance.

With the introduction of Eli Whitney's cotton gin in 1793 the economics of slavery in the United States underwent a dramatic change. Whitney's invention permitted the profitable cultivation of short staple cotton and thus gave rise to the expansion of plantation slavery in order to meet the growing demand for raw cotton that came from textile manufacturers in both New England and Great Britain. Economic historian Gavin Wright has argued that the economy of the antebellum South was not backward but was, rather, dependent. He makes a good point, for the development of the plantation economy brought considerable profits. To suggest that plantation slavery was essential to the health of the American economy throughout the first half of the nineteenth century is no exaggeration. By 1860, 67 percent of Americans with estates valued at or more than $100,000 lived in the South. During the antebellum period, moreover, Southern cotton provided the foundation for American economic growth. In the early decades of the nineteenth century cotton exports alone accounted for between 50 and 60 percent of total American exports, with Southern planters and Northern merchants alike enjoying handsome returns. Planters invested their capital to acquire additional land and more slaves in an effort to keep up with the growing demand for cotton.

Beguiled by the apparent strength of their economy, Southerners mistakenly, and in the end disastrously, concluded that "Cotton was King." It was not. Rather, cotton, however great the profits it could generate, was in reality a pawn on the world market. The slaveholding planters of the South never controlled the demand for cotton. They prospered when demand was high but endured prolonged and severe depressions when demand evaporated.

Moreover, although slavery seemed a source of infinite wealth, it actually retarded the eco-

nomic development of the South. Slavery might have initiated economic growth, but it could not promote or sustain economic diversification. Because planters invested their profits in land and slaves, the South retained an overwhelmingly agricultural economy and lacked the capital necessary to foster the development of commerce and industry. Compared to its Northern counterpart, the Southern economy was sluggish, backward, and inefficient, which proved a disaster for the Confederacy during the Civil War when Southern manufacturing could not keep pace with the war matériel that, by comparison, poured from Northern factories.

Worth repeating is the fact that the prosperity of the slaveholding South depended almost entirely on demand for cotton on the world market. Since the international market for single commodities was notoriously fickle, Southern affluence and wealth remained forever precarious. Until the eve of the Civil War, the world market for raw cotton and cotton textiles grew at an exponential rate despite periodically severe depressions. This sustained growth led Southern planters mistakenly to believe that the expansion of the cotton economy was limitless.

Like the slaveholding colonies in Latin America and the Caribbean, the South exhibited impressive rates of economic growth for long periods of time. Yet, the South failed the test of economic development, which alone could have guaranteed the political viability of the region. The economy of the antebellum South might have grown and even prospered, but it never developed or diversified and was, therefore, condemned to underdevelopment, stagnation, and eventually to economic as well as political disaster.

In any slave economy, even one as strong as that of the antebellum South, the investment of capital can take only two meaningful forms: land and slaves. Herein lay the paradox of economic growth without economic development. Capital investment in the South brought additional acres planted in cotton and more slaves to work those fields. It did not encourage economic diversification as it did in the North. At issue was the flexibility of the slave system, its ability to reallocate resources and investments when faced with depression in vital sectors of the economy. Could and would Southern planters shift capital away from land and slaves when the cotton economy fell into a depression and profitable opportunities awaited elsewhere?

The slaveholders of the South were no fools. They were not, in fact, really capitalists at all. Their political power and social status, to say nothing of their wealth, rested on the theoretical assertion of absolute power over other human beings. They could, therefore, never blithely sacri-

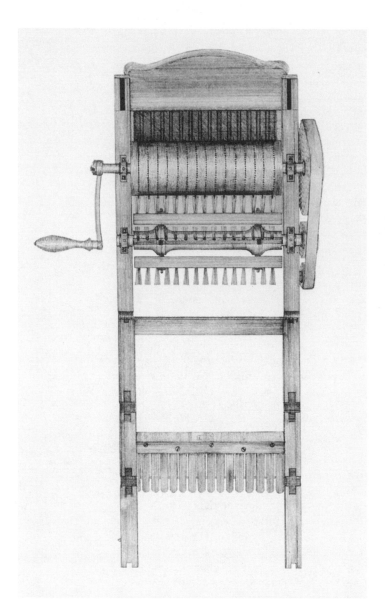

Drawing of Eli Whitney's cotton engine

(Eli Whitney Papers, Manuscript and Archives, Yale University Library, New Haven, Conn.)

ECONOMIC IMPACT

fice the foundation of their social, political, psychological, and moral lives to a mere balance sheet of profits and losses, credits and debits. Slaveholders operated in, but were not of, the burgeoning capitalist world of the nineteenth century. Their economic interests and political ideology were, indeed, increasingly at odds with the interests and ideology of capitalism.

Under such circumstances, the economic viability of the slaveholders' regime reduces to questions of political and military power. Was the economy strong enough to secure Southern independence and protect slavery in the event of a political and military crisis? Situating the economic history of the South within a political context reveals that a lengthy economic crisis was unlikely to generate the transfer of resources to other sectors, however attractive or promising they might have appeared. It could, instead, be expected to engender a political cri-

sis as the advocates of slavery endeavored with intensifying ardor to preserve their way of life.

Southern slaveholders felt themselves increasingly besieged during the three decades before the Civil War. Their commitment to slavery isolated them and their society from most of the rest of the world and threw them collectively on the defensive. Bound to agriculture and slavery, Southerners could not take full advantage of the astonishing transformation of the national economy that occurred during the first half of the nineteenth century. Unlike the North, the South did not demonstrate the ability to attract and absorb abundant and cheap immigrant labor, to lure investment capital from abroad, to encourage technological innovation, or to launch and sustain an industrial and market revolution capable of propelling a nation to world power. However much the Southern slave economy grew, each passing year exposed its structural weaknesses and added to the political and military disabilities that burdened the ruling elite.

The economy of the antebellum South, like those of other slaveholding countries in the Western Hemisphere, could thus not lay the foundation for continuous economic growth and development. Nowhere did a slave regime advance science and technology, create expanding home markets adequate to encourage economic diversification, accumulate the capital necessary to finance industrialization, or foster entrepreneurship. Slave economies in the South and elsewhere might from time to time have produced spectacular profits in response to external demand for their staple commodities— whether they were sugar, coffee, tobacco, or cotton—but slavery simultaneously ensured economic stagnation and decline once that demand was withdrawn. In addition, slavery also closed the road to industrialization, which was the single economic development that could have set the slaveholders on an equal economic footing with their enemies.

As a consequence of this failure, all slave societies of the New World, including the South, met the same dire fate. The South, though, displayed special characteristics. In striking contrast to the slaveholding regimes of the Caribbean and in partial contrast to Brazil, the antebellum South produced a slaveholding class capable of seizing regional political power and deeply influencing the course of national politics for more than fifty years. The systemic economic difficulties that troubled the South, therefore, did much more than create painful readjustments once the world demand for cotton slackened. These economic shortcomings confronted a proud and powerful slaveholding elite with the prospect of military defeat and political disaster.

Had the Confederates won their war for independence, the triumphant South would have in all likelihood remained an economic colony of the North. An independent South, determined to compete militarily, politically, and economically with the leading nation-states of the nineteenth century, could not have avoided undertaking a program of rapid industrialization and capitalist development. To accomplish these objectives, Southerners would have had before long to emancipate their slaves, or else they would have sentenced themselves to the perpetual economic retardation and dependence of a second-rank power. Perpetuating slavery doomed the slaveholders to become, at best, economic clients of Northern capital, however wealthy certain individuals within their ranks might have become. The loss of economic power would have gradually eroded the slaveholders' political influence at home and abroad. Although an independent nation, the Confederate States of America would then have fallen more completely than ever before under the political, economic, and cultural hegemony of the capitalist world.

—MARK G. MALVASI,
RANDOLPH-MACON COLLEGE

Viewpoint:
No. Slavery was a viable economic institution that generated substantial rates of return for slaveholders.

The controversial issue of Southern backwardness is not simply a point of dispute between contemporary historians; it has a long history that goes back at least to the American Revolution (1775–1783). In fact, modern historians rest many of their arguments upon the criticisms and conclusions of nineteenth-century observers. What is particularly interesting about this issue, however, goes beyond historians' choice of evidence and probes the heart of how people approach the idea of history. In other words, the issue of Southern economic development involves the most basic ways people think about the past.

Immediately following the American Revolution, amateur historians began writing detailed histories of their towns and states. Their endeavors resulted partly from the pride of winning the war against Great Britain, but Revolutionary-era historians also sought ways of explaining their specific state's contribution to independence and

the forging of American liberty. Jeremy Belknap of New Hampshire was one of the first scholars to write a state history. Most often these historians glorified their state at the expense of significant contributions made by others. For instance, New Englanders were particularly proud that they began a process of ending slavery after the Revolution. They enjoyed writing about liberty-loving New England states that fought the Revolution to expand human freedom and of Southern states that were only concerned with maintaining their local privilege and control, never mind that slavery in their region had lost its economic viability or that New Englanders had profited from the slave trade and had sold most of their slaves down South.

By the early nineteenth century, historians influenced by German idealism introduced the idea of inevitable progress into their historical analysis. This concept meant that history moved in linear phases toward a universal goal, such as the United States becoming increasingly democratic. Some early historians, however, claimed that the South did not follow the same trajectory as the rest of the country. Historian and ardent abolitionist Richard Hildreth argued that slavery caused the South to be socially and economically backward. His sentiment was echoed by many observers both in the North and in the South, such as Frederick Law Olmsted, David Ramsay, and Lydia Maria Child. Many people in the South accepted the assertion of backwardness and campaigned for economic diversification. All of them in one form or another claimed slavery retarded economic development by fostering a preoccupation with the production of staple crops. One common denominator united these observers. They all believed the South was out of step with progress, which they measured through the lens of industrialization. Their appraisals ultimately faltered because they equated an industrial economy with efficiency and economic diversity with capitalism.

Modern historians who believe the South fell behind the North economically rarely challenge these assumptions. Though they define capitalism as a means of exchange, they often refer to it as a system that develops according to changes in the means of production. Economies appear to develop in stages, and each subsequent step must be better than what preceded it. The smartest people in this scenario are those with the foresight to control the next means of production rather than simply being able to predict and account for consumer demand. Furthermore, these stages of change are inevitable. These scholars discerned a regular pattern: people stop chasing animals and settle down to farm; they move on to complex forms of agriculture and then to primitive industry; and finally,

THE MOST CONTEMPTIBLE INSIGNIFICANCE

The publication of Hinton Rowan Helper's The Impending Crisis of the South: How to Meet It *in 1857 caused much controversy. The North Carolina writer used U.S. Census records to demonstrate how slavery damaged the Southern economy and society. Although no friend of African Americans, Helper advocated the abolition of slavery because it would help the nonslaveholding white majority in the long run. As may be expected, his book was ill received in the South, where some states banned it, but approximately one hundred thousand copies were sold in the North during the presidential campaign of 1860:*

. . .The causes which have impeded the progress and prosperity of the South, which have dwindled our commerce, and other similar pursuits, into the most contemptible insignificance; sunk a large majority of our people in galling poverty and ignorance, rendered a small minority conceited and tyrannical, and driven the rest away from their homes; entailed upon us a humiliating dependence on the Free States; disgraced us in the recesses of our own souls, and brought us under reproach in the eyes of all civilized and enlightened nations—may all be traced to one common source . . . *Slavery!*

Reared amidst the institution of slavery, believing it to be wrong both in principle and in practice, and having seen and felt its evil influences upon individuals, communities and states, we deem it a duty, no less than a privilege, to enter our protest against it, and to use our most strenuous efforts to overturn and abolish it! . . . We are not only in favor of keeping slavery out of the territories, but, carrying our opposition to the institution a step further, we here unhesitatingly declare ourself in favor of its immediate and unconditional abolition, in every state in this confederacy, where it now exists! Patriotism makes us a freesoiler; state pride makes us an emancipationist; a profound sense of duty to the South makes us an abolitionist; a responsible degree of fellow feeling for the negro, makes us a colonizationist.

. . . Nothing short of the complete abolition of slavery can save the South from falling into the vortex of utter ruin. Too long have we yielded a submissive obedience to the tyrannical domination of an inflated oligarchy; too long have we tolerated their arrogance and self-conceit; too long have we submitted to their unjust and savage exactions. Let us now wrest from them the sceptre of power, establish liberty and equal rights throughout the land, and henceforth and forever guard our legislative halls from the pollutions and usurpations of pro-slavery demagogues.

. . . It is not so much in its moral and religious aspects that we propose to discuss the question of slavery, as in its social and political character and influences. To say nothing of the sin and the shame of slavery, we believe it is a most expensive and unprofitable institution; and if our brethren of the South will but throw aside their unfounded prejudices and preconceived opinions, and give us a fair and patient hearing, we feel confident that we can bring them to the same conclusion. Indeed, we believe we shall be enabled—not alone by our own contributions, but with the aid of incontestable facts and arguments which we shall introduce from other sources—to convince all true-hearted, candid and intelligent Southerners . . . that slavery, and nothing but slavery, has retarded the progress and prosperity of our portion of the Union; depopulated and impoverished our cities by forcing the more industrious and enterprising natives of the soil to emigrate to the free states; brought our domain under a sparse and inert population by preventing foreign immigration; made us tributary of the North, and reduced us to the humiliating condition of mere provincial subjects in fact, though not in name.

Source: *Hinton Rowan Helper,* The Impending Crisis of the South: How to Meet It, *edited by George M. Fredrickson (New York: Burdick Brothers, 1857; Cambridge, Mass.: Belknap Press of Harvard University Press, 1968), pp. 21–33, 40–41.*

ECONOMIC IMPACT

an industrial revolution takes place that not only changes an economy but also introduces new forms of political and social relations.

Assessing economic evolution provides modern historians with a way to place the South in the broad context of American national development. Its culture and labor system placed the South outside of what historians think was the inevitable move of the United States toward industry, democracy, and progress. These historians conclude that slavery must have been unprofitable; that it caused economic retardation; that the South formed a distinctly different society antithetical to authentic American values based on individualism and commercialism; and that the South must have been so different that it could not harmoniously coexist with industrial, capitalist, liberal America. A classic historiographical drama then develops in which an energetic South emerges in colonial North America, reaches the pinnacle of its wealth and stature by the Revolution, only to fall tragically by shunning the inevitable progress of free labor and industrial development. This story rests not on hard evidence but on assumptions. Little doubt exists that distinctive cultural traits separated the antebellum South, North, and West, but the prevalence of entrepreneurial vigor, the availability of business enterprise, and a commitment to developing markets were not among them.

The interpretive error made by advocates of the backwardness myth involves two things. First, they deny that money flows to those economic sectors where it is used to secure the best returns. At any given moment, one may not receive a higher return on investing in industry than in agriculture. Profits are determined by how well an entrepreneur meets consumer demand, not by his or her choice of a specific form of production. Consumer willingness to pay more for greater quantities of one product is a subjective and indeterminable variable of economics. The second mistake follows the first in that industrialization is equated with progress. Industrial society has vastly improved the human condition, but a society does not need to be industrial in order to enjoy the benefits of industrialization. Trade, especially foreign, alleviates the need for every society to be industrial. Self-sufficiency does not mean a society is progressive, it only means that the people have accepted greater costs by refusing to trade with other people.

Even if the South was not backward in a strict economic sense, specific criticisms and evidence deserve a close inspection. Signs of economic backwardness usually include the following criteria: debt peonage, soil exhaustion, lack of industrialization, and poor labor productivity. Historians typically attribute the presence of these things to Southerners being so obsessed with investing in slaves that they did so at the expense of other kinds of investments. They argue that the lure of romantic plantation life proved too strong for masters to resist purchasing more and more slaves, each time sinking further into debt. In an effort to stretch their investment in slaves, planters used intensive agricultural practices that depleted soil nutrients. Extracting the greatest yields from their plantations required debt-ridden masters to brutalize their slaves, which subsequently lowered productivity and any hope of financial gain. In the end, Southerners would have been better off had they invested their money in industry and nonstaple agriculture.

Planters who borrowed to increase their slave workforce and landholdings were far from caught in a vicious cycle. Rather, they normally chose the soundest investments, which returned profits that exceeded their interest payments. This choice was a sign of financial acuity, not captivity to slavery. The best estimates indicate that a single slave provided his or her owner a 6 to 8.5 percent rate of return over his or her lifetime. Female slaves in the cotton belt of the Gulf South brought the highest rates. Thus, even an indebted planter could expect a modest return of 2 percent on his investment after paying an average 4 to 6 percent interest.

Soil exhaustion in the Old South should not be blamed on slavery or staple production. Problems of soil fertility plagued Northern farmers just as it did Southerners, and though Southern farmers could count on more labor to work the land, they used farming methods similar to those found in the North. The only difference was that the longer growing season in the South permitted a focus on staple crops and the highest returns. The real culprits of soil exhaustion included heavy rains that leached the soil, erosion-prone terrain, and above all, the ready availability of land. Cheap land meant most slaveowners could expend less capital by moving to virgin lands than by diverting workers to improve their current soil. When market conditions changed or enough planters could not afford to move, they practiced good stewardship such as manuring their fields.

Crop diversification and industrial development also depended upon market conditions rather than slavery. Capital went to slaves and land because people received the highest rates of return while exerting the least amount of time and effort. Slavery diverted little new capital investment from industry, particularly after the closing of the international slave trade to the United States. Despite repeated demonstrations of the usefulness of slavery in factories, staple agriculture provided security whereas factories, railroads, and transportation companies offered risk. Admittedly, cultural factors played an important role. Those who accumulated capital typically invested in land and slaves either because of prestige or because they valued the life of a planter. This attitude was true across the South as bankers, traders, and other businessmen became planters after amassing their fortunes in other ventures.

Another argument made against slavery with regard to economic development rests on the position that free labor was more productive than slave labor. It does not follow, however, that individual examples of poor productivity translated into economic retardation overall. Here again the problem concerns fundamental

ECONOMIC IMPACT

economic beliefs, not slavery. Even if slavery could be proved to be unproductive throughout the antebellum economy, it would only hamper economic growth if labor served as the primary building block of an economy. One might strengthen this argument somewhat by suggesting slavery "tied up" capital at the expense of economic development. Yet again, capital must be the foundation of growth. As unlikely as it may appear, the important work of economists such as Simon Kuznets and Peter T. Bauer in the field of Third World economic development suggests that neither labor nor capital plays a crucial role in economic growth. Instead, the key ingredients are innovation and technology, two areas in which the South typically excelled.

Many American inventors found their start on farms or plantations that used slave labor. Eli Whitney comes first to mind with the cotton gin, but leading innovators included Cyrus McCormick and Thomas Jefferson. In the areas of literature, scholarship, and culture Southern intellectuals such as William Gilmore Simms, David Ramsay, A. B. Longstreet, and Edgar Allan Poe earned recognition. Theologians such as James H. Thornwell and Robert L. Dabney, legal theorists such as St. George Tucker and T. R. R. Cobb, and social thinkers such as Henry Hughes reached national prominence. In the area of science and exploration the South boasted the accomplishments of Meriwether Lewis, Thomas Clingman, Joseph Le Conte, and Matthew Maury. In political theory and economics, Americans from all regions recognized such Southern intellectuals as John Taylor, Jacob N. Cardozo, Thomas Cooper, John Calhoun, Henry Clay, George Fitzhugh, and John Randolph. One should not forget the Founding generation, among whom slaveholders carried extensive prominence: James Madison, Jefferson, George Washington, John Hancock, and Patrick Henry to name only a few. Approximately 80 percent of the signers of the Declaration of Independence were directly connected with slavery.

In agriculture, however, their area of economic specialization, Southerners stood at the pinnacle of innovation and technology. The antebellum plantation system represented an enormous improvement over earlier agricultural practices. For example, planters devised managerial innovations such as the gang-and-task system to improve worker productivity. Agricultural reformers such as John Taylor, Edmund Ruffin, and Hill Carter of Virginia; James H. Hammond of South Carolina; and Martin W. Phillips of Mississippi used the latest scientific advances to improve soil fertility, labor management, and the profitability of their plantations. In most Southern states, planter conventions, societies, and journals developed extensive networks to dispense the latest information about sound agricultural techniques.

Even on the issue of the incompatibility of slavery with industrialization, strong evidence suggests that slavery would have remained viable even had the South experienced industrial growth. Repeated experiments in places such as the Tredegar Iron Works in Richmond, Virginia, showed how easily slaves could be trained for factory work. Some Southerners condemned the use of slaves in factories because they opposed all industrialization; others believed only white labor should be used in factory work. Great numbers of slaves were not used in factories because of competition for labor presented by profitable staple production.

To claim that the South was not economically backward does not mean that Southern slave owners were free from economic distress. Many farmers and planters, but never most, mortgaged their property in an effort to live a grand life or to mimic the extravagance of their neighbors. Cultural practices, not slavery, were to blame for the high rate of Southern debt. Furthermore, the boom times that tempted so many Southerners into debt could be attributed to inflationary banking practices common in all parts of the country, not to slavery.

In the end, the question of backwardness relies on accepting a specific understanding of the nature of history. It is an epistemological problem that forces the scholar to adopt culturally specific criteria to the neglect of basic economic rules. A different way of asking the question might generate different answers. For example, one could question the degree to which capital mobility was free, given laws preventing manumission, or how productive slaves were, given statutes making slave education illegal. Instead of framing the question as one of agriculture versus industry or specialization versus diversification, a better approach would be to ask if the Southern economy was truly free. The answer would probably be "no"; however, the same answer would also apply to the North and West.

–CAREY ROBERTS,
ARKANSAS TECH UNIVERSITY

References

Peter T. Bauer, *Dissent on Development: Studies and Debates in Development Economics* (London: Weidenfeld & Nicolson, 1971).

Robert William Fogel, *Without Consent or Contract: The Rise and Fall of American Slavery* (New York: Norton, 1989).

ECONOMIC IMPACT

Fogel and Stanley L. Engerman, *Time on the Cross: The Economics of Negro Slavery,* 2 volumes (Boston: Little, Brown, 1974).

Eugene D. Genovese, *The Political Economy of Slavery: Studies in the Economy & Society of the Slave South* (New York: Pantheon, 1965).

Genovese and Elizabeth Fox-Genovese, *The Fruits of Merchant Capital: Slavery and Bourgeois Property in the Rise and Expansion of Capitalism* (New York: Oxford University Press, 1983).

Simon Kuznets, *Modern Economic Growth: Rate, Structure, and Spread* (New Haven: Yale University Press, 1966).

Peter J. Parish, *Slavery: History and Historians* (New York: Harper & Row, 1989).

Francis Butler Simkins and Charles Pierce Roland, *A History of the South,* fourth edition (New York: Knopf, 1972).

Mark M. Smith, *Debating Slavery: Economy and Society in the Antebellum American South* (Cambridge & New York: Cambridge University Press, 1998).

Kenneth M. Stampp, *The Peculiar Institution: Slavery in the Ante-Bellum South* (New York: Knopf, 1956).

Harold D. Woodman, *King Cotton and His Retainers: Financing and Marketing the Cotton Crop of the South, 1800–1925* (Lexington: University of Kentucky Press, 1968).

Gavin Wright, *The Political Economy of the Cotton South: Households, Markets, and Wealth in the Nineteenth Century* (New York: Norton, 1978).

ECONOMIC IMPACT

EMANCIPATION

Did emancipation improve the conditions of former slaves in the United States?

Viewpoint: Yes. Freedom offered African Americans the opportunity to improve their lot, although immediate political, economic, and social improvements were limited.

Viewpoint: No. Despite having escaped slavery, African Americans still faced racial prejudice and legal discrimination; the promise offered by emancipation faded when blacks, impoverished, illiterate, and disadvantaged, experienced continuing exploitation in the labor market.

Scholars have long debated the consequences of emancipation in the United States. Freed from bondage by war, the former slaves occupied an ambiguous position in Southern society. For the most part, the freedmen rejected their dependence and celebrated their freedom. Yet, they also sought to assert and maintain it, "to make sure," as Peter Kolchin has written, "that they were *really* free, not just free in name." Determined to escape subservience, the freed blacks desired most of all to work for themselves and to acquire land. They opposed the return to gang labor or to any other arrangement characteristic of slavery. Landownership remained an unrealized ambition for most blacks in the South, though they forced changes in economic relations that enhanced their independence.

Blacks, for example, refused to work under the supervision of overseers. They also exacted concessions from anxious planters fearful of losing their services to a rival who offered more-generous terms. During the years immediately following the Civil War (1861–1865), blacks did not effect revolutionary changes in Southern society. Rather, they essentially fought their former masters to a stalemate, a remarkable accomplishment in itself, considering the many disadvantages under which they operated even in the favorable political climate of Reconstruction (1865–1877). As a people, blacks, incapable of achieving complete freedom, nevertheless prevented themselves from being transformed into a wholly servile agricultural labor force. Although the sharecropping system that came to prevail in the postwar South bred dependence, it also allowed blacks greater autonomy over their work and their lives. Since they had a direct economic stake in producing a good crop, freedmen worked hard, but did so on their own terms and without supervision. In addition, sharecroppers saw themselves as partners in a joint economic venture, not as wage laborers subject to the whim and will of an employer. "I am not working for wages," explained Bernard Houston, an Alabama sharecropper, in a letter to George S. Houston on 3 August 1867, "but am part owner of the crop and as I have all the rights that you or any other man has I shall not suffer them abridged."

Yet, after emancipation, blacks arguably faced worse instances of racism, discrimination, and violence than they had endured under slavery. Southern whites tried systematically to deny freedom to blacks. Southern state legislatures enacted Black Codes designed to return blacks to a status approximating slavery by limiting their right to own land, to enter certain occupations, or to gain access to the courts. The authorities also coerced blacks to agree to labor contracts with white landlords if the blacks could not document residence or employment. The continued social, economic, and political subordination of blacks has suggested to some historians that emancipation did not significantly alter the lives or improve the lot of the former slaves.

Emancipation did not work miracles. Exploitation, poverty, and racism remained prominent and disturbing aspects of Southern life. Although blacks asserted their freedom and took advantage of every opportunity to remake their lives, they did so within a restrictive legal, political, and cultural framework. Then, too, blacks acquiesced in and, in some ways, even welcomed racial segregation. Whites, of course, sought to keep blacks separate and subordinate. Blacks' purposes were more complex. They retreated from the white world not only because they felt unwelcome and often unsafe but also because they embraced a new sense of community and self-reliance.

By the 1870s, however, even the hope and promise of establishing an interracial society had faded. The end of slavery created such magnified and grandiose expectations that disappointment and disillusionment became almost inevitable. Even under ideal conditions, intractable economic, social, political, and cultural realities would have rendered so exalted and diverse a set of desires remote and unattainable. Nevertheless, historian Eric Foner concluded, "like a massive earthquake, the Civil War and the destruction of slavery permanently altered the landscape of Southern life." Amid adversity and failure, Foner argued, the era of emancipation and Reconstruction nonetheless inaugurated "America's unfinished revolution."

Viewpoint:
Yes. Freedom offered African Americans the opportunity to improve their lot, although immediate political, economic, and social improvements were limited.

At the end of the Civil War (1861–1865) Republican Representative Thaddeus Stevens of Pennsylvania proposed that the U.S. government confiscate 394,000,000 acres of land from approximately seventy thousand Confederates and parcel it out in 40-acre allotments to every adult male freedman. The remainder, Stevens argued, ought to be sold to pay the public debt, fund pensions for disabled Union veterans, and compensate loyal Unionists in the South whose property had been damaged or destroyed during the war. Congress, however, rejected Stevens's Confiscation Plan; many members of the Republican Party found its attack on private property too radical.

The failure of Stevens's program meant that Reconstruction (1865–1877) would have only a limited economic content and would, therefore, not sustain the freedom that the former slaves had won. As a consequence, from the outset blacks' political and civil rights rested on precarious foundations. Had Republicans understood the need to give the freedmen economic support, they might have enabled both black and white farmers to gain a measure of economic independence. Had Southern planters lost their land and control of their labor force, there could have been no revival of the plantation economy as occurred in the South even before the end of Reconstruc-

tion. Finally, had black and white farmers been able to practice subsistence agriculture and to produce for local markets instead of growing cash crops such as cotton for wealthy landowners, they might not have been drawn into the international depressions of the 1870s and 1890s that ruined their chances for a better life.

At the dawn of the twentieth century most blacks in the South remained bound to whites as sharecroppers or tenant farmers. Few blacks owned, or even managed to rent, land, and thus they remained poverty-stricken and propertyless, both dependent on and subordinate to whites. Even then, complained one planter, sharecropping "is wrong policy; it makes the laborer too independent; he becomes a partner, and has a right to be consulted."

With the help of the federal government, and for a time sympathetic state governments, blacks had gained a measure of political power during Reconstruction. The United States was the only society in which freed slaves, within a few years of emancipation, had acquired significant political rights, which opened the doors of opportunity that were never again completely closed. Yet, without a solid economic foundation, this revolutionary experiment in freedom and democracy proved impossible to maintain.

Former Confederate general Robert V. Richardson, treasurer of the American Cotton Planters' Association, anticipated the limits of Reconstruction when he wrote in December 1865: "The emancipated slaves own nothing, because nothing but freedom has been given to them." Like many of his contemporaries, whether Congressmen or freedmen, Richardson knew that freedom defined merely as self-ownership was limited, for it threw blacks into society poor, uneducated, and disadvantaged in countless

BY THE PRESIDENT OF THE UNITED STATES OF AMERICA.

A Proclamation.

Whereas, on the twenty-second day of September, in the year of our Lord one thousand eight hundred and sixty-two, a proclamation was issued by the President of the United States, containing, among other things, the following, to wit:

"That on the first day of January, in the year of our Lord one thousand eight hundred and sixty-three, all persons held as slaves within any State or designated part of a State, the people whereof shall then be in rebellion against the United States, shall be then, thenceforward, and forever, free; and the Executive government of the United States, including the military and naval authority thereof, will recognize and maintain the freedom of such persons, and will do no act or acts to repress such persons, or any of them, in any efforts they may make for their actual freedom.

"That the Executive will, on the first day of January aforesaid, by proclamation, designate the States and parts of States, if any, in which the people thereof, respectively, shall then be in rebellion against the United States; and the fact that any State, or the people thereof, shall on that day be in good faith represented in the Congress of the United States, by members chosen thereto at elections wherein a majority of the qualified voters of such State shall have participated, shall, in the absence of strong countervailing testimony, be deemed conclusive evidence that such State, and the people thereof, are not then in rebellion against the United States."

Now, therefore, I, ABRAHAM LINCOLN, PRESIDENT OF THE UNITED STATES, by virtue of the power in me vested as commander-in-chief of the army and navy of the United States, in time of actual armed rebellion against the authority and government of the United States, and as a fit and necessary war measure for suppressing said rebellion, do, on this first day of January, in the year of our Lord one thousand eight hundred and sixty-three, and in accordance with my purpose so to do, publicly proclaimed for the full period of one hundred days from the day first above mentioned, order and designate as the States and parts of States wherein the people thereof, respectively, are this day in rebellion against the United States, the following, to wit: ARKANSAS, TEXAS, LOUISIANA, (except the Parishes of St. Bernard, Plaquemines, Jefferson, St. John, St. Charles, St. James, Ascension, Assumption, Terre Bonne, Lafourche, St. Mary, St. Martin, and Orleans, including the City of New Orleans,) MISSISSIPPI, ALABAMA, FLORIDA, GEORGIA, SOUTH CAROLINA, NORTH CAROLINA, AND VIRGINIA, (except the forty-eight counties designated as West Virginia, and also the counties of Berkeley, Accomac, Northampton, Elizabeth City, York, Princess Ann, and Norfolk, including the cities of Norfolk and Portsmouth,) and which excepted parts are for the present left precisely as if this proclamation were not issued.

And by virtue of the power and for the purpose aforesaid, I do order and declare that all persons held as slaves within said designated States and parts of States are and henceforward shall be free; and that the Executive government of the United States, including the military and naval authorities thereof, will recognize and maintain the freedom of said persons.

And I hereby enjoin upon the people so declared to be free to abstain from all violence, unless in necessary self-defence; and I recommend to them that, in all cases when allowed, they labor faithfully for reasonable wages.

And I further declare and make known that such persons, of suitable condition, will be received into the armed service of the United States, to garrison forts, positions, stations, and other places, and to man vessels of all sorts in said service.

And upon this act, sincerely believed to be an act of justice warranted by the Constitution upon military necessity, I invoke the considerate judgment of mankind and the gracious favor of Almighty God.

In witness whereof I have hereunto set my hand and caused the seal of the United States to be affixed.

[L. S.] Done at the CITY OF WASHINGTON this first day of January, in the year of our Lord one thousand eight hundred and sixty-three, and of the Independence of the United States of America the eighty-seventh.

By the President:

Abraham Lincoln

William H. Seward Secretary of State.

A true copy, with the autograph signatures of the President and the Secretary of State.

Jno G Nicolay

Prte. Sec. to the President.

ways. A writer for the Louisville *Democrat* knew it, too, for he asserted that the former slave needs to understand that "he is *free,* but only to labor," and that he must, therefore, be prevented from obtaining access to land. Blacks, on the contrary, believed they were entitled to land, if for no other reason than the contributions they had already made to American economic development and prosperity. In a powerful speech delivered in 1866 and cited in Eric Foner's *Nothing but Freedom: Emancipation and Its Legacy* (1983), freedman Bayley Wyat proclaimed that blacks:

> has a right to the land where we are located. For why? I tell you. Our wives, our children, our husbands, has been sold over and over again to purchase the lands we now locates upon; for that reason we have a divine right to the land. . . . And den didn't we clear the land, and raise de crops ob corn, ob cotton, ob tobacco, ob rice, ob sugar, ob everything. And den didn't dem large cities in de North grew up on de cotton and de sugars and de rice dat we made? . . . I say dey had grown rich, and my people is poor.

To mean anything, freedom had to mean more than merely the end of slavery. Freedmen such as Wyat insisted that it did; Richardson and other members of the Southern planter aristocracy contended that it did not.

The end of slavery destroyed the social system of the South, but for many people the old order died hard. Members of the Southern slave-owning elite, to say nothing of the slaves themselves, struggled to understand, adjust, accept, and forgive. For those whites who had shaped the Southern ruling class, the defection of so many slaves marked the end of their world. No blacks could any longer be trusted. Yet, with the end of slavery, some whites felt themselves emancipated from the burdens of having to care for their slaves. Those who could not accept the reality that blacks had been freed simply burned their slave quarters and ordered the former slaves off the land, threatening to kill them if they lingered. Others responded more cautiously, hoping to convince the blacks to remain with them and to work for wages. Still others despaired, not for the blacks but for themselves. They wondered how they could survive without slaves to cultivate their land, care for their houses, cook their meals, nurture their children, and satisfy their whims. No matter what the response of the whites, blacks had attained their freedom, but as a consequence they were now on their own with the odds, and increasingly the law, stacked against their success.

The political, economic, and social condition of blacks in the United States did not immediately improve with emancipation. Daniel H. Chamberlain, the last Republican governor of South Carolina during Reconstruction, summed up the situation, explaining to former abolitionist William Lloyd Garrison that "the uneducated negro was too weak, no matter what his numbers, to cope with the whites." Freed blacks endured legal discrimination in the form of the Black Codes and such rulings as *Plessy* v. *Ferguson* (1896), in which the Supreme Court of the United States declared constitutional state laws mandating segregation, and *Cumming* v. *County Board of Education* (1899), in which the Court determined that laws establishing separate schools for white children were constitutional even if there were no schools for blacks comparable to the white schools from which they were now legally excluded. If the law by chance failed to limit access to public facilities or to proscribe the activities of blacks, custom and practice did not. The editor of the Richmond *Times* conveyed the prevailing sentiments when he wrote:

> It is necessary that this principle [of segregation] be applied in every relation of Southern life. God Almighty drew the color line and it cannot be obliterated. The negro must stay on his side of the line and the white man must stay on his side, and the sooner both races recognize this fact and accept it, the better it will be for both.

Blacks also confronted intimidation, violence, and disfranchisement that compromised their liberty, robbed them of their citizenship, and threatened their dignity as human beings, to say nothing of their lives. Yet, whatever its limitations, freedom was better than nothing, and whenever opportunities for action arose, blacks seized the initiative to strike a blow in the cause of liberty. As slaves, blacks had lived for a long time with oppression and exploitation, and they proved more than willing to fight and die for freedom, as the approximately 209,000 who took up arms against the Confederacy demonstrated.

In Eugene D. Genovese's *From Rebellion to Revolution: Afro-American Slave Revolts in the Making of the Modern World* (1979), one of these soldiers, Corporal Prince Lambkin, provides an eloquent and unforgettable statement of blacks' determination to put an end to bondage. Rising to address his fellow soldiers of the First South Carolina Volunteers, one of the celebrated all-black regiments of the Union Army, Lambkin declared:

> Our mas're dey hab lib under de flag, dey got dere wealth under it, and ebryting beautiful for dere chilen. Under it dey hab grind us up, and put us in dere pocket for money. But de fus' minute dey tink dat ole flag mean freedom for we colored people, dey pull it right down, and run up de rag ob dere own. But we'll neber desert de ole flag, boys, neber; we had lib under it for *eighteen hundred sixty-two years,* and we'll die for it now.

It is no small irony that those men and women who were denied their freedom did their share and more to preserve the birthright of every American. Gabriel Prosser, Denmark Vesey, Nat Turner, Lambkin, and countless others whose names history does not record, knew the value and the meaning of freedom. Because they had withstood and overcome slavery, they also knew what freedom cost.

The failure of Reconstruction, the survival of the plantation system, and the ongoing exploitation of blacks obscure the drama of emancipation. For blacks, the end of slavery marked the fundamental turning point in their individual and collective lives, whatever hardships they encountered as a result. Testifying before a Senate committee in 1883, Reverend E. P. Holmes of Georgia, a former house servant, made plain the importance that freedom had for black people. "Most anyone ought to know that a man is better off free than as a slave," Holmes said, "even if he did not have anything. I would rather be free and have my liberty. I fared just as well as any white child could have fared when I was a slave, and yet I would not give up my freedom."

—MARK G. MALVASI,
RANDOLPH-MACON COLLEGE

Viewpoint:
No. Despite having escaped slavery, African Americans still faced racial prejudice and legal discrimination; the promise offered by emancipation faded when blacks, impoverished, illiterate, and disadvantaged, experienced continuing exploitation in the labor market.

The end of slavery might have destroyed the social system of the Old South, but it did nothing to eliminate racism. As early as 1865 legislatures in all Southern states except North Carolina enacted Black Codes designed to control blacks and to restrict their civil rights. Although these regulations varied from state to state, the most common provisions included the establishment of racial segregation in public places, the prohibition of interracial marriage, and the legal recognition of marriages between blacks. Black Codes also prevented blacks from serving on juries or from testifying against whites in court, though they could give testimony against other blacks. In some states, such as Mississippi, these laws reinstituted many of the criminal provisions of the slave codes. The Mississippi law, for example, declared that "all

penal and criminal laws now in force describing the mode of punishment of crimes and misdemeanors committed by slaves, free negroes, or mulattoes are hereby reenacted, and decreed to be in full force against all freedmen, free negroes, and mulattoes."

The Black Codes in general forbade blacks from entering any but agricultural employment. In Mississippi they prevented blacks from buying or renting farmland and required them to sign an annual labor contract with a white employer; in South Carolina they made it illegal for blacks to purchase or own city lots and compelled them to pay a tax of between $10 and $100 to enter an occupation other than farming or domestic service. Blacks were also prohibited from leaving the plantation, or from entertaining guests upon it, without permission. If blacks could not give evidence of being employed, they could be detained under a charge of vagrancy and fined, or bound to work for a white landowner if unable to pay. The vagrancy statute imposed involuntary labor as punishment for a wide array of persons deemed antisocial, including:

> rogues and vagabonds, idle and dissipated persons, beggars, jugglers, or persons practicing unlawful games or plays, runaways, common drunkards, common night-walkers, lewd, wanton, or lascivious persons, . . . common railers and brawlers, persons who neglect their calling or employment, misspend what they earn, or do not provide for the support of themselves or their families, or dependents, and all other idle and disorderly persons, including all who neglect all lawful business, habitually misspend their time by frequenting houses of ill-fame, gaming houses, or tippling shops.

Apprenticeship laws authorized the state to bind out to white employers black children whose parents could not support them or who were "not teaching them habits of industry and honesty; or are persons of notoriously bad character."

Although either the Federal Army, the Freedmen's Bureau, or the Civil Rights Act (1866) invalidated most of the Black Codes, these laws reveal what the contours of social and race relations in the post–Civil War South would have been if left entirely in the hands of whites. As African American historian W. E. B. Du Bois observed, the Black Codes represented "what the South proposed to do to the emancipated Negro, unless restrained by the nation." Black Congressman Josiah Walls warned that the Black Codes indicated what Southern Democrats would do "if they should ever again obtain control of this Government." In essence, whites intended these laws to keep blacks a propertyless, rural, laboring class, slaves in everything but name.

With the adoption of the Black Codes, the freedmen, indeed, found themselves cruelly thrust back into much the same position they

EMANCIPATION

had occupied as slaves. The laws that had recognized their citizenship and their rights disappeared. Some freedmen nonetheless protested their mistreatment. A letter to the governor of Mississippi from a group of freedmen asked that if "Mississippi has abolished slavery, . . . does she mean it or is it a policy for the present?" Further, they pointed out that "now we are free, we do not want to be hunted by negro runners and their hounds unless we are guilty of a criminal crime."

Most blacks sensibly realized that their protests would have little effect on the situation and might in some ways even make it worse. A writer in one African American newspaper declared that the Black Codes "express an average of the justice and humanity which the late slaveholders possess." He felt assured, though, that with the aid of the federal government "the right will prevail and truth [will] triumph in the end." For the time being, the government appeared to respond sympathetically to the plight of blacks, suspending the Black Codes in several states. Some Southern state legislatures repealed the harshest laws on their own. While the Codes were thought "dead," however, the forces that had created them were very much alive.

With the failure of the Black Codes, Southern whites tried to curb the freedom and power of blacks through intimidation, violence, and terror, with the largest number of violent acts arising from the attempts of blacks to assert their rights. Freedmen were assaulted and, in some cases, murdered for not satisfying their employers, for trying to buy or rent land, or for simply trying to leave the plantations on which they had once been enslaved. One Tennessee newspaper reported that white "regulators" were "riding about whipping, maiming and killing all the negroes who do not obey the orders of their former masters, just as if slavery existed." Many former black soldiers who had fought for the Union returned home only to find cinders and ashes. The rising tide of racist violence prompted one Louisiana freedman to declare: "I would say to every colored soldier, 'Bring your gun home'." Other blacks wearily realized that out of the ruin of the Civil War another conflict was smoldering. Whites knew it, too, for a former governor of North Carolina remarked "with reference to Emancipation, we are at the beginning of the war."

Perhaps the greatest threat to the freedmen was the appearance of a new organization determined to unnerve and overpower blacks and their white supporters: the Ku Klux Klan. Organized in 1866 in Pulaski, Tennessee, the Klan set out to restore white supremacy throughout the South. Klansmen rode about the Southern countryside wearing white masks and robes, issuing threats, harassing blacks, and on occasion engaging in destruction, violence, and murder. During their brief career, the Klan and similar groups such as the Knights of the White Camellia and the White League "whipped, shot, hanged, robbed, raped, and otherwise outraged Negroes and Republicans across the South in the name of preserving white civilization."

Congress struck back at the Klan with three Enforcement Acts passed in 1870 and 1871. The first of these measures made it a federal offense to interfere with any citizen's right to vote. The second placed the election of Congressmen under the supervision of federal election officials and marshals. The third, the so-called Ku Klux Klan Act, made it illegal to engage in conspiracies, to wear disguises in public, and to resist, threaten, or in any way intimidate officials of the courts or the government.

Federal mandates and prosecutions weakened the Klan, but such societies as the Mississippi Rifle Club and the South Carolina Red Shirts continued to harass blacks and white Republicans, enabling conservative whites gradually to reassume control of government and society in one Southern state after another. Republicans fell out of power in Virginia and Tennessee in 1869 and Georgia and North Carolina in 1870, even though the "Old North State" had a Republican governor until 1876. Republicans held on longer in the states of the Deep South, which had larger black populations than those in the upper South. In the elections of 1876, however, voters dismissed the Republicans from office in South Carolina, Louisiana, and Florida, the three remaining states where they held sway.

Northern support for Reconstruction (1865–1877) had begun to wane with the Panic of 1873. Economic hard times distracted Northerners from the problems of the former slaves and made Reconstruction programs seem an expensive luxury. Even whites who favored racial equality usually thought in terms of legal equality, which they believed would naturally follow from emancipation. Yet, for freedom to be meaningful and equality assured, the federal government had to guarantee the physical safety of black men and women and support their liberty by giving them land. When the government failed to do so, Reconstruction faltered and then collapsed.

For a brief period during the 1870s and 1880s greater flexibility and tolerance had characterized race relations in the South. The former slave owner, wrote a South Carolina newspaper editor, "has no desire to browbeat, maltreat, and spit upon the colored man." There lingered among many white Southerners feelings of benevolence and paternalism toward blacks, and in any event most did not regard blacks as a threat to the existing social and political order.

EMANCIPATION

HE WAS ALWAYS RIGHT

The following account is that of Henry Blake, an African American born into slavery in Arkansas; he made these statements when he was interviewed by a representative of the Works Progress Administration in the 1930s:

After freedom, we worked on shares a while. Then, we rented. When we worked on shares, we couldn't make nothing—just overalls, and something to eat. Half went to the white man, and you would destroy your half, if you weren't careful. A man that didn't know how to count would always lose. He might lose anyhow. The white folks didn't give no itemized statements. No, you just had to owe so much. No matter how good account you kept, you had to go by their account, and—now, brother, I'm telling you the truth about this—it's been that way for a long time. You had to take the white man's words and notes on everything. Anything you wanted you could get, if you were a good hand. If you didn't make no money, that's all right; they would advance you more. But you better not try to leave and get caught. They'd keep you in debt. They were sharp. Christmas come, you could take up twenty dollars in somethin'-to-eat and much as you wanted in whiskey. You could buy a gallon of whiskey—anything that kept you a slave. Because he was always right and you were always wrong, if there was a difference. If there was an argument, he would get mad and there would be a shooting take place.

Source: *George P. Rawick,* The American Slave: A Composite Autobiography, *volume 8 (Westport, Conn.: Greenwood Press, 1972), pp. 175–179.*

Such attitudes began to change in the early 1890s when the Populist, or People's, Party tried to organize black and white farmers into a political coalition to challenge for control of state governments throughout the South. "You are kept apart," Populist leader Tom Watson of Georgia told an audience of black and white farmers, "in order that you may be separately fleeced." Such language frightened those in power. They responded by appealing to the fears of Southern whites that the South would again come under "Negro domination," as they believed had been the case during Reconstruction.

Since competition for the black vote was growing, that relatively small group of men who dominated Southern politics at the end of the nineteenth century, known as the Bourbons, reasoned it was best to eliminate the black vote altogether. The Bourbons were members of the Democratic Party. As long as they could manipulate the black vote to their liking, they had no objection to blacks' going to the polls and selecting the Democratic candidate of their choice. It was, however, another matter entirely when their Republican, Independent, and especially Populist adversaries began striving to capture the black vote. Under those circumstances, the right of blacks to vote had to be withdrawn.

The Fifteenth Amendment (1870) made it impossible simply to disfranchise blacks, so the Bourbons devised other, less direct, means to keep them from voting. They instituted a poll tax that most blacks could not afford to pay and literacy tests that most blacks, and many whites, could not pass.

Mississippi led the way in the disfranchisement of blacks. At a state convention held in 1890, delegates modified the Reconstruction constitution of 1868, which had extended suffrage to blacks. First, Mississippi established a new residency requirement of two years in the state and one year in the election district that often prevented both black and white tenant farmers, who habitually moved every year, from voting. Second, the new provisions disqualified voters convicted of certain crimes such as vagrancy, to which blacks were uncommonly susceptible. Third, the reforms mandated that all taxes, including the poll tax, be paid by 1 February of election year. Even those rare blacks who could afford to pay their taxes either moved frequently or were not in the habit of keeping careful records. They had plenty of time to lose tax receipts before election day arrived in the fall and were thus barred from voting. Fourth, the new regulations instituted a literacy test. To assist illiterate whites who could not, for example, read a passage from the Constitution, most Southern states instituted what became known as the "understanding clause." An election official read a portion of the Constitution to a potential white voter and then asked if he had understood it. If he answered "yes," he was permitted to vote.

Other states found different ways for whites to get around the literacy requirement. In 1895 the South Carolina legislature declared that owning property assessed at $300 qualified an illiterate voter. Many more whites than blacks met the prerequisite. Three years later the Louisiana state legislature invented the ingenious "grandfather clause," which enabled illiterates to vote if their fathers or grandfathers had been eligible on 1 January 1867, when all blacks in the state had been disfranchised. By 1910 the legislatures of Oklahoma, Alabama, Georgia, North Carolina, and Virginia had incorporated the grandfather clause into state election laws. Such restrictions were effective in limiting the black vote. In 1896, for example, 130,000 blacks registered to vote in Louisiana; by 1900 that number had fallen to 5,320. According to the census of 1900, Alabama had 121,259 literate black men over the

EMANCIPATION

age of twenty-one, all of whom ought to have been eligible to vote; only 3,742 were registered.

The federal government did little to rectify the situation. In 1890 the Senate, apparently not wishing to interfere in the internal affairs of the states, defeated a bill sponsored by Representative Henry Cabot Lodge (R.–Mass.) that would have authorized federal supervision of state elections to reexamine the qualifications of those excluded from voting. Lodge's bill marked the last significant attempt to protect black voters until Congress passed the Voting Rights Act (1965).

Despite their political limitations, blacks won a few major, if short-lived, victories, chief among them passage of the Civil Rights Act (1875). Although poorly enforced, the Act outlawed discrimination in transportation, theaters, restaurants, hotels, and other places of public accommodation. In 1883, however, the U.S. Supreme Court ruled, with only one dissent, that the Fourteenth Amendment (1868) prohibited state governments from discriminating on the basis of race but did not restrict private organizations, companies, or individuals from doing so. Hence, railroad and street-car companies, restaurants, hotels, theaters, private clubs, hospitals, and the like could legally keep blacks out if they wished.

The repeal of the Civil Rights Act of 1875 did not immediately rob blacks of their rights any more than its passage had guaranteed them. In 1885, for instance, blacks in South Carolina continued to ride in first-class railway cars apparently without exciting comment. As early as 1881, by contrast, the Tennessee state legislature had required railroads operating in the state to provide separate first-class cars for blacks and whites. Not until 1888 did Mississippi require separate railway cars for blacks and whites. When in 1890 Louisiana also established separate cars for blacks and whites, Homer Plessy, an octoroon (one-eighth black) convicted for refusing to leave an all-white car, challenged the constitutionality of the law in the U.S. Supreme Court.

The justices rendered their decision in the case of *Plessy* v. *Ferguson* in 1896, upholding state laws that mandated segregation. Writing the majority opinion, Justice Henry Brown Billings from Massachusetts declared that segregation laws "have been generally, if not universally, recognized as within the competency of state legislatures in the exercise of their police power." Separate seating arrangements, the majority of the Court concluded, thus did not deprive blacks of their constitutional rights. The sole dissenting voice came from Justice John Marshall Harlan, a former slaveholder and Unionist from Kentucky, who had also opposed repeal of the Civil Rights Act of 1875. "In my opinion," Harlan wrote, "the judgment this day rendered will, in time, prove to be quite as pernicious as the decision made by this tribunal in the Dred Scott Case." The ruling, Harlan predicted, would "stimulate aggressions, more or less brutal, upon the admitted rights of colored citizens."

Events made Harlan's words prophetic. Soon the principle of segregation extended to every aspect of life for blacks, from public accommodations to recreation and sports to health care and employment. The violence that Justice Harlan had foretold also became a reality. Between 1890 and 1899 the number of lynchings that occurred in the United States averaged 187.5 per year, 82 percent of which took place in the South. In 1892 black journalist and social activist Ida B. Wells launched what eventually became an international movement opposed to lynching when she wrote a series of articles about the lynching of three friends in Memphis, Tennessee. The antilynching movement attracted considerable support in all regions of the United States, including the South, much of it coming from white women. Wells's goal was the enactment of a federal antilynching law, which would empower the U.S. government to prosecute those responsible for lynchings when local and state governments failed or refused to do so.

The opposition to lynching, however, was an exception to the general support for white supremacy. Few whites, Northern or Southern, ever fully accepted the idea of racial equality with former slaves. In time, Northerners who feared the invasion of blacks into their states became increasingly sympathetic to the view of Southerners that black equality really meant the oppression of white people. The reality that blacks faced in both the North and the South during the last thirty years of the nineteenth century was the emergence of a racial caste system embodied in the laws of the United States and sustained by the attitudes and conduct of whites. Regrettably, the hopes that the majority of black Americans had long entertained for equality and integration remained unfulfilled.

–CHESTER J. WYNNE,
WASHINGTON, D. C.

References

Robert Cruden, *The Negro in Reconstruction* (Englewood Cliffs, N.J.: Prentice-Hall, 1969).

W. E. B. Du Bois, *Black Reconstruction: An Essay toward a History of the Part Which Black Folk Played in the Attempt to Reconstruct Democracy in America, 1860–1880* (New York: Harcourt, Brace, 1935).

EMANCIPATION

Eric Foner, *Nothing but Freedom: Emancipation and Its Legacy* (Baton Rouge: Louisiana State University Press, 1983).

Foner, *Reconstruction: America's Unfinished Revolution, 1863–1877* (New York: Harper & Row, 1988).

Eugene D. Genovese, *From Rebellion to Revolution: Afro-American Slave Revolts in the Making of the Modern World* (Baton Rouge: Louisiana State University Press, 1979).

Leon F. Litwack, *Been in the Storm So Long: The Aftermath of Slavery* (New York: Knopf, 1979).

Litwack, *Trouble in Mind: Black Southerners in the Age of Jim Crow* (New York: Knopf, 1998).

Benjamin Quarles, *The Negro in the Making of America,* second revised edition (New York: Collier / London: Collier-Macmillan, 1987).

George Brown Tindall, *America: A Narrative History,* second edition, volume 2 (New York: Norton, 1988).

Theodore B. Wilson, *The Black Codes of the South* (Tuscaloosa: University of Alabama Press, 1965).

C. Vann Woodward, *American Counterpoint: Slavery and Racism in the North-South Dialogue* (Boston: Little, Brown, 1971).

Woodward, *The Strange Career of Jim Crow,* third edition (New York: Oxford University Press, 1974).

EMANCIPATION

Were the conditions of slavery worse in the English colonies than in the Spanish and Portuguese colonies?

Viewpoint: Yes. Unlike Spanish and Portuguese statutes, English law deprived the slaves of all rights, rendering them utterly subject to the will of the masters.

Viewpoint: No. Slaves in the Spanish and Portuguese colonies were treated with barbaric cruelty, especially in rural areas, and laws enacted to protect them were ineffective and unenforceable.

In the late 1950s Stanley M. Elkins proposed that only a comparative study could yield adequate answers to the question of whether slaves were better off in Spanish and Portuguese colonies than in English colonies. It was no longer sufficient, Elkins contended, for historians merely to assert the universal inhumanity of slavery. Frank Tannenbaum's brief but suggestive volume titled *Slave & Citizen: The Negro in the Americas* (1946) established the contours of such a comparative study. Yet, it was the appearance of Elkins's *Slavery: A Problem in American Institutional and Intellectual Life* in 1959 that ignited a firestorm of debate. Elkins maintained that fundamental differences existed between the system and practice of slavery in North America and Latin America. Scholars such as Orlando Patterson, by contrast, have emphasized the underlying similarities that they believe defined slavery throughout the Western Hemisphere. The American South, Patterson wrote in *Slavery and Social Death* (1982), "shared with all slaveholding societies certain imperatives of the interaction between slaveholder and slave."

Elkins concluded, however, that no ideas, values, or institutions developed in the American South to inhibit the evolution of slavery and the emergence of plantation capitalism. Custom, law, and religion instead promoted the growth of a "total institution" that not only deprived slaves of their freedom and exposed them to unremitting coercion but also robbed them of their dignity and stripped them of their humanity. So overwhelming was the experience of slavery in the South that it "infantilized" its victims, producing a distinctive personality type that Elkins identified as "Sambo." Docile and compliant, tractable and submissive, childish and dependent, Sambo, a psychic casualty of inhumane repression, could offer little resistance to his enslavement. Sambos were made, not born. Slavery had destroyed their ability to function as emotionally mature adults. To make his point, Elkins likened the harm done to slaves on Southern plantations to that which the inmates of Nazi concentration camps had suffered.

Drawing on the work of Tannenbaum and Brazilian historian Gilberto Freyre, Elkins determined that slavery in North America and the British Caribbean was of a more severe character than slavery in the Spanish and Portuguese possessions of South America. British slaveholders, Elkins explained, were capitalists who sought to maximize their profits. In the Spanish and Portuguese provinces, on the contrary, the influence of the Catholic Church, the law, and an aristocratic, anticapitalist tradition combined to mitigate the worst aspects of slavery.

Eugene D. Genovese, Elkins's most insightful critic, acknowledged that his thesis raised subtle and intriguing questions that deepened and enriched the debate over the cruelty and inhumanity of slavery. At the same time, Genovese and other historians declared that Southern slaveholders were neither unrestrained capitalists nor sadistic SS guards intent on the debasement and torture of blacks. They further demonstrated that the benevolence of the church, the law, and aristocratic culture were weaker in practice than in theory. Genovese also charged that Elkins had underestimated the integrity of the slaves' personalities and their capacity for resistance. In addition, Genovese affirmed, Southern planters had relied less on coercion and violence to enforce discipline and elicit obedience than on paternalism, an intricate system of reward and punishment, flattery and rebuke, and kindness and brutality. Paternalism might have induced blacks to accept slavery even as it enabled them to resist its dehumanizing logic.

Viewpoint:
Yes. Unlike Spanish and Portuguese statutes, English law deprived the slaves of all rights, rendering them utterly subject to the will of the masters.

Slavery in the British colonies and later in the United States was uniformly severe. English law deprived slaves of all the rights of persons, property, and family and subjected them to the will of the master without recourse. In *Slavery: A Problem in American Institutional and Intellectual Life* (1959), Stanley M. Elkins gave the classic statement of this argument. "In the Spanish and Portuguese colonies," he wrote, "we are immediately impressed by the comparative lack of precision and logic governing the institution of slavery there; we find an exasperating dimness of line between the slave and free portions of society, a multiplicity of points of contact between the two, a confusing promiscuity of color, such as would never have been thinkable in our own country." Elkins went on to demonstrate that while the Spanish and Portuguese recognized the basic humanity of their slaves, the British and Americans did not. "Certain assumptions were implied . . . which made it impossible that the slave in [Latin American] culture should ever be quite considered as mere property, either in law or in society's customary habits of mind. . . . These assumptions . . . were, in effect, that he was a man, that he had a soul as precious as any other man's, that he had a moral nature, that he was not only susceptible to sin but also as eligible for grace as his master—that master and slave were brothers in Christ." English and American law, according to Frank Tannenbaum, another preeminent historian of slavery, refused to acknowledge the moral personality of the slave, denying to "the Negro the moral status requisite for effective legal freedom" as well as "the moral competence" necessary to become "a man."

The changing status of blacks in the Chesapeake Bay region during the seventeenth and eighteenth centuries offers a case in point. Although not spared the ruthless exploitation that almost all propertyless men in Virginia faced during the seventeenth century, the blacks who managed to survive joined whites in the scramble for land, servants, and status. The frontier conditions that prevailed throughout much of the Chesapeake enabled many blacks to set the terms of their own labor, establish relatively stable family lives, and occasionally barter for their freedom. In the seventeenth century black freedmen in the Chesapeake owned land, held servants, voted, and even occupied minor political offices. They could sue and be sued and could give testimony in courts of law. They could own, buy, and sell property and could pass it on to their descendants. Until they were outlawed in 1691, interracial marriages between blacks and whites were permissible, if uncommon.

Blacks in the Chesapeake thus initially enjoyed many of the same legal rights and protections as other subjects of the English Crown, or at least were not systematically denied those rights and protections. However, a direct correlation existed between the growing numbers of blacks in the Chesapeake and the need for government officials to develop laws regulating black freedom. The condition of the slaves deteriorated as their numbers increased. By the middle of the seventeenth century the trend was clear. As the black population rose, the rights of black men and women, free and slave, diminished.

In the 1640s blacks in Maryland lost the right to bear arms. In the 1660s both Virginia and Maryland administered stern punishments for the crime of miscegenation (race mixing), which little more than a decade earlier colonial officials had ignored or treated as a minor offense. The Maryland legislature decreed in 1664 that all "freeborne English women forgetfull of their Condiciōn and to the disgrace of our Nation doe intermarry with Negro Slaues . . . shall Serue the master of such slaue dureing the life of her husband." During this period, too, the law acknowledged that masters could not discipline their slaves or coerce them to labor by threatening to take away their liberty. Since

SO MUCH RIGOR

Charles Ball was a slave who worked on plantations in Maryland, South Carolina, and Georgia:

In Maryland and Virginia, although the slaves are treated with so much rigor, and ofttimes with so much cruelty, I have seen instances of the greatest tenderness of feeling on the part of their owners. I, myself, had three masters in Maryland, and I cannot say now, even after having resided so many years in a state where slavery is not tolerated, that either of them (except the last, who sold me to the Georgians, and was an unfeeling man), used me worse than they had a moral right to do, regarding me merely as an article of property, and not entitled to any rights as a man, political or civil. My mistresses, in Maryland, were all good women; and the mistress of my wife, in whose kitchen I spent my Sundays and many of my nights, for several years, was a lady of most benevolent and kindly feelings. She was a true friend to me, and I shall always venerate her memory. . . .

If the proprietors of the soil in Maryland and Virginia, were skillful cultivators—had their lands in good condition—and kept no more slaves on each estate, that would be sufficient to work the soil in a proper manner, and kept up the repairs of the place—the condition of the colored people would not be, by any means, a comparatively unhappy one. I am convinced, that in nine cases in ten, the hardships and suffering of the colored population of lower Virginia, are attributable to the poverty and distress of its owners. In many instances, an estate scarcely yields enough to feed and clothe the slaves in a comfortable manner, without allowing anything for the support of the master and family; but it is obvious, that the family must first be supported, and the slaves must be content with the surplus—and this, on a poor, old, worn out tobacco plantation, is often very small, and wholly inadequate to the comfortable

sustenance of the hands, as they are called. There, in many places, nothing is allowed to the poor Negro, but his peck of corn per week, without the sauce of a salt herring, or even a little salt itself. . . .

The general features of slavery are the same everywhere; but the utmost rigor of the system, is only to be met with, on the cotton plantations of Carolina and Georgia, or in the rice fields which skirt the deep swamps and morasses of the southern rivers. In the tobacco fields of Maryland and Virginia, great cruelties are practiced—not so frequently by the owners, as by the overseers of the slaves; but yet, the tasks are not so excessive as in the cotton region, nor is the press of labor so incessant throughout the year. . . .

Flogging—though often severe and excruciating in Maryland, is not practiced with the order, regularity and system, to which it is often reduced in the South. On the Potomac, if a slave gives offense, he is generally chastised on the spot, in the field where he is at work, as the overseer always carried a whip—sometimes a twisted cow-hide, sometimes a kind of horse-whip, and very often a simple hickory switch or gad, cut in the adjoining woods. For stealing meat, or other provisions, or for any of the higher offenses, the slaves are stripped, tied up by the hands—sometimes by the thumbs—and whipped at the quarter—but many times, on a large tobacco plantation, there is not more than one of these regular whippings in a week—though on others, where the master happens to be a bad man, or a drunkard—the back of the unhappy Maryland slave, is seamed with scars from his neck to his hips.

Source: Charles Ball, *"Fifty Years in Chains; or, the Life of an American Slave (1858),"* in African American Voices: The Life Cycle of Slavery, *edited by Steven Mintz (St. James, N.Y.: Brandywine, 1999), pp. 94–96.*

slaves had already lost their freedom, the masters, in order to command obedience and labor, had to make them fear for their lives. Hence, colonial legislatures in both Virginia and Maryland moved to protect masters and other whites from criminal prosecution for killing a slave.

Social practice in the Chesapeake, of course, did not always adhere to the letter of the law. Some free blacks continued to prosper and to live as respected members of their communities.

Yet, according to historian Donald R. Wright, the dike holding back the flood of legislation and social practice that condemned blacks to unmitigated slavery broke when the importation of large numbers of Africans began after 1680. In short order, blacks in the Chesapeake lost their remaining freedoms and found themselves completely set apart from whites.

The *Statutes of Virginia* of 1705 both codified and illustrated the transformation. Defining the rights of white English servants, the *Statutes* declared:

> And also be it enacted, by the authority aforesaid, and its is hereby enacted, That all masters and owners of servants, shall find and provide for their servants, wholesome and competent diet, clothing, and lodging, by the discretion of the county court; and shall not, at any time, give immoderate correction; neither shall, at any time, whip a chrisitan white servant naked, without the order from a justice of the peace: And if any, notwithstanding this act, shall presume to whip a christian servant naked, without such an order, the person so offending, shall forfeit and pay for the same, forty shillings sterling to the party injured: To be recovered, with costs, upon petition without the formal process of an action. . . .

White servants had rights. Their master could not punish them without direct legal permission from the appropriate authorities. Servants could even sue their masters if they violated their rights.

The same rules did not apply to slaves. According to the *Statutes:*

> If any slave resist his master, or owner, or other person, by his or her order, correcting such a slave, and shall happen to be killed in such correction, it shall not be accounted a felony; but the master, owner, and every such other person so giving correction, shall be free and acquit of all punishment and accusation for the same, as if such accident never happened. And also, if any negro, mulatto, or Indian, bond or free, shall at any time, lift his or her hand, in opposition against any christian, not being negro, mulatto, or Indian, he or she so offending, shall, for every such offence, proved by the oath of the party, receive on his or her bare back, thirty lashes, well laid on, cognizable by a justice of the peace for that county wherein such offence shall be committed.

The slaves by law had no rights that whites were obligated to respect. As the slave population in the Chesapeake grew, the laws governing slavery became more rigid and the punishment for wrongdoing more severe. In the 1780s, Jacob, a slave owned by Martha Flint of Lancaster County, Virginia, stood trial with his owner and another white woman for stealing tobacco and food. Each woman received a whipping. The law dictated that Jacob be hanged for his actions, but the court showed mercy, or what passed for mercy in a slave society. Since he had acted in the company of "Christian white persons," Jacob, instead of facing execution for stealing sixpence worth of property, was made "to stand for an hour at the pillory, to have each ear nailed to the pillory and then cut off close to the head." Afterward, he also suffered a "full whipping."

Many travel accounts dating from the eighteenth and nineteenth centuries attest that Latin American slaves enjoyed greater leisure, less discipline, and more freedom than their counterparts in British America. Slaves in Latin America faced no legal barriers to marriage, education, and gradual emancipation and enjoyed legal protections from cruel and oppressive treatment. Finally, they did not endure the stigma attached to race in British America. In 1856 the English traveler Thomas Ewbank noted that in Brazil he had "passed black ladies in silks and jewelry, with male slaves in livery behind them. . . . Several have white husbands. The first doctor in the city is a colored man; so is the President of the Province." The differences that Ewbank and others found in the condition and status of slaves in Latin America and British North America arose from two primary factors. First, Latin culture de-emphasized the profit motive, and second, the Roman Catholic Church insisted on the rights of slaves to marry, to worship freely, and to be accorded the basic respect due to all human beings.

In Latin America, moreover, civil and church law were not at odds. The Spanish legal tradition recognized freedom as the natural condition of man and thus granted slaves certain rights and protections. Not only the Church but the law entitled slaves to marry, to seek redress from abusive masters, and to purchase their freedom. Similarly, Portuguese authorities issued edicts intended to prevent the mistreatment of slaves in Brazil.

After 1750 the Portuguese, Spanish, and French became intensely concerned with reforming imperial administration. Under the influence of the Enlightenment, statesmen sought to make government not only more efficient but also more humane. In Portugal the Marquis de Pombal initialed reforms designed to protect slaves and to bring about a greater equality between the races throughout the vast Portuguese Empire. King Charles III of Spain (reigned 1759–1788) supported a series of enlightened reforms intended to improve both the benevolence and competence of the Spanish Empire. The *Real Cédula* (Royal Decree) of 1789 bore the imprint of the Enlightenment ideals of rationality and efficiency combined with the more traditional outlook of Spanish Catholicism.

The *Real Cédula* had three objectives. First, it was designed to reinvigorate the colonial economy. Second, it was to prevent insurrection and idleness among blacks and compel them to productive labor. Third, it was to shield blacks from cruelty and abuse and to encourage the acceptance of Catholic religion and morality among the slave population of the Spanish Empire. The law also provided for the registering of, and keeping records on, slaves and the punishment of masters who denied their slaves adequate provisions or prevented them from obtaining religious instruction. As a substitute for the *Code Noir* (Black Code) of 1685, the *Real Cédula* in many ways represented a genuine advancement in the enlightened and humane treatment of bondmen and bondwomen.

Among the blacks in the Spanish and Portuguese colonies were skilled craftsmen, soldiers, musicians, poets, priests, and judges. "I am accustomed to seeing many [blacks] engaged in all manner of careers," remarked a delegate to the Cortes of Cádiz in 1811. The opportunities and rights that blacks enjoyed in Latin American society existed before the abolition of slavery. It was thus not surprising that emancipation, when at last it came to Latin America, was brought about, as Frank Tannenbaum long ago made clear, "without violence, without bloodshed, and without civil war."

–MARK G. MALVASI,
RANDOLPH-MACON COLLEGE

Viewpoint:
No. Slaves in the Spanish and Portuguese colonies were treated with barbaric cruelty, especially in rural areas, and laws enacted to protect them were ineffective and unenforceable.

No doubt there is some truth in the idyllic picture of Latin American slavery in which slaves and masters prayed, drank, and loafed together and in which masters ignored their ledgers and account books and preferred instead to frolic with slave girls. Planters in the British West Indies and in North America also idealized their system of bondage, portraying their slaves as indolent and carefree and characterizing their slave laws as benevolent and humane. Yet, both of these stereotyped images of mild servitude and racial harmony are questionable.

Spain was the most powerful nation in Europe during the fifteenth and sixteenth centuries. The Spanish determined that it was their Christian duty to take under their guidance and protection the backward natives whom they encountered in the New World. As a consequence, they introduced them not only to Spanish culture and Roman Catholicism but also to forced labor in the mines, torture, rape, murder, diseases such as smallpox, and artificially induced famine. The generosity of the Spanish and the blessings of the Spanish God reduced the native population of Hispaniola (meaning "Little Spain") from 500,000, and perhaps as many as 1 million, to 60,000 in only fifteen years.

The Dominican priest Bartolomé de Las Casas pleaded for the abolition of native slavery in Hispaniola and for more humane treatment of the Indians. He reported extensively on the horrors of Spanish rule and displayed a genuine sympathy for those whose misfortune it was to fall under their enlightened sway. In his now famous *Short Account of the Destruction of the West-Indians Lands,* published in 1522, he lamented that:

> The Spaniards attacked [the Indians'] cities and towns showing no regard for either children or graybeards. They spared neither pregnant women nor women about to give birth, but tore open their bellies and hacked everything to pieces. The Indians were attacked like lambs resting in their pens. The Spaniards took bets among each other that they could cut people in half with one blow of their swords or split someone's head or rip his intestines from his body with their pikes. . . . They also made wide gallows in such a manner that the victims' feet almost touched the earth and, every time, they hung thirteen Indians on each in honor and for the glory of the Redeemer and the Twelve Apostles; and put wood and fire underneath the gallows so as to burn their victims alive. Others again they bound tight and wrapped dry straw around their bodies, lit it and burnt them alive. Others they let live specifically so they could cut off both of the victim's hands and hang them around their necks, saying, "Go spread the news about this and tell your countrymen who have fled to the mountains."

As a result of Las Casas's efforts the Spanish Crown abolished forced labor in law even while the colonists maintained it in fact. Tormented by the prospect of the total annihilation of the native peoples within a single generation, Las Casas devised a plan to import more robust blacks from Africa to perform the most arduous labor. In 1517 the new king of Spain, Charles I (reigned 1516–1556), authorized the export of 15,000 African slaves to Hispaniola.

It is also significant that the portrait of Brazilian slavery as benign originated in the late eighteenth and early nineteenth centuries, when the sugar plantations were in decline. The conditions that prevailed during the sugar boom of the seventeenth century, the mining boom of the eighteenth century, and the coffee boom of the nineteenth century bring a much harsher vision of slavery into focus. So severe were working conditions in Brazil during the sugar boom that on average slaves lived only seven years after arriving from Africa.

The interpretation of Brazilian slavery as generally mild compared with slavery in the British colonies of the Caribbean and North America owes much to Gilberto Freyre who, in his important and provocative book *The Masters and the Slaves: A Study in the Development of Brazilian Civilization* (1943), emphasized the paternal relations that existed on the sugar plantations of northeastern Brazil. The conditions that Freyre described, however, usually applied to house slaves who occupied a privileged position and not to field hands. During harvesttime and when the sugar mills were grinding the cane, slaves commonly worked around the clock. The masters and overseers who supervised their labor imposed discipline with such brutality that punishment often degenerated into a festival of sadistic cruelty.

Slaves who ran away and were recaptured were branded with an *F* for *fugao* (fugitive) and had their ears slashed as an identifying mark. Chronic offenders received a severe whipping. It was a commonly accepted practice to punish the most recalcitrant with a *novena* or a *trezena* during which the slave was bound hand and foot, placed facedown on a table, and beaten for between nine and thirteen consecutive nights. The cuts that the whips left on the body were sometimes teased with a razor or rubbed with a mixture of salt and urine. During the middle of the eighteenth century Brazilian masters welcomed new slaves to their plantations with a vicious whipping of one hundred lashes or more without cause and then worked them in the fields without rest. Portuguese and later Brazilian law did not command masters to treat their slaves in this way; nor did the law prohibit such conduct. How well or poorly a slave fared depended entirely on the whim of the master.

The invention of other methods and instruments of torture must have taxed the imagination and ingenuity of even the most sadistic. Constructed of iron or wood, the *tronco* held a slave's ankles fastened in one place for several days. The *libambo* held the arms in place in a fashion similar to the *tronco*. The law, of course, protected slaves from excessively cruel masters and overseers, but authorities found the statutes difficult to administer and enforce. A decree of the Portuguese Crown in 1700 denounced the barbarity with which both male and female slave owners treated their slaves. The document singled out for special condemnation the practice of many female slave owners who forced their female slaves into prostitution. Admirable as these sentiments might have been, the law did little to assist the slaves, for colonial officials were helpless to end the practice.

The Catholic Church also exerted minimal influence on behalf of the slaves. On the plantations a chaplain, paid and housed by the landowner, represented the Church. His chief role was to acquaint the slaves with the teachings of Scripture and to remind them that disobedience to their master was a sin. The slaves of Brazil doubtless found no comfort in such words, however well intentioned they might have been. The frequency of suicide among them speaks volumes about their condition.

The situation was better in the cities, where officials could enforce the laws that protected slaves and punish those who violated them. In cities, too, slaves had greater opportunities to earn money with which to purchase their freedom, especially if they had learned a skill. Yet, urban slavery presented its own set of restrictions and dangers. In Cartagena, for instance, slaves were subject to repressive police regulations. Punishments for various sorts of misbehavior ranged from cutting off the hands, ears, or penis to execution. In 1755 the city councillors of Mariana demanded that the right of slaves to buy their freedom be withdrawn, and that slaves who tried to escape be crippled for life, either by having part of a foot amputated or by having an Achilles tendon severed, rendering them still fit for labor but not for flight. As a message to their other slaves, masters posted the heads of recaptured fugitives on spikes along the main road leading into the Brazilian mining district of Minas Gerais.

Throughout Latin America and the Caribbean, slaves had no legal defense against physical assault. Spanish law might have endowed them with certain rights, but it also left them completely subject to their master's will and categorized the murder of slaves as a minor offense punishable by a fine. Similarly, the Portuguese government issued edicts intended to prevent the abuse of slaves in Brazil. Yet, Brazilian law was a notoriously chaotic tangle of contradictory rules, codes, and decrees. To complicate matters, the lawyers and magistrates in Brazil who interpreted the law were celebrated for their dishonesty and corruption. Even had the law been clearly defined and fairly applied, it would probably have done the slaves little good. They were spread over an immense area, often beyond the reach of a distant government and, for all intents and purposes, subject wholly to the will of their masters.

Although British provinces had a reputation for fostering a particularly ruthless brand of slavery, Parliament for decades pressured colonial legislatures to enact stricter penalties for assaulting or killing a slave. With the exception of a few British colonies such as Barbados, colonial governments by the early nineteenth century had enacted statutes that made the willful killing of a slave a felony punishable by death. The same trend occurred in the new United States. As early as 1791, the courts in North Carolina classified such a crime as murder. By 1816 the laws of Georgia contended that maiming or killing a slave was the same as maiming or killing a free white person. Both states also granted slaves what was then the extraordinary right of a trial by jury.

Stung by attacks from British abolitionists, the colonial assembly of Jamaica made the rape of slave women a crime that carried the death penalty. A committee of the Jamaican assembly

went so far as to endorse the view that slaves fell under the protection of English common law save in cases where its application was limited by statute. This doctrine implied that the rights of slaves and the rights of freeborn English subjects were approximately the same and that the legal status of slavery involved only the express disabilities that specific legislation had imposed. Although this view ran counter to all conceptions of chattel slavery, it gained widespread acceptance, especially in the United States.

As Bryan Edwards, an apologist for slavery, pointed out, one reason that Jamaican planters were willing to tolerate more stringent laws protecting slaves was their recognition that slaves could not testify against white men. Extending the protections of common law to slaves thus carried no grave danger as long as courts and juries were composed of slaveholders or men sympathetic to their interests. Since slaves themselves could give no evidence in court, even the meanest planter had little to fear.

These qualifications notwithstanding, the government of the United States abolished the slave trade in 1808, and the British Parliament outlawed slavery throughout the British Empire in 1833. Meanwhile, Spain and Portugal, as well as Brazil upon gaining independence, resisted all efforts to suppress the slave trade. During the

1830s, the decade in which the British abolished slavery, Brazilian planters imported more than 400,000 slaves from Africa. In addition, North American planters were fond of comparing the fertility of their own slaves with the low birth and high mortality rates of slaves in the West Indies and Latin America. Since the slaves of the Southern United States were the only slave population in the New World to reproduce itself by natural means, Southern planters concluded that theirs was the milder and more humane system. A slave who endured seven years on the sugar plantations of the West Indies or the mines of Latin America had lived a long time.

In 1800, for example, about 1 million slaves lived in both Brazil and the United States. Subsequent importations into Brazil were three times greater than those into the United States. Yet, by 1860 there were about 3.5 million slaves in the United States and only 500,000 in Brazil. Three factors explain this divergence. First, the number of slave men far exceeded the number of slave women in the West Indies and Latin America. This imbalanced sex ratio hampered natural reproduction. Second, the high incidence of communicable diseases and the chronic occurrence of ailments such as tetanus, which was particularly lethal to infants, exacted a heavier toll on the slave populations of Latin America and the West

Drawing of the Rua do Valongo, a notorious slave market in Rio de Janeiro, Brazil, circa 1800

(from Hugh Thomas, The Slave Trade, *1997)*

ENGLISH COLONIES

Indies. Third, poorer nutrition and sanitation throughout Latin America and the West Indies contributed to generally higher mortality rates.

Such allowances, however, neither explain nor excuse the callous disregard that the planters of Latin America and the West Indies showed toward human life. Their attitude originated less from cultural than from economic considerations. When the life expectancy of a slave was at most a relatively few years, there was little economic incentive to improve living and working conditions. Planters in Latin America and the Caribbean (including the British West Indies) took a short-term view of their labor needs and accepted the axiom that it made sense to work their slaves to death and then purchase others to replace them.

Whatever the law might have allowed, prohibited, or circumscribed, in almost every colony in Latin America and the Caribbean slaves were subjected to a variety of punishments including being boiled alive or roasted in furnaces. Such acts were almost invariably illegal; nevertheless, they occurred. The *Real Cédula* (Royal Decree) of 1789 might have acknowledged the humanity of the slaves, but at the same time, it decreed that the slaves must work from dawn until dusk and that their employment must be confined to agriculture so that they offered no competition to white artisans. The law prevented slaves from testifying in court and acquiring property except for the benefit and with the permission of their masters. All blacks, whether slave or free, were barred from receiving an education and were required at all times to be respectful of, and submissive to, whites. Any black or mulatto who contradicted a white person or who spoke in a haughty voice received a severe whipping. The penalties increased for raising a hand against a white but diminished in accordance with the lightness of the offender's skin color.

By 1789 there were far more enlightened and humane proposals under discussion for the government of slaves in Great Britain, France, and the United States than in Portugal, Spain, or Brazil. It is, therefore, unwarranted to conclude that the treatment and condition of slaves was substantially better in Latin America and the Spanish Caribbean than it was in the English colonies of the New World. Spanish and Portuguese planters shared with their counterparts in Barbados, Jamaica, Virginia, South Carolina, and other English slave-holding colonies a deep antipathy toward blacks, an abiding fear of slave insurrection, and a growing hostility to education and even religious instruction for the slaves. All imposed unwavering discipline and, even with the approach of emancipation, made no effort to prepare their slaves for freedom. Everywhere slaves were property, and nowhere does the evidence suggest that masters undertook willingly and peacefully to alter that circumstance.

—MEG GREENE,
MIDLOTHIAN, VIRGINIA

References

Ira Berlin, *Many Thousands Gone: The First Two Centuries of Slavery in North America* (Cambridge, Mass.: Belknap Press of Harvard University Press, 1998).

Michael Craton, *Sinews of Empire: A Short History of British Slavery* (Garden City, N.Y.: Anchor/Doubleday, 1974).

David Brion Davis, *The Problem of Slavery in the Age of Revolution, 1770–1823* (Ithaca, N.Y.: Cornell University Press, 1975).

Carl N. Degler, *Neither Black nor White: Slavery and Race Relations in Brazil and the United States* (Madison: University of Wisconsin Press, 1986).

Seymour Drescher, *Capitalism and Antislavery: British Mobilization in Comparative Perspective* (New York: Oxford University Press, 1987).

Richard S. Dunn, *Sugar and Slaves: The Rise of the Planter Class in the English West Indies, 1624–1713* (New York: Norton, 1973).

Stanley M. Elkins, *Slavery: A Problem in American Institutional and Intellectual Life* (Chicago: University of Chicago Press, 1959).

David Eltis, *The Rise of African Slavery in the Americas* (New York: Cambridge University Press, 2000).

Thomas Ewbank, *Life in Brazil, or the Land of the Cocoa and the Palm* (New York: Harper, 1856).

Gilberto Freyre, *The Masters and the Slaves: A Study in the Development of Brazilian Civilization*, second revised edition, translated by Samuel Putnam (New York: Knopf, 1964).

Eugene D. Genovese, *From Rebellion to Revolution: Afro-American Slave Revolts in the Making of the Modern World* (Baton Rouge: Louisiana State University Press, 1979).

William Walter Henning, *The Statutes at Large: Being a Collection of All the Laws of Virginia from the First Session of the Legislature in the Year 1619,* 13 volumes (Richmond, Va.: W. Gray, 1819–1823).

Winthrop Jordan, *White over Black: American Attitudes toward the Negro, 1550–1812* (Chapel Hill: University of North Carolina Press, 1968).

Herbert S. Klein, *Slavery in the Americas: A Comparative Study of Virginia and Cuba* (Chicago: University of Chicago Press, 1967).

Bartolomé de Las Casas, *The Devastation of the Indies: A Brief Account* (New York: Seabury, 1974).

Edmund S. Morgan, *American Slavery, American Freedom: The Ordeal of Colonial Virginia* (New York: Norton, 1975).

Philip D. Morgan, *Slave Counterpoint: Black Culture in the Eighteenth-Century Chesapeake and Low Country* (Chapel Hill: University of North Carolina Press, 1998).

Thomas Morris, *Southern Slavery and the Law, 1619–1860* (Chapel Hill: University of North Carolina Press, 1996).

Peter J. Parish, *Slavery: History and Historians* (New York: Harpers, 1989).

Orlando Patterson, *Slavery and Social Death: A Comparative Study* (Cambridge, Mass.: Harvard University Press, 1982).

Willie Lee Rose, ed., *A Documentary History of Slavery in North America* (New York: Oxford University Press, 1976).

Philip J. Schwarz, *Twice Condemned: Slaves and the Criminal Laws of Virginia, 1705–1865* (Baton Rouge: Louisiana State University Press, 1988).

Frank Tannenbaum, *Slave & Citizen: The Negro in the Americas* (New York: Vintage, 1946).

Donald R. Wright, *African Americans in the Colonial Era: From African Origins through the American Revolution* (Arlington Heights, Ill.: Harlan Davidson, 1990).

ENGLISH COLONIES

FREE SOCIETY

Did proslavery theorists in the United States offer a cogent critique of free society?

Viewpoint: Yes. By the late antebellum period Southern thinkers believed that free society in the North was an experiment that had failed; they concluded that some form of bound labor would have to be reimposed to maintain social and economic order.

Viewpoint: No. Proslavery theorists offered no convincing argument because they relied on racism to justify slavery in the American South.

The proslavery ideology was not a simple expression of Southern guilt or paranoia; neither was it a psychological mechanism adapted to justify the oppression of blacks or a political weapon of short-lived usefulness during the sectional conflict. Rather than dismissing the Southern defense of slavery as a moral and intellectual failing or as a political expedient, historians have recently come to see it as the key to understanding a wider pattern of beliefs and values in the antebellum South, the basis of a coherent Southern world-view. "Slavery," writes the historian Drew Gilpin Faust, "became a vehicle for the discussion of fundamental social issues—the meaning of natural law, the conflicting desires for freedom and order, the relationship between tradition and progress, the respective roles of liberty and equality, dependence and autonomy." In 1856 George Frederick Holmes, among the leading advocates of slavery, anticipated Faust's interpretation, declaring: "The question of slavery is implicated with all the great problems of the current age."

Although Southern thinkers acknowledged early on that slavery was a political, though not a moral, evil, by the 1820s they increasingly emphasized the benefits of a social order based on slavery. The defense of slavery that developed after 1820 was thus not the product of Southern guilt. It evolved, instead, into a cogent ideology that systematically challenged the efficacy, supremacy, and morality of what Southerners referred to as the "free-labor system." By the 1830s Southerners were less troubled about whether slavery was right than about precisely why it was right and how they could best demonstrate its rectitude, benevolence, and justice. Despite the "speculative doubts by which the slaveowners were troubled," Holmes argued, "the general sentiment among them . . . had always tenaciously maintained the sanctity and inviolability of slavery, but they have not arrived at a clear comprehension of the reasons by which slavery is justified and proved to be right and expedient, without the aid of the . . . treatises which the controversy still raging has called forth."

During the 1840s and 1850s secular thinkers such as Virginia lawyer and journalist George Fitzhugh and theologians such as South Carolina Presbyterian clergyman James Henley Thornwell agreed that slavery alone provided the basis for a Christian social order in the modern world. Yet, proslavery theorists such as Fitzhugh and Thornwell were no mere reactionaries celebrating feudalism, serfdom, and the Middle Ages. Rather, they and their compatriots strove to fashion an alternate vision of social, political, and moral order to counter what in their minds constituted the immoral and unchristian dominance of free labor and free markets. Fed, clothed, housed, and protected, the slaves, Southerners believed, were better off than Northern factory workers, whose employers had no interest in their health, welfare, happiness, or survival. Free in name only, Southerners observed, Northern workers were often at liberty to starve. The humanitarian arrangements of slavery, Southerners proclaimed, contrasted favorably with the avaricious materialism of the Northern "free" society. The Yankees cared only about money and profits, while Southerners had accepted the daunting responsibility for the human beings whom God had entrusted to their care.

How persuasive such arguments were, even in the years before the Civil War (1861–1865), remains questionable. Southerners seem to have sensed that they engaged principally in conversation with each other. "We think hardly to be expected," admitted Holmes in 1843, "that anything which can be said at this late date will at all diminish the wrongheaded fanaticism and perverse intolerance of the Northern abolitionists," who were "past the cure of argument." Holmes could not have known that it would be neither in pamphlets, essays, and books nor in debating societies and parlors that the enemies of slavery would demonstrate the worthlessness of proslavery thought and the superiority of free society.

Viewpoint:
Yes. By the late antebellum period Southern thinkers believed that free society in the North was an experiment that had failed; they concluded that some form of bound labor would have to be reimposed to maintain social and economic order.

Slavery provided the basis of status, wealth, and power in the antebellum South. The slaveholding class dominated blacks and also exercised power over non-slaveholding whites, as, in *The Impending Crisis of the South: How to Meet It* (1857), Hinton Rowan Helper recognized and lamented. A minority of the white population, slaveholders commanded such esteem and wielded such authority that they, and not yeomen, formulated the Southern worldview and shaped the Southern way of life. Planters set the tone of Southern politics, society, culture, thought, and religion. The traditional Southern emphasis on family, community, honor, elegance, leisure, learning, and faith was the pride and province of this class of aristocratic slave owners. Slavery unified Southern civilization, created a social ideal that the non-slaveholding yeoman farmers aspired to emulate, and consolidated the economic and political power of the gentry. Moreover, the generation of Southern thinkers who came of age between 1815 and 1850 recognized the plight of the modern world arising directly from the system of free labor and the character of free society and posited slavery as an alternative.

Antebellum Southern thinkers denounced free society for promoting a brutal, immoral, irresponsible wage slavery in which the masters of capital impoverished and exploited their workers without assuming personal responsibility for their welfare. Along with German political and economic theorists Karl Marx and Friedrich Engels, proslavery theorists regarded capitalism as the most revolutionary and destructive force in modern history—the force primarily responsible for the dissolution of traditional social relations. In *The Communist Manifesto* (1848), Marx and Engels had written:

> Our epoch, the epoch of the bourgeoisie, possesses . . . this distinctive feature: it has simplified the class antagonisms. . . . The bourgeoisie, wherever it has got the upper hand, has put an end to all feudal, patriarchal, idyllic relations. It has pitilessly torn asunder the motley feudal ties that bound man to his "natural superiors," and has left remaining no other nexus between man and man than naked self-interest, than callous "cash payment." It has drowned the most heavenly ecstasies of religious fervor, of chivalrous enthusiasm, of philistine sentimentalism, in the icy water of egotistical calculation. It has resolved personal worth into exchange value. . . . In one word, for exploitation, veiled by religious and political illusions, it has substituted naked, shameless, direct, and brutal exploitation.

At this point, of course, the similarity ended. Marx and Engels praised capitalism precisely for its destructive work; Southerners condemned it.

Although they shared the widespread confidence that material progress was inevitable, Southern thinkers during the first half of the nineteenth century acknowledged that progress had always and everywhere depended on the servile labor of the masses. This arrangement could mean, and often had meant, untold misery for hundreds of thousands. Believing that human suffering calculated the costs of material progress, Southerners defended slavery as the surest bulwark against what they regarded as a destructive, immoral, and unchristian social and economic system and its cruel and reckless labor market. They agreed with European socialists that the capitalist world of the nineteenth century was on the threshold of a protracted crisis from which it would not recover.

FREE SOCIETY

**Antebellum proslavery
cartoon
comparing the
English working class
and American slaves**

*(Granger Collection,
New York City)*

Slavery alone thus seemed to ensure progress without the attendant social dislocation, political upheaval, and moral confusion. For those who took seriously the biblical injunction to be their brothers' keepers, slavery was the best, if not the only, means of preserving a Christian social order in the modern world.

Certainly, slavery was flawed, as were all earthly institutions requiring men to cope as best they could with the wages of sin. The relative merits of various systems of society and government, their comparative success in dealing with the evil inherent in human nature, rec-

ommended or condemned them. Chancellor William Harper of South Carolina wrote in *Memoir on Slavery, Read Before the Society for the Advancement of Learning, of South Carolina, at its Annual Meeting at Columbia* (1838) that "the condition of our whole existence is but to struggle with evils—to compare them—to choose between them and so far as we can, to mitigate them. To say that there is evil in any institution, is only to say that it is human." Yet, for Harper, slavery was far from a "peculiar institution." It existed, he pointed out, "over far the greater portion of the inhabited earth," and "within a very few centuries, it may be said to have existed over the whole earth—at least in all those portions of it which had made advances toward civilization. We may safely conclude then, that it is deeply founded in the nature of man and the exigencies of human society." Human beings were always and everywhere born to subjugation, Harper contended, and slavery alone provided the social, political, and institutional structures in which morally frail human beings could live together in peace, each free to serve God according to their abilities and their station.

Among the Christian duties of masters was the responsible management of property, which Southerners deemed part of man's social nature. Yet, Southerners expressly denied the bourgeois concept of property that gave owners an absolute right to do with it as they pleased. Secular and religious law required that the masters of slaves protect, nurture, and govern all their household dependents, including their human chattel. Perhaps it had always been necessary that one class of men labor for the benefit of another, as proslavery theorists reasoned. A genuinely Christian slavery, however, organized and institutionalized inequality and exploitation to correspond to the ethical canons of the Bible, and thus alone made possible material progress without the terrible economic, social, political, and moral disturbances that plagued the North and Europe.

Yet, for growing numbers of Southern thinkers, slavery had no future in the Western world. The laws of political economy indicated that sooner or later the costs of maintaining free labor would fall below those of maintaining slave labor. When free labor became less expensive, it would inspire a retreat from slavery, which would become a casualty of the economic progress it had helped to generate.

Political economists and historians, such as George Tucker and Thomas Roderick Dew, were far from sanguine about the consequences of emancipation, not only for the slaveholders and the former slaves but for free workers as well. With the abolition of slavery, brought on by the decreasing cost of free labor, the standard of living for workers and their families would decline to mere subsistence, and in times of extreme economic hardship would fall below that level. Tucker, Dew, and a host of other proslavery economic and social theorists predicted that the end of slavery would condemn the great mass of humanity to live amid unremitting squalor, to face pitiless exploitation, and to endure the constant presence of death. "Surely no one," historian Paul K. Conkin has observed, "ever offered a gloomier reason for eventual emancipation."

Mindful of their Christian offices, Southerners recoiled in horror at the prospect of this human waste and wreckage. No people who tolerated such afflictions could justly think themselves civilized. The savage abuse that the laboring classes were certain to endure also invited political disaster. Workers in the United States and from around the world would not forever submit to these wretched conditions. They would destroy themselves in a furious class struggle, but perhaps not before exacting terrible vengeance on their oppressors.

Southern thinkers took the measure of the French Revolution (1789–1799) and the more dangerous radicalism that it presaged on both sides of the Atlantic Ocean and anticipated insurrection, anarchy, and the consequent imposition of tyranny to restore social and political order. Commenting on unrest among wage workers in the United States, James Hervey Smith of Beaufort, South Carolina, reflected that "we have already seen some symptoms of this evil . . . while wages are twice or three times as high as in Great-Britain, and provisions more abundant; what will be the condition of our manufacturers when these circumstances shall vary—when the population in our manufacturing towns shall become dense and poor . . . ?"

The history of revolution also conditioned Dew's vision of the future. The *Jacquerie* in France (1358) and the Peasants' Revolt in England (1381) both brought short-term advantages for the participants, until the ruling classes overwhelmed them and did their worst to the survivors. "Power can never be dislodged from the hands of the intelligent, the wealthy, and the courageous, by any plans that can be formed by the poor, the ignorant, and the habitually subservient," Dew wrote; "history scarce furnishes an example." The implications of the French Revolution were more serious and its significance more complex and profound.

Although he deplored the Reign of Terror (1793–1794), Dew hailed the French Revolution as among the "grandest epochs in the history of man." The ancien régime had been socially, politically, and economically oppressive, and Dew interpreted the Revolution in its initial stages as an uprising of respectable but subjugated property owners against a dominant ruling elite of clerics, aristocrats, and kings that had outlived its usefulness. Members of the rebellious bourgeoisie had wealth but, as Dew noted, lacked the social prestige and political influence concomitant with their economic status. Many sought to remove the impediments that limited their advancement, for no doubt, Dew inferred, they resented a social system that valued birth more than merit. "It became necessary," Dew wrote, "either to roll back the tide

FREE SOCIETY

of civilization or else fit the government, by timely changes, to the constant revolutions which were taking place in the several organizations. France . . . was no longer fitted for the institutions of feudalism, and change or revolution became absolutely necessary."

The French Revolution had departed from its original aims of liberating property and respecting talent during the several *journees* when Parisian mobs redirected its course. Enthralled with the possibility of remaking society, the sans-culottes (meaning "without breeches"; the radical republicans) forced events to move in a more radical direction than the propertied revolutionaries of the bourgeoisie had wanted to take them. The demands of the lower classes for economic security, social equality, and political democracy first turned violent and then barbarous. A similar expansion of equality and democracy in the United States provoked Dew to sobering and melancholy reflections. Whatever blessings might accompany the rise of equality and the spread of democracy, their growth afforded demagogues an unmistakable opportunity to pander to the lower classes and, in effect, to engage in a democratic politics of envy and resentment. In an essay published in the *Southern Literary Messenger* in 1836, Dew considered that

> the tumults and riots at the elections in our great cities—the lawless mobs of the north which have already set the civil authority at defiance, and have pulled down and destroyed the property of the citizen—all are but the premonitory symptoms of the approaching calamity—they are but the rumbling sound which preceded the mighty shock of the terrible earthquake. If these things happen now, what may we expect hereafter?

Circumstances had muted this tension somewhat, for in Jacksonian America upward social mobility was still a viable prospect. American workers entertained reasonable expectations of entering the ranks of the propertied classes, if not for themselves then at least for their children. By the 1830s, however, Dew had begun to fear that such opportunities would not last forever. Territorial expansion would reach its limit, population density would increase, and Dew's question, "what may we expect hereafter?", would reassert itself. Dew thought he glimpsed the future:

> The time must come . . . when millions shall be crowded into our manufactories and commercial cities—then will come the great and fearful pressure upon the engine—then will the line of demarkation stand most palpably drawn between the rich and the poor, the capitalist and the laborer—then will thousands, yea, millions arise, whose hard lot it may be to labor from morn till eve through a long life, without the cheering hope of passing from

that toilsome condition in which the first years of their manhood found them, or even of accumulating in advance that small fund which may release the old and infirm from labor and toil, and mitigate the sorrow of declining years.

Dew had no illusions about the reaction of these workers to their fate. They would arise and demand protection and succor from the propertied classes and the state. In his magnum opus, *A Digest of the Laws, Customs, Manners, and Institutions of the Ancient and Modern Nations,* published posthumously in 1853, seven years after Dew's untimely death, he concluded:

> When the day shall come that this class shall form the numerical majority, as it did in France, then will the high pressure come on our institutions; and the reign of terror in France has presented, I fear, too faithful a picture of what a government *may be,* that shall fall *exclusively* into such hands.

Fortunately no social system, Dew wrote, was "better calculated to ward off [these] evils" than that of the South. Slavery alone ensured steadfast resistance to such "dangerous vices."

Nevertheless, like Tucker, Dew contemplated the end of slavery when economic conditions no longer favored its existence. His supposition that slavery would decline and eventually vanish anticipated a catastrophe not only for the United States but also for Western civilization—a catastrophe that other Southern thinkers thought they saw on the horizon by the time of Dew's death. For Dew the unattractive contours of this disaster had already assumed identifiable shape in the 1830s. He did not envision a socialist future resting upon the dictatorship of the proletariat. More plausibly, he thought the ruling class, or perhaps certain debauched and unscrupulous elements within it, would impose a vulgar and remorseless tyranny to shield private property and to arrest the descent into anarchy that the intensifying class struggle had unleashed. Frightened property owners would have no choice but to submit.

Could a people who believed themselves devoutly Christian accept the masses sinking to a despair so deep and unremitting that it robbed them of their chance to attain salvation? Conversely, could any Christian people worthy of the name acquiesce in the revolutionary violence that those hopeless souls were sure to perpetuate? To ask these questions was to answer them, and, by the 1850s, Southern thinkers did not hesitate. Free society was finished; everywhere some form of personal servitude would have to be reinstituted to save the laboring classes and to avert the destruction of class warfare.

—MARK G. MALVASI,
RANDOLPH-MACON COLLEGE

FREE SOCIETY

**Viewpoint:
No. Proslavery theorists offered no convincing argument because they relied on racism to justify slavery in the American South.**

Recently, historians have become intrigued by the proslavery arguments that antebellum Southern intellectuals offered. Until the late 1960s many scholars viewed the arguments as aberrations. Southerners, so the arguments go, had alienated themselves from national and human progress by holding onto slavery as the Western world was abolishing it. In rejecting this Whiggish view of history, modern historians have explained the proslavery arguments in a variety of ways: as attempts to unify Southern society, as part of the broader transatlantic conservative movement, as a way of developing an exclusively Southern social vision, or as a devastating critique of free society. There were many proslavery arguments circulating in the Old South. In general, the various proslavery arguments did not offer compelling critiques of free society because of a reliance on racism to defend both slavery and the use of legal and social coercion to organize and discipline labor.

Proslavery theorists presented slavery as necessary for the advance of civilization and moral progress, two goals advanced by proponents of free labor as well. Virginia jurist and novelist Nathaniel Beverley Tucker in 1844 argued that the master-slave relation involved whites and blacks in a "state of steadily progressive advancement in the comforts of civilization, and in the moral and intellectual improvement that civilization imparts." Chancellor William Harper of South Carolina, echoing Virginian Thomas Roderick Dew, president of the College of William and Mary, believed not only that "the institution of Slavery is a principal cause of civilization" but also that it was the "sole cause" of civilization. Harper thought that because sinful man avoided the labor necessary to improve human life and build civilization, the "coercion of Slavery alone" was "adequate to form man to habits of labour." All societies, he added, built their prosperity on slavery. Virginia lawyer and journalist George Fitzhugh agreed. He maintained that slavery had caused the South to flourish "like the bay tree, while Europe," after abolishing slavery, "starves." For proslavery theorists, a slave society had done what free societies could not—achieved a stable, prosperous, and moral social order.

The proslavery theorists ultimately relied on racism to justify the South's "progressive" form of slavery. In his famous defense of slavery, Dew asserted that the black slave "is not only *economi-*

cally but *morally* unfit for freedom." South Carolina novelist and social thinker William Gilmore Simms believed that blacks were an "inferior race," a view that Harper echoed when he called blacks "an inferior variety of the human race." Harper and other proslavery thinkers argued that free society, which was based on the notion of equality, had simply missed or ignored the fact of inherent inferiority in the human race. He portrayed blacks as dull children whose initial savagery, derived from their African homeland, had been tamed by the benign influence of Southern slavery. Harper insisted that "nothing but the coercion of slavery" could overcome blacks' "propensity to indolence." Proslavery theorists discounted the prospect of equality because they observed that nature had not endowed all with equal talents. They did not seek a meritocracy to determine the social order according to talent, but settled for subordination on the basis of race. Regardless of their individual merits, these theorists contended, blacks as a people were best suited for slavery. Simms argued that the black African race was "destined . . . to final obliteration, unless rescued from incapacity and sloth by the coercive vigor of some conquering race, which shall compel him to the work of self-development." Slavery had helped an inferior race progress in morals, whereas free society, by insisting upon equality, had overseen and encouraged the corruption of public morality. Harper exclaimed, "Tell me of an evil or abuse; of an instance of cruelty, oppression, licentiousness, crime or suffering, and I will point out, and often in five fold degree, an equivalent evil or abuse in countries where Slavery does not exist!" The insistence on the racial inferiority of blacks and the progressive moral effect of slavery led Tucker to maintain that slavery was necessary for freedom. Whites could use coercion of inferior peoples to protect freedom, or, as Tucker put it to his friend Simms in 1851: "If we will not *have* slaves, we must *be* slaves." "Inferior" blacks got protection and security from their condition while whites received liberty.

Proslavery theorists argued that a free society based its liberty on a ruthless competition for money that exploited workers rather than on a familial view that protected inferior laborers and shielded them from the uncertainty and brutality of the market. Fitzhugh posited that free societies required "selfishness, rivalry, and competition" for success. This system placed the weak at a disadvantage. In a slave society, "which is a series of subordinations" and "is consistent with christian morality," the strong could perform their duties toward the weak without feeling threatened. The order that prevailed was familial, and "the golden rule," not competition, guided conduct. Harper contended that slavery provided lifelong security, that is, care from birth to

FREE SOCIETY

THE SOUTH'S EFFECTIVE WEAPON

The following editorial appeared in an Alabama newspaper at the beginning of the Civil War (1861–1865):

The total white population of the eleven States now comprising the confederacy is 6,000,000, and therefore to fill up the ranks of the proposed army (600,000) about ten percent of the entire white population will be required. In any other country but our own such a draft could not be met, but the Southern States can furnish that number of men, and still not leave the material interests of the country in a suffering condition. Those who are incapacitated for bearing arms can oversee the plantation, and the Negroes can go on undisturbed in their usual labors. In the North, the case is different; the men who joined the army of subjugation are the laborers, the producers and the factory operatives. Nearly every man from that section, especially those from the rural districts, leaves some branch of industry to suffer during his absence. The institution of slavery in the South alone enables her to place in the field a force much larger in proportion to her white population [than] in the North. The institution is a tower of strength to the South, particularly at the present crisis, and our enemies will be likely to find that the "moral cancer" about which their orators are so fond of prating, is really one of the most effective weapons employed against the union by the South.

Source: Montgomery Advertiser, 6 November 1861.

---

death—something that was denied to wage laborers who worked only as long as they brought profits to their employers. He even argued that the sale of slaves was better than the firing of a wage laborer because the slave's "means of subsistence are secure" with his new owner, while the worker was left to starve. Proslavery theorists did not consider that employers in a free society might believe that they had a moral duty toward their employees, much like the slave owner felt toward his slaves. Instead, in proslavery tracts capitalists appeared only as greedy exploiters.

Proslavery ideologues did not merely critique free society but rejected it. Harper wrote: "The love of liberty is a noble passion—to have the free, uncontrolled disposition of ourselves, our words and actions. But alas! it is one in which we know that a large portion of the human race can never be gratified." Again, theories of racial inferiority supported the rejection of freedom, for Harper believed that blacks, not whites, lacked the capacity for freedom. Proslavery

theorists further agreed that free society was a myth. In free societies, capital "enslaved" free laborers. Fitzhugh noted that those in "free society" were "actively engaged in the slave-trade under more odious and cruel forms than were ever known before." Jeffersonian theorist John Taylor of Caroline remarked in 1805 that the "paper system" (the capitalist economy based on paper money and credit) of "indirect slavery extorts from the laboring people of England far greater profit than direct slavery has ever produced in Virginia." Free society was simply another form of slavery. With the exception of Fitzhugh's work, Southern proslavery arguments boiled down to a rejection of individual freedom—as well as political, social, and economic freedom—on racial grounds. Proslavery writers wanted freedom and prosperity for whites but subordination and paternalistic protection for blacks. They accepted the fruits of a free society but wanted slavery to limit the risks of the free choices of individuals.

The attempts to condemn free society could take absurd routes, such as the one explored by Harper regarding sexual immorality. In rejecting the characterization of Southern society as "one wide stew for the indulgence of unbridled lust," Harper acknowledged that sex between white men and black female slaves occurred, but insisted that such sexual dalliances were a part of all human societies. Slavery, however, mitigated the harsh consequences of such behavior in the South. Harper compared the unwed mother in Northern and European cities to the unwed slave mother. He found that an unwed mother in a free society "is an outcast" and is driven to prostitution. In the South, however, the black slave knows that her master will care for her child, regardless of its parentage. Thus, the female slave was at least materially better off than the poor, abandoned, unwed mother in a free society. Furthermore, Harper believed that the wide availability of slave women, and the fact that their offspring would be cared for, discouraged prostitution in the South and made illicit sexual intercourse as benign as possible. The sexual indiscretions of young white males with "enslaved females is less depraving in its effects, than when it is carried on with females of their own caste." Because the white youth saw the slave as an inferior, the "intercourse is generally casual." The white youth "is less liable to those extraordinary fascinations, with which worthless women sometimes entangle their victims, to the utter destruction of all principle, worth, and vigor of character." Such arguments reveal the base nature of slavery, the open exploitation of women under slavery, the reliance of the proslavery theorists on racism, and their failure to criticize free society convincingly.

FREE SOCIETY

Proslavery ideologues recognized the instability in free societies caused by the fluctuation of capital, but their proposed solution was a coercive society that would allow whites to profit from the labor of an "inferior" race. The proslavery argument pushed aside the Jeffersonian libertarian ideal in the name of social order. It did not ably critique free society but sought to appropriate the goods of free society to some and deny them to others based on race. For the most part, proslavery theorists did not argue their points using scientific data about free society in the North but instead based their arguments on their perceptions of the North as a corrupt, greedy society. Northern society, however, produced reformers who attempted to alleviate the sufferings of workers and the poor while preserving freedom. The proslavery argument, based on myth and misinformation, could not supplant the strengths of a free society.

–ADAM L. TATE,
STILLMAN COLLEGE

References

George D. Armstrong, *The Christian Doctrine of Slavery* (New York: Scribner, 1857).

Mark Blaug, *Economic Theory in Retrospect*, fifth edition (Cambridge & New York: Cambridge University Press, 1997).

Paul K. Conkin, *Prophets of Prosperity: America's First Political Economists* (Bloomington: Indiana University Press, 1980).

Thomas Roderick Dew, "Abolition of Negro Slavery," in *The Ideology of Slavery: Proslavery Thought in the Antebellum South, 1830–1860*, edited by Drew Gilpin Faust (Baton Rouge: Louisiana State University Press, 1981), pp. 21–77.

Dew, *A Digest of the Laws, Customs, Manners, and Institutions of the Ancient and Modern Nations* (New York: Appleton, 1853).

Clement Eaton, *The Mind of the Old South* (Baton Rouge: Louisiana State University Press, 1964).

E. N. Elliott, ed., *Cotton is King and Pro-Slavery Arguments* (Augusta, Ga.: Pritchard, Abbott & Loomis, 1860).

Faust, "The Proslavery Argument in History," in *Southern Stories: Slaveholders in Peace and War* (Columbia: University of Missouri Press, 1992), pp. 72–87.

George Fitzhugh, "Southern Thought," in *The Ideology of Slavery: Proslavery Thought in the Antebellum South, 1830–1860*, edited by

Faust (Baton Rouge: Louisiana State University Press, 1981), pp. 272–299.

George M. Fredrickson, *The Black Image in the White Mind: The Debate on Afro-American Character and Destiny, 1817–1914* (New York: Harper & Row, 1971).

Eugene D. Genovese, *The Political Economy of Slavery: Studies in the Economy & Society of the Slave South* (New York: Pantheon, 1965).

Genovese, *The Slaveholders' Dilemma: Freedom and Progress in Southern Conservative Thought, 1820–1860* (Columbia: University of South Carolina Press, 1992).

Genovese, *The World the Slaveholders Made: Two Essays in Interpretation* (New York: Pantheon, 1969).

Genovese and Elizabeth Fox-Genovese, "Slavery, Economic Development, and the Law: The Dilemma of the Southern Political Economists, 1800–1860," *Washington & Lee Law Review*, 41 (Winter 1984): 1–29.

William Harper, *Memoir on Slavery, Read Before the Society for the Advancement of Learning, of South Carolina, at its Annual Meeting at Columbia* (Charleston: Burges, 1838).

Hinton Rowan Helper, *The Impending Crisis of the South: How to Meet It* (New York: Burdick, 1857).

James C. Hite and Ellen J. Hall, "The Reactionary Evolution of Economic Thought in Antebellum Virginia," *Virginia Magazine of History and Biography*, 80 (1972): 476–488.

William Sumner Jenkins, *Pro-Slavery Thought in the Old South* (Chapel Hill: University of North Carolina Press, 1935).

Allen Kaufman, *Capitalism, Slavery, and Republican Values: American Political Economists, 1819–1848* (Austin: University of Texas Press, 1982).

Thomas Robert Malthus, *An Essay on the Principle of Population* (London: Johnson, 1798).

Stephen Scott Mansfield, "Thomas Roderick Dew: Defender of the Southern Faith," dissertation, University of Virginia, 1968.

James Oakes, *Slavery and Freedom: An Interpretation of the Old South* (New York: Knopf, 1990).

D. P. O'Brien, *The Classical Economists* (Oxford: Clarendon Press, 1975).

Michael O'Brien, ed., *All Clever Men, Who Make Their Way: Critical Discourse in the Old South* (Fayetteville: University of Arkansas Press, 1982).

The Pro-Slavery Argument, as Maintained by the Most Distinguished Writers of the Southern States: Containing Several Essays, on the Subject, of Chancellor Harper, Governor Hammond, Dr. Simms, and Professor Dew (Charleston: Walker, Richards, 1852).

David Ricardo, *On the Principles of Political Economy, and Taxation* (London: Murray, 1817).

William Gilmore Simms, "Miss Martineau on Slavery," *Southern Literary Messenger,* 3 (November 1837): 641–657.

Tipton R. Snavely, *George Tucker as Political Economist* (Charlottesville: University Press of Virginia, 1964).

John Taylor to Timothy Dwight, September 1805, reprinted in "A Sheaf of Old Letters," edited by David R. Barbee, *Tyler's Quarterly Historical and Genealogical Magazine,* 32 (October 1950): 84–86.

Larry E. Tise, *Proslavery: A History of the Defense of Slavery in America, 1701–1840* (Athens: University of Georgia Press, 1987).

William P. Trent, *William Gilmore Simms* (Boston & New York: Houghton, Mifflin, 1892).

Nathaniel Beverley Tucker, "An Essay on the Moral and Political Effect of the Relation between the Caucasian Master and the African Slave," *Southern Literary Messenger,* 10 (June & August 1844): 329–339, 470–480.

Robert C. Tucker, ed., *The Marx-Engels Reader,* second edition (New York: Norton, 1978).

HEALTH

Were the slaves in the United States in good health?

Viewpoint: Yes. The United States had the only slave population in the Western Hemisphere to increase by reproduction. That ability suggests the slaves were generally in good health and that the masters provided at least the essentials in diet, housing, clothing, and medical care.

Viewpoint: No. Despite their ability to reproduce, the slaves were generally in poor health and received inconsistent medical care. Slaves suffered from chronic ailments; harsh labor conditions, poor sanitation, and nutritional deficiencies combined to produce high mortality rates.

Eager to demonstrate the benevolence of their regime, slaveholding planters of the South took a personal interest in the lives of their slaves. Although slavery was far from humane, many, though by no means all, slave owners accepted the biblical injunction to be their brothers' keepers. As a consequence, during the fifty years before 1861 the material condition and the health of slaves in the United States substantially improved. If slaves did not consume a nutritionally balanced diet, they at least enjoyed one adequate to their needs. American slaves, after all, did not endure the famines that, as late as the mid nineteenth century, periodically haunted the poor in Europe and around the world. The weekly ration of a peck (eight quarts) of cornmeal and between two and four pounds of pork became standard fare for adult field hands. The slaves, of course, supplemented this diet with opossum, squirrel, rabbit, chicken, fish, and shellfish as well as fruits and vegetables.

Plentiful food helped to sustain the slaves' reasonably good health. Yet, slaves also suffered from deficiencies in important vitamins that, especially in infants and children, caused the spread of illness and elevated mortality rates. Debilitating as they could be, the inadequacies of the slaves' diet had more to do with the limited knowledge of nutrition in the nineteenth century than with the exploitive character of slavery. From a nutritional standpoint, whites also had bad diets. A mortality rate among the slaves of thirty per one thousand was higher than that of Southern whites but lower than that for most Caribbean slaves and on a par with that of many western Europeans. Endowed with the sickle-cell trait, blacks largely escaped malaria but died with greater frequency from cholera, tetanus, and various infant and childhood maladies.

The medical care that slaves received was not substantially worse than that of Southern whites, and in some instances may even have been marginally better. Masters generally took every precaution, made every effort, and spared no expense to protect the health of their valuable investments. Doctors regularly visited some plantations but came to others only in the event of serious illness. Larger estates might have had a hospital on the premises where slaves went for treatment and recuperation. Remedies that doctors administered to the slaves, which included bleeding and emetics, did not differ appreciably from the care that whites received. Given the rigors that such correctives entailed, however, it is not surprising that blacks resisted or avoided them and preferred instead to rely on their own brand of traditional folk medicine. Nineteenth-century medical practice may have killed as many as it cured, and it certainly did not improve the health and longevity of the slaves.

**Viewpoint:
Yes. The United States had the only slave population in the Western Hemisphere to increase by reproduction. That ability suggests the slaves were generally in good health and that the masters provided at least the essentials in diet, housing, clothing, and medical care.**

The health of slaves has not received from historians the attention it is due. This relative neglect is partly the result of a lack of quantitative data. Further complicating efforts to produce an accurate picture of slaves' health is the great variety of diet and medical care provided to slaves by their owners. As historian Eugene D. Genovese has noted, "the wide range in practice among slaveholders meant that even if most slaves received good care, a large number of others did not. And the poor quality of the medical profession may well have resulted in worse conditions for slaves with concerned masters who provided physicians than for those who had to rely on folk medicine and trust to nature." With so much uncertainty, it should come as no surprise that historians have vigorously debated the health of slaves. Yet, the available evidence suggests that slaves in the United States were not significantly less healthy than white Americans and that they were considerably healthier than slaves in the Caribbean. An examination of the evidence also clearly shows that whatever differences existed between the health of white and black Americans likely were not the result of slavery.

Robert W. Fogel and Stanley L. Engerman have observed that "while the quality of slave medical care was poor by modern standards, there is no evidence of exploitation in the medical care typically provided for plantation slaves. The inadequacy of medical care arose not from intent or lack of effort on the part of masters, but from the primitive nature of medical knowledge and practices in the antebellum era." By modern standards the medical care received by white Southerners was also quite poor, but most slaveholders made an honest attempt to provide good medical services for their slaves. The reasons for slaveholders' concern were threefold: "slaves represented a financial investment which required protection; many masters felt a true humanitarian commitment toward their slaves; and whites realized that certain illnesses could easily spread to their own families if not properly treated and contained." Many slaveholders spent substantial sums to provide medical care for their sick or injured slaves, even in cases in which economics does not seem to have been a factor.

Most slaveholders were also conscientious about providing their slaves with a healthy diet. "The belief that the typical slave was poorly fed is without foundation in fact," write Fogel and Engerman. Though there were seasonal variations and some masters were more generous than others, the average slave consumed an ample amount of calories and most nutrients. According to an article by Kenneth F. Kiple, "There was neither hunger in the slave cabins nor outright starvation as slaves sometimes experienced in the West Indies." On average, slaves consumed far in excess of twentieth-century daily recommended levels of many important nutrients, including proteins, calcium, iron, thiamin, riboflavin, niacin, and vitamins A and C. Their intake of proteins exceeded the twentieth-century recommendation by 110 percent. Their intake of calcium was 20 percent greater; of riboflavin, 50 percent greater; of niacin, 70 percent greater; of iron, 230 percent greater; of vitamin C, 150 percent greater; and of thiamin, 375 percent greater than twentieth-century recommendations. American slaves also ate more meat than most Europeans or their counterparts in the Caribbean. In the nineteenth century, masters generally provided a daily ration of a half-pound of meat. English and French laborers seldom enjoyed meat more than once a week. In addition to their daily ration of meat, which was usually pork, slaves also received good rations of cornmeal, molasses, and seasonal fruits and vegetables. Many slaves supplemented this basic diet by hunting, fishing, or cultivating a small garden. Compared to the average diet of all Americans in 1879, slaves consumed at least 10 percent more calories. Because of their better diet, slaves in the United States attained greater physical stature than slaves elsewhere in the Western Hemisphere.

One means by which one can quantify the health of slaves is to compare their life expectancy and mortality rates to those of populations with which they were contemporary. As Philip D. Curtin has carefully documented, slaves in the United States were much healthier than their counterparts in the Caribbean. Slave deaths regularly outnumbered births on the unhealthy Caribbean plantations. In most regions of British North America, by contrast, slave births outpaced deaths by the early eighteenth century. "By the end of the eighteenth century," Curtin

COLD BACON AND CORN CAKE

In the following account, Solomon Northrup describes working and living conditions on a Louisiana plantation during the antebellum period:

The hands are required to be in the cotton field as soon as it is light in the morning, and, with the exception of ten or fifteen minutes, which is given them at noon to swallow their allowance of cold bacon, they are not permitted to be a moment idle until it is too dark to see, and when the moon is full, they often times labor till the middle of the night. They do not dare to stop even at dinner time, nor return to the quarters, however late it be, until the order to halt is given by the driver.

The day's work over in the field, the baskets are "toted," or in other words, carried to the gin-house, where the cotton is weighed. No matter how fatigued and weary he may be—no matter how much he longs for sleep and rest—a slave never approaches the gin-house with his basket of cotton but with fear. If it falls short in weight—if he has not performed the full task appointed him, he knows that he must suffer. And if he has exceeded it by ten or twenty pounds, in all probability his master will measure the next day's task accordingly. So, whether he has too little or too much, his approach to the gin-house is always with fear and trembling. Most frequently they have too little, and therefore it is they who are not anxious to leave the field. After weighing, follow the whippings; and then the baskets are carried to the cotton house, and their contents stored away like hay, all hands being sent in to tramp it down. If the cotton is not dry, instead of taking it to the gin-house at once, it is laid upon platforms, two feet high, and some three times as wide, covered with boards or planks, with narrow walks running between them.

This done, the labor of the day is not yet ended, by any means. Each one must then attend to his respective chores. One feeds the mules, another the swine—another cuts the wood, and so forth; besides, the packing is all done by candle light. Finally, at a late hour, they reach the quarters, sleepy and overcome with the long day's toil. Then a fire must be kindled in the cabin, the corn ground in the small hand-mill, and supper, and dinner for the next day in the field, prepared. All that is allowed them is corn and bacon, which is given out at the corncrib and smoke-house every Sunday morning. Each one receives, as his weekly allowance, three and a half pounds of bacon, and corn enough to make a peck of meal. That is all—no tea, coffee, sugar, and with the exception of a very scanty sprinkling now and then, no salt. . . .

An hour before daylight the horn is blown. Then the slaves arouse, prepare their breakfast, fill a gourd with water, in another deposit their dinner of cold bacon and corn cake, and hurry to the field again. It is an offense invariably followed by a flogging, to be found at the quarters after daybreak. Then the fears and labors of another day begin; and until its close there is no such thing as rest. . . .

Source: Solomon Northrup, Twelve Years a Slave: Narrative of Solomon Northup, a Citizen of New-York, Kidnapped in Washington City in 1841, and Rescued in 1853, from a Cotton Plantation near the Red River, in Louisiana *(Auburn, N.Y.: Derby & Miller / Buffalo, N.Y.: Derby, Orton & Mulligan, 1853).*

---

notes, "North American slave populations were growing at nearly the same rate as that of the settler populations from Europe." Partly as a result of its healthier plantation regime, the United States possessed about one-third of the total African American population in 1950, notwithstanding that fewer than 5 percent of the slaves imported to the New World came to North America. The Caribbean, by comparison, had only 20 percent of the African American population despite importing more than 40 percent of the slaves to the New World.

Slaves in the United States had an average life expectancy of 36 years in 1850. This figure is not significantly less than the average life expectancy of white Americans, which in 1850 was 40 years. The life expectancy of American slaves was the same as that of people living in Holland and France during the 1850s. More telling, American slaves could expect to live significantly longer than white urban populations. Free residents of Boston, New York, and Philadelphia in 1830 could expect to live only to the age of 24, as could residents of Manchester, England, in 1850.

HEALTH

Regardless of race, life in the agricultural South was healthier than in cities, though Southern blacks and whites both suffered a higher mortality rate than Northerners.

Furthermore, if masters were keeping their slaves in poor health, one would expect the racial disparity in life expectancy to diminish after emancipation, but this result was manifestly not the case. In fact, the gap between black and white life expectancy actually widened after blacks attained their freedom. Thirty-five years after the Civil War (1861–1865) the difference between black and white life expectancy had grown to more than 14 years. The mortality rate of Southern blacks rose after emancipation. White Americans born in 1900 could expect to live 47.6 years; blacks born in the same year could expect to live only 33 years. White Americans born in 1929 could expect to live 58.6 years; blacks born in that year had a life expectancy of only 46.7 years. Though this racial disparity has decreased as the American life expectancy has increased, white Americans still outlive blacks. In 1999 the average life expectancy for whites was 77.3 years, while for blacks it was only 71.4 years. The persistence in the difference between white and black life expectancy points to causes other than slavery for whites' greater longevity.

One sees this trend repeated when examining infant mortality rates. By modern standards a horrific percentage of antebellum children, white and black alike, died before their first birthday. Of every 1,000 children born to whites in 1850, 146 died within the first year. Black children born the same year died at a rate of 183 per 1,000. As with life expectancy rates, the racial disparity in the survival rate of children has also persisted long after the abolition of slavery. Indeed, the black infant mortality rate actually went from being 20 percent higher than that of whites in 1850 to 50 percent higher than white infant mortality during most of the twentieth century. Of white children born in 1960, an average of 22.9 of every 1,000 died within the first year. Yet, an average of 44.3 out of 1,000 black children born the same year did not live to their first birthday. In 1970 the infant mortality rate for whites was 17.8 deaths per 1,000 and 32.6 for blacks; in 1980 the infant mortality rate for whites was 11 deaths per 1000 and 21.4 for blacks. Again, the increased divergence between white and black infant mortality rates during the twentieth century points toward factors other than slavery as the cause of slave infants dying more often than white infants.

Because of local and seasonal variations and the fact that some masters treated their bondmen better than others, it is all too easy to find anecdotal evidence of slaves who were not healthy. Moreover, when viewed from a modern perspective neither whites nor blacks in the antebellum United States were very healthy. Yet, when one looks at the average slave's diet or mortality statistics for slaves in the United States, clearly slaves were nearly as healthy as white Americans and healthier than most other contemporary populations. As Kiple has observed, "the health of adult slaves in the antebellum Southern United States was almost as good (or bad) as that of their white masters." The majority of masters provided their slaves with a good diet and the best medical care available. Any inadequacy of care was far more likely to be the result of limited medical knowledge than maliciousness.

–SEAN R. BUSICK,
KENTUCKY WESLEYAN COLLEGE

Viewpoint:
No. Despite their ability to reproduce, the slaves were generally in poor health and received inconsistent medical care. Slaves suffered from chronic ailments; harsh labor conditions, poor sanitation, and nutritional deficiencies combined to produce high mortality rates.

The extent to which slaves in the South enjoyed good health was of considerable variation. Certainly most slaves in the British North American colonies, and later the United States, fared better than their counterparts in the West Indies. Yet, recent scholarship suggests that the high mortality rates traditionally attributed to the Caribbean have also been exaggerated. Slaves in all American societies, it seems, enjoyed a life expectancy well beyond the proverbial seven years assumed in most histories. As with other aspects of their lives, however, the slaves' health was precarious, for the need to extract as much labor from the slaves as possible while providing only minimal necessities proved debilitating.

Slaveholders, of course, animated by both interest and sentiment, congratulated themselves that they had done everything in their power, and more, to ensure the good health of their slaves. Most retained a physician to attend to the slaves at an average annual cost of $3 per slave. They sometimes spent hundreds of dollars to provide care for slaves who had fallen ill. These efforts notwithstanding, the general health of the slaves remains an issue of considerable disagreement. Practices diverged widely, and for every slave who received good, or at least adequate, medical attention, there was a slave who did not. Then, too, the dubious nature of the treatments prescribed and the uneven quality of physicians may have left those slaves who got medical care in a worse condition than those who indulged in folk remedies or who let nature take its course.

Dietary deficiencies frequently compounded the problem of slave health. The standard weekly ration for the slaves on James Henry Hammond's South Carolina plantation, Silver Bluff, was three pounds of meat (usually pork), a peck of cornmeal, and molasses. Although this diet provided the slaves with a sufficient caloric intake, it was deficient in protein, calcium, magnesium, iron, and other essential vitamins and minerals. The slaves, of course, did not subsist solely on the fare their master tendered but supplemented their diets in many ways. Hammond gave evidence of such ingenuity, lamenting that his slaves stole food from his larder, along with sheep and hogs, and took potatoes directly from the ground. Hammond, indeed, despaired of ever harvesting a potato crop.

Although some slaves probably did not get enough to eat, there is little evidence to suggest that slaves in the South were habitually underfed and malnourished. However, Richard Carruthers, a former slave from Texas, is quoted in Eugene D. Genovese's *Roll, Jordan, Roll: The World the Slaves Made* (1974) as saying:

> If they didn't provision you 'nough, you just had to slip round and get a chicken. That easy 'nough, but grabbin' a pig sure 'nough problem. . . . That ain't stealin', is it? You has to keep right on workin' in the field, if you ain't allowanced 'nough, and no nigger like to work with his belly groanin'.

Even some slaveholders admitted that slaves stole food because they were hungry. "The very best remedy for hog stealing," a Virginia planter wrote, "is to give the rougues [sic] a plenty of pork to eat."

The harsh conditions of slavery combined with nutritional deficiencies and questionable medical care to produce a higher level of mortality in blacks than whites during the nineteenth century. To be sure, Hammond, like other slaveholders, was deeply concerned about the health of his slaves, if only to protect his investment, and so kept himself informed about current medical theories and practices of the day. Even by the standards of the nineteenth century, the slaves on Hammond's plantation were extraordinarily unhealthy. According to Hammond's biographer, Drew Gilpin Faust, between 1831 and 1835 the slaves' annual mortality rate was 6.5 percent, more than twice the rate that historical demographers have calculated for the entire slave population in the United States in 1830. Faust calculates

that between 1831 and 1841, 72 percent of children born at Silver Bluff died before they reached the age of five. These mortality rates are not only incompatible with present expectations but also were exceptional in comparison to other North American slave communities.

Hammond was appalled at the mortality rate. The slaves' ill health affected his economic prospects, but of equal significance it posed a distressing challenge to his image of himself as an effective and benevolent master. "One would think," he recorded in his plantation diary, " . . . that I was a monster of humanity." Hammond tried everything to improve his slaves' health, drawing on all the current trends in medicine. He first relied on the so-called heroic practice, which required blistering ointments, purgatives to induce vomiting and diarrhea, the ingestion of calomel (a mercurial compound that is poisonous), and bleeding to rid his slaves of pathogens in the blood.

When these extreme methods failed, often killing more than they cured, Hammond abandoned them in favor of the supposedly less severe methods of "Botanic" or "Thomsonian" practice. Named for the health reformer Samuel Thomson, Thomsonian medicine used only herbal remedies and steadfastly rejected the application of such chemical compounds as calomel and such dangerous practices as bleeding. At the same time Thomsonianism recommended such treatments as steam baths that could be debilitating and enemas laced with cayenne pepper that, to say the least, could be painful. By the 1850s both heroic and botanic practices had fallen out of favor, and Hammond discontinued them and instead embraced homeopathy. Homeopathic practitioners theorized that if artificially induced weaker symptoms of a disease replaced the more virulent strains, then the body would respond by healing itself.

Whatever Hammond's current medical enthusiasm, his slaves continued to grow ill and die at an alarming rate. Faust has suggested that hereditary syphilis existed among certain slave families on Hammond's plantation and contributed to a high rate of miscarriage and infant mortality. The pattern of familial death seems to confirm her suspicions. Other of Hammond's slaves died from tuberculosis, infections that resulted from poor sanitary conditions, which Hammond worked hard to improve, and scrofula, a form of tuberculosis that affects the lymphatic glands in the neck. Still others died from a disease unknown to nineteenth-century medicine: sickle-cell anemia. In the malarial lowlands of South Carolina, where Hammond's plantation was located, the sickle-cell trait provided resistance to malaria.

Although the chronically poor health of some of Hammond's slaves is probably not rep-

Photograph of Renty, a
field hand from a South
Carolina plantation, 1850

*(Peabody Museum, Harvard
University, Cambridge,
Mass.)*

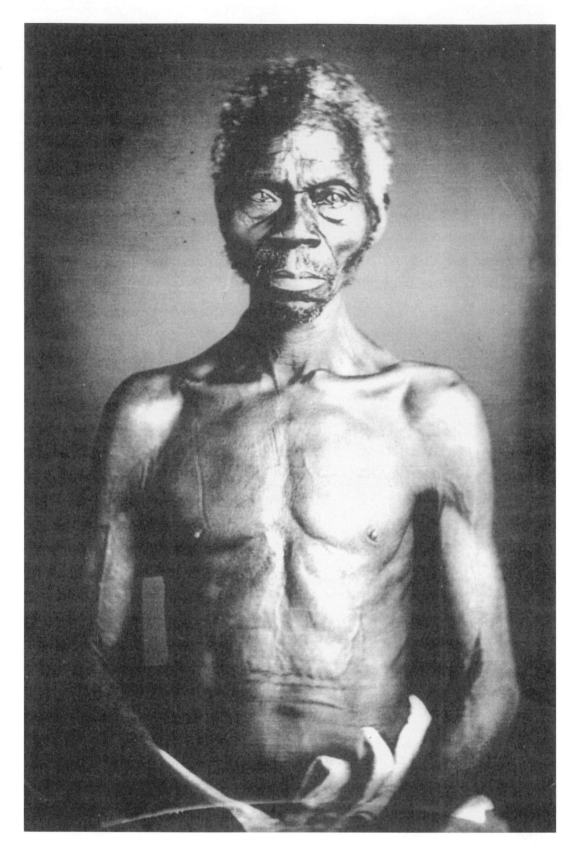

resentative of slave health in general, their condition does suggest that despite persistent efforts the physical welfare of the slaves was always fragile. Moreover, like slaves throughout the South, those on Hammond's plantation resisted his exertions in their behalf. They concealed their illnesses to avoid unpleasant and sometimes deadly treatments and continued to practice trusted African folk cures and remedies. When, in 1851, Hammond discovered that an alternate system of medicine thrived among his slaves, he subjected both the practitioners and their patients to severe punishment, but to no avail. A system of African folk medicine flourished on Hammond's plantation as it did on many others, for slaves were determined to control their own bodies and look after their own health.

Since the medical profession during the nineteenth century did not enjoy an impeccable reputation, many planters, unlike Hammond, accepted and even welcomed the presence of slave doctors. Several states and localities tried to prevent blacks from practicing medicine, but such attempts had little chance of success, especially in the quarters. The law could deny black doctors the right to treat white patients, a practice that had been quite common during the eighteenth century, but it could rarely keep black doctors from attending slaves, with or without permission from the master. In many instances the slaves' mistrust of white physicians evoked sympathy from their masters, who often found such doctors unreliable if not dangerous. "It is seldom that I call in a physician," wrote John Hamilton of Louisiana to his brother. "We Doctor upon the old woman slave and have first-rate luck." This skepticism on the part of masters and slaves alike was not surprising if the description that Fanny Kemble gave of the infirmary on her husband Pierce Butler's Georgia rice plantation indicates the general state of the medical treatment afforded the slaves and the general state of slave health:

How shall I describe to you the spectacle which was presented to me on entering . . . ? But half the casements, of which there were six, were glazed, and these were obscured with dirt, almost as much as the other windowless ones were darkened by the dingy shutters, which the shivering inmates had fastened to in order to protect themselves from the cold. In the enormous chimney glimmered the powerless embers of a few sticks of wood, round which, however, as many of the sick women as could approach were cowering, some on wooden settlers, most of them on the ground, excluding those who were too ill to rise; and these last poor wretched lay prostrate on the floor, without bed, mattress, or pillow, buried in tattered and filthy blankets, which, huddled round them as they lay strewed about, left hardly space to move upon the floor. And here, in their hour of sickness and suffering, lay those whose health and strength are spent in unrequited labor for us . . . , whose produce was to buy for us all the luxuries which health can revel in, all the comforts which can alleviate sickness.

Kemble found women unattended in the throes of childbirth and others who had recently miscarried or delivered stillborn infants. The slaves also suffered from rheumatism, fevers, influenza, and a variety of other ailments. "All were in the same deplorable condition," she complained, amid the "dirt, noise, and stench" they suffered "every aggravation of which sickness is capable. . . . In all, filth, disorder, and misery abounded. . . ." When Kemble voiced her outraged over the condition of the hospital and its patients to the overseer, he told her that "it was a matter of indifference to the owners," and so had remained in the same deplorable condition "for the last nineteen years and upward."

Much of the favor shown black doctors rested upon disdain for the ignorance and incompetence of their white counterparts, though Southern doctors continued to care for the slaves. Concerned about the health of their slaves, the masters nonetheless recognized the inadequacies of standard medical practice. The slaves themselves took an even more disparaging view. They may have appreciated the efforts of their masters and mistresses to attend to their welfare, but when illness struck they relied on African folk remedies to provide the cure. "Oh, de people never didn' put much faith to de doctors in dem days," recalled Josephine Bacchus, a former slave from South Carolina. "Mostly, dey would use de herbs in de fields for dey medicine." Frederick Douglass, by contrast, attributed the widespread popularity of slave medicine precisely to the failure of the slaveholders to dispense adequate care.

The methods that slave doctors employed sometimes worked and sometimes did not. They were, in any event, no worse than the theories of white doctors. Slaves ate green figs and salt to cure cholera, with predictable results. They ingested cat soup, boiled cockroaches, and several other antidotes that did not revolutionize medical science. When the slaves survived these correctives, just as they had the purging and the bleeding in which white physicians engaged, they were convinced that the doctor who had attended them was a genius and that his methods had effected their recovery. Thus, whatever motive prompted slaves to undertake the practice of medicine, and whatever the effectiveness of that practice, it represented an admirable effort on their part to care for themselves and each other.

—MARTINA NICHOLAS,
YOUNGSTOWN STATE UNIVERSITY

References

Philip D. Curtin, *The Atlantic Slave Trade: A Census* (Madison: University of Wisconsin Press, 1969).

Stanley L. Engerman, "Demography," in *Dictionary of Afro-American Slavery*, revised edition, edited by Randall M. Miller and John David Smith (Westport, Conn.: Praeger, 1997), pp. 182–186.

Paul D. Escott and David R. Goldfield, eds., *Major Problems in the History of the American South: Documents and Essays*, volume 1, *The Old South* (Lexington, Mass.: D. C. Heath, 1990).

Drew Gilpin Faust, *James Henry Hammond and the Old South: A Design For Mastery* (Baton Rouge: Louisiana State University Press, 1982).

Robert William Fogel and Stanley L. Engerman, *Time on the Cross: The Economics of American Negro Slavery*, 2 volumes (Boston: Little, Brown, 1974).

Eugene D. Genovese, *Roll, Jordan, Roll: The World the Slaves Made* (New York: Pantheon, 1974).

Kenneth F. Kiple, "Diet," in *Dictionary of Afro-American Slavery*, revised edition, edited by Miller and Smith (Westport, Conn.: Praeger, 1997), pp. 186–191.

Kiple, "Health and Disease," in *Dictionary of Afro-American Slavery*, revised edition, edited by Miller and Smith (Westport, Conn.: Praeger, 1997), pp. 308–312.

National Center for Health Statistics, *Health, United States, 2001* (Hyattsville, Md.: U.S. Dept. of Health and Human Services, Public Health Service, Centers for Disease Control, National Center for Health Statistics, 2001).

William Dosite Postell, *The Health of Slaves on the Southern Plantations* (Baton Rouge: Louisiana State University Press, 1951).

Todd L. Savitt, "Health Care," in *Dictionary of Afro-American Slavery*, revised edition, edited by Miller and Smith (Westport, Conn.: Praeger, 1997), pp. 312–317.

Savitt, *Medicine and Slavery: The Diseases and Health Care of Slaves in Antebellum Virginia* (Urbana: University of Illinois Press, 1978).

Richard B. Sheridan, "Mortality and the Medical Treatment of Slaves in the British West Indies," in *Race and Slavery in the Western Hemisphere: Quantitative Studies*, edited by Engerman and Genovese (Princeton: Princeton University Press, 1975), pp. 285–310.

Richard H. Shryock, "Medical Practice in the Old South," *South Atlantic Quarterly*, 29 (April 1930): 172–182.

Kenneth M. Stampp, *The Peculiar Institution: Slavery in the Ante-Bellum South* (New York: Knopf, 1956).

HOUSE SERVANTS

Did the house servants, slave drivers, and other privileged slaves in the United States collaborate with the slaveholding regime?

Viewpoint: Yes. From the beginning of slavery in the New World, some slaves occupied positions of influence, authority, and privilege; these persons served the master's interests at the expense of their fellow slaves.

Viewpoint: No. House servants, drivers, and other privileged slaves emerged as authority figures on their plantations and were often instrumental in inspiring, organizing, and leading slave rebellions when the opportunity arose to do so.

Overstatement about the social differences between privileged and ordinary slaves is the source of common misconceptions about the nature of slavery. Of course, privileged and skilled slaves always stood apart from field hands, and the masters valued the former for their special expertise. The shortage of labor on the Southern frontier, for example, prompted masters to employ slaves as guides, hunters, and lumberjacks, while also depending on their detailed knowledge of rice cultivation on plantations in coastal South Carolina and Georgia. In the North and in cities slaves often worked at skilled professions or engaged in domestic service. On the large estates of the Chesapeake Bay, the low country, and later the Deep South, planters increasingly encouraged their slaves to learn a trade, trained many others for service in the Big House (the master's dwelling), and turned to slave drivers to supervise labor in the fields.

Most slaveholders, however, owned too few slaves to have the luxury of differentiating between polished and advantaged house servants, drivers, and craftsmen and average field hands. Small slaveholders needed workers, and they expected everyone to do his or her share. In addition, bonds of friendship and kinship often united field workers with house servants, craftsmen, and drivers. Finally, although they might have occupied different stations, all slaves felt a common oppression. Masters did not necessarily accord house servants, craftsmen, or drivers better treatment than other slaves received. The benefits they received came at the price of diminished privacy and heightened scrutiny. Greater responsibilities also brought elevated expectations, and thus increased the chances of displeasing master or mistress and, consequently, experiencing his or her wrath.

Historians are now in the process of learning more about the complex and ambivalent role and status of the so-called privileged slaves. Did they accommodate their master's will and foster intimacy with whites for the purpose of self-aggrandizement or so they could conspire against the regime? Did they abuse and exploit other slaves or mediate between masters and fellow slaves, inflicting punishment when necessary but at the same time protecting their fellow bondmen and bondwomen from even worse torment? Did they use what power and influence they had acquired to buttress slavery or to make it more bearable, until an opportunity arose to strike a blow against it?

Viewpoint:
Yes. From the beginning of slavery in the New World, some slaves occupied positions of influence, authority, and privilege; these persons served the master's interests at the expense of their fellow slaves.

Although constituting only a small minority, house servants and drivers were something of an elite among the slave population of the antebellum South. However unintentionally and perhaps unwittingly, these slaves could not help but contribute to the survival and success of plantation society. The masters certainly encouraged pride in their house servants, raising social divisions between them and the field hands and thereby dividing the slave community against itself. Some house servants openly confessed their contempt. "We house slaves thought we was better'n the others what worked in the field," declared one former slave. "We really was raised a little different, you know." To be sure, many house servants identified with their master and his family and felt superior even to poor whites. Rosa Starke, a former house servant, cited in George P. Rawick's *The American Slave: A Composite Autobiography,* volume 3, *South Carolina Narratives* (1972), insisted that:

> A house nigger man might swoop down and mate wid a field hand's good lookin' daughter, now and then, for pure love of her, but you never see a house gal lower herself by marryin' and matin' wid a common field-hand nigger. Dat offend de white folks, 'specially de young misses, who liked de business of match makin' and matin' of de young slaves.

House servants were reputed to enjoy better food, clothing, and housing than their counterparts who worked in the field. Fredrika Bremer, who visited many plantations, thought that the slaves who lived and worked in the Big House (the master's dwelling) fared far better than hired servants in Europe. Not only did house servants receive special consideration from the master and his family, but if they did not get what they wanted or thought was their due, they were in a position to take it. House slaves also had greater protection against being sold. The training that they had received and the affection that whites felt for them made it much less likely that their master or mistress would sell them. If by some chance they were sold, they commonly went on the market as a family.

The most elusive and yet important of the house servants was the Mammy, who, because of such romantic antebellum defenses of slavery as

Edward A. Pollard's *Black Diamonds Gathered in the Darkey Homes of the South* (1859) and such nostalgic twentieth-century novels as Margaret Mitchell's *Gone with the Wind* (1936), has become the most prominent figure in the legend of the Old South. Annie Laurie Broidrick of Vicksburg, Mississippi, summarized the image:

> Consequential, important, and next in authority to the owners were the old "black mammies," who raised and superintended the care of the children. As they grew old they were exempt from hard work, and ruled white and black with impartial severity. Our old "mammy Harriet" raised two or three generations of children. We had the greatest love for her, but it was tempered with fear, for she never overlooked a fault and was ready to tell "old miss" how "de chillun was carrying on. . . ."

Revered by all, the Mammy reigned over black and white alike. Yet, the Mammy also accepted the mutual obligations that bound master to slave and as such reinforced the paternalist social order of the plantation South.

The intimacy with whites that the Mammy and the other house servants experienced made it more difficult for them to repudiate slavery. Writing of her beloved Mammy Maria, Susan Dabney Smedes proclaimed that Mammy "had come to love the white family better than her own blood and race." The house servants, suggests historian Eugene D. Genovese, became "the great 'integrationists' in the black community, culturally as well as politically." Benjamin Drew, a former slave, was less charitable. In *A North-side View of Slavery* (1856), he wrote that house servants "are just the same as white men. Some of them will betray another [slave] just to curry favor with the master."

Equally ambiguous was the position of slave drivers. Supervising the slave-labor gangs, drivers were often the most important and valued slaves on the plantation. Masters depended on them to keep other slaves at work and to maintain discipline. Throughout the South black drivers even operated plantations for absentee owners. Writing in *De Bow's Review,* a South Carolina rice planter described the responsibilities of the driver:

> Drivers are, under the Overseer, to maintain discipline and order on the place. They are responsible for the quiet of the negro-houses, for the proper performance of tasks, for bringing out the people early in the morning, and generally for the immediate inspection of such things as the Overseer only generally superintends.

Whatever desires they might have entertained to stand up for their fellow slaves, drivers ultimately served the master's interests and, like the faithful servants of the Old Testament, added wealth to his coffers.

HOUSE SERVANTS

Respected for their intelligence, experience, and ability, the drivers earned the accolades of their masters. "The head driver . . . is to be treated with more respect than any other negro," wrote South Carolina planter James Henry Hammond. Duncan Clinch Heyward remembered one valued driver: "March was then in his prime, being in his forty-third year, tall and straight and of powerful build. Intelligence and understanding showed in his face, and force in his every movement. He looked indeed like one born to command." In a letter to his sister, William S. Pettigrew of North Carolina revealed the qualities that he sought in a driver, believing he had identified them in a slave named Glasgow, who was "honest, industrious, not too *talkative* . . . a man of good sense, a good hand

himself, and has been hitherto faithful in the discharge of whatever may have been committed to his care." Good drivers knew their business and enjoyed the master's confidence and loyalty because they had proven themselves adept, proficient, and reliable. They became his agents of order and discipline in the quarters and in the fields. They enforced the rules that he imposed and punished those who disobeyed. Many, no doubt, went further and identified their interests with his.

The privileges accruing to drivers were many and varied but typically included additional food, clothing, tobacco, and whiskey. They may also have lived in more spacious and comfortable lodgings than ordinary field hands and perhaps received a cash bonus at Christmas. Then, too,

HOUSE SERVANTS

most drivers did far less work than other slaves, though some labored in the fields. Yet, even those who performed field work could avoid the most arduous tasks. Perhaps more important, they could protect members of their family from the ordeal of working in the fields and could generally keep the whip off their backs. Some drivers also culled the sexual favors of slave women, either through bribery or force. A driver could make a woman's life easy or miserable, depending on her attitude toward his sexual advances. On her husband's Georgia plantation, Frances Anne Kemble reproached Sophy for having given birth to the driver's child out of wedlock. In Kemble's *Journal of a Residence on a Georgian Plantation in 1838–1839,* edited by John A. Scott (1961), Sophy replied: "Oh yes, missis, we know—we know all about dat well enough; but we do any thing to get our poor flesh some rest from de whip; when he made me follow him into de bush, what use me tell him no? He have strength to make me." A chastened Kemble could only lament: "I have written down the woman's words; I wish I could write down the voice and look of abject misery with which they were spoken."

Slave narratives are replete with similar tales of the drivers' inhumanity. Jane Johnson, a former slave from South Carolina, recalled that the driver on her plantation was "de meanest man, white or black, I ever see." Henry Cheatam described his black driver as "de meanest devil dat ever lived on de Lord's green earth. I promised myself when I growed up dat I was a-goin' to kill dat nigger if it was de last thing I ever done." The drivers, many former slaves complained, behaved worse than the masters. Some took advantage of their station to exact personal vengeance. Dan Josiah Lockhart, a driver who eventually escaped to Canada, declared that his master whipped him for being too hard on the slaves. An enraged Kemble described the severity with which the drivers often subjugated the slaves:

> The command of one slave to another is altogether the most uncompromising utterance of insolent truculent despotism that it ever fell to my lot to witness or listen to. "You nigger—I say, you black nigger—you no hear me call you—what for you no run quick? . . . Hi! You boy!" and "Hi, you girl!" shouted in an imperious scream, is the civilest mode of apostrophizing those at a distance from them; more frequently it is "You, nigger, you hear? Hi! you nigger." And I assure you no contemptuous white intonation ever equaled the *prepotenza* of the despotic insolence of this address of these poor wretches to each other.

In the Caribbean, even more than in the United States, drivers warranted their reputation for cruelty and barbarism, and the enmity of the slaves that accompanied it. Yet, it is worth considering Genovese's argument that the drivers found themselves in a complicated, if not impossible, situation. Genovese wrote that:

> A good driver had to mediate: to keep the slaves working as steadily as possible, especially during the harvest season, and to remonstrate with master and overseer not to demand what they could not get without brutality if indeed at all. To the extent that the driver succeeded in this mediation he played a decisive role in instilling a more modern work discipline in his people, and, at the same time, he offered some protection—for better or worse—against factorylike regimentation.

Although they may not have been docile pawns or vicious sadists, the drivers did their master's bidding. If they wished to maintain their status and their privileges, they had little choice but to impose discipline on, and exact labor from, their fellow slaves. To the extent that they did so, they promoted deference to the master's authority and accommodation to the slaveholding regime.

—MARK G. MALVASI,
RANDOLPH-MACON COLLEGE

**Viewpoint:
No. House servants, drivers, and other privileged slaves emerged as authority figures on their plantations and were often instrumental in inspiring, organizing, and leading slave rebellions when the opportunity arose to do so.**

The drivers were privileged slaves. They lived better, ate better, dressed better, and had more freedom than the slaves over whom they exercised authority. Black drivers summoned the slaves to their work, often assigned them their daily tasks, and made certain that they completed their assignments. They settled disputes between slaves, administered discipline when necessary, and represented the master's interests and power in the quarters. P. J. Laborie, a Caribbean coffee planter, argued that effective drivers "ought to possess fidelity, affection, intelligence, sobriety, discretion, justice, and severity. They should know to preserve distance and authority . . . give attention to every thing and render account of every thing to the master. Lastly, to be perfectly skilled in work of every kind." According to historian Robert L. Paquette, "the stability and prosperity of tobacco, cotton, coffee, indigo,

PANCAKE STICKS

In a 6 April 1830 letter, Angelina Grimké Weld, daughter of a South Carolina Supreme Court judge, described the treatment meted out to house slaves in Charleston:

This lady used to keep cowhides, or small paddles, (called "pancake sticks,") in four different apartments in her house; so that when she wished to punish, or to have punished, any of her slaves, she might not have the trouble of sending for an instrument of torture. For many years, one or other, and *often* more of her slaves, were flogged *every day;* particularly the young slaves about the house, whose faces were slapped, or their hands beat with the "pancake stick," for every trifling offence—and often for no fault at all. But the floggings were not all; the scoldings and abuse daily heaped upon them all, were worse: "fools" and "liars," "sluts" and "husseys," "hypocrites" and "good-for-nothing creatures," were the *common* epithets with which her mouth was filled, when addressing her slaves, adults as well as children. Very often she would take a position at her window, in an upper story, and scold at her slaves while working in the garden, at some distance from the house . . . and occasionally order a flogging. I have known her thus on the watch, scolding for more than an hour at a time, in so loud a voice that the whole neighborhood could hear her. . . .

The utter disregard of the comfort of the slaves, in *little* things, can scarcely be conceived by those who have not been a *component part* of slaveholding communities. . . . In South Carolina mosquitos swarm in myriads, more than half the year—they are so excessively annoying at night, that no family thinks of sleeping without nets of "mosquito bars" hung over their bedsteads, yet slaves are never provided with them, unless it be the favorite old domestics who get the cast-off pavilions; and yet these very masters and mistresses will be so kind to their *horses* as to provide them with *fly nets.* Bedsteads and bedding too, are rarely provided for any of the slaves—if the waiters and coachmen, waiting maids, cooks, washers, &c., have beds at all, they must generally get them for themselves. Commonly they lie down at night on the bare floor, with a small blanket wrapped around them in winter, and in summer a coarse osnaburg sheet, or nothing. Old slaves generally have beds, but it is because when younger *they have provided them for themselves.*

Only two meals a day are allowed the house slaves—the *first at twelve* o'clock. If they eat before this time, it is by stealth, and I am sure there must be a good deal of suffering among them from *hunger,* and particularly by children. Besides this, they are often kept from their meals by way of punishment. . . .

Chambermaids and seamstresses often slept in their mistresses' apartments, but with no bedding at all. I know an instance of a woman who has been married eleven years, and yet has never been allowed to sleep out of her mistress's chamber.—This is a *great* hardship to slaves. When we consider that house slaves are rarely allowed social intercourse during *the day,* as their work generally *separates* them; the barbarity of such an arrangement is obvious.

Source: *Richard O. Curry and Joanna Dunlap Cowden, eds.,* Slavery in America: Theodore Weld's American Slavery As It Is *(Itasca, Ill.: Peacock, 1972), pp. 37–38, 41–42.*

rice, and sugar plantations, among the more sophisticated enterprises of their day, hinged to a great extent on [the driver's] performance."

History has not treated the drivers kindly. Abolitionist writers such as Harriet Beecher Stowe portrayed them as vile, merciless, and sadistic. She described Sambo and Quimbo, the drivers on Simon Legree's Red River cotton plantation in *Uncle Tom's Cabin Or, Life Among the Lowly* (1852), as "gigantic negroes" with "coarse, dark, heavy features" and a "barbarous, guttural, half-brute intonation," educated "in savageness and brutality." The black driver, Stowe continued, "is always more tyrannical than the whites. . . . The slave is always a tyrant, if he can get a chance to be one." The image endured. The saintly Uncle Tom dies from the savage beating that Sambo and Quimbo inflict upon him. In *David Walker's Appeal: In Four Articles, Together with a Preamble, to the Colored Citizens of the World . . .* (1829), black abolitionist David Walker characterized drivers as traitors for whom he reserved a special contempt. The whites "take us, (being ignorant,) and put us as drivers over the other, and make us afflict each other as bad as they themselves afflict us—and to crown the whole of this catalogue of cruelties, they tell us that we . . . are an inferior race of beings!" Antislavery novelists in Latin America offered much the same image of the driver. In Cirilo Villaverde's *Cecilia Valdés* (1881), which many scholars consider the *Uncle Tom's Cabin* of Cuba, the drivers are ferocious in disciplining their fellow slaves. Anselmo Suárez y Romero wrote in *Francisco: El ingenio, ó, las delicas del campo* (Francisco: The Sugar Mill, or, the Delights of the Country, 1838) that the slave driver held his position because he "obeys religiously" the commands of his white superiors and is barbarous "in cracking the lash and his inhumanity in treating the other [slaves], his brothers and comrades."

The historians of slavery have perpetuated the image of the driver as "the master's man." In his classic study of Cuban slavery, *Hampa Afro-Cubana: Los Negros Esclavos: Estudio Sociológico y de Derecho Publico* (Afro-Cuban Underworld: The Negro Slaves: Sociological and Public Right Study, 1916), Fernando Ortiz cited contemporary accounts that depicted the *contramayoral* (driver) as "a figure more terrible" than the white overseer, "the most dreaded adversary, a slave like the others, and therefore hard and cruel toward his fellow slaves, especially with those from a tribe hostile to his. Then he becomes ferocious, implacable with the spirit of revenge." C. L. R. James, in *The Black Jacobins: Toussaint L'Ouverture and the San Domingo Revolution* (1938), characterized drivers as "giving stinging blows to all who, worn out by fatigue, were compelled to take a rest—men and women, young and old." Privileged drivers, James wrote, "had strong attachment to their masters" and were "permeated with their vices." In *Slave Society in the British Leeward Islands at the End of the Eighteenth Century* (1965), Elsa V. Goveia quoted travelers' accounts for a representation of the drivers as "mostly black or mulatto fellows of the worst dispositions" who used the lash unsparingly "wherever they see the least relaxation from labour; nor is it a consideration with them, whether it proceeds from idleness or inability, paying at the same time, little or no regard to age or sex." Orlando Patterson summarized the general conception of the driver in his study of slavery in Jamaica, writing that "it was not unusual for 'the great villain' to occupy the post. . . . These drivers often abused their authority. They had their own favorites, especially among the women; and if they bore a grudge against any of the slaves they could easily take it out on them in the field."

Until recently students of slavery in the United States shared this vision of the driver. In the first edition of *The Negro in Our History*

(1922), Carter G. Woodson wrote that the condition of the slaves "was not any better when [they] were placed under a Negro driver" than when they had endured the rancor of a white overseer. For the fourth edition (1927) Woodson added the sentence: "Some say it was worse." Between 1947 and 1994, in seven editions of *From Slavery to Freedom: A History of African Americans* (1994), the standard textbook for African American history, John Hope Franklin and Alfred A. Moss Jr. reiterated that "on some plantations a slave called the driver was selected to assist the owner or overseer in getting work out of the slaves. The other slaves frequently resented this delegation of authority to one among them, and the driver was sometimes viewed as a traitor, especially if he took his duties seriously." According to Kenneth M. Stampp, the drivers could be faithful, diligent, and effective managers who were also "notoriously severe taskmasters and, when given the power, might whip more cruelly than white masters." In *Slavery: A Problem in American Institutional and Intellectual Life* (1959), Stanley M. Elkins likened the driver to the Jewish prisoner in a Nazi concentration camp who was "placed in a supervisory position over his fellow inmates [and] who outdid the SS in sheer brutality."

Southern historian Clement Eaton anticipated a change in the scholarly treatment of the driver in the second edition of *The Mind of the Old South* (1967). Eaton rejected what he called the "abolition stereotype" of the driver as the master's bestial agent of discipline, punishment, and order among the slaves. He emphasized instead the driver's intelligence, his ability to mediate between the Big House and the slave quarters, and the respect he frequently commanded in the black community. During the 1970s, Robert Starobin, Robert William Fogel, Stanley L. Engerman, Eugene D. Genovese, Leslie Howard Owens, Randall Miller, and William L. Van Deburg substantially revised the image of the driver, in effect elaborating on Eaton's original insight. Yet, even these revisionist historians tended to view drivers as acquiescing in slavery and accommodating to the regime. Genovese observed that "in a few cases drivers led plots to murder masters or raise insurrections" but "rarely did they use their moral authority in the quarters to promote direct resistance and insurrection. The brutal and hated drivers of the Caribbean led or at least participated in insurrections much more readily." In *The Slave Drivers: Black Agricultural Labor Supervisors in the Antebellum South* (1979) Van Deburg concluded that "there is little evidence to show that drivers sought to engage in conspiracies or widespread insurrectionary activity aimed at overthrowing the slave system."

Since the 1980s, historians of slavery have altered the image of the driver still further, showing that during the eighteenth and nineteenth centuries, as Paquette has written, "the driver played a vital role in many, perhaps the majority, of the most significant conspiracies and revolts in the history of the Americas, including the United States." In November 1733 two *bombas* (drivers) named Claes and Kanta led the first major slave uprising to erupt on St. John in the Danish Virgin Islands. The final outbreak of organized slave violence in the Virgin Islands took place in St. Croix in 1848 under the command of "Gotlieb Bordeaux, alias General Buddoe, formerly the driver on [the] La Grange estate." Carolyn E. Fick has determined that *commandeurs* (drivers) played a major role in launching the slave revolt in Saint Domingue (Haiti) in 1791. The leaders of the most destructive slave rebellion in Cuban history, which occurred during the summer of 1825, were three *contramayorales* (drivers), two of whom were free persons of color.

Hilary Beckles, the authority on the slave insurrection that took place in Barbados in 1816, found that of nineteen leading conspirators whose occupations he could identify, fourteen were drivers. Chief among these was Bussa, the driver on the Bailey estate, after whom the rebellion is named. Beckles, in fact, referred to the Barbadian uprising as a "slave-drivers' war." Transcripts of the trials that took place in the aftermath of the rebellion in Demerara in 1823 contain the remarkable testimony of a slave named Paris, who revealed the degree to which drivers and house servants not only participated in the uprising but also organized and led it. Paris recounted that:

> Barre the butcher carried letters from Jack to Sam, the Governor's servant in town, and to the head driver at Herstelling [plantation], who was to be the leader of the east side of the river; at Rome [plantation], the head driver [was the leader]; at Providence, the head driver and Mr. Blake's cook; at Ruimveld, the head and the second drivers; at Le Penitence, the head driver and the manager's cook; but the head driver at Herstelling was to be the head of the whole; on Filleen's estate, the attorney's butler; on Best, the second driver, who was also to be the leader on the west side, and to send over the whole of the Negroes from that side to take the town, which was our grand object; Colin, at Mr. Meerten's; head driver at Belle Vue; west coast, Rotterdam first and second drivers, head men of the west coast . . . ; Good Success, first driver; Essequibo, Annandale, first driver, who was to have passed over to Belle Plaine, with one thousand Bush negroes, and from thence to have found his way to town. Columbia, first driver and butler; Hampton Court, first driver and d[itt]o; Main Stay, first driver and head butler; Tarsus, first driver and head butler; Caledonia, first and second drivers; Sophienberg, first driver; Hobabo, Julius, Mr. Edmonstone's head driver.

Finally, drivers initiated the violence in St. James parish that grew into the Jamaican Christmas revolt of 1831, which ultimately involved as many as fifty thousand slaves and destroyed hundreds of estates.

Slave revolts in the United States were fewer in number and of a lesser magnitude than those that erupted in Latin America and the Caribbean. In the conspiracies of Gabriel Prosser (1800) and Denmark Vesey (1822) and in the rebellion of Nat Turner (1831), the three most celebrated examples of collective slave resistance in American history, the drivers were not preeminent. Yet, these instances hardly exhaust the record of slave plots in the United States. Celeb, a black overseer on the Simkinses' plantation, planned an uprising in Virginia during 1792, which, involving thousands of slaves, was reputed to be larger than Gabriel's Rebellion. Drivers and house servants on the tobacco and indigo plantations outside of New Orleans were the principals in devising what came to be known as the Point Coupée Conspiracy (1795). Similarly, the drivers on low-country plantations near Savannah, Georgia, masterminded an insurrectionary scheme in 1806 that authorities uncovered and foiled. In 1811 the largest slave revolt in the United States began in the parishes of Saint Charles and Saint John the Baptist, located upriver from New Orleans. The leader of the uprising was a mulatto driver named Charles Deslondes.

Some drivers were a scourge to their fellow slaves. They worked them hard and punished them severely. Meanwhile, the drivers rewarded their favorites, and abused their power. New research, however, has suggested that the image of the driver as "the master's man" or "the great villain" is misleading and must be modified if not discarded. Drivers were not habitual revolutionaries any more than they were the sycophants of the master. More accurately, the drivers, along with other so-called privileged slaves, were important and respected men in the slave community, to whom the slaves often looked for counsel and leadership. The drivers occupied a difficult and ambiguous position and did their best to placate both masters and slaves without accommodating fully to the desires and demands of either. They may have cracked the whip when necessary, but they also more often than not looked the other way when slaves evaded their duties or performed with less enthusiasm than the master expected. Many drivers were also uncommonly good managers, demonstrating that blacks were anything but incompetent and stupid. And if drivers, at least in the United States, did not lead their people in rebellions against slavery often enough to satisfy the historians who judge them, it is because the drivers knew that such ventures amounted to suicide. As Solomon Northup, who had been a driver on a Louisiana plantation, explained:

> Such an idea as insurrection . . . is not new among the enslaved population of Bayou Boeuf. More than once I have joined in serious consultation, when the subject has been discussed, and there have been times when a word from me would have placed hundreds of my fellow-bondsmen in an attitude of defiance. Without arms or ammunition, or even with them, I saw such a step would result in certain defeat, disaster and death, and always raised my voice against it.

Northup's was not the voice of a traitor to his people or that of a collaborator with their enemies.

–JACOB W. FOX,
RICHMOND, VIRGINIA

References

Herbert Aptheker, *American Negro Slave Revolts* (New York: Columbia University Press / London: King & Staples, 1943).

Hilary Beckles, "The Slave-Drivers' War: Bussa and the 1816 Slave Rebellion," *Boletín de estudios Latinoamericanos y del Caribe*, 39 (December 1985): 85–109.

Beckles, *White Servitude and Black Slavery in Barbados, 1627–1715* (Knoxville: University of Tennessee Press, 1989).

Michael Craton, *Testing the Chains: Resistance to Slavery in the British West Indies* (Ithaca, N.Y.: Cornell University Press, 1982).

Benjamin Drew, *A North-side View of Slavery* (Boston: Jewett / New York: Sheldon, Lamport & Blakeman, 1856). Reprinted as *A North-Side View of Slavery: The Refugee: Or, The Narratives of Fugitive Slaves in Canada Related by Themselves . . .* (New York: Negro Universities Press, 1968).

Clement Eaton, *The Mind of the Old South*, revised edition (Baton Rouge: Louisiana State University Press, 1967).

Stanley M. Elkins, *Slavery: A Problem in American Institutional and Intellectual Life*, third edition (Chicago: University of Chicago Press, 1976).

Carolyn E. Fick, *The Making of Haiti: The San Domingue Revolution from Below* (Knoxville: University of Tennessee Press, 1990).

Fisk University, *Unwritten History of Slavery: Autobiographical Accounts of Negro Ex-Slaves* (Nashville: Social Science Institute, Fisk University, 1945).

Robert William Fogel and Stanley L. Engerman, *Time on the Cross: The Economics of American Negro Slavery*, 2 volumes (Boston: Little, Brown, 1974).

John Hope Franklin and Alfred A. Moss Jr., *From Slavery to Freedom: A History of African Americans*, seventh edition (New York: McGraw-Hill, 1994).

Eugene D. Genovese, *Roll, Jordan, Roll: The World the Slaves Made* (New York: Pantheon, 1974).

Elsa V. Goveia, *Slave Society in the British Leeward Islands at the End of the Eighteenth Century* (New Haven: Yale University Press, 1965).

Neville A. T. Hall, *Slave Society in the Danish West Indies: St. Thomas, St. John, and St. Croix*, edited by B. W. Higman (Baltimore: Johns Hopkins University Press / Mona, Jamaica: University of the West Indies Press, 1992).

Duncan Clinch Heyward, *Seed from Madagascar* (Chapel Hill: University of North Carolina Press, 1937).

C. L. R. James, *The Black Jacobins: Toussaint L'Ouverture and the San Domingo Revolution*, revised edition (New York: Vintage, 1963).

Frances Anne Kemble, *Journal of a Residence on a Georgian Plantation in 1838–1839*, edited by John A. Scott (New York: Knopf, 1961).

William Luis, *Literary Bondage: Slavery in Cuban Narrative* (Austin: University of Texas Press, 1990).

Randall Miller, "The Man in the Middle: The Black Slave Driver," *American Heritage*, 30 (October–November 1979): 40–49.

Solomon Northup, *Twelve Years a Slave*, edited by Sue Eakin and Joseph Logsdon (Baton Rouge: Louisiana State University Press, 1968).

Leslie Howard Owens, *This Species of Property: Slave Life and Culture in the Old South* (New York: Oxford University Press, 1976).

Robert L. Paquette, "The Drivers Shall Lead Them: Image and Reality in Slave Resistance," in *Slavery, Secession, and Southern History*, edited by Paquette and Louis A. Ferleger (Charlottesville: University Press of Virginia, 2000), pp. 31–58.

Orlando Patterson, *The Sociology of Slavery: An Analysis of the Origins, Development, and Structure of Negro Slavery in Jamaica* (London: MacGibbon & Kee, 1967).

George P. Rawick, ed., *The American Slave: A Composite Autobiography,* first and second series, 19 volumes (Westport, Conn.: Greenwood Press, 1972); first supplemental series, 12 volumes (Westport, Conn.: Greenwood Press, 1977); second supplemental series, 10 volumes (Westport, Conn.: Greenwood Press, 1979).

William Kauffman Scarborough, *The Overseer: Plantation Management in the Old South* (Baton Rouge: Louisiana State University Press, 1966).

Susan Dabney Smedes, *Memorials of A Southern Planter,* edited by Fletcher M. Green (New York: Knopf, 1965).

Kenneth M. Stampp, *The Peculiar Institution: Slavery in the Ante-Bellum South* (New York: Knopf, 1956).

Robert Starobin, "Privileged Bondsmen and the Process of Accommodation: The Role of House Servants and Drivers as Seen in Their Own Letters," *Journal of Social History,* 5 (Fall 1971): 46–70.

Harriet Beecher Stowe, *Uncle Tom's Cabin Or, Life Among the Lowly* (Boston: Jewett, 1852).

William L. Van Deburg, *The Slave Drivers: Black Agricultural Labor Supervisors in the Antebellum South* (Westport, Conn.: Greenwood Press, 1979).

David Walker, *David Walker's Appeal: In Four Articles, Together with a Preamble, to the Coloured Citizens of the World . . . ,* edited by Charles M. Wiltse (New York: Hill & Wang, 1965).

Carter G. Woodson, *The Negro in Our History* (Washington, D.C.: Associated Publishers, 1922).

HOUSE SERVANTS

LEGAL DEFINITION

Were slaves legally regarded as human beings in the United States?

Viewpoint: Yes. Slaves were legally defined as human beings who owed labor and obedience to their owners. The reference to slaves as "property" commonly alluded to a legal claim on their labor, not fundamentally different from the claim that an employer had on the labor of an indentured servant or a free worker.

Viewpoint: No. Slave laws did not consistently define slaves as human beings; slaves were a form of property that could be sold, transferred, or inherited.

The ambivalent principles of a slave society engendered contradictory judicial rulings. Some judges determined that slaves were persons who enjoyed the protection of the law and whose will the law could not disregard. Others, on the contrary, reasoned that slaves were property wholly at the disposal of their master. This legal confusion exposed the deception on which slavery rested. Once the law showed even a modicum of respect for the personality of the slave, it revealed that the master's domination was not total and thereby unintentionally but unavoidably created opportunities for subsequent assertions of the slaves' humanity.

Southern slave law never reconciled the competing definitions of slaves as persons and property. As a consequence, the courts hesitated to intervene in the master-slave relation. Its deficiencies notwithstanding, the legal system of the South afforded slaves a measure of security. Many historians have argued that the slave codes of Catholic countries extended greater rights and protections to their slaves than did the laws of the United States. The role and function of the law in Portuguese and Spanish America, however, did not derive from the ethos in which the law itself originated. Prevailing standards of efficiency, order, and discipline meant that the laws, although more limited, were better enforced in the United States than in such slaveholding societies as Brazil or Cuba. In Brazil, power effectively remained in the hands not of the authorities but of the *senhores de engenbo* (wealthy sugar planters) who often ignored the statutes and did as they pleased. The slogan *¡Obedezco, pero no cumplo!* (I obey, but I do not comply!) reveals the essential Spanish attitude toward enforcement of the law. In addition, officials in distant metropolitan capitals had formulated the slave law of Portuguese and Spanish America and imposed it upon resistant slaveholders. The slave law of the South, by contrast, emanated from the slaveholders themselves and thus more accurately reflected both their conception of right and wrong and their agreement about the extent to which they would circumscribe their power.

Southern slaveholders, of course, violated the law with impunity. Such transgressions, though, marked them as hypocrites and frauds in the eyes of their slaves, weakening their prestige and with it their authority. Even the master's transgressions, therefore, could be made to serve the slaves' interest. His conduct permitted them to see that he was not a saint or a god, sanctified and omnipotent, but a man who, however powerful, was subject to the same appetites, passions, frailties, and sins as other men. Moreover, slaves could insist on masters' living up to their own standards and respecting the slaves' humanity, a demand that, as historian W. E. B. Du Bois observed, frequently made the practice of slavery in the South less oppressive and ruthless than the laws that governed it.

Viewpoint:
Yes. Slaves were legally defined as human beings who owed labor and obedience to their owners. The reference to slaves as "property" commonly alluded to a legal claim on their labor, not fundamentally different from the claim that an employer had on the labor of an indentured servant or a free worker.

To ask whether slaves were human beings under law is not to argue that slaves could enjoy the same rights and privileges of free persons but whether the courts acknowledged the slaves' legal personality, which then entitled them to the protection of the state. Clouding this question is the fact that not all free people in antebellum America enjoyed the same rights and privileges. Free persons of color had different rights from slaves, as well as from whites; white women had fewer rights than white men. Although by 1857 the U.S. Supreme Court ruled that slaves were not entitled to the Constitutional rights of citizens, state courts recognized the humanity of slaves without conceding that slaves were citizens. Slave law acknowledged foremost the master's right to protect chattel and real property, but it also clearly defined a slave's right to life and limb.

In general terms all of the various slave codes read that a slave was chattel, that is, transferable property. Yet, as with all issues regarding slavery, that simple definition did not bring clarity but immediately degenerated into a complex tangle. Chattel slaves had no rights, and for the most part the slave codes made this fact plain. However, there were also instances in colonial, and later state, law that recognized slaves as human beings under law, albeit within a highly restricted context. Ultimately, the rights of slaves as human beings under law were circumscribed not only by their status as enslaved beings but also by the majority opinion in *Dred Scott* v. *Sandford* (1857). The Dred Scott decision established that slaves were not citizens but "property, to be used in subserviency to the interests, the convenience, or the will, of his owner," and "without social, civil, or political rights." The decision also established that comity did not apply in the case of the slaves: the rights slaves might enjoy within the

borders of one state did not automatically transfer across state lines. Moreover, having rights in a state did not imply that slaves had rights as citizens of the United States.

Laws describing slaves in the New World as "conveyable property" appeared as early as 1680, but within the complexities of these laws slaves were also defined as beings subject to punishment or protection. Legal precedent set by French and British colonial law established slaves as personal property that could be moved, sold, or rented according to the will and needs of the master. Slaves eventually had to abide by a separate set of laws that regulated their movements and limited their freedom. They could not travel unescorted or without permission. They could not carry weapons, own dogs or property, preach to or "harangue" an assembly, buy or sell liquor, engage in any trade, exercise any public office, tutor, practice law, be a witness in civil or criminal matters (unless specifically excepted by law), or engage in civil marriage. Slave owners, political theorists, and jurists struggled with the meaning of slavery within this evolving legal framework. They spilled much ink trying to define a slave and to determine what kind of property a slave represented, how that form of property was taxable, and what, if any, rights slaves had. Slave codes were not uniform from state to state, and the result was a complex morass of legislation and regulations that shared general principles but were not universally applicable.

Apologists for and opponents of slavery alike wrote extensively on the right of property in man. Implicit in some of these discussions, even those that came from proslavery theorists, was the recognition that, although technically classified as chattel, slaves were also human beings and as such were entitled to guarantees of protection and maintenance in return for their labor. This notion, indeed, formed the underpinning of paternalism. Political theorist Francis Lieber, while serving as professor of history and political economy at the University of South Carolina during the 1840s, tried to circumvent the problem of slaves' humanity by equating the ownership of human beings with the command of their labor power.

> "Properly speaking," Lieber wrote, "the slave himself is not property, but his labor is. Property involves the idea of free disposal over the thing owned, or, as the ancient civilians expressed it, the exclusive right of use and

LEGAL DEFINITION

abuse. . . . We possess no such right over the slave and never claimed it. We own the labor of the slave and this cannot be done without keeping the person performing the labor thus owned, in bondage . . . at the same time the slave remains a person. Slavery is an institution of property so far as the labor is concerned, but it is also an institution which established a status."

Similarly, proslavery essayist E. N. Eliot wrote: "Slavery is the duty and the obligation of the slave to labor for the mutual benefit of both the master and the slave, under a warrant to the slave of protection and a comfortable subsistence, under all circumstances. The person of the slave is not property . . . but the right to his labor is property and may be transferred like any other property." Albert Taylor Bledsoe, professor of mathematics at the University of Virginia and defender of Southern culture, further asserted that slaveholders could "lay no claim to the soul of a slave . . . only a right to the labor and lawful obedience of the slave." However, it was patently

obvious to all that the labor power of the slave could not be owned independently from his or her body, and abolitionists ridiculed the notion of owning only the slave's labor but not the body and the soul.

According to the Virginia courts, "Slaves are not only property, but they are rational human beings, and entitled to the humanity of the court, when it can be exercised without invading the rights of property. . . ." The slippery slope of defining what rights, if any, the slaves had kept legislators and jurists wary of skidding too close to the line that protected the master's property rights and maintained his legal dominion over the slaves. Even when lawmakers and judges recognized slaves as human beings before the law, they made it clear that the slave was first and foremost property, that the master's best interests and the slave's general welfare were irrevocably bound together, and that neither the courts nor the legislature could interpose themselves between the master and his slaves. On the contrary, the master-slave relation had to remain inviolate.

The greater part of slave codes was devoted to regulating the conduct of slaves, but these codes also included provisions that defined the responsibilities of masters. According to Article 173 of the 1824 Louisiana Slave Code, for example, "the slave is entirely subject to the will of his master, who may correct and chastise him, though not with unusual rigor, nor so as to maim him, or to expose him to the danger of loss of life, or to cause his death." Similarly, Section 2043 of the Alabama Slave Code of 1852 reads: "The master must treat his slave with humanity, and must not inflict upon him any cruel punishment; he must provide him with a sufficiency of healthy food and necessary clothing; cause him to be properly attended during sickness, and provide for his necessary wants in his old age." Article VII of the Alabama code further concerned explicit offenses against the slaves. Anyone who caused the death of a slave by cruel punishment with "malice aforethought" was guilty of murder in the first degree. Any person who had the right to correct a slave and through those punishments caused the death of the slave without any premeditated intention to kill was guilty of murder in the second degree but was also liable to be charged with murder in the first degree. Any master who permitted cruel punishments or who failed in any way to provide for the slave as required by law could be fined not less than $25 and not more than $1,000. Anyone indicted for any of these crimes was entitled to a trial by jury, two-thirds of whom would be slaveholders. Yet, whatever the intent of the law, with testimony from slave witnesses inadmissible, even the meanest slaveholders had little to fear.

In North Carolina during the colonial period, as in other British mainland provinces, slaves were legally regarded as chattel and valuable assets to their owners. The colonial assembly did not pass laws intended to protect them from cruel punishments and murder until 1774. According to this legislation, the first offense carried a penalty of a twelve-month term of imprisonment; the second, execution. This law was amended in 1791 to read that if a person was convicted of "maliciously killing a slave" he was guilty of murder and would suffer the same punishment as if he had killed a freeman. The law made no provisions for lesser charges. The Act of 1791 was overturned in *State* v. *Boon* (1801) because the section that described the penalty was considered too vague—there were several ways to punish a freeman for murder. In 1817 the state legislature decided that killing a slave was homicide and "shall partake of the same degree of guilt, when accompanied with the like circumstances, that homicide now does

at common law." Determining what this law meant was tested through various court cases. Although the law read that persons convicted of maliciously killing a slave would be charged with murder, it remained to be decided how far a white could go before his attacks were deemed malicious and whether slaves could justly defend themselves against such attacks.

In *State* v. *Tackett* (1820), the court ruled that the homicide of a slave "extenuated by a legal provocation" would result in a charge of manslaughter. Legal provocation meant that a slave had been "turbulent . . . insolent and impudent to white persons." In 1823 the North Carolina Supreme Court ruled that although unprovoked battery on a slave was indictable, every battery on a slave was not indictable "because the person making it may have the matter of excuse or justification, which would be no defence for committing a battery on a free person." This rendering of the law was upheld in the verdict in *State* v. *Hale* (1823), in which the court ruled that "a battery committed on a slave, no justifying circumstances being shown, was an indictable offense," but circumstances that would not justify battery on a free person justified them on a slave. The Chief Justice wrote of these crimes: "The offenses are usually committed by men of dissolute habits, hanging loose on society, who, being repelled from association with well-disposed citizens, take refuge in the company of colored persons and slaves whom they deprave by their example, embolden by their familiarity, and then beat, under the expectation that a slave dare not resent a blow from a white man."

Although slaves had, at least in theory, some expectation of protection from brutal and excessive force, *State* v. *Mann* (1829) addressed the issue of how the rights of the master weighed against this expectation. North Carolina judge Thomas Ruffin wrote, "the master is not liable to an indictment for a battery upon his slave. . . . The power of the master must be absolute to render the submission of the slave perfect. . . ." Ruffin also conceded that "I most freely confess my sense of harshness of this proposition . . . and as a principle of moral right every person in his retirement must repudiate it."

The master's right to strike a slave was further differentiated from his right to kill a slave in *State* v. *Will* (1834) in which Judge William Gaston of the North Carolina Supreme Court wrote:

> It is certain that the master has not the right to slay his slave and I hold it equally certain that the slave has a right to defend himself against the unlawful attempt of his master to deprive him of life . . . there is no legal limitation to the master's power of punishment

except that it shall not reach the life of the offending slave. It is for the legislature to remove this reproach from amongst us, if, consistently with public safety it can be removed. . . . If a slave, in defense of his life, kills an overseer, the homicide is by such circumstances, mitigated to manslaughter. It seems that the law would be the same, with respect to killing a master or a temporary owner, under similar circumstances.

How the North Carolina courts would consider the circumstances if a master punished a slave with no intent of killing him and the slave died anyway was argued in *State* v. *Hoover* (1839). It was decided that "the law would tenderly regard every circumstance," but if it was apparent that the punishment was "barbarously immoderate" and that the master was determined to kill the slave, then he would be found guilty of murder.

Generally, the court could not and would not consider white-on-slave battery to be the same as or equal in severity to slave-on-white battery, the underlying assumption being that punishment was an essential aspect of slave management. In addition, the courts acknowledged that masters could not hope to discipline their slaves by threatening to take away their liberty, which was already forfeit, but only by making them fear for their lives. However, in *State* v. *Caesar* (1849) the slave was deemed to have the right to defend himself against an assault from a person who had no authority over him: "if a white man wantonly inflicts upon a slave, over whom he has no authority a severe blow or repeated blows, under unusual circumstances and the slave at the instant, strikes and kills . . . he is only guilty of manslaughter giving due weight to the motives of policy and the necessity for subordination. . . ." While this decision can be interpreted as a peculiar right granted to slaves to defend their master's property, at the same time, the right to self-defense was accorded to all other persons and thus suggests that on some level the law recognized the slaves as legal persons even if those persons had dual identities as chattel. According to *State* v. *Caesar* and *State* v. *Will*, slaves had the right of self-defense, but their status predisposed them routinely to receive beatings and other assaults that were regarded as legal and necessary. In 1850 Judge Richard Pearson reaffirmed that "insolent language from a slave is equivalent to a blow by a white man, in its legal effect, as an excuse for battery."

The enforcement of these laws was irregular. The legal system of the slave South clearly and unequivocally favored the owners, while the prevailing concept of property rights also obstructed the routine punishment of crimes against slaves. Since slaves were property, circumstances had to be extreme before the courts or anyone else intervened in master-slave rela-

tions. Persons who were prosecuted were usually only fined and subject to public censure. In 1799 a white man shot and killed a slave who had shoved him to the ground. The North Carolina Supreme Court found the white man guilty of manslaughter but could not assign any penalty for the crime since the Act of 1791 had no provision for punishing manslaughter. In 1810 a Tarboro planter accused his slave of stealing $70 from him and gave the slave nearly three hundred lashes in an effort to extract a confession. The slave died from the whipping; after the master was acquitted, a writer in the *Raleigh Star* complained, "this was too flagrant a violation of humanity to pass unnoticed. . . . The man was arraigned at the bar, but he was acquitted; though not without murmur from many of the bystanders." In 1822 Jacob Pope of Halifax County suspended a female slave from a tree, tied her legs around its trunk, and whipped her to death. His punishment was a $200 fine plus court costs.

Since slave owners were tried by a jury of their peers and since the courts did not admit slave testimony, verdicts more serious than manslaughter were rare, and the death of practically any slave could be described as accidental. Sufficiently mitigating circumstances and inventive legal interpretations usually combined to save a slave owner who had killed a slave from the extreme penalties extended to those convicted of capital offenses. Slave owners whose barbaric habits and practices were aired in court often aroused contempt from their peers, as was the case in 1849 with a South Carolina jury of inquest investigating the death of a slave who had allegedly been severely disciplined for insolence. The master had whipped the slave, who was a cripple, wet his clothes, shackled his wrists, chained him by the neck, and left him in an open outhouse on a freezing February night. The next morning the slave was found dead; he had lost consciousness and slipped, which caused the chain around his neck to choke him, and had also subsequently frozen on what jury member Thomas Chapin called a "very cold and freezing" night. Although the jury managed to find the death to be accidental, Chapin wrote afterward that he believed the slave was murdered, that his neighbor was a "demon in human shape," and that his verdict would have been that the man had "deliberately but unpremeditatedly murdered" the slave. Even when confronted with circumstances as horrific as these, juries proved incapable of arriving at verdicts that would compromise the social order. Slaves were recognized as human beings under law, but the South was a slaveholding society not constructed to allow for the routine application of the law. To do so would have jeopardized the Southern social and political structure.

The law established the slave as a human being, and the courts interpreted the law in a manner that supported the concept of a slave's humanity within the law. Recognition of the slave's humanity accomplished several purposes. It assuaged some of the conflicted sensibilities of the enlightened element of the slave-owning aristocracy as they tried to balance the necessity of slave labor against the moral discomforts of owning slaves. They viewed themselves differently from their more common slave-owning neighbors, as the comments from *State* v. *Hale* obliquely suggest, and considered themselves to be more capable, prudent, and benevolent masters. They might have owned slaves, but they did not believe themselves to be barbarians. The laws that they crafted reflected an attitude shaped by their social position, prevailing political theory, and a desire to ensure the survival of a controversial institution in an increasingly egalitarian and democratic society. The recognition of the slaves' value as human beings was also another way to acknowledge the masters' Christian beneficence and demonstrate the legitimacy of their authority. By recognizing the humanity of the slaves, the law, which served the masters' interests, also reassured the slave owners that their dominance did not rest on the exercise of raw power.

Slaves were, after all, expensive investments. Their masters had the right to discipline them and, the courts reasoned, should have enough sense not to murder them since to do so would be to destroy their own property. Persons who had no authority over a slave should not, by the same token, have the right wantonly to kill a slave, just as they had no right to kill a freeman. Slaves, ironically, had the right to defend themselves if only to protect their master's investment.

—PAULA STATHAKIS,
CHARLOTTE, NORTH CAROLINA

Viewpoint:
No. Slave laws did not consistently define slaves as human beings; slaves were a form of property that could be sold, transferred, or inherited.

Personal relations between masters and slaves were of far less importance than economic necessities. Ensuring the unquestioned obedience of slaves to their masters and overseers thus became the paramount consideration in all the slave societies of the New World. To the extent that slaveholders wished their plantations to operate efficiently and profitably, they had to exercise absolute control over the bodies of the slaves. Although total domination remained elusive in practice, the law of slavery guaranteed the master virtually unlimited power. Recognizing that slaveholders could not impose discipline by threatening to deprive slaves of their liberty, which they had obviously already lost, the law granted masters the right to make the slaves fear for their lives. A Virginia statute of 1669, for example, accounted it no felony if a master or overseer killed a slave who resisted punishment:

> Whereas the only law in force for the punishment of refractory servants resisting their master, mistris or overseer cannot be inflicted upon negroes, nor the obstinacy of many of them by other than violent means supprest, *Be it enacted and declared by this grand assembly,* if any slave resist his master (or other by his masters order correcting him) and by the extremity of the correction should chance to die, that his death shall not be accompted Felony, but the master (or that other person appointed by the master to punish him) be acquit from molestation, such it cannot be presumed that prepensed malice (which alone makes murther Felony) should induce any man to destroy his own estate.

Similarly, the South Carolina slave code of 1712 outlined the punishments to be inflicted for offering "any violence to any christian or white person, by striking, or the like." For a first offense the slave suffered a whipping. Branding repaid a second offense. After a third instance of defiance the master could put the slave to death. Should the white man whom the slave assaulted be injured, maimed, or killed, the state automatically imposed a death sentence. The slave law of colonial South Carolina inflicted similar penalties for running away: whipping for a first attempt; branding for a second; severing ears for a third; and castration for a fourth.

The law also fixed the slaves' status as chattel. By the late seventeenth century, the law of most English slaveholding colonies had classified slaves in the same way that it categorized household goods and other personal property. The Virginia statutes of 1705 qualified slaves as a form of real estate, while the revisions of 1726 delineated them "chattels." The South Carolina code of 1740 rendered slaves "chattels personal, in the hands of their owners and possessors and their executors, administrators and assigns, to all intents, constructions, and purposes whatsoever. . . ." The application of such legal definitions automatically dispossessed slaves of their human rights, or at least rendered them indefensible and, therefore, meaningless under law. English law, in other words, did not recognize the humanity of slaves.

AN EXCEPTION

U.S. Supreme Court Associate Justice Benjamin R. Curtis dissented in the Dred Scott Case (1857). By using historical facts and legal precedent, he argued that blacks could be citizens of the United States and that Congress had the power to prohibit slavery from expanding into the territories:

It would not be easy for the Legislature to employ more explicit language to signify its will that the *status* of slavery should not exist within the Territory, than the words found in the act of 1820, and in the ordinance of 1787. . . .

I have thus far assumed, merely for the purpose of the argument, that the laws of the United States, respecting slavery in this Territory, were constitutionally enacted by Congress. It remains to inquire whether they are constitutional and binding laws.

. . . it is insisted, that whatever other powers Congress may have respecting the territory of the United States, the subject of negro slavery forms an exception.

The Constitution declares that Congress shall have power to make "*all* needful rules and regulations" respecting the territory belonging to the United States.

The assertion is, though the Constitution says all, it does not mean all—though it says all, without qualification, it means all except such as allow or prohibit slavery. It cannot be doubted that it is incumbent on those who would thus introduce an exception not found in the language of the instrument, to exhibit some solid and satisfactory reason, drawn from the subject-matter or the purposes and objects of the clause, the context, or from other provisions of the Constitution, showing that the words employed in this clause are not to be understood according to their clear, plain, and natural signification. . . .

. . . [In] eight distinct instances, beginning with the first Congress, and coming down to the year 1848, . . . Congress has excluded slavery from the territory of the United States; and six distinct instances in which Congress organized Governments of Territories by which slavery was recognised and continued, beginning also with the first Congress, and coming down to the year 1822. These acts were severally signed by seven Presidents of the United States, beginning with General Washington, and coming regularly down as far as Mr. John Quincy Adams, thus including all who were in public life when the Constitution was adopted.

If the practical construction of the Constitution contemporaneously with its going into effect, by men intimately acquainted with its history from their personal participation in framing and adopting it, and continued by them through a long series of acts of the gravest importance, be entitled to weight in the judicial mind on a question of construction, it would seem to be difficult to resist the force of the acts above adverted to. . . .

Looking at the power of Congress over the Territories as of the extent just described, what positive prohibition exists in the Constitution, which restrained Congress from enacting a law in 1820 to prohibit slavery north of thirty-six degrees thirty minutes north latitude?

The only one suggested is that clause in the fifth article of the amendments of the Constitution which declares that no person shall be deprived of his life, liberty, or property, without due process of law. . . .

Slavery, being contrary to natural right, is created only by municipal law. This is not only plain in itself, and agreed by all writers on the subject, but is inferable from the Constitution, and has been explicitly declared by this court. . . .

Is it conceivable that the Constitution has conferred the right on every citizen to become a resident on the territory of the United States with his slaves, and there to hold them as such, but has neither made nor provided for any municipal regulations which are essential to the existence of slavery?

Is it not more rational to conclude that they who framed and adopted the Constitution were aware that persons held to service under the laws of a State are property only to the extent and under the conditions fixed by those laws; that they must cease to be available as property, when their owners voluntarily place them permanently within another jurisdiction, where no municipal laws on the subject of slavery exist; and that, being aware of these principles, and having said nothing to interfere with or displace them, . . . and having empowered Congress to make all needful rules and regulations respecting the territory of the United States, it was their intention to leave to the discretion of Congress what regulations, if any, should be made concerning slavery therein?

. . . I am of opinion that so much of the several acts of Congress as prohibited slavery and involuntary servitude within that part of the Territory of Wisconsin lying north of thirty-six degrees thirty minutes north latitude, and west of the river Mississippi, were constitutional and valid laws.

Source: *William E. Gienapp, ed.,* The Civil War and Reconstruction: A Documentary Collection *(New York & London: Norton, 2001), pp. 43–46.*

In addition, the law ignored the integrity of the slave "family" and deprived slave "marriages" of any legal or moral standing. Attendance to the immortal souls of the slaves, so much in evidence in Spanish colonies, also rapidly disappeared from English legal considerations. A series of laws enacted between 1667 and 1671 made it clear that conversion of a slave to Christianity did not require emancipation from bondage. The Maryland law of 1671, for instance, decreed that any Christian slave

> is, are and shall att all tymes hereafter be adjudged Reputed deemed and taken to be and Remayne in Servitude and Bondage and subject to the same Servitude and Bondage to all intents and purposes as if hee shee they every or any of them was or were in and Subject vnto before such his her or their Becomeing Christian or Christians or Receiving of the Sacrament of Baptizme any opinion or other matter or thing to the Contrary in any wise Notwithstanding.

The humanity of the slaves was subject to no customary protections, nor was it the concern of the government. Neither did the churches exert much influence among the faithful to encourage them to honor the rights of slaves. If ministers persisted in admonishing slaveholders about their Christian obligations to the slaves, they risked arousing suspicions that they opposed slavery and thereby hindered the effectiveness of their mission.

Historian Stanley M. Elkins identified four categories that defined the legal status of slaves in the United States: "'term of servitude', 'marriage and the family', 'police and disciplinary powers over the slave', and 'property and other civil rights'." By the late seventeenth century, slavery had become both a perpetual and an inherited status. Once the law had redefined slavery, the statutes proceeded to decimate slave marriages and families. In custom and practice humanitarian sentiments doubtless prevailed, but Southern slaveholders failed to translate those considerations into laws that might have ensured the inviolability of the slave family and the sanctity of slave marriage. On the contrary, in every confrontation between property and humanity, slave law accommodated the interests of the former. The law could never allow slave marriages or families an independent legal existence without compromising the power of the master. The ruling in the case of *Howard* v. *Howard* (1858) stated what had by that time become the long-standing principle: "The relation of master and slave is wholly incompatible with even the qualified relation of husband and wife, as it is supposed to exist among slaves. . . ."

The astute legal scholar T. R. R. Cobb of Georgia also denied slave marriages status under law. "The contract of marriage not being recognized among the slaves," Cobb wrote, "none of its consequences follow. . . ." Daniel Dulany, attorney general of Maryland, noted that "a slave has never maintained an action against the violator of his bed. A slave is not admonished for incontinence, or punished for fornication or adultery; never prosecuted for bigamy, or petty treason for killing a husband being a slave, any more than admitted to an appeal for murder." In 1858 a North Carolina judge clarified the nature of slave "marriages," writing that "the relation between slaves is essentially different from that of man and wife joined in lawful wedlock. . . . with slaves it may be dissolved at the pleasure of either party, or by the sale of one or both, depending on the caprice or necessity of the owners."

As the offspring of these precarious unions, children had no legal security against separation from their parents. The single exception, as Frederic Bancroft pointed out in *Slave-Trading in the Old South* (1931), was the idiosyncratic law of Louisiana. This "least American of the Southern States," Bancroft wrote, was also the "least inhuman. . . . It forbade sale of mothers from their children less than ten years of age (and *vice versa*) and bringing into the State any slave child under ten years of age without its mother, if living. The penalty for violating either prohibition was from $1,000 to $2,000 and the forfeiture of the slave." Slave children, of course, also derived their legal condition from their mother. Had the children's legal status followed their father's condition, children born of free black or, more disturbing, of white fathers would have been free. Not only would this situation have created a free mulatto population throughout the South, it would also have deprived masters of additional slave property. Yet, the law rendered the fathers of slave children nonentities. The decision in *Frazier* v. *Spear* (1811) established the legal precedent, stating that "the father of a slave is unknown in our law."

However humanely enforced, justice, discipline, and punishment rested solely in the hands of the master. The law granted him complete power. "On our estates," explained Southern journalist and political economist J. D. B. De Bow, "we dispense with the whole machinery of public police and public courts of justice. Then we try, decide, and execute the sentences in thousands of cases, which in other countries would go into the courts." Southern slave law deplored "cruel and unusual punishment," but the great weakness of the legal system was the universal prohibition against permitting slaves to testify in court, save against each other. Confronted with the indictment of a master "for cruelly beating his own slave," a Virginia judge declined to adjudicate the case of *Commonwealth* v. *Turner* (1827). "Without any proofs that the common law did ever protect the slave against minor injuries from the hand of the master," he reasoned, ". . . where are we to look for the power which is now claimed of us?" "The battery of a slave, without special enactment," Cobb concurred, "could not be prosecuted criminally." The reason was self-interest. What master in his right mind would willfully destroy a valuable piece of his own property? This assumption had permeated the Virginia statute of 1669, which read in part, "It cannot be presumed that prepensed malice (which alone makes murther Felony) should induce any man to destroy his own estate." Admitting that slavery was morally vulnerable on this point of law, Cobb similarly resolved that "where the battery was committed by the master himself, there would be no redress, for the reason given in Exodus 21:21, 'for he is his money.' The powerful protection of the master's private interest would of itself go far to remedy this evil."

This same logic prompted Judge Thomas Ruffin of North Carolina to render one of the most famous decisions in Southern judicial history in the case of *State* v. *Mann* (1829). A lower court had ruled that the law vouchsafed a master to be charged with battery upon a slave, much as a parent could be charged with child abuse for administering an excessively severe punishment. Ruffin dissented, arguing that the relation between master and slave was unlike the relation between parent and child inasmuch as the law must give masters absolute authority whereas it restricted parental authority. The power of the master, Ruffin insisted, must never be allowed to fall within the purview of the law or come under the jurisdiction of the courts. In his opinion Ruffin brilliantly encapsulated the dehumanizing logic of American slave law:

> There is no likeness between the cases. They are in opposition to each other and there is an impassable gulf between them—the difference is that which exists between freedom and slavery—and a greater cannot be imagined. In the one the end in view is the happiness of the youth born to equal rights with that governor on whom the duty devolves of training the young to usefulness in a status which he is afterward to assume among free men.

Slavery, Ruffin continued, was an entirely different matter:

> With slavery it is far otherwise. The end is the profit of the master, his security and public safety; the subject, one doomed in his own person, and his posterity, to live without knowledge, and without the capacity to make anything his own, and to toil that another may reap the fruits. What moral considerations, such as a father might give to a son, might be addressed to such a being, to convince him what, it is impossible but that the most stupid must feel and know can never be true–that he is thus to labour upon a principle of natural duty, or for the sake of his own personal happiness, such services can only be expected from one who has no will of his own; who surrenders his will in implicit obedience to that of another. Such obedience is the consequence only of uncontrolled authority over the body. There is nothing else which can operate to produce the effect. The power of the master must be absolute to render the submission of the slave perfect. I must freely confess my sense of the harshness of this proposition, I feel it as deeply as any man can. And as a principle of moral right, every person in his retirement must repudiate it. But in the actual condition of things, it must be so. There is no remedy. This discipline belongs to the state of slavery.

A man of genuinely humane temperament, Ruffin must surely have understood that no people who thought themselves civilized and Christian could long endure the implications of such a verdict.

Even the willful and unprovoked murder of a slave, which was a criminal offense, strained the parameters of the law. "It would seem that from the very nature of slavery, and the necessarily degraded social position of the slave," Cobb asserted, "many acts would extenuate the homicide of a slave, and reduce the offence to a lower grade, which would not constitute a legal provocation if done by a white person." A North Carolina law of 1798 had earlier specified the restrictions on what constituted the murder of a slave. The law prohibited "maliciously killing a slave" but did not apply to a runaway, to a slave killed "in the act of resistance to his lawful owner," or to a slave "dying under moderate correction." According to Cobb, the law in South Carolina mandated that, in the absence of competent and credible witnesses to the killing of a slave, an affidavit from the accused declaring his innocence was admissible in his defense at trial.

Southern law denied the slaves their humanity. Not only could husbands not be husbands, wives not be wives, and parents not be parents, but the law, as Ruffin understood, required that slaves have no will of their own. Slaves had no right to their own persons, nor to those of their husband, wife, children, or parents. Slaves could not own, inherit, or bequeath property without the master's consent. Slaves could enter into no contracts or agreements, including marriage, for their word and their bond had no legal validity. Slaves under law were wholly dependent upon, and submissive to, their master, the perfect instrument of his will. In the case of *Brandon* v. *Planters' and Merchants' Bank of Huntsville* (1828), Alabama Supreme Court Justice Crenshaw made explicit the legal definition of slavery when he proclaimed that "a slave is in absolute bondage; he has no civil right, and can hold no property, except at the will of the master.... Slaves have no legal rights in things, real or personal; but whatever they may acquire, belongs, in point of law, to their masters." The fundamental, undeniable, inescapable fact of slavery was that the slaves were property, designated under law as "chattels personal ... to all intents, constructions and purposes whatsoever." The judicial alchemists of the Old South had done something more extraordinary than turn lead into gold; they had transformed men, women, and children into things.

–SHERMAN GREENE,
OAKLAND, CALIFORNIA

References

Frederic Bancroft, *Slave-Trading in the Old South* (Baltimore: Furst, 1931).

John Spencer Bassett, *Slavery and Servitude in the Colony of North Carolina* (Baltimore: Johns Hopkins University Press, 1896).

Bassett, *Slavery in the State of North Carolina* (Baltimore: Johns Hopkins University Press, 1899).

William Hand Browne, ed., *Archives of Maryland*, 72 volumes (Baltimore: Maryland Historical Society, 1883–1972).

Philip Alexander Bruce, *Economic History of Virginia in the Seventeenth Century* (New York & London: Macmillan, 1895).

Helen Tunnicliff Catterall, ed., *Judicial Cases Concerning American Slavery and the Negro*, 5 volumes (Washington, D.C.: Carnegie Institution, 1926–1937).

T. R. R. Cobb, *An Inquiry into the Law of Negro Slavery in the United States of America: To Which Is Prefixed an Historical Sketch of Slavery* (Philadelphia: T. & J. W. Johnson / Savannah: W. T. Williams, 1858).

Thomas Cooper and David J. McCord, eds., *The Statutes at Large of South Carolina*, 10 volumes (Columbia, S.C.: Johnston, 1836–1841).

David Brion Davis, *The Problem of Slavery in Western Culture* (Ithaca, N.Y.: Cornell University Press, 1966).

Stanley M. Elkins, *Slavery: A Problem in American Institutional and Intellectual Life* (Chicago: University of Chicago Press, 1959).

Eugene D. Genovese, *Roll, Jordan, Roll: The World the Slaves Made* (New York: Pantheon, 1974).

William Goodell, *The American Slave Code in Theory and Practice: Its Distinctive Features Shown by Its Statutes, Judicial Decisions, & Illustrative Facts* (New York: American & Foreign Anti-Slavery Society, 1853).

Oscar Handlin and Mary Handlin, "Origins of the Southern Labor System," *William & Mary Quarterly*, third series 7 (April 1950): 199–222.

William Waller Hening, *The Statutes at Large: Being a Collection of All the Laws of Virginia, from the First Session of the Legislature in the Year 1619*, 13 volumes (Richmond, Va.: Samuel Pleasants, 1809–1823).

John Codman Hurd, *The Law of Freedom and Bondage in the United States*, 2 volumes (Boston: Little, Brown, 1858, 1862).

Thomas D. Morris, *Southern Slavery and the Law, 1619–1860* (Chapel Hill: University of North Carolina Press, 1996).

Willie Lee Rose, ed., *A Documentary History of Slavery in North America* (New York: Oxford University Press, 1976).

Thomas Ruffin, *The Papers of Thomas Ruffin*, 4 volumes, edited by J. G. deRoulhac Hamilton (Raleigh: North Carolina Historical Commission, 1918–1920).

Philip J. Schwarz, *Twice Condemned: Slaves and the Criminal Laws of Virginia, 1705–1865* (Baton Rouge: Louisiana State University Press, 1988).

Mark V. Tushnet, *The American Law of Slavery, 1810–1860: Considerations of Humanity and Interest* (Princeton: Princeton University Press, 1981).

Julius Yanuck, "Thomas Ruffin and the North Carolina Slave Law," *North Carolina Historical Review*, 21 (November 1955): 456–475.

LEGAL DEFINITION

MAROON COMMUNITIES

Were maroon communities an effective means of resistance to slavery?

Viewpoint: Yes. Maroon settlements throughout the New World gave slaves an opportunity to reclaim their freedom; by provoking desertions and rebellions, maroons had a destructive impact on slavery.

Viewpoint: No. Although concerned with the welfare of bondmen and bondwomen, maroons generally accepted the legitimacy of slavery and frequently held slaves themselves.

Palenques, quilombos, mocambos, cumbes, mambises, and *laderias* emerged everywhere that slavery existed in the New World. In time these communities of runaway slaves came to be known simply as maroons, derived from the Spanish word *cimarrón,* which means "fugitive." Some maroon communities were small and lasted only a year or two, while others encompassed thousands of persons and endured for generations. Maroon communities flourished wherever there existed a black majority of predominantly African-born slaves. The proximity of an inaccessible hinterland also aided the development of maroon societies, providing the slaves not only with a place to which they could flee but also one that they could fortify and defend against attack. The relative absence of these demographic and geographical conditions in North America inhibited the emergence of large maroon settlements there. More than two thousand runaways and their descendants did manage to survive in the Dismal Swamp, located along the border of Virginia and North Carolina. Yet, this community paled by comparison to Palmares in Brazil, the most famous of the maroon settlements, which boasted a population of twenty thousand.

Maroons unleashed havoc against the slaveholding regimes of Latin America and the Caribbean. They raided plantations and settlements and encouraged slave desertion and rebellion. So disruptive and threatening was maroon activity that colonial governments formed special military units (*rancheadores* in Spanish territory; *capitões-do-mato* in Brazil) to combat and destroy these communities. When armed efforts failed to dislodge or annihilate the maroons, colonial officials in Brazil, Colombia, Cuba, Ecuador, Jamaica, Mexico, and Surinam negotiated agreements with them in an effort to restore peace. These treaties commonly recognized the autonomy of the maroons and granted them important territorial concessions in exchange for ending hostilities, returning runaway slaves, and aiding in the suppression of slave rebellions. To the extent that they honored their commitments and collaborated with the authorities, the maroons acquiesced in the perpetuation of slavery.

Although they plagued every slaveholding society in the New World, the maroons often had diffident and equivocal relations with the slaves themselves. The maroons sought to withdraw from slaveholding societies and to restore as many of the patterns of African culture and kinship as they could. They did not invariably challenge the existence of slavery itself.

Viewpoint:
Yes. Maroon settlements throughout the New World gave slaves an opportunity to reclaim their freedom; by provoking desertions and rebellions, maroons had a destructive impact on slavery.

By whatever means available, slaves everywhere in the Western Hemisphere resisted their enslavement. This opposition took various and complex forms. Escape constituted one of the most direct and effective means of defiance. Slaves deserted their masters to protest exceedingly cruel treatment or newly imposed restrictions, to elude a sudden change in the rules of work, or to avoid a harsh punishment. The mountainous terrain of Hispaniola, Jamaica, Cuba, and other Caribbean islands offered runaway slaves protection from capture. In the mountains they could establish inaccessible sanctuaries and defend themselves, if necessary, against a military onslaught. The formation of these maroon communities generally had a corrosive effect on slavery, for they inspired slaves to disaffection, desertion, and, on occasion, rebellion.

By the early seventeenth century, for example, Jamaican maroons had established extensive settlements in the mountains of the eastern and western portions of the island, which the Spanish tried for years unsuccessfully to destroy. The English continued the struggle after they took control of Jamaica in 1655. Far from being contained or eradicated, the Jamaican maroons actually increased their numbers, persuading other slaves to join them. They kept up a steady series of raids on the plantations, seizing food and other provisions as well as encouraging slaves to run away.

In Jamaica a general state of warfare prevailed between the maroons and the English colonial government. So powerful and troublesome had the maroons become that in 1738 the English negotiated a formal peace treaty with them. This momentous document recognized the freedom of the maroons, granted them land and hunting rights, and waived their obligation to pay taxes. In return the maroons agreed to submit to the jurisdiction of colonial courts in all interracial disputes, to ally themselves with the government in wars against foreign enemies, to lure no more slaves out of bondage, to harbor no new runaways, and to help suppress slave uprisings should they occur. Maroon settlements such as the one in Jamaica plagued every slaveholding society in the Caribbean and Latin America in which the terrain provided a hinterland into which slaves could flee. They gave enslaved Africans an opportunity to reclaim the freedom that they had lost.

Unlike the Jamaicans, most maroons did not have the good fortune to come to a political settlement with the authorities governing the regime. Their communities remained small units of dozens or hundreds of persons, sometimes in loose alliance and sometimes culturally and politically hostile to each other. As long as they remained outside the established colonial order, maroons sympathized with the fate of those still enslaved, if for no other reason than their own guerilla activities required intelligence and supplies from informants and supporters on the plantations. Everywhere in the Western Hemisphere, maroons, at one time or another, provoked desertions and slave revolts. They fought and often defeated the military expeditions sent to destroy them. Their success in such endeavors conveyed more to those who remained in bondage about the courage and prowess of black people than any abolitionist pamphlet ever could have.

Short of encouraging escape or rebellion, maroons retaliated to protect slaves from harsh treatment. In the Dutch colony of Surinam, for example, a rebellious leader of the maroon community rebuked an emissary of the government during peace negotiations in 1757, asking how Europeans could so cruelly abuse the slaves. He then offered some advice:

> We desire you to tell the governor and your court that in case they want to raise no new gangs of rebels, they ought to take care that the planters keep a more watchful eye over their own property, and do not trust them so frequently to the hands of drunken managers and overseers, who . . . are the ruin of the colony and wilfully drive to the woods such numbers of stout, active people, who by their sweat earn your subsistence, without whose hands your colony must drop to nothing, and to whom at last, in this disgraceful manner, you are glad to come and sue for friendship.

Brazilian slaves wrote perhaps the most impressive and heroic chapter in the history of maroon resistence to slavery. From the earliest days of slavery in Brazil some Africans regained their freedom by running away. Thousands of runaway camps, called *quilombos* and *mocambos,* sprang up between the sixteenth and the nineteenth centuries. The largest and most famous of the Brazilian maroon settlements was formed at the beginning of the seventeenth century in Pernambuco, one of the most productive and profitable centers of sugar production. It was called Palmares.

For the better part of a century, between 1605 and 1695, runaway slaves and their descendants, swelling to an estimated population of twenty thousand, defended their reconstituted

MAROON COMMUNITIES

MACANDAL

The maroons of Saint Domingue represented a disruptive force to French colonial administration. One of the more notorious runaways was Macandal, who caused fear throughout the island colony in the late 1750s:

It was at the plantation of M. Le Normand de Mézy in Limbé that the negro Macandal, born in Africa, belonged. His hand being caught in the mill, it had been necessary to cut it off, and he was made a herder of animals. He ran away.

During his period of hiding, Macandal made himself famous for the poisonings which spread terror among the negroes and which made them all obey him. He kept an open school for this execrable art. He had agents in all the corners of the colony, and death flew in at his slightest signal. Finally, in his comprehensive plan, he had conceived the infernal project of making all the men who were not blacks disappear from the surface of Saint Domingue. Also, his successes, which went on increasing, had spread an alarm which assured that there would be more. Not the watchfulness of the magistrate, not that of the Government, nothing could come up with the means of catching this wretch. Efforts punished by an almost sudden death served only to terrify the people even more.

One day the negroes of the Dufresne plantation in Limbé had arranged for a big dance there. Macandal, who had gone unpunished for a long time, came to join in the dance.

One young negro, perhaps because of the impression that the presence of this monster had produced on him, came to notify M. Duplessis a surveyor, and M. Trévan, who were on the plantation. They distributed tafia so profusely that the negroes all became drunk and Macandal, in spite of his caution, lost his good sense.

They went to arrest him in a slave hut, from which they led him to a room in one of the ends of the big house. They tied his hands behind his back and for want of irons put on a piece of bridle harness. The two whites wrote to the Cape to tell of the capture and with two negro domestics they kept guard over Macandal, with loaded pistols on the table, where there was a light.

The guards went to sleep. Macandal, perhaps aided by the two blacks, unfastened his hands, put out the candle, opened a window of a gable, threw himself into the prairie, and reached some coffee plants, leaping like a magpie.

The land breeze which was rising made the window hook rattle and woke people up. There was a great uproar. They searched for Macandal, whom the dogs soon found, and recaptured him.

Macandal, who could have escaped if he had used the two pistols on the table instead of fleeing was condemned to be burned alive. This was by an order of the Superior Council, 20 January 1758. Since he had boasted several times that if taken he would escape in different forms, he declared that he would take the shape of a fly to escape from the flames.

Fate having willed that post to which his chain was fastened be rotten, the violent efforts which he made because of the torments of the fire pulled out the screw ring and he leaped out over the funeral pyre.

The blacks cried out: "Macandal is saved!" The panic was wild. All the gates were shut. The detachment of Swiss guards who were on duty at the place of execution had the enclosure cleared out. The jailer Massé wanted to kill him with a sword thrust, but upon the order of the King's Attorney he was bound to a plank and thrown back into the fire.

Although the body of Macandal had been incinerated, many negroes believed even now that he did not die in this torture.

The memory of this creature, for whom epithets are inadequate, still awakens equally sinister ideas. The slaves call both poisons and poisoners "macandals," and this name has become one of the cruelest insults which they can address to each other.

Source: *Médéric-Louis-Elie Moreau de Saint-Méry, A Civilization that Perished: The Last Years of White Colonial Rule in Haiti, translated and edited by Ivor D. Spencer (Lanham, Md.: University Press of America, 1985), pp. 247–256.*

African community against first the Portuguese and then the Dutch, two of the greatest military powers of the age. The Dutch twice sent armies against Palmares and the Portuguese more than a dozen times before they finally destroyed it.

Politically and economically, Palmares was a remarkable achievement for the fugitive slaves of Brazil. It grew into a complex political organism governed by a king with assistance from a minister of justice and various subordinate military officials and civil servants. With power concentrated in relatively few hands, the authorities devised a system of law and justice in which such crimes as treason and murder, but also robbery and adultery, were punishable by death. The penalties for such offenses as robbery and adultery were so extreme because conflicts over property or women could cause internal dissension that might compromise security or tear the community apart.

In the initial years of settlement the Palmarinos endured shortages of virtually all essential goods and provisions. They solved these economic problems by marauding, raiding towns, plantations, and Indian villages in the interior of the country to acquire the supplies they needed. Gradually, they developed a more efficient and productive agricultural and commercial economy. Like other maroon communities throughout Latin America and the Caribbean, the inhabitants of Palmares began to trade with nearby towns and plantations. They exchanged agricultural produce, such as beans, bananas, and sugar cane, for utensils, guns, and ammunition. In time Palmares became more economically diverse and self-sufficient, even managing to support the labor of skilled mechanics and craftsmen.

Militarily, Palmares was a defensive stronghold. Each community within the larger settlement was a veritable fortress, invulnerable to attack. Until the protracted struggle against the Portuguese and the Dutch, the Palmarinos spread themselves across a vast area. The dispersal of the community served them well against the initial incursions, since the attacking forces could not launch coordinated assaults against each enclave. In addition, the destruction of one or more hamlets was not devastating to Palmares as a whole. The Palmarinos simply reorganized themselves and resumed the guerilla war that eventually wore their enemies out.

In 1678, however, the Portuguese inflicted terrible casualties on the Palmarinos, whose king, called the *ganga-zumba,* sued for peace. The Portuguese offered terms that they considered generous, including formal recognition of Palmares and freedom for its residents, the appointment of the *ganga-zumba* as a royal field commander in the Portuguese military, and the acknowledgment that the Palmarinos owned the land on which they lived—land that had long attracted the interest of Portuguese planters and merchants. In exchange, the Palmarinos agreed to give up some of the territory now under their control, to return all runaway slaves, and to help suppress Indian uprisings and slave rebellions.

The treaty divided the Palmarinos into factions, one of which, under the leadership of the war chief, who was called the *zumbi,* repudiated the agreement, assassinated the *ganga-zumba,* and resumed the struggle. Whatever his motives for renewing the conflict, the decision of the *zumbi* to stake everything on a war to the death against the Portuguese resulted in the slaughter of his staunchest followers, the enslavement of countless others, and the destruction of the independent community that he had sought to preserve.

During the final phase of the war the Portuguese crushed the Palmarino communities one by one. The beleaguered Palmarinos concentrated their forces at Macaco but at last succumbed to a combined frontal assault of Portuguese troops and their Indian allies. A formidable threat to the Portuguese slaveholding regime in Brazil for nearly a century, the maroon community at Palmares fell only after a long, expensive, and bloody campaign that, if nothing else, weakened the regime by creating internal dissension among the colonists and requiring the expenditure of resources that might more profitably have been spent to fund economic and social development.

In the British North American colonies and later the United States, small maroon communities harassed the slaveholders of the South from the seventeenth century until the end of the Civil War (1861–1865). Authorities in Virginia, for example, expressed concern in the 1670s over the possibility of a slave revolt but were even more disturbed about reports that maroons operated in every part of the colony. During the eighteenth century, Virginians suppressed a vigorous maroon community located in the Blue Ridge Mountains but had constant trouble with others in the Dismal Swamp, which they could not root out.

The area in and around the Dismal Swamp, situated along the border between Virginia and North Carolina, provided runaway slaves with the most favorable location in which to build houses, plant crops, and raise pigs and fowl. Toward the end of the seventeenth century the maroon communities established there had grown larger and more stable, evoking fears among whites of a general slave insurrection. Punitive expeditions destroyed these maroon settlements and prevented the runaways from consolidating guerrilla bases. By the late antebellum period the maroon problem in Virginia had diminished. In Georgia and South Carolina, however, a similar scenario developed, with small groups of maroons waging sporadic warfare, suffering defeat, and regrouping without ever managing to consolidate their forces, as had their counterparts in Jamaica, Brazil, Surinam, Cuba, Saint Domingue, and elsewhere throughout Latin America and the Caribbean. During the nineteenth century the center of maroon activity in the United States shifted to the southwestern frontier, especially Louisiana, and to Florida, where the Seminole Indians offered refuge to runaway slaves and staged a major confrontation with the American government.

From the earliest days of slavery, whites expressed concern about the collaboration of blacks and Indians and took measures to prevent it. White fears rested on some evidence of mutual sympathy and support among blacks and Indians. During the seventeenth and eighteenth centuries various tribes ignored treaty obligations to return runaway slaves and, instead, provided them refuge. In the nineteenth century, runaways sought and received protection from some Indian communities, especially in the Southwest.

The Second Seminole War (1835–1842) in Florida was the most dramatic and important venture in black and Indian cooperation. Runaway slaves established small colonies within the political framework of the Seminole nation and gradually insinuated themselves into Indian life. The Second Seminole War had several causes, but among the most vital was the unwillingness of the Indians to surrender the blacks whom they had come to regard as members of their families and communities. Blacks fought with such tenacity that American officers thought them the most fierce and determined enemies they encountered and depicted the campaign against the Seminoles as a struggle with black maroons and their Indian allies. By itself, the Second Seminole War was the most expensive Indian war in American history. Although the United States prevailed, the war cost approximately 1,600 American lives and a staggering $20 million. With victory came the galling admission that the government could hound blacks and Indians but could neither intimidate them nor impose its will upon them. American peace negotiators had to make the major concession of permitting the blacks to migrate westward with those Seminoles who chose to depart for Indian Territory.

In its scope and its heroism black participation in the Second Seminole War deserves to rank with that of the maroon conflicts in Jamaica, Surinam, and Brazil. The maroons of the United States, as Eugene D. Genovese has

suggested, might have failed the slaves by being too few in number to spark a general rebellion, but like maroons everywhere they contributed to the slaves' effort to make a better life for themselves in bondage and held out the hope for an eventual escape from slavery. Those who deserted the plantations and took to the woods, swamps, and highlands compelled masters to accord their slaves better treatment, if only to avoid further losses. Less tangibly, the maroons provided a constant reminder not only that slaves could flee but that they could also offer armed resistance.

—MEG GREENE,
MIDLOTHIAN, VIRGINIA

**Viewpoint:
No. Although concerned with the welfare of bondmen and bondwomen, maroons generally accepted the legitimacy of slavery and frequently held slaves themselves.**

Maroons occupied an ambiguous position in the slaveholding colonies and nations of the Western Hemisphere. They challenged the power of the slaveholding regimes but did not consistently oppose slavery itself. They assimilated elements of American and European culture, but in different ways and to varying degrees sought to restore as much of African life as they could recall. Fighting for their survival, they cultivated close relations with slaves, upon whom they often relied for food, supplies, and information, and whom they trusted to remain silent. In time, though, relations between maroons and slaves became strained.

Two circumstances deepened this antagonism. First, colonial authorities sometimes offered valuable incentives, such as peace treaties, land, or guarantees of freedom, to the maroons in exchange for capturing runaways or helping to crush slave rebellions. If maroon communities sometimes met their treaty obligations with indifference, or allowed them to slip altogether, they also, at other times, honored their commitments and did their part to contain or quell slave unrest. Ample evidence exists of such collaboration with whites.

In 1738, for example, the British governor of Jamaica, Edward Trelawney, proposed to negotiate a settlement with rebellious maroons. The "Articles of Pacification with the Maroons of Trelawney Town, concluded March 1, 1738" granted freedom and autonomy to the maroons

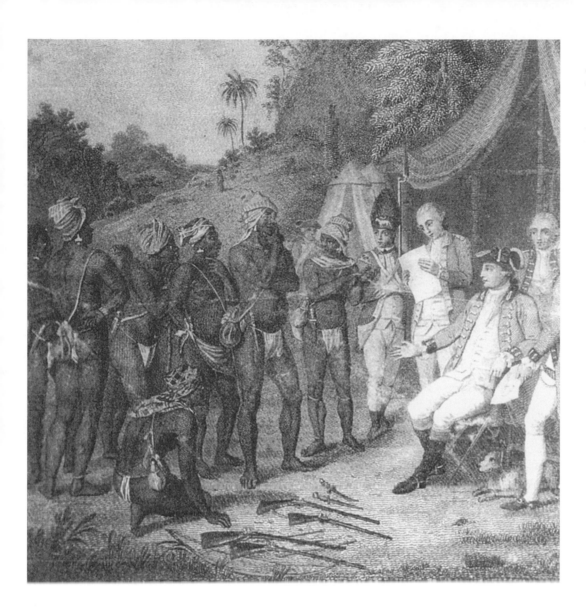

along with possession of designated lands, which they could cultivate as they wished as long as they agreed to sell the produce only in accordance with prescribed commercial regulations. In addition, the maroons obtained hunting rights. They agreed to pay homage to the royal governor, to submit to the jurisdiction of the white courts in all interracial disputes, and to petition the government for permission to execute a death sentence on one of their own. Two white men whom the governor appointed were to live among the maroons and function as governors-general to ensure that the maroons complied with the peace accords. Simultaneously, Captain Cudjoe, the maroon leader, attained official recognition as an officer of the British Crown.

More important than these territorial, economic, legal, and ceremonial achievements, the Jamaican maroons agreed to help the English repel foreign invasion and to capture and return all recent runaway slaves to their rightful owners.

More ominously from the slaves' point of view, the "Articles" required that

> The said Captain Cudjoe and his successors do use their best endeavors to take, kill, suppress, or destroy either by themselves, or jointly with any other number of men, commanded on that service by his excellency, the Governor, or commander in chief for the time being, all rebels wheresoever they be, throughout the island, unless they submit to the same terms of accommodation granted to Captain Cudjoe and his successors.

This compromise initiated a new stage in the relations between the maroons and the slaves as support gave way to animosity. The maroons upheld their part of the arrangement. They ruthlessly tracked down runaways, killing so many that the British at last offered a bounty for all taken alive. The maroons also attacked and destroyed new colonies of runaways with such efficiency that they jeopardized their own political cohesion and survival. British authorities frequently voiced their conviction that the military prowess of the maroons was instrumental in discouraging slave rebellions.

The full consequences of these actions became apparent only in 1795 when the Trelawney maroons themselves staged an uprising. Growing maroon suspicions about changes in British administration and intensifying quarrels over land ownership were the sources of the crisis. The incident that triggered it, however, was the arrest of two maroons. As punishment for their offenses the magistrate ordered them to be whipped, with slaves administering justice. The maroons were outraged. They cared nothing for the culprits, whom they themselves would probably have hanged, but they could not tolerate the degradation of having slaves carry out the sentence. "Do not subject us to insult and humiliation," the maroons complained to the British, "from the very people to whom we are set in opposition." During the Maroon War of 1795–1796 the Trelawney maroons had to fight the British without allies. They received no sympathy from the slaves and no help from other groups of maroons. The Accompong maroons, in fact, assisted the British in subduing the Trelawney rebels. The British policy of "divide and rule" had once more worked to perfection.

Other reasons existed for tension between maroons and slaves in addition to the tactics of colonial governments. The growing number of Creole, or native-born, slaves during the nineteenth century and the widening recess that opened between them and African-born maroons was the second cause of hostilities. African-born slaves had been instrumental in founding maroon communities, and the societies they built reflected those origins. Although Creoles sometimes became important leaders in a maroon community, they accounted for far fewer maroons than did Africans. Creoles' knowledge of the masters' language and their familiarity with the culture and customs enabled them to hide out in towns and cities, blending in more readily with the free black population if one existed. Native-born runaways had options, limited though they might have been, and did not always need to join maroon communities to assert and preserve their freedom.

Even when maroons expressed concern for the welfare of the slaves, they also revealed a willingness to leave slavery intact. Maroons might have challenged the abuses of slaveholders, and clearly did not wish to live as slaves themselves. At the same time, however, they accepted the legitimacy, or at least the reality, of slavery as a matter of course. Indeed, the maroons themselves sometimes held slaves. They seem to have practiced the mild form of slavery reminiscent of the kind ostensibly practiced in Africa. Without the testimony of the bondmen and bondwomen, it is impossible to determine just how benign a form of slavery existed in the maroon communities. The slaves themselves might have seen the matter a little differently.

In regions where the police power of the regime faltered and the influence and power of the maroons spread, as happened throughout Latin America and the Caribbean, the maroons offered slaves a measure of protection from abuse and brutality. The police power in the United State remained overwhelming, and as a consequence the maroons there found themselves constantly on the defensive.

Maroons and Indians sometimes established alliances against whites, but more commonly they remained strangers to one other. The blacks who entered the Indian communities could neither reconstruct an African world, as had the maroons in Jamaica and Brazil, nor could they fashion in any meaningful sense an Indian-African society. Either blacks acculturated to Indian ways, becoming Indians in essential respects, or they lived as inferiors, standing in relation to the Indians much as they stood in relation to whites. The Indian settlements that did absorb runaway slaves provided little opportunity for the development of an African American alternative to plantation slavery, thereby diminishing the chances for the emergence of a large-scale maroon community. The great centers of maroon activity and strength, such as Brazil, Jamaica, Surinam, Saint Domingue, and Cuba, either had few Indians or Indians so hostile to blacks that the blacks had to rely entirely on their own resources to survive.

Like the British Crown, the government of the United States implemented a classic policy of "divide and rule" to erode whatever solidarity had ripened between blacks and Indians. A mutual understanding among blacks, Indians, and even some poor whites had emerged during the seventeenth century, when Indians and blacks endured enslavement and many whites labored as indentured servants under conditions that rivaled those of the slaves. From time to time this sympathy flowered into collaboration. Yet, as Indian slavery and white indentured servitude waned, blacks became increasingly isolated in colonial society. Blacks and Indians sometimes established alliances against whites but more commonly were estranged from one another.

By the same token, slaves benefited from the hostility that existed between whites and Indians, sometimes earning their freedom by fighting with whites against native peoples. In Virginia under the English and in Louisiana under the French, slaves went into battle against Indians who were fighting to prevent the advance of

European settlement. The participation of blacks in these campaigns helps to explain the Indians' characterization of black troops as "black white men." Meanwhile, Native Americans, especially those in South Carolina and Louisiana, helped to hunt down runaways and extinguish slave rebellions. Effective white manipulation of both Indians and blacks significantly reduced possibilities for the organization of stable maroon communities in the North American colonies and later in the United States. In the South these small groups of runaway slaves, which may be called "maroons" only as a courtesy, often degenerated into bands of outlaws who preyed upon blacks, whites, and Indians without discrimination. Slaves refused to betray them, not from a sense of concord and solidarity but from fear of savage and terrifying reprisals.

Maroons everywhere defied the power of the masters and attempted to compel them to treat their slaves with greater humanity. Equally certain, however, as Eugene D. Genovese has shown, is that the ambiguous course the maroons followed inhibited the development of a revolutionary ideology in the quarters that might have inspired slaves to challenge the legitimacy of slavery itself. Immediate survival was paramount; enduring freedom would have to wait.

—MARK G. MALVASI,
RANDOLPH-MACON COLLEGE

References

Roger Bastide, *African Civilization in the Americas* (New York: Harpers, 1972).

Gilberto Freyre, *The Masters and the Slaves: A Study in the Development of Brazilian Civilization,* translated by Samuel Putnam, second revised edition (New York: Knopf, 1964).

Eugene D. Genovese, *From Rebellion to Revolution: Afro-American Slave Revolts in the Making of the Modern World* (Baton Rouge: Louisiana State University Press, 1979).

Barbara Kopytoff, "The Development of Jamaican Maroon Ethnicity," *Caribbean Quarterly,* 22 (June–September 1976): 33–50.

Kopytoff, "The Early Political Development of Jamaican Maroon Societies," *William & Mary Quarterly,* 35 (April 1978): 287–307.

Kopytoff, "Jamaican Maroon Political Organization: The Effects of the Treaties," *Social and Economic Studies,* 25 (June 1976): 87–105.

Sidney Mintz, *Caribbean Transformations* (Chicago: Aldine, 1974).

Edmund S. Morgan, *American Slavery, American Freedom: The Ordeal of Colonial Virginia* (New York: Norton, 1975).

Gerald W. Mullin, *Flight and Rebellion: Slave Resistance in Eighteenth-Century Virginia* (London: Oxford University Press, 1972).

Orlando Patterson, "Slavery and Slave Revolts: A Socio-Historical Analysis of the First Maroon War, 1655–1740," *Social and Economic Studies,* 19 (September 1970): 289–325.

Patterson, *The Sociology of Slavery: An Analysis of the Origins, Development, and Structure of Negro Slave Society in Jamaica* (London: Associated University Presses, 1967).

Richard Price, ed., *Maroon Societies: Rebel Slave Communities in the Americas* (Garden City, N.Y.: Anchor, 1973).

Vera Rubin and Arthur Tuden, eds., *Comparative Perspectives on Slavery in New World Plantation Societies* (New York: New York Academy of Sciences, 1977).

Stuart B. Schwartz, *Sugar Plantations in the Formation of Brazilian Society* (Cambridge: Cambridge University Press, 1985).

Frank Tannenbaum, *Slave & Citizen: The Negro in the Americas* (New York: Vintage, 1946).

MASTER-SLAVE RELATIONS

Was the relationship between masters and slaves characterized by cruelty?

Viewpoint: Yes. Relations between masters and slaves were of necessity based on harsh discipline, punishment, and degradation.

Viewpoint: No. Paternalism defined relations between masters and slaves. Although paternalism grew out of the need for discipline, slaves used the paternalist ethos to insist that the masters live up to their obligations to care for them and to recognize their humanity.

Slaves in the antebellum South faced a variety of circumstances. Some lived and worked on large plantations with hundreds of other slaves; most resided on small farms and labored in the fields alongside their masters. Some slaves rarely laid eyes on the man who owned them; others knew their master and his family intimately. A relatively small number of slaves lived and worked in cities, enjoying a freedom of movement and association about which their counterparts on isolated farms and plantations could only dream. The existence of such wide variations has made it nearly impossible for historians to generalize about the nature of slavery and the treatment of slaves.

Masters were neither uniformly cruel nor universally kind. Slaves usually did not live in constant fear and torment, though they never forgot—indeed, their masters never allowed them to forget—that they were not free. The close personal relations that often existed between masters and slaves in the South engendered both kindness and cruelty, both affection and hatred. Historian Eugene D. Genovese has characterized relations between masters and slaves as "paternal." Genovese, however, was careful to indicate that paternalism did not automatically or necessarily imply benevolence. Paternalism, as Genovese defined and applied it, meant that slave owners acted the part of the father to their slaves, taking a personal interest in their lives, supervising their labor, looking after their welfare, disciplining their excesses, and punishing their transgressions. Like any responsible parents, the masters offered guidance and protection to their "children" but in return expected work, obedience, gratitude, devotion, and even love. In *The Religious Instruction of the Negro in the United States* (1842), Reverend Charles Colcock Jones Sr. summarized the paternalist ethos, writing that the slaves "were placed under our control . . . not exclusively for our benefit but theirs also. . . . We cannot disregard this obligation thus *divinely imposed,* without forfeiting our humanity, our gratitude, our consistency, and our claim to the spirit of christianity [*sic*] itself."

Not all slaveholders, even those who believed that they knew what was best for their slaves and so interfered in every aspect of their lives, took seriously admonitions such as the one that Jones had issued. These efforts to control their slaves frequently led to resentment, cruelty, and violence. As many historians have pointed out, the slaveholders were a varied lot, running the gamut from humanitarians to sadists, with the majority falling somewhere between these two extremes. Regarding the slaves as perpetual children, most masters assumed that they had to threaten them and on occasion to make good on their threats by inflicting some form of corporal punishment. At the same time, most slaveholders tried to avoid excessive severity and did not make a habit of punishing slaves randomly or for trivial offenses. Yet, masters also did not shrink from making an example of a wayward or unruly slave when they deemed such instruction necessary to send a message to the individual and the community. The threat of punishment was real and constant, and few slaves could entirely shield themselves from it.

Viewpoint:
Yes. Relations between masters and slaves were of necessity based on harsh discipline, punishment, and degradation.

To argue that relations between masters and slaves were not cruel would be morally uncomfortable for most people, requiring an acknowledgment that the relationship was not adversarial and that slavery was morally acceptable within the context of a free society. The experience of slavery, for both black and white, was not monolithic. Slaves and masters reacted and responded to the institution in different ways, each as unique as the individual. Some slaves responded by being the "model" servant: docile, obedient, industrious, and loyal. Some masters were kind, generous, benevolent, and paternalistic. Others reacted in the opposite extreme: as crafty and insolent slaves or as indifferent and unreasonable masters. Many personalities would have fallen into the large chasm of possibilities between, fashioning a variety of coping mechanisms to survive the experience of being someone's property or of owning human chattel.

Through decades of extensive research, scholars have exposed much about the day-to-day experience of slave life. A slave's routine required hard work, long hours, harsh living conditions, unsatisfactory food, and minimal shelter and clothing. Slaves were expected to work long days, or as one former slave put it, "from dark to dark." Field hands stayed in the fields all day; there they ate their midday meal, took whatever breaks they were allowed, and worked in good weather and bad. Former slave and abolitionist leader Frederick Douglass wrote: "We worked in all weathers. It was never too hot or too cold; it could never rain, blow, hail, or snow too hard for us to work in the field. Work, work, work was scarcely more the order of the day than of the night. The longest days were too short for him [his master] and the shortest nights too long for him." Another former slave recalled, "we worked in the fields all the light hours, plowing and planting and sech like, and at nights we would shell corn for the fowls, and do other things.

When the moon shine some nights we would work in the fields all night."

Their meals consisted mostly of cornmeal, pot liquor (a broth left over from cooking), buttermilk, molasses, and sometimes pork, although many slaves did not have the opportunity to eat meat except during holidays. Some masters allowed their slaves to tend their own gardens in the summer. Masters usually provided their slaves with one set of clothes for each season and a pair of shoes each year. Unfortunates who outgrew or wore out their shoes and clothes usually went without until it was time to get new ones, regardless of the weather or the season. As soon as children were old enough to be useful, they worked in the fields with their parents, sharing in the long hours and hard labor. At the end of the workday they returned to their small frame cabins, which often had dirt floors and were sparsely furnished, and, as Hector Godbold, a former slave whose testimony was recorded during the Great Depression, remembered, "My Gawd, sleep right dere on de floor."

This routine was personally supervised by an overseer whom the owner hired to make sure that everyone was awake and reporting for work on time, that they stayed at work all day, and that they remained on the plantation. Since overseers often handled the dirty work, such as whippings and other forms of discipline, on some plantations the master could maintain the image of being a good man since someone else executed his expectations. Former slaves sometimes recalled that they had good masters, but they never praised their overseers.

However, long hours, hard work, privation, and child labor were common problems for all laborers in the nineteenth century in America and elsewhere. These factors, as unpleasant as they are, do not necessarily establish cruelty as the basis of relations between masters and slaves. Slave owners and apologists for slavery were fond of saying that although their slaves had to work hard, they were treated better than most free workers in America and Europe. In the antebellum period, industrial workers in New England worked twelve-hour shifts under the constant scrutiny of a shift supervisor, and their living quarters, diets, and material possessions were often scarcely better than those provided for slaves. Child labor was as common in other parts of the country and in Europe as it was in

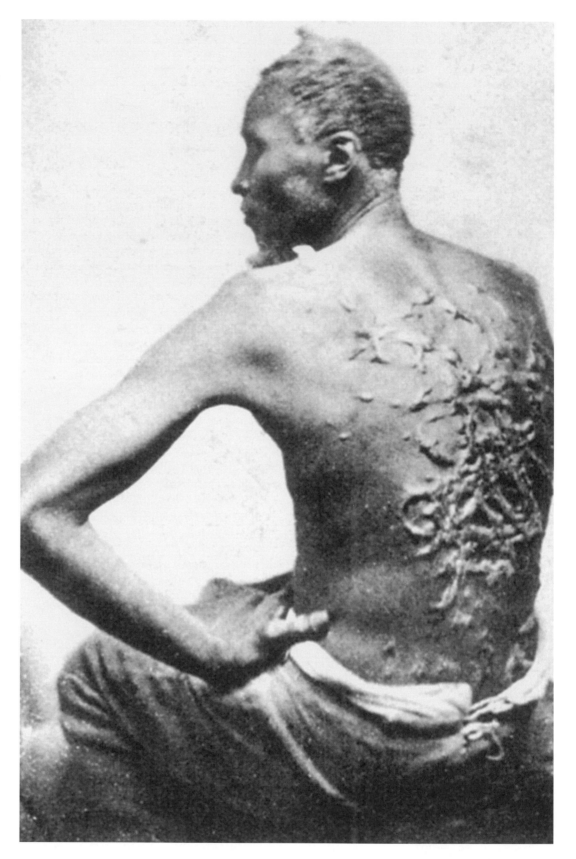

Photograph of Gordon, an escaped slave from Mississippi, with scars from whippings, 1863

(Illinois State Historical Library, Springfield)

MASTER-SLAVE RELATIONS

the American South. Most poor Southern whites were materially no better off than slaves. For many Southerners at the time, this argument seemed cogent and compelling. Slavery, they could reassure themselves, was a beneficial condition for the slave because it provided for his needs, but beyond that it taught him the virtues of industry, self-discipline, and productive labor. Introducing their chattel to Christianity, they argued, was the crowning achievement of this civilizing beneficence.

However, substantial differences existed among the factory worker, the poor white, and the slave. The factory worker was a free laborer who could in theory bargain to improve his circumstances. He could work where he pleased and earn a wage, however meager it might be. He was far more likely to be literate or to have the opportunity to become literate. Members of the working class might have had a low socio-economic status, but unlike slaves they were not universally despised and reviled as subhuman. Northerners had their own elaborate hierarchy of categories in which to position newly arrived ethnic groups. The stigma that had attached to the Irish in the middle of the nineteenth century eventually transferred to the Italians, Portuguese, Greeks, and southern and eastern Europeans by the end of the century as the descendants of Irish immigrants began to enter mainstream American society. The stigma of being a slave and of being black, however, never disappeared.

Many Americans, whether they owned slaves or not, assumed that blacks were inherently inferior to whites. Religious leaders often cited scriptural references proving that the God of the white man was not the God of the black man. Or they asserted that sin, the devil, and blackness had an inexorable connection. Even enlightened men such as third president of the United States, Thomas Jefferson, believed that blacks were naturally the physical, intellectual, and moral inferiors of whites. Senator John C. Calhoun of South Carolina asserted that freedom would be a mental burden to slaves. His conclusion was based on 1840 census data from which he extrapolated that there was a higher incidence of insanity among free blacks in the North than among slaves in the South. At best, many slave owners argued, slaves were child-like and stupid; at worst, they represented evil in human form or were a race denounced by a highly particular God.

These stereotypes were irrational, but deliberately so. Despite contentions that slaves were naturally child-like, a common complaint among slave owners was how cunning slaves could be or how maliciously clever they were at avoiding work. If slaves were the agents of sin and the devil, they were certainly brought into perilously intimate proximity to the master and his family. If they were the race rejected by God, slave owners discouraged the practice of black folk religions and instead lavished upon their slaves the more submissive teachings of Christianity. In contradiction to the argument that slaves were mentally inferior, the masters tried to prevent them from learning how to read and write, a prohibition that could only be based on the assumption that with instruction the slaves were as capable as anyone else of becoming literate. Therefore, it was necessary for white society to create a separate set of laws with harsh penalties to force blacks to remain in a condition of servitude. According to town ordinances for free and enslaved blacks published in 1864 in the *Western Democrat,* a North Carolina newspaper, free blacks caught fraternizing with slaves at night or on Sundays were fined, or whipped if they could not pay the fine. Slaves could not roam after dark without permission. If caught, they were jailed and beaten. No black, free or slave, could carry a firearm or any other type of weapon. Such laws further marginalized the slaves.

Masters knew that their slaves were not one-dimensional beings who were merely extensions of their own wills; in part, the complex morass of laws, conventions, and punishments evinced as much. Slave owners frequently had to intervene in disagreements that occurred among slaves over work, personality, or family conflicts. Masters sometimes lamented in their diaries that their slaves were obstinate, "sassed" them, or were too smart for their own good. Perhaps the most egregious aspect of the relationship between masters and slaves was that to maintain order and the upper hand in the arrangement, the masters had to caricature the slaves in an effort to make them seem less than human, thereby legitimizing the system of bondage. This belief and the practice that followed from it established cruelty as the basis of master-slave relations. There is no other explanation to justify the "benevolent" master taking slave children away from their mothers and selling them to speculators, who would in turn resell them in distant markets, guaranteeing that mother and child would never see each other again. Slave auctions were degrading and terrifying by design. William Wells Brown was leased to a slave trader who required him to manage and organize his human wares in the "Negro pen," the holding area in which slaves about to be sold were kept before the auction began. Brown had the unpleasant task of presenting the slaves for the buyers' scrutiny, making sure that they were dressed and situated in several artificial scenes: "Some were set to dancing, some to jumping, some to singing and some to playing cards. This was done to make them appear happy. My business was to see that they were placed in those situations before the arrival of purchasers, and I have often set them to dancing when their cheeks were wet with tears." Buyers approached the slaves as though they were livestock: "They 'xamined you just like they do a horse; they look at your teeth and pull your eyelids back and look at your eyes and feel you just like you was a horse."

How could a slave owner rationalize excessive punishments for a variety of offenses such as expressing an opinion, not wanting to work in grueling conditions, or running away? Whippings were always brutal and humiliating. Henry Lewis McGaffey remembered, "Old marse was hard on his slaves; he made 'em work hard and I seed him many times tie his slaves and strip dem ter de waist an' beat 'em til de skin would break. Once I saw him whip my mammy an' de blood run down her bare back an' den he put salt on it. I cried and he said iffen I didn't shut up he would beat me, den I went behind the kitchen to cry." Others described being beaten by a cabin paddle, which had forty holes in it designed to raise blisters; a cat-o'-nine-tails (a whip of nine knotted cords) was then used to break the blisters, which was followed by a bath of salt water to remove the loose flesh from the slave's back. Many slaves recalled masters or overseers capable of exacting fifty lashes for minor offenses. Whippings were a routine and demeaning part of life for adult slaves. One former slave related, "Well, during slavery, they had a whipping every Thursday . . . everybody got one on Thursday whether you had been bad or not during the week." Slaves knew that if they were disobedient, obstinate, or lazy, they were liable to be punished. Beyond this constant threat was the capricious nature of the punishment. Former slaves recalled whippings for incidents as trivial as dropping and breaking a plate or spilling milk.

What of the slaves who claimed they loved their master, however, or that their master was good to them and always treated them fairly? These comments are usually followed by explanations of having plenty to eat, a good place to live, going to the occasional camp meeting with other slaves, or celebrating the Fourth of July with a picnic and a dance. In some instances slaves might have become the favorites of the master or the mistress who then acted as their advocate, but it was always clear that they were never really part of the family nor would their status change because they were favorites. Feeding and housing one's slaves was the absolute least one could do; the kudos former slaves offered in this area perhaps suggested more about their penury at the time of their inter-

view than about the benevolence of their former masters. Any study of postbellum rhetoric shows the former master's keen interest in his own uncertain welfare and none at all for that of the freedman.

Relations between masters and slaves were cruel by definition because masters willfully participated in a social system deliberately designed to deprive other human beings of the freedom they themselves enjoyed as a birthright. The system required them to vilify, humiliate, and caricature slaves in order to compel their obedience. Douglass described the process of losing his dignity and sense of self as a slave: "I was broken in body, soul, and spirit. My natural elasticity was crushed, my intellect languished, the disposition to read departed, the cheerful spark that lingered about my eye died; the dark night of slavery closed upon me, and behold a man transformed into a brute."

Maintenance of the system required brutal, and often depraved, measures. Slaves were routinely subjected to ill treatment that ranged from verbal abuse to beatings and torture. Families and family life were often deliberately disrupted based on the owners' economic self-interest. When slaves were sold, they were rounded up like livestock and groped and prodded with no regard to the embarrassment or fear that such treatment caused them. Such measures created a legacy of racism that persisted long after slavery ended, which prevented blacks from entering mainstream American society and compelled them instead to live on the margins.

Slave owners and their agents acted to justify and preserve the Southern socio-economic status quo. Many slave owners were in all likelihood fundamentally reasonable people who did not relish the things they had to do to maintain the slave system. Yet, they did them anyway because these actions ultimately served their interests. Although some historians have suggested that slaveholders merely acted according to the mindset and ethos of their time, the antislavery and abolition movements suggest the possibility of alternatives. Planters would not have persisted in their efforts to maintain a troublesome and increasingly inefficient system if they had believed that it was not profitable to do so. Perhaps the main benefit of slavery from the masters' point of view was the preservation of the planter class as the ruling elite of the South. To preserve their status, and the wealth and power that accompanied it, Southern slaveholders, willingly or not, compromised the physical and psychological welfare of the slaves.

–PAULA STATHAKIS,
CHARLOTTE, NORTH CAROLINA

MASTER-SLAVE RELATIONS

Viewpoint:
No. Paternalism defined relations between masters and slaves. Although paternalism grew out of the need for discipline, slaves used the paternalist ethos to insist that the masters live up to their obligations to care for them and to recognize their humanity.

During the last several decades, historians have studied and debated the nature of master-slave relations in the antebellum South. Some scholars, such as Kenneth M. Stampp and Stanley M. Elkins, argued that masters dominated the slaves and that physical and psychological cruelty characterized master-slave relations. Elkins, in fact, concluded that enslavement was so severe that it deprived blacks of their personalities, wills, and culture. Other historians, on the contrary, have maintained that, like slavery itself, the master-slave relation was complex and rife with contradictions. In *Roll, Jordan, Roll: The World the Slaves Made* (1974), Eugene D. Genovese wrote that the "Old South, black and white, created a historically unique kind of paternalist society." African American poet and playwright Imamu Amiri Baraka (neé LeRoi Jones) agreed, adding that slavery was "most of all, a paternal institution." Genovese, however, was careful to point out that paternalism had little to do with a master's feelings of kindness, compassion, or generosity toward his slaves. Rather, Genovese suggested, paternalism emerged from the necessity "to discipline [the slaves] and morally justify a system of exploitation." Paternalism was thus Janus-faced, alternating from kindness, affection, and even love to cruelty, exploitation, and hatred.

The sense of paternalism that prevailed among the slaveholders evolved in part from the paternalist tradition of the Middle Ages. Reciprocal obligations that had bound landlords and serfs in medieval Europe dictated that each estate had certain rights and expectations that the other dare not violate or abridge. At the same time, each had duties toward the other that had to be honored and fulfilled. In the plantation society of the antebellum South, the masters depended upon their slaves not only to work but also to reproduce a labor force. According to the paternalist ethos, the slaves, in exchange for security and sustenance, owed their masters loyalty, obedience, and productive (as well as reproductive) labor. Paternalism, of course, served the material and psychological interests of the master class, enabling the slaveholders to justify an arrangement that otherwise might be exposed as cruel and ruthless exploitation. One may ask what ideology does not serve the interests of those who articulate and perpetuate it? Yet, paternalism also operated in the other direction. It gave the slaves a standard by which to measure, and a means by which to alter, the conduct of their masters. Paternalism, in short, provided the slaves a way to demand that the masters live up to their own best principles and recognize the humanity of the slaves. If the masters wished not only to prosper but also to legitimize their authority, they had little choice but to comply. As Genovese has noted, paternalism thus represented an attempt to acknowledge and to nullify what was perhaps the most troubling contradiction of American slavery. "For the slaveholders," Genovese declared,

> paternalism represented an attempt to overcome the fundamental contradiction in slavery: the impossibility of the slaves' ever becoming the things they were supposed to be. Paternalism defined the involuntary labor of the slaves as a legitimate return to their masters for protection and direction. But, the masters' need to see their slaves as acquiescent human beings constituted a moral victory for the slaves themselves. Paternalism's insistence upon mutual obligations—duties, responsibilities, and ultimately even rights—implicitly recognized the slaves' humanity.

Masters saw their slaves not just as workers but also as extended members of their families. This view in important respects connected with the slaves' expectations about the treatment they ought to receive and ran counter to the legal definition of their status as chattel. The slaves demanded—often implicitly, sometimes explicitly—that their masters treat them as men and women, as human beings, and not as property. The masters' acknowledgment—often implicit, sometimes explicit—of the slaves' humanity fostered an intimacy between them that permeated every aspect of their lives. Again, however, recognition of the slaves' humanity also served the interests of their masters. If nothing else, paternalism reinforced the need on the part of the slaveholders to maintain discipline and control.

On every well-managed plantation the master and, if there was one, the overseer kept order by crafting an intricate regime of work, rewards, and punishments. An elaborate set of rules and regulations also governed every aspect of slave life, although masters rarely, if ever, achieved the total control they sought. The slaveholders, nonetheless, tried to determine and manage even the most trivial aspects of daily living, from the time the slaves awoke, to when and what they ate, to the hour they went to bed—matters that free men and women could assume were individual and private. Many masters doubtless believed that they acted to ensure the slaves' welfare. It

BELLS AND HORNS

John Brown, a slave who lived in Virginia, Georgia, and Louisiana, describes how one of his owners used to discipline him.

To prevent my running any more, Stevens fixed bells and horns on my head. This is not by any means an uncommon punishment. I have seen many slaves wearing them. A circle of iron, having a hinge behind, with a staple and padlock before, which hang under the chin, is fastened round the neck. Another circle of iron fits quite close round the crown of the head. The two are held together in this position by three rods of iron, which are fixed in each circle. These rods, or horns, stick out three feet above the head, and have a bell attached to each. The bells and horns do not weigh less than twelve to fourteen pounds. When Stevens had fixed this ornament on my head, he turned me loose, and told me I might run off now if I liked.

I wore the bells and horns, day and night, for three months, and I do not think any description I could give of my sufferings during this time would convey anything approaching to a faint idea of them. Let alone that their weight made my head and neck ache dreadfully, especially when I stooped to my work. At night I could not lie down to rest, because the horns prevented my stretching myself, or even curling myself up; so I was obliged to sleep crouching. Of course it was impossible for me to attempt to remove them, or to get away, though I still held to my resolution to make another venture as soon as I could see my way of doing it.

Source: *John Brown,* Slave Life in Georgia: A Narrative of the Life, Sufferings, and Escape of John Brown, A Fugitive Slave, Now in England, *edited by L. A. Chamerovzow (London: Watts, 1855).*

was, of course, also good business to make sure that the plantation workforce was well fed and adequately housed.

Then, too, the effort to dictate even the mundane details of life was among the most potent and painful indications of what it meant to be a slave. Unlike the periodic breakup of a family or a brutal beating suffered for some offense against the established order, the day-to-day regimentation of the slaves offered a perpetual and humiliating reminder of how far the master's power extended and how completely the freedom of the slaves was denied.

The slaveholders, naturally, tried to temper interference and discipline with benevolence. They allotted extra rations or bestowed new clothing as acts of generosity for which slaves ought to have been grateful. However mixed their owner's motives might have been, the slaves benefited from the additional food and new clothes. They might even have felt gratitude for the master's largesse at the same time that they recognized their own dependence. From the master's point of view, better and more abundant food and clothing not only confirmed the sense of his own munificence but also increased the likelihood of creating and sustaining a healthy, contented, and productive workforce. Such acts of charity and kindness, however, did not show the slaveholders of the Old South to be exceptionally humane but rather exceptionally powerful. That reality could not have been lost on the slaves.

For their part, the slaves deeply resented the master's continual interference in their lives. The imposition of punishment, in particular, raised their ire. The slaves considered masters who punished frequently or arbitrarily to be "bad," for they violated the unspoken agreement that existed between masters and slaves about what was acceptable behavior. To counter such effrontery, the slaves slowed the pace of work, destroyed property, broke tools, abused animals, stole items, and feigned illness. If the perceived injustices were sufficiently severe, they ran away, burned down plantation buildings, or, on rare occasions, committed murder. Prudent masters understood when their actions had disrupted the fragile balance that characterized their relations with the slaves, and, without making any concessions, simply ignored future infractions until order was restored. Others, though, resorted to the whip. While slaveholders throughout the South decried the use of the lash, the majority had to punish their slaves far more than they cared to admit. If nothing else, corporal punishment served as a visceral reminder of the powerlessness of the slaves before their master's will.

The paternalism that slaveholders of the South practiced thus embodied the dualism inherent in slavery itself. The masters were both cruel and kind, and the slaves both docile and defiant. In time, the tension in this ideology became even more pronounced as slaveholders, in order to protect their property and preserve their way of life, adopted more-repressive slave laws. At the same time, they tried to uphold their obligations as Christian masters to nurture and protect their slaves. Even as the slaveholders reinforced slavery and strengthened their regime, they worked to reform slavery by making it more humane. Had civil war not intervened to cut short their efforts, the reforms might still have failed for the strain within the system might have become unbearable.

The contradictions inherent in slavery probably doomed it to destruction and, in any event, did not go unnoticed by the slave owners, even as they grew more militant and defiant throughout the 1840s and 1850s. Struggling to maintain control over their slaves, many masters began to sense what to them must have been a frightening realization: that the power they wielded was arbitrary and that the potential for abuse of that power was great. They consoled themselves with the thought that the majority of slaveholders were good and humane and that the abuse of slaves was a rarity carried out only by sadists and savages whom no gentleman would tolerate.

Notwithstanding the cruelty and exploitation at the heart of master-slave relations, paternalism enabled the slaves to assert their humanity in ways that the masters had to respect. Profound, complex, ambivalent, and contradictory human emotions characterized the master-slave relation, and no master ever completely controlled his slaves either through paternalism or punishment. As a result, the slaves used paternalism as a way in which to resist bondage, to reject their own dehumanization, to avoid falling into despair, and to keep alive love for one another, faith in God, and hope for the future.

–MEG GREENE,
MIDLOTHIAN, VIRGINIA

References

John F. Bayliss, ed., *Black Slave Narratives* (New York: Macmillan, 1970).

John W. Blassingame, *The Slave Community: Plantation Life in the Antebellum South,* revised edition (New York: Oxford University Press, 1979).

David Brion Davis, *The Problem of Slavery in the Age of Revolution, 1770–1823* (Ithaca, N.Y.: Cornell University Press, 1975).

Stanley M. Elkins, *Slavery: A Problem in American Institutional and Intellectual Life* (Chicago: University of Chicago, 1959).

Fisk University, *Unwritten History of Slavery: Autobiographical Accounts of Negro Ex-Slaves* (Nashville, Tenn.: Social Science Institute, Fisk University, 1945).

George M. Fredrickson, *The Arrogance of Race: Historical Perspectives on Slavery, Racism, and Social Inequality* (Middletown, Conn.: Wesleyan University Press, 1988).

Eugene D. Genovese, *The Political Economy of Slavery: Studies in the Economy and Society of the Slave South* (New York: Pantheon, 1965).

Genovese, *Roll, Jordan, Roll: The World the Slaves Made* (New York: Pantheon, 1974).

Charles Colcock Jones, Sr., *The Religious Instruction of the Negro in the United States* (Savannah, Ga.: Purse, 1842).

Peter Kolchin, *American Slavery, 1619–1877* (New York: Hill & Wang, 1993).

Leslie Howard Owens, *This Species of Property: Slave Life and Culture in the Old South* (New York: Oxford University Press, 1976).

George P. Rawick, ed., *The American Slave. A Composite Autobiography,* first and second series, 19 volumes (Westport, Conn.: Greenwood Press, 1972); first supplemental series, 12 volumes (Westport, Conn.: Greenwood Press, 1977); second supplemental series, 10 volumes (Westport, Conn.: Greenwood Press, 1979).

Kenneth M. Stampp, *The Peculiar Institution: Slavery in the Ante-Bellum South* (New York: Knopf, 1956).

John Woolman, *Some Considerations on the Keeping of Negroes, 1754: Considerations on Keeping Negroes, 1762* (Northampton, Mass.: Gehenna Press, 1970).

MEANS OF RESISTANCE

Did slaves effectively resist their enslavement?

Viewpoint: Yes. Slaves were troublesome property; they ran away, stole, slowed the pace of work, broke tools or pretended not to know how to use them, abused farm animals, and on occasion resorted to arson and murder to resist their masters' power.

Viewpoint: No. Running away, stealing, arson, murder, and other acts of resistance disrupted the plantation routine, but they did nothing to challenge or weaken the master's power and frequently incited retribution.

Outnumbered and outgunned, slaves in the United States faced long odds against the success of any form of resistance, whether individual or collective, manifest or covert. Yet, the slaves did not idly acquiesce in bondage. Often without disrupting the stability and security of the slave-holding regime, the slaves conducted acts of sabotage guaranteed to aggravate even the most benevolent and tranquil master. Slaves worked slowly and inefficiently. They also broke tools, injured or abused farm animals, pretended to misunderstand or "disremember" instructions, and feigned illness. Such actions were neither violent nor dramatic, and they by no means challenged the existence of slavery. At the same time such clandestine gestures enabled the slaves to express their discontent without risking severe punishment for themselves or others. Their conduct, though no doubt irritating to the master, did not defy his authority even while revealing its limitations.

Running away offered a less ambiguous means of resistance and defiance. Drawn to freedom in the northern United States and Canada, most runaways made the perilous journey alone. Approximately one thousand fugitives escaped every year, though many more tried and failed. The majority of runaways, however, stayed nearer to home, hiding in the woods, caves, and swamps within a few miles of where they lived. In time, the masters, overseers, or slave patrols recaptured most of them, or else they returned on their own, never having intended to escape permanently.

Fewer slaves dared a violent confrontation with their master. Some did conspire to murder a hated master or overseer, who then met with an unfortunate "accident," but more often violence against whites arose from opportunity and impulse rather than intrigue. Incited by some intolerable provocation, the assault on a master also prompted flight to evade the anticipated punishment. It is probably impossible for historians to determine the number and frequency of violent encounters between masters and slaves. Such occurrences were common enough to alarm whites, who took careful precautions against, and inflicted severe correction for, such audacity.

The circumstances of slave life that prevailed in the South dictated that acts of resistance were individual rather than cooperative. Under most conditions slave rebellion was sure to fail and elicit swift and merciless reprisals that fell indiscriminately upon the guilty and the innocent. Slaves did collaborate; to bring food and other necessities to runaways hiding in the district; to engage in thievery, arson, and murder; and to protect those guilty of such offenses. Even this cooperation was individual; slaves did not usually make the decision as a community to resist or defy the master. Although they set limits to their own oppression, the slaves remained slaves. Even if slaves were not docile and pliant, even if most were not loyal to their masters, they were also not suicidal. Slaves may have found a variety of ways to irritate their masters and to resist slavery, but most, quite sensibly, proved unwilling to bear the severe punishments meted out to those who disobeyed the rules. They thus submitted, however reluctantly, to the slaveholder's authority, knowing that any attempt to resist could bring terrible retribution not only against those who had roused the master's anger but also against all who were subject to his power and his rage.

Viewpoint:
Yes. Slaves were troublesome property; they ran away, stole, slowed the pace of work, broke tools or pretended not to know how to use them, abused farm animals, and on occasion resorted to arson and murder to resist their masters' power.

Slaves defied the authority and resisted the power of their masters in a variety of ways, most of which stopped short of violence and insurrection. They slowed the pace of work; they broke tools or pretended to have forgotten how to use them; and they injured, neglected, and abused the farm animals entrusted to their care. On occasion they expressed their disaffection more dramatically by stealing or running away. Less frequently, they resorted to arson and murder. Of necessity, the slaves accepted what they could not change, and slavery was one of the miseries about which they could do nothing, or next to nothing. They accommodated to slavery while resisting its ultimate logic, which, had they fully accepted it, would have left them dehumanized and overwhelmed by feelings of guilt and self-hatred. Yet, daily resistance implied acceptance of the status quo rather than a challenge to the existence of slavery. The slaves who chose to burn down plantation buildings, to run away, or to kill embodied a new and more determined, or perhaps a more desperate, form of insubordination.

Most whites in the antebellum South thought blacks were born thieves. Even on the best-managed plantations, plunder was a way of life. Slaves stole as much as they could lay their hands on and carry off, including hogs, chickens, cattle, rice, potatoes, vegetables, and alcohol. Many slaveholders acquiesced in the slaves' thievery. Convinced that blacks were so congenitally predisposed to steal that little could be done to prevent it, masters simply did their best to keep theft within reasonable proportions. The historian Joe Gray Taylor remarked in *Negro Slavery in Louisiana* (1963) that from the master's point of view "thieving habits on the part of the slave were not unforgivable. . . . The slave-

holder might look with a relatively tolerant eye on thefts from the smokehouse or his larder so long as the black thief consumed his loot, but was less tolerant when goods were purloined for trading purposes." Judge John Belton O'Neall made the same point: "Occasional thefts among the tolerably good slaves may be expected."

Stealing, however, was not merely a game the masters allowed the slaves to play. It could, and did, have serious repercussions, especially when financial losses began to accumulate. Slaves, however, had other ideas, and their own sense of right and wrong. The landscape architect Frederick Law Olmsted, who traveled extensively in the South, explained:

> It is told me as a singular fact, that everywhere on the plantation the agrarian notion has become a fixed point of the negro system of ethics: that the result of labor belongs of right to the laborer, and on this ground, even the religious feel justified in using "massa's property" for their own temporal benefit. This they term "taking," and it is never admitted to be a reproach to a man among them that he is charged with it, though "stealing," or taking from another man than their master, and particularly from one another, is so. They almost universally pilfer from the household stores when they have a safe opportunity.

Slaves stole because they were hungry but more often because they were dissatisfied with their diet. In Eugene D. Genovese's *Roll, Jordan, Roll* (1974), Walter Rimm of Texas is quoted as saying: "We has some good eats, but has to steal de best things from de white folks." The slaveholders acknowledged as much. A Virginia planter explained to Olmsted that it was "bad economy, not to allow an abundant supply of food to 'a man's force.' If not well provided for, the negroes will find a way to provide for themselves." Writing in the *Southern Agriculturalist*, another Virginia planter stated that "the very best remedy for hog stealing is to give the rougues [*sic*] a plenty of pork to eat." White standards of morality must have seemed hypocritical if not utterly sardonic to the slaves. Brudder Cotney, a Gullah preacher, asked an embarrassing question as reported in Genovese's *Roll, Jordan, Roll:* "Ef bukra [the white man] neber tief, how come nigger yer [here]? . . . How about de

Notice posted in the
Richmond Examiner
announcing a reward for
a runaway slave, 4
November 1800

(Library of Virginia, Richmond)

Ten Dollars Reward.

RANAWAY on the twelfth day of April laft, GABRIEL, a flave the property of Mrs Mary Bolling, of Peterfburg; obtained leave of abfence for 15 days to go to Mr. Benjamin Marable's in Gloucefter County—and the faid flave not having returned yet, and there being good reafon to believe that he is ftill lurking in that neighbourhood—the above fum will be paid for having him confined in jail fo that his owner gets him again, or a reward of Twenty Dollars, exclufive of what the law allows if brought home. Gabriel is a black man, about 30 years old, long vifage, about 6 feet high, fond of drink, and by trade a weaver. He was purchafed from the eftate of the late Colonel Peyton, and is well known in that part of the country. All perfons are forewarned from harbouring, employing or carrying the faid fellow out of the State.

Richeson Booker.

Peterfburg, October 30, 1800. eotf

tief dat steal nigger not from e mossa [master], but fum e fadder [father] an mudder [mother]?"

Historians such as Herbert Aptheker and Kenneth M. Stampp were among the first to recognize stealing as a form of resistance to slavery. Without making an absolute virtue of theft and deception, Aptheker and Stampp argued that the slaves, like other oppressed peoples, had the right to use any means available to them, including theft, to protect themselves, their families, and their communities from aggression and tyranny.

To an even greater extent than stealing, arson was a practical and impressive instrument of revenge and defiance. "Next to theft," Stampp plausibly affirmed in *The Peculiar Institution* (1956), "arson was the most common slave 'crime,' one which the slaveholders dreaded almost constantly. . . . More than one planter thus saw the better part of a year's harvest go up in flames." Since arson was often difficult to prove, there will forever remain doubts about how many fires the slaves set. Yet, whites, especially in times of political turmoil, sectional tension, or insurrectionary conspiracy, routinely assumed the worst. At the same time no slaveholder wanted to believe the slaves on his plantation capable of such acts of terrorism.

Although economically damaging and psychologically devastating to the master, arson was a mixed blessing to the slaves. An angry slave who burned down the corncrib, the smokehouse, or the distillery deprived his or her fellow slaves of food and drink to pilfer. If fire destroyed the Big House or the cotton crop, the master and his family undoubtedly suffered, but reprisals against the slaves were terrible and often merciless. The master who confronted financial ruin might sell a portion of his slaves to recover his losses. Bankruptcy effected the dispersal of the entire slave community. Nevertheless, those who suspected arson could not but acknowledge the militant defiance of the slaves, even as they remained bewildered about the ingratitude that had motivated such perverse attitudes and actions.

The majority of slave owners, however, insisted that they did not fear their slaves. Most professed to believe that no harm would come to them from their slaves, and that their slaves would protect them if the necessity arose to do so. To be sure, the slaves did not often resort to murder. They killed just often enough to make the masters doubt their convictions about slave loyalty and to justify their insecurity. When young Virginia Frost reproached a slave for impudence, the slave shot her to death. If determined to commit murder, slaves preferred to poison their victims, for no other reason than, in the days before sophisticated forensic science, such crimes regularly escaped detection. There were, of course, other effective but less disguised methods. On 21 September 1861, Mary Boykin Chesnut lamented in her diary about just such an instance:

Last night when the mail came in, I was seated near the lamp. Mr. Chesnut, lying on a sofa at a little distance, called out to me, "Look at my letters and tell me about them."

I began to read one aloud: it was from Mary Witherspoon—and I broke down. Horror and amazement was too much for me. Poor Cousin Betsey Witherspoon was murdered! She did not die peacefully, as we supposed, in her bed. Murdered by her own people. Her negroes.

A few days later Chesnut added in an entry dated 24 September:

William and Cousin Betsy's old maid, Rhody, [are] in jail. Strong suspicion, no proof of their guilt yet. The neighborhood is in ferment. . . . Lynching proposed! . . . Hitherto I have never thought of being afraid of negroes. I had never injured any of them. Why should they want to hurt me? Two-thirds of my religion consists of trying to be good to negroes because they are so in my power, and it would be so easy to be the other thing. Somehow today I feel that the ground is cut away from under my feet. Why should they treat me any better than they have done Cousin Betsy Witherspoon?

Sometimes the slaves did not act alone but conspired to murder their master or overseer. However infrequent, and whether spontaneous or planned, the murder of a white person by a slave left a deep and enduring impression. Presumably, the slaves aimed to eliminate individuals who had brutalized them. But taking the life of a kind and indulgent master or mistress, such as the unfortunate Mrs. Witherspoon, suggests the slaves were attacking slavery itself.

The most intrepid slaves delivered the hardest blows against the regime: they ran away. Since the introduction of slavery in the seventeenth century, slaveholders had dealt with runaways. Until the 1830s they had remained comparatively untroubled by the problem. Samuel A. Cartwright, a celebrated physician, announced that slaves who habitually deserted the plantation were, in fact, ill. They were unusually susceptible to a disease that he called "drapetomania," the compulsion to run away from home. Olmsted reported that Cartwright

believes that slaves are subject to a peculiar form of mental disease, termed by him *Drapetomania*, which, like a malady that cats are liable to, manifests itself by an irrestrainable propensity to *run away;* and in a work on the diseases of negroes . . . highly esteemed at the South for its patriotism and erudition, he advises planters of the proper preventative and curative measures to be taken for it.

He asserts that, "with the advantage of proper medical advice, strictly followed, this troublesome practice of running away, that many negroes have, can be almost entirely prevented. Its symptoms and the usual empirical practice on the plantations are described: "Before negroes run away, unless they are frightened or panic-struck, they become sulky and dissatisfied. The cause of this sulkiness and dissatisfaction should be inquired into and removed, or they are apt to run away or fall into the negro consumption." When sulky or dissatisfied without cause, the experience of those having most practice with *drapetomania*, the Doctor thinks, has been in favour of "whipping them *out of it.*" It is vulgarly called, "whipping the devil *out of them.* . . ."

Reassured by the learned Dr. Cartwright, the slaveholders did not begin to regard running away as a serious threat to the regime until confronted by the disturbances that the abolitionists raised. By the 1850s, however, the slaveholders were very nearly overwrought. They had good reason to be. Throughout the 1850s approximately one thousand slaves annually escaped to the northern United States, Canada, or Mexico. The slaveholders expended considerable sums trying to recover them.

Slaves commonly fled in response to specific provocations, to evade or decry a cruel punishment, to protest a change in the rules of work or the routine of plantation life, to reunite with loved ones from whom they had been forcibly separated, or to prevent themselves from retaliating in anger against a master or an overseer. The majority remained nearby, relying on their fellow slaves for food and information. In time, they returned of their own accord. These actions paralleled strikes by free workers who sought to gain concessions rather than to challenge the system itself. Those who left intending to strike for their freedom were of a different order. Typically unattached males between the ages of sixteen and thirty-five, they, unlike other runaways who for one reason or another sought a respite from their master's discipline or a restoration of previous norms, had obviously decided to repudiate slavery altogether, despite the long odds against success. They had determined that there were alternatives to slavery, and they permitted neither the masters nor the slaves whom they left behind to forget it. Choosing to risk their lives in a desperate attempt to win their freedom, the runaways offered the most effective resistance to slavery possible under the circumstances. In his autobiography Frederick Douglass spoke for all of them when he described his ordeal:

> I felt assured that, if I failed in this attempt, my case would be a hopeless one—it would seal my fate as a slave forever. I could not hope to get off with anything less than the severest punishment, and being placed beyond the means of escape. It required no very vivid imagination to depict the most frightful scenes through which I should pass, in case I failed. The wretchedness of slavery, and the blessedness of freedom, were perpetually before me. It was life and death with me.

—MARK G. MALVASI, RANDOLPH-MACON COLLEGE

Viewpoint:
No. Running away, stealing, arson, murder, and other acts of resistance disrupted the plantation routine, but they did nothing to challenge or weaken the master's power and frequently incited retribution.

A significant contribution of the most recent scholarship on slavery has been to establish the slaves as fully human, complex beings. Historians no longer accept the image of the slaves as contented workers either cheerfully adapted to slavery or too brutalized by the experience to challenge it. The prevailing image of the slave as the happy "darkey" singing in the fields and ultimately realizing that the correct response was obsequious obeisance to the master lasted until well after the Civil War (1861–1865). Any suggestion of slave personality or individuality was explained in that slaves suffered from many innate foibles and unfortunate idiosyncrasies and that they could not survive without strict institutional regimentation.

Subsequent studies in the later twentieth century revised the old image by illustrating that slaves had a sophisticated understanding of their predicament and that they learned how to navigate and exploit the system to their best advantage. Actions such as running away, theft, arson, and murder fall into the category of "day-to-day resistance" and are considered separate from the organized rebellions, infamous in the antebellum period. Mere mention of the Stono rebellion (1739), Gabriel's plot (1800), or Nat Turner's uprising (1831) made the blood of white slaveholding Southerners run cold. Fear of a violent slave insurrection was the dark side to the popular image of contented slaves that planters and apologists wished to convey. Few rebellions were actually executed, and most conspiracies were thwarted before they could be implemented. The fact that a few plots were successful, and that other unsuccessful plots were periodically conceived and discovered, was enough to terrify Southern slaveholders into a pattern of increased regimentation through stringent legislation and social and moral codes. As the slave's life became more restricted, it became more essential to create a variety of coping strategies to survive the experience. That laws and codes were continually stretched, tested, and broken attests to many fractures within Southern society. Slaves persistently resisted slavery through these behaviors, which engaged slave owners in the perpetual mission of redefining the legal and social parameters in which slaves, masters, and non-slave owners coexisted.

The slaveholding population viewed these coping strategies as patterns of misbehavior that needed to be preempted or foiled by constant vigilance. These behaviors ranged from offenses as minor as absconding for the day or stealing food to more serious actions as running away to freedom and sometimes even murder. Some of the better recent works on this subject clearly show that while acts such as these were widespread throughout the South, there was no absolute consensus among the general slave population regarding their validity, appropriateness, or necessity, although the majority of slaves who expressed an opinion on deeds such as these generally understood the rationale behind them.

There is no question that slaves resisted slavery. It is abundantly clear that the arrangement was not satisfactory for them, as the old school of historiography would have one believe, but it is questionable as to whether their resistance was effective or in what way one may define what could be effective under these circumstances.

If one says that these actions served to mitigate the worst aspects of slavery, and that running away, stealing, and so forth were emotionally, intellectually, or morally satisfying, even if only for a brief period, and often even in spite of the reality that anyone caught engaging in these actions was subjected to immediate and sometimes brutal punishment, then it is arguable that these methods were effective only as a palliative. If these actions were futile expressions of anger, frustration, humiliation, alienation, and hatred against the totality of a system in which the slaves were entirely enclosed and which they had no hope of destroying, then these actions were not effective means of resistance.

It is arguable that these were ineffective means of resistance for the following reasons: they represented different approaches intended to realize different ends, and thus did not create a collective consciousness that inspired effective group action to dismantle slavery. In addition, every instance of day-to-day resistance met with increased legal and social sanctions to control slave behavior.

An evaluation of these acts of defiance will clarify whether they were effective methods of resistance. Slaves used a variety of means to express their discontent with their condition, their masters, or their overseers. These patterns were practiced throughout the South but still did not engender a regionwide or nationwide movement that resulted in the collapse of slavery. The repetition of these patterns is easily explained by a variety of agencies, not the least of which were the sale or transfer of slaves (and behaviors) from one part of the region to another as well as the commonality of human response to repressive, harsh, and brutal circumstances.

The actions commonly recognized in the catalogue of day-to-day resistance are absenteeism, feigning illness, carelessness at work, arson, theft, running away, murder, infanticide, self-mutilation, and suicide. These acts are regarded as day-to-day resistance because they differ from the concept of the full-scale rebellion planned and organized to accomplish the destruction and overthrow of the slave-owning culture and to liberate those held in bondage. The intent, execution, and result of these deeds ran the gamut from innocuous to serious and from useful to capricious. Some of the acts of day-to-day resistance were well planned; some were spontaneous. Some were intended to damage or destroy the slave owner economically, while others were intended to satisfy the immediate material or emotional needs of the perpetrator. With the successful completion of some of these exploits, the greater good of the slave community might be served; with others, only individual motives and needs were satisfied.

Absenteeism, sometimes also called absconding or lying out, was not the same as running away. Absenteeism usually occurred when a slave was fed up with the drudgery of the routine and decided to take the day off to fish, hunt, visit family, or drink. Masters generally accepted this conduct as a part of the give-and-take of managing slaves; most did little about it and seemed to recognize it as a safety valve. When planters discussed these instances in their diaries, they often referred to the absentees in the same way one may regard a petulant child. For example, one planter described a truant slave as an "old scamp," indicating mild displeasure but also suggesting the confidence that the slave would soon return and resume his duties. These instances also allowed the owner to exercise his paternal role, acknowledging that every now and then some slaves would test his patience and that it was an inevitable behavior to expect from those who were supposedly child-like and irresponsible. His duty as the authority figure, the patriarch, who could choose benevolence over punishment was to find the appropriate and effective method to manage his slaves in all circumstances. This particular circumstance, irritating as it must have been, was not worthy of stringent measures in the view of the majority of owners. Absenteeism provided a temporary respite from slavery but did not effectively change the reality of the slave's life or challenge the power of the master.

Masters also usually overlooked the slaves who feigned illness because most were loathe to work a slave who might genuinely be ill; the consequences could be expensive or disastrous if the slave were sick enough to die. This plan was only advantageous for the slave who successfully managed to deceive his master and overseer. Success for one meant more work for the others since the routine of the plantation went on without them. Although most slaves may have engaged in this behavior at some point in their experience, it does not appear to have been a popular method within the group that had to support the persons pretending to be sick because it had adverse consequences for those who could not enjoy its advantages.

Carelessness at work and going slow were ways in which slaves controlled the pace and production demands of work. Many slaves were accused of being apathetic about their tasks to the extent that planters and overseers complained that they broke tools, ruined parts of the crop, abused or killed livestock, destroyed plantation property, and pretended to be too clumsy or incapable of learning new methods, especially those that were supposed to be more efficient. Slaves also learned to set their own pace in the fields; there was no reward for working hard and being efficient, as the overseer would expect it daily, and it would create an even more stressful work environment. If the entire gang worked at the same slow, reasonable pace, even the overseer would have to accommodate it. The destructive aspect of this behavior was defiant and was meant to communicate to the overseer and the master that there were areas of the slave experience that were pointless to try to control. Breaking tools and the like did not seriously disrupt the rhythm of plantation production, but it was aggravating nonetheless as it required the purchase of new tools or repeating a task until it was done properly, but it did not alter the amount or type of work that slaves performed.

Arson was more common in urban than in rural areas, but it was relatively common for a corncrib, smokehouse, or woodlands to go up in flames. In rare instances the master's house was the target of the hostility. Arsonists were seldom caught because the crime was easy to hide: it involved few people and it was difficult to determine what caused a fire or exactly who had set it. In areas or periods characterized by acute social tensions, all fires were blamed on disgruntled slaves, whether it was plausible the fire was arson or not. Arsonists could inflict serious economic damage if they destroyed a crop or storage buildings, but this damage would ultimately adversely affect them if it impaired the owner's ability to keep slaves. They might be sold or rented out and then perhaps find themselves in even worse circumstances than they already endured.

Theft is one of the best-documented and most suggestive aspects of resistance. Historians have documented many motives that explain the slaves' penchant for theft. Food was the single most stolen article on plantations. Some slaves claimed they stole food simply because they were hungry, or because they wanted more food and believed they were entitled to a share of what they labored to produce. Slaves rarely ate meat unless they pilfered from the henhouse or the hog lot. Most masters regarded this situation as inconvenient but petty thieving and yet further proof of the child-like and careless nature of slaves. They tried to prevent it but appeared resigned to the fact that theft was another one of those immature responses that were a natural aspect of slave behavior. Slave owners debated why slaves stole, what accounted for their apparent propensity to steal, and what should be done about it. Most slave owners arrived at the comfortable conclusion that stealing was an innate characteristic of black people, but it was not a natural outgrowth of slavery. Slaves also rationalized theft, as they believed that they themselves were stolen goods, and that every time their family members were sold away from them, their master had stolen from them so any theft against the master was justifiable.

Punishments for theft varied according to what was stolen and why. The generic punishment for stealing, as with most transgressions, was a whipping. One woman remembered the beating and salting she received for stealing a hog: "When dey get through wid you, you wouldn't wan' to steal no mo'—if you see a pig a mile off you'd feel like runnin' from him." Despite the severity of the punishment for stealing, it was a poor deterrent, as theft was the most persistent problem owners faced. Other slaves claimed they stole partly out of necessity but mostly for the satisfaction of getting something over on the master. Theft was the primary transgression that won admiration within the slave quarters, because it was the only act of defiance with potential to do the greatest good for the greatest number.

A slaveholder's ire was particularly roused if a slave sold or traded stolen plantation goods on the open market. Many laws were passed in an effort to curtail this behavior. Slaves seemed determined to risk commerce in stolen goods as long as they knew they had willing buyers, who were usually nonslaveholding white merchants. The severity of the laws concerned with illicit trading with slaves punished those who purchased the goods more than the slaves who sold them. This type of resistance was at its most effective: slaves using theft with the potential economically and socially to damage planter dominance. It is not clear to what extent slaves contrived this outcome and to what extent they were simply satisfied with the pure remunerative aspects of these transactions.

Arson was destructive and dangerous while carelessness was universally practiced as a means of preserving some semblance of a humane work schedule, and lying out and absenteeism only benefited the truant. Yet, theft was morally satisfying for the thief as well as for onlookers since it was an insidious and tidy blow against the master, and it provided immediate gratification in the form of more food or money. The only other potentially effective form of resistance to slavery was running away, but it was also the most difficult to execute successfully.

There were two forms of running away: running off for a few days to avoid a whipping, or running away permanently, to rejoin family from which one had been separated or to try to get North to freedom. Planters often complained in their journals about slaves they knew were hiding in the woods, and their rankled tone suggested that this was yet another behavioral problem they were saddled with that they were not sure how to handle, especially since whippings did not resolve the matter: "I have a negro in the woods he may attempt to go back though I cannot tell. It is Dick. I undertook to whip him a few days ago and when I called him up—he took to the woods. He is a great rascal. If I ever get him, I will sell him—for I believe he will spoil every negro we have if I keep him." Running away to hide and perhaps wait out a master's fury to escape punishment rarely worked, since the master's anger grew in proportion to the duration of a slave's absence, and their return was greeted with a severe beating or some other grim punishment.

Runaways who had no intention of coming back were the ones who merited advertisements in local papers. Their owners usually knew them well enough to understand what motivated their flight. Most advertisements for runaway slaves describe the fugitives as male, often a skilled laborer, who was articulate, "artful and sensible," and who might be able to pass as a free person. Most owners also knew their slaves well enough to predict where the escapee might go. For example, Harry, who escaped from Richard Harris in 1829, was an "intelligent ingenious fellow, well calculated to pass himself for a free man, which he will no doubt attempt to do; he is well known in this county, particularly in this and the neighborhood of the late Lemmon Ruffin, Esq. Where he has a wife. . . ." Isaac, a literate carpenter, ran away in 1826, and according to his master, "I expect he will try to pass for a free man, and get to a non slave holding state, as he has four or five years back had an 'itching' that way."

Running away was a most serious offense, and the slave-owning class made every effort to find and restore slaves to their owner's custody. The damaging implications of running away were legion. Successful runaways might encourage the slaves left behind. Their departure constituted a capital loss, and every successful runaway slave became fodder for abolitionist literature designed to generate a negative public image of slave own-

NOT SUSPECTING THE LEAST ATTEMPT

An uprising by enslaved persons was the fear of all slave-ship captains. In the 1730s a particularly bloody revolt occurred on the English slaver Don Carlos. James Barbot Jr., a sailor on the vessel, left this vivid account:

About one in the afternoon, after dinner, we, according to custom caused them, one by one, to go down between decks, to have each his pint of water; most of them were yet above deck, many of them provided with knives, which we had indiscreetly given them two or three days before, as not suspecting the least attempt of this nature from them; others had pieces of iron they had torn off our forecastle door, as having premeditated a revolt, and seeing all the ship's company, at best but weak and many quite sick, they had also broken off the shackles from several of their companions feet, which served them, as well as billets they had provided themselves with, and other things they could lay hands on, which they imagin'd might be of use for this enterprize. Thus arm'd, they fell in crouds and parcels on our men, upon the deck unawares, and stabb'd one of the stoutest of us all, who receiv'd fourteen or fifteen wounds of their knives, and so expir'd. Next they assaulted our boatswain, and cut one of his legs so round the bone, that he could not move, the nerves being cut through; others cut our cook's throat to the pipe, and others wounded three of the sailors, and threw one of them over-board in that condition, from the forecastle into the sea; who, however, by good providence, got hold of the bowline of the foresail, and sav'd himself . . . we stood in arms, firing on the revolted slaves, of whom we kill'd some, and wounded many; which so torrif'd the rest, that they gave way, dispersing themselves some one way and some another between decks, and under the fore-castle; and many of the most mutinous, leapt over board, and drown'd themselves in the ocean with much resolution, shewing no manner of concern for life. Thus we lost twenty seven or twenty eight slaves, either kill'd by us, or drown'd; and having master'd them, caused all to go betwixt decks, giving them good words. The next day we had them all again upon deck, where they unanimously declar'd, the Menbombe slaves had been the contrivers of the mutiny, and for an example we caused about thirty of the ringleaders to be very severely whipt by all our men that were capable of doing that office. . . .

Source: James Barbot Jr., "A Supplement to the Description of the Coasts of North and South Guinea," in Awnsham and John Churchill, Collection of Voyages and Travels (London: Printed by assignment from Messrs. Churchill, 1732).

ers and their society through the horrific personal accounts of slave life and the dangers of escape as told by the slaves themselves. As a consequence, hunting fugitive slaves was serious business. Slave patrols, both municipal and private, intervened to avert many attempted escapes. Patrols manned by planters were usually more humane than those organized by poor, nonslaveholding whites, who were usually more interested in brutalizing their captives than in returning them in any condition to be useful. Apprehended fugitives could expect to be beaten at the time of their capture and again upon their return to their master. Less fortunate ones were killed in the struggle to remain at large either by the slave hunters or by their dogs, known as Negro Dogs and universally feared for their viciousness. The use of dogs to bring in slaves was often criticized since the dogs regularly dismembered the slaves they tracked and captured. Running away was effective and inspiring if it was undertaken successfully. If the runaway was captured, the consequences were horrendous. Although many slaves thought it worth the risk, the majority did not.

Murder, infanticide, self-mutilation, and suicide were uncommon and constituted the most extreme forms of day-to-day resistance. For whites, the most upsetting of these was murder, clearly the most intolerable of all acts of defiance. Although rare, when slaves murdered their masters or overseers, the details of the event lived in infamy for decades afterward. Murderers were hunted down and captured with as much fervor as were runaways, and the punishments were always more severe. Apprehended murderers were lucky if they were merely hanged; more often vengeful whites insisted on prolonging death through various tortures. Several documented cases exist of mothers killing their children to spare them the agonies of a slave's life, or of persons cutting off their own fingers, hands, or feet to make themselves worthless as slaves, and there are fewer recorded cases of suicides. These measures were excessive reactions to the experience of slavery and suggest more about the profundity of an individual's personal despair and the individual's ultimate inability to engage in any meaningful act of resistance.

Individual acts of defiance and resistance demonstrate that slaves were not powerless within the system of slavery. Through acts of day-to-day resistance they manipulated the system, often to their advantage, but these actions also shaped the system, often to their disadvantage. Every act of resistance was met with either physical punishment or the creation of new or modified laws and unwritten social codes designed to limit their experience outside of slavery and to increase the distance between themselves and freedom. Did these acts of resistance weaken the institution of slavery? No, for it seems that most acts of resistance strengthened the resolve of slave owners to reassert their personal, social, and economic dominance. Day-to-day resistance was effective only in mitigating some of the worst of the quotidian

experiences of slavery, but it did not enable the slaves to be the agents of its destruction.

–PAULA STATHAKIS,
CHARLOTTE, NORTH CAROLINA

References

Herbert Aptheker, *American Negro Slave Revolts* (New York: Columbia University Press, 1943).

Raymond A. Bauer and Alice H. Bauer, "Day to Day Resistance to Slavery," *Journal of Negro History,* 27 (1942): 388–419.

Helen Tunnicliff Catterall, ed., *Judicial Cases Concerning American Slavery and the Negro,* 5 volumes (Washington, D.C.: Carnegie Institution, 1926–1937).

Frederick Douglass, *Narrative of the Life of Frederick Douglass, an American Slave, Written by Himself* (New York: Norton, 1997).

John Hope Franklin and Loren Schweninger, *Runaway Slaves: Rebels on the Plantation* (New York: Oxford University Press, 1999).

George M. Fredrickson and Christopher Lasch, "Resistance to Slavery," *Civil War History,* 13 (1967): 315–329.

Eugene D. Genovese, *Roll, Jordan, Roll: The World the Slaves Made* (New York: Pantheon, 1974).

Alex Lichtenstein, "'That Disposition to Theft, with Which They Have Been Branded': Moral Economy, Slave Management and the Law," *Journal of Social History,* 21 (1988): 413–440.

Frederick Law Olmsted, *The Cotton Kingdom* (New York: Modern Library, 1984).

Freddie L. Parker, ed., *Stealing A Little Freedom: Advertisements for Slave Runaways in North Carolina, 1791–1840* (New York: Garland, 1994).

Kenneth M. Stampp, *The Peculiar Institution: Slavery in the Ante-Bellum South* (New York: Vintage, 1956).

Stampp, "Rebels and Sambos: The Search for the Negro's Personality in Slavery," *Journal of Southern History,* 37 (1971): 367–392.

Joe Gray Taylor, *Negro Slavery in Louisiana* (Baton Rouge: Louisiana Historical Association, 1963).

William E. Wiethoff, *The Insolent Slave* (Columbia: University of South Carolina Press, 2002).

C. Vann Woodward, ed., *Mary Chesnut's Civil War* (New Haven, Conn.: Yale University Press, 1981).

MEANS OF RESISTANCE

MIDDLE PASSAGE

Did the treatment of slaves during the Middle Passage produce excessively high mortality rates?

Viewpoint: Yes. In the 350-year history of the slave trade, an estimated 1.8 million slaves died on the Middle Passage.

Viewpoint: No. Although the Middle Passage had an initial high mortality rate for slaves and transporters alike, it steadily declined because traders and ship captains undertook measures to maintain the health of their slaves and to achieve maximum profits.

The Middle Passage, the voyage across the Atlantic Ocean, was the notorious second stage of the journey that Africans experienced as they moved from freedom to bondage. Under ordinary circumstances Portuguese ships could sail from Angola to Pernambuco in thirty-five days, to Bahia in forty days, and to Rio de Janeiro in fifty days. During the 1670s British vessels leaving Guinea took forty-four days to reach the Caribbean, while Dutch ships took as long as eighty days to arrive in Curaçao. French slavers needed seventy days to cross the Atlantic from Africa. By the end of the eighteenth century, improvements in ship construction had reduced the average time for all voyages to thirty days, except those of French ships sailing from Madagascar and Mozambique. These vessels first called at the Mascarene Islands in the Indian Ocean; from there they made their way to the Caribbean, returning to France via Saint Domingue (Haiti). These complex expeditions generally required several years to complete.

Crossing the "green sea of darkness," as medieval Arabs called the Atlantic Ocean, endowed the Middle Passage with its drama and its terror. Horrifying and traumatic, the Middle Passage exposed slaves to nearly unremitting cruelty. Shackled, often naked, and confined below deck in a space too small for an adult to sit upright, the slaves endured the deadening heat; the oppressive stench of perspiration, excrement, vomit, and blood; and the appalling illnesses that invariably accompanied such overcrowded, unsanitary conditions. In *Slave and Citizen: The Negro in the Americas* (1946), historian Frank Tannenbaum provided a chilling account:

> On the ship itself the men and women were crowded between decks, with little air and less ventilation except such as filtered through narrow ventilators. There they were kept at least fifteen or sixteen hours a day—on good days, that is—in darkness, without modern systems of sanitation, and without running water, naked, and with chains about their ankles. Two men were chained together, as a rule the right ankle of one to the left ankle of another. And, thus crowded and bound hand and foot, they were allowed a space barely larger than a grave—five feet six inches long, sixteen inches broad, and two to three feet high, not high enough to sit up in.

The slaves did not submit passively to their fate. Scholars now agree that more than 450 recorded shipboard insurrections or attacks against slaving vessels occurred during the journey to the New World. The crews were heavily armed and enforced discipline through punishment and torture.

Was the Middle Passage a virtual death sentence for a substantial minority of the slaves? Between 10 million and 11 million Africans came as slaves to the New World. Estimates suggest mortality rates of between 10 percent and 20 percent, with approximately 1.8 million slaves dying on the Atlantic crossing during the 350-year history of the slave trade. Slaves died from disease, malnutrition, dehydration, and suicide. Others succumbed to wounds or beatings. Dreadful as the death toll was, revisionist historians have argued that it might have been worse had the crews of slave ships not made efforts to deliver a reasonably healthy cargo to the slave markets of Latin America and the Caribbean. In any event, revisionists point out, the sailors died at about the same rate as the slaves.

Viewpoint:
Yes. In the 350-year history of the slave trade, an estimated 1.8 million slaves died on the Middle Passage.

The Atlantic slave trade was exceedingly cruel. Although its historical accounts are biased, coming as they did from those opposed to slavery, it is fair to point out that the abolitionists alone identified and denounced the inhumanity of the slave trade. Others remained impervious to it. An "opaqueness to human suffering and sorrow grew upon those engaged in [the slave trade]," wrote Frank Tannenbaum in his classic study *Slave and Citizen: The Negro in the Americas* (1946), "that would be hard to believe if the record were not full beyond conjecture." If descriptions of the slave trade and the Middle Passage seem to emphasize only the brutality, it is perhaps so not because the sources are distorted but because there was so little else worthy of note. Not every story has two sides.

The slaves' ordeal began long before the slave traders herded them aboard ships bound for the New World. The rigorous and traumatic journey from the interior of Africa to the Atlantic coast was itself often tantamount to a death sentence. Suffering from disease, malnutrition, injury, and perhaps wounds suffered in battle, the slaves began their trek to the coast in an already weakened condition. To complicate matters, as they moved across the African countryside the slaves encountered volatile epidemiological environments to which they had not previously been exposed, thus greatly enhancing the possibility of contracting a disease against which they had developed no immunity.

On the trail the slaves' diets also deteriorated, further impairing their health. In his history of the Angolan slave trade, *The Way of Death: Merchant Capitalism and the Angolan Slave Trade, 1730–1830* (1988), Joseph C. Miller indicates that slaves, having virtually no access to fresh fruit, vegetables, and meat, subsisted almost entirely on manioc, an edible root with a high starch content. Prevailing racialist theories of medicine only compounded the slaves' afflic-

tions, for physicians believed that blacks needed less food than whites and could survive for days on a few millet heads and a kola nut. "The slaves who died along the path," Miller concluded, "must have suffered malnutrition to a degree approaching sheer starvation." The supply of water was also inadequate, doubly so since slave drivers preferred to travel in the dry season when fewer sources of water were available. Slave caravans did not usually carry much water with them, stopping instead to drink at pools and streams, some of which had doubtless become contaminated with parasites during the summer months.

Under these conditions scurvy, dysentery, typhus, typhoid, and smallpox were rampant. Exposed to the chill of higher elevations, the damp nights, and the lack of adequate clothing and shelter, many slaves developed respiratory ailments that the Portuguese called *constipações* (chills). Miller estimates the death rate from the Angolan slave trade to have reached the astronomic level of between 400 and 600 per 1,000. During the second half of the eighteenth century, slave traders anticipated losing 40 percent of their captives—some to flight, most to death—between the time they acquired them in the African interior and the time they drove them to the African coast. "That estimate," Miller writes, "would mean that 25 percent of the slaves died en route to the coast. Such a figure would imply a mean death rate between time of purchase and time of arrival in the towns of 500 per 1,000 per year."

In the slave pens, called barracoons, located in and on the outskirts of West African port cities, conditions were nearly as deplorable. Hundreds of naked, hungry, and sick slaves lived in squalor and slept in their own excrement, with scarcely enough room to lie down or move about. Yet, their diets, although far from adequate, improved over what they had been receiving, and they had more frequent opportunities to bathe. As a consequence, some slaves began to regain a modicum of good health, just in time to ascend the auction block. Nevertheless, the mortality rate in the slave pens still ranged between 10 percent and 15 percent, at least among the slaves in Angola upon whom Miller reports. In the absence of countervailing evidence there is no reason to assume that mortality rates were substantially lower elsewhere. The number of slave deaths declined throughout the eighteenth century, except in periods of drought and famine. In the final analysis, however, the exodus from the African interior to the coast constituted nothing less than a demographic catastrophe. Miller surmises that:

> Of 100 people seized in Africa, 75 would have reached the marketplaces in the interior; 85 percent of them, or about 64 of the original 100, would have arrived at the coast; after losses of 11 percent in the barracoons, 57 or so would have boarded the ships; of those 57, 51 would have stepped onto Brazilian soil, and 48 or 49 would have lived to behold their first master in the New World. The full "seasoning" period of 3–4 years would leave only 28 or 30 of the original 100 alive and working. A total "wastage" factor of about two-thirds may thus be estimated for the late-eighteenth-century Angolan trade, higher earlier in the trade, probably a bit lower by the 1820s. . . .

These deaths, too, must be accounted part of the slave trade, a deadly prelude to the Middle Passage.

Abolitionists such as Sir Thomas Fowell Buxton, a member of the British Parliament who helped to form the British and Foreign Anti-Slavery Society in 1823, enumerated the hazards of the Middle Passage. Buxton first complained that the ships used in the slave trade were too small, inadequate "in point of tonnage" as he put it, to accommodate the number of slaves they were made to transport. This deficiency not only left the slaves cramped and uncomfortable but also rendered them miserable and exposed to illness, injury, and death. Alexander Falconbridge, who had served as the surgeon aboard several different slaving vessels, confirmed Buxton's judgment. Describing how crews arranged the slaves in preparation for the journey to the New World, Falconbridge wrote:

> The men Negroes, on being brought aboard ship, are immediately fastened together two and two, by handcuffs on their wrists, and by irons riveted on their legs. . . . They are frequently stowed so close as to admit of no other posture than lying on their sides. Neither will the height between decks, unless directly under the grating, permit them the indulgence of an erect posture, especially where there are platforms, which is generally the case.

The slaves "had not as much room as a man in his coffin," Falconbridge testified before a Parliamentary committee of inquiry in 1790. "Their confinement in this situation was so injurious, that he has known them to go down apparently in good health at night, and be found dead in the morning." Falconbridge also observed

that a vessel sailing from Liverpool with 700 slaves was

> so crowded, that they were even obliged to lie upon one another. This occasioned such a mortality among them, that, without meeting with unusual bad weather, or having a longer voyage than common, nearly one-half of them died before the ship arrived in the West Indies.

The crew laid the sick and injured on bare planks, by which means "those who are emaciated frequently have their skin, and even their flesh, entirely rubbed off, by the motion of the ship, from the prominent parts of the shoulders, elbows, and hips, so as to render the bones in those parts quite bare." The victims of such care writhed in excruciating pain for weeks if, Falconbridge added ruefully, they happened to live that long. Not surprisingly, though, few withstood "the fatal effects of it."

Twenty-two days after leaving Mozambique in 1815, thirteen of the slaves aboard the Portuguese slave ship *St. Joaquim* had died and ninety-two were suffering from "the flux" (dysentery). All the slaves, healthy and ill alike, were cramped together below deck, "perfectly naked," in a space not more than two feet high. Olaudah Equiano, one of the few slaves who had the opportunity and inclination to recount his experience crossing the Atlantic, verified these wretched conditions, which he found "absolutely pestilential":

> I was soon put down under the decks, and there I received such a salutation in my nostrils as I had never experienced in my life, so that, with the loathsomeness of the stench, and crying together, I became so sick and low that I was not able to eat. . . . The closeness of the place, and the heat of the climate, added to the number in the ship, which was so crowded that each had scarcely room to turn himself, almost suffocated us. This produced copious perspirations, so that the air became unfit for respiration, for a variety of loathsome smells, and brought on a sickness amongst the slaves, of which many died, thus falling victims to the improvident avarice, as I may call it, of their purchasers.

The slaves added to these death tolls by committing suicide, usually by refusing food or jumping into the sea. Equiano related tales of blacks taking their own lives by hurling themselves into the ocean rather than accepting enslavement, and more than once he expressed a desire to join them. Noting the powerful attachment that Africans had to their homeland and the inconsolable sorrow they felt at being torn from it, French entrepreneur Jacques Savary wrote at the end of the seventeenth century that

> From the moment that the slaves are embarked, one must put the sails up. The rea-

SHACKLES AND LAMENTATIONS

British surgeon Alexander Falconbridge provided an account of the treatment of slaves during the Middle Passage:

About eight o'clock in the morning the Negroes are generally brought upon deck. Their irons being examined, a long chain, which is locked to a ring-bolt fixed in the deck, is run through the rings of the shackles of the men and then locked to another ring-bolt fixed also in the deck. By this means fifty or sixty and sometimes more are fastened to one chain in order to prevent them from rising or endeavoring to escape. If the weather proves favorable they are permitted to remain in that situation till four or five in the afternoon when they are disengaged from the chain and sent below.

The diet of the Negroes while on board, consists chiefly of horse beans boiled to the consistency of a pulp; of boiled yams and rice and sometimes a small quantity of beef or pork. The latter are frequently taken from the provisions laid in for the sailors. They sometimes make use of a sauce composed of palm-oil mixed with flour, water and pepper, which the sailors call slabber-sauce. Yams are the favorite food of the Eboe [Ibo] or Bight Negroes, and rice or corn of those from the Gold or Windward Coast; each preferring the produce of their native soil. . . .

They are commonly fed twice a day; about eight o'clock in the morning and four in the afternoon. In most ships they are only fed with their own food once a day. Their food is served up to them in tubs about the size of a small water bucket. They are placed round these tubs, in companies of ten to each tub, out of which they feed themselves with wooden spoons. These they soon lose and when they are not allowed others they feed themselves with their hands. In favorable weather they are fed upon deck but in bad weather their food is given them below. Numberless quarrels take place among them during their meals; more especially when they are put upon short allowance, which frequently happens if the passage from the coast of Guinea to the West Indies islands proves of unusual length. In that case, the weak are obliged to be content with a very scanty portion. Their allowance of water is about half a pint each at every meal. It is handed round in a bucket and given to each Negro in a pannekin, a small utensil with a straight handle, somewhat similar to a sauceboat. However, when the ships approach the islands with a favourable breeze, the slaves are no longer restricted.

Upon the Negroes refusing to take sustenance, I have seen coals of fire, glowing hot, put on a shovel and placed so near their lips as to scorch and burn them. And this has been accompanied with threats of forcing them to swallow the coals if they any longer persisted in refusing to eat. These means have generally had the desired effect. I have also been credibly informed that a certain captain in the slave-trade, poured melted lead on such of his Negroes as obstinately refused their food.

Exercise being deemed necessary for the preservation of their health they are sometimes obliged to dance when the weather will permit their coming on deck. If they go about it reluctantly or do not move with agility, they are flogged; a person standing by them all the time with a cat-o'-nine-tails in his hands for the purpose. Their music, upon these occasions, consists of a drum, sometimes with only one head; and when that is worn out they make use of the bottom of one of the tubs before described. The poor wretches are frequently compelled to sing also; but when they do so, their songs are generally, as may naturally be expected, melancholy lamentations of their exile from their native country.

The women are furnished with beads for the purpose of affording them some diversion. But this end is generally defeated by the squabbles which are occasioned in consequence of their stealing from each other.

On board some ships the common sailors are allowed to have intercourse with such of the black women whose consent they can procure. And some of them have been known to take the inconstancy of their paramours so much to heart as to leap overboard and drown themselves. The officers are permitted to indulge their passions among them at pleasure and sometimes are guilty of such excesses as disgrace human nature.

Source: Alexander Falconbridge, An Account of the Slave Trade on the Coast of Africa *(London: Phillips, 1788).*

MIDDLE PASSAGE

son is that these slaves have so great a love for their country that they despair when they see that they are leaving it forever; that makes them die of grief, and I have heard merchants who engage in this commerce say that they die more often before leaving the port than during the voyage. Some throw themselves into the sea, others hit their heads against the ship, others hold their breath to try and smother themselves, others still try to die of hunger from not eating . . . .

Other perils besides overcrowding, injury, disease, malnutrition, and suicide threatened slaves on the Middle Passage. The onset of foul weather or the attack of pirates took their toll on cargo and crew alike. "If they meet with bad weather, in rounding the Cape," declared famous English captain James Cook, "their sufferings are beyond description; and in some instances one-half of the lives on board are sacrificed." In 1706 the Danish ship *Kron-Printzen* sank in a storm with 820 slaves onboard; all of them drowned. Among the more disgraceful episodes occasioned by foul weather took place in 1738 when the Dutch vessel *Leuden* ran aground off the coast of Surinam near the mouth of the Marwowijne River. To avert pandemonium, the crew closed the hatches on the slave decks and, taking with them 14 slaves, abandoned ship leaving 702 slaves to drown. An even more notorious incident occurred in 1783 when Luke Collingwood, captain of the slaver *Zong*, ordered his crew to throw 132 slaves overboard because insurance covered death from drowning but not from illness or starvation.

With a crew of 14, the *Zong* had departed São Tomé, located off the coast of West Africa, on 6 September 1781, laden with 440 slaves. By the time the *Zong* reached Jamaica on 29 November, 60 slaves and 7 crewmen had died, with many more gravely ill and near death. A seasoned veteran of the slave trade, Collingwood realized that he could not even sell the remaining healthy slaves. Potential buyers would fear that these slaves would also fall ill and die. The voyage was a total loss. To salvage a meager return for the owners of the *Zong* and those who had invested in the expedition, the captain disposed of the ill slaves by throwing them into the sea. He then sold the rest of his cargo and sailed for Liverpool, whereupon the owners filed an insurance claim to recover the financial losses they had sustained from the drowned slaves—a claim on which they eventually collected.

Equiano discovered the truth about what had taken place on the *Zong* and helped to bring these outrages to the attention of a stunned and horrified English public. Equiano alerted British abolitionist Granville Sharp, who recorded the episode in his *Memoirs* (1820):

the master of the ship called together a few of the officers, and stated to them that, if the sick slaves, died a natural death, the loss would fall on the owners of the ship; but, if they were thrown alive into the sea, on any sufficient pretext of necessity for the safety of the ship, it would be the loss of the underwriters, alleging at the same time, that it would be less cruel to throw sick wretches into the sea, than to suffer them to linger out a few days under the disorder with which they were afflicted.

Some members of the crew, notably first mate James Kelsal, objected, but Collingwood's arguments at length prevailed. Accordingly, Sharp continued, Collingwood "chose out from the cargo 132 slaves, and brought them on deck, all or most of whom were sickly, and not likely to recover, and he ordered the crew by turns to throw them into the sea." He first had 54 slaves chained together and cast into the water. The next day Collingwood drowned 42 more, and on the third day, 36, the last 10 victims, as Sharp wrote, springing "disdainfully from the grasp of their tyrants, defied their power, and leaping into the sea, felt a momentary triumph in the embrace of death. . . ."

Students of the slave trade need not resort to such incredible and ghastly occurrences as those that transpired onboard the *Leuden* and the *Zong* to document the abysmal conditions and high mortality rates that the Middle Passage habitually engendered. Before 1700 approximately 20 percent of the slaves died while crossing the Atlantic. On 194 voyages between 1680 and 1688 the Royal Africa Company lost 24 percent of its slaves. After 1700 the mortality rates declined to about 5 percent for a voyage that lasted from between four and six weeks. Even then, however, some voyages could sustain losses as high as 30 percent or 40 percent. The improvement may at first seem dramatic, as indeed it was, but had that same mortality rate prevailed among the populations of England or France during the eighteenth century, contemporaries would have regarded them as an indication of an epidemic. Additionally, although the mortality rates of immigrants, soldiers, and convicts approached those of the slaves during the eighteenth century, by the nineteenth century they had fallen to less than 1 percent for transatlantic voyages. The death rate for slaves, by contrast, never dipped below 5 percent. Whatever refinements Europeans may have made in the transport of slaves across the Atlantic, there was a minimum death rate that they never managed to curtail. This grim calculus provides one more indication of the consequences that arise from robbing men and women of their humanity and regarding them as property to be bought and sold, to be abused, exploited, and brutalized beyond the limits of endurance.

-MEG GREENE,
MIDLOTHIAN, VIRGINIA

**Viewpoint:
No. Although the Middle Passage
had an initial high mortality rate for
slaves and transporters alike, it
steadily declined because traders
and ship captains undertook
measures to maintain the health
of their slaves and to achieve
maximum profits.**

Mortality rates for Africans and Europeans during the Middle Passage were approximately equal. In fact, if Africans survived the Middle Passage, they fared better than did Europeans. The annual death rate for Europeans newly arrived in the West Indies was 125 per 1,000; for Africans, it was only 30 per 1,000.

During much of the seventeenth century the mortality rate for slaves on the Middle Passage was approximately 20 percent. Shipboard arrangements were deficient in every respect, and, consequently, the Atlantic crossing yielded high death tolls. Conditions improved after 1700, however, significantly raising the number of slaves who survived the voyage. Average morality rates dropped to 10 percent during the first half of the eighteenth century, and by 1775 they had declined to around 5 percent, at which level they remained until the slave trade came to an end. The statistics discredit the older view that posited catastrophic mortality among slaves during the Middle Passage. Contemporary evidence notwithstanding, it now seems clear that most captains of slave vessels did not engage in the reckless destruction of life. Every slave death represented a financial loss to them as well as to their employers.

The Dutch believed that their ships were the best managed and most efficient. A contemporary description indicated that:

> Though the number [of slaves] sometimes amounts to six or seven hundred, yet by . . . careful management . . . they are so regulated that it seems incredible: and, in this particular, our [Dutch] nation exceeds all other Europeans; for the French, Portuguese and English slave ships are always foul and stinking; on the contrary, ours are for the most part clean and neat.

The Frenchman Jean Barbot, on the contrary, thought the Portuguese the most humane among the European slave traders. In the sixteenth century, King Manuel of Portugal ordered that wooden beds be installed in all slave ships and insisted that crews provide slaves with shelter from the elements. Manuel sought to assure that every vessel also carried adequate supplies of food, water, and other necessary provisions. The Law of 1684 implied that slaves ought at least to enjoy minimum comforts during the Middle Passage. Barbot thus affirmed that the Portuguese slave traders were:

> commendable, in that they bring along with them to the coast a sufficient quantity of coarse thick mats to serve as bedding under the slaves aboard, and shift them every fortnight or three weeks with fresh mats which, besides it is softer for the poor wretches to lie upon than the bare deals or decks, must also be much healthier for them, because the planks or deals contract dampness more or less, either from the deck being washed so often to keep it clean and sweet, or from the rain that gets in now and then . . . and even from the very sweat of the slaves; which being so crowded in a low place, is perpetual.

Testifying before the Privy Council in 1790, Swedish mineralogist Christian Wadström echoed Barbot, declaring that "the Portuguese slave ships are never overcrowded and the sailors are chiefly . . . *negros ladinos,* who speak their language and whose business it is to comfort and attend the poor people on the voyage. The consequence is that they have little or no occasion for fetters, so constantly used in the other European slave ships, and that they perform their voyage from Angola, etc., to Brazil with very little mortality." Each Portuguese seaman had charge of approximately fifteen slaves and was paid a bounty for every one who arrived at the destination in good health.

As tempting as it might be to take these comments uncritically, there is no evidence to suggest that any one European power was better than its rivals at treating the slaves with kindness or at keeping them alive. The decrease in slave mortality resulted from systematic changes in the conduct of the slave trade that all European nations adopted and applied to a greater or less extent. First, merchants and companies engaged in the transport of slaves began to acquire ships specifically constructed for that purpose. By 1750 slavers averaged two hundred tons. The larger ships, although still smaller than those used in other forms of commerce, offered more room and additional ventilation, thereby creating healthier conditions for the slaves, even as traders continued to fill their ships to capacity. The Portuguese reasoned that the slave deck "ought to be at least five and a half or six feet high, the more airy and convenient for such a considerable number of human creatures; and consequently far more healthy for them." This change, of course, did not imply that the slaves now traveled in luxury or even in comfort.

Second, eighteenth-century traders of nearly all European countries inoculated slaves against smallpox, instituted better hygiene and sanitation practices, and improved the quality of

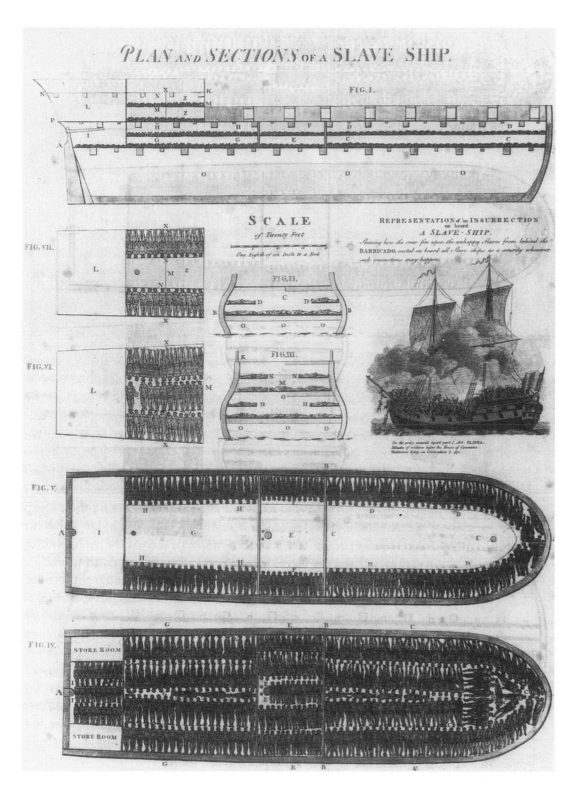

MIDDLE PASSAGE

medical care. "Thrice a week," wrote Barbot, "we perfume betwixt decks with a quantity of good vinegar in pails, and red hot bullets in them, to expel the bad air, after the place has been well scrubbed with brooms; after which, the deck is cleaned with cold vinegar." Increasingly, surgeons established hospital quarters onboard ship that enabled them to examine and minister to slaves who had fallen ill.

Third, slave traders carried larger quantities of provisions with which to feed the slaves. Although still often inadequate, the slaves' diet on the Middle Passage improved throughout the eighteenth century and was by no means appreciably inferior to food that the crew ate. The fare was simple, consisting of manioc, maize, oats, rice, millet, kidney beans, plantains, yams, potatoes, coconuts, limes, and oranges. Slaves typically received a ration of ten ounces of yams, ten ounces of biscuit, three-and-one-half ounces of beans, two ounces of flour, and perhaps even a small portion of salt beef or dried turtle meat. The Law of 1684 decreed that all Portuguese vessels had to carry a supply of water ample enough to give each slave a daily *canada* (1.5 pints). On ships departing from Liverpool, crews provided the slaves with two pints of water per day, and crews on those slavers leaving from Nantes dispensed three pints. After 1750, when physicians recognized a deficiency of vitamin C as the cause of scurvy, slaves often got a mouthwash of vinegar and lime juice each morning. The Dutch fed their slaves "'three time a day with indifferent good victuals and much better than in their own country.'" The English varied this practice, feeding the slaves twice daily, at ten o'clock in the morning and at five o'clock in the evening. Barbot recorded that at "each meal we allowed each slave a full coconut shell of water and, from time to time, a dram of brandy." Taken together, these innovations explain the marked decline in slave mortality rates.

Yet, despite advancements and precautions, slaves continued to die during the Middle Passage. Various gastrointestinal ailments seem to have been the main culprits. Tainted food and fetid water caused dysentery, or the "bloody flux." In all likelihood dysentery, and the dehydration that resulted from it, killed more slaves than any other single disorder. The cataclysmic mortality rates that haunted some voyages resulted from outbreaks of smallpox, measles, influenza, or other highly communicable diseases that quickly reached epidemic proportions and were unrelated to food, water, hygiene, or medical care. Over such epidemiological events even the most capable, effective, and proficient captains and crews had little control.

The length of a voyage did not generally correlate with higher mortality, with one notable exception. Even as mortality fell throughout the eighteenth century, the East African slave trade, which was 33 percent longer than the West African routes, suffered a greater number of deaths. Wadström, who had testified to the humanity of the Portuguese slave traders, at the same time noted that "some slave merchants were sending a few ships to Mozambique for slaves. They told me that, though in the long, cold and stormy voyage around the Cape of Good Hope, many more of the slaves died than even in the passage from Guinea to the West Indies, yet . . . their cheapness in Mozambique fully compensated for the increased mortality."

Similarly, several studies, such as Herbert S. Klein's *The Middle Passage: Comparative Studies in the Atlantic Slave Trade* (1978), have concluded that no relation existed between the practice of "tight-packing" and high mortality. Tightly packed vessels did not have substantially higher death rates than those on which there were fewer slaves. The disadvantage of tight packing evidently was not that it led to the greater incidence and easier spread of disease but that it reduced the space available to store food and water for the voyage, shortages that resulted in malnutrition and dehydration. These factors, and not overcrowding, were more often the principal causes of illness and death.

Brutality toward the slaves during the Middle Passage was neither ordinary nor inevitable, and crews often did what they could to keep up the morale of the slaves. It was, after all, in the interest of captain and crew to deliver the slaves in good, saleable condition. Testifying before the Hutt Committee of the House of Commons in 1848, Thomas Tobin, a slave captain from Liverpool, stated that he "endeavoured, by keeping them [the slaves] in a good humour, to knock perhaps a dozen out of these irons on a morning; then the next morning the same; the men took it in good heart and they used to draw lots themselves to see who should be let out the next morning, until they were about half out, and then we let them all out." The entire company of his ship, Tobin said, was "constantly employed . . . making everything [as] comfortable as could possibly be for the slaves. . . . They came up at about eight o'clock in the morning, and people were appointed over the hatchways with cloths, and they were rubbed down by themselves." Instructions from the directors of the Dutch Middleburg Company exhorted that sailors "not permit any Negroes, slaves, or slave women to be defiled or mistreated," and went on to insist that "care be taken that the doctor and supercargo check the mouths and eyes of the slaves every morning." Barbot recommended that kindly treatment of the slaves inhibited and soothed "their brutish temper" and also abated "the deep sense of their lamentable condition, which many are sensible enough of, whatever we may think of their stupidity. . . . [A]ll possible care is taken to preserve and subsist them in the interest of the owners."

With an increasing degree of success, slave traders endeavored to maintain the health and welfare of the slaves during the course of the Middle Passage. Their livelihood, and the prosperity of their employers, depended upon such efforts. For as Miller has observed, "it was literally, and sadly, true that 'if few die the profit is certain, but if many are lost so also is their owner.'"

–MARK G. MALVASI,
RANDOLPH-MACON COLLEGE

References

Roger Anstey, *The Atlantic Slave Trade and British Abolition, 1760–1810* (Atlantic Highlands, N.J.: Humanities Press, 1975).

Willem Bosman, *A New and Accurate Description of the Coast of Guinea: Divided into the Gold, the Slave, and the Ivory Coasts* (London: Knapton and others, 1705).

Thomas Fowell Buxton, *The African Slave Trade and Its Remedy* (London: Clowes & Sons, 1840).

Philip D. Curtin, *The Atlantic Slave Trade: A Census* (Madison: University of Wisconsin Press, 1969).

Olaudah Equiano, *The Interesting Narrative of the Life of Olaudah Equiano,* edited by Robert J. Allison (Boston: Bedford Books of St. Martin's Press, 1995).

P. E. H. Hair, Adam Jones, and Robin Law, eds., *Barbot on Guinea: The Writings of Jean Barbot on West Africa, 1678–1712,* 2 volumes (London: Hakluyt Society, 1992).

Herbert S. Klein, *The Middle Passage: Comparative Studies in the Atlantic Slave Trade* (Princeton: Princeton University Press, 1978).

Joseph C. Miller, *The Way of Death: Merchant Capitalism and the Angolan Slave Trade, 1730–1830* (Madison: University of Wisconsin Press, 1988).

David Northrup, ed., *The Atlantic Slave Trade,* second edition (Boston: Houghton Mifflin, 2002).

Johannes Menne Postma, *The Dutch in the Atlantic Slave Trade, 1600–1815* (Cambridge & New York: Cambridge University Press, 1990).

James A. Rawley, *The Transatlantic Slave Trade: A History* (New York: Norton, 1981).

Frank Tannenbaum, *Slave and Citizen: The Negro in the Americas* (New York: Knopf, 1946).

Hugh Thomas, *The Slave Trade: The Story of the Atlantic Slave Trade, 1440–1870* (New York: Simon & Schuster, 1997).

NEW CULTURE

Did the slaves develop a new culture under slavery?

Viewpoint: Yes. Through a long, slow, uneven process, Africans transformed themselves into African Americans and created a distinctive culture that was an amalgam of African, European, and American customs, beliefs, and practices.

Viewpoint: No. Forcibly detached from their homeland and kinship networks, set down in a strange environment, surrounded by an alien and hostile people, and herded together with other Africans with whom they had little or nothing in common, slaves had neither the means nor the opportunity to form a distinctive African American culture.

The historical understanding of slave life and culture underwent many changes during the twentieth century. The inability or unwillingness to take black people or black culture seriously marred the otherwise sophisticated and insightful analyses of historian Ulrich B. Phillips, who dominated the study of slavery during the first half of the twentieth century. Phillips viewed blacks as naturally inferior, backward, and submissive. Even historians who shared neither Phillips's racial biases nor his benevolent view of slavery continued to emphasize the docility of the slaves. They were, according to Kenneth M. Stampp in *The Peculiar Institution: Slavery in the Ante-Bellum South* (1956), a "culturally rootless people."

In *Slavery: A Problem in American Institutional and Intellectual Life* (1959), Stanley M. Elkins characterized slaves as the helpless victims of a "closed system" and a "total institution." The enslavement of Africans, Elkins suggested, had much in common with the experience of Jews in Nazi concentration camps during the Holocaust. Robbed of their African culture and prevented from creating a meaningful alternative, slaves became infantile "Sambos" who identified completely with white norms, values, and standards and who, as a consequence, had no independent life of their own.

The so-called Elkins thesis provoked stinging retorts. Scholars countered that Elkins had accumulated little empirical evidence to support his conclusions. They found, on the contrary, that the slaves had established a vibrant culture that enabled them to sustain their psychic independence and emotional equilibrium, and thereby to resist oppression and exploitation. To rebut Elkins's contention that slaves were passive, tractable, and obedient, historians writing in the 1960s and 1970s began to focus on the slaves themselves rather than on the treatment that they had received from whites. In the work of Eugene D. Genovese, Robert W. Fogel, Stanley L. Engerman, Herbert Gutman, John W. Blassingame, Lawrence W. Levine, and a host of others, slaves for the first time became historical actors in their own drama. No longer were they the mere objects of either white brutality or white affection. "The world the slaves made" became a viable subject for historical investigation.

The achievements of this generation of historians fundamentally altered the understanding of slave life and culture. Instead of portraying the slaves as victims, Genovese, Fogel, Engerman, Gutman, Blassingame, and Levine emphasized their resilience, ingenuity, and autonomy. Perhaps in their urgency to demonstrate that the slaves were not the casualties of their master's despotism, these historians overstated the case for slave independence. Younger scholars have already begun to challenge the judgment that the slaves managed somehow to escape the worst ravages of slavery. Nevertheless, the effort to rebut Elkins made it forever impossible to imagine the slaves as utterly bereft of identity and culture and totally subject to, and dependent upon, the will of the master.

Viewpoint:
Yes. Through a long, slow, uneven process, Africans transformed themselves into African Americans and created a distinctive culture that was an amalgam of African, European, and American customs, beliefs, and practices.

When the first African slaves arrived in North America more than four centuries ago, they brought little with them. Stripped of earthly possessions and in many cases even of their names, they had only their memories and cultural traditions to sustain them. In time, these bits and pieces of cultural inheritance, drawn from many different sources, came together to create a new and vibrant cultural force throughout the Americas. This culture has endured and flourished with little sign of disappearing.

For decades historians have fiercely debated the notion that African American slaves developed their own culture. Earlier generations of scholars flatly denied that an African American slave culture existed. One of the strongest arguments came from Melville J. Herskovits during the 1940s. Herskovits argued that a people without a past had no reliable connections to their history, which some historians of slavery and the South took as proof of the absence of slave culture. Further, these scholars also believed that any people without a history were, according to John Michael Vlach in *By The Work of Their Hands: Studies in Afro-American Folklife* (1991), "more easily looked upon as a commodity or tools," suggesting that the slaveholders' collective conscience was somewhat comforted by the idea that the slaves were little more than blank tablets to be inscribed as they saw fit. The belief among slaveholders that slaves were a people without a culture and a history thus made them easier to abuse and exploit. This pattern continued well into the twentieth century. The publication of sociologist E. Franklin Frazier's groundbreaking *Negro Family in*

the United States (1939) seemed to confirm the prevailing conceptions about the cultural and historical background in which blacks lived. Frazier argued that African American family life was more the product of white domination than of any historical tradition that existed among the slaves or their ancestors. To suggest, however, that slaves preserved nothing of their African heritage and developed no culture of their own in the New World is to do blacks a grave disservice. Even under the rigors of slavery blacks forged a culture from disparate elements that offered them both a measure of solace and autonomy.

Herskovits was among the first scholars to identify the presence of what he termed *Africanisms,* or elements of African origin and influence present in African American culture. Although many scholars initially dismissed Herskovits's theories, they rushed to judgment. Herskovits's initial findings helped lay the groundwork for future research that examined more closely the traits and materials from which African American culture derived. Still, Herskovits wrote despairingly about the possibility that any African customs, beliefs, and practices had survived the journey from Africa intact:

> It is apparent that African forms . . . had but a relatively slight chance of survival. Utensils, clothing, and food were supplied the slaves by their masters. . . . Thus African draped cloths were replaced by tailored clothing, however ragged; the short-handled, broad-bladed hoe gave way to the longer-handled, slimmer-bladed implement of Europe; and such techniques as weaving and ironworking and wood carving were almost entirely lost.

In his introduction to *By the Work of Their Hands,* Vlach has gone beyond Herskovits's initial conclusions to show that Africanisms were not, in fact, "an isolated cultural element but an assertive proof of an alternative history" that provides "a link to an unwritten past." Anthropologist Paul Bohannon gives further credence to this idea, particularly in reference to African American cultural expressions such as folktales. He states that all elements present in any culture are determined twice: once in reality and once in the mind. Thus, an African American folktale has

NEW CULTURE

BIBLE, SIEVE, AND GRAVEYARD DUST

Jacob Stroyer, a former slave in South Carolina and later a minister, recalls life in the slave quarters:

The slaves had three ways of detecting thieves, one with a bible, one with a sieve, and another with graveyard dust. The first way was this:—four men were selected, one of whom had a bible with a string attached, and each man had his own part to perform. Of course this was done in the night, as it was the only time they could attend to such matters as concerned themselves. These four would commence at the first cabin with every man of the family, and one who held the string attached to the bible would say, "John or Tom," whatever the person's name was, "you are accused of stealing a chicken or a dress from Sam at such a time," then one of the other two would say, "John stole the chicken," and another would say, "John did not steal the chicken." They would continue their assertions for at least five minutes, then the man would put a stick in the loop of the string that was attached to the bible, and holding it as still as they could, one would say, "Bible, in the name of the Father and of the Son and of the Holy Ghost, if John stole that chicken, turn," that is, if the man had stolen what he was accused of, the bible was to turn around on the string, and that would be a proof that he did steal it. This was repeated three times before they left that cabin, and it would take those men a month sometimes when the plantation was very large, that is, if they did not find the right person before they got through the whole place.

The second way they had of detecting thieves was very much like the first, only they used a sieve instead of a bible; they stuck a pair of scissors in the sieve with a string hitched to it and a stick put through the loop of the string and the same words were used as for the bible. Sometimes the bible and the sieve would turn upon names of persons whose characters were beyond suspicion. When this was the case they would either charge the mistake to the men who fixed the bible and the sieve, or else the man who was accused by the turning of the bible and the sieve, would say that he passed near the coop from which the fowl was stolen, then they would say, "Bro. John we see dis how dat ting work, you pass by de chicken coop de same night de hen went away." But when the bible or the sieve turned on the name of one whom they knew often stole, and he did not acknowledge that he stole the chicken of which he was accused, he would have to acknowledge his previously stolen goods or that he thought of stealing at the time when the chicken or dress was stolen. Then this examining committee would justify the turning of the bible or sieve on the above statement of the accused person.

The third way of detecting thieves was taught by the fathers and mothers of the slaves. They said no matter how untrue a man might have been during his life, when he came to die he had to tell the truth and had to own everything that he ever did, and whatever dealing those alive had with anything pertaining to the dead, must be true, or they would immediately die and go to hell to burn in fire and brimstone, so in consequence of this, the graveyard dust was the truest of the three ways in detecting thieves. The dust would be taken from the grave of a person who died last and put into a bottle and water was put into it. Then two of the men who were among the examining committee would use the same words as in the case of the bible and the sieve, that is, one would say, "John stole that chicken," another would say, "John did not steal that chicken;" after this had gone on for about five minutes, then one of the other two who attended to the bible and the sieve would say, "John, you are accused of stealing that chicken that was taken from Sam's chicken coop at such a time," and he would say, "In the name of the Father and the Son and the Holy Ghost, if you have taken Sam's chicken don't drink this water, for if you do you will die and go to hell and be burned in fire and brimstone, but if you have not you may take it and it will not hurt you." So if John had taken the chicken he would own it rather than take the water.

Sometimes those whose characters were beyond suspicion would be proven thieves when they tried the graveyard dust and water. When the right person was detected, if he had any chickens he had to give four for one, and if he had none he made it good by promising him that he would do so no more. If all the men on the plantation passed through the examination and no one was found guilty, the stolen goods would be charged to strangers. Of course these customs were among the negroes for their own benefit, for they did not consider it stealing when they took anything from their master.

***Source**: Jacob Stroyer,* My Life In the South, *revised edition (Salem, Mass.: Salem Observer Book and Job Print, 1885), pp. 59–62.*

NEW CULTURE

two purposes. First, it is a form of entertainment and perhaps of instruction. Second, it is a cultural artifact that keeps alive customs, practices, beliefs, and memories. Given this broadened description of what constitutes "culture," historians, anthropologists, and archaeologists can use virtually any artifact—from pottery to utensils, from stories to songs, and even a particular architectural style—to indicate the existence of an African American culture.

In its origins and evolution, African American culture responded to two different sources: Africa and Europe. Although some scholars have maintained that any group coming to America drew on similar resources, African Americans have a special history. They were the only people systematically brought to the New World against their will and forcibly placed in servitude. Because of this circumstance, it is not too much to say that African Americans in a sense had European culture forced upon them and that they were expected to conform to it. Yet, despite the shock of capture, the ordeal of the Middle Passage, the hardship of slavery, and the coerced cultural immersion that they endured, blacks managed to retain important elements of the African past, in however fragmentary a way.

This situation prompted among African Americans the development of another important and enduring aspect of their culture and personality: improvisation, the ongoing creativity of an enslaved and downtrodden people who, from a position of weakness and vulnerability, sought to make the most of what they kept. African American scholar and essayist Cornel West has recognized in this tendency toward improvisation one of the defining qualities of what he describes as "the cultural hybrid character" of African American life. To explain this distinctive outlook, West turned to the metaphor of jazz, "not so much," as he wrote:

> as a term for a musical art form, as for a mode of being in the world, an improvisational mode of protean, fluid, and flexible dispositions toward reality suspicious of "either/or" viewpoints, dogmatic pronouncements, or supremacist ideologies. . . . The interplay of individuality and unity is not one of uniformity and unanimity imposed from above but rather of conflict among diverse groupings that reach a dynamic consensus subject to questioning and criticism. As with a soloist in a jazz quartet, quintet, or band, individuality is promoted in order to sustain and increase the *creative* tension with the group—a tension that yields higher levels of performance to achieve the aim of the collective project.

African American culture in slavery and freedom was thus continually a work in progress; one that was adapted, molded, and changed as various situations required. This particular aspect of African American culture has in large measure made it exceptional and vibrant.

Vlach, too, recognized the improvisational quality of African American culture in a trait that he called "stylistic consistency." For instance, Vlach pointed out, storytelling, an African legacy, evolved into something more African American, with characters changed to fit the situations common to slaves' lives, such as the clever trickster outwitting the powerful master. The content of the slave tale might be different from the African original, revealing the improvisational aspect of the culture, but it was clearly connected in tone, style, and meaning to the African oral tradition, marking the element of continuity essential to all cultures.

In the realm of material culture, slave women fashioned quilts that, although a distinctly European form, distinguished themselves by their bright colors and unmistakably African design patterns. African motifs were also incorporated into the intricate wrought-iron gates, grilles, balconies, and fences that adorn private dwellings and public buildings from Charleston, South Carolina, to New Orleans. Moreover, architectural styles from Africa, such as the familiar shotgun house, long a building staple throughout the South, reveal an African sensibility in spatial design. At the same time, Southern vernacular architecture drew on local or regional building traditions, thereby producing an American style that shows the distinctive characteristics of the African and African American tradition in architecture.

The contours of African American culture in slavery and freedom have become of increasing interest to scholars since the 1960s. Still, the subject is ripe for more serious study. In his essay "African Influence on the Art of the United States" Robert Farris Thompson wrote, "mankind must applaud Afro-American art in the United States for its sheer existence, a triumph of creative will over the forces of destruction." Through the acknowledgment and exploration of African American culture, historians and others may better understand how African Americans perceived the world into which they were brought as slaves and how they survived in bondage and in freedom. Even as old customs, practices, folkways, and beliefs disappear, change, or diminish in importance, remnants survive, waiting to be rediscovered and reinvented, as when a people forced into bondage came together to create a new way of existing in a world that treated them with hostility and degradation.

—MEG GREENE,
MIDLOTHIAN, VIRGINIA

NEW CULTURE

**Viewpoint:
No. Forcibly detached from their homeland and kinship networks, set down in a strange environment, surrounded by an alien and hostile people, and herded together with other Africans with whom they had little or nothing in common, slaves had neither the means nor the opportunity to form a distinctive African American culture.**

Two arguments have dominated the study of slavery in the United States. The first emphasized the misery and devastation that slavery caused; the second emphasized the development of African American culture and the slaves' resistance to exploitation. The older tradition probably originated with the abolitionists. In the United States, Theodore Dwight Weld's *American Slavery as It Is: Testimony of a Thousand Witnesses* (1839) marked the first systematic effort to chronicle the brutality and degradation of slavery. Twentieth-century sociologist E. Franklin Frazier argued that blacks emerged from slavery without feelings of self-esteem, a sense of group identity, a collective purpose, or a culture. He not only denied the existence of an African American culture but also found nothing in the African heritage that could assist blacks in making the necessary adjustments to American society. The passage of time, the process of acculturation, and the dynamics of racial oppression, Frazier asserted, had obliterated any traces of African culture and had, in fact, precluded the emergence and development of an African American alternative. Similarly, Abram Kardiner and Lionel Ovesey wrote in *The Mark of Oppression: A Psychosocial Study of the American Negro* (1951) that the slave had "no intrapsychic defenses—no pride, no group solidarity, no tradition." Even after emancipation "the marks of his previous status were still upon him socially, psychologically, and emotionally. And from these he has never since freed himself."

During the second half of the 1950s such neo-abolitionist historians as Kenneth M. Stampp and Stanley M. Elkins continued and extended this line of inquiry, in part to challenge the conclusions of Ulrich Bonnell Phillips, the recognized authority on the subject since the appearance of *American Negro Slavery* (1918), that slavery was relatively gentle and the plantation regime comparatively benign. Stampp and Elkins tried to show that the opposite had been true. Slavery, they agreed, was founded on relations of authority and subordination, cruelty and

violence. In *The Peculiar Institution: Slavery in the Ante-Bellum South* (1956) Stampp wrote:

> Most masters . . . would have been gratified if their slaves had willingly shown proper subordination and wholeheartedly responded to the incentives offered for efficient labor. They found, however, that some did not respond at all, and that others responded only intermittently. As a result, slaveholders were obliged to supplement the lure of rewards for good behavior with the threat of punishment for bad. . . . Without the power to punish, which the state conferred upon the master, bondage could not have existed. By comparison, all other techniques of control were of secondary importance.

Elkins maintained that slavery was a "closed system" and a "total institution" that "infantilized" its victims, stripping them of their personalities and cultures and rendering them utterly dependent upon the master. He suggested that slavery had produced a "Sambo" personality type who was childish, lazy, irresponsible, carefree, self-deprecating, and submissive. Sambos, Elkins insisted, were made, not born. The shock of capture, the removal from their homeland, the detachment from native culture, and the subordination to absolute authority had destroyed the slaves' sense of self and their ability to function as mature adults. The typical slave was thus broken in spirit, docile, irresponsible, unstable, alienated, dependent, and degraded. To dramatize his conclusions, Elkins compared the devastation that slavery had wrought with the dehumanization that took place in the Nazi concentration camps during the Holocaust, which was, in Elkins's view, "a special and highly perverted instance of human slavery." "The only mass experience that Western people have had within recorded history comparable in any way with Negro slavery," he continued, "was undergone in the nether world of Nazism." To critics who accused him of portraying slaves only as helpless victims, Elkins responded:

> I can only suggest that it is still possible to romanticize the spaces in the system. There was a time when Ulrich Phillips was rightly censured for doing something not unlike this, and one might still unwittingly do much the same thing for purposes quite different from Phillips. [Slavery] was, after all, a very hard system, and we would do well not to forget it. I would concede that there must have been room in it for the virtuosos, the master opportunists, the ones who "played it cool." But how much room? And how much of the system's infinite variety of coercions could the individual slave absorb without his finally internalizing the very role he was being forced to play?

Beginning in the 1960s, amid the agitation for civil rights, the scholarly pendulum swung in the other direction. Several historians high-lighted slave resistance and the evolution of African American culture, which in itself, they argued, constituted a form of resistance. Theirs was a quest to discover how blacks had survived under slavery, withstood its harshest dictates, and kept their dignity and humanity. Most had little to say about the damage that slavery inflicted upon its victims. None was as concerned to examine the physically and psychologically devastating aspects of slavery as Stampp and Elkins had been.

In *The Slave Community: Plantation Life in the Antebellum South*, published initially in 1972 and substantially revised in 1979, John W. Blassingame maintained, contra Elkins, that slavery did not annihilate the personality of the slave. Slavery was not, according to Blassingame, "a total institution" that rendered its victims "submissive, infantile, and docile." The slaves were, on the contrary, "dangerous, insubordinate, bold, evil, restless, turbulent, vengeful, barbarous, and malicious," or at least whites feared them to be so. Slave life was vibrant and diverse, he contended, with family, community, religion, music, and folklore combining to provide instruments of resistance to the emotionally crippling potential of the system. "The most remarkable aspect of the whole process of enslavement," Blassingame wrote, "is the extent to which the American-born slaves were able to retain their ancestors' culture." Blacks were thus not the "pathological," "dehumanized," and "infantile" victims of slavery, deprived of history, community, or identity.

Lawrence W. Levine echoed these themes in *Black Culture and Black Consciousness: Afro-American Folk Thought from Slavery to Freedom* (1977). Levine was intent to render articulate a people whom historians had consigned to silence, but who, in their own lifetimes, had often told their own story in their own way. It was misleading and wrong, Levine wrote, to "conceive of slavery as a closed system which destroyed the vitality of the Negro and left him a dependent child." Slaves were not "pure victims" who experienced only "unrelieved suffering and impotence." Even in the midst of "the brutalities and injustices of the antebellum and postbellum racial systems black men and women were able to find the means to sustain a far greater degree of self-pride and group cohesion than the system they lived under even intended for them to be able to do." Slavery was not benign, Levine contended; rather, human beings were more resilient than historians had realized. Levine stated his thesis succinctly and cogently:

Upon the hard rock of racial, social, and economic exploitation and injustice black Americans forged and nurtured a culture: they formed and maintained kinship networks, made love, raised and socialized children, built a religion, and created a rich expressive culture in which they articulated their feelings and hopes and dreams.

Music and song, both sacred and secular, were distinctive expressions of the nascent African American community and collective consciousness. African American folktales, as Levine presents them, are less satisfactory as indications of communal life. The trickster tales schooled vulnerable men and women about how to live in a world of duplicity and power. Many of the trickster's antics do, indeed, arise from the need for self-defense against those who are bigger and stronger than he. The pranks of a trickster such as Br'er Rabbit, however, are often unwarranted and mean-spirited. He steals from and cheats not only those more powerful than himself but those who are weaker. He exacts ruthless vengeance against those who frustrate his will. The trickster, in short, is an inveterate hustler. His main objective is survival at any cost. He is not the agent of community, at least when it is not to his advantage to be so. Family, community, friendship, trust, compassion, and love are unaffordable luxuries in a world dominated by the seven deadly sins. If this sort of cunning was the psychological adjustment that slavery demanded, then blacks paid a high price to create and sustain a measure of cultural independence.

Herbert Gutman, in *The Black Family in Slavery and Freedom, 1750–1825* (1976), rejected the notion that slavery debilitated black family life. He insisted, on the contrary, that stability and continuity were its paramount attributes. Gutman did not merely imply that the black family, exposed to the rigors of slavery, managed to survive to console the downtrodden and oppressed—he went further. In his analysis the black family under slavery was, and could only be, strong and resilient. It grew more vibrant and autonomous while the authority, coercion, and prejudice of whites receded into the background and while the influence of slavery itself declined. Gutman's model of the black family, therefore, made no provision for debility, infirmity, or disintegration, as if slavery in the end had hardly touched it at all.

At the heart of Eugene D. Genovese's study of slavery, *Roll, Jordan, Roll: The World the Slaves Made* (1974), is the concept of paternalism, which established the dialectic of accommodation and resistance as the mechanism for dealing with bondage. Unlike Gutman, Genovese confirmed the power of the master class while at the same time allowing slaves the autonomy necessary to fashion their own culture and religion, to say nothing of an embryonic black nationalism, within the confines of a despotic system that

African American banjo and gourd fiddle, nineteenth century

(from Edward D. C. Campbell Jr., ed., Before Freedom Came, *1991)*

of their slaves, providing them with food, clothing, and shelter that were on a par with, or better than, what average workers in the North and Europe received. Slaveholders also allegedly promoted stable, monogamous families among their bondmen and bondwomen and rarely broke those families apart through sale unless extreme economic hardship dictated. Whippings and other harsh forms of punishment were infrequent, since the masters were not sadists but entrepreneurs; rewards were far more effective than discipline at inducing the slaves to work hard. As capitalist businessmen, the slaveholding planters of the Old South found cruelty and bloodshed unnecessary and deplorable. For their part, the slaves emerge from the pages of *Time on the Cross* as dutiful members of the bourgeoisie fully endowed with the Protestant work ethic. Fogel and Engerman hoped "to strike down the view that black Americans were without culture, without achievement, and without development for their first two hundred years on American soil," to destroy, as they wrote, "the myth of black incompetence."

Blacks never quite warmed up to the idea that their ancestors had made excellent slaves. Would Fogel and Engerman "recommend a return to slavery?" asked Kenneth Clark in an interview on the *Today Show*. Economists and historians questioned not only the authors' purposes but also their methods. As Elkins explained, by the time the critics had finished with *Time on the Cross*, "they had rendered doubtful the procedures by which every one of the book's major assertions had been reached."

An original variation on the "culture thesis" came from Sterling Stuckey. In *Slave Culture: Nationalist Theory and the Foundations of Black America* (1987), Stuckey proposed that disparate African peoples had forged a common culture on the plantation—a culture that had insulated itself from European and American influences and remained in important respects essentially African. It was, ironically, the "common horror" of slavery that bred this African cultural nationalism and unity in the New World, something that Africans themselves have never accomplished.

The extensive historiography of slavery makes it undeniable that blacks developed a new culture under slavery. Whatever flaws mar the historical literature on slave culture, the overwhelming evidence contained in that impressive body of work renders it impossible to suggest otherwise. The "Elkins thesis" that slavery robbed blacks of culture and personality is vulnerable on many fronts, not least of which is the lack of empirical evidence to support the elegant theory that slavery was a "total institution" against which resistance was limited or nonexistent. Yet, has the discovery of slave culture, how-

they could neither escape nor abolish. For the slaveholding planters, paternalism humanized what would otherwise have been gross exploitation. Paternalism imposed the social and moral responsibility to nurture the slaves in body and soul. In exchange for this care, the slaves owed their masters fidelity, obedience, and labor. The obligations on both were mutual and binding. Although it implied acquiescence in slavery, paternalism also demanded an affirmation of the slaves' humanity.

Robert W. Fogel and Stanley L. Engerman went further. Not only did they assert that slavery was efficient and lucrative but also that it was progressive and humane. In *Time on the Cross: The Economics of American Negro Slavery* (1974) Fogel and Engerman avowed that the majority of slaveholders paid close attention to the welfare ever much it has deepened and enriched the understanding of slavery, blinded historians to certain elemental realities? African American novelist Toni Morrison has perhaps offered the most telling rendition of the atrocities of slavery in *Beloved* (1987), a tale in which the ghosts of slavery literarily haunt blacks. Morrison explores the interior lives and personal histories of former slaves to show that slavery was terrifying and malevolent not because it exposed a whole people to violence, rape, murder, and other indignities but because these outrages happened to individual men and women. She demonstrates that the cruelties visited on men and women one by one rippled through an entire community and touched a whole people. "Not a house in the country ain't packed with some dead Negro's grief," Sethe, the main character in *Beloved*, tells her mother-in-law, Baby Suggs, as both women struggle to forget what can never be forgotten.

Any person or group dispossessed of liberty, home, and identity will find some mechanism of defense and perseverance. Men and women living under intolerable circumstances will marshal all their resources—material and spiritual, individual and collective—in an effort to survive, to make life not only bearable but also predictable and intelligible. Cultures blended in such a crucible offer some protective covering, though they are not necessarily the most wholesome or healthy. They may even contain an excess of deformity and perversion. No study of slave culture, therefore, can any longer fail to acknowledge, and in some sense to answer for, the people whom slavery assaulted, the lives that slavery mangled, the souls that slavery destroyed.

–MARTINA NICHOLAS,
YOUNGSTOWN STATE UNIVERSITY

References

John W. Blassingame, *The Slave Community: Plantation Life in the Antebellum South,* revised edition (New York: Oxford University Press, 1979).

Paul Bohannon, "Rethinking Culture: A Project for Current Anthropologists," *Current Anthropology,* 14 (1973): 136.

Stanley M. Elkins, *Slavery: A Problem in American Institutional and Intellectual Life* (Chicago: University of Chicago Press, 1959).

Robert William Fogel and Stanley L. Engerman, *Time on the Cross: The Economics of American Negro Slavery,* 2 volumes (Boston: Little, Brown, 1974).

E. Franklin Frazier, *The Negro Family in the United States* (Chicago: University of Chicago Press, 1939).

Frazier, *Race and Culture Contacts in the Modern World* (New York: Knopf, 1957).

Eugene D. Genovese, *Roll, Jordan, Roll: The World the Slaves Made* (New York: Pantheon, 1974).

Herbert Gutman, *The Black Family in Slavery and Freedom, 1750–1825* (New York: Pantheon, 1976).

Melville J. Herskovits, *The Myth of the Negro Past* (New York & London: Harper, 1941).

Abram Kardiner and Lionel Ovesey, *The Mark of Oppression: A Psychosocial Study of the American Negro* (New York: Norton, 1951).

Lawrence W. Levine, *Black Culture and Black Consciousness: Afro-American Folk Thought from Slavery to Freedom* (New York: Oxford University Press, 1977).

Toni Morrison, *Beloved* (New York: Knopf, 1987).

Ulrich Bonnell Phillips, *American Negro Slavery: A Survey of the Supply, Employment and Control of Negro Labor as Determined by the Plantation Regime* (New York & London: Appleton, 1918).

Kenneth M. Stampp, *The Peculiar Institution: Slavery in the Ante-Bellum South* (New York: Knopf, 1956).

Sterling Stuckey, *Slave Culture: Nationalist Theory and the Foundations of Black America* (New York: Oxford University Press, 1987).

Robert Farris Thompson, "African Influence on the Art of the United States," in *Black Studies in the University: A Symposium,* edited by Armstead L. Robinson, Craig C. Foster, and Donald H. Ogilvie (New Haven: Yale University Press, 1969), pp. 128–177.

John Michael Vlach, *By The Work of Their Hands: Studies in Afro-American Folklife* (Charlottesville: University Press of Virginia, 1991).

Theodore Dwight Weld, *American Slavery as It Is: Testimony of a Thousand Witnesses* (New York: American Anti-Slavery Society, 1839).

Cornel West, *Race Matters* (Boston: Beacon, 1993).

NEW CULTURE

NEW WORLD VISION

Did slavery compromise the image of the New World as an Edenic land?

Viewpoint: Yes. Many intellectuals and statesmen in Europe and the United States believed that the existence of slavery compromised, if not destroyed, the promise of the New World to revitalize and purify civilization and humanity.

Viewpoint: No. Slavery was essential to the economic success of the New World, which was a basic element of the promise America offered.

How were Europeans to reconcile the existence of slavery with the image of America as a land of promise, an earthly paradise? Was the New World to be the setting for the regeneration or the degradation of humanity? For more than two hundred years Europeans did not torment themselves with such questions, remaining largely indifferent to the plight of African slaves and to their own complicity with an evil that they chose to rationalize or evade rather than to confront and resolve.

The problem of slavery had engaged thinkers since antiquity. Only in the eighteenth century, however, did they find it imperative to accommodate the reality of slavery with ideas of morality and progress. By the nineteenth century, as historian David Brion Davis has argued, intellectuals in both Europe and the United States had come to regard slavery as the repudiation of natural law, Christian ethics, progress, enlightenment, reason, and democracy.

Emancipation of the slaves, by contrast, was, in the words of American poet and essayist Ralph Waldo Emerson, "an event singular in the history of civilization; a day of reason; of the clear light; of that which makes us better than a flock of birds and beasts; a day, which gave the immense fortification of a fact,—of gross history—to ethical abstractions." Emerson and others of his age believed in the inevitability of moral progress. At the beginning of the twenty-first century people are less inclined to share their views, however much they may appreciate and even admire the effort to recognize slavery as a moral problem implicated in the meaning of America.

**Viewpoint:
Yes. Many intellectuals and
statesmen in Europe and the United
States believed that the existence of
slavery compromised, if not
destroyed, the promise of the New
World to revitalize and purify
civilization and humanity.**

Americans, as historian David Brion Davis has maintained, were and are embarrassed when they recall that a slaveholder wrote the Declaration of Independence (1776) and that slavery was a legal institution in the Thirteen Colonies at the beginning of the American Revolution (1775–1783). During the struggle for independence many American leaders admitted that slavery was contrary to the principles for which they fought, and several reformers warned that the Revolution could not be justified unless Americans rid the land of slavery. The irony of slaveholders fighting for liberty and the rights of man was only part of a larger paradox that historians have seldom understood in its full magnitude and dimensions. The ideology of the American Revolution was grounded in the belief that the United States was a regenerative force, the new hope for a tired world. To fulfill its historic destiny, America had to free itself from the decadence, perversion, and corruption of Europe.

From the time of the earliest discoveries, Europeans had projected visions of liberation and perfection into the vast and, to their eyes, vacant spaces of the New World. Explorers approached the uncharted coasts with vague preconceptions of discovering the mythical Atlantis or El Dorado. Naked savages, living in apparent splendor, freedom, and innocence awakened hopes of what historian Hugh Honour has characterized as a "new Golden Land." Even Christopher Columbus—as practical, hardheaded, and unsentimental a man as ever was—fell under the spell of the golden-skinned natives whom he encountered living at their leisure amid the bounty of nature. In August 1498, when he lay at anchor in the Gulf of Paria (between Venezuela and Trinidad) during his third voyage to the New World, Columbus wrote that he had arrived on the "nipple" of the earth, which, he thought, reached closer to Heaven than any other part of the world. He believed that the Garden of Eden must be nearby.

A growing literature celebrated America as a natural world, free from the avarice, luxury, corruption, sinfulness, and materialism of Europe. To the promoters of colonizing expeditions America was a virgin land, a place for solving all the problems and satisfying all the desires of life.

In America, they maintained, things would be better, for America was the new Promised Land. This long-held tradition, culled from a mixture of classical and biblical sources, also later helped to shape Americans' image of themselves as the "New Adam," a creature unencumbered by the fears, superstitions, and sins of a moldering civilization, a wise innocent dwelling in an earthly paradise. The American was at once the happy farmer, content to enjoy the blessings of a simple rural life, and the adventurous pioneer, expansive and confident of his ability to conquer and improve the world. By the time of the American Revolution (1775–1783) European liberals and radicals looked to America as the only hope for the future of humanity. It was in America, they declared, that social and political institutions were most clearly modeled on the rational plan of nature and God. By reconciling the natural order with human progress, Americans had at last fulfilled the ancient dream of creating "a more perfect union."

What, though, was the meaning of slavery in this earthly paradise? In *Histoire philosophique et politique des éstablissements et du commerce des Européens dans les deux Indies* (Philosophical and Political History of the European Trading Establishments in the Two Indies), published in 1770 and publicly burned in 1781, Abbé Guillaume-Thomas-François de Raynal, the French historian and philosopher, was among the first scholars to attempt an answer to this question.

Like most other thinkers associated with the Enlightenment, Raynal thought slavery contrary to nature. He conceded that relations of subordination and authority had once been necessary to the progress of civilization, but slavery offered evidence only of human greed and selfishness. Raynal believed that the advance of society enhanced rather than mitigated its worst evils. The lust for wealth, power, and luxury, he argued, had corrupted the modern world and brought slavery to entire peoples.

For Raynal, an incomprehensible cruelty and violence had characterized European expansion into the New World from the outset. The early voyages to America had unsettled the European mind and imagination, creating a new breed of men insatiable in their quest for wealth and power. Far from being a land of hope and redemption, the Americas had provided virtually unlimited opportunities for savage exploitation. Although the Enlightenment had improved European morals, the slave trade to the Americas gave constant stimulus to the worst passions and vices of humanity.

Was this result, Raynal wondered, the necessary outcome of American development? He could not easily accept that conclusion. Yet, Raynal conceded, the colonies of the New

LIBERTY, EQUALITY, FRATERNITY,

DEDICATED TO THE SMARTEST NATION IN ALL CREATION.

World would not have been prosperous without slaves. He summarized his views, writing: "without this labor, these lands, acquired at such a high cost, would remain uncultivated." As a committed enemy of slavery, his only response was a flourish of despair. "Well then," he wrote, "let them lie fallow, if it means that to make these lands productive, man must be reduced to brutishness, whether he be the man who buys, or he who sells, or he who is sold."

Although Raynal recognized that slavery was, from the beginning, intimately bound up with the meaning of the New World, he did not abandon the traditional idea that America was also a land of promise. The inhabitants of the New World, he suggested, although corrupted by slavery, had an opportunity to create a new society based on the principles of reason. If they should one day succeed in ridding the world of the evil that enveloped them, they might become a great people, united in their dedication to advancing the freedom of humanity. After having been devastated by the Europeans, the New World might still rise to prominence and liberate the rest of mankind from oppressive customs, institutions, and practices.

In Raynal's view, as Davis has argued, the promise of America could never be fulfilled without the abolition of slavery, which was not readily forthcoming. Between the potential mission to save the world and the actual state of corruption there lay an unbridgeable gap. Such an interpretation of the American dilemma carried overtones of the Christian conception of the human condition as sinful but capable of redemption. Raynal, however, had no faith in the power of Christianity to remove this burden of sin, especially since the Roman Catholic Church had long both tolerated and enacted the worst forms of barbarism and inhumanity. His faith in the efficacy of reason was only slightly greater. Were there not, he asked, any inherent forces at work in America that would lead to the eradication of slavery and thus free the land to fulfill its providential mission? Was slavery in America an historical accident, or was it part of the essential and substantive nature of the New World?

Raynal gave no definite answers. He acknowledged that in the ancient world slavery had coexisted with affluence, republican government, and advancing civilization, and that the advent of Christianity had left it unaffected. Slavery had come to an end in Europe only when economic and political conditions favored emancipation. Finally, Raynal pointed out that slavery had been associated with the development of the Americas from the earliest Portuguese and Spanish settlements. He thus implied that slavery was intrinsic to America.

In the end Raynal indicated that slavery would be eradicated only through some cataclysmic upheaval, such as a massive slave rebellion led by a black Spartacus (a slave and gladiator who led a revolt against Rome in 73–71 B.C.E.) who would be an instrument in the hands of God for punishing the blind avarice of Europeans and their descendants who peopled the New World. Raynal's enthusiasm for such blood atonement revealed his lack of faith in any interior force for gradual emancipation and peaceful reform. America, it seemed, could not realize without agony its promise to redeem the world.

Antislavery Quaker John Woolman of New Jersey reached similar conclusions. Woolman declared that God had opened the New World and, as with Israel of old, had blessed his chosen people with abundance and freedom. Instead of being humbled by their success and grateful for their bounty, they had succumbed instead to greed and had become absorbed in the pursuit of luxury and power. If Americans continued to be unfaithful to their high calling to redeem the world, Woolman prophesied, they and their descendants would surely face the awful retribution of God's justice.

Virginia statesman Thomas Jefferson recoiled from this vision, perhaps because he feared it would come to pass. "Indeed I tremble for my country when I reflect that God is just," Jefferson wrote in *Notes on the State of Virginia* (1785), "that his justice cannot sleep forever: that considering numbers, nature, and natural means only, a revolution of the wheel of fortune, an exchange of situation, is among possible events: that it may become probable by supernatural interference!" In this famous passage from Query XVIII, Jefferson's rational control over the problem of slavery broke down. Like Woolman, he predicted a servile revolt instigated by God. Jefferson here appealed not to the serene Deity of the Enlightenment but to the Old Testament God of Wrath.

According to Jefferson, the slaves, although a distinctly inferior people, were an alien and menacing presence in America. They had the potential to destroy the beautiful harmony of his image of America as an earthly paradise. Jefferson believed that all virtue came from the land. "Those who labor in the earth," he asserted, "are the chosen people of God, if ever he had a chosen people, whose breasts he has made his peculiar deposit for substantial and genuine virtue." If this assessment were true, then the slaves who worked the land had logically to be at least as virtuous as their masters, and perhaps more so. Jefferson could not make this concession, nor could he conceive of the slaves as linking their masters to the soil. The blacks were too different ever to enable the masters to project an image of themselves as bound to the soil through their slaves. As a consequence, Jefferson regarded blacks as obstacles that stood between their masters and the earth, which, it bears repeating, was for him the source of all virtue.

At the same time, the masters demanded absolute obedience from their slaves, who, in essence, were extensions of the master's will. Jefferson, though, wrestled with the notion that the masters had rendered themselves dependent upon their slaves, not only for their material welfare, which originated from slave labor, but also for their definition of themselves as masters. The identity of the master as a master depended on the willingness of the slaves to acknowledge him as master. Subtly, unwittingly, yet unmistakably the logic of this relation opened the possibility that the slaves had some measure of autonomy and independence and were not simply the instruments of their master's will.

Jefferson sensed the problem. The masters of slaves were not self-sufficient or independent, which for Jefferson were two of the characteristics that ensured a virtuous people and a healthy commonwealth. Jefferson had to confront the unpleasant prospect that his beloved Virginia, America, and the entire New World were as corrupt and as evil as Europe. Americans did not live in harmony with nature as God intended but attempted to dominate not only nature but human nature through their exploitation of the slaves. In the end Jefferson's intuition about the future was as apocalyptic as the expectations of Raynal and Woolman, and utterly confounded his vision of the New World as an earthly paradise. In *Notes on the State of Virginia* Jefferson was nearly prophetic about the end that the Confederacy would meet in the Civil War (1861–1865) when Union soldiers devastated the Southern New Canaan.

–MEG GREENE,
MIDLOTHIAN, VIRGINIA

Viewpoint:
No. Slavery was essential to the economic success of the New World, which was a basic element of the promise America offered.

The presence of slavery did not confound the image of the New World as an earthly paradise, though it did complicate that vision. One of the earliest attempts to reconcile the reality of slavery with the image of the New World as a paradise came from Virginia planter Robert Beverley, whose remarkable work, *The History and Present State of Virginia*, was published in London in 1705. Beverley offered an ecstatic and sensuous vision of the garden of Virginia. The second part, titled "of the NATURAL *Product and conveniences* of VIRGINIA; in its Unimprov'd STATE before the *English* went thither," is a fertility hymn in praise of the waters, fish, fowl, soil, vegetation, herbs, and grains of Virginia.

When Beverley considered "the Husbandry and Improvements of the Country," the development of farms and plantations, he nearly described ecstacy. To blend the delights of nature and plantation, Beverley found a memorable symbol in the summerhouse of William Byrd I, his father-in-law. Beverley wrote:

> Have you pleasures in a Garden? All things thrive in it, most surprisingly [*sic*]; you can't walk by a Bed of Flowers, but besides the entertainment of their Beauty, your Eyes will be saluted with the charming colors of the Humming Bird, which revels among the Flowers, and licks off the Dew and honey from their tender Leaves, on which it only feeds. . . . Colonel Byrd, in his Garden, which is the finest in that Country, has a Summer-House set

round with the *Indian* Honey-suckle, which all the summer is continually full of sweet Flowers, in which these Birds delight exceedingly. Upon these Flowers, I have seen ten or a dozen of these beautiful Creatures together, which sported about me so familiarly, that with their little Wings they often fann'd my Face.

In his desire to describe the harmony of Virginia as a natural and improved garden, Beverley fashioned a poetic image of the plantation summerhouse and almost totally ignored the concrete details of plantation life. Yet, in Beverley's evocation originated the idea that the plantation was at the center of the Garden of the New World. The glimpse of a planter such as Byrd seated amid the honeysuckle and the hummingbirds in that faraway summer foreshadowed the image of the plantation situated in the timeless South, a secure world redeemed from the ravages of time and history, a place of both independence and permanence.

At the time Beverley published *The History and Present State of Virginia*, the significance of the plantation as a symbol of the independence and permanence that characterized the South was only beginning to emerge in literature and thought. The transformation of this natural paradise into "paradise improved" occurred specifically in the mind and imagination of William Byrd II of Westover.

Byrd was among the most prominent Virginia planters during the first half of the eighteenth century. In three letters Byrd clarified the image of Virginia as a New World garden. Lately returned from what proved to be his last journey to England, Byrd wrote to his old friend the earl of Orrery in 1726 to explain the benefits of life in Virginia, about which he had only one reservation:

> Besides the advantage of a pure air, we abound in all kinds of provision without expense (I mean we who have plantations). I have a large family of my own, and my doors are open to everybody, yet I have no bills to pay, and half-a-crown will rest undisturbed in my pockets for many moons together. Like one of the patriarchs [of the Old Testament], I have my flock and herds, my bondmen and bondwomen, and every sort of trade amongst my own servants, so that I live in a kind of independence on everyone but Providence. However, though this sort of life is without expense, yet it is attended with a great deal of trouble. I must take care to keep all my people [his slaves] to their duty, to set all the springs in motion, and to make everyone draw his equal share to carry the machine forward. But then 'tis an amusement in this silent country and a continual exercise of our patience and economy. . . . Thus, My Lord, we are happy in our Canaans if we could but forget the onions and fleshpots of Egypt.

In Byrd's letter to Lord Orrery he presented a vision of an earthly paradise realized exclusively in the plantation society of Virginia. That society he identified with Canaan, the promised land of Exodus. The plantations of Virginia were "New Canaans," which offered complete salvation from a land (Europe) in which the allure of evil was as oppressive as it was ubiquitous. The most significant aspect of Byrd's vision, however, was his identification of this new way of life with the master's supervision of "bondmen and bondwomen."

As historians Stanley M. Elkins and Edmund S. Morgan have shown, there was nothing "natural" about the introduction of slavery into the colonial South. Slavery had no necessary connections with either a tropical climate or the crops grown in such a locale. In Virginia, Maryland, and the other North American colonies where slavery took root and flourished, the climate was hardly tropical, and the staple crop, tobacco, could be grown as far north as Canada. Nor had slavery in the past been limited to a particular people or defined by skin color. Even the planters of seventeenth-century Virginia had preferred white laborers from England, Scotland, and Ireland to black slaves from Africa.

The introduction of slavery also was not a matter of legal precedent. English colonists who settled in the Chesapeake Bay region had no legal category comparable to "slave." Slavery had existed for centuries, but nothing in these earlier forms of bondage compelled slavery to develop in North America. In crucial respects, then, the colonists did not import slavery from elsewhere but re-created it in America. When colonial Virginians committed themselves to slavery, they broke with their own past and, as evinced in Byrd's letter to Lord Orrery, sought to incorporate slavery into the myth of the New World as earthly paradise. At this stage the effort was comparatively painless, involving no more than the invention of a literary image of slave society as a patriarchal garden in which a kind, benevolent, and wise master presided over his "people" amiably at work in the tobacco fields or the Big House.

As the population of "Ethiopians" increased, however, Byrd became conscious of the growing difficulty of assimilating slavery into the vision of the New World as earthly paradise. In 1736, ten years after he had written to Lord Orrery, Byrd confided to another correspondent, the earl of Egmont, that slaves

blow up the pride and ruin the industry of white people, who, being a rank of poor creatures below them, detest work for fear it should make them look like slaves. Then that poverty, which will ever attend upon idleness, disposes them as much to pilfer as it does the Portuguese, who account it much more like a gentleman to steal than to dirty their hands with labor of any kind.

Byrd also feared that masters who had to discipline large numbers of slaves would from time to time have to be severe with them. This necessity, he wrote to Egmont, was "terrible to a good-natured man, who must submit to be either a fool or a fury." The most dreadful prospect that Byrd envisioned was servile insurrection. This possibility led him to wonder whether Parliament should not consider the abolition of slavery or at least a ban on the further importation of slaves into the North American colonies.

These concerns, although evident in Byrd's writing, did not become overriding considerations for him. He belonged to a world in which slavery had become a necessity—a world in which men equated necessity with destiny. Accepting that slavery was indispensable, Byrd continued to explore the relation of slavery to the image of the New World as earthly paradise. The most significant evocation of this image came in a 1736 letter to Peter Beckford of Jamaica. Byrd tried to entice Beckford to visit Westover, probably hoping to sell him some land:

We live here in Health & in Plenty, in Innocense & Security, fearing no Enemy from Abroad or Robbers at home. Our Government too, is so happily constituted that a Governour must first outwit us before he can oppress us. . . . Our negroes are not so numerous or so enterprizeing as to give us any apprehension or uneasiness nor indeed is their Labour any other than Gardening & less by far what the poor People undergo in other countries. Nor are any crueltys exercized upon them, unless by great accident they happen to fall into the hands of a Brute, who always passes here for a monster. . . .

Perhaps the most important aspect of Byrd's letter is his description of the role of the slaves. They were the gardeners in this "New World Garden" of Virginia. Yet, Byrd declared that there were not many slaves and they rarely suffered harsh treatment. Compared to the situation in Jamaica, Byrd's observations were accurate. In making such pronouncements, however, he concealed that the number of slaves in Virginia was rapidly increasing and that, as a result, their rights and status were declining.

Byrd's recognition that in the plantation garden the slaves, not the master, were accorded the role of gardeners remains one of the most momentous insights into the intellectual and cultural history of the South. Byrd rehearsed poetically an anxiety that was already beginning to haunt Virginia planters during the first half of the eighteenth century. European peasants actually and imaginatively belonged to the land. They were under the control of the landlord whom they served, but he did not exercise absolute power over them. The landlord had an obligation to protect and nurture both the land and the people whom God had entrusted to his care.

IMPROVING A WILDERNESS

Quaker and abolitionist John Woolman, in a 1757 letter to fellow Quakers settling in North Carolina, advised his readers to avoid employing slaves:

While I write, the youth come fresh in my way. Dear young people, choose God for your portion; love His truth, and be not ashamed of it; choose for your company such as serve him in uprightness; and shun as most dangerous the conversation of those whose lives are of an ill savour; for by frequenting such company some hopeful young people have come to great loss, and been drawn from less evils to greater, to their utter ruin. In the bloom of youth no ornament is so lovely as that of virtue, nor any enjoyments equal to those which we partake of in fully resigning ourselves to the divine will. These enjoyments add sweetness to all other comforts, and give true satisfaction in company and conversation, where people are mutually acquainted with it; and as your minds are thus seasoned with the truth, you will find strength to abide steadfast to the testimony of it, and be prepared for services in the church.

And now, dear friends and brethren, as you are improving a wilderness, and may be numbered amongst the first planters in one part of a province, I beseech you, in the love of Jesus Christ, wisely to consider the force of your examples, and think how much your successors may be thereby affected. It is a help in a country, yea, and a great favour and blessing, when customs first settled are agreeable to sound wisdom; but when they are otherwise the effect of them is grievous; and children feel themselves encompassed with difficulties prepared for them by their predecessors.

As moderate care and exercise, under the direction of true wisdom, are useful both to mind and body, so by these means in general the real wants of life are easily supplied, our gracious Father having so proportioned one to the other that keeping in the medium we may pass on quietly. Where slaves are purchased to do our labour, numerous difficulties attend it. To rational creatures bondage is uneasy, and frequently occasions sourness and discontent in them; which affects the family and such as claim the mastery over them. Thus people and their children are many times encompassed with vexations, which arise from their applying to wrong methods to get a living.

I have been informed that there is a large number of Friends in your parts who have no slaves; and in tender and most affectionate love I beseech you to keep clear from purchasing any. Look, my dear friends, to divine Providence, and follow in simplicity that exercise of body, that plainness and frugality, which true wisdom leads to; so may you be preserved from those dangers which attend such as are aiming at outward ease and greatness.

Treasures, though small, attained on a true principle of virtue, are sweet; and while we walk in the light of the Lord there is true comfort and satisfaction in the possession; neither the murmurs of an oppressed people, nor a throbbing uneasy conscience, nor anxious thoughts about the events of things, hinder the enjoyment of them.

When we look towards the end of life, and think on the division of our substance among our successors, if we know that it was collected in the fear of the Lord, in honesty, in equity, and in uprightness of heart before Him, we may consider it as His gift to us, and, with a single eye to His blessing, bestow it on those we leave behind us. Such is the happiness of the plain ways of true virtue.

Source: John Woolman, A Journal of the Life, Gospel Labours, and Christian Experiences of that Faithful Minister of Jesus Christ *(Philadelphia: Crukshank, 1774).*

It was different, symbolically and legally, with the masters. The slaveholders of the New World owned property not only in land but also in the human beings who worked the land. Thus arose the fear, which racial prejudice compounded, that slavery threatened the source of social order: the rational mind. Masters could hardly attribute the power of reason or imagination to the slaves. To do so would be tacitly to admit that the slaves had minds of their own and were not merely possessions that functioned as instruments of the master's will. If the slaves had their own narrative to recount, their own interpretation of slavery to put forth, they could expose the vision of an early paradise embodied in the plantation society of Virginia and the New World as a fraud.

Confronted with the growing opposition to slavery, the generation of Southern thinkers who came of age in the nineteenth century had either to reject slavery or embrace it. In time, they committed themselves to a defense of slavery not as a "necessary evil" but as a "positive good," the only reliable basis upon which to establish and preserve a Christian social order in the modern world.

Like many of his contemporaries, South Carolina poet Henry Timrod believed that the slave South would save the world. Slavery, Timrod insisted, provided the model for a humane and Christian social order. During the meeting of the first Confederate Congress, which took place in Montgomery, Alabama, in February 1861, Timrod composed "Ethnogenesis" to celebrate the birth of a nation dedicated to bringing this new world into being. The final stanza best conveys his faith in the redemptive power of slavery:

But let our fears—if fears we have—be still
And turn us to the future! Could we climb
Some mighty Alp, and view the coming time,
The rapturous sight would fill
    Our eyes with happy tears!

Not only for the glories which the years
Shall bring us; not from lands from sea to sea
And wealth, and power, and peace, through these
    Shall be;

But for the distant peoples we shall bless,
And the hushed murmurs of a world's distress:
For, to give labor to the poor,
    The whole sad planet o'er,

And save from want and crime the humblest door,
Is one among the many ends for which
    God makes us great and rich!

In "Ethnogenesis" Timrod not only anticipated Southern victory in the coming war but contemplated an exceptional role for the South in history. The powerful forces of nature and the guiding hand of God would serve the cause, enabling Southerners to rout their enemies and establish an enduring civilization that would forever end the torment and distress of the human condition. At the conclusion of "Ethnogenesis" Timrod imagined a vast Southern empire from which war, crime, and poverty had been eliminated and earthly life at last brought to perfection. For Timrod, the slave South was the New Zion.

The existence of slavery thus modified, but did not destroy, the vision of America as an earthly paradise. It took the "mighty scourge of war," as President Abraham Lincoln wrote, to accomplish that.

—MARK G. MALVASI,
RANDOLPH-MACON COLLEGE

References

Robert Beverley, *The History and Present State of Virginia*, edited by Louis B. Wright (Chapel Hill: University of North Carolina Press, 1947).

William Cohen, "Thomas Jefferson and the Problem of Slavery," *Journal of American History*, 56 (December 1969): 503–526.

J. Hector St. Jean de Crèvecœur, *Letters from an American Farmer* (London: Davies, 1782).

David Brion Davis, *The Problem of Slavery in the Age of Revolution, 1770–1823* (Ithaca, N.Y.: Cornell University Press, 1975).

Davis, *The Problem of Slavery in Western Culture* (Ithaca, N.Y.: Cornell University Press, 1966).

Richard Beale Davis, *Intellectual Life in Jefferson's Virginia, 1790–1830* (Chapel Hill: University of North Carolina Press, 1964).

Davis, *Intellectual Life in the Colonial South, 1585–1763*, 3 volumes (Knoxville: University of Tennessee Press, 1978).

Stanley M. Elkins, *Slavery: A Problem in American Institutional and Intellectual Life* (Chicago: University of Chicago Press, 1959).

Hugh Honour, *The New Golden Land: European Images of America from the Discoveries to the Present Time* (New York: Pantheon, 1975).

Thomas Jefferson, *Notes on the State of Virginia*, edited by William Peden (New York: Norton, 1954).

R. W. B. Lewis, *The American Adam: Innocence, Tragedy, and Tradition in the Nineteenth Century* (Chicago: University of Chicago Press, 1955).

Mark G. Malvasi, *The Unregenerate South: The Agrarian Thought of John Crowe Ransom, Allen Tate, and Donald Davidson* (Baton Rouge: Louisiana State University Press, 1997).

Pierre Marambaud, *William Byrd of Westover, 1674–1744* (Charlottesville: University Press of Virginia, 1971).

John Chester Miller, *The Wolf by the Ears: Thomas Jefferson and Slavery* (New York: Free Press, 1977).

Edmund S. Morgan, *American Slavery, American Freedom: The Ordeal of Colonial Virginia* (New York: Norton, 1975).

NEW WORLD VISION

OUTCOME OF REBELLIONS

Were slave rebellions effective in the struggle for abolition?

Viewpoint: Yes. Slave rebellions plagued virtually every slaveholding regime, pressuring authorities to reevaluate their position on slavery.

Viewpoint: No. Most slave rebellions failed, resulting in the execution of the conspirators and savage reprisals against, and greater oppression of, the slaves.

Rebellion offered the most dramatic expression of the slaves' discontent with slavery and desire for freedom. The largest and most successful uprisings took place in Latin America and the Caribbean. Outnumbered and outgunned, the slaves of North America were understandably reluctant to engage in actions that amounted to suicidal folly. When uprisings did occur, the military quickly suppressed them and carried out brutal reprisals against the participants. In the United States, slave conspiracies and insurrections terrified whites but did little to endanger the slaveholding regime.

Throughout Latin America and the Caribbean, by contrast, slave rebellions became increasingly commonplace and menacing. In Barbados, Brazil, Cuba, Demerara (present-day Guyana, formerly British Guiana), Jamaica, Saint Domingue (Haiti), Surinam, the Virgin Islands, and elsewhere, slave uprisings were not only more frequent than in North America but also more violent and destructive. Slaveholders throughout the Western Hemisphere tried to prevent news of these incidents from reaching their slaves, fearing that it would inspire similar audacity and defiance among them. At the same time, however, the rebellions prompted many in both the colonies and metropolises to question the continued viability of slavery.

Only in Saint Domingue did a slave revolt effect immediate emancipation. Except in Jamaica, where British colonial authorities negotiated treaties that guaranteed the freedom of the rebels, insurrections usually ended in the defeat and indiscriminate massacre of the slaves. Although most slave uprisings failed, it is hard to deny the contribution that they made to the struggle for abolition. The Christmas Rebellion of 1831 in Jamaica, for example, influenced passage of the Emancipation Act of 1833, which freed approximately 500,000 slaves in the British Empire. Nowhere did slaveholders as a class voluntarily liberate their slaves. They did so only when coerced by overwhelming political and military force. Refusing to be mere victims of oppression, slave rebels entered boldly into the Jamaican fight and thereby helped to ensure the freedom of their people.

Viewpoint:
Yes. Slave rebellions plagued virtually every slaveholding regime, pressuring authorities to reevaluate their position on slavery.

A slave revolt is a struggle for freedom. Resistance to slavery occurred everywhere that slavery existed, but slave insurrections, rebellions, and revolutions marked a special kind of challenge and thus required a special kind of heroism in the face of extraordinary circumstances. Nothing could be more naive or more arrogant than for historians to ask why a slave uprising did not occur on every plantation throughout the Western Hemisphere. As the odds against the success of such revolts become clear, it is less difficult to understand their infrequency and still less to appreciate the rebels' courage and resourcefulness, to say nothing of the impact of their actions on the course of history.

A violent confrontation with injustice was at the core of any and every revolt against slavery. For a long time, however, as historian Eugene D. Genovese has argued, slave revolts had an isolationist and a restorationist, rather than a revolutionary, character. Even the rebellious slaves perceived their actions as an effort to withdraw from society and reconstitute a lost African world, not to challenge the system of slavery itself. In this context the revolt against slavery generally took the form of a rejection of unbearable exploitation or the alteration of customary arrangements that had clarified relations between masters and slaves. When slave uprisings did not lead to heroic sacrifice, bloody defeat, and harsh oppression, they led to the retreat from colonial society and to the establishment of maroon communities.

Many slave rebellions began as more or less spontaneous acts of desperation directed against the withdrawal of privileges, the imposition of brutal punishments, the affliction of gross injustice, the pain of hunger, or similar deprivations. These rebellions, as well as the guerrilla wars that the maroons waged in various slaveholding colonies, aimed at withdrawing individuals from slave society and resurrecting a social order perceived as traditionally African. Toward the end of the eighteenth century, however, slave revolts shifted decisively from attempts to secure freedom from slavery to efforts to overthrow slavery as a social system and win for blacks a place in the modern community of nations. As historian C. L. R. James demonstrated, the great slave uprising in Saint Domingue (Haiti), which began during the 1790s, marked the turning point. There were, of course, hints of this revolutionary outlook in earlier slave insurrections. Just as certainly, the restorationist character of many of the early rebellions colored those that occurred after the revolution in Saint Domingue.

The first major slave rebellion on record in the New World occurred in Hispaniola ("Little Spain") in 1522 and was easily suppressed. Yet, from that time until the moment of emancipation, violent slave uprisings became a fact of life for the masters. The British colony of Barbados, for example, experienced a series of dramatic but abortive rebellions in 1649, 1675, and 1692. The first was a relatively minor affair, but the rebellion of 1675 resulted in the arrest of 110 slaves. Authorities executed 17 leaders: 11 were beheaded and 6 burned alive. The conspiracy of 1692 demonstrated sophisticated planning, with the formation of a military chain of command at least three months before the revolt took place. The slaves planned to seize control of the entire island. Informants, however, betrayed the rebels, and colonial officials detained some 300 conspirators. They executed 19 of them, including the leaders Sampson, Ben, Hammon, and Sambo.

The most restive slaves in the Caribbean lived in Jamaica. Rebellions occurred there at regular intervals after 1670. The last and most serious revolt was the Christmas Rebellion of 1831, when approximately 20,000 slaves in the western parishes rose up against their masters. The terrified planters responded with their full might and eventually managed to reestablish control over the island. Their victory was temporary and costly. The bloody upheaval hastened the passage of the British Emancipation Act of 1833, which ended slavery throughout the British Empire.

The largest slave revolt in the history of the United States took place in Louisiana in 1811. Although the details remain somewhat obscure, evidence suggests that between 180 and 500 slaves (the lower estimate is probably closer to the actual number) armed with axes, pikes, knives, and a few guns struck toward New Orleans. The slaveholders, supported by a militia composed of free blacks and reinforced by federal troops under the command of General Wade Hampton, quickly smashed the uprising. The slaves' military inexperience and lack of suitable weapons had not prevented them from manifesting a degree of organization and prowess sufficient to make the slaveholders fearful of the future.

As soon as the slaves' ranks had broken, vengeful whites began an indiscriminate slaughter, although the rebels had killed only two or three whites and had restricted themselves to burning plantations. Whites, by contrast, summarily executed 66 blacks and subsequently killed 16 leaders of the rebellion. The executioners beheaded their victims, put the heads on spikes, and used them to adorn the road from New Orleans to the plantation where the revolt had begun.

Detail of an 1831 woodcut of Nat Turner's Rebellion

(Library of Congress, Washington, D.C.)

The revolt in Louisiana occurred on the frontier and thus had less impact on Southern society than three others that also took place early in the nineteenth century, although two of the three never came to fruition. The abortive revolts of Gabriel Prosser in Richmond, Virginia (1800), and of Denmark Vesey in Charleston, South Carolina (1822), along with the bloody rampage of Nat Turner through Southampton County, Virginia (1831), terrified the country.

Prosser, Vesey, and Turner had much in common. Each could read and write and had developed special skills that elevated them above ordinary field hands. Prosser was a blacksmith, with a militant political and religious temperament that placed him in a long succession of revolutionary artisan slaves. Turner was a jack-of-all-trades who worked as a field hand. He was also an exhorter whom other slaves believed to have special religious powers. Like Prosser, though perhaps to an even greater extent, Turner emerged as a messianic Christian prophet who skillfully combined the language of the Bible with the rhetoric of the American War for Independence (1775–1783). Vesey had purchased his freedom in 1800 after winning a lottery. While a slave, he worked as a seaman and visited many countries, including Haiti. He spoke several languages and read widely in philosophy and politics. Each of these remarkable men blended religious appeals to the slaves with the themes of the Declaration of Independence (1776) and the Declaration of the Rights of Man and Citizen (1789). Prosser, Turner, and Vesey projected an interpretation of Christianity that emphasized the God-given right to freedom for all persons.

Vesey formulated perhaps the most subtle and sophisticated appeal. He quoted the Bible, but relied on one of his trusted lieutenants, an Angolan slave named Jack Pritchard but more commonly known as "Gullah Jack," to reach those slaves who had not yet converted to Christianity, whose conversions were superficial, or who were hostile to a faith that they regarded as the religion of their masters. In merging elements of Christian belief and African culture, Vesey, Pritchard, and their followers drew together the sources that had combined to form a distinct African American worldview and to stiffen the resolve of men and women who faced overwhelming odds against the success of their enterprise.

The strategic objectives of these revolts remain somewhat unclear, save perhaps in Vesey's case, apart from the obvious aim of securing the freedom of as many slaves as possible. Prosser apparently sought to seize control of Richmond, which was a realistic prospect given its indifferent defenses. Possibly he intended to win political recognition for an independent black state or hoped to win freedom for blacks within the existing political framework of Southern society. More likely, he improvised, intending to take advantage of whatever opportunities developed.

Vesey seems to have entertained the possibility of conquering Charleston and the surrounding hinterland and establishing there an independent black republic modeled on Haiti. He had undoubtedly calculated the odds against success and seems also to have had serious expectations of sailing to Haiti with as many former slaves as survived the initial engagements.

Turner's goals remain the most obscure. He may have thought of raising blacks throughout the Virginia countryside en masse to strike for freedom, or he may have expected to found a large maroon community in the Dismal Swamp, located along the boundary of North Carolina. Of all the major slave plots and insurrections in the United States, Turner's displayed the least evidence of careful planning, preparation, and foresight. In one sense at least this deficiency may have served him well, for unlike Prosser and Vesey, Turner was not betrayed from within his own ranks.

By the time of Prosser, Vesey, and Turner, slave revolts in the South, one way or another, amounted to a virtual death sentence. Only the most heroic souls, even as measured by the highest standards of self-sacrifice, could contemplate such a desperate course. The wonder then is not that slave revolts were few and their success limited but that they occurred at all. Whatever their limitations and failures, slave rebels compelled the slaveholders to pay a steep price in blood and treasure to keep them in bondage, and by their actions rather than their accomplishments repeatedly demonstrated to the world the impossibility of extinguishing their determination to be free.

–MARK G. MALVASI,
RANDOLPH-MACON COLLEGE

Viewpoint:
No. Most slave rebellions failed, resulting in the execution of the conspirators and savage reprisals against, and greater oppression of, the slaves.

All slaves wanted their freedom. Historians such as Herbert Aptheker have understandably entertained a romantic fascination with the image of the slaves liberating themselves through violence. Yet, the principal outcome of slave insurrections in all but a few cases was not freedom but heightened oppression and mass execution of blacks. Contrary to the views of Orlando Patterson, the fact that blacks, particularly in the United States, did not rise up to end their subjugation offers no evidence of their cowardice. Most slave rebellions were suicidal adventures, as the fates of Gabriel Prosser, Denmark Vesey, Nat Turner, and countless others demonstrated.

Even in Latin America and the Caribbean, where the conditions necessary to produce slave insurrections were far more favorable than in the United States, the results admitted little variation. The British government was the first to emancipate the slaves under its jurisdiction. An examina-

tion of the role that slave rebellions played in that process, therefore, presents a viable test case to determine the general success of slave uprisings in effecting the abolition of slavery.

The slaves on the English sugar colony of Barbados rebelled on Easter Sunday night, 14 April 1816, after 115 years of apparent docility. Twenty thousand slaves from seventy-five estates participated, and within a few hours they had taken possession of the southeastern portion of the island. They sent whites fleeing from their homes, but were otherwise restrained. The slaves did not kill the whites who were at their mercy or engage in widespread destruction of property. Instead, they established a defensive perimeter around Bridgetown and invited the leaders of the colony to negotiate.

White Barbadians soon disabused the slaves of such civilized foolishness. The acting governor declared martial law and ordered an army composed of regular troops, including the all-black First West India Regiment, and local militiamen into the field. The commander, Colonel Codd, encouraged his men to kill all the slaves who refused to surrender and also instructed them to raze the slave quarters. Yet, even Codd had to admit in his official report that "Under the irritation of the Moment and exasperated at the atrocity of the Insurgents, some of the Militia of the Parishes in Insurrection were induced to use their Arms rather too indiscriminately in pursuit of the Fugitives." The rebellious slaves killed one white civilian and one black soldier. The army, by contrast, took the lives of 50 slaves in battle and summarily executed 70 others. In addition, 300 captives were put on trial in Bridgetown. Of that number 144 were executed and 132 deported to other English colonies.

The slave rebels misjudged the strength, determination, unity, and power of the colonial regime and exaggerated the sympathy they were likely to receive from the opponents of slavery in Parliament. The uprising, in fact, horrified the champions of the antislavery cause, who made every effort to deflect public criticism from themselves for having contributed to its outbreak. Far from coming to the aid of the slaves in Barbados, William Wilberforce, leader of the abolitionist forces, advised his emancipationist colleagues in Parliament to denounce the rebellion and to avoid trying to turn it to their political advantage. Frightened that his enemies might hold him responsible for the insurgency, Wilberforce delivered a speech before the House of Commons so contrite and apologetic that it angered others in the abolitionist movement. The slave revolt in Barbados thus momentarily debilitated rather than energized the crusade against slavery in the British Empire.

OUTCOME OF REBELLIONS

COMMENCE THE WORK OF DEATH

Nat Turner, leader of an 1831 slave rebellion in Southampton County, Virginia, in which more than fifty whites were murdered, recounted his activities after he was captured:

Hark got a ladder and set it against the chimney, on which I ascended, and hoisting a window, entered and came down stairs, unbarred the door, and removed the guns from their places. It was then observed that I must spill the first blood. On which armed with a hatchet, and accompanied by Will, I entered my master's chamber; it being dark, I could not give a death blow, the hatchet glanced from his head, he sprang from the bed and called his wife, it was his last word. Will laid him dead, with a blow of his axe, and Mrs. Travis shared the same fate, as she lay in bed. The murder of this family five in number, was the work of a moment, not one of them awoke; there was a little infant sleeping in a cradle, that was forgotten, until we had left the house and gone some distance, when Henry and Will returned and killed it; we got here, four guns that would shoot, and several old muskets, with a pound or two of powder.

We remained some time at the barn, where we paraded; I formed them in a line as soldiers, and after carrying them through all the manoeuvres I was master of, marched them off to Mr. Salathul Francis', about six hundred yards distant. Sam and Will went to the door and knocked. Mr. Francis asked who was there, Sam replied it was him, and he had a letter for him, on which he got up and came to the door; they immediately seized him, and dragging him out a little from the door, he was dispatched by repeated blows on the head; there was no other white person in the family.

We started from there for Mrs. Reese's, maintaining the most perfect silence on our march, where finding the door unlocked, we entered, and murdered Mrs. Reese in her bed, while sleeping; her son awoke, but it was only to sleep the sleep of death, he had only time to say who is that, and he was no more. From Mrs. Reese's we went to Mrs. Turner's, a mile distant, which we reached about sunrise, on Monday morning. Henry, Austin, and Sam, went to the still, where, finding Mr. Peebles, Austin shot him, and the rest of us went to the house; as we approached, the family discovered us, and shut the door. Vain hope! Will, with one stroke of his axe, opened it, and we entered and found Mrs. Turner and Mrs. Newsome in the middle of a room almost frightened to death. Will immediately killed Mrs. Turner, with one blow of his axe. I took Mrs. Newsome by the hand, and with the sword I had when I was apprehended, I struck her several blows over the head, but not being able to kill her, as the sword was dull. Will turning around and discovering it, dispatched her also. A general destruction of property and search for money and ammunition, always succeeded the murders.

By this time my company amounted to fifteen, and nine men mounted, who started for Mrs. Whitehead's, (the other six were to go through a by way to Mr. Bryant's, and rejoin us at Mrs. Whitehead's,) as we approached the house we discovered Mr. Richard Whitehead standing in the cotton patch, near the lane fence; we called him over into the lane, and Will, the executioner, was near at hand, with his fatal axe, to send him to an untimely grave. As we pushed on to the house, I discovered some one run round the garden, and thinking it was some of the white family, I pursued them, but finding it was a servant girl belonging to the house, I returned to commence the work of death, but they whom I left, had not been idle; all the family were already murdered, but Mrs. Whitehead and her daughter Margaret. As I came round to the door I saw Will pulling Mrs. Whitehead out of the house, and at the step he nearly severed her head from her body, with his broad axe. Miss Margaret, when I discovered her, had concealed herself in the corner, formed by the projection of the cellar cap from the house; on my approach she fled, but was soon overtaken, and after repeated blows with a sword, I killed her by a blow on the head, with a fence rail. By this time, the six who had gone by Mr. Bryant's, rejoined us, and informed me they had done the work of death assigned them.

Source: "The Confessions of Nat Turner: The Insurrection," From Revolution to Reconstruction—an .HTML Project <http://odur.let.rug.nl/~usa/D/1826–1850/slavery/confes05.htm>.

On 18 August 1823 nearly 30,000 slaves on sixty estates arose in rebellion in Demerara (present-day Guyana, formerly British Guiana). Although restrained in their conduct, they refused to negotiate, informing the colonial governor that "God had made them of the same flesh and blood as the whites, that they were tired of being Slaves to them, that their good King had sent Orders that they should be free and they would not work any more." As in Barbados, the slaves proved no match for the colonial military. At Bachelor's Adventure plantation, 2,000 slaves battled 300 imperial troops. Badly outnumbered, the soldiers still managed to kill between 100 and 150 rebels, while themselves suffering only 2 wounded. They then proceeded to execute 60 slaves without trial and an equal number in accordance with the judgment of a military court. In all, 250 slaves died. Authorities also arrested Reverend John Smith of the London Missionary Society and pastor of Bethel Chapel on Le Resouvenier plantation. Charged with complicity and incitement, Smith was convicted under martial law and sentenced to death. He died in prison from tuberculosis on 6 February 1824, a week before King George IV commuted his sentence but ordered him deported from the colony.

When in early October 1823 news of the slave revolt in Demerara reached London, it stunned the opponents and heartened the defenders of slavery. Thomas Fowell Buxton, who had assumed leadership of the abolitionists in the House of Commons from an ailing Wilberforce, was compelled to repudiate the actions of the slaves. Buxton's opposition to the decision of Foreign Secretary George Canning to withdraw measures designed to ameliorate the condition of the slaves made him, as he admitted, "'the most unpopular man in the House.'" Neither Buxton, Wilberforce, nor anyone else dared offer a public endorsement of the Demerara rebellion. The trial, imprisonment, and death of Smith, however, provided the abolitionists with a cause célèbre. Like other missionaries, Smith had been careful not to discuss politics with the slaves. He was intent on preaching the gospel and advised them to work hard and obey their masters. The conspicuous attack on Christianity, as Buxton noted at the time, "'changed the current of public opinion.'" Even the abolitionists seemed to have forgotten the 250 dead slave rebels, hailing Smith as the "Demerara Martyr." They rebuked the planters of Demerara not for butchering hundreds of their slaves but for taking the life of a saintly minister of Christ.

The largest slave revolt in the British Caribbean erupted in Jamaica in December 1831. At the end of the Christmas holiday on 27 December thousands of slaves throughout the island refused to return to work. Samuel Sharpe, the preeminent leader of the rebellion, had urged the slaves to pledge "not to work after Christmas as slaves, but to assert their claim to freedom, and to be faithful to each other." The uprising spread rapidly. Soon two hundred plantations and perhaps as many as 60,000 slaves were involved. On 29 December the rebels defeated the militia in a skirmish at Montpelier and sent whites fleeing to coastal towns while the slaves controlled the interior. The slaves hoped to negotiate a truce with the colonial government that would have ended the fighting and guaranteed their freedom, but it was not to be. Lord Belmore, the colonial governor, declared martial law and instructed Sir Willoughby Cotton, the commander of military forces in Jamaica, to crush the rebellion. General Cotton carried out his orders with a ruthless efficiency, allowing the militia to exact savage vengeance. Imperial troops and militiamen killed 200 slaves in the fighting and subsequently executed no fewer than 340 others. The colonists also conducted a pogrom against both the "Native" Baptist preachers, such as Sharpe, as well as white Baptist missionaries, whom they blamed for inciting the slaves to participate in what became known as the "Baptist War." Sharpe was hanged on 6 February 1832.

Once more, public opinion in England centered on the persecution of white missionaries rather than the death of black slaves. To most members of the House of Commons, however, neither the fate of the missionaries nor that of the slaves was of primary importance. A protracted war between the slaves and their masters in the colonies threatened the prosperity of the imperial economy, and hence the stability of the empire. Economic and political, rather than moral, questions engaged the attention of Parliament. More accurately, participants in these events could not effectively separate moral from political and economic considerations, altruism from self-interest. Perhaps unrest among the slaves helped to bring these issues into sharper focus, but the slave rebellions, disconcerting as they were, remained only one factor in a complex series of developments that ultimately led to emancipation.

During the eighteenth and nineteenth centuries, for example, Great Britain and the United States, which were at the forefront of the struggle against slavery, experienced extraordinary rates of economic growth. Free labor, it seemed, contributed directly to economic progress and, in fact, may have been indispensable to its realization. Although both Great Britain and the northern United States continued to profit from slavery and the slave trade, neither society had more than a modest stake in preserving the system and had, in essence, already committed to the ideology of free labor. Those who became the enemies of slavery argued freedom and prosperity were reciprocal rather than exclusive. They no longer believed that prosperity required the sacrifice of freedom to order. They had evidence to the contrary from their own experience, for it seemed that the more freedom a society attained the more prosperity it enjoyed. By limiting freedom, slavery not only violated the rights of man, it also retarded economic advancement.

At the same time, secular opponents of slavery in the eighteenth and nineteenth centuries feared slave rebellions. Such uprisings were too menacing, violent, and destructive of life and property to champion. They did not so much cultivate independent moral objections to slavery as they became convinced that the institution was a social and economic anachronism. Even had the slaves never rebelled, the majority of men and women who sought abolition would have come to the conclusion that slavery had to go. As increasing numbers of citizens determined that slavery was an economic liability, as well as a moral embarrassment, slavery became vulnerable in ways that it had not previously been. Under the right set of circumstances, its adversaries could dismantle it. Before the eighteenth century the idea that slavery could be obliterated had not occurred to many persons. Slavery was a fact of life that had to be accepted and endured. Then, in large part because of the economic transformation that occurred during the eighteenth and nineteenth centuries, people discovered that they could get along without it. Once the economic justification for slavery ceased to be persuasive, the political, social, and moral justifications were sure to suffer rejection as well.

As expressions of sheer courage in the face of overwhelming odds, the slave rebellions showed whites that they could not easily delude themselves that blacks were docile, stupid, timid, or content. In a more important sense, however, the slave rebellions were failures. They did not effect emancipation, and the uprisings in Barbados and Demerara actually hurt the antislavery cause. The Emancipation Act of 1833, which freed the slaves throughout the British Empire, was part of a widespread initiative to liberalize politics and society that followed more closely from the Reform Bill of 1832 than from the Jamaican Christmas Rebellion. Even the successful revolution that ended slavery in the French colony Saint Domingue (Haiti) ironically led to the expansion of slavery elsewhere. Among the reasons Napoleon Bonaparte agreed to sell the Louisiana Territory to the United States was the loss of Haiti, and with it the hope of establishing a French Empire in the Western Hemisphere. The slave revolutionaries of Saint Domingue thus in large part made possible the American acquisition of Louisiana, which, in turn, led to the expansion and entrenchment of slavery in the Deep South. Whatever else they may have accomplished, the rebellious slaves did not abolish slavery.

—CHESTER J. WYNNE,
WASHINGTON, D.C.

References

Herbert Aptheker, *American Negro Slave Revolts* (New York: Columbia University Press, 1943).

Hilary Beckles, "The Slave-Drivers' War: Bussa and the 1816 Slave Rebellion," *Boletin de Estudios Latinoamericanos y del Caribe,* 39 (December 1985): 85–109.

Lerone Bennett Jr., *Before the Mayflower: A History of Black America,* fifth edition (Chicago: Johnson, 1982).

Robin Blackburn, *The Overthrow of Colonial Slavery, 1776–1848* (London & New York: Verso, 1998).

Michael Craton, "Slavery Revolts and the End of Slavery," in *The Atlantic Slave Trade,* second edition, edited by David Northrup (Boston: Houghton Mifflin, 2002), pp. 188–200.

Craton, *Testing the Chains: Resistance to Slavery in the British West Indies* (Ithaca, N.Y.: Cornell University Press, 1982).

Craton, James Walvin, and David Wright, eds., *Slavery, Abolition, and Emancipation: Black Slaves and the British Empire* (London & New York: Longman, 1976).

Emilia Viotti Da Costa, *Crowns of Glory, Tears of Blood: The Demerara Slave Rebellion of 1823* (New York: Oxford University Press, 1994).

David Brion Davis, *The Problem of Slavery in the Age of Revolution, 1770–1823* (Ithaca, N.Y.: Cornell University Press, 1975).

Eugene D. Genovese, *From Rebellion to Revolution: Afro-American Slave Revolts in the Making of the Modern World* (Baton Rouge: Louisiana State University Press, 1979).

Genovese, *Roll, Jordan, Roll: The World the Slaves Made* (New York: Pantheon, 1974).

C. L. R. James, *The Black Jacobins: Toussaint L'Ouverture and the San Dominge Revolution,* revised edition (New York: Vintage, 1963).

Orlando Patterson, *The Sociology of Slavery: An Analysis of the Origins, Development, and Structure of Negro Slave Society in Jamaica* (London: MacGibbon & Kee, 1967).

Kenneth M. Stampp, *The Peculiar Institution: Slavery in the Ante-Bellum South* (New York: Knopf, 1956).

David Turley, *The Culture of English Antislavery, 1780–1860* (London & New York: Routledge, 1991).

Eric Williams, *Capitalism and Slavery* (Chapel Hill: University of North Carolina Press, 1944).

OUTCOME OF REBELLIONS

PECULIAR INSTITUTION

Was slavery in the Western Hemisphere a peculiar institution?

Viewpoint: Yes. Modern slavery was a peculiar institution, having largely disappeared from Europe in the centuries before it was reintroduced into the New World. The revitalization of slavery violated custom and law.

Viewpoint: No. Slavery had a long history in Europe, and even after it was eliminated other forms of bound labor remained.

Was slavery a peculiar institution, and if it was, how and when did it become so? Slavery had existed in the ancient world among the Greeks and Romans as well as among the Egyptians, Hebrews, Christians, and Muslims. Agricultural slavery persisted into the early Middle Ages but declined by the ninth century. Moreover, slavery began to reappear in Europe, first in Spain, where both Christians and Muslims enslaved prisoners of war, and then in Italy during the second half of the fourteenth century in response to the labor shortage that resulted from the Black Death (1347–1351). The Portuguese and Spanish also introduced slavery into the colonies they held in the mid-Atlantic, such as the Madeira and Canary Islands. Far from being peculiar, slavery had long been a common practice in the Mediterranean world. It required little imagination to transfer slavery from its European setting to the New World.

Yet, there was something disturbingly different about New World slavery: black Africans eventually became its sole victims. Failed attempts to enslave Native Americans and other Europeans prompted the enslavement of Africans as a logical, economical, and efficient solution to the labor shortages that colonists faced. Once introduced, slavery proved almost impossible to eliminate. The ancients, as nineteenth-century French writer Alexis de Tocqueville pointed out, had not encountered such difficulties. They could rid themselves of the problem of slavery merely by freeing their slaves, who were often of the same race as their masters. The former slaves, so similar to their masters in appearance, education, and manners, in a short time became indistinguishable from them. In the modern world, by contrast, masters could emancipate their slaves, but they could not eliminate the burden of racial prejudice that prevented the recognition of blacks as equals.

Viewpoint:
Yes. Modern slavery was a peculiar institution, having largely disappeared from Europe in the centuries before it was reintroduced into the New World. The revitalization of slavery violated custom and law.

"Generally speaking," wrote nineteenth-century French writer Alexis de Tocqueville, "it requires great and constant efforts for men to create lasting ills; but there is one evil which had percolated furtively into the world: at first it was hardly noticed among the usual abuses of power; it began with an individual whose name history does not record; it was cast like an accursed seed somewhere on the ground; it then nurtured itself, grew without effort, and spread with the society that accepted it; that evil was slavery." By the time Europeans reintroduced slavery into the New World, it had largely disappeared from Europe. Europeans had, of course, known slavery from antiquity, and so the coming of slavery to the New World was in one sense nothing new. Yet, the slavery that developed in the New World was different from its ancient predecessor.

Typically, in the ancient world two types of slavery existed. Slaves worked as domestics or artisans to serve a system of household production. They also worked in gangs to furnish goods for an international market economy. Large-scale agricultural slavery existed into the early Middle Ages, but by the ninth century it, too, had disappeared from Europe; domestic and artisanal slavery followed two centuries later. The rise of slavery in the New World thus involved the revival of a system of labor that had been dormant in Europe for nearly five hundred years.

Europeans who journeyed to the New World initially sought to develop other forms of labor and adopted slavery with reluctance, only after exhausting all other options. The Spanish devised various means of organizing Native American labor as alternatives to slavery. The Spanish government, for example, enacted regulations to protect the Indians of New Spain, declaring them subjects of the Crown whom colonists were not to enslave. Despite modifications in these rules that permitted the enslavement of natives captured in war or those already held as slaves by other native groups, the royal government, in 1542, declared illegal the enslavement of all natives.

The *encomienda* was the earliest attempt to rescue the native population from enslavement at the hands of Spanish colonists. In exchange for instructing the Indians in Christianity and permitting them to work their lands to provide for their own sustenance, the *encomienda* obliged the Indians to pay tribute to the colonists in the form of either goods or labor. Designed as another alternative to chattel slavery, the *mita* also exacted forced labor from the Indians but prevented the Spanish from holding them in bondage.

Despite the good intentions of Spanish officials, the Indians, quickly and often ruthlessly enveloped by the *encomienda* system, became a source of labor vital to colonial interests. With impunity, Spanish colonists circumvented or ignored royal decrees outlawing the enslavement of the native population, who, from their perspective, had merely traded Aztec and Incan exploitation for Spanish. To address this situation, the government abolished the *encomienda* in 1550 and replaced it with the *repartimiento,* a system that permitted those settlers who could demonstrate a need for labor to compel natives to work for them during a fixed period of time. The law required the Spanish to ensure that the Indians had decent working conditions and to pay them a wage. Practice, though, once more diverged from law, and the Spanish government ended the *repartimiento* system except in mining.

However feebly, the Spanish resisted brutalizing and enslaving the Indians, but they could do nothing to keep them from dying. Isolation from the rest of the world had kept Native Americans from being exposed to many diseases that were endemic elsewhere. When diseases common in the Old World entered the New, the mortality rate was staggering. Modern estimates place the native population before the arrival of Europeans at anywhere from 13.3 to 112 million. By 1650 the native population had declined to between 4.5 and 10 million. The culprits included measles, malaria, plague, influenza, and especially smallpox.

Europe, Asia, and parts of Africa formed a common disease pool. In those regions, smallpox was a childhood disease that, although serious, was rarely fatal. Victims usually recovered and acquired immunity against recurrence. When smallpox entered the New World, it affected a population previously unexposed and thus without natural immunity. The devastation was massive and widespread.

The Spanish conquerors also imposed new political and economic structures on Native American society that displaced many persons from their traditional patterns of social organization and habits of life and work. The insecurity and upheaval that these disruptions created weakened the native populations psychologi-

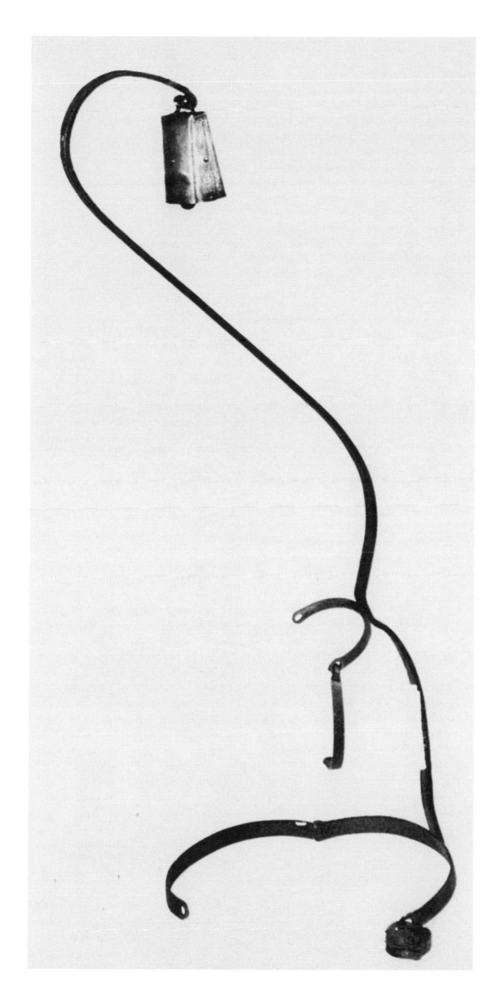

PECULIAR INSTITUTION

cally and physiologically and further impaired their ability to withstand disease.

Confronted with restrictions on the use of native labor and hampered by a rapidly declining native population, Spanish colonists in the New World began to look elsewhere for workers. Like the Portuguese—and later the English, French, Dutch, and Danish—the Spanish believed that Africans offered several advantages over Indians. Many Africans were accustomed to the labor discipline that large-scale agricultural production required. They also came from regions that shared a disease pool with Europeans and were less susceptible to illnesses that were exterminating the natives. Perhaps the most important advantage from the Spanish point of view was that Africans were not under the protection of the Crown. As a consequence, they were subject to a degree of exploitation from which the Indians were legally shielded.

The English, however, initially favored white indentured servitude rather than slave labor and did not even establish formal legal definitions of slavery until the early eighteenth century. In return for transportation across the Atlantic Ocean, an outfit of clothes, a steady and adequate diet (including a generous supply of alcohol), and decent housing, English settlers hoping to make a better life for themselves signed a legal contract called an indenture that bound them to work for a master for four to seven years. Approximately 50 to 67 percent of all Englishmen (few women migrated) who arrived in Virginia until 1680 were indentured servants.

Indentured servitude, according to historian Edmund S. Morgan, was a temporary status that was perfectly acceptable everywhere in English colonial society. Most indentured servants were young men between the ages of fifteen and twenty-five. Some were kidnapped or otherwise coerced into servitude, but the majority entered into the agreement voluntarily. Lured by the potential benefits of a new life in a place where labor was in high demand, indentured servants had a real opportunity to acquire freedom and land after relatively few years of servitude. In the New World there seemed boundless opportunities for upward social mobility. Impoverished Englishmen could redeem themselves, enrich the mother country, and spread English influence abroad.

During the 1630s, when the high mortality rate in Virginia at last began to decline, many indentured servants stood on the threshold of realizing their ambitions. Having fulfilled the terms of their contracts, they settled along the great rivers of Virginia, established farms, and began planting corn, raising livestock, and cultivating tobacco, the staple cash crop of the region. The image of Virginia as "Earth's only paradise," forecast in English poet Michael Drayton's ode "To the Virginian Voyage" (1606), seemed to have become a reality:

> And cheerfully at sea,
> Success you still entice,
> To get the pear and gold,
> And ours to hold,
> Virginia,
> Earth's only paradise.
>
> Where nature hath in store
> Fowl, venison, and fish,
> And the fruitful'st soil
> Without your toil
> Three harvests more,
> All greater than your wish.

From the success of the Virginia colony, however, new problems arose. After 1640, as the mortality rate continued to decline and the population to increase, former indentured servants suddenly found it more difficult to acquire property. As people began living longer, Morgan has shown, there appeared in Virginia a growing number of freed servants who could not now afford to purchase land except on the frontier, which was unprotected from Indian attack, or in the unfertile interior. By 1676 an estimated 25 percent of Virginians were without land and, worse, without the prospect of obtaining any.

The presence of a class of impoverished former servants frightened the planter elite. Young, single, and propertyless, they had nothing invested in the community and, therefore, had nothing to lose by attacking it. Even more ominously, they were armed. Sir William Berkeley, royal governor of Virginia, feared a revolt of these dispossessed men. His fears were justified, for in 1676 rebellion swept Virginia. Known as Bacon's Rebellion, this uprising was the largest civil disturbance in the colonies before the American War for Independence (1775–1783) a century later. Although Bacon's Rebellion subsided quickly, the causes did not immediately disappear. Greater numbers of indentured servants arrived in Virginia every year to man the plantations. When they attained their freedom, most could still not afford to buy land. It was under these circumstances that slave traders began to bring large numbers of slaves to Virginia. Costing only £20 in 1700, about twice as much as it cost to engage an indenture servant, a slave was bound to the master for life. With the decline in mortality, slaves, although more expensive than servants, became more profitable investments.

The unexpected social benefits of slavery proved as great as the economic benefits, for the slaves were less dangerous than the freed servants had become. No slave rebellion in

American history ever approximated the magnitude or success of Bacon's Rebellion. Slaves fell permanently under the control of their masters and could be denied rights that Englishmen, indentured or free, could traditionally demand. There was a limit beyond which the abridgment of English rights and liberties could not go. The English, by comparison, subjected slaves to harsh punishments without recourse to the courts. They could keep slaves unarmed, unorganized, and ignorant. The color of the slaves' skin marked their probable status and made escape more difficult. By enslaving Africans, Virginia planters stopped adding to the band of indigent white free men who threatened to disrupt the fragile social order of the colony. If large numbers of Africans had not been available, Morgan surmises, English colonial planters would probably have found it impossible to keep the former servants in their place. The continued abuse of English subjects might have resulted in the outbreak of another rebellion or, more likely, in a Parliamentary ban on the continued importation of servants. The attempted enslavement of Englishmen would have caused greater disorder than it remedied. In violation of all custom and law, English colonists evidently thought the enslavement of Africans an expedient solution to the problem of organizing a reliable and disciplined labor force and, quite unexpectedly, of establishing and maintaining social and political order.

The Spanish, English, and other Europeans came to regard slaves brought from Africa as essential to the settlement of the New World. Slavery existed throughout North and South America and the Caribbean, stretching from the St. Lawrence River basin in Canada to the Rio de la Plata in Brazil. It was indispensable to the economies of the colonies that Europeans most valued. As Tocqueville recognized, in reviving a most "peculiar institution," which their ancestors had long ago abolished, Europeans had fastened a permanent evil upon the modern world.

—MARK G. MALVASI,
RANDOLPH-MACON COLLEGE

Viewpoint:
No. Slavery had a long history in Europe, and even after it was eliminated other forms of bound labor remained.

Slavery in the Mediterranean world dated to antiquity. Even after it was abolished, other types of bound labor, such as serfdom, remained. The ancient Hebrews had practiced slavery; a family of substance might own two or three slaves, who engaged chiefly in domestic service. Considered members of their master's household and family, Hebrew slaves were afforded the protection of the law. If their master injured them, they were freed. If he killed them, he faced punishment. Some slaves inherited their master's property or married into his family, thereby gaining their freedom. The Hebrew state also owned slaves whom it obtained as prisoners of war. These slaves worked either in the temples, mines, fields, or commercial enterprises of the kings.

Like the Hebrews, the Mycenaean Greeks were slave owners, also commonly holding in bondage those whom they had captured in war. There were, for instance, five hundred women listed as slaves from Asia who harvested and prepared flax to be woven into cloth. Slaves were abundant in the Hellenistic world, with an average of ten thousand slaves a day passing though the slave market at Delos. Hellenistic slaves worked in domestic and government service, mining, farming, and textile manufacturing. Slave women often became concubines. The Romans employed slaves in their households. Slaves also toiled as domestic servants for those Muslims who could afford to purchase and maintain them.

The occupation of these domestic slaves was largely noneconomic. They frequently acted as servants, guards, and sexual partners. Their primary function in many cases was to demonstrate the wealth and status of their owners. There were exceptions. Slave artisans carried out the production of goods for local consumption, often working side by side with their masters. Collectively, the contributions of these slaves made a significant impact on the economy of the ancient world. His defense of slavery notwithstanding, William Harper of South Carolina correctly pointed out that slavery was far from a "peculiar institution." It existed, Harper wrote in 1837, "over far the greater portion of the earth," and "within a very few centuries, it may be said to have existed over the whole earth."

Slavery began to reappear in Europe during the second half of the fourteenth century, first in Spain, where both Christians and Muslims enslaved prisoners of war during the *reconquista* (reconquest), and then in Italy. The reemergence of slavery occurred in large part as a response to the labor shortage that resulted from the Black Death (1347–1351). Estimates suggest the plagues that ravaged Europe throughout the fourteenth century claimed between 25 and 40 percent of the population. This dramatic reduction in the number of people enabled survivors to command higher wages and attain a better standard of living. To reduce labor costs, house-

ARISTOTLE ON SLAVERY

Fourth-century B.C.E. Greek philosopher Aristotle comments on slavery:

Let us first speak of master and slave, looking to the needs of practical life and also seeking to attain some better theory of their relation than exists at present. . . . Property is a part of the household, and the art of acquiring property is a part of the art of managing the household; for no man can live well, or indeed live at all, unless he be provided with necessaries. And so, in the arrangement of the family, a slave is a living possession, and property a number of such instruments; and the slave is himself an instrument which takes precedence of all other instruments. . . .The master is only the master of the slave; he does not belong to him, whereas the slave is not only the slave of his master, but wholly belongs to him. Hence we see what is the nature and office of a slave; he who is by nature not his own but another's man, is by nature a slave; and he may be said to be another's man who, being a human being, is also a possession. And a possession may be defined as an instrument of action, separable from the possessor.

But is there any one thus intended by nature to be a slave, and for whom such a condition is expedient and right, or rather is not all slavery a violation of nature? There is no difficulty in answering this question, on grounds both of reason and of fact. For that some should rule and others be ruled is a thing not only necessary, but expedient; from the hour of their birth, some are marked out for subjection, others for rule. . . . Again, the male is by nature superior, and the female inferior; and the one rules, and the other is ruled; this principle, of necessity, extends to all mankind.

Where then there is such a difference as that between soul and body, or between men and animals (as in the case of those whose business is to use their body, and who can do nothing better), the lower sort are by nature slaves, and it is better for them as for all inferiors that they should be under the rule of a master. For he who can be, and therefore is, another's and he who participates in rational principle enough to apprehend, but not to have, such a principle, is a slave by nature. Whereas the lower animals cannot even apprehend a principle; they obey their instincts. And indeed the use made of slaves and of tame animals is not very different; for both with their bodies minister to the needs of life. Nature would like to distinguish between the bodies of freemen and slaves, making the one strong for servile labor, the other upright, and although useless for such services, useful for political life in the arts both of war and peace. But the opposite often happens—that some have the souls and others have the bodies of free men. And doubtless if men differed from one another in the mere forms of their bodies as much as the statues of the gods do from men, all would acknowledge that the inferior class should be slaves of the superior. It is clear, then, that some men are by nature free, and others slaves, and that for these latter slavery is both expedient and right.

There is a slave or slavery by law as well as by nature. The law of which I speak is a sort of convention—the law by which whatever is taken in war is supposed to belong to the victors. But this right many jurists impeach, as they would an orator who brought forward an unconstitutional measure: they detest the notion that, because one man has the power of doing violence and is superior in brute strength, another shall be his slave and subject. Even among philosophers there is a difference of opinion. The origin of the dispute, and what makes the views invade each other's territory, is as follows: in some sense virtue, when furnished with means, has actually the greatest power of exercising force; and as superior power is only found where there is superior excellence of some kind, power seems to imply virtue, and the dispute to be simply one about justice (for it is due to one party identifying justice with goodwill while the other identifies it with the mere rule of the stronger). If these views are thus set out separately, the other views have no force or plausibility against the view that the superior in virtue ought to rule, or be master.

Others, clinging, as they think, simply to a principle of justice (for law and custom are a sort of justice), assume that slavery in accordance with the custom of war is justified by law, but at the same moment they deny this. For what if the cause of the war be unjust? And again, no one would ever say he is a slave who is unworthy to be a slave. Were this the case, men of the highest rank would be slaves and the children of slaves if they or their parents chance to have been taken captive and sold. Wherefore Hellenes do not like to call Hellenes slaves, but confine the term to barbarians. Yet, in using this language, they really mean the natural slave of whom we spoke at first; for it must be admitted that some are slaves everywhere, others nowhere. The same principle applies to nobility. Hellenes regard themselves as noble everywhere, and not only in their own country, but they deem the barbarians noble only when at home, thereby implying that there are two sorts of nobility and freedom, the one absolute, the other relative.

Source: *"Documents on Greek Slavery, c. 750–330 BCE,"* Ancient History Sourcebook <http://www.fordham.edu/halsall/ancient greek-slaves.html>.

holders, especially in Italy, turned to slavery. In 1363, for example, the government of Florence authorized the unlimited importation of foreign slaves.

Italian slaves performed a variety of functions. In the cities slaves worked at skilled trades, producing handcrafted goods for their masters, just as had their counterparts in antiquity. They also served as nursemaids and playmates. Fiammetta Adimari, for example, wrote to her husband in 1469: "I must remind you that when Alfonso [their son] is weaned we ought to get a little slave-girl to look after him, or else one of the black boys to keep him company." Wealthy Florentine merchants commonly owned two or three slaves, sometimes using the females as concubines. Francesco Datini, for instance, fathered an illegitimate daughter by Lucia, his twenty-year-old slave. His wife, Margherita, who could not bear children, reluctantly brought the child into their household and raised her as her own. Most illegitimate children of slaves, however, were not so fortunate. Their fathers either sold them away from their mothers or simply abandoned them.

Slaves obtained in Italian markets came principally from the eastern Mediterranean or the region surrounding the Black Sea. Included among their number were Tartars, Russians, Albanians, and Dalmatians. Italians also acquired slaves in Africa, either Moors or Ethiopians, and purchased Muslims from the Spanish. Merchants grew rich from the commerce in slaves. During the early fifteenth century, between 1414 and 1423, ten thousand slaves were sold on the Venetian market alone and brought handsome profits. Most were female, many of them children or teenagers.

Yet, by the end of the fifteenth century, slavery was beginning to disappear from Italian cities. Moral and religious considerations prompted some masters to free their slaves, while others not motivated by conscience found the acquisition of slaves more difficult and more costly when the Turkish conquest of the Byzantine Empire in 1453 closed the Black Sea market to Italian traders. As a consequence, the price of slaves rose dramatically, further reducing demand. Italians had also begun to fear that slaves, or the "domestic enemies" as they called them, constituted a dangerous presence and were worth neither the trouble nor the expense to acquire and maintain. During the sixteenth century, therefore, slaves were in evidence only in princely courts of Italian city-states, where they were little more than novelties and curiosities, especially if they had dark skin.

The Italians' disaffection with slavery did not mean that Europeans were finished with it. Although the large-scale use of slaves in agriculture had disappeared from medieval Europe, in the fifteenth century the Castilians and the Portuguese established sugar plantations on the islands of the eastern Atlantic Ocean and worked them with slave labor. These plantations became the models for the similar enterprises that emerged in the New World during the sixteenth century.

The origin of sugar cultivation in Europe dates from the eleventh century, when the first Crusaders encountered Muslims growing sugarcane on plantations in Syria and Palestine. In the thirteenth century, after the Muslims toppled the last states that the Crusaders had erected, Europeans transplanted the sugar culture to Cyprus, Crete, and Sicily. By the fifteenth century the Castilians and the Portuguese had brought sugar production to the Atlantic islands they had conquered. Only there did European sugar planters come to rely almost exclusively on slave labor, as would their counterparts in the Americas a century later.

During the 1450s, at the same time the Italians were divesting themselves of their slaves, the Portuguese began to use slaves on sugar plantations in the Madeira Islands. The slaves came largely from Morocco, located in North Africa, and the neighboring Canary Islands. There were limits on the number of slaves the Portuguese could profitably employ, for Madeiran sugar plantations were small in comparison with those that later developed in Latin America and the Caribbean.

In the initial phase of their conquest of the Canary Islands the Castilians had enslaved the native peoples and sold them in Spain and in the Madeira Islands. The Spanish pressed those who remained into domestic service. Household service and not agriculture was, in fact, the most common occupation for slaves in the Canary Islands. In part the use of slaves in domestic service rather than in agriculture arose because the people of the Canaries had developed neither an agricultural economy nor a commercial network by the time the Castilians arrived in the fourteenth and fifteenth centuries.

Politically, the island populations organized themselves into various bands. The Castilians made treaties with some of these groups while they fought against others. A royal decree made it legal to enslave only those who resisted the Spanish incursion. It was illegal to enslave members of the bands who cooperated with, and submitted to, the Spanish, but they could enslave as prisoners of war members of allied bands who rebelled or refused to honor the terms of their agreements. The natives of the Canary Islands, however, did not make a substantial or enduring addition to the international slave trade. The population of the islands was small, and it declined steadily as the result of disease after the Castilians arrived. Thus, by the early sixteenth century the Canarian slave trade to Europe had ceased, and the surviving natives increasingly intermarried with the colonists and assimilated to Iberian culture.

Since natives did not satisfy the labor needs of the Castilians in the Canary Islands, they recruited free workers from Portugal, Castile, and other parts of Spain. They welcomed Moors from North Africa and brought American Indians from the New World until the Spanish Crown outlawed the trade. In time, slaves brought from West Africa came to constitute the most significant element in the workforce of the Canary Islands. By the sixteenth century the Spanish had imported approximately ten thousand slaves into the Canary Islands, 67 to 75 percent of whom came from Africa. Slaves accounted for between 10 and 12 percent of the population. As with the transatlantic slave trade to the New World, males vastly outnumbered females, 62 to 38 percent.

The tasks these slaves performed encompassed all aspects of economic life in the colony, but they were especially vital to sugar production. By the early seventeenth century, slavery had become equally important to the economies of Latin America and the Caribbean. That development ought not to be surprising. In their conquest and exploitation of the Atlantic islands, the Portuguese and the Spanish had already laid the foundation for the expansion of the plantation system and the introduction of slavery into the New World. The slaves who came to the Americas participated in an institution that already had a long history in Europe.

–MEG GREENE,
MIDLOTHIAN, VIRGINIA

References

Pierre Bonnassie, *From Slavery to Feudalism in Southwestern Europe,* translated by Jean Birrell (Cambridge & New York: Cambridge University Press / Paris: Editions de la Maison des sciences de l'homme, 1991).

C. R. Boxer, *The Portuguese Seaborne Empire, 1415–1825* (London: Hutchinson, 1969).

M. E. Bradford, *A Better Guide Than Reason: Federalists and Anti-Federalists* (New Brunswick, N.J.: Transactions, 1994).

K. R. Bradley, *Slavery and Rebellion in the Roman World, 140 B.C.–70 B.C.* (Brussels: Latomus, 1984).

David Brion Davis, *The Problem of Slavery in Western Culture* (Ithaca, N.Y.: Cornell University Press, 1966).

David Eltis, *The Rise of African Slavery in the Americas* (Cambridge & New York: Cambridge University Press, 2000).

M. I. Finley, *Ancient Slavery and Modern Ideology* (New York: Viking, 1980).

William Harper, "Memoir on Slavery," in *The Ideology of Slavery: Proslavery Thought in the Antebellum South, 1830–1860,* edited by Drew Faust (Baton Rouge: Louisiana State University Press, 1981), pp. 78–135.

Bernard Lewis, *Race and Slavery in the Middle East: An Historical Enquiry* (New York: Oxford University Press, 1990).

Edmund S. Morgan, *American Slavery, American Freedom: The Ordeal of Colonial Virginia* (New York: Norton, 1975).

J. H. Parry, *The Spanish Seaborne Empire* (London: Hutchinson, 1966).

Frank M. Snowden Jr., *Blacks in Antiquity: Ethiopians in the Greco-Roman Experience* (Cambridge, Mass.: Belknap Press of Harvard University Press, 1970).

Barbara L. Solow, ed., *Slavery and the Rise of the Atlantic System* (Cambridge & New York: Cambridge University Press, 1991).

John Thornton, *Africa and Africans in the Making of the Atlantic World, 1400–1680* (Cambridge & New York: Cambridge University Press, 1992).

Alexis de Tocqueville, *Democracy in America,* translated by George Lawrence, edited by J. P. Mayer and Max Lerner (New York: Harper & Row, 1966).

Joseph Vogt, *Ancient Slavery and the Ideal of Man,* translated by Thomas Wiedemann (Oxford: Blackwell, 1974).

PROFITS

Was slavery profitable?

Viewpoint: Yes. Slavery generated extraordinary profits and huge fortunes for the slaveholding planters and those connected with the slave trade.

Viewpoint: No. Slavery caused extensive structural weaknesses in the economies of all slaveholding regimes that retarded economic development.

The pursuit of commercial agriculture in the South gave rise to an economy dependent on slave labor. Although the slave economy generated extraordinary profits, historians continue to debate its viability. Could slavery not only sustain economic growth but also contribute to economic development? Could the slave South compete effectively with the free-labor system emerging in the northern United States and western Europe, which had given rise to an industrial and a market revolution?

The market, of course, also underlay the Southern economic relations and activity. Yet, the Southern market was, and had long been, confined to the sale of tobacco, indigo, rice, cotton, and other agricultural commodities. Unlike in the North and Western Europe, in the South a market in labor power was virtually nonexistent. To be sure, the slaveholders of the Old South participated extensively in a variety of commercial transactions. They sold their produce, bought items for personal consumption and for use on their farms and plantations, and borrowed money with which to purchase additional land and slaves. The market thus governed exchange but not production. Historian James Oakes has explained that "a highly developed market economy was a precondition to the emergence of any slave society. Yet master and slave formed what was, at bottom, a nonmarket relationship."

The question, however, remains: did slavery pay? In important respects the social and economic history of the South paralleled that of the North. During the thirty or forty years before the Civil War (1861–1865), Southerners, like Northerners, moved westward, acquired land, established farms, and prospered from the sale of their agricultural produce. Measured in per capita income (the output of goods and services divided by population) Southern economic growth between 1840 and 1860 exceeded that of the North. "If we treat the North and South as separate nations and rank them among the countries of the world," argued historian Robert W. Fogel, "the South would stand as the fourth most prosperous nation of the world in 1860, . . . more prosperous than France, Germany, Denmark, or any of the countries in Europe except England."

Fogel's conclusion, though technically correct, is flawed and misleading. To the historian, the Southern economy presents the paradox of economic growth without economic development. Impressive as it was, Southern economic growth rested on a precarious foundation: the continuous expansion of staple-crop agriculture. By bringing ever more land under cultivation, Southerners could generate increased profits. At the same time, they failed to promote the sorts of economic diversification and development that were taking place in the North and in western Europe. The extraordinary prosperity that

169

Southern planters enjoyed depended on their ability to produce and market a highly desired and valuable commodity. A severe crop shortage or a sudden fall in the demand for, and thus the price of, cotton, jeopardized Southern prosperity and thrust the South into an economic crisis. Although by no means moribund, the slave economy of the South, like the slave economies elsewhere in the Western Hemisphere, endured structural weaknesses that rendered it permanently backward and underdeveloped in comparison with economic systems predicated upon freedom.

Viewpoint:
Yes. Slavery generated extraordinary profits and huge fortunes for the slaveholding planters and those connected with the slave trade.

Answering the question of the profitability of slavery may appear to be an easy task at first. One could merely cite the pioneering work of such historians as Alfred H. Conrad, John R. Meyer, Robert W. Fogel, or Stanley L. Engerman, all of whom studied slave prices, production yields, plantation expenses, and investment returns. They concluded that, over the long term, a typical antebellum slaveowner could expect returns equal to those from other kinds of investments. The profitability question, however, involves more than an accumulation of case studies designed to measure how well a particular slave owner ran his business.

The profitability issue raises questions about how markets in general operate and to what degree slave labor was compatible with a capitalist economy. Historians and economists who deny the profitability of slavery normally rest their case on two different criteria. On one hand, some argue that Southern slavery as a system of labor characterized a "precapitalist" order threatened by the spread of free-labor ideology and commercial enterprise. Because of their precarious and inevitably declining position, slaveholders closed ranks to defend their social order much as had the European landed elite of the eighteenth and nineteenth centuries. Coming from a different direction, libertarians, on the other hand, claim the inherent inefficiency of slave labor forced slaveowners to rely on government regulations to protect the institution. Though these opponents share little else, together they insist that the inherent weaknesses of slavery precluded real profit. To address both of their concerns, it is important for students of Southern slavery to step back and define exactly what is meant by terms such as "capitalism" and "profit."

At its most basic level capitalism is a means of exchange, whereby people trade something they have for something they want. Over time humanity discovered ways to improve exchange,

the most important of which occurred in antiquity when people started using money rather than bartering a variable amount of goods. Money simplified the process of exchange and enabled individuals more accurately to weigh their costs and calculate their profits. Items in high demand but in short supply commanded a higher price than items that were readily available or less desired. If people produced and sold an item at a higher price than their costs, they made a profit.

Profits, however, depend upon many criteria, some of which are beyond the producer's or seller's control. For Southern slave owners, the profits they realized from using slave labor depended on factors such as climate, soil, length of the growing season, farm technology, capital improvements, and not least, demand for their crops and livestock. Calculating profitability thus required slaveholders to pay attention to more than the productivity of labor. For this reason, Fogel and Engerman's contention in *Time on the Cross: The Economics of American Negro Slavery* (1974) that slaves were highly productive workers failed to win the acceptance of many historians. One can argue, as Gavin Wright has done in *The Political Economy of the Cotton South: Households, Markets, and Wealth in the Nineteenth Century* (1978), that the profits reaped on Southern plantations during the antebellum period were largely the result of the demand for cotton (and rice and sugar), not a reliance on slave labor. However, like all entrepreneurs, slave owners who made the greatest profits managed to meet market demand while keeping costs down, especially labor costs. So the question must be, were labor sources available that were cheaper than slavery? Was there a more profitable alternative whereby the demand for cotton could be met? After all, tobacco farmers in the Chesapeake Bay region had realized substantial returns from using indentured servants during the seventeenth and eighteenth centuries.

In more ways than one, the American South's shift toward the use of slave labor rather than indentured servants signified the desire of planters to reap higher profits. The term of indentured servitude was temporary; as the supply of willing Europeans dried up during the seventeenth century, the costs of hiring indentured labor increased. Over the long term, the economic benefits of slavery surpassed those of

PROFITS

BRANDING A NEGRESS

indentured labor in terms of reliability, consistency, and lower costs. The sharp rise in slave prices throughout the nineteenth century confirms that demand for slaves increased rather than stagnated. Above all, if there was one economic consideration that plagued Southern slave owners throughout the existence of slavery, it was labor shortages, not surpluses. In general, few slave owners complained about boarding and clothing their slaves or taking care of those who were sick, indigent, and elderly. Such costs were trifling when compared to the benefits to be reaped. Even in areas where staple-crop agri-culture declined, masters rented or leased their slaves to city dwellers or labor-deficient farmers.

Critics argue the capitalization of slaves (what the master invested to purchase a slave) necessarily reduced the master's profit because he could have received higher rates of return on other investments. Hence, so this argument goes, lost interest must be weighed as an operating cost. Additional costs must be factored in to cover injuries, deaths, and other unexpected risks. Historian Kenneth M. Stampp answered this objection in *The Peculiar Institution: Slavery in the Ante-Bellum South* (1956) by explaining

PROFITS

how risks naturally caused the price of slaves to be discounted. A healthy, energetic male slave commanded a much higher price than a middle-aged female. A slave with a history of rebellion or scars from harsh punishment could be purchased at a much lower price than a slave known to be docile. Stampp further explained that the cost of purchasing a slave

> was merely the payment in a lump sum of a portion of what the employer of free labor pays over a period of years. The price of a slave, together with maintenance, was the cost of a lifetime claim to his labor; it was part of the wage an employer could have paid a free laborer. The price was what a master was willing to give for the right to maintain his workers at a subsistence level, and to gain full control over their time and movements.

Maintaining control over slaves was not without its costs, which often eroded a master's potential profits. Here again, costs depended upon many conditions, most of which would not have been alleviated by a reliance on free labor. Truly, masters routinely complained about their slaves' work habits and laziness. As historian Eugene D. Genovese showed in *Roll, Jordan, Roll: The World the Slaves Made* (1974), slaves practiced subtle forms of resistance that hindered their productivity. Slaves ran away during peak harvests, broke tools, feigned illness, and followed other strategies to relieve themselves of the work. One would expect such behavior from people denied the fruits of their own labor. There is no question that slavery impacted the slaves in psychological, physical, and economic terms, but the master who relied upon force to eke out the labor of his slaves was bound to lose money over time. For this reason, planters devised ways of sidestepping the use of force whenever possible.

Plantation management became an obsession to many profit-seeking planters who knew the poor productivity of their slaves could be improved. One can argue that a significant amount of low slave productivity depended on the dismal performance of overseers, whose handling of slaves rarely struck a balance between severity and leniency. The same can be said of Northern factory managers in handling free workers. However, planters devised methods of increasing productivity while providing overseers with strict criteria by which to judge slave performance. For example, large cotton plantations relied on a gang system of labor to ensure that slave time was filled with work. Rice plantations often used the task system whereby slaves were given a certain number of chores to complete and then were left to themselves. In each case, masters offered slaves a variety of incentives that resembled those found in free-labor situations.

Those slaves who picked the most cotton received special rewards. Slaves who completed their tasks early could work in their own gardens and sell the surplus. In short, even the most devoted defender of slave labor resorted to using free-labor methods of encouragement.

The efficiency of slave labor, then, is a testament to the capability of Southern entrepreneurs and African American laborers, not to the advantages of slavery over free labor. What does this situation tell historians about the two main criticisms of slaveholders: being more concerned with social control than profit, and the inefficiency of labor requiring government intervention? In many ways social control, or "paternalism," coincides with institutional means of enforcement. Whether slavery encouraged this development must be examined in terms of the motivation of the slaveholders. Did they seek social control because they wished to protect their property and potential profits or because they hoped for a hierarchical social order based on paternalism and deference?

While some historians see masters as profit-oriented businessmen, others view them as a self-conscious landed elite. There is no question that many large planters exhibited paternalistic qualities, especially in the tidewater areas of Maryland, Virginia, and North Carolina, or in Western areas settled by tidewater planters. Not only were slaves thought of as extended family members in these areas, but under legal codes existing prior to the nineteenth century, slaves also were treated as real property as opposed to chattel. Being classified as realty subjected slaves to the same entail provisions that covered land. Preventing slave holdings from being broken up meant many generations of slaves were owned by the same family. Paternalism naturally developed; or rather, the paternal connection between slaves and slave owners intensified within a culture where paternalism already existed. Not only did paternalistic relations characterize the English society from which many tidewater planters came, but it was also evident in their interaction with indentured servants in the New World. Furthermore, deference continued to be exhibited toward upper-class tidewater planters by lower-class whites and slaves well into the nineteenth century.

Observers of planter behavior face quite a few problems when extrapolating from obvious examples of paternalism to Southern society at large. First, large slaveholders represented only a minority of slave owners and only a fragment of larger white society. By 1860 only about 25 percent of white Southerners owned slaves. Of these, only a few hundred could be classified as large planters. Second, many masters with small holdings exhibited a much more individualistic

PROFITS

attitude toward society, the market, and their slaves than did planters. Though the upward mobility of small slave owners can be exaggerated, a case could be made that they focused on market conditions to a greater extent than larger planters. Providing enough work for large slaveholdings typically meant masters planted staples regardless of price fluctuations. Small owners could vary the slaves' working habits and could shift their crops to corn or foodstuffs when staple prices declined. In effect, small farmers could better react to market conditions to maximize their profits than many large-scale planters. Third, even large planters sold their slaves during lean times, and the planter who refused generally did so to his or to his family's regret. Even the Virginian gentry, faced with the dismal financial conditions during the War of 1812, broke up their slave families and sold them west or further south. Paternalism notwithstanding, economic viability and profits still determined a master's ultimate relationship with his slave. Finally, paternalism and profit seeking are not mutually exclusive. One can be both paternal and acquisitive; in fact, one could naturally lead to the other. A prudent master thus always looked for ways to increase his slaves' productivity.

Though paternalism failed to diminish a slave owner's position as a businessman, there is one challenge to the profitability argument that deserves attention. One must concede that slaveholders used political institutions to counter free-market conditions that might have proved devastating to slavery. Slaveholders relied upon state regulations for police powers and patrols to prevent rebellions and monitor slaves who traveled the countryside. Legal codes regulated inheritance, protected slave property, and in many cases prevented educating slaves to rise above their condition. In areas where depressed market conditions prompted anxious masters to sell their slaves, manumission was forbidden so as to prevent the price of slaves from dropping to market levels. Considerations about social control were present in restricting manumission, but social control also conformed to masters wishing to keep slave prices high. After all, potentially unmanageable property depreciated over time. Masters even relied on federal authorities to fulfill the fugitive slave clause of the Constitution (1787). At all levels government protected slavery. No wonder that Illinois senator Stephen A. Douglas's Freeport Doctrine (1858) of "unfriendly local legislation," as Avery Craven described it in *The Coming of the Civil War* (1942), met extensive resistance in the South.

However, to claim that benefits reaped from antimarket activity were not profits goes too far. Simply because political institutions are used to appropriate an unwarranted transfer of money,

goods, or services from person A to person B does not mean that person B receives no profit. On the contrary, person B seeks institutional arrangements that govern the inappropriate transfer precisely because he deems it profitable. One can argue that non-market-produced income is illegitimate, immoral, or harmful to society in general, but that does not mean it is unprofitable. As Southern conservatives pointed out, when Northern manufacturers benefited from high tariffs, which protected them from market competition, one did not claim their businesses were unprofitable. Perhaps a tighter definition of terms is in order. Slavery was a form of "rent-seeking" whereby political institutions were used to transfer wealth from the slaves to the slave owners, but those who benefited still received great wealth and a return on their investments.

All of these points are somewhat arbitrary and apply generally rather than specifically. Any one slaveholder might have been a better entrepreneur than another. Furthermore, one could own hundreds of slaves, as Virginia planter and statesman Thomas Jefferson did, but be such a poor farmer that profits were rarely realized.

–CAREY ROBERTS,
ARKANSAS TECH UNIVERSITY

Viewpoint:
No. Slavery caused extensive structural weaknesses in the economies of all slaveholding regimes that retarded economic development.

There has been a long history of observation and analysis on the efficiency of slavery. The answer of most scholars has been that slavery is definitely not an efficient manner in which to organize the labor in society. Most also agree that slavery is exploitative. Finally, the balance of opinion is that slavery does not pay in the long run, even when viewed only from the perspective of the slave owner who obtains the windfall benefit of uncompensated slave labor.

Members of the classical school of economics, for example, were unanimous in their opinion of the unprofitability of slavery. Scottish political economist Adam Smith studied the entire scope of human history to determine which institutions—in particular, which labor institutions—best contributed to the wealth of nations. *An Inquiry into the Nature and Causes of the Wealth of Nations* (1776) concludes that

THE PRESENT HIGH PRICE

In a letter to his brother dated 5 January 1835, Henry A. Tayloe of Walnut Grove, Alabama, discusses slave prices and offers advice:

George and myself only made 30 bales and George about the same. I wish you may visit me early this Spring to make some arrangements about your Negroes. If they continue high I would advise you to sell them in this country on one and two years credit bearing 8 per ct interest. The present high price of Negroes can not continue long and if you will make me a partner in the sale on reasonable terms I will bring them out this Fall from VA and sell them for you and release you from all troubles. On a credit your negroes would bring here about $120 to $130, bearing 8 per ct interest. My object is to make a fortune here as soon as possible by industry and economy, and then return to enjoy myself. Therefore I am willing to aid you in any way as far as reason will permit. You had better give your land away if you can get from $6 to $800 round for your Negroes—and if you will incur the risk with me, and allow me time to pay you, I will give a fair price for one half bring them to this country sell the whole number and divide the proceeds of the sale equally. It is better to sell on time as by so doing good masters may be obtained. . . . I have rented land for your negroes and Henry Key's, and shall attend to them faithfully. Gowie ran off about the 18th of December and has not been heard of. I hope to hear of him in a few days that I may put him to work. He went off without any provocation. I expect he is a deceitful fellow.

Source: *Alabama Department of Archives and History, "Letter from Henry Tayloe on the domestic slave trade," in* Africans in America *<http://www.pbs.org/wgbh/aia/part4/4h3138t.html>.*

PROFITS

The experience of all ages and nations, I believe, demonstrates that the work done by slaves, though it appears to cost only their maintenance, is in the end the dearest of any. A person who can acquire no property, can have no other interest but to eat as much, and to labour as little as possible. Whatever work he does beyond what is sufficient to purchase his own maintenance, can be squeezed out of him by violence only, and not by any interest of his own. In ancient Italy, how much the cultivation of corn degenerated, how unprofitable it became to the master when it fell under the management of slaves, is remarked by both Pliny and Columella. In the time of Aristotle it had not been much better in ancient Greece.

Smith notes that slaves, unlike free laborers, do not have the incentive to work efficiently. Slave labor requires the additional expense of violence and is, indeed, an entirely different form of management that in the end does not pay:

Under such different management, the same purpose must require very different degrees of expence to execute it. It appears, accordingly, from the experience of all ages and nations, I believe, that the work done by freemen comes cheaper in the end than that performed by slaves. It is found to do so even at Boston, New York, and Philadelphia, where wages of common labour are so very high.

In *A Treatise on Political Economy* (1803), French political economist Jean-Baptiste Say agreed with Smith that slavery was unprofitable. However, Say added to Smith's analysis by showing that slave labor negatively impacted not only the slave but the owner as well. Slavery, according to Say, was an asymmetric relationship that destroyed the work incentive of the slave, while at the same time hampering the entrepreneurial ability of the master. American economist Robert E. Gallman made a similar point in his presidential address "Slavery and Southern Economic Growth" (1979), delivered to the Southern Economic Association.

From the first economic theorist, Richard Cantillon, to later contributors such as John Stuart Mill and John Elliott Cairnes, the classical school of economists found slavery defective. These men all lived and wrote in the age when slavery was still in practice. Indeed, they openly opposed slavery, and thus Romantics such as English writer John Ruskin, who supported the traditional institutions of society, dubbed the political economy of the classical economists the "dismal science."

A review of the vast historical literature on the economics of slavery raises an important point. Simple calculations of maintenance costs versus the wages of free labor naturally can result in slave labor costing less than free labor, but economists, including German political philosopher Karl Marx, found that the real economic costs were many and substantial. In an important socio-economic sense, slavery is similar to criminal activity: slavery can pay for an individual slave owner or a group of owners during a particular period or under special circumstances, but it does not pay in the larger economic sense and, therefore, is eventually eliminated or society is shattered. A common source of error is to claim that slavery is profitable in a particular time and place when special circumstances are actually responsible for prosperity. Ulrich B. Phillips was an important historian of slavery who pointed out many, but not all, of these types of these errors.

Highly ironic is the claim that slavery pays, a claim that made its most dramatic resurgence in the antebellum South at a time when slavery was dying as an institution, both economically and politically, around the world. European governments, which had previously supported the slave trade, now sought its demise for economic, political, ideological, and religious reasons. Slave systems in South America and the Caribbean were collapsing at a sure and steady rate. After the American Revolution (1775–1783), Northern states eliminated slavery, and many of their slaves were moved south. The late antebellum South was, therefore, the only remaining true "showcase" for the profitability of slavery.

Economic historians such as Kenneth M. Stampp, Alfred H. Conrad, John R. Meyer, Robert W. Fogel, Stanley L. Engerman, and their followers resurrected the case for profitable slavery in the late antebellum South when slave prices increased dramatically. They found that farms in the South were relatively efficient compared to farms in the North and nonslave farms in the South. Fogel and Engerman in *Time on the Cross: The Economics of American Negro Slavery* (1974) were at some pains to explain the difference in farm efficiency between the Old South and the New South. Despite resorting to nonslave explanations for this difference in efficiency, they seem undisturbed by the fragility of their conclusions regarding the causal relations between profitability and slavery, nor do they seem highly attuned to the fact that the world was going through the Industrial Revolution, that America was rapidly expanding into an economic superpower, and that all of these world-shaking developments found one of its axes in the American South.

Possibly the only thing more dramatic than the economic development of the antebellum South was the firestorm of intellectual criticism levied at Fogel and Engerman's book. Every single issue put forth in this book was critiqued and criticized at various levels and from a variety of viewpoints. These criticisms themselves have generated a literature of their own, the results of which have been nicely summarized by historians Elizabeth Fox-Genovese and Eugene D. Genovese in *Fruits of Merchant Capital: Slavery and Bourgeois Property in the Rise and Expansion of Capitalism* (1983):

> The economic interpretations of the slave economies of the New World, as well as those social interpretations which adopt the neoclassical economic model but leave the economics out, assume everything they must prove. By retreating from the political economy from which their own methods derive, they ignore the extent to which the economic process permeates the society. They ignore, that is, the interaction between economics, narrowly defined, and the social relations of production on the one hand and state power on the other.

This literature has been further extended to address the central theme of *Time on the Cross,* that the "enslaved and their owners performed as actors and actresses in a drama written, directed, and produced by the 'free market,'" to show that slavery is not an institution of the market process but can only logically result from government intervention and can only be sustained by government intervention.

The complex issues involved in the choice between slavery and free labor have been unfortunately simplified to the single issue of profit, which is a theoretical concept that explains the reallocation of resources in the market economy. The profitability-of-slavery thesis provides various calculations of estimated accounting profits of antebellum cotton plantations that employed both free and slave labor during the Industrial Revolution. One would certainly expect to see profitable farms during this tumultuous period. However, the important question is what factors account for this profitability. Was it the rapid increase in the demand for cotton, cheap fertile land, entrepreneurial management, slavery, or some other combination of these factors? While this issue is difficult to resolve precisely, the case for slave labor can be easily dismissed.

The fact that Fogel and Engerman found that slave efficiency was apparently higher in the older Southern states than in the newer Southern states immediately suggests that the issue of cheap, fertile land was an important explanation for "relative efficiency," profitability, and the demand for slaves. The number of acres of land per slave increased and the percentage of land devoted to cotton also increased. The exploding world demand for cotton generated by the boom of the Industrial Revolution also served to bolster the slave economy.

Most important is the dynamic nature of the Southern economy during the decades prior to the Civil War (1861–1865). In 1830 the lower South was a lightly populated section with a primitive economy, with agricultural production and settlements largely limited to the coastline and rivers. By 1860 the population and land under cultivation had greatly increased; a rail system had been built; and interior cities had been established, while industry to serve the needs of the agricultural economy had been created. This dynamic "disequilibrium" period must also account for some of the "relative efficiency," profitability, and high prices of slaves. The wages of free labor were also abnormally high in the Southwestern states.

In addition to the natural factors that explain the apparent prosperity of slavery, there are also some important artificial factors that helped slavery to survive. Various government policies enacted in the Southern states were instrumental in moving the cost of slave management from the slave owner to society at large, in effect creating a large but hidden subsidy to slavery. Public-work projects, such as railroad con-

PROFITS

struction, also provided a significant but not permanent advantage to slave owners.

The first of these artificial factors was the slave codes. Each slave state had a legislated code that established rules for slave management. While these rules are often decried as limiting slave activities, the purpose of the codes was to prevent successful escape and slave rebellions. Prohibitions against reading and writing, for example, were designed to prevent slaves from writing their own permission slips to be away from the plantation, reading maps and signs, and communicating with slaves on other plantations.

Manumission laws restricted the freeing of slaves. Normally, in a market economy slave owners find it advantageous to sell slaves their freedom, grant freedom for courageous or meritorious behavior, or to bequeath freedom to a slave in the owner's will for a lifetime of obedient service. While beneficial to the individual slave owner, manumission of slaves is, at the same time, a disadvantage to owners in general because a large free black population makes the control and security of the slave population more difficult. Manumission laws therefore reduced the security cost of slavery by making all slaves black and all blacks slaves.

Southern statutes required that white males be drafted into a patrol service that enforced the slave codes, patrolled roads and slave quarters, and tracked down runaway slaves. This policy served to intimidate slaves from running away because patrols were random and patrollers were often abusive of slaves. The patrol statutes served to shift the security cost of slave ownership from the slave owner to the general community and thus provided slaveholders with a subsidy for what otherwise was the most unique and most expensive part of slave management. This artificial addition to the market economy supported the relative efficiency of slave labor in the antebellum South.

Massive public-works projects were undertaken in the antebellum South that had direct economic effects on slave ownership. These projects included the clearing of the Mississippi River and the building of a network of railroads equal to that of the Northeast or the Northwest. River clearing was subsidized and conducted by the federal government, while most railroads were built by city or state governments or were heavily subsidized by them, to say nothing of massive federal grants of public land. Slaves were an important source of labor for railroad construction and maintenance, while railroads opened up new fertile land to cotton cultivation and gave interior plantations better access to markets so they could be self-sufficient and more effectively pursue their comparative advantage in cotton. The massive public subsidy created a frenzied effort to complete railroads, further buoyed the market for slaves, and caused higher slave prices in the short run.

Finally, the capitalist nature of slavery must be thoroughly scrutinized because slave owners borrowed vast sums and paid large amounts of interest to acquire their slaves. Many slave owners had lost money or gone bankrupt during downturns in the economy such as the Panics of 1819 and 1837. Furthermore, many scholars have argued that the massive investment in slaves distorted capital investment and was a great hindrance to both economic growth and development. It certainly is not a contradiction to argue that a fast-growing, developing economy could have grown even faster had its economic institutions been improved.

Admittedly, slavery was profitable for some slave owners, especially under certain conditions, during certain periods, or when aided by the right combination of subsidies. However, slavery was not the best course even under these special circumstances. The general case is: slavery does not pay when measured on a level playing field. Independent of special conditions and subsidies, it benefits slave owners to sell slaves their freedom because slavery is at odds with both humanity and economic rationality. As twentieth-century political economist Ludwig von Mises reminds us: "experience has shown that these methods of unbridled brutalization render very unsatisfactory results. Even the crudest and dullest people achieve more when working of their own accord than under the fear of the whip," and this condition is, in fact, a matter of the nature of man, not special conditions and circumstances.

–MARK THORNTON,
LUDWIG VON MISES INSTITUTE
AND
–MARK A. YANOCHIK,
GEORGIA SOUTHERN UNIVERSITY

References

Robert V. Anderson and Robert E. Gallman, "Slaves as Fixed Capital: Slave Labor and Southern Economic Development," *Journal of American History*, 64 (June 1977): 24–46.

Fred Bateman and Thomas Weiss, *A Deplorable Scarcity: The Failure of Industrialization in the Slave Economy* (Chapel Hill: University of North Carolina Press, 1981).

Alfred H. Conrad and John R. Meyer, "The Economics of Slavery in the Ante-Bellum South," *Journal of Political Economy*, 66 (1958): 95–130.

Avery Craven, *The Coming of the Civil War,* second edition (Chicago: University of Chicago Press, 1957).

Haywood Fleisig, "Slavery, the Supply of Agricultural Labor, and the Industrialization of the South," *Journal of Economic History,* 36 (September 1976): 572–597.

Robert William Fogel and Stanley L. Engerman, *Time on the Cross: The Economics of American Negro Slavery,* 2 volumes (Boston: Little, Brown, 1974).

Elizabeth Fox-Genovese and Eugene D. Genovese, *Fruits of Merchant Capital: Slavery and Bourgeois Property in the Rise and Expansion of Capitalism* (New York: Oxford University Press, 1983).

Robert E. Gallman, "Slavery and Southern Economic Growth," *Southern Economic Journal,* 45 (April 1979): 1007–1022.

Herbert G. Gutman, *Slavery and the Numbers Game: A Critique of Time on the Cross* (Urbana: University of Illinois Press, 1975).

David M. Levy, *How the Dismal Science Got Its Name: Classical Economics and the Ur-text of Racial Politics* (Ann Arbor: University of Michigan Press, 2001).

Robert A. Margo, *Wages and Labor Markets in the United States, 1820–1860* (Chicago: University of Chicago Press, 2000).

Ludwig von Mises, *Human Action: A Treatise on Economics,* third edition (Chicago: Regnery, 1966).

James Oakes, *The Ruling Race: A History of American Slaveholders* (New York: Knopf, 1982).

Peter J. Parish, *Slavery: History and Historians* (New York: Harper & Row, 1989).

Ulrich B. Phillips, *American Negro Slavery: A Survey of the Supply, Employment and Control of Negro Labor as Determined by the Plantation Regime* (New York & London: Appleton, 1918).

Jean-Baptiste Say, *A Treatise on Political Economy,* translated from fourth French edition by C. R. Prinsep (Boston: Wells & Lilly, 1821).

Francis Butler Simkins and Charles Pierce Roland, *A History of the South,* fourth edition (New York: Knopf, 1972).

Adam Smith, *An Inquiry into the Nature and Causes of the Wealth of Nations,* edited by Edwin Cannan (New York: Modern Library, 1937).

Mark M. Smith, *Debating Slavery: Economy and Society in the Antebellum American South* (Cambridge & New York: Cambridge University Press, 1998).

Kenneth M. Stampp, *The Peculiar Institution: Slavery in the Ante-Bellum South* (New York: Knopf, 1956).

Richard Sutch and Edward Saraydar, "The Profitability of Ante Bellum Slavery—Revisited," *Southern Economic Journal,* 31 (April 1965): 365–383.

Mark Thornton, "Slavery, Profitability, and the Market Process," *Review of Austrian Economics,* 7 (1994): 21–47.

Nathaniel A. Ware, *Notes on Political Economy as Applicable to the United States* (New York: Leavitt, Trow, 1844).

Harold D. Woodman, "The Profitability of Slavery: A Historical Perennial," *Journal of Southern History,* 29 (August 1963): 303–325.

Gavin Wright, *The Political Economy of the Cotton South: Households, Markets, and Wealth in the Nineteenth Century* (New York: Norton, 1978)

Mark A. Yanochik, "Essays on the Economics of Slavery," dissertation, Auburn University, 1997.

Yanochik, "The Patrol System and Its Effect on the Profitability of Ante-bellum Slavery," M.A. thesis, Auburn University, 1993.

Yanochik, Brad Ewing, and Mark Thornton, "A New Perspective on Antebellum Slavery: Public Policy and Slave Prices," *Atlantic Economic Journal,* 29 (September 2001): 330–340.

Yanochik, Thornton, and Ewing, "Railroad Construction and Antebellum Slave Prices," *Social Science Quarterly* (forthcoming).

PROFITS

RACISM

Did slavery result from racism?

Viewpoint: Yes. Europeans justified the enslavement of Africans, and argued for the perpetuity of slavery, because they believed blacks were innately inferior to whites.

Viewpoint: No. European prejudice against blacks developed long before slavery and continued long after it was abolished.

Was slavery the child of racism? Predisposed to view African peoples as inferior to themselves, Europeans found that enslaving them presented no special logical, ethical, or moral difficulties. Yet, not all systems of slavery in the New World emphasized race to the same extent or even defined it in the same way. Slavery was a racist institution in Latin America, but because the Portuguese and Spanish laws of slavery were based on Roman rather than English antecedents, it remained nonracist in its rules and application. The English, by contrast, had no direct legal experience with slavery. As a consequence they fashioned a legal system with race as the chief organizing principle.

The slaveholders of the American South, for example, celebrated the bonds of affection that existed between masters and slaves. According to historian Stanley M. Elkins, however, they developed "the most implacable race-consciousness yet observed in virtually any society. It was evolved in the Southern mind . . . as a simple syllogism, the precision of whose terms paralleled the precision of the system itself. All slaves are black; slaves are degraded and contemptible; therefore all blacks are degraded and contemptible and should be kept in a state of slavery." It thus became nearly impossible for Southerners in particular, and for Americans in general, to think of blacks, whether slave or free, as other than loathsome and debased. Such attitudes help to explain the racist underpinnings of much public policy in the United States as well as peculiarly American social taboos, such as laws strictly prohibiting manumission and the outrage and disgust at miscegenation.

Nevertheless, proslavery Southerners could not permit racism to blind them to historical reality or biblical truth. They knew that the meaning of race had changed over time and that "race" was thus not an immutable category but varied with context and circumstance. Legal scholar T. R. R. Cobb, for instance, went out of his way to demonstrate that most of the "foreign" (that is, non-Hebrew) slaves of the Israelites had been black. He knew better and in the end had to admit that even when the slaves were black the same derogatory significance did not attach to skin color in the ancient world as in the modern South. Similarly, many Southern thinkers, religious as well as secular, rejected the notion that blacks were the products of a separate creation that rendered them subhuman. As devout Christians they could accept no belief that contradicted the teachings of Scripture. They had, therefore, to conclude that blacks, although inferior to whites, were human beings whom God had endowed with immortal souls. As alluring as the argument of innate racial inferiority must have been to proslavery Southerners, they had to develop another rationale to justify the enslavement of blacks. Even in the South, it seems, racism had its limits.

Viewpoint:
Yes. Europeans justified the enslavement of Africans, and argued for the perpetuity of slavery, because they believed blacks were innately inferior to whites.

Were early Americans racist in that they automatically considered Africans inferior because of their color and used this alleged inferiority to justify enslaving them? Or did American slavery develop primarily in response to labor, economic, and social forces, and only later was the Africans' blackness associated with New World slavery? The issue of which came first, racism or slavery, is more than just an academic question. By examining what has become known as the "origins debate," one can further understand the evolution of racist ideology in early American society and its subsequent impact on race relations in modern America.

In addressing why early Americans enslaved black Africans, certain economic and social factors are generally acknowledged: an increasing demand for labor in the late-seventeenth-century Chesapeake area and a corresponding decline in white indentured servants migrating to the region; the increased availability of slaves after 1672 with England's creation of the Royal Africa Company to ship Africans to British America; and a growing number of armed, landless, and angry former servants threatening Virginia's political and social order. Black labor unexpectedly solved these economic and social problems. It was permanent, unarmed, self-perpetuating, and, in the long run, less expensive.

These economic and social explanations for the emergence of American slavery have some merit, but they do not explain why Southern planters enslaved only black Africans, and did so long before the emergence of assorted problems with the white labor supply. Nor do they explain why New England, which did not have the economic needs of the South and suffered no uprisings from the white underclass, also adopted slavery. What was it about Africans that made them special candidates for enslavement? Why was slavery in America exclusively a status based on race and color? Only racism, which transcends profits and social caste, can adequately answer these critical questions.

Any fruitful discussion of the relation between racism and American slavery must begin with a definition of the term. Modern scholars define racism as "a dogmatic belief in the inherent behavioral and intellectual differences between races which allows hierarchical rankings of peoples." It is important to emphasize, how-ever, that racism is not a static belief system; it is constantly evolving. Indeed, not until the early nineteenth century did American racism develop into a sophisticated and dogmatic ideology. Yet, its early inchoateness did not make it any less virulent and pernicious. The pivotal question, therefore, is not whether early white Americans held to a fully developed racist ideology prior to the emergence of slavery, but whether their racial discrimination against black people was strong enough to have been a significant cause, rather than primarily a product, of slavery.

The virulence of European racism is seen as early as the fifteenth century when Spaniards began categorizing Africans as a biologically inferior people soon after they began trafficking African slaves to Spain. Their ranking of Africans as inferior was based not only on race but also on culture, which early modern Europeans associated with race. The Africans' darker skin, eating habits, dress, sexual conduct, and even body odor were all marks of inferiority to Europeans who perceived their culture as the embodiment of civilization. Europeans linked any abnormal cultural, social, and religious systems with permanent characteristics such as skin color. In this way skin color, a badge of race, became an "indelible marker of cultural, and thus racial, inferiority." Thus, even before settling the New World, Europeans held racist attitudes toward Africans that made them ideal candidates for enslavement. It is no coincidence that slavery in Spain paralleled the development of this antiblack sentiment.

Similarly, the enslavement of Africans in North America lay in racial attitudes that took shape in England during the early 1500s when the English began acquiring firsthand accounts of West Africans. Measured against English standards of civilization, these Elizabethan texts described Africans as "blacke, brutish, savage, monstrous & rude," a people of "beastly lyving without a God, lawe, religion, or common wealth" who "bore more than a passing similarity to animals." This English animalization of Africans is perhaps most clearly revealed in their early descriptions of black women whose "breasts hang down below their navels," as wrote one observer, "so that when . . . weeding, they hang almost to the ground, that at a distance you would think they had six legs." One "cannot know a man from a woman but by their breasts," echoed another Englishmen in describing the inhabitants of Guinea in 1555, "which in the most part be very foule and long, hanging downe low like the udder of a goate." English narratives further dehumanized African women by depicting them as promiscuous beasts who bit off the penises of their sexual partners, copulated with apes, experienced no pain at childbirth, breast-fed over their shoulder, and allowed their children to run about naked. Such

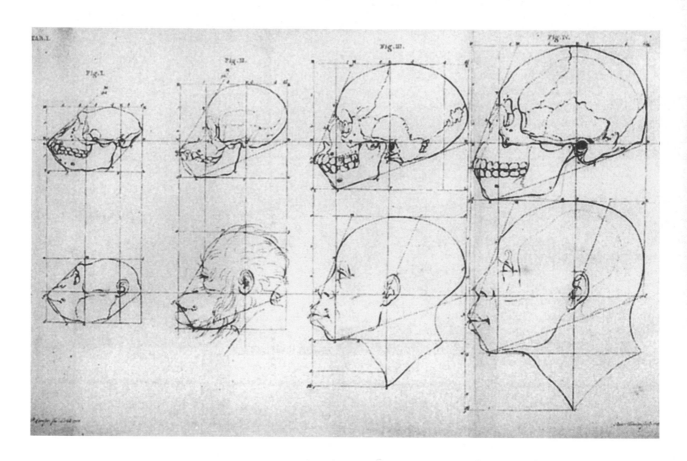

Measurement of facial angles from a copper engraving in *Verhandeling Van Patrus Camperi,* a treatise on black inferiority, 1791

(British Library, London)

animal-like appearance and behavior justified their "domestication" and enslavement in English eyes. Additionally, African women's apparent propensity for easy childbirth and breast-feeding convinced colonizers that they could easily perform hard labor in the Americas. The fact that by the mid 1500s the Portuguese and Spanish were transporting thousands of African slaves to America only reinforced among the English the "growing connection between color and bondage."

More than anything else, it was the Africans' blackness that repelled the English. Indeed, the concept of blackness in Elizabethan England was loaded with pejorative meaning. Black meant dirty, foul, ugly, malignant, and evil. In contrast, white represented purity, virginity, virtue, beauty, and goodness. The English people's negative attachments to the color black, according to one modern scholar, deeply prejudiced their assessment of West Africans. The English assumed that if the color black epitomized baseness and evil, then those same characteristics must belong to black-skinned people. English writers, playwrights, and poets propagated such contemptuous characteristics by frequently associating African blackness with barbarism, physical monstrosity, and immorality. Such attitudes of Africans as a dark and, therefore, an inferior and subhuman people further justified their enslavement in the English mind. So by the time the first Africans arrived in North

America in 1619, the racial attitudes of the English were already firmly fixed.

Without a doubt, it was the English people's pervasive racial prejudice toward the Africans' race and blackness, and not economic or social factors, that served as the primary determinant for the development of American slavery. From the first arrival of Africans in North America, English settlers relegated blacks to the lowest rung of society and never treated them as the equals of white men, whether servant or free. Indeed, evidence strongly suggests that from the outset early Virginians held blacks as slaves. In Virginia's 1624 census, for example, the twenty-two blacks enumerated lack a last name, and nearly half are recorded with no name at all. If these Africans were free, the enumerators would have listed them with full names as they did white servants. Additionally, most blacks entering the colony were not listed with their age and date of arrival, information that was crucial for determining the length of service for indentured servants. That such information was not recorded for these black emigrants suggests that they were sold into service without a written contract of indenture for a specified period of time, but instead were held in servitude either for as long as the purchaser desired or for life. Even the inventories of early Virginia planters—which listed all blacks, even children, as more valuable than any white servant—clearly show that Africans were targeted for enslavement from their earliest arrival in North America.

Court rulings in early Virginia further illustrate the deep racial prejudice held by white settlers toward blacks, a sentiment reflecting the latter's singularly debased status in Chesapeake society. In 1624, just five years after the first Africans arrived, the local court logged the following ruling: "John Phillip a negro Christened in England 12 yeers since, sworne and exam sayeth, that beinge in a ship with Sir Henry Maneringe, they took a Spanish ship about cape Sct Mary, and caryed her to Mamora." Despite its brevity this ruling reveals that from the beginning Virginia law was guided by a theory of racial subordination. Had it not been, the court would have simply referred to Phillip by name alone, without mentioning his race or religion, just as it had done with the white defendants in the case. If blackness did not "carry the stigma of inferiority," as historian A. Leon Higginbotham has noted, Phillip's color and religion "would *not* be material to the determination of whether his testimony was admissible in court because the blemish of his race would *not* need to be washed clean by the grace of the Christian religion." Phillip's inferior status was implicit in that his race alone was identified.

The Virginia court reaffirmed the prevailing view of black inferiority in 1630 when it ordered a white man, Hugh Davis, to receive a whipping before a group of blacks for "abus[ing] himself" and "defil[ing] his body by lying with a negro" to the "shame of Christianity." The racist language of this ruling suggests that Davis was punished for having intercourse with someone thought to be inferior, someone considered less than human. In other words, his crime "was not fornication, but bestiality." Davis committed a crime not only against nature, however, but also against Christianity, which, at least in the eyes of the Virginia court, implied that the Africans' inferiority was decreed by God.

Ten years later the Virginia court further revealed the racist character of white society in a ruling involving a racially mixed group of runaway servants, two of whom were white and another black. For violating their contract, the two white servants received thirty lashes and had their terms of service extended for one year. The black servant, by contrast, was ordered to serve his master for the rest of his life. In effect, he was reduced to slavery because of his color alone.

These judicial cases are important not only because they laid the foundation for the legal enslavement of Africans but also for what they reveal about racism in early America. English settlers already considered blackness a stigma of inferiority. The courts simply reflected this racist attitude by treating people from the two races

differently. Granted, early Americans did not possess a well-developed racist ideology; this belief system would not come until the early nineteenth century when it became more popular to classify humans according to race. Still, the absence of a fully articulated ideology of racial superiority does not dilute the virulence of anti-black sentiment among early Americans and its singularly destructive impact on African Americans. More than anything else, it was the Africans' blackness, and the stigma of inferiority that whites attached to it, that allowed for their exploitation "in ways that colonists never considered for white slaves or servants." American slavery was molded by the early colonists' racial discrimination against Africans; it was their discriminatory attitude and behavior toward blacks that conditioned the form slavery would take. To argue that early Anglo-Americans were not racist, maintains one authority on the subject, "sanitizes their attitudes and policies towards blacks and thereby distorts racism's baneful role in the seventeenth century and beyond."

–KEITH KRAWCZYNSKI,
AUBURN UNIVERSITY AT MONTGOMERY

Viewpoint:
No. European prejudice against blacks developed long before slavery and continued long after it was abolished.

For reasons that historians may perhaps never fully understand, the skin color of Africans became their defining characteristic and aroused the deepest interest among Europeans. To the Portuguese and Spanish, Africans were "negroes." To the French, they were "noirs." To the English, they were "blacks." In all four languages and among all four peoples the different words carried the same connotations of meanness, filth, ugliness, corruption, contempt, and evil. In European legend, folklore, and history, there was black magic, blackmail, blacklists, blackguards, black knights, and the Black Death. Throughout the pages of European literature there were countless tales of white men turning black from sin. For the European imagination, white, by contrast, indicated purity, justice, beauty, joy, and holiness.

Early in the seventeenth century Jean Mocquet, a French traveler to Africa, America, and the West Indies, confirmed these judgments, observing that blacks, "it might be properly said . . . came out of Hell, they are so burnt, and dreadful to look upon." In the eighteenth century English writer John Atkins agreed that "the Black Colour

GIVE ME AN EVERLASTING WAR

Sergeant Reuben A. Pierson of the Ninth Louisiana Infantry served in the Virginia theater of operations during the Civil War (1861–1865). Below are two letters that he wrote to his father, explaining his views on the conflict, slavery, and the North:

Camp C, Virginia

January 31, 1862

The young men who have not ambition and moral courage to fight for the preservation of that rich legacy bequeathed to them—and purchased for them by the blood of their ancestors will be scoffed at and looked upon as base cowards unworthy [of] the name of southern man and unfit for the enjoyment of our glorious institution [of slavery]. The day is now dawning and will soon open bright and clear as a May morning, when we will be acknowledged as one of the best governments that holds a place in the catalogue of the nations of the earth. Let the unholy and base legions of Lincolndom pour forth their fury and rage in all its power—we will meet them [on the field and] we will defeat them or perish upon the soil of our loved and cherished southern republic. That is what southern men have vowed by their acts and not by words. Let us die a soldiers death or live a freemans life.

Orange County, Virginia

March 22, 1864

I for one am unwilling to accept anything short of a final separation from the fiendish barbarians with whom we have been so long associated. It is true I love peace but give me an everlasting war in preference to a union with a people who condescend to equalize themselves with the poor, ignorant & only half civilized negro. Such a people is base, vile, & altogether unworthy of the proud name of Americans. I will not dwell upon this theme. Such thoughts are always exciting my passions of revenge and veng[e]ance.

Source: *Thomas W. Cutrer and T. Michael Parrish, eds.,* Brothers in Gray: The Civil War Letters of the Pierson Family *(Baton Rouge: Louisiana State University Press, 1997), pp. 77, 228.*

---

happy with the color of their skin and considered Europeans to be less attractive than themselves. Thomas Phillips, a seventeenth-century Welsh sea captain engaged in the slave trade, echoed Browne's observations. Phillips could not "imagine why they [blacks] should be despised for their colour, being what they cannot help. . . . I can't think there is any intrinsic value in one colour more than another, that white is better than black, only we think it so, because we are so, and are prone to judge favourably in our own case. . . ." Richard Ligon went further than Browne and Phillips. Visiting the Cape Verde Islands and Barbados, Ligon was captivated by the beauty of the blacks whom he saw, especially the women. "The young Maids," he remarked, "have ordinarily very large breasts, which stand strutting out so hard and firm, as no leaping, jumping, or stirring, will cause them to shake any more, than the brawns of their arms."

During the seventeenth, eighteenth, and nineteenth centuries several other European travelers to Africa or the Americas, and even the captains of slave ships, also wrote generous descriptions of blacks. They marveled at blacks' agility, grace, and beauty. Moreover, Europeans who published accounts of their journeys to Africa or the New World commented on the radiance of blacks' teeth and the cleanliness of their bodies. Samuel Purchas, a seventeenth-century writer, also noted their good manners. Purchas was not alone in confessing that, although Africans seemed untroubled by their nakedness, which shocked Europeans, "yet it is holden shame with them to let a fart, which they wonder at in the Hollanders, esteeming it a contempt."

Yet, the problem of Africans' black skin remained. There emerged among educated Europeans of the sixteenth, seventeenth, and eighteenth centuries two prevailing theories about the nature and meaning of black skin. The first was biblical, the second scientific.

A long tradition of biblical exegesis associated black skin and slavery with the sin of Ham and the curse laid upon his son, Canaan. According to scripture, Ham, one of the sons of Noah, had intercourse with his wife aboard the ark, contrary to God's injunction. For this sin his descendants were cursed. Black skin was the mark of their forebear's infidelity and transgression. In another version of the story Ham sinned by looking upon his drunken father's nakedness. The results were the same. Canaan and his entire line were cursed and condemned to perpetual slavery. "Cursed be Canaan," cried Noah in Genesis 9:25. "A servant of servants shall he be unto his brethren." There were few more powerful justifications for the enslavement of Africans than the association of black skin with sinfulness and the notion that slavery was the punishment for that sin.

---

and wooly Tegument of these *Guineans,* is what first obtrudes itself on our Observations, and distinguishes them from the rest of Mankind." The mysterious and sinister power of blackness pervaded the European mind. It was embodied in Africans who were, from the European perspective, "children of darkness."

Despite these negative associations, other Europeans, such as English writer Sir Thomas Browne, argued that standards of beauty were a matter of custom and prejudice, not of universal law. Africans, Browne asserted, were no doubt

The obvious appeal of this argument notwithstanding, most proslavery theorists, especially those infused with orthodox Protestantism, were reluctant to apply it as a justification for enslavement. For Presbyterian theologian James Henley Thornwell of South Carolina, race was not in the final analysis the basis for slavery. Although Thornwell regarded blacks as inferior to whites, he rejected the scientific racism that characterized blacks as the products of a separate creation. Scripture, he declared, did not endorse racial slavery but rather the principle of slavery in general, without regard to race. Thornwell rested the theological defense of slavery on his conviction of the innate sinfulness of man rather than on a biblical curse applied exclusively to blacks. An anonymous writer in the Richmond *Enquirer* put the matter succinctly: "While it is far more obvious that negroes should be slaves than white, for they are only fit to labor, not to direct; yet the principle of slavery itself is right, and does not depend upon difference of complexion."

When Dr. Josiah Nott of Mobile, Alabama—the foremost Southern proponent of ethnology, or the science of racial differences—attempted to justify slavery by proving that blacks constituted a "separate, distinct, and unequal species," he incited the wrath of orthodox Southerners. Although Nott made heroic efforts to reconcile his views on race with the teachings of Scripture, his overt challenge to biblical literalism could not but offend large numbers of his fellow Southerners. The scientific validation of blacks' natural inferiority offered an apparently irrefutable and alluring argument in defense of slavery. Yet, most antebellum Southern thinkers rejected it. George Frederick Holmes, long a professor at the University of Virginia, was also long sympathetic to the notion that race was a major determinant of civilization and history. Nonetheless, he advised that the theories of ethnology remained "enveloped in all the mist of obscurity." Proslavery writer George Fitzhugh of Port Royal, Virginia, declared more bluntly that if forced to choose between ethnology and the Bible, Southerners had best adhere to the Holy Writ.

Southern concerns notwithstanding, ideas about race had, and would continue, to operate in defense of slavery. It was, for example, one of the unremarked tragedies of history that Europeans found blacks living in proximity with apes. Although many scholars and theologians, even those who defended slavery, rejected the hypothesis that black skin originated with the curse placed on Ham and Canaan, they entertained the theory that blacks descended from apes. The idea that blacks evolved from apes, or at least that they were the products of a separate creation from the rest of humanity, was the innovation of radicals, freethinkers, charlatans, and heretics

such as sixteenth-century German physician and alchemist Paracelsus and the Italian philosopher Giordano Bruno, the latter of whom the Catholic church executed in 1600.

Only with the growth of the international slave trade did theories of innate black inferiority gain widespread currency. Many writers on the subject magnified the physical and intellectual differences between blacks and whites and explained them with reference to science rather than to Scripture. It was, of course, in the interest of slave traders and slave owners to propagate the belief that blacks were not fully human, and they had a rich tradition on which to draw in fashioning this argument. European folklore was replete with stories of ape men and the monstrous offspring that resulted from every imaginable sort of bestiality. The fantastic tales of early explorers and chroniclers had only multiplied the variety and grotesqueness of such creatures.

Since the Renaissance, Europeans had viewed themselves as having been made in the image of God. European myth, however, had always acknowledged an uneasy connection between man and beasts. Europeans believed in fixed and distinctive species but held simultaneously to another ancient belief in the continuity of creation, which they called the Great Chain of Being. According to this doctrine there were infinite and subtle variations between every form of life that linked all creation in one vast, hierarchical continuum. God, the Creator of the universe, was alone atop the Chain, followed by various gradations of angels, then humans, and, last, the beasts.

In the late seventeenth century, European scientists thought they had discovered one link between man and apes in the Hottentots, a people from South Africa whose brutish appearance and bestial customs provided the basis for the familiar stereotype of blacks well into the twentieth century. By the eighteenth century, several European scholars and scientists, particularly in France, began to argue systematically that blacks were a separate species and that they constituted a link between human beings and animals. The scientific debate raged over whether blacks were a separate species or whether there was unity to the human race and that the differences between blacks and whites were superficial, principally resulting from their environments. Even those theorists who concluded that Africans and Europeans had the same origin and were members of the same species believed that the white man was the human standard and blacks the deviation. Europeans thus came to regard blackness as a kind of aberration or disease. As a consequence of climatic conditions or chemical agents trapped between the layers of the skin, Africans had degenerated from their white ancestors. This hypothesis was nothing less than a secular, scien-

RACISM

tific version of Ham's curse, with biology replacing divine judgment.

Representative of this outlook was Virginia planter and statesman Thomas Jefferson, who professed to abhor slavery but believed that on the scale of the Great Chain of Being blacks were morally, intellectually, and physically inferior to whites. He maintained that all species had fixed characteristics that they could not alter. "Every race of animals," he wrote, "seems to have received from their Maker certain laws of extension at the time of their formation. Their elaborative organs were formed to produce this, while proper obstacles were opposed to its further progress. Below these limits they cannot fall, nor rise above them. . . . All the manna of heaven would never raise the Mouse to the bulk of the Mammoth." Nor, he might have added, transformed blacks into the equals of whites. Convinced that blacks' inferiority was an immutable principle of natural history, Jefferson advanced "it . . . that the blacks, whether originally a distinct race, or made distinct by time and circumstances, are inferior to whites in the endowments of both body and mind." When Jefferson contemplated the abolition of slavery, therefore, he found it impossible to conceive of emancipation without colonization. He believed that the freed slaves, inferior to whites in every way, could never live in peace with their former masters. Their presence, he contended, was degrading to the society as a whole.

Jefferson combined a virulent racism with a genuinely antislavery rhetoric because he incorrectly assumed that race was a fixed, observable, physical reality. Race is not a biological fact; it is an idea, an ideological construct, and an historical phenomenon. Jefferson's predecessors and contemporaries knew as much. In the heyday of the Atlantic slave trade both merchants and their customers understood that the cargoes of the slave ships included Africans of vastly different national, cultural, and linguistic backgrounds. To traders and planters, not all Africans were the same and did not constitute a single group. They could discourse at length on the differences among the Coromantees, Mandingoes, Foulahs, Congoes, Angolas, Eboes, Nagoes, Pawpaws, Gabbons, and a host of other African peoples. Experienced buyers and sellers of slaves could distinguish members of these groups from one another by sight, and set prices accordingly.

Ideas about skin color derived their meaning and importance from the context in which Europeans encountered Africans. Europeans made use of whatever reference points were readily at hand in assimilating their unprecedented experience with blacks. Africans' skin color became a highly visible sign by which to identify this unfamiliar and perhaps frightening people who inhabited what for Europeans was a mysterious and exotic continent. To be sure, Europeans' racial ideology conditioned their evolving perceptions of and attitudes about blacks, but it often distorted or concealed as much as it clarified and illuminated. Travelers to Africa, for example, who knew Africans to be diverse people of many subtle variations of skin color (reality) spoke of black Africans (ideology). Slave traders who enjoyed the amenities that their African hosts provided (reality) spoke of savage Africans (ideology). Missionaries acquainted with both Muslim and Christian Africans (reality) spoke of pagan Africans (ideology). Planters who feared slave insurrection (reality) spoke of docile, child-like, and stupid Africans (ideology). The ideology of race enabled Europeans to develop ideas and a language with which to think and talk about Africans while, at the same time, it prevented them from understanding their own experiences.

The reality of Africa and Africans was far more complex than the European racial ideology allowed. Did racism, then, cause slavery? The simple answer is "no," for the European prejudice against blacks antedated slavery. Europeans exhibited racial prejudices against blacks long before, and long after, they moved to enslave them. Without question that bias, and the conviction of racial superiority that accompanied it, facilitated the development of slavery, which for centuries bound together two peoples in bitter antagonism.

–RICK KAAT,
SAN FRANCISCO, CALIFORNIA

References

John Atkins, *A Voyage to Guinea, Brasil, and the West-Indies. . . .* (London: Ward & Chandler, 1735).

Thomas Browne, *Pseudodoxia Epidemica,* in *The Works of Sir Thomas Browne,* volume 3, edited by Geoffrey Keynes (London: Faber & Gwyer, 1928).

David Brion Davis, "Constructing Race: A Reflection," *William & Mary Quarterly,* third series 54 (January 1997): 7–17.

Davis, *The Problem of Slavery in the Age of Revolution, 1770–1823* (Ithaca, N.Y.: Cornell University Press, 1975).

Davis, *The Problem of Slavery in Western Culture* (Ithaca, N.Y.: Cornell University Press, 1966).

Carl N. Degler, *Neither Black nor White: Slavery and Race Relations in Brazil and the United States* (Madison: University of Wisconsin Press, 1971).

RACISM

Degler, "Slavery and the Genesis of American Race Prejudice," in *Interpreting Colonial America: Selected Readings,* second edition, edited by James Kirby Martin (New York: Harper & Row, 1978), pp. 124–139.

Stanley M. Elkins, *Slavery: A Problem in American Institutional and Intellectual Life* (Chicago: University of Chicago Press, 1959).

David Eltis, *The Rise of African Slavery* (Cambridge & New York: Cambridge University Press, 2000).

George M. Fredrickson, *The Black Image in the White Mind: The Debate on Afro-American Character and Destiny, 1817–1914* (New York: Harper & Row, 1971).

A. Leon Higginbotham, "The Ancestry of Inferiority (1619–1662)," in *How Did American Slavery Begin?: Readings,* edited by Edward Countryman (Boston: Bedford Books of St. Martin's Press, 1999), pp. 85–98.

Thomas Jefferson, *Notes on the State of Virginia,* edited by William Peden (Chapel Hill: University of North Carolina Press, 1954).

William Sumner Jenkins, *Pro-Slavery Thought in the Old South* (Chapel Hill: University of North Carolina Press, 1935).

Winthrop D. Jordan, *Black Over White: American Attitudes Toward the Negro, 1550–1812* (Chapel Hill: University of North Carolina Press, 1968).

Jordan, *The White Man's Burden: Historical Origins of Racism in the United States* (New York: Oxford University Press, 1974).

Peter Kolchin, *Unfree Labor: American Slavery and Russian Serfdom* (Cambridge, Mass.: Belknap Press of Harvard University Press, 1987).

Richard Ligon, *A True & exact history of the island of Barbadoes. . . .* (London: Moseley, 1657).

Russell Menard, "From Servants to Slaves: The Transformation of the Chesapeake Labor System," *Southern Studies,* 16 (Winter 1977): 355–390.

Jean Mocquet, *Travels and Voyages into Africa, Asia, and America, the East and West-Indies, Syria, Jerusalem, and the Holy-Land. . . ,* translated by Nathaniel Pullen (London: Newton, 1696).

Edmund S. Morgan, *American Slavery, American Freedom: The Ordeal of Colonial Virginia* (New York: Norton, 1975).

Morgan, "Slavery and Freedom: The American Paradox," *Journal of American History,* 59 (1972): 5–29.

Jennifer L. Morgan, "Some Could Suckle Over Their Shoulder: Male Travelers, Female Bodies, and the Gendering of Racial Ideology, 1550-1770," *William & Mary Quarterly,* third series 54 (January 1997): 167–192.

Donald L. Noel, "Slavery and the Rise of Racism," in *The Origins of American Slavery and Racism,* edited by Noel (Columbus, Ohio: Merrill, 1972), pp. 153–170.

Frederick Law Olmsted, *The Cotton Kingdom* (New York: Modern Library, 1984).

Orlando Patterson, *Slavery and Social Death: A Comparative Study* (Cambridge, Mass.: Harvard University Press, 1982).

Thomas Virgil Peterson, *Ham and Japheth: The Mythic World of Whites in the Antebellum South* (Metuchen, N.J.: Scarecrow Press, 1978).

Thomas Phillips, *A Journal of A Voyage Made in the* Hannibal *of London, Ann. 1693, 1694. . . .* (London: Lintot & Osborn, 1732).

Samuel Purchas, *Purchas his Pilgrimage: In Five Books. . . .* (London: Stansby, 1625).

Raymond Starr, "Historians and the Origins of British North American Slavery," *Historian,* 36 (November 1973): 1–18.

James H. Sweet, "The Iberian Roots of American Racist Thought," *William & Mary Quarterly,* third series 54 (January 1997): 143–166.

Alexis de Tocqueville, *Democracy in America*, translated by George Lawrence, edited by J. P. Mayer and Max Lerner (New York: Harper & Row, 1966).

Alden T. Vaughan, "Blacks in Virginia: A Note on the First Decade," *William & Mary Quarterly,* third series 29 (October 1972): 469–478.

Vaughan, "The Origins Debate: Slavery and Racism in Seventeenth-Century Virginia," *Virginia Magazine of History and Biography,* 97 (July 1989): 311–354.

Vaughan and Virginia Mason Vaughan, "Before Othello: Elizabethan Representations of Sub-Saharan Africans," *William & Mary Quarterly,* third series 54 (January 1997): 19–44.

Eric Williams, *Capitalism and Slavery* (Chapel Hill: University of North Carolina Press, 1944).

Betty Wood, *The Origins of American Slavery: Freedom and Bondage in the English Colonies* (New York: Hill & Wang, 1997).

RELIGION OF LIBERATION

Did conversion to Christianity improve the lives of the slaves?

Viewpoint: Yes. Christianity was among the slaves' most important weapons in resisting the dehumanization inherent in slavery.

Viewpoint: No. Although Christianity comforted the slaves and served as a defense against their brutalization, it significantly muted the impulse toward rebellion.

Until the 1740s not only the slaves but also their masters resisted the conversion of blacks to Christianity. Most slaves embraced traditional African religious customs, beliefs, and practices, and most whites were indifferent to the spiritual lives of the slaves. Some masters, however, were adverse to evangelizing to slaves, fearing that the Christian message of equality before God would entice the slaves to rebel. Even as late as the nineteenth century most white Southerners would not have disagreed with the South Carolina planter Whitemarsh B. Seabrook, who insisted that "anyone who wanted slaves to read the entire Bible belonged in a lunatic asylum."

The distrust of Christianity among masters and slaves began to abate during the late 1730s and early 1740s with the advent of the Great Awakening, the first in a series of religious revivals to erupt in the British North American colonies. Of even greater significance in bringing the slaves to Christianity were the evangelical revivals of the 1770s and 1780s. Although initially opposed to slavery, evangelical clergymen did not engender an abolitionist movement. Instead, as historian Donald G. Mathews has shown, they convinced the planters that it was their Christian obligation to acquaint the slaves with the truth of the Gospel. Evangelical clergymen had the courage of their convictions, welcoming black converts and regarding them as the spiritual, but not the social or political, equals of whites. Although this attitude provoked suspicion and hostility among many whites, "the half-century following 1740," as historian John B. Boles in *Masters & Slaves in the House of the Lord: Race and Religion in the American South, 1740–1870* (1988) has explained, "was the critical period during which some whites broke down their fears and inhibitions about sharing their religion with the slaves in their midst, and some blacks—only a few at first—came to find in Christianity a system of ideas and symbols that was genuinely attractive."

Historians generally agree that by the 1830s, Christianity had become an important element of slave culture. For many slaves, Christianity imparted a message of deliverance. Slave Christianity was also more emotional and ecstatic than its staid white counterparts, expressing the joy that blacks felt in life, community, and God. Even white Baptists and Methodists could not match the enthusiasm that blacks displayed at worship; Presbyterians and Episcopalians, meanwhile, found such unrestrained conduct scandalous and vulgar. However distinct were the black and white variants of Protestant Christianity in the South, crucial similarities remained. Whatever antagonism existed between them, religion linked the masters and slaves in Christian fellowship and brotherhood. This sense of spiritual connection with whites produced ambiguous and contradictory results. It may have offered a sense of relief and security to the slaves who hoped that a devoutly Christian master would be less prone to resort to violence or cruelty against those with whom he shared a religious bond. At the same time, acceptance of Christianity may have rendered the slaves more obedient and less inclined to challenge earthly authority. To be sure, Christianity could encourage the appearance of a Nat Turner, determined to avenge himself and his people. Christianity, however, also muted resistance to slavery by permitting slaves to resign themselves to their fate without also succumbing to despair. They prayed for freedom and awaited its coming, trusting in God to rescue them from bondage in his own time and his own way.

Viewpoint:
Yes. Christianity was among the slaves' most important weapons in resisting the dehumanization inherent in slavery.

Religion was at the heart of African American culture. As Albert J. Raboteau and many other historians have demonstrated, Africans came to the New World with old and powerful religious beliefs, customs, and practices. Under slavery, this African religious heritage did not completely disappear but neither did it remain static. Circumstances required its modification, and it thus continued to evolve as a living tradition, putting down roots in a new soil, bearing new fruit as a unique hybrid of African, European, and American origins.

Slavery and racism undermined blacks' sense of worth as individuals and as a people, reinforcing their dependence on, and subordination to, whites. Resisting the dehumanizing logic of slavery as best they could, slaves found that the most important weapon in their arsenal of defense was a partially autonomous religious life that taught them to value and love each other, to take a critical view of their masters, to reject the rationale for their enslavement, and to await the judgment of God and the blessings of salvation. The religion of the slaves consisted of an imaginative blending of disparate ideas, beliefs, rituals, practices, and traditions into an intricate worldview that combined acceptance of what had to be endured (slavery) with resistance to the feelings of despair that slavery engendered. Three important elements of slave religion—the doctrines of sin, salvation, and the soul—reveal how the slaves accommodated to slavery while they resisted its harshest dictates.

One aspect of the biblical defense of slavery maintained that the enslavement of blacks fulfilled the biblical curse on the descendants of Ham. A son of Noah, Ham, ignoring God's prohibition, engaged in sexual intercourse while on the Ark. In another version of the story, Ham looked upon his naked father while Noah was drunk and disoriented. Either way, Ham had to be punished. Black skin was the mark of Ham's

sin, and slavery was the curse that God imposed upon his progeny.

The slaves developed a concept of sin but never believed that their predicament was the fulfillment of Ham's curse. In their view, slavery was not punishment for the collective sin of black people. The assertion that blacks suffered from the curse of Ham, which even many whites found theologically dubious, had few, if any, echoes in the quarters. On the contrary, blacks frequently rendered biblical stories in ways that directly challenged whites' conclusions. According to historian Eugene D. Genovese, Charity Moore remembered her father explaining how sin had come into the world. The story is familiar, except for one key alteration: Adam was so horrified by his sin, said Moore, that he turned white. Sin and white people thus entered the world at precisely the same moment. Like countless other slaves, Moore offered an exegesis of scripture and an interpretation of Christianity that hardly justified the enslavement of blacks. Rather, such revisions enabled blacks to understand that, although they themselves were beloved of God, they lived temporarily under conditions that were evil.

Even the slaves who embraced Christianity, however, had at best only a vague concept of original sin. There is, in fact, no equivalent of the Christian doctrine of original sin in any of the prominent religions that developed in West or Central Africa. For the slaves, therefore, sin meant wrongdoing, an act for which individuals were themselves directly responsible. Sin involved some sort of injustice or a violation of accepted moral and ethical standards. Traditional African theology had only the most obscure notion of the one doctrine that might have prompted blacks to think that their enslavement was justified. African American religion in general, and the African American version of Christianity in particular, emphasized a sense of shame rather than a sense of guilt. Enslavement might have been a shameful indication of weakness, but it was not sinful, and it did not provoke in blacks the conviction that they were receiving just punishment from the God whom they had offended.

In 1852, a slave preacher told his congregation as much within earshot of whites who heard and reported his every word, but who did not

A Bill for the better regulation of the conduct of negroes, slaves, and free persons of colour —

Be it enacted by the General Assembly of the State of North Carolina, and it is hereby enacted by the authority of the same; that it shall not be lawful under any pretence for any free negro, slave, or free person of colour to preach or exhort, or in any manner to officiate as a preacher, and if any free negro, or free person of colour shall be thereof duly convicted on indictment before any court having jurisdiction thereof he shall for each offence receive not exceeding thirty nine lashes on his bare back, and where any slave shall be guilty of a violation of this act, he shall on conviction before a single Magistrate receive not exceeding thirty nine lashes on his bare back —

RELIGION OF LIBERATION

comprehend their significance. On the day of the Last Judgment, the preacher exclaimed, Jesus would separate the goats from the lambs. The goats, who had sinned, he would gather with his left hand and cast into hell. The lambs, who had obeyed his Father's commandments, he would gather with his right hand and take into heaven. Jesus would return, the preacher assured his congregation, and in his own time and his own way would mete out justice to the righteous and the unrighteous alike. The chorus of "Amen!," "Hallelujah!," and "Praise Jesus!" that greeted the preacher's words left the whites in attendance to marvel at the quaint and simple faith of their black brothers and sisters in Christ.

Little did the white spectators realize that the black preacher had communicated to his audience both a religious and a political message. He had told them that Jesus loved them and would look after them. If they followed his laws and kept faith with him, he would never abandon them in this world or the next. He would, in the meantime, visit his wrath upon the greedy, lecherous, sinful, goat-footed white devils. The wooly-headed blacks, the flock of which he was the Shepherd, would, by contrast, one day sit at his right hand and enjoy the full bounty of Paradise.

The slaves' beliefs about salvation, heaven, and the afterlife were, if anything, even more ambiguous than their doctrine of sin. Some slaves thought that heaven was a place beyond earthly torment, where whites could never again harm them. Others believed that heaven meant a return to Africa. For many, heaven was anywhere blacks could love one another and live without fear. Such ambivalence should not be surprising. After all, as Genovese has pointed out, men and women who aspire to freedom rarely make the effort to fit their dreams into simple, organized categories.

In its most fundamental and accessible form, the slaves' vision of heaven counteracted the depression and despair that they experienced in life and contributed to their consciousness as a people. If they were not much in this world, the slaves reasoned, the next world held out the promise of freedom, justice, and equality. From this idea of heaven, blacks deduced a sense of individual and collective worth that helped to diminish the stature and power of the white men who dominated them. The converse of this vision of heaven was a vision of hell and the special torment that Satan had reserved for the slaveholders. Faith in the life to come thus consoled the slaves during their long years of affliction and compensated them for the miseries that they had to suffer on Earth.

Less directly, the slaves manipulated the Christian ideas of salvation, heaven, and the afterlife in ways both aggressive and defensive. The slaves took Jesus at his word that his kingdom was not of this world. They understood Jesus to mean that earthly arrangements did not prevail in heaven. What was so in this life was not always so in the next. This insight enabled slaves to render ironic but penetrating judgments of their masters. Former slave Andrew Moss of Georgia, quoted in *The American Slave: A Composite autobiography* (1972), proclaimed that "de white folks what owned slaves thought that when dey go to Heaven de colored folks would be dere to wait on 'em." Frances Anne Kemble reported in *Journal of a Residence on a Georgian Plantation in 1838–1839* (1863) that when her young daughter asked a house servant named Mary whether she knew that "some persons are free and some are not," Mary replied: "Yes missus, *here,* I know it is so here, in this world."

The slaves merged the orthodox Christian with the traditional African conception of the soul. Although slaves believed that the soul, or essence, of a person was unique, they also believed that human beings were not the only creatures that had souls. For reincarnated spirits returning to this world, the human body offered only one of many possible hosts. Yet, the soul remained synonymous with the inner life, with the elemental personality of the individual that could, over the course of many lifetimes, inhabit several corporeal forms. The soul could also exist independently of the body while the body still lived. It could wander freely throughout the world, return to the past, or travel to the future. Africans and many African Americans believed that dreams marked the journeys of the soul. When people dreamed of visiting with dead relatives, returning to Africa, or escaping from bondage, they were experiencing the various migrations of the soul, which they recalled upon waking. If the slaves' bodies existed in bondage, their souls, the essence of their being, lived in freedom. No master could chain them down.

African American scholar W. E. B. Du Bois estimated that only about one-sixth, or approximately 17 percent, of the adult slave population in the United States formally converted to Christianity. The influence of Christianity in the slave community, however, far exceeded the numbers of slaves who sought to be baptized. Slaveholders, of course, used the teachings of Christianity to keep slaves in their place and to reconcile them to their fate; that is, to render them docile and obedient. The slaves, of course, had other uses for Christianity, which they transformed into a religion of spiritual, though rarely political, defiance. Christianity enabled the slaves to retain their faith in earthly deliverance and yet to accept their enslavement. Christianity empowered slaves to instill a spirit of love and even pride into their community and yet to quell the desire for vengeance and rebellion that would have proved suicidal. Christianity helped the slaves to acknowledge whites as their brothers and sisters in Christ and yet to renounce the sense of their own degradation that would have plunged them into self-hatred and despair.

Religion in general, and Christianity in particular, gave a moral coherence to slave life. The slaves' dynamic religious worldview furnished discipline, reinforced a sense of collective identity and individual worth, and helped to safeguard the slaves if not from the physical then certainly from the psychological trauma that slavery engendered. Armed with their faith, the slaves asserted their humanity, struggled to improve their lot and, when opportunities arose, to throw off the yoke of bondage. Christianity may have strengthened their ties to whites and even compelled them to acquiesce in slavery, rendering unto Caesar that which belonged to Caesar, but Christianity also narrowed considerably what Caesar, in fact, could legitimately claim. The souls of black folk belonged not to man but to God. The slaves thus transformed the Christian promise of personal salvation into a hope of collective deliverance in this world and the next.

—MEG GREENE,
MIDLOTHIAN, VIRGINIA

Viewpoint:
No. Although Christianity comforted the slaves and served as a defense against their brutalization, it significantly muted the impulse toward rebellion.

When masters and slaves shared the same faith and prayed to the same God, inciting the slaves to rebellion was often difficult. It was not impossible, for Christianity had a revolutionary potential. Led by black preachers, the slaves of the South did not simply adopt Christianity as their masters presented it and intended them to understand it. Instead, they blended it with their own African folk beliefs to create a faith that, according to Eugene D. Genovese in *From Rebellion to Revolution: Afro-American Slave Revolts in the Making of the Modern World* (1979), "served as a bulwark against the dehumanization inherent in slavery" and that promised their ultimate release from bondage. Yet, throughout Latin America and the Caribbean, masters could boast that their Christian slaves provided greater security against slave insurrection than the military. "As Christian profession became a symbol of being civilized," writes Genovese, "it narrowed the apparent gulf between master and slave,

white and black; in precisely the same way, it weakened the unity of the quarters."

In the Caribbean, African religion manifested itself in two forms, Obeah and Myalism, which were not entirely compatible. The adherents to Obeah (a form of shamanism or sorcery) focused on private welfare and vengeance. The ability of Obeah priests to heal and to kill was legendary; their reputation extended as far as Europe and North America. The practices of Obeah scandalized Christian missionaries, for the devotees aspired to harm and punish others, including fellow slaves, who had wronged them. Both the leaders and followers of Obeah were predominantly African born. As a consequence, the influence of Obeah declined as the number of native-born slaves increased.

By the second half of the eighteenth century, Myalism was well established among the slaves of the Caribbean. The disciples of Myalism concerned themselves with the welfare of the slave community rather than with carrying out personal vendettas. Like Obeah, however, Myalism was resolutely anti-Christian and hostile to the slaveholding regime. Myalists at the least restrained the impulse to accommodate and at the most encouraged slaves to revolt. More politically dangerous than Obeah, Myalism was frequently associated with slave rebellions. It was deeply implicated, for instance, in the slave uprising of 1760 that occurred in Jamaica. The oaths that the Myalists swore and the rituals they performed steeled them against the exigencies of political resistance and warfare. Among other beliefs, they thought themselves immune to the white man's bullets and assumed that if they happened to be killed they would be reincarnated in Africa.

When, during the nineteenth century, missionaries sought to convert the slaves to Christianity, many Myalists became Methodists. In truth, they never entirely abandoned their folk religion but rather created an African-Christian hybrid. Not until the 1840s, following emancipation, did Christianity begin to predominate among the former slaves of Jamaica. After seizing the island in 1655, the English worked hard to eradicate the vestiges of African religion. Nevertheless, as historian Philip D. Curtin has argued, distinctly African religious beliefs and practices survived longer in Jamaica than did any other aspect of African culture. Similarly, historian Eric Williams declared that African religious cults remained widespread throughout the Caribbean into the middle of the twentieth century. In the Dutch colonies of Demerara and Surinam the indifference to converting the slaves and the extraordinary barbarism that they endured combined to encourage the continuance of African religions and to keep both settlements in a perpetual state of unrest.

TWO CHURCHES

Peter Randolph, a slave from Virginia who received his freedom in 1847, noted significant differences in the nature of the Christianity taught by the masters and that taught by the slaves:

Many say the Negroes receive religious education—that Sabbath worship is instituted for them as for others, and were it not for slavery, they would die in their sins—that really, the institution of slavery is a benevolent missionary enterprise. Yes, they are preached to, and I will give my readers some faint glimpses of these preachers, and their doctrines and practices.

In Prince George County there were two meeting-houses intended for public worship. Both were occupied by the Baptist denomination. These houses were built by William and George Harrison, brothers . . . that their slaves might go there on the Sabbath and receive instruction, such as slave-holding ministers would give. The prominent preaching to the slaves was, "'Servants, obey your masters.' Do not steal or lie, for this is very wrong. Such conduct is sinning against the Holy Ghost, and is base ingratitude to your kind masters, who feed, clothe and protect you. . . ." I should think, when making such statements, the slaveholders would feel the rebuke of the Apostle and fall down and be carried out from the face of day, as were Ananias and Sapphira, when they betrayed the trust committed to them, or refused to bear true testimony in regard to that trust.

There was another church, about fourteen miles from the one just mentioned. It was called "Brandon's church," and there the white Baptists worshiped. . . .

There was one Brother Shell who used to preach. One Sabbath, while exhorting the poor, impenitent, hard-hearted, ungrateful slaves, so much beloved by their masters, to repentance and prayerfulness, while entreating them to lead good lives, that they might escape the wrath (of the lash) to come, some of his crocodile tears overflowed his cheek. . . . But, my readers, Monday morning, Brother Shell was afflicted with his old malady, hardness of heart, so that he was obliged to catch one of the sisters by the throat, and give her a terrible flogging.

The like of this is the preaching, and these are the men that spread the Gospel among the slaves. Ah! such a Gospel had better be buried in oblivion, for it makes more heathens than Christians. Such preachers ought to be forbidden by the laws of the land ever to mock again at the blessed religion of Jesus, which was sent as a light to the world. . . .

Not being allowed to hold meetings on the plantation, the slaves assemble in the swamps, out of reach of the patrols. They have an understanding among themselves as to the time and place of getting together. This is often done by the first one arriving breaking boughs from the trees, and bending them in the direction of the selected spot. Arrangements are then made for conducting the exercises. They first ask each other how they feel, the state of their minds, etc. The male members then select a certain space, in separate groups, for their division of the meeting.

Preaching in order, by the brethren; then praying and singing all round, until they generally feel quite happy. The speaker usually commences by calling himself unworthy, and talks very slowly, until, feeling the spirit, he grows excited, and in a short time, there fall to the ground twenty or thirty men and women under its influence. Enlightened people call it excitement; but I wish the same was felt by everybody, so far as they are sincere.

The slave forgets all his sufferings, except to remind others of the trials during the past week, exclaiming: "Thank God, I shall not live here always!" Then they pass from one to another, shaking hands, and bidding each other farewell, promising, should they meet no more on earth, to strive and meet in heaven, where all is joy, happiness and liberty. As they separate, they sing a parting hymn of praise.

Sometimes the slaves meet in an old log-cabin, when they find it necessary to keep a watch. If discovered, they escape, if possible; but those who are caught often get whipped. Some are willing to be punished thus for Jesus' sake. Most of the songs used in worship are composed by the slaves themselves, and describe their own sufferings. Thus:

"Oh, that I had a bosom friend,
To tell my secrets to,
One always to depend upon
In everything I do!"

"How do I wander, up and down!
I seem a stranger, quite undone;
None to lend an ear to my complaint,
No one to cheer me, though I faint."

Some of the slaves sing—

"No more rain, no more snow, No more cowskin on my back!"

Then they change it by singing—

"Glory be to God that rules on high."

In some places, if the slaves are caught praying to God, they are whipped more than if they had committed a great crime. The slave holders will allow the slave to dance, but do not want them to pray to God. Sometimes, when a slave, on being whipped, calls upon God, he is forbidden to do so, under threat of having his throat cut, or brains blown out. Oh, reader! this seems very hard—that slaves cannot call on their Maker, when the case most needs it. Sometimes the poor slave takes courage to ask his master to let him pray, and is driven away, with the answer, that if discovered praying, his back will pay the bill.

Source: *Peter Randolph, Slave Cabin to the Pulpit (Boston: Earle, 1893), pp. 196–199, 202–204.*

RELIGION OF LIBERATION

Most of the slaves in the French colony of Saint Domingue (Haiti) were born in Africa, obtained little or no formal religious instruction from their masters or other whites, including the Catholic clergy, and had every reason to associate Roman Catholicism with greed, corruption, decadence, vice, and brutality. They instead identified themselves with Vodûn (voodoo), though they blended it with elements of Roman Catholicism. When the revolution erupted in 1791, Vodûn priests commanded the slaves to rise in a holy war against their Catholic masters. To a much greater extent than Catholicism, Vodûn demanded militant insurgency. As such, it fundamentally and irrevocably separated the slaves from the slaveholders, but the revolutionary character of Vodûn took shape less as a result of theological differences with Catholicism. It inspired political hostility to the regime and infused strength and courage into oppressed people who at last had an opportunity to fight back.

The Catholic Church in Brazil could do little to end slavery or the slave trade. Embedded in the medieval system of social hierarchy and having adapted that system to its own organization, the Church regarded slavery as one more consequence of original sin. As David Brion Davis noted in *The Problem of Slavery in Western Culture* (1966):

> It was . . . a traditional belief that total subordination was man's natural and legal condition after the Fall of Adam. If the absolute sovereignty of God stood behind all legitimate power, the completeness of creation, as well as divine justice, demanded an absolute subjection—in a spiritual sense, of all Christians; in a worldly sense, of the lowest ranks on the social scale. The essence of both sin and slavery was a denial of self-sovereignty, a negation of the natural ability to will that which was just and lawful. All men were condemned by Adam's sin to sweat for their bread; and some men . . . were required to sweat more than others. Sin and the necessities of Providence qualified the belief in the equality of men before God, and sanctioned the enslavement and transportation to America of millions of Africans.

In addition, the priests who served the plantations were more dependent upon the planters than they were upon the bishop and were, as Gilberto Freyre, the great historian of slavery in Brazil, has pointed out, often members of the planter's family. Even if not blood relatives, the status of priests depended on pleasing the *senhor* (lord or master), who was the absolute ruler of his world.

Yet, historian Frank Tannenbaum was surely correct to suggest that the activity and law of the Church vastly improved the lives of the slaves. Without directly challenging slavery, the Church encouraged manumissions. The Church repeatedly condemned the slave trade and, more specifically, Catholics' participation in it, though these prohibitions, coming from Rome, were ineffective in Portuguese Brazil. Even the Church, however, did not obtrude where individuals had been born, or sold themselves, into slavery or had become slaves through capture in a just war or conviction by a legitimate court. The prevailing assumption against the slave trade was that it forced men, women, and children into slavery outside the law and against their will. The Church also taught that master and slave were brothers in Christ. The master had an obligation to protect and care for the slave, just as the slave had an obligation to work and obey. In Eph. 4: 5, 9 St. Paul had enumerated these mutual responsibilities: "Servants, be obedient to them that are your masters according to the flesh with fear and trembling, in singleness of your heart, as unto Christ. . . . And, ye, masters, do the same things unto them, forbearing threatening, knowing that your Master also is in heaven; neither is there respect of persons with him."

Full participation and communion in the Catholic Church afforded slaves greater security than they would have otherwise enjoyed. It also significantly limited the possibilities of rebellion. Consequently, in Brazil, as elsewhere in Latin America and the Caribbean, African religions intertwined with Christianity. Candomble in Bahia, Xangô in Pernambuco, and Macumba in Rio de Janeiro appeared in organized and coherent movements of explicitly West African origin. Yet, each also displayed the unmistakable influence of Catholicism. Similarly, Brazilian slaves transformed the cult of Saint George into the cult of Ogun, the African god of war and vengeance. The adherents to the Ogun cult, whom Freyre called the "fighting aristocracy of the slave population," ignited many street fights and riots. Freyre indicated, however, that rulers often redirected and neutralized the rebelliousness of the oppressed. Such reactionary tendencies notwithstanding, non-Christian or anti-Christian religions also nurtured a genuinely revolutionary potential. For, as historian Roger Bastide argued, religion did not merely adorn slave uprisings, it was at "the very heart of the revolt."

Nowhere is the truth of Bastide's insight more fully demonstrated than in the impressive slave rebellions that took place in Bahia between 1807 and 1835, when Muslim slaves rose up against their white, Christian masters. These uprisings were not ordinary slave rebellions. To be sure, the participants resented their status, and many preferred death to surrender. In their minds, though, they were conducting a holy war against the Christian slaveholding regime. Throughout the Americas, Muslim slaves had earned a special reputation for defiance. Their religious heritage did not permit them easily to accept enslavement to Christian infidels whom Allah had commanded them to resist at all cost.

The Hausa (a West African people living largely around present-day Nigeria) assumed leadership of the early Bahian revolts. Muslim penetration of Hausa territory in Africa dated from at least the fourteenth century. Although the great majority of persons in this region continued to practice traditional African religions, they were already conditioned to follow Muslim leadership by the time they had arrived in the New World as slaves. In Bahia, therefore, Islam united disparate African peoples. The Yoruba, who had fought against the Hausa and the Fulani (who were also Muslim) in Africa, now joined them, setting aside their former rivalry to battle a common enemy. Muslim leaders of the slave revolts in Bahia forged alliances among peoples previously estranged from one another and imposed steadfast discipline in order to hold those alliances together, which proved indispensable during this protracted struggle that assumed both a political and a religious character.

The rebellions culminated in January 1835 when Brazilian officials uncovered a plot to stage a massive uprising. Although they took every precaution to avert it, they failed. The slaves suffered defeat, but not until hundreds of persons, white and black, Christian and Muslim, had been wounded or killed. Perhaps the finest testament to the courage and prowess of the captured slave leaders was that, instead of being hanged as criminals and rebels, they were shot with full military honors.

Wherever a non-Christian or an anti-Christian religion—such as Myalism, Vodûn, or Islam—prevailed among the slaves, their struggle, by its nature, took on something of the character of a holy war. Under such circumstances, religion drove an impenetrable wedge between the slaves and their masters, provoking the slaves to rise not only against those who held them in bondage but also against those who were enemies of their faith.

–MARK G. MALVASI,
RANDOLPH-MACON COLLEGE

References

John B. Boles, ed., *Masters & Slaves in the House of the Lord: Race and Religion in the American South, 1740–1870* (Lexington: University of Kentucky Press, 1988).

David Brion Davis, *The Problem of Slavery in Western Culture* (Ithaca, N.Y.: Cornell University Press, 1966).

Gilberto Freyre, *The Masters and the Slaves: A Study in the Development of Brazilian Civilization,* second English-language edition, translated by Samuel Putnam (New York: Knopf, 1956).

Eugene D. Genovese, *From Rebellion to Revolution: Afro-American Slave Revolts in the Making of the Modern World* (Baton Rouge: Louisiana State University Press, 1979).

Genovese, *Roll, Jordan, Roll: The World the Slaves Made* (New York: Pantheon, 1974).

Frances Anne Kemble, *Journal of a Residence on a Georgian Plantation in 1838–1839,* edited by John A. Scott (New York: Knopf, 1961).

Donald G. Mathews, *Religion in the Old South* (Chicago: University of Chicago Press, 1977).

Thomas Virgil Peterson, *Ham and Japheth: The Mythic World of Whites in the Antebellum South* (Metuchen, N.J.: Scarecrow Press, 1978).

Albert J. Raboteau, *Slave Religion. The "Invisible Institution" in the Antebellum South* (New York: Oxford University Press, 1978).

George Rawick, ed., *The American Slave: A Composite Autobiography,* first and second series, 19 volumes (Westport, Conn.: Greenwood Press, 1972); first supplemental series, 12 volumes (Westport, Conn.: Greenwood Press, 1977); second supplemental series, 10 volumes (Westport, Conn.: Greenwood Press, 1979).

Mechal Sobel, *Trabelin' On: The Slave Journey to Afro-Baptist Faith* (Westport, Conn.: Greenwood Press, 1979).

Sterling Stuckey, *Slave Culture: Nationalist Theory and the Foundations of Black America* (New York: Oxford University Press, 1987).

Frank Tannenbaum, *Slave and Citizen: The Negro in the Americas* (New York: Knopf, 1946).

RELIGION OF LIBERATION

REPARATIONS

Should the descendants of the slaves receive reparations from the United States government?

Viewpoint: Yes. Slavery was a gross violation of human rights, and justice demands that the descendants of the slaves be compensated for the exploitation of their ancestors.

Viewpoint: No. Compensation for the injustice of slavery might have been due to the slaves themselves, but the descendants of the slaves, who did not themselves endure bondage, are due nothing.

Will paying reparations to the descendants of slaves at last balance the ledger between black and white Americans, ending centuries of racial animosity that has tortured and disgraced the United States? Many whites feel guilt about slavery even while they resent the accusations of racism leveled against them. Some advocates of reparations, however, do not invoke past injustice or even enduring racism to justify seeking monetary damages. Rather, they regard the struggle to obtain reparations as a way of negating the political authority that they believe whites exercise over blacks.

Even the most degraded whites, these critics maintain, enjoy a status that is higher than that of the most exalted blacks. Militant proponents of reparations thus espouse the dissolution of the white community as a political and economic force and see reparations as an efficient and effective way of accomplishing that goal. If every white person in the United States, along with the white-dominated federal government and white-owned corporations, had to contribute to the reparations trust fund, the massive redistribution of power and wealth that resulted would destroy the privilege of being white.

Those who object to reparations, by contrast, insist that the welfare programs in place since the 1960s already constitute the payment of reparations from which blacks have benefited for two generations. Besides, opponents argue, no one alive today, black or white, had anything to do with slavery. They cannot, therefore, profit from or take responsibility for a past that they had no part in making.

The antidote for past wrongs is restitution, explained English philosopher Owen Barfield. The antidote for feelings of guilt is repentance. Yet, who remains to repent of slavery? And if white Americans did try to make restitution, would surrendering all that they now own be sufficient to clear the account?

Viewpoint:
Yes. Slavery was a gross violation of human rights, and justice demands that the descendants of the slaves be compensated for the exploitation of their ancestors.

Slavery was a horrendous crime that Europeans and later Americans perpetrated against Africans. The time has come for those whose ancestors profited from slavery to make restitution to those whose ancestors endured it. The time has come for a show of contrition, of repentance, of justice. According to David Brion Davis, a renowned historian of the international movement to abolish slavery, nearly everyone in the West was in some way connected to slavery and the slave trade. The entire Western Hemisphere, Davis suggests, was "enmeshed in slavery." By capturing millions of their own people and offering them for sale, Davis concedes, Africans themselves abetted slavery and the slave trade. European and American merchants, entrepreneurs, and planters, however, exploited the situation to enrich their colonies, their nations, and themselves. Even those individuals not directly involved in buying and selling slaves invested in the slave trade, including such unlikely figures as English philosopher John Locke and French writer Voltaire. New Englanders, whose descendants came to abhor slavery, were not only responsible for carrying slaves to the New World, but they also shipped food, shoes, clothing, and other items to the South and the slaveholding colonies of the West Indies. They financed slave-trading expeditions, insured both slave traders and planters against loss, and constructed many of the ships in which the slaves were transported. Finally, Davis points out, even those Europeans and Americans who might have found slavery repugnant, bought and used the products of slave labor: sugar, tobacco, cotton, rice, indigo, hemp, and rum. From the outset, slavery in the United States was a national phenomenon.

Slavery was legal in the Thirteen Colonies at the time of the American War for Independence (1775–1783). The Constitution of the United States (1787) sanctioned slavery, protected slave property, and extended additional representation to the Southern states based on their slave populations. As a consequence, slaveholders dominated the national government until the outbreak of the Civil War (1861–1865). In Davis's view, with the exception of the Adamses, even the nonslaveholding presidents from the North, Martin Van Buren and Millard Fillmore

of New York, Franklin Pierce of New Hampshire, and James Buchanan of Pennsylvania, catered to Southern demands. With few exceptions, American foreign policy also consistently favored slaveholding interests. Successive administrations, Davis argues, invariably "refused to cooperate with efforts by Britain to suppress the international slave trade, even though the United States had defined the African slave trade in 1820 as piracy, a capital crime."

This extraordinary set of circumstances had come about not only because Southerners were powerful but also because slavery was profitable. In the decades before the Civil War, cotton became the principal export of the United States. Slavery thus made possible the development of textile manufacturing, shipbuilding, banking, and insurance in New England; paid for American imports; and attracted investment capital from abroad. In addition, slavery enhanced land values throughout the South, especially in such southwestern states as Alabama, Mississippi, Louisiana, and Texas. Except for the land itself, slaves represented the single largest capital asset in the nation. "In 1860," Davis writes, "the value of Southern slaves was about three times the amount invested in manufacturing or railroads. . . . Not surprisingly, the richest Americans were concentrated in the South."

The Confederacy lost the war for Southern independence and yet won a tremendous ideological victory that enabled Southerners to diminish the importance of slavery in American history, and even, as Davis contends, "somehow remove [it] as a cause of the war." Slavery became, in effect, an unfortunate if benign accident that had little enduring influence on American society and life. Yet, national reconciliation demanded acquiescence in white supremacy and black subordination, a formula that, in turn, inaugurated a long era of racial discrimination and violence. The continued oppression and exploitation of African Americans offers a powerful argument for reparations. In *The Debt: What America Owes to Blacks* (2000) social activist Randall Robinson maintains that the legacy of slavery and racism has made the payment of reparations not only just but also necessary. Robinson believes any progress that African Americans have made is incidental. They have a right, he insists, to present a bill to America for centuries of unremunerated toil from which neither they nor their ancestors received a fair return. "America's socio-economic gaps between the races remain," Robinson has written, "like the aged redwoods rooted in a forest floor, going nowhere, seen but not disturbed, simulating infinity, normalcy. Static."

Despite the accomplishments of the Civil Rights movement in ending legal discrimina-

REPARATIONS

Family of
African American
sharecroppers after
the Civil War

*(Valentine Museum,
Richmond, Va.)*

tion, poverty continues to haunt black America. Those African Americans who have advanced into the middle class have lost their connection with poor blacks, who are now left to fend for themselves. Those who have fallen victim to poverty command reparations to fund improvements in health care, housing, jobs training, and education. In addition, Robinson asserts, racism remains "unbowed" and is, indeed, the principal cause of poverty among blacks, to say nothing of the despair that pervades much of the black community. "Modern observers," Robinson suggests, "now look at the canvas as if its subjects were to be forever fixed in a fore-ordained inequality. Of the many reasons for this inequality, chief of course is the seemingly incurable virus of *de facto* discrimination that continues to poison relations between the races at all levels." He intends reparation payments not only to compensate for past injustice but, more importantly, to remedy this lingering damage.

Slavery and racism have done even worse than mire blacks in a debilitating poverty. Together they have robbed blacks of their dignity, identity, and humanity. "Since this nation's inception," Robinson declares,

> taxpayers—white, black, brown—have spent billions on museums, monuments, memorials, parks, centers for the performing arts, festivals, and commemorative occasions. Billions have been spent on the publication of history texts, arts texts, magazines, newspapers, and history journals. Formulaic television and large-screen historical fiction treatments virtually defy count. Almost none of this spending, building, unveiling, and publishing has been addressed to the needs of Americans who are not white.

Robinson traces the poverty and despair that are presently ravaging the black community to a "sense of rootlessness" that arose from systematic efforts to deprive blacks in America of knowledge about their African origins, culture, and history. Wrenched from their African homeland, blacks, Robinson observes, are "history's amnesiacs." They have never found a place in American society because "the armaments of culture and history that have protected the tender interiors of peoples from the dawn of time have been premeditatively stripped from the black victims of American slavery. . . . Far too many Americans of African descent believe their history starts in America with bondage and struggles forward from there toward today's second-class citizenship."

There have, of course, always been individual blacks who managed to overcome the impediments that hindered African Americans, those special few who succeeded against all odds. They are, in Robinson's estimation, exceptions to the rule, less ideals than aberrations. How many other blacks who merited recognition and advancement, Robinson wonders, have been impaired by the "static, unarticulated, insidious racial conditioning . . . to which all Americans are subject?" No matter how hard they strive, there is no ladder for the majority of blacks to climb to the top of American society, from whence, Robinson concludes, emerges the need for reparations.

To determine the viability of offering reparations to blacks, Democratic Representative John Conyers of Michigan introduced House Resolution 40, the "commission to Study Reparation Proposals for African-Americans Act." In the meantime, celebrated defense attorney Johnnie Cochran and Harvard law professor Charles Ogletree headed a group of black lawyers who initiated class-action suits against the federal government and several private corporations that had profited from slavery. Filed on behalf of the thirty-five million descendants of slaves, the initial suits named Aetna Inc., the FleetBoston Financial Corporation, and the CSX Corporation as defendants. Aetna, the suit alleged, insured slave traders and slaveholders against the deaths of their slaves. The suit accused FleetBoston of acquiring a bank in Rhode Island that once lent money to slave traders. CSX purportedly bought companies that had used slave labor in the construction of railroads. The lawsuits claimed, however, that as many as one thousand American corporations benefited from, or in some way helped to perpetuate, slavery between 1619 and 1865. The charges read in part that "the practice of slavery constituted an immoral and inhumane depravation of Africans' life, liberty, African citizenship rights, and cultural heritage and it further deprived them of the fruits of their own labor."

For many blacks, the proposal of HR 40 and the appeal to the courts are a mere prologue. "Once and for all," Robinson has announced, "America must face its past. . . . Slavery . . . hulled empty a whole race of people with intergenerational efficiency. Every artifact of the victim's past, every custom, every ritual, every god, every language, every trace element of a people's whole inherited identity, was wrenched from them and ground into a sharp choking dust." The government, the corporations, and all white Americans must acknowledge their responsibility for this catastrophe. They must apologize for inflicting more than four hundred years of degradation and misery upon blacks. They must pay, until all traces of racism have been eradicated from American society and the human heart.

–MARGARET BARNES,
MIDLOTHIAN, VIRGINIA

Viewpoint:
No. Compensation for the injustice of slavery might have been due to the slaves themselves, but the descendants of the slaves, who did not themselves endure bondage, are due nothing.

"The fundamental problem of American democracy in the 21st century," writes Manning Marable, director of the African-American Studies Program at Columbia University, "is the problem of 'structural racism': the deep patterns of socio-economic inequality and accumulated disadvantage that are coded by race, and constantly justified in public discourse by both racist stereotypes and white indifference." For Marable, as for other leaders of the African American community—including Democratic Representative John Conyers of Michigan, social activist and author Randall Robinson, attorney Johnnie Cochran, Harvard law professor Charles Ogletree, and Reverend Al Sharpton—reparations, along with an ample dose of white racial guilt, are the solution. Provoking guilt over slavery and racism is essential, for without it neither corporations nor the government have any inducement to pay. Robinson admitted as much when he wrote that "once the record is fleshed out and made fully available to the American people, I think companies will feel some obligation."

What exactly is "the record" to which Robinson referred? Few today would deny that the enslavement of approximately eleven million Africans was an evil of audacious proportions. But what is to be done about it now? Slavery ended in the United States in 1865 and in the Western Hemisphere in 1888, when the government of Brazil at last abolished it. Justice demands that the slave traders, the slaveholders, and any who profited directly from slavery make restitution to the slaves for exploiting and brutalizing them. Jews and other victims of the Nazi Holocaust, Europeans whom the Nazis forced into slave labor, and the Japanese interred in the United States during World War II (1939–1945) have received similar compensation. The problem with applying corresponding settlements to slavery is that both the victims and the perpetrators of this enormity are dead, and so justice is beyond mortal reach.

This fact hardly deters the advocates of reparations for blacks, although they are not always clear about who should pay and from where the money will come. When they indicate that the federal government ought to foot the bill, they really mean the American taxpayers. Are those

Americans liable whose ancestors came to the United States long after slavery had been abolished? What about those who trace their lineage to a forebear who fought, and perhaps died, to free the slaves? To complicate matters, should the descendants of those blacks who themselves owned slaves pay or receive reparations? Then, too, ought Congress to subpoena representatives from the various Arab, European, and African states that participated in the slave trade and wring from their struggling economies contributions to the reparations trust fund?

Such questions do not much trouble the proponents of reparations, who expect never to have to answer them. They are, indeed, not even preoccupied with having their day in court, for they do not expect to prevail in the legal proceedings that they have initiated against such companies as Aetna, Inc., CSX Corporation, and FleetBoston Financial Corporation. Rather, they hope to arrive at out-of-court settlements with these and other firms by appealing to the guilty consciences of CEOs and boards of directors and by threatening national boycotts and bad publicity that make stockholders pulse with fear. "Let's just say you'll pay because it's in your interest to pay," fictional Senator Pat Geary tells Mafia boss Michael Corleone in *The Godfather: Part II* (1974). The same attitude prevails among the supporters of reparations. To some, these tactics may seem the appropriate rejoinder to centuries of discrimination and injustice. Others, such as editorialist John Leo, who are more clear-sighted and clearheaded, see them for what they are: "a racial shakedown."

The procedure is already well established. In *Shakedown: Exposing the Real Jesse Jackson* (2002) Kenneth Timmerman shows that corporations, frightened at being branded racist, routinely accede to the demands of black activists who challenge their goodwill on racial issues. Nike is, perhaps, the most notable exception, while the Ford Motor Company, which for decades spent a fortune to prop up languishing minority-owned dealerships, represents the norm. Many corporations thus succumbed to what amounts to racial extortion. Ward Connerly and Edward Blum, who are leading the fight against racial preferences, noted that "Texaco, Denny's, Coca-Cola, and others have settled specious bias claims rather than have Mr. Sharpton, Mr. Jackson, and members of the Congressional Black Caucus call for a nationwide boycott of their companies." Blacks have also targeted prominent universities. Harvard, Yale, Princeton, Brown, and the University of Virginia all have a connection to slavery and the slave trade. It is only a matter of time before angry and idealistic students, white and black, begin to denounce their schools and

A TROJAN HORSE

African American journalist and political analyst Juan Williams comments on reparations for slavery:

If reparations become a reality, black Americans already battling presumptions of inferiority (they are less hardworking, less intelligent and less patriotic, according to whites questioned by pollsters) will also bear the weight of being demeaned as less able than any Mexican immigrant or Bosnian refugee. The newcomers, after all, are not asking for reparations—they only want a chance to make it in America. The result will be a further segregation of low-income black people from the mainstream.

On a political level, the cost of reparations may be even higher. Reparations will mean an end to the moral responsibility that all Americans, especially white Americans, have for the history of slavery, legal segregation and the continuing racism in our national life. That white guilt opens the door to the idea of national obligation to repair the damage of racism. Once the first reparations check is written, that moral responsibility will disappear, and the door will shut on all claims for affirmative action in private industry, government and academia. It may also bring a collapse of the already tenuous support for social-welfare programs that are a key to repairing the horrors of public schools in big cities, high rates of poverty among children, and jails overflowing with young black men.

Democrats as well as Republicans have rejected efforts to raise the reparations issue in Congress for a dozen years, and polls show that nearly 70% of whites stand in opposition to even an apology for slavery. The minute any company starts writing reparations checks all the collective white guilt that fuels support for social policy to help poor black people will be exhausted. The debt will be paid and forgotten.

Given the devastating consequences contained in this Trojan Horse, why does the reparations movement march on?

On a simple level, it is about the alluring possibility of a bonanza payday for some of the lawyers involved. And there are still people who think they might get a check for thousands of dollars if some company somewhere issues a reparation check. The IRS is dealing with increasing numbers of people who have been duped into believing that they can claim a "Slavery Rebate" on their tax forms. (Last year 80,000 taxpayers made that claim.)

But greed aside, the reparations movement is also evidence of the growing strength of black America. Some of the best-educated, most affluent black people in world history are properly flexing their political muscles. Randall Robinson, author of a best-selling book calling for reparations, has told interviewers that the key issue is that black people have "decided for ourselves that they are our due."

In a diverse nation, the demands of a strong and vocal black community cannot be ignored. No matter how farfetched the legal claim may be, there will be press conferences and college conferences to review the horrors of slavery. The devastation that slavery visited on black people is beyond debate, and so is the history of exploitation of former slaves once they were set free without compensation for their labor.

But that sound argument is now being contorted into claims that black America is still feeling the impact of slavery. That stretch is necessary for the lawyers behind the reparations movement to support the idea that there are victims of slavery alive to serve as plaintiffs in a lawsuit. But while racist attitudes persist, it's hard to make the case that slavery is the issue when black Americans are enjoying record levels of educational attainment and income.

One intriguing way to look at reparations is as an effort by the rising black middle class to take control of the massive budgets dedicated to social-welfare policy. In the current lawsuits the money from reparations is designated for a treasury that would be controlled by a black elite and used as they see fit to improve life in black America. What is now national policy for dealing with black poverty would become a matter of a black nationalist agenda.

That is as sure a road to racial separatism as you can get. Scandals are sure to follow as money goes to black entrepreneurs who may be friends of the people handing out the money. And inevitably some black nationalists will complain that those controlling the money are addressing the wrong needs. Even without infighting and scandals it is obscene to think of this modern generation of black Americans profiting from the blood money drawn nearly 140 years ago from the exploitation of slaves.

Source: *Juan Williams, "Slavery Isn't the Issue: Reparations Would Be Bad for America,"* Wall Street Journal *(14 April 2002), in* FreeRepublic.com *<http://www.freerepublic.com/focus/news/665707/posts>.*

REPARATIONS

administrations as racist and insist that reparations be paid from the burgeoning endowments.

The moral horror at slavery notwithstanding, 75 percent of Americans, and 90 percent of whites, oppose reparation payments. Assuming for the moment that those who espouse reparations could entice or cajole these men and women into abandoning their disapproval, there remains another objection that argument and intimidation cannot so easily dismiss or overcome. Since the 1960s the government of the United States has, in effect, been furnishing reparations to blacks. Although this compensation has not enabled the majority of blacks to escape poverty, welfare has provided billions of dollars to poor blacks. Even more important, it has created jobs for those who managed the welfare bureaucracy and who, ironically, have become the principal beneficiaries of the system. Political scientists Michael K. Brown and Steven P. Erie, for example, estimated that President Lyndon B. Johnson's "Great Society" programs created two million government jobs, most of them on the state and local level but with payrolls funded by federal grants. A disproportionately high ratio of these positions went to blacks. According to the statistics that Brown and Erie compiled, the number of blacks at work in the welfare sector increased by 850,000 between 1960 and 1976. In addition, blacks also found employment in local transportation authorities and law enforcement agencies. By 1970, 57 percent of black male and 72 percent of black female college graduates worked for the government. Nearly forty years ago the federal welfare system initiated the government jobs program that reparations are in part designed to generate.

Any plan to pay reparations must include arrangements for assisting poor blacks while training them to enter the workforce. The federal government in conjunction with the states has already implemented such welfare-to-work policies, rendering superfluous the demands of those who advance the cause of reparations. Equally redundant is the claim that money ought to be allocated to permit inner-city blacks to buy homes. Again, an agency is already in operation; the Community Development Corporation has for years enabled blacks who live in urban ghettos to enjoy the benefits of home ownership. A portion of the reparations fund is also designated to encourage banks to lend capital to blacks to start small businesses. Since 1977 the Community Reinvestment Act has provided the guidelines and incentives to various financial institutions to make such start-up money available. Finally, affirmative action, which John McWhorter, an African American professor of linguistics at the University of California at Berkeley, has characterized as "a reparative policy if ever there was one," addresses racial injustices past and present. The injuries that blacks have suffered are real but so too is the compensation that they have been receiving for years through an array of government programs.

The idea of paying reparations to blacks is not new. Boris I. Bittker, a white law professor, offered the first extended analysis of the question in *The Case for Black Reparations*, published in 1973. Although Bittker recommended that some blacks collect reparations, he concluded that not all should be eligible. Only those blacks compelled to attend segregated schools ought to be compensated, for they had endured verifiable discrimination and thus merited relief. Bittker explicitly rejected the notion of making skin color alone ("blackness") the basis of reparations. To do so, he thought, would revive and promote the same arbitrary conception of race that had originally justified slavery and discrimination. He also resisted paying reparations directly to black organizations and institutions to distribute as they saw fit. Given the diversity of the black community, Bittker maintained that it was impossible to determine which associations represented the majority of black Americans. Writing in a day when the Black Power movement was at its zenith, Bittker wondered who was "to decide whether a group that claims to be the vanguard is really only a body of stragglers because the army is moving in the opposite direction? . . . Among American blacks today, differences in economic status, geographical origin and current locations, outlook, organizational ties, and educational background are powerful centrifugal forces that black nationalist groups have not succeeded in neutralizing."

Bittker made a reasonable and compelling legal and moral case that black Americans who had actually experienced discrimination warranted redress. Those currently endorsing reparations are pursuing a different and more ambitious agenda, which Marable has specified as "closing the socioeconomic gap between blacks and whites." Reparations now amount to nothing less than a revolutionary redistribution of money and property along racial lines. Yet, money and property are of secondary importance. The real issue that underlies the debate over reparations is power—the power, as Sam Francis writes, to bring about

the delegitimization of the old white, European, and Eurocentric America and the legitimization of a new, nonwhite, non-European and even anti-white and anti-European America. The money for reparations is largely just a teaser; the real payoff is the racial power that reparations and the acknowledgment of white guilt and white illegitimacy would bring.

Francis may exaggerate the case, but his assessment ought to call to mind nineteenth-century French writer Alexis de Tocqueville's reflections on the tragic history of slavery and race relations in the United States, which, as usual, Tocqueville ascertained with a remarkable and disturbing clarity: "If freedom is refused to the Negroes . . . , in the end they will seize it themselves; if it is granted them, they will not be slow to abuse it."

–MARK G. MALVASI,
RANDOLPH-MACON COLLEGE

References

Boris I. Bittker, *The Case for Black Reparations* (New York: Random House, 1973).

Michael K. Brown and Steven P. Erie, "Blacks and the Legacy of the Great Society: The Economic and Political Impact of Federal Social Policy," *Public Policy,* 29 (Summer 1981): 299–330.

David Brion Davis, "The Enduring Legacy of the South's Civil War Victory," *New York Times,* 26 August 2001, pp. 1, 6.

Sam Francis, "Abolishing America: Reparations as Power Grab" (3 September 2001) <http://www.vdare.com/francis/power_grab.htm>.

"Lawsuits seeking slavery reparations," *Richmond Times-Dispatch,* 27 March 2002, pp. A1, A4.

Nicholas Lemann, *The Promised Land: The Great Black Migration and How It Changed America* (New York: Knopf, 1991).

John Leo, "Shakedown Artists Plan to Pick Deep Pockets of Corporations," *Richmond Times-Dispatch,* 14 April 2002, p. E6.

John McWhorter, "Against Reparations," *New Republic* (23 July 2001): 32–38.

Randall Robinson, *The Debt: What America Owes to Blacks* (New York: Dutton, 2000).

Kenneth Timmerman, *Shakedown: Exposing the Real Jesse Jackson* (Washington, D.C.: Regnery, 2002).

Alexis de Tocqueville, *Democracy in America,* edited by J. P. Mayer (Garden City, N.Y.: Anchor, 1969).

Walter Williams, "Reparations . . . Who Would Get Them? Who Should Pay?" *Richmond Times-Dispatch,* 7 February 2001, p. A13.

REPARATIONS

RHYTHM OF WORK

Did slaves control the rhythm and pace of their work?

Viewpoint: Yes. For all the tendencies toward modern work discipline, plantation labor remained bound to the rhythms of nature and traditional ideas of time and work. The slaves worked hard, but they resisted the regularity and routine of work characteristic of industrial capitalism.

Viewpoint: No. The planters of the South and elsewhere regulated the labor of their slaves according to the discipline of the clock, and in the process created a time-based form of plantation capitalism that emphasized order and efficiency in the management of slave labor.

In recent years the debate has intensified over whether slaves controlled the rhythm and pace of their work. The widely accepted interpretation has long been that the masters struggled and failed to impose industrial work discipline on their slaves. Field work, however arduous, continued to be governed by the diurnal and seasonal rhythms of nature and premodern notions of time. Historians have begun to question such conclusions, proclaiming the emergence and importance of mechanical time in the South after 1830. The more conscious of time the masters became, the more fully they compelled their slaves to obey the relentless dictates of the clock. To the extent that the clock came to regulate life on the plantation, the slaves lost the ability to manage the pace of their labor. Arguments pronouncing the ascendancy of mechanical time implicitly raise questions about the efficacy of slave resistance. Slaves may not have internalized time-discipline, but they could not avoid submitting to it. Vulnerable to their master's will and power, supported as it was by the force of law and the fear of punishment, the slaves had little choice but to acquiesce. They were, as one historian has put it, "mastered by the clock."

On the other side of this discussion are historians who maintain that the traditional attitudes and values of blacks were hard to overcome. Slaves had a work ethic of their own that was at once a defense against exploitation and an assertion of such premodern values as a sense of joy in life and beauty of creation—values often antagonistic to the Protestant work ethic that dominated American society. The slaves were not lazy. Rather, they rejected the work ethic that the masters tried to perpetrate upon them and fashioned ideas of work and leisure that enabled them to resist their master's will and, at the same time, to sustain a connection with their African cultural inheritance. Unlike whites, blacks simply did not see work as a moral duty. The great African American historian W. E. B. Du Bois noted that the slaves were not easily reduced to mechanical draft animals, as European workers became. Blacks, Du Bois concluded, could be driven only so hard and so far. Not subject to the discipline of the clock, they worked slowly and carelessly even under the most severe compulsion if they "did not find the spiritual returns adequate." Du Bois contended, "The Negro laborer has not been trained in modern organized industry but rather in a different school."

**Viewpoint:
Yes. For all the tendencies toward modern work discipline, plantation labor remained bound to the rhythms of nature and traditional ideas of time and work. The slaves worked hard, but they resisted the regularity and routine of work characteristic of industrial capitalism.**

The extent to which slaves influenced the plantation regime has long been a matter of contention among historians. In his influential *Slavery: A Problem in American Institutional and Intellectual Life* (1959) Stanley M. Elkins argued that with their brutal exploitation of blacks, Southern masters fashioned a plantation order that resembled the Nazi concentration camps. Masters entirely broke down slaves' personalities, rendering them submissive, infantile "Sambos." However, such a view greatly underestimates blacks' strength of character, resourcefulness, and endurance, while simultaneously overestimating whites' mastery.

Since the appearance of Elkins's book, historians such as Eugene D. Genovese, Robert William Fogel, Stanley L. Engerman, William W. Freehling, and Charles Joyner have refuted his concentration-camp thesis. They have shown that slaves did indeed preserve the will and the ability to resist their masters in subtle, and sometimes not so subtle, ways. Not only did the plantation require slaves to accommodate masters but masters also were sometimes forced to accommodate their slaves. Through the careful employment of strategies of resistance and accommodation, slaves managed to retain their identities and to stamp their personalities onto the plantation world. Slaves "successfully resisted becoming extensions of their masters' wills" and "achieved a degree of psychological and cultural autonomy," Genovese contended.

One of the principal means of resistance that slaves employed was working slowly and badly. "The slave's weapon was deceit," explains Freehling. "Power was achieved by playing childish parts maladroitly. . . . Slaves constantly misunderstood orders, broke tools, abused mules, missed weeds." Frederick Law Olmsted, a Northern critic of slavery and the South, described how the slaves on one Virginia plantation dragged out their work by playing childish parts. "During three hours, or more, in which I was in company with the proprietor, I do not think there were ten consecutive minutes uninterrupted by some of the slaves requiring his personal direction or assistance." Slaves thwarted

their masters' anger by playing the childish, ignorant Sambo when confronted about their slow and negligent work. Never quite certain whether slaves were deliberately lazy and deceitful or simply incapable of satisfactory labor, masters were never sure of the appropriate response. Frustrated slave owners, unsure whether to encourage or punish their slaves, wanted to believe their bondpeople were, if not happy, at least contented. The alternative was too frightful to contemplate. No master wanted to think his slaves were on the verge of open revolt. Therefore, they chose to believe their slaves were naturally lazy and stupid. Carefully calculating the risk of punishment, slaves adroitly manipulated their masters' prejudices.

Much of slaveholders' reticence to recognize slow and bad work as resistance to their authority can be attributed to what Genovese identified as a paternalistic society. Southern paternalism "grew out of the necessity to discipline and morally justify a system of exploitation." Though paternalism represented something different to masters and slaves, both accepted it as the basis of their relationship. For slaveholders, "paternalism defined the involuntary labor of the slaves as a legitimate return to their masters for protection and direction. But, the masters' need to see their slaves as acquiescent human beings constituted a moral victory for the slaves themselves. Paternalism's insistence upon mutual obligations—duties, responsibilities, and ultimately even rights—implicitly recognized the slaves' humanity." Paternalism answered masters' psychological need to believe their slaves were contented and, in the philosophy of mutual obligation, provided slaves an effective tool of resistance. Olmsted's Virginia planter and his slaves knew their parts and played them well. Olmsted observed that the master's demeanor toward his slaves was "paternal—familiar and kind; and they came to him like children who have been given some task, and constantly are wanting to be encouraged and guided, simply and confidently." In Maryland he observed slaves whose work was so slow, stupid, and dilatory that their master "would frequently take the duty off their hands into his own, rather than wait for them, or make them correct their blunders."

By exploiting their exploiters' sense of paternalism, slaves successfully exerted considerable influence over the rhythm and pace of work on the plantation. Slaves often parried their owners' best efforts to exert mastery. For example, masters encouraged their slaves to sing happy, up-tempo songs while they worked in the fields. Spirited singing neatly fit slaveholders' paternalistic image of themselves as the beneficent masters of happy slaves. They also entertained the hope that up-tempo singing would hasten the pace of work. However, slaves responded by sing-

Photograph of slaves planting sweet potatoes on a plantation on Edisto Island, South Carolina, 1863

(New-York Historical Society, New York City)

ing, and working to the pace of, slow tunes that frequently expressed sorrow and longing for freedom. These songs, which W. E. B. Du Bois called "the greatest gift of the Negro people," "are the music of an unhappy people, of the children of disappointment." "It is impossible to conceive of a greater mistake," wrote former slave and abolitionist Frederick Douglass, than the supposition that slaves sang because they were happy. Nevertheless, paternalistic masters patiently accepted slaves setting a slow pace of work with their singing. They even found the singing reassuring. As historian Mark M. Smith has explained, masters found slave singing illustrative of their "imagined plantation Elysium" and evidence "that not only was all right with their world but their world, in fact, was all right."

Slaves in the Carolina and Georgia low country controlled the rhythm and pace of their work even more directly than slaves in other regions. There, slaves and conditions compelled their masters to adopt the "task system," under which slaves were given a specific task to complete each day and after it was finished the remainder of the day belonged to them. Thus, slaves directly controlled the rhythm and pace, if not necessarily the volume, of their work. Yet, even here, while undoubtedly appreciating their relatively greater auton-

omy, slaves resisted the individualistic ethos of the task system. They preferred the communal work patterns of Africa to being treated as individuals. As Joyner explained in *Down by the Riverside: A South Carolina Slave Community* (1984), "moving across the fields in a row hoeing side-by-side to the rhythm of work songs, the slaves imposed a group consciousness on their field work."

Slaves also controlled the rhythm and pace of their work by resisting the attempts of enterprising planters to impose upon them a modern, capitalist, clock-time discipline. Africans arriving in America knew only natural time, which corresponds to the cyclical patterns of days and seasons. Slaves resisted, and were sometimes able to ignore, their masters' efforts at running the plantation on clock time. Their partial success resulted from paternalistic masters being quick to believe their child-like slaves incapable of comprehending clock time and because planting and harvesting are necessarily governed by the seasonal cycles of natural time. In the predominantly agricultural South, according to Smith, "naturally defined time remained important to African Americans even after the Civil War."

Masters chose to believe that slaves sang because they were happy and that they worked slowly and resisted clock time because of racial inferiority. Therefore, slaves often controlled the rhythm and pace of work even though planters recognized that condescension carried a high price. As South Carolina writer William Gilmore Simms explained to Nathaniel Beverley Tucker, paternalistic masters often indulged slaves even when they could ill afford to do so. "Our planting interest, though considerable, like that of too many of our race & neighbours, has not been profitable; and my habits are somewhat expensive," he wrote. In fact, he admitted that his habits were too expensive to be borne by "the resources of a Cotton plantation which has been too frequently mismanaged, and where an undue indulgence of the slaves is permitted." Fellow South Carolinian Mary Boykin Chesnut agreed that, by accepting slow and bad work, planters paid a high price for paternalism: "A hired man would be a good deal cheaper than a man whose father and mother, wife and twelve children have to be fed, clothed, housed, and nursed, their taxes paid, and their doctor's bills, all for his half-done, slovenly, lazy work," she confided to her diary. The indifferent labor of the slaves is one of the few subjects on which Olmsted and the proslavery polemicist, George Fitzhugh, would have agreed. "Considering his indolence and unskilfulness," Fitzhugh argued in *Sociology for the South, or, The Failure of Free Society* (1854), "the slave enjoys more of the farm's profits than he is entitled to by his labor."

As Genovese has argued, the rhythm and pace of work on each plantation was the result of a compromise that had to be hammered out between the slaves and their master. Granted, one party to the compromise was bound in chains. However, the other was bound by the paternalistic ethos of Southern slave society. Astute slaveholders also recognized the practical limits to their mastery. The harder they pushed their slaves, the more likely they were to resist, rebel, or run away. Slaveholders also knew that kindness and incentives were as likely as the lash to increase productivity. Therefore, when slaves chose to resist by setting a slow pace, masters, according to Genovese, "decided that blacks could not work steadily and so concluded that they ought not to expect them to." Masters could generally cajole or compel enough labor to keep their plantations running as profitable enterprises, but that was all they got out of their slaves. Through slow and sloppy work, slaves successfully "resisted that regularity and routine which became the *sine qua non* for industrial society and which the planters . . . tried to impose upon them."

—SEAN R. BUSICK,
KENTUCKY WESLEYAN COLLEGE

Viewpoint:
No. The planters of the South and elsewhere regulated the labor of their slaves according to the discipline of the clock, and in the process created a time-based form of plantation capitalism that emphasized order and efficiency in the management of slave labor.

Slaves may have attempted to control the rhythm and pace of work by slowing down, by abusing the animals in their charge, by breaking tools, or by pretending to have forgotten how to use them. All their efforts were to no avail. Through the threat of punishment and violence and, more commonly, the repetition of such sounds as the chiming of bells or blowing of horns, masters and overseers countered these tendencies and imposed upon slaves an external obedience to mechanical time that took from them much of their ability to determine the tempo at which they worked. The slave-owning planters thus regulated the labor of their slaves by enforcing the discipline of the clock.

Documenting the attitudes toward mechanical time among the slaveholders of the antebellum South, historian Mark M. Smith found that, in 1865, nearly 70 percent of Southern heads of households owned either a clock or a watch. In the plantation district of Laurens County, South Carolina, the number of slaveholders who owned clocks and watches increased from 5 percent in the late 1780s to 75 percent by 1865. During the 1830s Southern slaveholders had already begun to embrace mechanical, or clock, time and to redefine the work habits of their slaves, reflecting their growing concern with punctuality, efficiency, order, and productivity. The appeal of "scientific agriculture" also prompted slaveholders to apply the discipline of clock time to the cotton fields.

Southern agricultural journals such as the *Farmer's Register* reminded planters that "time is money" and quoted with approbation Benjamin Franklin's aphorisms about the perils of wasting time. Unlike Southerners, complained John Forsyth in *De Bow's Review* in 1854, the Northern businessman "has no time for shooting a beef at the cross-roads or the grocery. With him life is too short to lose a moment; every hour has its business." Forsyth recommended that Southerners imitate Northerners "in all their good and valuable qualities." In 1843 C. T. Botts, editor of the *Southern Planter*, considered that no laborer, slave or free,

should have his attention distracted or his time occupied in thinking about what he should do next; the process of thought and arrangement should devolve wholly upon the superinten-dent, and the manual laborer, to be most effec-tive, should by constant repetitions perform mechanically, and almost without the effort, his daily task.

Countless slaveholders evidently took this advice to heart. In 1852, for example, an "Alabama planter" had written in *De Bow's Review* that he required his slaves to

> rise in time to be at their labour by light. Their breakfast hour is eight o'clock . . . which requires fifteen minutes. . . . In the winter they have one hour, and summer three to rest, in the heat of the day. . . . I require them to retire at nine o'clock precisely. The foreman calls the roll at that hour, and two or three times during the night, to see that all are in their places. . . . By pursuing this plan with my servants they become attached to me, and have respect for my orders.

Other planters communicated time to their field hands by ringing bells or blowing horns. In his instructions to a new overseer, Virginia planter St. George Cocke explained that he wished to use a horn to schedule work and other planta-tion activities. He wrote:

> It is strictly required of the manager that he rise at the dawn of day every morning; that he blow a horn for the assembling of the hands; require all hands to repair to a certain and fixed place in ten minutes after the blowing of the horn, and there himself see that all are present, or notice absentees. . . . There will be stated hours for the negroes to breakfast and dine, and those hours must be regularly observed. Breakfast will be at eight o'clock, and dinner at one o'clock. . . . A horn will be sounded every night at nine o'clock, after every negro will be required to be at his quarters.

Another planter, who called himself "Agricola," utilized a large cow bell "that could be heard two miles [away] . . . as a signal for bed time, for get-ting up of a morning, for ceasing work at noon and resuming it after dinner. Where the distance is not so great a common bar of steel . . . may be struck with a hammer, and will answer in place of a bell."

Former slaves interviewed during the 1930s verified the regimentation of work on the planta-tion, an arrangement that admitted little variation in routine. In *The American Slave: A Composite Autobiography* (1977), Laura Montgomery, who had been a slave in Mississippi, is cited as saying that when it was time to go to the field, "marse would blow [his horn] dat hour every mornin' an' we had to git out right now and start dat work." Prince Johnson, a former slave from Oklahoma, echoed Montgomery's account: "Every morning about four o'clock we could hear that horn blow for us to get up and go to the field."

A mechanical sense of time seems to have been alien to West African cultures. For slaves in colonial America, evidence suggests that African time sensi-bilities were largely unaltered. It is also misleading to suggest that the African consciousness of time disappeared as soon as slaveholders introduced clock time on the plantation. Masters, after all, did not make clocks or watches readily available to the slaves, who still relied on the sun or the stars to esti-mate the time of day. As recorded in *The American Slave*, "We didn't own no clocks dem days," reflected Jane Simpson, a former slave from Mis-souri, "we just told de time by de sun in de day and de stars at night. If it was clouded we didn't know what time it was." Planters, in fact, concealed from the majority of their slaves the mysterious, almost magical, secret of telling time, reserving that knowl-edge for themselves and those few slaves—such as house servants, cooks, and drivers—whose duties required it. James Bolton, a former slave from Georgia, remembered that his mistress "done larned the cook to count the clock, but none of the rest of our niggers could count the clock," as reported in *The American Slave*. Tob Davis spoke for the majority of slaves, however, when he said, "Dey don't have de watches dem deys fo' de nigger so dey can't tell de time." Simpson added with a rueful sarcasm that "De white folks didn't want to let de slaves have no time for der self."

Despite their unfamiliarity with and their resistance to mechanical time, plantation slaves did not escape the rigors of labor regulated by the clock. Slaves may have clung to their traditional sense of time, but in the fields they were com-pelled to obey the master's watch, depriving them of the ability to work at their own pace. "When I growed up they give me so many rows of cotton to hoe or pick," explained Mose Smith in *The Ameri-can Slave*. "I work my own rows and they timed me so I had to hurry to get the work done, and when they send me off the farm to do a chore they time me on that." Holding the slaves to a strict timetable in the performance of their assigned tasks enabled the masters to exert greater control over the pace of their work and thus to ensure greater efficiency and productivity.

Bells and horns used to mark the passage of time were just as effective instruments of disci-pline as was the physical presence of the master or the overseer and the threat of punishment that their presence implied. "Bells and horns! Bells for this and horns for that!" lamented Charely Williams. "All we knowed was go and come by bells and horns." Dave Walker, a former Missis-sippi slave, elaborated in *The American Slave*: "We wuz trained to live by signals of a ole cow horn. Us knowed whut each blow meant. All through de day de ole horn wuz blowed, to git up in de mo'nings, to go to de big kitchen out in Mars' back yard ter eat, to go to de fields, an' to come in an' on lak dat all day." Other former slaves testi-fied to the frenetic pace of life and work that they

INVALIDS AND AN IDLE ROGUE

Matthew Gregory Lewis, a planter on Jamaica, made the following observations about slaves avoiding work:

The hospital has been crowded, since my arrival, with patients who have nothing the matter with them. On Wednesday there were about thirty invalid, of whom only four were cases at all serious; the rest had "a lilly pain here, massa," or "a bad pain me no know where, massa," and evidently only came to the hospital in order to sit idle and chat away the time with their friends. Four of them the doctor ordered into the field peremptorily: the next day there came into the sick-house six others; upon this I resolved to try my own hand at curing them; and I directed the head-driver to announce that the presents which I had brought from England should be distributed to-day, that the new-born children should be christened, and that the negroes might take possession of my house, and amuse themselves till twelve at night. The effect of my prescription was magical; two-thirds of the sick were hale and, hearty, at work in the field, on Saturday morning, and to-day not a soul remained in the hospital except the four serious cases. . . . On my arrival I found that idle rogue Nato, as usual, an inmate of the hospital, where he regularly passes at least nine months out of the twelve. He was with infinite difficulty persuaded at the end of a fortnight to employ himself about the carriage-horses for a couple of days; but on the third he returned to the hospital, although the medical attendants, one and all, declared nothing to be the matter with him, and the doctors even refused to insert his name in the sick-list. Still he persisted in declaring himself to be too ill to do a single stroke of work: so on Thursday I put him into one of the sick-rooms by himself, and desired him to get well with the doors locked, which he would find to the full as easy as with the doors open; at the same time assuring him that he should never come out till he should be sufficiently recovered to cut canes in the field. He held good all Friday; but Saturday being a holiday, he declared himself to be in a perfect state of health, and desired to be released. However, I was determined to make him suffer a little his lying and obstinacy, and would not suffer the doors to be opened for him till this morning, when he quitted the hospital, saluted on all sides by loud huzzas in congratulation of his amended health, and which followed him during his whole progress to the cane-piece.

Source: *Matthew Gregory Lewis,* Journal of a Residence among the Negroes in the West Indies *(London: Murray, 1845), pp. 64, 153–154.*

associated with the sound of the bells and horns and the discipline of clock time. "Wuk started on place in mawnins 'bout fo' 'clock," said Robert Young. "Overseer would ring a bell an' I member hearin' feets hot de flo' on right atter 'nother when de bell would ring. All de darkies got out to field as fast as they could."

The compulsion to obey the sound of the bell or horn and submit to what slaves called "plantation time" arose in part because the master had a virtual monopoly not only over the instruments for telling time but also over the instruments for punishing disobedience. Slaves' respect for the clock was thus born of fear. According to a former slave named William Byrd, as recorded in *The American Slave:*

Master, he had [a] great iron piece hanging just out side his door and he hit that every morning at 3:30. The negroes they come tumbling out of their beds. If they didn't master he come round in about thirty minutes with that cat-o-nine tails and begins to let [the] negro have that and when he got through they knew what bell was the next morning.

Yet, the fear of punishment notwithstanding, slaves devised subtle means of resistance to contest the imposition of the clock. By feigning ignorance or confusion about how to tell time, slaves could inconvenience their master's family and guests. As documented in her *Retrospect of Western Travel* (1838), Harriet Martineau, while visiting a plantation, was awakened and summoned to breakfast "half dressed" only to discover the meal had "been served an hour too early, because the clock stopped, and the cook . . . ordered affairs to her own conjectures." According to Catherine Cooper Hopley, an English visitor to the Millbank plantation in Virginia:

Dinner . . . is dependent entirely on the arrangements or rather accidents of the negroes. . . . The Millbank servants were very irregular. We never knew until the dinner-bell rang whether it would be before twelve, or after three, or any intermediate hour.

Such instances of resistance notwithstanding, on Southern plantations the clock was another weapon in the hands of the master. By the clock he

RHYTHM OF WORK

could regulate the pace of slave labor and engender in his slaves a new awareness of, and a relentless obedience to, time.

–RICK KAAT,
SAN FRANCISCO, CALIFORNIA

References

Mary Boykin Chesnut, *A Diary from Dixie, as Written by Mary Boykin Chesnut, Wife of James Chesnut, Jr., United States Senator from South Carolina, 1859–1861, and Afterward an Aide to Jefferson Davis and a Brigadier-General in the Confederate Army,* edited by Isabella D. Martin and Myrta Lockett Avary (New York: Appleton, 1905).

Frederick Douglass, *Narrative of the Life of Frederick Douglass, An American Slave* (Boston: Anti-Slavery Office, 1845).

W. E. B. Du Bois, *The Souls of Black Folk: Essays and Sketches* (Chicago: McClurg, 1903).

Stanley M. Elkins, *Slavery: A Problem in American Institutional and Intellectual Life* (Chicago: University of Chicago Press, 1959).

George Fitzhugh, *Sociology for the South, or, The Failure of Free Society* (Richmond, Va.: Morris, 1854).

Robert William Fogel and Stanley L. Engerman, *Time on the Cross: The Economics of American Negro Slavery,* 2 volumes (Boston: Little, Brown, 1974).

John Forsyth, "The North and the South," *De Bow's Review,* 17 (1854): 361–378.

William W. Freehling, *The Road to Disunion,* volume 1, *The Secessionists at Bay, 1776–1854* (New York: Oxford University Press, 1990).

Eugene D. Genovese, *The Political Economy of Slavery: Studies in the Economy and Society of the Slave South* (New York: Pantheon, 1965).

Genovese, *Roll, Jordan, Roll: The World the Slaves Made* (New York: Pantheon, 1974).

Catherine Cooper Hopley, *Life in the South from the Commencement of the War, Being a Social History of Those Who Took Part in the Battles, from a Personal Acquaintance with Their Homes, from the Spring of 1860 to August 1862,* 2 volumes (London: Chapman & Hall, 1863).

Charles Joyner, *Down by the Riverside: A South Carolina Slave Community* (Urbana: University of Illinois Press, 1984).

David S. Landes, *Revolution in Time: Clocks and the Making of the Modern World* (Cambridge, Mass.: Belknap Press of Harvard University Press, 1983).

Harriet Martineau, *Retrospect of Western Travel,* 2 volumes (London: Saunders & Otley, 1838).

Earl McKenzie, "Time in European and African Philosophy," *Caribbean Quarterly,* 19 (1973–1974): 77–85.

Frederick Law Olmsted, *A Journey in the Seaboard Slave States: With Remarks on Their Economy* (New York: Dix & Edwards / London: Sampson Low, Son, 1856).

Michael O'Malley, "Time, Work and Task Orientation: A Critique of American Historiography," *Time and Society,* 1 (1992): 341–358.

George P. Rawick, ed., *The American Slave: A Composite Autobiography,* first and second series, 19 volumes (Westport, Conn.: Greenwood Press, 1972); first supplemental series, 12 volumes (Westport, Conn.: Greenwood Press, 1977); second supplemental series, 10 volumes (Westport, Conn.: Greenwood Press, 1979).

William Gilmore Simms, *Letters of William Gilmore Simms,* volume 3, edited by Mary C. Simms Oliphant, Alfred Taylor Odell, and T. C. Duncan Eaves (Columbia: University of South Carolina Press, 1954).

Mark M. Smith, *Listening to Nineteenth-Century America* (Chapel Hill: University of North Carolina Press, 2001).

Smith, *Mastered by the Clock: Time, Slavery, and Freedom in the American South* (Chapel Hill: University of North Carolina Press, 1997).

Smith, "Old South Time in Comparative Perspective," *American Historical Review,* 101 (December 1996): 1432–1469.

Smith, "Time, Slavery and Plantation Capitalism in the Ante-Bellum American South," *Past & Present: A Journal of Historical Studies,* 150 (February 1996): 142–168.

Mechal Sobel, *The World They Made Together: Black and White Values in Eighteenth-Century Virginia* (Princeton: Princeton University Press, 1987).

E. P. Thompson, "Time, Work-Discipline and Industrial Capitalism," *Past & Present: A Journal of Historical Studies,* 38 (December 1967): 56–97.

Ivor Wilks, "On Mentally Mapping Greater Asante: A Study of Time and Motion," *Journal of African History,* 33 (1992): 175–190.

SAINT DOMINGUE

Was the slave insurrection on Saint Domingue (Haiti) a turning point in the modern history of slavery?

Viewpoint: Yes. The Haitian Revolution not only freed the slaves on Saint Domingue but also established the first independent African American nation and began the process by which blacks in the Western Hemisphere acquired the rights of citizenship.

Viewpoint: No. After gaining their freedom, the former slaves of Haiti exchanged white masters for black and mulatto masters, and Haiti sunk into poverty and corruption.

By the last decades of the eighteenth century, the population of Saint Domingue (Haiti) consisted of approximately 450,000 slaves, 40,000 whites, and 28,000 free blacks and mulattoes. This French colony was the most prosperous in the Western Hemisphere, the aggregate value of its exports greater than that of the British North American colonies. The outbreak of the French Revolution in 1789 reshaped the political and social relations of Saint Domingue. The elite, composed of 10,000 aristocrats, opposed the revolution and supported the Crown, while the 30,000 white shopkeepers and artisans who constituted the middle class (along with most of the free blacks and mulattoes) espoused the revolutionary doctrines of the Jacobins. The quarrels and conflicts that divided the whites presented an opportunity for the slaves, who, in 1791, under the leadership of a Vodûn priest named Boukman, rose in rebellion.

By 1793, the slave uprising had become a full-scale war. Those whites who championed the revolution battled the elite who did not. The British and Spanish sent troops, ostensibly to quell the slave rebellion but also hoping to wrest control of Saint Domingue from the French. Amid the tumult François Dominilque Toussaint L'Ouverture emerged as the leader of the slave rebels. Initially fighting with the Spanish against the French, Toussaint L'Ouverture switched sides when the revolutionary government in France abolished slavery. By 1795 he had helped the French to expel the Spanish from the colony and in 1796 came to rule Saint Domingue as governor-general. During the next four years, between 1796 and 1800, Toussaint L'Ouverture defeated both the British forces and his domestic enemies. In 1801 he invaded and conquered Santo Domingo, the portion of the island that had remained under Spanish control, and compelled the Spanish to withdraw. Toussaint L'Ouverture proclaimed himself the ruler of Saint Domingue for life, but at the same time he eschewed independence and declared his allegiance to France.

When, in 1801, Napoleon Bonaparte became First Consul of France, he sought to oust Toussaint L'Ouverture from power and reestablish slavery in Saint Domingue. Napoleon's agents captured Toussaint L'Ouverture, whom Napoleon then imprisoned in France. Yet, Jean-Jacques Dessalines and Henri Christophe, two of Toussaint L'Ouverture's most trusted subordinates, defeated the army that Napoleon sent against them, banished the remaining whites from the island, and changed its name from *Saint*

Domingue to *Haiti,* which means "land of the mountains." Dessalines and Christophe established the independent republic of Haiti on 1 January 1804.

From its inception, political turmoil and economic hardship afflicted the new nation, whose present continues to be marred by unremitting poverty and factional violence. The Haitian Revolution, however, had far-reaching implications. Slaveholders in the Caribbean, Latin America, and the United States trembled at the image of slaves embarked upon a murderous rampage and did all they could to prevent the fever of slave revolution from spreading. Such fears were not misplaced, for the accomplishments of the slaves on Saint Domingue did inspire slave rebels elsewhere. Gabriel Prosser in Virginia (1800) and Denmark Vesey in South Carolina (1822), both of whom staged unsuccessful slave uprisings, found a source of pride and hope in the Haitian Revolution. Perhaps the supreme irony of the Haitian Revolution, though, is that in defeating the French, the former slaves put an end to Napoleon's dream of reconstituting a New World empire for France. The loss of Haiti prompted Napoleon to sell the Louisiana Territory to the United States in 1803, thereby opening the way for the establishment of one of the most extensive and powerful slaveholding regimes in history.

Viewpoint:
Yes. The Haitian Revolution not only freed the slaves on Saint Domingue but also established the first independent African American nation and began the process by which blacks in the Western Hemisphere acquired the rights of citizenship.

The French revolutionaries dreamed of creating a world in which everyone could enjoy the benefits of *liberté, égalité, et fraternité* (liberty, equality, and fraternity). They envisioned all people rising in majesty to shake off the oppression of the past. Inspired by the ideals of the French Revolution (1789–1799), a brilliant former slave named Toussaint L'Ouverture claimed for his enslaved brothers and sisters a share of the *liberté, égalité, et fraternité,* to say nothing of the human dignity, that the French revolutionaries affirmed for themselves.

Toussaint L'Ouverture led the slave uprising on the French colony of Saint Domingue (Haiti), which was the only successful slave revolt in modern history. The Haitian Revolution transformed thousands of slaves into a people able to defeat the most powerful armies of Europe in what must surely rank as one of the great epic dramas of modern history. The uprising, which began in 1791, lasted for twelve years. Before it ended, 350,000 persons had died, and Haiti, the first independent nation in the Caribbean and the first African American state in the world, had been born.

The Treaty of Ryswick, signed in 1695 by representatives of France and Spain, gave the French legal title to the western half of the island of Hispaniola, which Christopher Columbus had claimed for the Spanish Crown in 1492. Renaming their portion of the island Saint Domingue,

the French colonists prospered. The land was fertile, and France provided a good market for the cash crops, such as cocoa, indigo, cotton, sugarcane, and coffee, that they cultivated. At first the French relied on indentured servants, whom they called *engagés,* to work in the fields. Bound to a master for a set number of years, the *engagés* regained their freedom when their terms of service expired. The harsh working conditions and the unhealthy climate of the island as well as the improving economic opportunities in France induced fewer and fewer whites to journey to Saint Domingue as indentured servants. The settlers began to clamor for slaves, and traders brought them all they could buy.

By 1789 Saint Domingue was the richest colony in the world. Trade with Saint Domingue supplied approximately 67 percent of French overseas commerce. Saint Domingue was also the largest market for slaves in the Western Hemisphere. At the end of the eighteenth century there were at least 7,000 plantations situated throughout the island. Hailed as the "pearl of the Antilles," Saint Domingue was the pride of France, the envy of her imperial rivals, and an integral component of European economic life. The success of the colony rested on the labor of 500,000 slaves. For them Saint Domingue was a hell on earth.

During the night of 22 August 1791, as historian Martin Ros described the scene, a wall of fire rose on the horizon in northern Saint Domingue. It swept across the plain and seemed to spread in all directions, moving at once toward the mountains and the sea. The immense flames created enormous gusts of wind that drove the fire on, causing it to rage through the forests, the fields thick with indigo, cotton, sugarcane, and coffee, the warehouses, the sugar mills, and the plantation homes. Fifty thousand slaves, under the leadership of a Vodûn priest named Boukman, had arisen in rebellion. With painted faces and bare chests smeared with ashes

Drawing of Toussaint L'Ouverture, leader of the slave rebellion on Saint Domingue (Haiti), circa 1795

(Bibliotheque Nationale de France, Paris)

and blood, they took vengeance on whites for centuries of humiliation, torture, and murder. This terrible festival of violence lasted for days. In that time the rebellious slaves killed 2,000 whites, destroyed 180 sugarcane plantations and 800 coffee plantations, and inflicted damages estimated at 2 million francs.

The whites retaliated with a counterattack that was even more gruesome and indiscriminate. During the next three weeks they slaughtered between 15,000 and 20,000 blacks and mulattoes. On 3 September the colonial assembly met in Cape François, the capital of Saint Domingue, to enact measures designed to prevent future slave insurrections. The army, composed of only 2,500 men, though supported by heavy artillery and bolstered by the arrival of British troops from Jamaica, had already restored order throughout the island. The rebellious slaves retreated, and the white ruling elite survived the largest, bloodiest, and most frightening slave insurrection ever to take place in the Western Hemisphere. Despite the revolutionary fervor in France, *liberté, égalité, et fraternité* had limits that were, if necessary, to be ruthlessly enforced.

The rebellion, however, did not end, and by 1792 Toussaint L'Ouverture had become its recognized leader. After the slaves on Saint Domingue won their freedom in 1793, Toussaint L'Ouverture and his forces joined with the French to drive the English from the island in 1798. He invaded the eastern half of the island, called Santo Domingo, which the Spanish still governed, and in 1801 freed the slaves there. After the defeat of the Spanish, Toussaint L'Ouverture was sole master of Saint Domingue. His administration was firm, but efficient and just, and staunchly resistant to the efforts of Napoleon Bonaparte, the new ruler of France, to reinstate slavery. In 1802, however, Napoleon's brother-in-law, General Charles Leclerc, commander of French troops in Saint Domingue, set a trap for Toussaint L'Ouverture, captured him, charged him with treason, and deported him to France, where he died in prison in 1803.

Despite Toussaint L'Ouverture's ignominious and tragic fate, the slave revolt on Saint Domingue marked a turning point in the modern history of slavery. Toussaint L'Ouverture introduced a new constitution for Saint Domingue that proclaimed the former slaves to be "free and French." That expression was more than a mere rhetorical declaration of independence or a wish to transform African Americans into Europeans. By inserting the phrase "free and French" into the constitution, Toussaint L'Ouverture sought to identify his cause and his people with the revolutionaries in France who aspired to establish *liberté, égalité, et fraternité* for all. He understood that the assertion of freedom for blacks was not enough. Freedom meant nothing separate from the laws, institutions, and traditions that made men free.

Before the slave revolution in Saint Domingue, Eugene D. Genovese has contended, all slave uprisings, from those of the Roman Empire to the massive rebellions that took place throughout the Americas, had been essentially defensive. The rebellious slaves, sometimes numbering in the thousands, longed only to withdraw from slave society and to restore as much of the traditional African way of life as they could remember.

Some of these rebellions succeeded. Maroons in Jamaica forced the British to sign treaties that guaranteed their autonomy. Communities of former slaves in Surinam secured similar rights from the Dutch. In Brazil during the seventeenth century runaway slaves founded a huge colony that eventually numbered twenty thousand at Palmares. The Palmarinos resisted both the Dutch and the Portuguese for nearly a century before succumbing to superior force. As courageous as these efforts were, none of them challenged slavery as a system. Many of the former slaves, whether in Jamaica, Surinam, Brazil, or elsewhere, held slaves themselves.

In Saint Domingue, by contrast, the slave rebellion passed into a national revolution aimed not at reconstructing a lost African world but at ending slavery and, further, at erecting a modern, independent, black nation-state. Toussaint L'Ouverture's phrase "free and French" offered the former slaves of Saint Domingue a new definition of themselves. Those words proclaimed that the citizens of this new nation-state were to enjoy the same benefits of freedom and equality that the revolutionaries in France had demanded for themselves.

Haiti, as the victorious former slaves renamed Saint Domingue, was a small country with a big revolution. The Haitian Revolution did not constitute just one more uprising of slaves. It formed, instead, part of a continuum with the American and French Revolutions that signaled the beginning of a new era in history, destined irrevocably to remake the modern world. After the slave revolution in Haiti, everything changed. The slave uprisings that followed indicated a fateful departure from the earlier pattern of insurrection. Blacks had entered modern history. No longer did they desire only to withdraw from society into some half-forgotten African past. Rather, blacks now aspired to end their isolation and oppression and to earn a place for themselves among the community of nations.

The creation of an independent black republic in Haiti exposed as folly the attempts of the ruling classes in Europe and the United States to impose their will upon the world. Toussaint L'Ouverture understood that in a fundamental sense the world was becoming unified. He saw at the end of the eighteenth century that a global economy was emerging, and with it a world political community from which no people could effectively isolate themselves. The most impressive aspect of the blacks' triumph in Haiti was not the magnificent discipline, unity, and power that they showed in the face of implacable foes. It was rather their superior intelligence and the acute insight into the course of world events that they, and their extraordinary leader, displayed.

Toussaint L'Ouverture's vision of freedom, equality, and independence for blacks combined with a revolutionary enthusiasm in France for the universal "rights of man and citizen." Together these ideas exposed the growing vulnerability of the slaveholders in the European colonies of the New World as well as the United States. This reactionary class could not hope to survive forever in a world increasingly dominated by a liberal bourgeoisie such as the one that had come to power in France, a class, among other things, committed to free trade and free labor. Toussaint L'Ouverture appreciated that the best prospects for blacks lay in worldwide recognition of their citizenship, not just of their freedom. To that end, he demanded respect for the rights of blacks as individuals, struggled to ensure their equality before the law, and insisted upon their participation as citizens in the politics of the emerging democratic world.

–MEG GREENE,
MIDLOTHIAN, VIRGINIA

Viewpoint:
No. After gaining their freedom, the former slaves of Haiti exchanged white masters for black and mulatto masters, and Haiti sunk into poverty and corruption.

On the surface the slaves of Saint Domingue (Haiti) made stunning achievements in their long struggle for freedom and equality. They humiliated the Spanish and the English, and they made Haiti a graveyard for Napoleon Bonaparte's magnificent army and put an end to his imperial ambitions in the New World. However, their accomplishments seemed too good to be true.

The former slaves of Haiti exchanged white masters for black and mulatto masters. Toussaint L'Ouverture and his successors, Jean-Jacques Dessalines and Henri Christophe, imposed such a harsh regime of forced labor upon the former slaves that the economy never recovered from their ministrations, and Haiti quickly became what it is today: the most impoverished, backward, and wretched country in the Western Hemisphere.

Toussaint L'Ouverture, and after him Dessalines and Christophe, sent the former slaves back to the plantations and dealt swiftly and decisively with those who refused to work. Toussaint L'Ouverture aimed at restoring sugar production and rebuilding the once profitable export sector of the Haitian economy, for he understood that the new black state would recede into abject poverty and cultural barbarism unless it could restore industry and construct schools, churches, cultural institutions, and all the other accoutrements of a modern civilized nation. He knew that nothing would be possible for Haiti in isolation and that firm political and military alliances with revolutionary France were essential to national survival. Toussaint L'Ouverture also realized that economic and cultural reconstruction on such a massive scale, as well as continued support from France, had to be paid for. Payment required restoration of the sugar economy oriented toward the world market, which, in turn, required labor, discipline, and hard work.

In time, however, this severe policy yielded to a complex peasant revolution that, under the guise of ending dictatorship and establishing democracy, resulted in the division of the land among the weary and poor former slaves. They abandoned Toussaint L'Ouverture's efforts to revitalize the export sector and slipped instead into a subsistence economy, thus creating the most thoroughgoing peasant country in the Caribbean. The dream of a modern, independent black state died in the scramble of the former slaves for scraps of land to call their own and for a chance to live according to the old ways. Predictably, these people turned not to democratic and representative but to authoritarian government to protect their claims to independent proprietorship.

On 8 December 1804, less than a year after founding it, Dessalines abolished the Haitian republic and declared himself Emperor Jacques I. He confiscated the remaining white-owned property to distribute among the land-hungry masses and encouraged his followers to rid Haiti of the white scourge by massacring all the whites who remained on the island. Dessalines's lieutenants, Christophe and Alexandre Sabès Pétion, conspiring to put an end to his dictatorship and, at the same time, to restore order to Haiti, assassinated him on 17 October 1806.

BEFORE THE BUSINESS ENDS

News of the upheaval in Saint Domingue (Haiti) traveled quickly to the United States. The following account appeared in a Philadelphia newspaper in late 1791:

AUTHENTIC PARTICULARS Of the late Disturbances at S. Domingo, received from a gentleman at Cape François, in a letter to his friend in this city.

Cape François, Wednesday evening, Aug. 24.

YESTERDAY morning the Volunteers were all ordered out by order of the Assembly, who convened at an early hour. I was not acquainted with the case till near 9 o'clock, at which time a draft from every company was made, together with a large party of the Cape regiment, to march immediately to the plains, and but a few miles from town, where it seems the Negroes of a number of plantations had rebelled, assembled in a body, and killed the Overseer of one plantation, and a gentleman belonging to this town. In the afternoon reports began to circulate, and the alarm became general. Several thousands of the Negroes had assembled, and committed some ravages by burning several habitations, which they continued doing all last night, in spite of the troops which went to stop their depredations. Many Negroes were yesterday killed, indeed all that could be met with. . . .

The causes of this dreadful insurrection I dare not conjecture; but it is said, the tyranny of some of the Overseers is not the least of the causes. A plot to burn the town and the shipping in the road, has been discovered, and which was to have been attempted the night before last. Many will be the sacrifices before the business ends, and doubtless the conspirators of so infernal a piece of work, will soon meet their just reward. Some are taken up on suspicion of supplying the incendiaries with the means, and some have been caught in attempting to execute the infernal project.

Nothing has been done in town these two days, but keeping the volunteers and militia in arms, and every store and ship is obliged to be kept shut. In fine, all is fear, suspicion, jealousy! And every one has an interest in watching even the looks of the people of color.

Sunday, 28 August.

Since writing the foregoing, numerous have been the most cruel murders and massacres,—and numberless plantations, with the buildings and crops, destroyed by fire. . . . If the infernal devils were content with this destruction, it would be happy for the Colonists; but they add the cruelty of savages to their incendiary conduct, inhumanly murdering all the whites they catch, sparing neither age nor sex.—I cannot enter into particulars; it would take more time than I have to spare.—Suffice it to say, that our troops are not able to check the ferocity of the Blacks, who are continually increasing in numbers. As many as 5,000 are assembled in a body, about 6 miles from town, and now and then the artillery has a chance to throw a few shot among them. Upwards of a thousand have already been killed on different plantations, and in different manners. If any are taken, they are commonly put to death on the spot. . . .

Sunday morning, September 11th.

We are every day expecting succors from Jamaica. The letters of our Assembly to the Governor and Assembly of that island, requesting a supply of troops, are published in some of the papers which I send you.

At present our fears for the safety of the towns are subsided, and every exertion making to quell the insurrection, and for putting a stop to the depredations of the blacks. The volunteers have been continually upon duty, who go to the camp in rotation, and are relieved every two or three days from those in town. In general they are very much harassed by the intense heat. The free Mulattoes and Negroes are all armed by the government, and in many instances have behaved bravely against the Negroes.

In the situation of affairs at present, it is next to impossible to tell when the troubles will end. The Negroes keep themselves embodied in different places, and when attacked, they immediately fly and scatter. This method of theirs harasses our troops in such a manner that, without effecting any thing essential, they get quite worn out, and are obliged to be immediately relieved. In fine, if I may be allowed to hazard a conjecture, it appears, that several months will elapse before the insurrection will be quelled, and it will require years to reinstate this part of the colony in the flourishing situation that it was in 3 weeks ago. . . .

Source: The Pennsylvania Gazette, *Philadelphia, 12 October 1791.*

SAINT DOMINGUE

Yet, Christophe and Petion quickly fell to squabbling with each other. In 1811 Christophe established himself as King Henri I and took over northern Haiti. Four years earlier, in 1807, Petion had founded the independent republic of Haiti in the south, in which he served as president. Christophe's declaration of a kingdom in northern Haiti prompted a bloody but indecisive civil war that lasted for seven years. Between 1811 and 1818 political, economic, and cultural development in Haiti virtually came to a halt. The war ended only with Petion's death in 1818. Two years later, however, Christophe suffered a paralytic stroke and shot himself. These events inaugurated a long era of instability in Haiti, the tragic consequences of which are today all too familiar.

What became of Toussaint L'Ouverture himself? His sad fate in many respects mirrored that of the revolution he came to lead and in which he had placed all his hopes for the future of his country and his people. In 1802 General Charles Leclerc, the commander of French troops in Haiti, captured Toussaint L'Ouverture by a shameless act of treachery and shipped him off to France. He advised Napoleon that "you cannot keep Toussaint L'Ouverture at too great a distance from the sea and put him in a position that is too safe. This man has raised the country to such a pitch of fanaticism that his presence would send it up again in flames."

Mistreated, disgraced, and harassed by his jailers, Toussaint L'Ouverture never received the news that would have eased the suffering of his last days. All the blacks and mulattoes in Haiti were now free and were marching against the French in an alliance that could no longer be defeated. Toussaint L'Ouverture had no knowledge of these events when, from his prison cell, he appealed to his new master, Napoleon, who was on his way to becoming the master of France and Europe. On 17 September 1802 Toussaint L'Ouverture wrote:

> If I committed any crime while I did my duty, it was definitely unintentional. If I committed an offense by boldly drafting a constitution at an early date, this was done as a result of my great desire to do right by the people and still please the government. I had the misfortune of seeing your wrath descend on me, but my conscience is clear because I remained faithful and honest. You never had a more honest servant. I have now been wretchedly ruined and dishonored. You are too noble and just to delay making a decision about my fate. In the report that I sent you, I have opened my heart to you.

When no answer arrived from Napoleon, Toussaint L'Ouverture wrote again on 29 September:

> Allow me, First Consul, to say to you with all due respect the government had been completely misled with regard to Toussaint Lou-verture, one of the most diligent and courageous servants the government ever had in Haiti. I toiled long and hard to win honor and fame from the government and to earn the respect of my fellow citizens. And now I am being rewarded with thorns and gross injustice. I do not deny the mistakes that I may have made and I ask forgiveness for these. But those failings do not deserve even one-fourth the punishment that is meted out to me, nor the treatment to which I am being subjected.

Toussaint L'Ouverture reiterated that he had served France and the people of Haiti faithfully and well and that his loyalty was beyond question or reproach. "I am not a learned man," he admitted, "and there are not many things I can do. But my father . . . taught me to walk the path of virtue and honor; my conscience is at ease on this point. If I had not been faithful to the government, I would not be here—that is a fact. . . . Ever since August 10, 1790, I have continuously been at the service of this country. Now I am a prisoner and powerless." Toussaint L'Ouverture asked for his freedom so that he could continue his work. "I hope that you, who are a great man and a genius, will make a decision about my fate! May you relent," Toussaint L'Ouverture entreated Napoleon, "and your heart be touched by my wretched condition."

Toussaint L'Ouverture died in a cold dungeon high in the Jura Mountains on 7 April 1803 at the age of fifty-seven. Napoleon never responded to his letters. He apparently assumed that he had broken Toussaint L'Ouverture's spirit. Yet, after his final defeat at Waterloo, when he himself was a prisoner on St. Helena, Napoleon confessed that he had blundered in not governing Haiti through Toussaint L'Ouverture. Even then, however, he seems to have regarded Toussaint L'Ouverture as an ungrateful slave, not a great leader or a free man.

From his perspective Napoleon was right. Toussaint L'Ouverture's willing submission to him confirmed Napoleon's own freedom and power. Although the revolution that Toussaint L'Ouverture had led ended in failure and although his own life came to a miserable end, his accomplishments may yet stand as a warning to the powerful that the conditions of dominance and submission, of slavery and freedom, are not as simple and clear as they may seem. The worst horrors and tragedies of slavery, as illustrated in the relations between Toussaint L'Ouverture and Napoleon, arose not from physical coercion or punishment but from psychological manipulation and spiritual terror. After all, even from his fortress prison in the Jura Mountains, Toussaint L'Ouverture could still think of himself as the first servant of the Republic of Haiti. He hoped and believed that he had won his own freedom and had established the independence of his people in alliance with revolutionary France.

In his letters Toussaint L'Ouverture reminded Napoleon of his years of honest and devoted service. He assured Napoleon of his continued allegiance and expected Napoleon, from a sense of justice, to acknowledge his autonomy and independence as a free man. Napoleon deceived Toussaint L'Ouverture, and Toussaint L'Ouverture's own hopeful naiveté reenslaved him. Napoleon's silence spoke volumes about his inability and unwillingness to acknowledge the freedom and autonomy, and hence the power, of others. Like millions of other enslaved men and women, Toussaint L'Ouverture could at last only call upon God to deliver him from bondage. He found to his sorrow that he could expect nothing from those who exercised worldly power.

–S. D. BLACK,
RICHMOND, VIRGINIA

References

David Brion Davis, *The Problem of Slavery in the Age of Revolution, 1770–1823* (Ithaca, N.Y.: Cornell University Press, 1975).

Carolyn Fick, *The Making of Haiti: The Saint Domingue Revolution from Below* (Knoxville: University of Tennessee Press, 1990).

Eugene D. Genovese, *From Rebellion to Revolution: Afro-American Slave Revolts in the Making of the Modern World* (Baton Rouge: Louisiana State University Press, 1979).

C. L. R. James, *The Black Jacobins: Toussaint L'Ouverture and the San Domingo Revolution,* second revised edition (New York: Vintage, 1963).

Thomas O. Ott, *The Haitian Revolution, 1789–1804* (Knoxville: University of Tennessee Press, 1973).

Martin Ros, *Night of Fire: The Black Napoleon and the Battle for Haiti* (New York: Sarpedon, 1994).

SAINT DOMINGUE

SEXUAL EXPLOITATION

Did masters generally countenance the sexual exploitation of slave women?

Viewpoint: Yes. The slaveholders' sexual exploitation of slave women destroyed the pretense of benevolent and harmonious relations between masters and slaves and revealed that the masters' legal power over them was absolute.

Viewpoint: No. Many Southerners deplored the sexual vulnerability of slave women and lamented the inadequate legal protection afforded them.

How common was the sexual abuse of slave women in the antebellum South? Recent historical scholarship suggests that it was frequent and widespread and that whites knew it to be so. Although public opinion never condoned the sexual exploitation of black women, some whites, such as William Harper of South Carolina, defended the practice. Lamenting sexual intemperance and debauchery, Harper nonetheless argued that the sexual license white men enjoyed with slave women mitigated "against the temptation to greater crimes, and more atrocious vices, and the miseries which attend them; against their own disposition to indolence, and the profligacy which is the common result." In Harper's view the presence of female slaves had virtually eliminated the scourge of prostitution from the South and yet had enabled young men to indulge in "licentious intercourse" that was "less depraving in its effects, than when it [was] carried on with females of their own caste." The act itself, Harper thought, was degraded. As a consequence, sexual encounters with a female slave were "generally casual," and the men involved were "less likely to receive any taint from her habits and manners . . . to the utter destruction of all principle, worth and vigor of character." Concerned with the effects of sexual incontinence on the manners and morals of whites, Harper failed to examine the psychological devastation that the victims of such "licentious intercourse" endured.

The best modern evidence suggests that rape victims experience a series of emotional reactions, which emerge, linger, and evolve over time. Women move from shock to fear, from an overwhelming sense of violation to a debilitating sense of helplessness, from uncontrollable rage to a loss of self-respect. Most slave women, however, had no opportunity to come to terms with a single incidence of rape, since their masters or other white men repeatedly and continually assaulted them for months and even years. Nor could they depend on much help or sympathy from white women, who often reserved their humiliation, anger, and resentment not for their husbands but for the slave mistresses. In addition, a slave woman's own "husband" had no legal standing and thus, according to historian Melton A. McLaurin, could not protect her "from the sexual advances of the man who owned them both."

Some slave women, of course, entered into long, voluntary, and mutual relationships with white men that essentially constituted common-law marriages. More frequently, slave women became the unwilling sexual partners of white men. Even when not the result of force, these misalliances rested on aggression and coercion, for only conscience restrained the master's exercise of power over his female slaves. The law remained silent, the women of

217

the slaveholding class hostile or powerless, and slave men determined but ineffectual. Yet, these disadvantages notwithstanding, slaves in general, and female slaves in particular, were not utterly defenseless against predatory masters. They fought back as best they could to combat the shameful indignities that they suffered—indignities from which no slave woman was safe.

**Viewpoint:
Yes. The slaveholders' sexual exploitation of slave women destroyed the pretense of benevolent and harmonious relations between masters and slaves and revealed that the masters' legal power over them was absolute.**

"We live surrounded by prostitutes," wrote Mary Boykin Chesnut of South Carolina in her diary on 18 March 1861. "God forgive us, but ours is a *monstrous* system and wrong and iniquity. Perhaps the rest of the world is as bad—this *only* I see. Like the patriarchs of old our men live all in one house with their wives and their concubines, and the mulattoes one sees in every family exactly resemble the white children—and every lady tells you who is the father of all the mulatto children in every body's household, but those in her own, she seems to think drop from the clouds or pretends so to think. . . ." If the law did not technically sanction the sexual exploitation of slave women in the antebellum South, the conventions governing sexuality, as Chesnut recognized, certainly broke down, although the absence of legislation designating the rape of slave women as a crime or protecting the sanctity of slave marriage renders even that concession dubious. "Even a cursory survey of slavery," writes historian Catherine Clinton, "indicates that this system fundamentally included sexual exploitation." Southerners granted dispensation to masters who became sexually involved with slave women while disavowing those who kept white mistresses. To be sure, few slaveholders went so far as James Henry Hammond, who acknowledged his slave mistress as the rival to his wife. Yet, many of his counterparts violated the rules of gentlemanly conduct and the vows of marital fidelity.

Hammond presents an important, if extreme, illustration of the sexual confusion associated with slavery in the South. The most striking incursion into the lives of slaves was the sexual interference of white men with slave women. At least two slave women at Silver Bluff, Hammond's plantation located on the Savannah River, served as his mistresses. They were the seamstress Sally Johnson and her daughter Lou-isa, whom Hammond had purchased together for $900 in 1838.

In separate studies of Hammond and his family, historians Drew Gilpin Faust and Carol Bleser have emphasized an emotional and revealing letter that Hammond wrote in 1856 to his son Harry in which he admitted these relationships. Hammond then asked his son to care for the two women and their offspring after his own death.

> In the last will I made left you . . . Sally Johnson the mother of Louisa & all the children of both. Sally says Henderson is my child. It is possible, but I do not believe it. Yet act on her's rather than my opinion. Louisa's first child *may* be mine. Take care of her & her children who are both of *your* blood if not of mine & of Henderson. The services of the rest will I think compensate for indulgence to these. I cannot free these people & send them North. It would be cruelty to them. Nor would I like that any but my own blood should own as slaves my own blood of Louisa. I leave them to your charge, beleiving [sic] that you will best appreciate & most independently carry out my wishes in regard to them. Do not let Louisa or any of my children or possible children be the slaves of strangers. Slavery *in my family* will be their happiest earthly condition.

For Hammond, certainly, these were more than casual relationships. He felt powerful, conflicting, and troubling emotions about Sally and Louisa Johnson and their children.

Even by the standards of the plantation society of the South, Hammond's tangled sexual alliances were complicated. In that world it was impossible to separate sexual relations from racial domination, oppression, and exploitation. Sally and Louisa Johnson not only were subject to Hammond's sexual demands and emotional needs but also faced the threat of coercion and perhaps violence if they did not comply, and scorn and ostracism from the slave community if they did. In addition, they no doubt experienced the bitter resentment of Hammond's wife, Catherine, who discovered his liaisons and attempted to end them by insisting the women involved be sold. Hammond refused, but neither did he ever permit the women to marry, thus isolating them further from their fellow slaves.

Hammond's sexual escapades may have been extraordinary, but in their disruption of life in his household and in the slave community they were typical. Slave women, moreover, had to contend with the advances not only of their masters but, as Hammond's letter implied, of their sons and other whites as well. Overseers frequently assumed that as representatives of the master's authority they had an implicit license to do as they pleased with slave women. As a consequence of these episodes, Elizabeth Fox-Genovese has argued in *Within the Plantation Household: Black and White Women of the Old South* (1988), "many southerners privately concurred with the harshest northern critics of slavery that the system suffered from sexual disarray."

In his popular novel *Swallow Barn, or A Sojourn in the Old Dominion* (1832), John Pendleton Kennedy made a similar point. He has the representative of the traditional South, Virginia planter Frank Meriwether, master of Swallow Barn, explain to his young Northern visitor that some of the abolitionists' criticisms of slavery are justified. Meriwether, in fact, thought it necessary to reform certain aspects of the slave system to mitigate its worst evils, among them the sexual abuse of slave women. Slave marriages, Meriwether said, ought to be protected by law not only so that husbands and wives could not be separated by sale or children taken from their parents but also to prevent white men from violating marital relations. Under present circumstances Southerners "are justly liable to reproach," he tells his guest, "for the neglect or omission of our lives to recognize and regulate marriages, and the relation of family amongst the negroes. We owe it to humanity and to the sacred obligations of Christian ordinances, to respect and secure the bonds of husband and wife, and parent and child. . . . The law should declare this. . . ." The legal recognition of slave unions also implied that slave women must be shielded from the predatory conduct of the master, his sons, his overseer, or other white men. The general disregard for "these attachments," Meriwether concludes, "has brought more odium upon the conditions of servitude than all the rest of its imputed hardships; and a suitable provision for them would tend greatly to gratify the feelings of benevolent and conscientious slaveholders, whilst it would disarm all considerate and fair-minded men, of what they deem the strongest objection to the existing relations of master and slave."

As many historians have demonstrated, the power of the master constituted the foundation of slavery. Interference from the state, whether through legislation or adjudication, limiting that authority carried grave implications. It was thus difficult to restrain those slave owners whose sexual exploits placed them beyond the realm of polite society. Fox-Genovese has asked

HER NAME IS SALLY

In an 1818 newspaper article, James T. Callender accused former president of the United States Thomas Jefferson of having fathered a son with his slave, Sally Hemings:

It is well known that the man, *whom it delighteth the people to honor,* keeps, and for many years past has kept, as his concubine, one of his own slaves. Her name is SALLY. The name of her eldest son is TOM. His features are said to bear a striking although sable resemblance to those of the president himself. The boy is ten or twelve years of age. His mother went to France in the same vessel with Mr. Jefferson and his two daughters. The delicacy of this arrangement must strike every person of common sensibility. What a sublime pattern for an American ambassador to place before the eyes of two young ladies!

If the reader does not feel himself *disposed to pause* we beg leave to proceed. Some years ago, this story had once or twice been hinted at in *Rind's Federalist.* At that time, we believed the surmise to be an absolute calumny. One reason for thinking so was this: A vast body of people wished to debar Mr. Jefferson from the presidency. *The establishment of this* SINGLE FACT would have rendered his election impossible. We reasoned thus; that if the allegation had been true, it was sure to have been ascertained and advertised by his enemies, in every corner of the continent. The suppression of so decisive an enquiry serves to show that the common sense of the federal party was overruled by divine providence. It was the predestination of the supreme being that they should be turned out; that they should be expelled from office by the *popularity* of character. . . .

Source: *"The President Again,"* Richmond Recorder, 4 August 1818.

the pertinent question: "If, as many jurists . . . insisted, the power of the master must be absolute, how could it be curtailed in domestic affairs, especially when its victims had no identity as women at law?" Southern slave law, of course, prohibited the murder of slaves, but not for accidental deaths that occurred in the course of administering correction and not in the case of sexual assault, which as a legal category did not exist. Jurists such as T. R. R. Cobb of Georgia, like Kennedy's fictional Meriwether, argued that the legal vulnerability of slave women had to be addressed, if only because failure to do so would further discredit the South and its institutions. Cobb stated explicitly that the rape of slave women ought to be a crime, but such a contention fell upon profoundly deaf ears. The sexual power of slave-owning men in the South followed from their social and political power, to which slave women were utterly exposed without protection or recourse.

The sexuality of slave women was not their own, any more than, from the master's point of view, were their bodies. In the South, writes Clinton, women, especially slave women, "bore total sexual accountability; white men enjoyed total sexual control." Nor could the "husbands" of slave women defend them against a master's promiscuous advances, at least not without risking their own lives, a cost that many slave women no doubt found unacceptable. If a master's conscience could not restrain him, then no power on earth could do so. Outside the South women were demanding and receiving greater control over their bodies and their lives, but the prevailing gender relations and sexual conventions were irrelevant under the circumstances of slavery. Slave women were neither ladies nor, properly speaking, were they women who merited the preservation of their virtue. In its underlying logic the slaveholders' sexual incontinence, declares Fox-Genovese, "did not differ significantly . . . from the separation of mothers and children, the assigning of women to 'men's' work, or physical brutality. All subjected slave women to a sense of atomization. As a slave woman and her master confronted each other, the trappings of gender slipped away. The woman faced him alone. She looked on naked power."

The law did nothing, or next to nothing, to restrain the masters of slaves. They exercised an authority that few in the South—white or black, male or female—could disregard or oppose. Despite occasional moments of affection, devotion, and even love between masters and their slave paramours, the masters' unbridled power meant their relations with slave women were predicated on a truculence from which white women were sheltered. In resisting the sexual dictates of their masters, therefore, slave women confronted a situation fraught with peril. They endangered themselves and their loved ones, not only their "husbands" but also their children. Yet, what other choice did they have? Exposed to indignities and outrages from which no one could shield them, slave women fought back with the means at hand. Some abandoned their children to escape their masters. Others resorted to abortion, infanticide, and murder. Neither custom nor law permitted them to become virtuous mothers and wives. It was thus not virtue that they sought, but victory.

—MARTINA NICHOLAS,
YOUNGSTOWN STATE UNIVERSITY

**Viewpoint:
No. Many Southerners deplored the sexual vulnerability of slave women and lamented the inadequate legal protection afforded them.**

Slaveholders abused and exploited slave women sexually without facing legal repercussions. Their dalliances, however, violated the customs, values, and mores of Southern society and frequently excited public condemnation. From the beginning of slavery, miscegenation was a problem. In the British North American colonies all sexual indiscretions brought reprimand and punishment, but interracial liaisons provoked uncommonly severe denunciation. In 1630 the court sentenced Hugh Davis, a white man, "to be soundly whipped before an assembly of Negroes and others for abusing himself to the dishonor of God and shame of Christians, by defiling his body in lying with a Negro, which fault he is to acknowledge next Sabbath day."

Not only white men endured such punishments. The Maryland legislature decreed in 1664 that all "freeborne English women forgetfull of their free Condiciōn and to the disgrace of our Nation doe intermarry with Negro Slaues . . . shall Serue the master of such slaves durieng the life of her husband. And that all the Issue of such freeborne woemen soe marryed shall be Slaues as their fathers were." White women who defied social convention and entered into sexual relationships with black men were widely thought of as aberrant and perverse. Their immorality was debased and depraved. Sacrificing the privileges of race and gender, they became permanent outcasts. That alliances between white men and black women, and more rarely between white women and black men, took place, there can be no doubt; that they were habitually disparaged is equally clear.

Another indication that whites in the South did not condone sexual relations between masters and slaves was the belief that one drop of black blood "polluted" white blood, which then ceased to be white. (The formula did not operate in reverse: one drop of white blood did not "purify" black blood, making it white.) Moral corruption explained the desire among whites for black sexual partners. Although he noted an alarming proliferation of race mixing in the South, the Reverend J. D. Long unequivocally decried the practice. "Amalgamation is increasing at a horrible rate throughout the slave states. . . . One of the reasons why wicked men in the South uphold slavery is that facility which it affords for a licentious life. Negroes tell no tales in courts of law of the violation by white men of

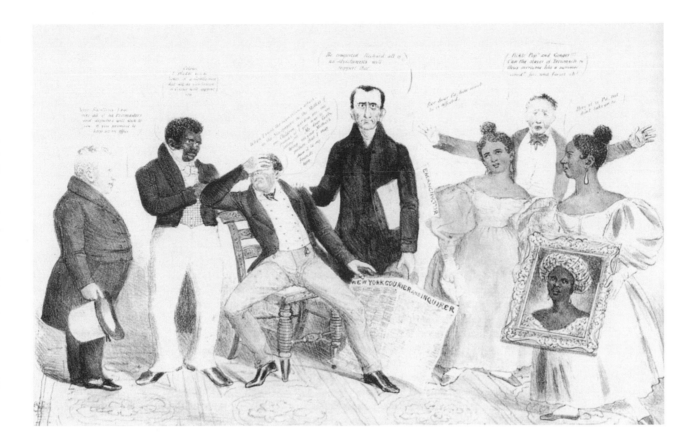

Political cartoon lampooning Vice President Richard M. Johnson and his biracial daughters, 1836

(Library Company of Philadelphia, Pa.)

colored females." Traveling in the West Indies and North America during the mid 1770s, Scotswoman Janet Schaw early questioned the motives that underlay miscegenation. "I sincerely believe," she wrote, that white men "are excited to that crime by no other desire or motive but that of adding to the number of their slaves." In Schaw's estimation greed rather than sexual indulgence had prompted the connections with black women, an act that she found disgraceful and abhorrent whatever its motive and purpose.

If not always contrite or ashamed of their sexual unions with female slaves, masters were prudent enough to conceal them in an effort to avoid the public scandal and embarrassment that was certain to follow from such revelations. Reverend Charles Colcock Jones Sr. of Georgia, on the contrary, exposed the perfidy of a houseguest who had sexual intercourse with Jones's family maid. A man of deep piety, Jones was enraged at such a wanton violation of a defenseless creature of God. Leroy Pope, a former governor of Alabama, "notoriously kept a mulatto girl with whom he associated as freely as with his wife." Needless to say, Mrs. Pope was humiliated and incensed, and the polite society of Huntsville was offended. Coming upon her husband and his mistress too often "in each others' embraces, the enraged Mrs. Pope made so much a fuss about it" that Mr. Pope had to send the slave to a distant plantation that he owned in Mooresville, Ala-

bama. When he began to spend more time in Mooresville, the wrath of the community allied with his wife's anger to force him to sell the slave. If Pope expected his friends and neighbors to ignore or defend his sexual improprieties, or to absolve him of guilt and responsibility, he experienced a rude awakening. Southerners did not look kindly on such indiscretions.

As the Pope case illustrates, sexual liaisons between masters and slaves, although tolerated in private, rarely survived public scrutiny. White men had to obey the abstemious sexual and racial conventions that governed society in the antebellum South. Bennet H. Barrow, a Louisiana planter, was outraged that some of his neighbors in West Feliciana Parish had taken up with slave mistresses. "The people submit to amalgamation [race mixing] in its worse form in this parish, Josias Grey takes his mulatto children with him to public places etc. and receives similar company from New Orleans." Inveighing against sexual relations between whites and blacks, Henry Hughes of Mississippi exclaimed: "Hybridism is heinous. Impurity of races is against the law of nature. Mulattoes are monsters. The law of nature is the law of God. The same law which forbids consanguinous amalgamation forbids ethnical amalgamation. Both are incestuous. Amalgamation is incest."

Thomas Foster Jr., also of Mississippi, brazenly pursued an affair with a slave named Susy to the neglect of his wife and the dismay of his

SEXUAL EXPLOITATION

family, friends, and community. He ignored his parents' insistence that he come to his senses and abandon the relationship. Threatening violence to his family, he vowed to kill his wife and to slit the throats of their children if she interfered with him. When he took to drink and began taunting his wife with his love for a "black wench," she left him and returned to her father's house. Falling seriously ill, Foster repented and summoned his wife to beg her forgiveness. She promised to return to him on one condition: that he deed to his father, in the presence of witnesses, ownership of Susy. He agreed but, after regaining his health, soon resumed his profligate ways. His father, though, refused to cooperate by turning Susy over to him and in December 1826 gave his son an ultimatum: "Either give up this girl Susy and go home to your wife and children . . . or declare your intention to the contrary." Foster answered his father on Christmas Day when he ran away with Susy. By abandoning his wife and family, Foster insulted Southern propriety and banished himself forever from respectable society. His conduct was looked upon as intolerable and dishonorable.

Richard M. Johnson of Kentucky also defied both public opinion and private morality by living openly with his mulatto "housekeeper," Julia Chinn. An admired statesman and military leader, Johnson had served honorably in the War of 1812 and became vice president of the United States in 1837. His private life, however, left Southerners aghast. Johnson never married. Chinn, the mistress of his household, bore him two daughters, Imogene and Adaline, whom he acknowledged as his offspring and for whom he provided amply. He saw that they were well educated, arranged commendable marriages for them to white men, and deeded his estates to them in 1832. As Johnson rose to national prominence in the Democratic Party, however, members of the press began to voice concern about his proximity to the White House. His relationship to Julia was considered unacceptable, despite its obviously reciprocal character. In 1831, two years before Johnson's beloved Julia died of cholera, a writer in the Washington *Spectator* reflected that:

> The colored will have an Esther at the foot of the throne, who may not only dictate modes and fashions to the female community, but may deliver her people from civil disabilities, break down the barrier of prejudice which separates the two races, and produce an amalgamation. . . . Such a consummation would be the means of an African jubilee throughout the country.

In different ways Foster and Johnson violated the sexual customs and ideals that defined proper relations between free white men and enslaved black women in the antebellum South. Historians of slavery will probably never know the frequency with which sexual partnerships occurred between masters and slaves. Yet, Southerners thoroughly disapproved of miscegenation, which they regarded as the exception rather than the norm. Historians Robert W. Fogel and Stanley L. Engerman concurred. In *Time on the Cross: The Economics of American Negro Slavery* (1974), they argued that between 1620 and 1865 only 7.7 percent of slaves were mulattoes. This figure, concluded Fogel and Engerman, "suggests that on average only a very small percentage of the slaves born in any given year were fathered by white men." (Census reports indicate that in 1860 approximately 13 percent of the African American population had white ancestry.) According to Fogel and Engerman, the planters rarely exploited their female slaves. They speculated that many more white men were deterred from having sexual intercourse with black women "by racist aversions" than were "tempted by the myth of black sexuality." Even when contemporaries implied a much greater incidence of miscegenation than Fogel and Engerman ascertained, they almost universally deplored the consequences: the appearance of a mixed-race population. "This evil [miscegenation] has extended so far," declared Lucius Verus Bierce, "that more than one half the slave population are mixed with whites."

White Southerners admitted but never countenanced the sexual exploitation of slave women. In any event, not all sexual unions between masters and slaves were exploitative. Evidence shows that some planters established long-term relationships with their slave partners. On occasion affection, and even love, prevailed. James Dallas Burrus, the first professor of mathematics at Fisk University, who was the son of a white father and a slave mother, recalled that his parents "lived together in affectionate and respectful companionship." In *Roll, Jordan, Roll: The World the Slaves Made* (1974), Eugene D. Genovese similarly observed that:

> Many white men who began by taking a slave girl in an act of sexual exploitation ended by loving her and the children she bore. They were not supposed to, but they did—and in larger numbers than they or subsequent generations of white and black southerners wanted to admit. The Supreme Court of Kentucky refused to judge insane a white man who wanted to marry the slave he had just emancipated. However repugnant, the court declared, such concubinage occurred too often to permit denial of the attraction.

Nevertheless, the sexual violation of slave women occurred regularly enough to constitute a scandal among whites and an affliction among blacks. The slaves, however, did not casually accept or dismiss the sexual aggression of white men and resisted it with enough success to keep it to a minimum. Most of the sexual encounters between whites and blacks on Southern plantations involved single women and typically fell somewhere in between forcible rape and willing seduction. Many planters who began an affair with a slave woman ended by caring about and for her. Although plantations do not appear to have been the brothels or harems of abolitionist fantasies, the tragedy of miscegenation lay not in the submission to lust and the dictates of exploitation but in the inability or unwillingness of whites and blacks alike to appreciate the affection that so often grew from sordid beginnings.

–OPHELIA V. LITTLE,
YORKTOWN, VIRGINIA

References

Terry Alford, *Prince among Slaves* (New York: Harcourt Brace Jovanovich, 1977).

Lucius Verus Bierce, *Travels in the Southland, 1822–1823*, edited by George W. Knepper (Columbus: Ohio State University Press, 1966).

Arthur W. Calhoun, *A Social History of the American Family from Colonial Times to the Present*, 3 volumes (Cleveland, Ohio: Clark, 1917–1919).

Catherine Clinton, "Caught in the Web of the Big House: Women and Slavery," in *The Web of Southern Relations: Women, Family, and Education*, edited by Walter J. Fraser Jr., R. Frank Saunders Jr., and Jon L. Wakelyn (Athens: University of Georgia Press, 1985), pp. 19–34.

Clinton, *The Plantation Mistress: Woman's World in the Old South* (New York: Pantheon, 1982).

Edwin A. Davis, ed., *Plantation Life in the Florida Parishes of Louisiana, 1836–1846, as Reflected in the Diary of Bennett H. Barrow* (New York: Columbia University Press, 1943).

Drew Gilpin Faust, *James Henry Hammond and the Old South: A Design for Mastery* (Baton Rouge: Louisiana State University Press, 1982).

Robert W. Fogel and Stanley L. Engerman, *Time on the Cross: The Economics of American Negro Slavery*, 2 volumes (Boston: Little, Brown, 1974).

Elizabeth Fox-Genovese, *Within the Plantation Household: Black and White Women of the Old South* (Chapel Hill: University of North Carolina Press, 1988).

Eugene D. Genovese, *Roll, Jordan, Roll: The World the Slaves Made* (New York: Pantheon, 1974).

James Henry Hammond, *Secret and Sacred: The Diaries of James Henry Hammond, a Southern Slaveholder*, edited by Carol Bleser (New York: Oxford University Press, 1988).

Henry Hughes, *Treatise on Sociology: Theoretical and Practical* (Philadelphia: Lippincott, Grambo, 1854).

John Pendleton Kennedy, *Swallow Barn, or A Sojourn in the Old Dominion* (Philadelphia: Carey & Lea, 1832).

Leland Winfield Meyer, *The Life and Times of Colonel Richard M. Johnson of Kentucky* (New York: Columbia University Press / London: King, 1932).

Joe M. Richardson, "A Negro Success Story: James Dallas Burrus," *Journal of Negro History*, 50 (October 1965): 274–282.

Willie Lee Rose, ed., *A Documentary History of Slavery in North America* (New York: Oxford University Press, 1976).

Janet Schaw, *Journal of a Lady of Quality: Being the Narrative of a Journey from Scotland to the West Indies, North Carolina and Portugal in the Years, 1774–1776*, edited by Evangeline Andrews and Charles McLean Andrews (New Haven: Yale University Press, 1921).

Deborah Gray White, *Ar'n't I a Woman: Female Slaves in the Plantation South* (New York: Norton, 1985).

Joel Williamson, *New People: Miscegenation and Mulattoes in the United States* (New York: Free Press, 1980).

C. Vann Woodward, ed., *Mary Chesnut's Civil War* (New Haven: Yale University Press, 1981).

Bertram Wyatt-Brown, *Southern Honor: Ethics and Behavior in the Old South* (New York: Oxford University Press, 1982).

SEXUAL EXPLOITATION

SISTERHOOD

Did a sense of sisterhood develop between slave and slaveholding women?

Viewpoint: Yes. White slaveholding women and black slave women developed a sense of solidarity, however truncated, in the face of common patriarchal oppression.

Viewpoint: No. The status, privileges, and wealth of slaveholding women rested on the ownership of slaves, a circumstance that precluded the emergence of solidarity with black slave women.

Long before the advent of feminist scholarship and women's history in the 1960s, the concept of gender was already an important category of analysis in writing about the South. W. J. Cash's *Mind of the South* (1941), for example, offered in many respects a "gendered" interpretation. To Cash, the "mind of the South" was unmistakably masculine. A "common brotherhood of white men" united the slaveholding planters, the yeoman farmers, and the poor whites. Cash anticipated the ways in which subsequent historians of the South, such as Bertram Wyatt-Brown and Joel Williamson, have related white supremacy (racism) to male domination (patriarchy).

The current wave of scholarly interest in Southern women originated with the publication of Anne Firor Scott's *The Southern Lady: From Pedestal to Politics, 1830–1930* (1970). Focusing on women of the planter class, Scott argued that many of them not only opposed slavery but were nascent abolitionists. In *The Plantation Mistress: Woman's World in the Old South* (1982), Catherine Clinton emphasized the despotic character of the white, male patriarchy to which all women were subjected, and insisted more ardently than Scott that most elite women not only felt guilty about slavery but steadfastly opposed it. Suzanne Lebsock's *Free Women of Petersburg: Status and Culture in a Southern Town, 1784–1860* (1984), a study of white and free black women in antebellum Petersburg, Virginia, uncovered a female culture of "personalism" that transcended the obstacles of both race and class, enabling women to challenge the dominance of the Southern patriarchy. Marli F. Weiner found substantial evidence that strong emotional bonds existed between plantation mistresses and their female house servants. In *Mistresses and Slaves: Plantation Women in South Carolina, 1830–80* (1998), Weiner determined that Southern women, slave and free, shared "deeply held fundamental assumptions about female behavior" that were grounded in the ideals of nineteenth- century domesticity. A decade earlier, Elizabeth Fox-Genovese had come to the opposite conclusion. She maintained in *Within the Plantation Household: Black and White Women of the Old South* (1988) that the women of the slaveholding class did not question or challenge the social system from which they derived so many benefits. Fox-Genovese thus rejected as desultory the evidence of hostility to slavery among white women of the planter class as well as of a feminist sisterhood linking mistresses and female slaves.

Although no consensus about the relation of female slaves to slaveholding women has emerged from more than three decades of scholarly ferment, the lines of debate are clear. Were female slaves and slaveholding women in the South united by gender or divided by race and class? Did women whose fathers and husbands owned slaves advocate or oppose slavery? Did they link the oppression of the slaves and the subjugation of women to a common white, male patriarchy, or did they accommodate to their subordination and relish the privileges that slavery brought them? Did the white women of planter families feel a sense of solidarity with their female slaves, or did they have reason to fear the slaves' hatred and vengeance?

Viewpoint:
Yes. White slaveholding women and black slave women developed a sense of solidarity, however truncated, in the face of common patriarchal oppression.

White and black women in the Old South needed one another. They were, in important respects, members of a single family. Like all families, theirs was often rife with tension, anxiety, and rage, but not always. Southern women—slave and free, black and white—shared all manner of life in the Big House. Black women delivered, cared for, and nursed white babies. White women sometimes reciprocated, aiding black women in childbirth and attending to mother and child afterward. Plantation mistresses shared their sorrows, trials, joys, and hopes with trusted female house servants. Women being women, the slaves doubtless reciprocated. Southern women, bound in relations of fundamental antagonism, yet enduring a common patriarchal oppression, still somehow managed to take solace from each other's presence.

Mistresses cared for and nurtured their female slaves, drawing closer to them, for example, by nursing them and members of their family back to health when they were ill. Although inconvenienced by having to care for ailing slaves at the same time that they were deprived of their services, plantation mistresses genuinely worried about them and grieved for them if they died. One mistress lamented the death of a treasured house slave, saying that she had been more of a mother to her than a servant. When Susan Davis Hutchinson visited a Mrs. Clarke, she found her nursing Cynthia, who was gravely ill, and caring for Cynthia's two children "as if they were her own." Illness and death awakened the plantation mistress to the mortality and the humanity of her female slaves and heightened the affection and love that she felt for those with whom she had for so long been intimate.

Often against their wills, mistresses and their female house slaves were trapped in relations of mutual dependence. The slaves relied upon the mistress's good will and protection; the mistress required not only her slaves' labor but also their obedience and love. Their intimacy was fervent, passionate, and frequently excruciating. Each, for

instance, knew all there was to know about the other's romantic aspirations, conquests, and disappointments. As cited in Eugene D. Genovese's *Roll, Jordan, Roll: The World the Slaves Made* (1974), Annie Laurie Broidrick of Mississippi confirmed that "many a romantic tale was confided by mistress and maid to each other during the hours the hair was being brushed and the soft wrapper donned." Female house servants could also be of immense help to a young mistress in these romantic intrigues, for they had access to information that the white woman could not as easily obtain. Genovese explained:

> If the beau lived on a nearby plantation, the servants of the two households probably knew each other or could arrange to know each other. The young lady's servants then became privy to the beau's private life and could report on his character, morals, and other love interests. They could learn much about his true feelings for their mistress. When he lived a bit farther away, this access to private information might even be enhanced, for an excuse could be found to send a servant to his home, and she would be likely to receive an invitation to spend the night among his house servants. Sometimes, the servants decided against a gentleman whose attentions their mistress fancied and were not bashful about saying so. The servants appropriated to themselves some of the duties and rights of Big Sister, not to say Mother.

Mistresses expected equal candor on the part of their female slaves. They wanted to know the identity of their current suitors, and, according to Genovese, did not hesitate to interfere in the affairs of engaged or married couples. The connection between mistresses and female slaves grew stronger with each confidence that passed between them, as did the pretensions of the slaves who felt a new importance, and perhaps a sense of equality, as a result of the secrets they carried. This mutual intimacy and dependence drew mistresses and female slaves closer together but at the same time inevitably aroused bitterness, hostility, anger, and even violence.

Usually, female slaves and their mistresses found ways to keep these emotions within acceptable and secure confines. Yet, many mistresses also discovered themselves unexpectedly subject to their slaves, who ran their households and arranged their lives. Ensnared in their dependence, the mistresses suddenly did not appear so formidable. An elderly former slave from Texas

SISTERHOOD

Nineteenth-century engraving of a Southern mistress berating two household servants

(Library of Congress, Washington, D.C.)

revealed, as quoted by Genovese, that after a while she no longer thought of herself as a slave "'cause I was really only ole Mis' housekeeper; kept house, took care of her money and everything; she was one o' these kinds [of] women that couldn't keep up with nothing, and I just handled her money like it was mine almost." This level of reliance made the female slaves valued and indispensable members of the plantation family and household. When white ladies could not pick up their own knitting needles or get themselves a glass of water, that same dependence must surely have attenuated their grandeur and power in the eyes of their slaves, who had come to know them too well to be overawed.

Despite their own repeated outbursts of anger and the frequent resort to cruelty, plantation mistresses often petitioned fathers and husbands to treat the slaves humanely. Recognizing, and no doubt exaggerating, the mistress's powers of intervention, male and female slaves alike frequently appealed to her to intercede for them with the master. The majority of slaves saw the master as the source of authority on the plantation but saw the mistress as a source of kindness and compassion, a potential ally in a time of crisis. Frances Anne Kemble, a British actress who married a Georgia slaveholder, recorded in her diary that when she arrived at one of her husband's plantations a female slave "went down on her knees, and uttered in a loud voice a sort of extemporaneous prayer of thanksgiving at our

advent." As Kemble recounted the incident, the old woman cried "tanks to de good Lord God Almighty that missus had come, what give de poor niggar sugar and flannel." From her extensive and detailed analysis of nineteenth-century slave narratives and twentieth-century WPA interviews with former slaves, Elizabeth Craven determined that:

> The slave generally saw the mistress of the plantation as a positive influence in the slave system. Those who were most likely to remember well of her were the house servants, the male slaves, and those who lived on large plantations. However, what influence the white mistress had was definitely in a subordinate position to the will of the master. . . . The mistress, by force of her personality and the social structure in which she lived, generally emerges in the slave narratives as a white woman who tried to live up to the responsibilities of her position. Accountable to her husband, she was surrounded by dependents. Her cruelties could make life miserable for some of the slaves; her kindness could cheer the entire plantation.

In *The Plantation Mistress: Woman's World in the Old South* (1982), Catherine Clinton argued that many mistresses saw themselves as the "conscience" of the plantation. They opposed the destruction of slave families through sale. Being mothers themselves, they were particularly determined to prevent slave mothers from being separated from their children. They lamented the brutality that lurked always beneath the surface of a slave society and that regularly exploded above the surface. When the overseer beat one of her female slaves, Maria Bryan despaired that Southern whites were inhumane and that slavery was a "cursed system." Writing to her sister, Julia, Maria exclaimed: "Today Jenny came in crying very much, her face bloody and swelled. She said that Fulton the overseer had beat her with his fist, because she had not spun a sufficient quantity. It would have distressed you to have seen her. Oh! How great an evil is slavery."

"Missus," however, was not "Massa." Slave and slaveholding women alike lived under the dominion of the master, whose authority commanded the plantation household. The master's supremacy, especially the abuse of his male prerogatives, brought misery to the lives of slave women and their mistresses. In subtle but important ways this situation created an emotional link between white and black women in the plantation South, although those connections as often as not manifested themselves in anger and violence as in tenderness and devotion. Yet, both were the victims of an oppressive, patriarchal system. Black and white women in the Old South were thus connected by shared experiences, common affections, and mutual adversity. In a document cited by Clinton, a slave in Texas, Mathilda Turner, wrote to her former mistress, Jane Gurley, in North Carolina: "Dear Mistress, I have been long wishing to ritc to you but had nott the oppertuity. . . . I have got a fine sun. His name is William Marcus. I named him after your little sun. I and all the balance of our people is all wall and give their bast love to you." At times, the bonds of womanhood could overcome slavery and racism, to say nothing of vast differences in education and wealth, and permit women to face each other as human beings.

–MARTINA NICHOLAS,
YOUNGSTOWN STATE UNIVERSITY

Viewpoint:
No. The status, privileges, and wealth of slaveholding women rested on the ownership of slaves, a circumstance that precluded the emergence of solidarity with black slave women.

Women of the planter class were elitist and racist. Although they shared an extraordinarily intense physical and emotional intimacy with their female slaves, these bonds of affection never evolved into a nascent sisterhood that would have allowed them to join forces against male oppression. Slaveholding women were privileged, and their status rested on the ownership of slaves. Their relations with their own slaves, however personally cordial, were by their nature antagonistic, and remained so as long as slavery exalted the one and subjugated the other. However apparently tranquil their relationships might have been, mutual tension, anger, and frustration prevailed between mistresses and their female slaves. Life in the Big House could be an endless battle of wits, a relentless war of nerves. Mistresses were exacting, and even cruel, taskmasters—often more so than fathers, husbands, and sons—and some were quick to reach for the whip or whatever instrument of punishment happened to be closest at hand. When slaves became impudent, disobedient, incompetent, or generally exasperating, mistresses first lost their patience and then lost their tempers. The slaves usually paid for this aggravation but seem to have regarded the beatings as the price of asserting their wills. Eliza Magruder wrote in her diary that her Aunt Olivia had whipped a slave named Annica for being stubborn and disrespectful. A year later Magruder reported that she herself had whipped her slave, Lavinia. She regretted these incidents and prayed for greater self-control, but that did not prevent a reprise of such unpleasant scenes. In *Within the Plantation Household: Black and White Women of the Old South* (1988), Elizabeth Fox-Genovese admirably illustrates the nature of these relationships by recounting a series of anecdotes about women who were evidently irascible and erratic mistresses:

> Ida Henry's unpredictable mistress could be either tolerant or mean. One day the cook was passing potatoes at table and "old Mistress felt of one and as it wasn't soft done, she exclaimed to de cook, 'What you bring these raw potatoes out here for?' and grab a fork and stuck hit in her eye and put hit out." Once Anna Dorsey, failing to hear her mistress call her, continued with her work until the mistress "burst out in a frenzy of anger over the woman not answering." Despite Anna Dorsey's protestations, her mistress "seized a large butcher knife and struck at Anna," who, "attempting to ward off the blow, . . . received a long gash on the arm that laid her out for some time." Hannah Plummer's mother's mistress "whipped her most every day, and about anything. Mother said she could not please her in anything, no matter what she done or how hard she tried." Once, the mistress returned from town especially angry and "made mother strip down to her waist, and then took a carriage whip an' beat her until the blood was runnin' down her back." Hannah Plummer's mother took to the woods, vowing never to come back.

Obviously, the familiarity that grew between mistresses and slaves invited strife as well as amity.

For their part the slave women who lived and worked in the Big House became experts on the foibles of their mistresses and knew just how

THE PLAIN TRUTH

In her memoirs former slave Harriet Ann Jacobs recalls her relationship with her master and mistress:

Yet I, whom she detested so bitterly, had far more pity for her than he had, whose duty it was to make her life happy. I never wronged her, or wished to wrong her; and one word of kindness from her would have brought me to her feet.

After repeated quarrels between the doctor and his wife, he announced his intention to take his youngest daughter, then four years old, to sleep in his apartment. It was necessary that a servant should sleep in the same room, to be on hand if the child stirred. I was selected for that office, and informed for what purpose that arrangement had been made. By managing to keep within sight of people, as much as possible during the day time, I had hitherto succeeded in eluding my master, though a razor was often held to my throat to force me to change this line of policy. At night I slept by the side of my great aunt, where I felt safe. He was too prudent to come into her room. . . . he deemed it necessary to save appearances in some degree. But he resolved to remove the obstacle in the way of his scheme; and he thought he had planned it so that he should evade suspicion. . . . During the day Mrs. Flint heard of this new arrangement, and a storm followed. I rejoiced to hear it rage. . . .

She handed me a Bible, and said, "Lay your hand on your heart, kiss this holy book, and swear before God that you tell me the truth."

I took the oath she required, and I did it with a clear conscience.

"You have taken God's holy word to testify your innocence," said she. "If you have deceived me, beware! Now take this stool, sit down, look me directly in the face, and tell me all that has passed between your master and you."

I did as she ordered. As I went on with my account her color changed frequently, she wept, and sometimes groaned. She spoke in tones so sad, that I was touched by her grief. The tears came to my eyes; but I was soon convinced that her emotions arose from anger and wounded pride. She felt that her marriage vows were desecrated, her dignity insulted, but she had no compassion for the poor victim of her husband's perfidy. She pitied herself as a martyr; but she was incapable of feeling for the condition of shame and misery in which her unfortunate, helpless slave was placed.

Yet perhaps she had some touch of feeling for me; for when the conference was ended, she spoke kindly, and promised to protect me. I should have been much comforted by this assurance if I could have had confidence in it; but my experiences in slavery had filled me with distrust. She was not a very refined woman, and had not much control over her passions. I was an object of her jealousy, and, consequently, of her hatred; and I knew I could not expect kindness or confidence from her under the circumstances in which I was placed. I could not blame her. Slave-holders' wives feel as other women would under similar circumstances. The fire of her temper kindled from small sparks, and now the flame became so intense that the doctor was obliged to give up his intended arrangement. . . .

The secrets of slavery are concealed like those of the Inquisition. My master was, to my knowledge, the father of eleven slaves. But did the mothers dare to tell who was the father of their children? Did the other slaves dare to allude to it, except in whispers among themselves? No, indeed! They knew too well the terrible consequences. . . .

Reader, I draw no imaginary pictures of southern homes. I am telling you the plain truth. Yet when victims make their escape from this wild beast of Slavery, northerners consent to act the part of bloodhounds, and hunt the poor fugitive back into his den, "full of dead men's bones, and all uncleanness." Nay, more, they are not only willing, but proud, to give their daughters in marriage to slaveholders. The poor girls have romantic notions of a sunny clime, and of the flowering vines that all the year round shade a happy home. To what disappointments are they destined! The young wife soon learns that the husband in whose hands she has placed her happiness pays no regard to his marriage vows. Children of every shade of complexion play with her own fair babies, and too well she knows that they are born unto him of his own household. Jealousy and hatred enter the flowery home, and it is ravaged of its loveliness.

Southern women often marry a man knowing that he is the father of many little slaves. They do not trouble themselves about it. They regard such children as property, as marketable as the pigs on the plantation; and it is seldom that they do not make them aware of this by passing them into the slave-trader's hands as soon as possible, and thus getting them out of their sight.

Source: *Harriet Ann Jacobs,* Incidents in the Life of a Slave Girl: Written By Herself, *edited by L. Maria Child (Boston: Privately printed, 1861), pp. 51–57.*

SISTERHOOD

to appease or aggravate them. The mistress dictated; the servants resisted, trying to determine how to thwart the mistress's will without at the same time incurring her wrath. The servants probed; the mistress retreated and did her best to maintain the upper hand in her own household. Slaveholding women repeatedly complained about the ineptitude, negligence, discourtesy, and impertinence of their female slaves. By their accounts the slaves were a constant source of annoyance, disappointment, torment, and grief. To their mistresses, the slaves were also selfish and lazy. In poignant self-reproach, Mary Henderson, the mistress of a North Carolina plantation, lamented that she had left her infant daughter in the care of her old nurse who, although experienced in child rearing, had callously neglected the girl. When the child died, Henderson, overwhelmed by sorrow, rebuked herself and poured out her rancor against the nurse in the pages of her diary.

Yet, because women of the master class frequently relinquished the most basic and tedious aspects of housekeeping and child care to their female slaves, they found themselves helplessly dependent upon them. Such feelings of weakness and inadequacy hardly inspired white women, who thought themselves innately superior to blacks, to behave with kindness, understanding, and charity toward their slaves. Not surprising, many slave women reported that their mistresses subjected them to incessant criticism. The efforts of white women to impose their will notwithstanding, female slaves often understood a great deal more than their mistresses about what needed to be done to ensure the smooth and efficient operation of the household. Plantation cooks were notoriously willful and independent. Tales abound of defiant black cooks ordering from the kitchen a mistress who knew little about what was involved in the preparation of a meal. In addition to cooking, female slaves also churned butter; washed, ironed, sewed, repaired, and altered clothing; changed bed linens; cleaned carpets and drapes; dusted and polished furniture; swept floors; tended gardens; and fed hogs, chickens, goats, and other barnyard animals. They also nursed the sick, suckled infants, minded children, and did whatever their mistresses wanted or needed them to do, freeing the white women to read, write, entertain guests, or visit family and friends. The leisure that white women enjoyed, however, came at the cost of being virtual strangers to the management of their own homes.

The struggles within the household were intensely personal. Mistresses and slaves, for instance, rarely agreed about the appropriate level of work and the suitable time frame in which it ought to be completed. If the mistress raged and insulted, an indignant female slave could grow sullen and malinger. With little recourse, the mistress either conceded defeat and worked out a compromise or punished the slaves, which only deepened their resentment. In retaliation for bad treatment, female slaves became inattentive to their household chores. They dissembled, pretending not to have heard their mistress's instructions or feigning to have misunderstood them. A vexed Frances Butler Leigh, the mistress of a Georgia plantation, revealed the method she had devised for supervising the work of her female slaves. First, she explained, she told them what to do. Next, she showed them how to do it. Finally, she did it herself. The aggravation of those incapable of doing for themselves must have been incomprehensible.

Mistresses had other reasons to be concerned about the attitude of their female slaves toward them. Slaves sometimes gave in to feelings of malice. One slave assigned to attend her seriously ill mistress kept hitting her in the face with a fan. Others abused the children left in their care. Efforts to discipline a slave could often take an unexpected and perilous turn. Slaves might become not simply disdainful but violent. Murder and arson, though rare, were not inconceivable. When Maria Morisett chastised her female slaves Sall and Creasy, they killed her and disposed of her body. Only when the remains were discovered did the two confess their crime. House slaves poisoned members of their mistress's family just often enough to make reasonable the fear of such an occurrence. To escape an anticipated whipping, Rhody helped to poison her mistress, Betsey Witherspoon; Witherspoon's cousin, South Carolinian Mary Boykin Chesnut, was distraught. On 7 October 1861 Chesnut tried to reassure herself that despite the obvious threat, she was safe:

> If they want to kill us, they can do it when they please—they are noiseless as panthers. . . . We ought to be grateful that anyone of us is alive. But nobody is afraid of their own Negroes. There are horrid brutes—savages, monsters—but I find everyone, like myself, ready to trust their own yard. I would go down on the plantation tomorrow and stay there, if there were no white person in twenty miles. My Molly and half a dozen others that I *know*—and all the rest I believe—would keep me as safe as I should be in the Tower of London.

(One may wonder whether the redoubtable Chesnut was being deliberately ironic or unselfconsciously revealing in selecting the Tower of London, in which countless prisoners awaited execution, as the image of her safe haven.) Nearly two weeks later, on 18 October, Chesnut recorded that her mother-in-law cried out at the supper table not to eat the soup. It tasted bitter to her, and she suspected the cook had administered poison. "Mrs. Witherspoon's death," Chesnut reflected, "has clearly driven us all wild."

Elizabeth Meriwether of Tennessee thought her slave Evelyn was devoted to her until Evelyn set the front porch ablaze because, as she dis-

SISTERHOOD

closed, she wanted to live in town. Despite Evelyn's actions, Meriwether continued to insist that Evelyn bore her no ill will. This protective artifice shielded Meriwether and other slaveholding women like her from the disquieting truth that they had many reasons to mistrust and fear their slaves. To keep their sanity, they had to deny that they lived amid constant danger from those closest to them.

Mistresses and slaves, united as women, were separated by race and class. They at once experienced a complex amalgam of intimacy and isolation, forbearance and impatience, affection and estrangement, love and hate. However much compassion mistresses might have felt at the plight of their slaves, they benefited from slavery and did nothing to challenge the system from which they derived so many prerogatives. Although perhaps as much the victims of patriarchy, white women of the slaveholding class were not oppressed in the same manner as their female slaves. White females, after all, were free to be women, to become wives and mothers, to abide by the prevailing gender conventions that were safeguarded in custom and law, and to enjoy their status as privileged members of the ruling elite.

–MEG GREENE,
MIDLOTHIAN, VIRGINIA

References

Catherine Clinton, *The Plantation Mistress: Woman's World in the Old South* (New York: Pantheon, 1982).

Elizabeth Fox-Genovese, *Within the Plantation Household: Black and White Women of the Old South* (Chapel Hill: University of North Carolina Press, 1988).

Eugene D. Genovese, *Roll, Jordan, Roll: The World the Slaves Made* (New York: Pantheon, 1974).

Frances Anne Kemble, *Journal of a Residence on a Georgian Plantation in 1838–1839,* edited by John A. Scott (New York: Knopf, 1961).

Suzanne Lebsock, *Free Women of Petersburg: Status and Culture in a Southern Town, 1784–1860* (New York: Norton, 1984).

Anne Firor Scott, *The Southern Lady: From Pedestal to Politics, 1830–1930* (Chicago: University of Chicago Press, 1970).

Brenda E. Stevenson, *Life in Black and White: Family and Community in the Slave South* (New York: Oxford University Press, 1996).

Marli F. Weiner, *Mistresses and Slaves: Plantation Women in South Carolina, 1830–80* (Urbana: University of Illinois Press, 1998).

Deborah Gray White, *Ar'n't I a Woman?: Female Slaves in the Plantation South* (New York: Norton, 1985).

White, "Female Slaves: Sex Roles and Status in the Antebellum Plantation South," *Journal of Family History,* 8 (Fall 1983): 248–261.

C. Vann Woodward, ed., *Mary Chesnut's Civil War* (New Haven: Yale University Press, 1981).

SISTERHOOD

SLAVE REBELLION

Were the prospects of slave rebellions less threatening in North America than in Latin America and the Caribbean?

Viewpoint: Yes. Slave uprisings in North America were infrequent because geographical and demographic conditions limited the possibilities of rebellions.

Viewpoint: No. Although slave insurrections might have been more difficult to stage in the United States than elsewhere, the fear of such uprisings constantly plagued the white community.

Slave uprisings were rare in the American South. Those that did take place were invariably local affairs and were quelled with relative ease. Authorities foiled the conspiracies of Gabriel Prosser in Richmond, Virginia (1800), and Denmark Vesey in Charleston, South Carolina (1822), even before they began. The existence of a well-armed white majority and the presence of a unified ruling class in the South combined to discourage slave insurrections. The dispersal and isolation of the slaves ensured that any outbreak of violence that did occur would be small compared to those that broke out in Latin America and the Caribbean, and thus more easily contained. Under these circumstances, attempting a massive slave revolt was utter madness. The incidence or rumor of a slave rebellion might panic whites and inspire blacks, but such events never endangered the survival of the regime.

The slaves of the South forged no revolutionary tradition comparable to that which slaves elsewhere in the Western Hemisphere developed. Estimates suggest that in 1763 no fewer than two thousand slaves rebelled in Berbice. Thousands rose in the series of revolts that took place in eighteenth-century Venezuela, while hundreds of slaves at a time participated in the Cuban insurgency of the nineteenth century. Jamaica distinguished itself as an arena of slave violence. According to the historical sociologist Orlando Patterson, Jamaican slave revolts averaged four hundred participants. Major uprisings exploded in Jamaica during the 1690s and almost every year between 1730 and 1740. One thousand slaves rebelled in 1760, while at the same time the British fought a protracted maroon war. The bloody Christmas Rebellion of 1831 was thus the culmination of a long heritage of revolutionary activity on the part of Jamaican slaves.

In the century before the abolition of slavery in the British Empire, at least eighteen separate rebellions erupted in Essequibo, Berbice, Demerara, and Barbados excluding abortive uprisings and maroon wars. The slaves of Barbados staged a general uprising on Easter Sunday, 1816, and in 1823 between ten thousand and twenty thousand slaves revolted in Demerara. Throughout the entire history of slavery in the Southern United States, the combined action of the slaves did not equal the magnitude of these two rebellions alone. Brazilian slaves were nearly as defiant, inciting at least six major revolts between 1807 and 1835. Conditions kept the slaves of the South from achieving comparable success. Yet, they were not the rank cowards for which some white contemporaries mistook them. They did their best, and one may forever wonder what they might have accomplished under more favorable circumstances.

Viewpoint:
Yes. Slave uprisings in North America were infrequent because geographical and demographic conditions limited the possibilities of rebellions.

Eugene D. Genovese has identified eight essential conditions that favored the outbreak of massive slave rebellions and protracted guerrilla wars. Rebellion and war were more probable first, when there was a greater degree of absentee ownership and cultural isolation of blacks from whites; second, when blacks substantially outnumbered whites; third, when slaves were concentrated in units of at least one hundred; fourth, when African-born slaves outnumbered native-born slaves; fifth, when autonomous black leadership emerged; sixth, when economic distress, famine, or both prevailed; seventh, when the white ruling class was divided either by warfare or internal political strife; and eighth, when geography made possible the formation of independent colonies of runaways. These conditions established a political and military balance of power between slaves and their masters, making it possible to contemplate slave insurrection without thinking the outcome suicidal. Slave uprisings, of course, might explode anywhere at any time with or without obvious provocation. For, as Herbert Aptheker sagely observed, the principal cause of slave revolts was slavery. Yet, the probabilities for a large-scale rebellion rested on the existence of the general conditions that Genovese delineated.

According to Genovese, fewer of these conditions prevailed in North America than in Latin America and the Caribbean. Consequently, the slaves of the antebellum South had a history that was fundamentally different from that of slaves elsewhere in the Western Hemisphere. In the South there were comparatively few instances of absentee ownership and cultural isolation. Most masters resided on their plantations for at least part of the year and, of necessity, had more extensive interaction with their slaves than did their counterparts in Latin America and the Caribbean. In addition, slaves in the South did not starve and, indeed, received a diet adequate to enable them to reproduce themselves by natural means. This situation arose in part because slavery in the United States entered a period of unprecedented economic importance and territorial expansion after the closing of the international slave trade in 1808. The prospect of making tremendous profits from cotton planted, tended, and harvested using slave labor persuaded the masters of the necessity to improve the material lives of their slaves in an effort to guarantee a healthy labor force in the present and adequate reproduction in the future. This development made

the lives of the slaves more bearable at the same time that it dimmed the prospects for rebellion.

The need to keep the slaves in reasonably good health led to the advent of paternalism, the conviction that reciprocal rights and obligations bound masters and slaves. The acceptance of paternalism virtually guaranteed the slaves a measure of physical comfort. Of equal importance, paternalism implied that the slaves could fashion relatively stable families and communities to accompany a rich spiritual life and a viable culture. It compelled masters, in short, to acknowledge the slaves not as mere property but also as human beings. In *Roll, Jordan, Roll: The World the Slaves Made* (1976), Genovese described the complex social relations that paternalism effected:

> A paternalism accepted by both masters and slaves . . . afforded a fragile bridge across the intolerable contradictions inherent in a society based on racism, slavery, and class exploitation that had to depend on the willing reproduction and productivity of its victims. For the slaveholders paternalism represented an attempt to overcome the fundamental contradiction in slavery: the impossibility of the slaves ever becoming the things they were supposed to be. Paternalism defined the involuntary labor of the slaves as a legitimate return to their masters for protection and direction. But, the masters' need to see their slaves as acquiescent human beings constituted a moral victory for the slaves themselves. Paternalism's insistence upon mutual obligations—duties, responsibilities, and ultimately even rights—implicitly recognized the slaves' humanity.

Paternalism, however, also limited the possibilities for rebellion. Instead, slaves in the United States practiced other forms of resistance appropriate to their situation, even if that resistance meant the continued acceptance of slavery.

Were the slaves in the United States unwilling or unable to rise up in large numbers to challenge the power of their masters? The easy answer is no; yet, it requires some explanation and elaboration. No evidence indicates that the slaves of the South ever lost their aspiration for freedom or were reduced to abject dependence and docility. Quite the contrary, they never abandoned their hope of deliverance from bondage and do not seem to have expected liberty to be handed to them without effort on their part. They found, however, only limited opportunities to stage successful insurrections, and so sensibly decided not to commit suicide. They instead forged alternate strategies not only of resistance and defiance but of survival.

In the United States blacks constituted a minority of the population in all but a few areas. Only in South Carolina and Mississippi did blacks have a narrow majority, ranging between 55 and 57 percent of the population. Elsewhere the proportion of slaves was 47 percent in Louisiana; 45 percent in Alabama; 44 percent in Georgia; 31

percent in Virginia; 25 percent in Tennessee; and 20 percent in Kentucky. Slaves, by contrast, constituted 90 percent of the population of British Guiana (Guyana). Jamaica, Saint Domingue (Haiti), and much of the Caribbean had huge black majorities, often amounting to more than 80 percent. Even with the level of miscegenation that took place in Brazil, blacks there still outnumbered whites. If Genovese is right that slaves required a large numerical preponderance to offset the enormous military advantages of their masters, then the slaves of the Caribbean and Latin America—the slaves of the Guianas, Jamaica, Saint Domingue, Cuba, Demerara, Antigua, Brazil, and elsewhere—could at decisive moments feel their strength. The slaves of the United States could not help but feel their weakness.

Moreover, Southern slaves were not concentrated in large numbers except in the rice districts of the Carolina and Georgia low country and on the sugar plantations of Louisiana. Even in those locales, the plantations were sufficiently spread out and the police apparatus sufficiently powerful to discourage attempts at a collective uprising. In addition, the slaves faced the white majority almost completely unarmed. To be sure, they did have access to a few crude weapons, or tools that they could transform into weapons. Those who worked in the cane fields, for instance, had knives large and sharp enough to decapitate a man with a single blow. Other slaves carried firearms while standing guard on the plantations. More slaves knew how to load, aim, and fire guns than the law allowed, for planters often gave trusted slaves permission to hunt with guns. Some doubtless shared this knowledge with fellow slaves to whom the master had not granted the privilege. A former slave interviewed for the Fisk University Slave Narrative Collection and quoted in Genovese's *From Rebellion to Revolution: Afro-American Slave Revolts in the Making of the Modern World* (1979) was candid in admitting that "Culled folks been had guns all their life. They kept them hid." Recent archeological excavations of the slave quarters on various plantation sites confirm that the old man had told the truth.

Nevertheless, slaves in the South were still outgunned. Even if the slaves had access to guns and knew how to operate them, few understood their tactical uses. White Southerners, by contrast, early taught their sons to shoot. Firearms had long been an important part of Southern male culture. It is no exaggeration to suggest that, for all intents and purposes, the white male population of the South constituted one giant militia, armed, experienced, resourceful, and capable of all the savagery that fear and hatred can inspire. In Genovese's 1979 work a former slave from Missouri is reported as saying that "I've seen Marse Newton and Marse John Ramsey shoot too often to believe they can't kill a nigger."

White Southerners also had the federal army to support them. Americans now think of the army of the United States fighting to destroy slavery, but in the decades before the Civil War (1861–1865) that same army was available to put down slave rebellions and restore civil order. To be sure, presidents rarely summoned the army for such missions. Dealing with slave uprisings was mainly the work of local and state militias. However, the army was available if needed, and that knowledge bolstered the confidence of the slaveholders and dampened the spirit of the slaves. Masters and slaves alike understood that imposing federal garrisons stood at the ready to reinforce state militia units should they happen to waver. Although federal troops under the command of General Wade Hampton entered the slave rebellion of 1811 in Louisiana only after the militia had reestablished order, their resolution and zeal reassured the slaveholders for the future and could not have escaped the notice of the slaves. Throughout Latin America and, to a lesser extent, the Caribbean, the colonial armies were notoriously unreliable. Mercenaries filled out their ranks, did no more than they had to, and often did less than circumstances warranted.

The slaveholders of the South were also politically unified, and in their unity was their strength. Unity did not always come so easily to slaveholders who resided in the colonies of warring European nations. For centuries almost the whole of the Caribbean comprised one grand theater of war. During brief intervals of peace Portuguese, Spanish, English, French, Dutch, and Danish slaveholders gladly offered military assistance to each other to quell slave disturbances large and small. In times of war, however, they left enemy slaveholders to fend for themselves and, perhaps, encouraged the slaves to rise up against them. Repeatedly, the French incited the slaves of the English who incited the slaves of the Spanish who incited the slaves of the French. The slaves themselves needed little provocation, though they welcomed evidence of powerful allies whatever their motives. The slaves, too, deftly remained loyal to whichever European power had the most to offer at any given moment.

After the American War of Independence (1775–1783) slaveholders in the South had no metropolitan capital in Europe to answer to, and, at the same time, enjoyed a considerable share of power in the new government of the United States. Southern slaves could thus entertain no reasonable expectation that the government would come to their aid. They experienced no other authority in their daily lives than that of their masters, who had insisted that the Constitution protect slave property and whose consent was required to modify those arrangements. The

RESISTANCE! RESISTANCE! RESISTANCE!

The young Presbyterian minister Henry Highland Garnet made a controversial speech at the National Negro Convention held in Buffalo, New York, in the summer of 1843. Although "An Address to the Slaves of the United States of America" shocked many of the seventy delegates for its justification of violence, it was rejected as an official convention statement only by a slim majority. One of the delegates who did not approve of Garnet's speech was the abolitionist leader Frederick Douglass.

Fellow-men! patient sufferers! behold your dearest rights crushed to the earth! See your sons murdered, and your wives, mothers, and sisters, doomed to prostitution! In the name of the merciful God! and by all that life is worth, let it no longer be a debatable question, whether it is better to choose LIBERTY or DEATH!

In 1822, Denmark Veazie, of South Carolina, formed a plan for the liberation of his fellow men. In the whole history of human efforts to overthrow slavery, a more complicated and tremendous plan was never formed. He was betrayed by the treachery of his own people, and died a martyr to freedom. Many a brave hero fell, but History, faithful to her high trust, will transcribe his name on the same monument with Moses, Hampden, Tell, Bruce, and Wallace, Touissaint L'Overteur, Lafayette and Washington. That tremendous movement shook the whole empire of slavery. The guilty soul thieves were overwhelmed with fear. It is a matter of fact, that at that time, and in consequence of the threatened revolution, the slave states talked strongly of emancipation. But they blew but one blast of the trumpet of freedom, and then laid it aside. As these men became quiet, the slaveholders ceased to talk about emancipation; and now, behold your condition to-day! Angels sigh over it, and humanity has long since exhausted her tears in weeping on your account!

The patriotic Nathaniel Turner followed Denmark Veazie. He was goaded to desperation by wrong and injustice. By Despotism, his name has been recorded on the list of infamy, but future generations will number him among the noble and brave.

Next arose the immortal Joseph Cinque, the hero of the Amistad. He was a native African, and by the help of God he emancipated a whole ship-load of his fellow men on the high seas. And he now sings of liberty on the sunny hills of Africa, and beneath his native palm trees, where he hears the lion roar, and feels himself as free as that king of the forest. Next arose Madison Washington, that bright star of freedom, and took his station in the constellation of freedom. He was a slave on board the brig Creole, of Richmond, bound to New Orleans, that great slave mart, with a hundred and four others. Nineteen struck for liberty or death. But one life was taken, and the whole were emancipated, and the vessel was carried into Nassau, New Providence. Noble men! Those who have fallen in freedom's conflict, their memories will be cherished by the true hearted, and the God-fearing, in all future generations; those who are living, their names are surrounded by a halo of glory.

We do not advise you to attempt a revolution with the sword, because it would be INEXPEDIENT. Your numbers are too small, and moreover the rising spirit of the age, and the spirit of the gospel, are opposed to war and bloodshed. But from this moment cease to labor for tyrants who will not remunerate you. Let every slave throughout the land do this, and the days of slavery are numbered. You cannot be more oppressed than you have been—you cannot suffer greater cruelties than you have already. RATHER DIE FREEMEN, THAN LIVE TO BE SLAVES. Remember that you are THREE MILLIONS.

It is in your power so to torment the God-cursed slaveholders, that they will be glad to let you go free. If the scale was turned, and black men were the masters, and white men the slaves, every destructive agent and element would be employed to lay the oppressor low. Danger and death would hang over their heads day and night. Yes, the tyrants would meet with plagues more terrible than those of Pharaoh. But you are a patient people. You act as though you were made for the special use of these devils. You act as though your daughters were born to pamper the lusts of your masters and overseers. And worse than all, you tamely submit, while your lords tear your wives from your embraces, and defile them before your eyes. In the name of God we ask, are you men? Where is the blood of your fathers? Has it all run out of your veins? Awake, awake; millions of voices are calling you! Your dead fathers speak to you from their graves. Heaven, as with a voice of thunder, calls on you to arise from the dust.

Let your motto be RESISTANCE! RESISTANCE! RESISTANCE!—No oppressed people have ever secured their liberty without resistance. What kind of resistance you had better make, you must decide by the circumstances that surround you, and according to the suggestion of expediency. Brethren, adieu. Trust in the living God. Labor for the peace of the human race, and remember that you are three millions.

Source: *Henry Highland Garnet,* An Address to the Slaves of the United States of America *(New York: Printed by J. H. Tubitt, 1848).*

SLAVE REBELLION

slaves of the British West Indies, by contrast, understood that Parliament could end the slave trade and abolish slavery almost at will, with or without the permission of colonial slaveholders. However much they might lord it over their slaves, colonial slaveholders had not the ability to resist such political coercion.

The antebellum South did endure internal social and political divisions, the most serious of which positioned slaveholders against nonslaveholders. Although such antagonisms deepened rather than abated during the sectional crisis of the 1850s, Southern whites set aside their differences when faced with a threat from their slaves and closed ranks to suppress it. "Like Metternich," Genovese writes, "they calculated that if the great and well-born would vigilantly man their posts, the people would not dare rise or would be speedily crushed if they did." White solidarity helped to deter slaves in the South from engaging in open rebellion. Southern slaves did not lack the will to rise up that their counterparts in Latin America and the Caribbean had so amply displayed. Rather, they had few opportunities to do so and only minimal prospects for success when they did.

–MEG GREENE,
MIDLOTHIAN, VIRGINIA

Viewpoint:
No. Although slave insurrections might have been more difficult to stage in the United States than elsewhere, the fear of such uprisings constantly plagued the white community.

Why did slaves in the South not rebel as often or as successfully as their counterparts in Latin America and the Caribbean? The question admits of no easy answers. In such innovative works as *American Negro Slave Revolts* (1943), Herbert Aptheker posited a revolutionary tradition among Southern slaves. There were, according to Aptheker, more than 250 slave revolts or conspiracies in the United States. "The first settlement within the present borders of the United States to contain slaves," he wrote, "was the locale of the first slave revolt." The uprising occurred in a Spanish settlement located along the Pee Dee River in contemporary South Carolina. When, in November 1526, the slaves rebelled and fled to a nearby Indian village, the Spaniards returned to Santo Domingo. They left, Aptheker declared, "the rebel Negroes with their Indian friends—as the first permanent inhabitants, other than the Indians, in what was to be the United States."

Although Aptheker exaggerated the case, he did uncover considerable evidence of insurrection and other forms of physical resistance to slavery, and was among the first to emphasize both the extent and the importance of such overt defiance, which other historians, such as Ulrich B. Phillips, had dismissed as trivial or nonexistent. It may be that the significance of slave rebellions in the United States does not lie in their frequency, magnitude, or intensity but in their occurrence, for the slaves in the United States faced nearly hopeless odds against success. Rather than disparaging slaves for staging few and sporadic uprisings, historians ought to applaud them for trying at all.

In 1657 slaves and Indians staged an uprising in Hartford, Connecticut. Another insurrection involving slaves and Indians took place in Newbury, Massachusetts, in 1690. An Indian slave and a black woman killed their master, his wife, and their five children in Queen's County, New York, in 1708. Four years later, in 1712, thirty African slaves rebelled in New York City, murdering nine whites. The insurrection in Stono, South Carolina, which took place in 1739, involved between fifty and one hundred slaves under the command of a rebel named Jemmy. They set fire to several buildings and tried to escape to Florida, which was then a Spanish colony. Before succumbing to a dominant force, Jemmy and his followers massacred twenty-five whites. Peter H. Wood, the leading historian of the Stono Rebellion, has argued that the combination of a black majority and the unsettled character of frontier society increased white anxiety. The more whites tried to control and circumscribe blacks, the more restive the slaves became, until at last the uprising ensued.

The largest slave rebellion in American history occurred in 1811 in St. John the Baptist Parish, Louisiana. Between 300 and 500 slaves, armed with pikes, hoes, and axes, marched on New Orleans. The rebels were well organized, having arrayed themselves into disciplined military units. They nonetheless disintegrated in combat against a militia joined by a company of free blacks and regular army troops led by General Wade Hampton. More famous, although smaller, than the Louisiana uprising were the revolts of Gabriel Prosser, Denmark Vesey, and Nat Turner.

A devout Christian, Prosser, with the help of his brothers Martin and Solomon, and his wife, Nancy, planned to attack Richmond, Virginia, during the spring or summer of 1800. He dreamed of creating a black state in the heart of the Old Dominion. Prosser arranged his band of slaves into three columns: the first was to attack the federal arsenal in Richmond and seize the arms and munitions stored there; the second was to take control of the powder house; and the third was to enter the town simultaneously from two directions and kill any whites who moved against the slaves, save

Frenchmen, Methodists, and Quakers. Prosser believed that the United States and France had gone to war, and he expected assistance from the French. After he had secured Richmond, Prosser intended to move against other towns and cities in the state. If he prevailed, he would become the king of Virginia. If his plot miscarried, he had ordered the slaves to retreat to the mountains and commence a protracted guerilla war.

Prosser selected 30 August 1800 as the day on which to launch the strike. While he finalized preparations, two slaves divulged his plans to their master, who in turn informed the authorities. Unaware of the betrayal, Prosser assembled his men, an estimated one thousand strong, six miles from Richmond. When a thunderstorm washed out the roads and bridges, making it impossible to get into the city, all was lost. Before Prosser could decide on what course of action to take, the militia attacked. Prosser and thirty-four of his men were arrested, tried, convicted, and hanged. At the trial of Gabriel's brother Solomon on 11 September, Ben, who, like Gabriel, was a slave of Thomas H. Prosser, divulged what was to have occurred:

> In the first place, Mr. Prosser and Mr. Johnson were to be killed and their arms seized upon; then they were to resort to and kill all the White Neighbours. This plan to be executed on Saturday night on which there was such a great fall of rain.... After Murdering the Inhabitants of the Neighbourhood, the assembly were to repair to Richmond and Seize upon the Arms and Ammunition—to-wit, the Magazine. Gabriel was to command at commencement of the business. ... 1,000 men was to be raised from Richmond, 600 from Ground Squirrel Bridge, and 400 from Goochland.... The Rain which fell on Saturday night, the 30th August, prevented the carrying the said plan into Execution.

The Richmond correspondent for the Boston *Chronicle* wrote that the slaves "could scarcely have failed of success, for, after all, we could only muster four or five hundred men, of whom not more than thirty had muskets."

Denmark Vesey had worked as a seaman until he won a lottery and purchased his freedom. During his twenty years as a slave he had traveled widely and learned to read, write, and speak several languages. In 1822 Vesey conceived an elaborate conspiracy to free the slaves and take over Charleston, South Carolina. Vesey and his chief lieutenant, a ship's carpenter named Peter Poyas, carefully laid out the details of the planned insurrection. They would begin by setting houses ablaze. When the townsmen rushed to put out the fires, their own servants were to murder them as soon as they stepped outside their homes. The slaves were then to kill the women and children. Amid the tumult, units of the slave army that Vesey had assembled were simultaneously to assail six locations, taking possession of the arsenals, the guardhouses, the powder maga-

zines, and the naval stores. Blacks were "fully able to conquer the whites," Vesey told his followers, if they "were only unanimous and courageous, as the St. Domingo [Haitian] people were." Vesey determined to proceed with the uprising even after discovering that a house servant had disclosed the outlines of the plot to Charleston officials. When a second slave came forward with more detailed information, however, authorities arrested Vesey and most of the other principal conspirators, numbering 131 in all. On 2 July he and five of his chief aides were hanged at Blake's Landing. The state also executed 30 others. In a letter published in the *Niles Weekly Register* on 7 September, Governor Thomas Bennett of South Carolina offered a reassuring assessment of the Vesey conspiracy. To allay the continuing panic that engulfed the state, Governor Bennett confidently asserted that black degradation and inferiority combined to ensure the inevitable failure of future slave plots. Although he doubtless said what his constituents wanted to hear, one may forgive thoughtful men and women for doubting the accuracy of his judgment:

> When we contrast the numbers engaged with the magnitude of the enterprize, the imputation of egregious folly or madness is irresistible: and supposing the attempt to have been predicated on the probability, that partial success would augment their numbers, the utmost presumption would scarcely have hazarded the result. Servility long continued, debases the mind and abstracts it from that energy of character, which is fitted to great exploits. It cannot be supposed, therefore, without a violation of the immutable laws of nature, that a transition from slavery and degradation to authority and power, could instantly occur. Great and general excitement may produce extensive and alarming effects; but the various passions which operate with powerful effect on this class of persons, impart a confident assurance of detection and defeat to every similar design.... [I]t is reasonable to conclude, that, in proportion to the number engaged, will be the certainty of detection; and that an extensive conspiracy cannot be matured in this state.

Prosser and Vesey died in silence. (Poyas, Vesey's lieutenant, admonished his comrades "do not open your lips. Die silent as you shall see me do.") Nat Turner, by contrast, revealed not only his plans but his hopes. In a statement made to Dr. Thomas Gray, a physician who visited him in prison, Turner confessed that the same Spirit which had guided and enlightened the Old Testament prophets had also instructed him to "arise and slay my enemies with their own weapons." An exhorter, a visionary, and a rebel, Turner assumed a messianic posture in the slave community of Southampton County, Virginia. He came to believe that he had a divinely ordained mission to lead his people out of bondage. Such, he thought, was his destiny. "Having soon discovered to be great, I must appear so," Turner explained, "and

Uprising of the Negroes in Jamaica, an engraving of the painting by Jacques-Louis David, eighteenth century

(from Seymour Drescher and Stanley L. Engerman, eds., A Historical Guide to World Slavery, *1998)*

therefore [I] studiously avoided mixing in society and wrapped myself in mystery, devoting my time to fasting and prayer." Immersing himself in Scripture, Turner found there a language of freedom. He also heard voices and saw visions that fired his imagination. He interpreted the occurrence of a solar eclipse, which appeared to him as "white spirits and black spirits engaged in battle," as a sign that he must lead a rebellion against slavery. When in the fields Turner "discovered drops of blood on the corn," he knew the time was at hand.

Turner selected four deputies, Henry Porter, Hark Travis, Nelson Williams, and Samuel Francis, and immediately began to make preparations to seize the nearby town of Jerusalem, Virginia, the county seat of Southampton. The biblical associations with the name could not have been lost on Turner, who had convinced himself that God was guiding his every step. He told Dr. Gray that he had set the date for the uprising as 4 July 1831, but he fell ill on that day and postponed the attack until 21 August. On that day he ordered his disciples to meet him in the woods near his master's plantation.

Starting with the family of his master, Joseph Travis, Turner planned to go from house to house killing all the whites in the district. At the outset of Turner's rebellion, his company consisted of seven men armed with a hatchet and a broadax. Without fanfare, the slaves killed Travis, his wife, and his two teenage children. They neglected an infant, but Turner ordered two of his men to return and kill the child; they did so. Turner's band moved swiftly and quietly through the darkness, leaving devastation in their wake. In all, fifty-seven whites died, and Turner's ranks swelled to seventy slaves. He told Dr. Gray, "I took my station in the rear, and, as it was my object to carry terror and devastation wherever we went, I placed fifteen or twenty of the best armed and most to be relied on in front, who generally approached the houses as fast as their horses could run. This was for two purposes—to prevent their escape, and strike terror to the inhabitants."

By morning Turner's men were within three miles of Jerusalem when, against Turner's better judgment, they stopped at the Parker farm. There a band of approximately twenty armed whites attacked them. The slaves drove them off and went in pursuit only to encounter a larger group coming from Jerusalem to join the fight. Forced to retreat, the slaves regrouped and again skirmished with whites the following day. After this second clash Turner's forces scattered, and he went into hiding.

SLAVE REBELLION

In addition to local citizens, three thousand Virginia militiamen and federal troops descended upon Southampton County to root out the insurgents and restore order. The editor of the *Richmond Whig* wrote that "men were tortured to death, burned, maimed and subjected to nameless atrocities. The overseers were called upon to point out any slaves whom they distrusted; and if any tried to escape they were shot down."

Turner himself remained a fugitive for almost two months. While at large, he spread panic and terror throughout Virginia, Maryland, and North Carolina. General W. H. Broadnax informed the governor of Virginia that "the consternation unfortunately was not confined to the county where the danger existed, but extended over all immediately about it. Not a white family in many neighborhoods remained at home, and many went to other counties, and the rest assembled at different points in considerable numbers for mutual protection." When captured at last, Turner was put on trial and executed on 11 November. During his interview with Turner, Dr. Gray asked him, "Do you not find yourself mistaken now?" to which Turner replied with a disturbing question of his own: "Was not Christ crucified?"

In carrying out a successful rebellion, the slaves of the South might have faced hopeless odds. That does not mean that such efforts ought to be regarded with disdain, as pitiable or vain attempts destined to fail and bring savage reprisals. Viewed from an alternate perspective, historians might do well to ponder the nature of slavery if the slaves had been completely docile and, lacking a rebellious spirit, had given their masters no reason to fear them. Any hint of a conspiracy or insurrection brewing among the slaves, however insubstantial, thrust whites into a hysteria. After reading a book and seeing a play about the Sepoy mutiny, Mary Boykin Chesnut confided to her diary fears that other Southern whites must certainly have entertained in their darkest moments:

> What a thrill of terror ran through me as those yellow and black brutes came jumping over the parapets! These faces were like so many of the same sort at home. To be sure, John Brown had failed to fire their hearts here, and they saw no cause to rise and burn and murder us all. . . . But how long would they resist the seductive and irresistible call "only rise, kill, and be free"?

There may be less evidence of a revolutionary tradition among the slaves of the antebellum South than among those of Latin America and the Caribbean. Yet, if the foiled conspiracies, the rumors of uprisings that never took place, and the rebellions that did take place counted for nothing, why did whites respond to them with such alarm and such fury? Whites could not deceive themselves. They knew that their slaves had cause to rise against them. If they thought such outbursts impossible or insignificant, they would not have found them so terrifying to contemplate. Southern whites tried to reassure themselves of the slaves' devotion, but "let . . . a single armed Negro be seen or suspected," wrote a correspondent for the *United States Gazette*, "and, at once, on many a lonely plantation, there were trembling hands at work to bar doors and windows that seldom had been even closed before, and there was shuddering when a grey squirrel scrambled over the roof, or a shower of walnuts came down clattering from the overhanging boughs."

–MARK G. MALVASI,
RANDOLPH-MACON COLLEGE

References

Herbert Aptheker, *American Negro Slave Revolts* (New York: Columbia University Press, 1943).

Lerone Bennett Jr., *Before the Mayflower: A History of Black America,* fifth revised edition (New York: Penguin, 1984).

John W. Blassingame, *The Slave Community: Plantation Life in the Antebellum South,* revised edition (New York: Oxford University Press, 1979).

David Brion Davis, *The Problem of Slavery in Western Culture* (Ithaca, N.Y.: Cornell University Press, 1966).

Stanley M. Elkins, *Slavery: A Problem in American Institutional and Intellectual Life,* third revised edition (Chicago: University of Chicago Press, 1976).

Eugene D. Genovese, *From Rebellion to Revolution: Afro-American Slave Revolts in the Making of the Modern World* (Baton Rouge: Louisiana State University Press, 1979).

Genovese, *Roll, Jordan, Roll: The World the Slaves Made* (New York: Vintage, 1976).

Willie Lee Rose, ed., *A Documentary History of Slavery in North America* (New York: Oxford University Press, 1976).

Kenneth M. Stampp, *The Peculiar Institution: Slavery in the Ante-Bellum South* (New York: Vintage, 1956).

Frank Tannenbaum, *Slave and Citizen: The Negro in the Americas* (New York: Vintage, 1946).

Peter H. Wood, *Black Majority: Negroes in Colonial South Carolina from 1670 through the Stono Rebellion* (New York: Knopf, 1974).

C. Vann Woodward, ed., *Mary Chesnut's Civil War* (New Haven: Yale University Press, 1981).

SLAVE REBELLION

SLAVEHOLDERS

Were the slaveholders capitalists?

Viewpoint: Yes. Driven by the profit motive, the slaveholders of the Old South developed a distinctive brand of agrarian capitalism.

Viewpoint: No. The economic choices, social values, political commitments, and moral convictions of slaveholders became increasingly estranged from, and hostile to, the capitalist ethos.

The slaveholders of the South were acquisitive; produced staple crops such as tobacco, sugar, and cotton for the world market; and made handsome profits in the process. Does it follow that they were capitalists? The debate about whether the slaveholders practiced an uncommonly successful agrarian capitalism has long engaged the minds and imaginations of historians. Robert W. Fogel and Stanley L. Engerman once suggested that had the Civil War (1861–1865) not intervened, the capitalist slaveholders of the Old South would have invested in industrial development as soon as it became profitable to do so. If the economic benefits of agriculture had continued to predominate, they would, alternately, have grown rich from cotton and other cash crops. Eugene D. Genovese, by contrast, has vigorously contended that the slaveholders were in but not of the capitalist marketplace and the capitalist world, and that during the antebellum period their social values and political convictions became increasingly hostile to the free-labor system. Other historians, such as James Oakes and William Dusinberre, have argued that since the implementation of commercial agriculture required considerable managerial and entrepreneurial skill, the slaveholders found no inherent contradiction between slavery and capitalism. Instead, they integrated these techniques in an effort to achieve economic modernization.

Lingering in the background of this controversy are questions about the causes of the Civil War. Was the war an irreconcilable conflict between two rival social, political, and economic systems dominated by competing ruling classes? Those historians who have maintained that the conflict emerged inevitably out of fundamental differences between the sections disagreed over whether moral, cultural, social, ideological, or economic issues were the primary causes. They were in general accord that the divergence between the North and South was at the heart of the matter. Other scholars, however, have questioned that conclusion and maintained instead that the issues separating Northern industrial capitalists and Southern agrarian capitalists were neither serious nor important enough to have initiated armed conflict.

Such questions continue to confound, provoke, and inspire. If the slaveholding planters of the Old South were capitalists who shared so much in common with their Northern counterparts, why did they secede from the Union and fight a bloody and tragic war? If the slaveholding planters were capitalists, why were they convinced that Northerners had grown implacably hostile to their social system, economic and political interests, values, morals, worldview, and way of life? If the slaveholding planters were capitalists, why by 1860 were the industrial capitalist North and the agrarian capitalist South incapable any longer of coexisting as a single nation?

Viewpoint:
Yes. Driven by the profit motive, the slaveholders of the Old South developed a distinctive brand of agrarian capitalism.

Of all the arguments tendered in defense of slavery, the rarest was that slavery profited the slaveholders. Proslavery theorists went out of their way to demonstrate that slave labor was neither efficient nor lucrative. Writing in *De Bow's Review* in 1849, South Carolina planter and statesman James Henry Hammond declared that "in an economical point of view slavery presents some difficulties. As a general rule, I agree that . . . free labor is cheaper than slave labor. . . . We must, therefore, content ourselves with . . . the consoling reflection, that what is lost to us is gained in humanity." Northern and European opponents of slavery tended to agree. Irish economist John E. Cairnes, American agricultural expert Solon Robinson, and the observant landscape architect Frederick Law Olmsted, who traveled extensively throughout the South, each concluded that slavery was more expensive and less profitable than free labor. Many historians, from Ulrich Bonnell Phillips to Jeffrey Rogers Hummel, have accepted this verdict. In *American Negro Slavery: A Survey of the Supply, Employment and Control of Negro Labor as Determined by the Plantation Regime* (1918) Phillips concluded that by the 1850s a relatively small number of planters made money "in spite of slavery rather than because of it." Hummel characterized slavery as a "deadweight loss" to the Southern economy, bringing meager returns on an enormous capital investment and expenditure.

If slavery were so unprofitable and if planters were simply not that interested in making money, historians need to explain not so much why Southerners continued to hold slaves (they had already invested too much in them to contemplate emancipation), but why slaves commanded such high prices and why Southerners continued to buy them. Perhaps, like gamblers, the slaveholders anticipated that one extended streak of good luck would make them wealthy beyond the dreams of avarice, and so in defiance of all reason, they maintained their slave labor force in that hope. Perhaps, on the contrary, the slaveholders were simply careless and inattentive businessmen who did not realize that their plantations bled money. Slavery may have also endured because it was already in place and its elimination would have been painful, difficult, and costly. Southerners feared that slaves, if

emancipated, would abuse their liberty, posing a threat to social order and civilization in the South. Slavery was thus indispensable to managing and humanizing race relations. Moreover, the ownership of slaves was fashionable and prestigious, even if not apparently useful.

The slaveholders were not concerned exclusively with economics when they defended their right to property in man. Yet, it does not follow that they were indifferent to considerations of profit and loss. "There is considerable evidence," wrote Robert W. Fogel and Stanley L. Engerman in *Time on the Cross: The Economics of American Negro Slavery* (1974), "that slaveowners were hard, calculating businessmen who priced slaves, and their other assets, with as much shrewdness as could be expected by any northern capitalist." Historians William Dusinberre and Richard Follett have demonstrated in separate studies that the rice planters of South Carolina and the sugar planters of Louisiana operated thriving capitalist enterprises, even while they clung to slavery. The sugar planters, Follett writes, "embraced the capitalist ideology of the burgeoning market revolution [of the nineteenth century], yet simultaneously retained a commitment to the organic ties of paternalism. Recasting the master-slave relationship to ensure optimal productivity, the sugar masters discovered that capitalist economic predilections coexisted quite harmoniously with pre-capitalist social relations of production." Both the sugar and the rice planters were capitalist entrepreneurs who welcomed technological innovation, such as steam-powered sugar mills, and who also attempted to impose upon their plantations the organizational efficiency of nineteenth-century factories. They valued industry, discipline, order, and system in the management of their estates. If slavery had been unprofitable, Southerners would have abandoned it, not from desire but from necessity. Simply put, they could not have afforded the expense of feeding, clothing, housing, and caring for slaves who brought only meager returns. The system was profitable, however, and during the late antebellum period the slave economy gave every indication of sustained and vigorous growth. Slave prices rose, and the demand for slaves was far greater than the supply. The slaveholding capitalists of the Old South could not have been more delighted or more confident. They were sufficiently convinced that slavery was economically viable to risk secession and war when they feared a hostile government endangered their property and their prosperity.

Critics of the notion that slaveholders were capitalists argue that they failed to diversify,

thereby ensnaring themselves in a vicious cycle by reinvesting their profits in additional land and slaves. Yet, what capitalist entrepreneur would not wish to finance the expansion of his business solely from his profits, without having to borrow and go into debt? Some planters, to be sure, accumulated intractable debts and were rewarded with bankruptcy, though obviously not all of them became insolvent. Many earned enough to meet their personal needs and those of their families, to pay the operating expenses of their plantations, and to accumulate a surplus for investment. In addition, the lure of profits rather than the constraints of slave labor induced planters to engage in the cultivation of a single staple crop, whether it was sugar, tobacco, or cotton.

Staple-crop agriculture, the massive investment in land and slaves, and the lack of economic diversification in the South, so some historians contend, prevented slaveholders from encouraging the development of commerce and industry. After the closing of the slave trade in 1808, however, the purchase of slaves required no additional outlay of capital. The domestic slave trade merely transferred existing resources from one individual to another. Those who profited from the sale of slaves could have invested in commerce and industry. Proslavery thinkers such as Virginia lawyer and journalist George Fitzhugh even wanted to employ slaves in industry as a means of making the South more economically independent.

Aside from spending luxuriantly and living extravagantly, the slaveholders did not put the bulk of their surplus capital into commerce and industry because they expected more sustained and substantial returns from agriculture. In other words, as befit good capitalists, they made a rational economic calculation. Southern planters invested in land and slaves not primarily because, in good Jeffersonian fashion, they regarded agriculture as a noble and virtuous calling or because they embraced the agrarian tradition. Rather, Southerners engaged in farming because, as Kenneth M. Stampp wrote in *The Peculiar Institution: Slavery in the Ante-bellum South* (1956), "the production of one of the staples seemed to be the surest avenues to financial success." The impediments that hampered Southern industry may also have dissuaded prudent capitalists from making sizable investments. In the decades before the Civil War (1861–1865) Southern manufacturers could not effectively compete with their Northern counterparts, who enjoyed easy access to larger markets, who benefited from lower production costs, and who had cheaper and better sources of power and transportation. "All of these factors," Stampp concluded, "destined the South, with or without slavery, to be a predominantly agricultural region—and so it continued to be for many years after emancipation."

Economic interests further shaped the masters' evaluation of the efficiency and the costs of

Engraving of a slave sale in Charleston, South Carolina, from the *Illustrated London News,* 29 November 1856

(Oberlin College Library, Oberlin, Ohio)

slave labor. Many contemporaries and historians have suggested that, except under close supervision, the slaves worked indifferently. In *The Slave Power: Its Character, Career, and Probable Designs: Being an Attempt to Explain the Real Issues Involved in the American Contest* (1862) Cairnes observed that the labor of the slave "is given reluctantly, and consequently the industry of the slave can only be depended on so long as he is watched. The moment the master's eye is withdrawn, the slave relaxes his efforts." Cairnes's assessment was probably correct, but how often did masters leave slaves unsupervised? Despite the slaves' efforts to resist, circumvent, or subvert their master's authority, the fear of punishment offered slaves a compelling incentive to be diligent in the performance of their duties. From the point of view of capitalist masters determined to make a profit, slavery possessed other competitive advantages over free labor. It cost less to purchase and maintain slaves than to employ free workers. The slaves in the United States also reproduced themselves, augmenting their master's supply of labor without incurring additional expense. The costs of raising slaves from childhood were more than offset by their productivity as adults. Slaves, in a sense, were a self-perpetuating resource, and masters could continue to benefit from their production and reproduction long after the initial purchase. "The price of a slave together with maintenance," wrote Stampp, "was the cost of a lifetime claim to his labor." Slaveholders large and small protected themselves against losses from illness, injury, death, or flight by taking out insurance policies on their slaves. Furthermore, slaves worked longer hours, were subjected to more severe labor discipline, and never went on strike.

Those historians who reject the judgment that slaveholders were capitalists point out the alleged rigidity of slave labor. They assert that in times of economic hardship merchants and manufacturers could lay off or fire those workers who were superfluous. Cutting labor costs was the quickest and most efficient means of reducing production costs and preserving acceptable profit margins. Slaveowners, however, did not have the luxury of trimming their workforce. They might sell a few slaves, but they could not dispose of them all, and they still had to provide for those who remained. In this respect, as some scholars are willing to concede, slavery might have been the more humane system, but it was also unquestionably the more expensive. Historians who argue against planter capitalism have failed to consider that rather than paying to maintain extraneous slaves, most planters faced an acute labor shortage. Only on rare occasions could they not find work to occupy their slaves throughout the year. Even in the midst of a depression—perhaps especially so—slaveholders expanded production to compensate for declining prices. Economic adversity, therefore, did not idle the slaves.

Despite the periodic and sometimes agonizing depressions that beset the Southern economy, slavery was a profitable enterprise from which the slaveholders derived substantial benefits. If not ordinary capitalists, the planters of the antebellum South acted much like capitalists elsewhere. They made rational economic decisions about the ventures in which to invest their money based on anticipated profits. They sought to pay the lowest prices for, and to extract the maximum productivity from, their workforce. They took seriously the moral obligation to care for their slaves, but, like other capitalists, seldom forfeited profits to considerations of humanity. Even when the masters expressed love for their slaves, it is unlikely that they singled out those who were lazy, unruly, or troublesome. It seems that the slaveholders always felt the greatest affection for those slaves who worked the hardest, who were the most efficient and productive, and who put the most money in their master's pocket.

—MARK G. MALVASI,
RANDOLPH-MACON COLLEGE

**Viewpoint:
No. The economic choices, social values, political commitments, and moral convictions of slaveholders became increasingly estranged from, and hostile to, the capitalist ethos.**

The slaveholding planters of the antebellum South were anomalies in the capitalist world of the nineteenth century. They were, as historian Eugene D. Genovese has argued, embedded in the capitalist world market at the same time that their political ethos, social values, cultural outlook, and moral sensibilities became increasingly and self-consciously antibourgeois and anticapitalist. Yet, if it is inaccurate to think of the Southern slaveholders as capitalists, it is equally misleading to identify them with the landed gentry of medieval Europe, with whom they nevertheless shared important commonalities. They had even less kinship with the nineteenth-century bourgeoisie, save that their production of commodities for market compelled them on occasion to think and act like businessmen, an occurrence that has beguiled many historians into believing them either potential or full-fledged capitalists. Long before the nineteenth century, no one who did not rely on a purely subsistence economy could escape the market, and the planters of the

South, who cultivated staple cash crops for sale and export, could never be mistaken for subsistence farmers. In Genovese's formulation the slaveholders of the South were "in but not of the capitalist world" and to the extent possible resisted the penetration of market relations and the emergence of a market society.

Adding to confusion over this question is the affirmation that the wealthiest slaveholding planters of the British Caribbean were capitalists. They typically did not reside in the colonies and had diverse interests in commerce, finance, and manufacturing, of which owning slave plantations in the West Indies was only one. Profit was their chief, and frequently their sole, motive for involving themselves with slavery. Southern planters were a different breed. They lived on their plantations and, along with their slaves, created what Genovese has described as a "paternalist society." A complex ideology, paternalism did not imply only tenderness and benevolence on the part of the slaveholders, although it could and did promote bonds of affection and even love. Whatever else it may have been, paternalism, from the master's point of view, was a means to ensure labor discipline among the slaves and to justify a system of exploitation that rested on coercion and often outright brutality. Paternalism also required masters to acknowledge the humanity of the slaves, to protect them from the worst abuses of the system, and to afford them a modicum of decent treatment. As Genovese made clear in his study of slavery, *Roll, Jordan, Roll: The World the Slaves Made* (1974):

> The slaveholders had to establish a stable regime with which their slaves could live. Slaves remained slaves. They could be bought and sold like any other property and were subject to despotic personal power. And blacks remained rigidly subordinated to whites. But masters and slaves, whites and blacks, lived as well as worked together. The existence of the community required that all find some measure of self-interest and self-respect. Southern paternalism developed as a way of mediating irreconcilable class and racial conflicts; it was an anomaly even at the moment of its greatest apparent strength. But, for about a century, it protected both masters and slaves from the worst tendencies inherent in their respective conditions. It mediated, however unfairly and even cruelly, between masters and slaves, and it disguised, however imperfectly, the appropriation of one man's labor power by another.

Southern society was thus unique. Neither feudal nor capitalist (nor precapitalist), the South was not merely a society with slaves, as was much of the Caribbean, but a slave society in which the master-slave relation suffused all aspects of life and even influenced relations between free men as well as those between white men and white women. This situation is not to suggest that the Southern economy failed to develop any of the institutions and apparatus ordinarily associated with capitalism, such as a banking system, a commercial network, and a credit structure. It is to propose that banking, commerce, and credit operated differently in the slave South than in the capitalist North. The existence of commerce, for example, does not imply the dominance of capitalism. Those historians who maintain the ascendancy of capitalism in the antebellum South have observed the extensive and multiple connections between the plantation and the market and have quite sensibly proposed that there was no cause for discord between the planters who grew cotton, the merchants who bought and sold it, and the manufacturers who produced yarn and cloth. Their thesis challenges the simplistic notion that the chief economic conflict dividing the United States before the Civil War (1861–1865) was the agrarianism of the South versus the industrialism of the North. Such an insight, however, does not prove the existence of a plantation capitalism. Even those Southerners who prospered from the commercial economy either invested their profits in land and slaves, and so became slaveholders themselves, or else found their businesses dependent upon the patronage of the slaveholding class.

Southern industrialists were in perhaps even worse straits. Nonslaveholding yeomanry did not enjoy the requisite purchasing power to sustain an extensive home market for manufactured goods, and the slaves restricted the market still further. The planters bought for the slaves only inexpensive clothing and cheap tools, most of which they could import from the North. Potential investors, therefore, had little incentive to apply their surplus capital to the development of Southern industry when so many lucrative opportunities awaited outside the South. Like the merchants, the industrialists were tethered to, and limited by, the plantation economy.

With economic power firmly in the hands of a planter elite indifferent, if not hostile, to industrialism, the South lagged far behind the North in the development of manufacturing. The political interests of the slaveholders also impeded the growth of industry. Slaveholders dreaded the emergence of an urban bourgeoisie that might make common cause with its Northern counterpart as well as an urban working class of uncertain social and political disposition. Along with the coming of industry the planters anticipated and disparaged the rise of cities, which they were convinced would become the focus of Southern social and political life, thereby depriving them of the local

SLAVEHOLDERS

STAPLE DEPENDENCE

A planter and slave owner from South Carolina, William J. Grayson comments on cotton agriculture and its effect on the plantations:

At that time and before people lived on their plantations and all useful and pleasant things flourished accordingly. Now plantations are cotton fields rearing a crop for foreign markets and little more. The fruits have almost disappeared. Oranges are rare, pomegranates formerly seen everywhere are seldom met with, figs are scarce and small. Few planters have a good peach or strawberry; worms destroy one and weeds choak the other. Formerly they were cultivated under the owner's eye and flourished accordingly. Even the fish and oysters of the coast and inlets were better of old or better looked after. They have become less abundant like the deer of the woods and the small game of the fields, or the people are less diligent in seeking them. The planter's whole attention now is absorbed by his cotton crop.

The cultivation of a great staple like cotton or tobacco starves everything else. The farmer curtails and neglects all crops. He buys from distant places not only the simplest manufactured article his brooms and buckets, but farm productions, grain, meat, hay, butter, all of which he could make at home. What is obtained in this way is sparingly consumed. If grain and hay are bought, horses, mules, cattle suffer from short supplies. Success or failure in the crop for market makes little difference in the supply of food. If the crop is short everything is put on half rations; if it succeeds, the planter seeks an additional enjoyment, a jaunt to the North, or a voyage to Europe, and mules, pigs, and cattle, fare little better than before. This is true in a greater or less degree of the whole cotton growing region. It is especially true of the low country planters in Georgia and Carolina. They devote themselves to their cotton fields. They buy their corn from North Carolina, their meat from Kentucky, their hay from New York, their butter from farmers a thousand miles away in a climate that makes it necessary to house and feed everything six months in the year. Under this system the country that might be the most abundant in the world is the least plentiful. The beef is lean, the poultry poor, the hogs a peculiar breed with long snouts and gaunt bodies, toiling all summer to keep themselves alive with partial success, and in the winter making a slender and uncertain return for the damage they have wrought to fields and fences.

Source: *William J. Grayson,* Witness to Sorrow: The Antebellum Autobiography of William J. Grayson, *edited by Richard J. Calhoun (Columbia: University of South Carolina Press, 1990), p. 43.*

---

influence, prerogatives, and status that they regarded as the quintessence of liberty. Finally, slaveholders and nonslaveholders alike resisted the imposition of a weighty tax burden to assist Southern industrialists—a tax burden that would surely become ever more oppressive as the need intensified to counter Northern and European economic advantages.

Rather than serving as the agent of an incipient capitalism, the banking system in the South also enhanced the plantation economy. In the commercial Northeast and the agrarian West, banks promoted economic expansion and diversification by extending credit to finance the development of agriculture, industry, and mining; the construction of roads, bridges, canals, and railroads; and the purchase of land. Southern banks, by contrast, were less speculative. They lent money to planters only to enable them to market their crops and to buy additional land and slaves. Credit in the South reinforced the economic domination of the planter elite and inhibited the maturation of alternate sectors of the economy. Like Southern merchants and manufacturers, Southern bankers could not function as independent capitalists, for they, too, were mere adjuncts of the plantation system.

The ideals, values, and worldview of the Southern planters were distinctly antibourgeois and anticapitalist. They emphasized honor, learning, refinement, leisure, family, and community, and decried what they considered the vulgar notion that profit and the cash nexus constituted the sine qua non of political, social, and moral life. In their minds the master-slave relation was fundamentally noneconomic. For the slaveholders, Genovese affirms, "paternalism provided the standard of human relationships, and politics and statecraft were the duties and responsibilities of gentlemen." Historians on both sides of the debate agree that the planters were acquisitive, no less so than their bourgeois rivals, but, again, acquisitiveness is not the equivalent of capitalism. In *The Political Economy of Slavery: Studies in the Economy and Society of the Slave South* (1965) Genovese explained that Southern principles were, in fact, antithetical to capitalism:

> The aristocratic spirit of the planters absorbed acquisitiveness and directed it into channels that were socially desirable to a slave society: the accumulation of slaves and land and the achievement of military and political honors. Whereas in the North people followed the lure of business and money for their own sake, in the South specific forms of property carried the badges of honor, prestige, and power. Even the rough parvenu planters of the South-western frontier—the "Southern Yankees"—strove to accumulate wealth in the modes acceptable to plantation society. Only in their crudeness and naked avarice did they differ from the Virginia gentlemen. They were a generation removed from the refinement that follows accumulation.

Physician William Henry Holcombe of Natchez, Mississippi, put it more succinctly: "The Northerner loves to make money, the Southerner to spend it."

Slavery was the source of the planters' wealth, status, and power, and it was they who established the character of Southern social, economic, cultural, and political life. Rather than being in decline in the years before the Civil War, the Southern planter aristocracy, though vulnerable, was on the rise, eager perhaps too eager to defend itself against a mounting challenge to their way of life, even at the expense of economic interest. Their sense of dignity and honor required nothing less.

—MEG GREENE,
MIDLOTHIAN, VIRGINIA

References

John E. Cairnes, *The Slave Power: Its Character, Career, and Probable Designs: Being an Attempt to Explain the Real Issues Involved in the American Contest* (London: Parker, Son & Bourn, 1862).

William Dusinberre, *Them Dark Days: Slavery in the American Rice Swamps* (New York: Oxford University Press, 1996).

Carville Earle, "The Price of Precocity: Technical Choice and Ecological Constraints in the Cotton South, 1840–1890," *Agricultural History*, 66 (Summer 1988): 25–60.

Robert W. Fogel and Stanley L. Engerman, *Time on the Cross: The Economics of American Negro Slavery*, 2 volumes (Boston: Little, Brown, 1974).

Robert Follett, "On the Edge of Modernity: Louisiana's Landed Elites in the Nineteenth-Century Sugar Country," in *The American South and the Italian Mezzogiorno: Essays in Comparative History*, edited by Enrico Dal Lago and Rick Halpern (Houndmills, U.K. & New York: Palgrave, 2002), pp. 73–94.

Elizabeth Fox-Genovese and Eugene D. Genovese, *The Fruits of Merchant Capital: Slavery and Bourgeois Property in the Rise and Expansion of Capitalism* (New York: Oxford University Press, 1983).

Genovese, *The Political Economy of Slavery: Studies in the Economy and Society of the Slave South* (New York: Pantheon, 1965).

Genovese, *Roll, Jordan, Roll: The World the Slaves Made* (New York: Pantheon, 1974).

Jeffrey Rogers Hummel, *Emancipating Slaves, Enslaving Free Men: A History of the American Civil War* (Chicago: Open Court, 1996).

James Oakes, *The Ruling Race: A History of American Slaveholders* (New York: Knopf, 1982).

Ulrich Bonnell Phillips, *American Negro Slavery: A Survey of the Supply, Employment and Control of Negro Labor as Determined by the Plantation Regime* (New York & London: Appleton, 1918).

Kenneth M. Stampp, *The Peculiar Institution: Slavery in the Ante-bellum South* (New York: Knopf, 1956).

SLAVERY

Did slavery cause racism?

Viewpoint: Yes. With the slave trade racism became rigidly defined in custom and law.

Viewpoint: No. Slavery followed from racism and reinforced existing perceptions of blacks' racial inferiority. Racism both preexisted and survived slavery.

The color of Africans' skin intrigued, frightened, and repelled Europeans. Exaggerating the physical and mental differences that allegedly separated blacks from whites, European writers conjectured that blacks had descended from apes or had emerged as the result of a biblical curse on the descendants of Canaan and Ham. With the expansion of the Atlantic slave trade toward the end of the seventeenth century, theories of black inferiority abounded. It was, after all, in the interest of slave traders and slave owners to propagate the myth that Africans were not human beings, or at least not fully human, a species different from the rest of humanity. Defined as brutish and bestial, heathen and savage, Africans seemed to Europeans as fit only for slavery.

It is not clear why Europeans fixated on the skin color of Africans. Perhaps they did so simply because the physical appearance of blacks was so markedly different from their own and, regarding themselves as superior beings, most Europeans associated a series of negative characteristics with blacks. This view of blacks preceded slavery and helped to justify it. At the same time, slavery deepened racism. The two seem to have existed in tandem.

During the eighteenth century some thinkers, notably Julien Offroy de La Mettrie, Baron de Montesquieu, Abbé Guillaume-Thomas-François de Raynal, and Adam Smith implicitly offered some hope for Africans by suggesting that environment rather than genetics determined the human personality. Scholars such as these suggested that one could remove the blacks from Africa, educate them in the customs of Western civilization, introduce them to the Christian faith, and they would become like white men. Abbé Raynal went so far as to assert that the longer Africans lived outside of Africa, the whiter their skin would become. Yet, despite the development of the environmentalist argument even thinkers sympathetic to blacks continued to believe them inferior to whites. Africans and Europeans may have been the products of a single creation, with only environment creating the variations that distinguished them, but from the European point of view, whites remained the standard and blacks the deviation.

Viewpoint:
Yes. With the slave trade racism became rigidly defined in custom and law.

In his classic study *Capitalism & Slavery* (1944), Eric Williams wrote:

> Slavery in the Caribbean has been too narrowly identified with the Negro. A racial twist has thereby been given to what is basically an economic phenomenon. Slavery was not born of racism: rather, racism was the consequence of slavery. Unfree labor in the New World was brown, white, black, and yellow; Catholic, Protestant, and pagan. . . . Here, then, is the origin of Negro slavery. The reason was economic, not racial; it had to do not with the color of the laborer, but the cheapness of the labor.

Asserting that slavery caused racism, Williams surely overstated his thesis. Although the relation of slavery to race has generated considerable debate, it has also produced undue confusion and false dichotomies. Some scholars, such as Carl N. Degler, have maintained that existing racial prejudice led to the enslavement of Africans. Others, such as Williams, have suggested that racism was an outgrowth of slavery itself. The available evidence sustains neither conclusion in its pure form but rather supports a revised version that is, in important respects, an amalgam of both. The appropriate questions, perhaps, are instead how slavery and racism become so completely intertwined as to define social relations in the slaveholding colonies of the New World.

Williams was correct in ascertaining that the European colonists' initial demands for labor were "color-blind." He argued that planters in the English colonies, for example, actually preferred to engage the labor of poor, white servants than that of either natives or Africans. Indentures, convicts, political and religious nonconformists, kidnapped children, and bushwhacked adults swelled the ranks of servants flooding the British Caribbean and North American colonies. Williams estimated that between 1654 and 1685, 10,000 servants sailed from Bristol alone and that more than 250,000 persons, constituting 50 percent of all English immigrants, came as servants to the New World.

More recently, historian Edmund S. Morgan has confirmed Williams's essential conclusion, while extending his analysis far beyond Williams's original formulation. The excessively high mortality rates that prevailed in Virginia until the 1630s made labor a scarce and valuable commodity. For those who could afford to do so the opportunity to enlarge their labor supply proved an irresistible temptation. As Morgan showed, in the Chesapeake region wealth and status early became synonymous with the extensive use of bound, but not necessarily slave, labor. White indentured servitude was legal everywhere in colonial society. Most servants were young men between the ages of fifteen and twenty-five. Some were kidnapped or otherwise coerced, but most voluntarily entered into their contracts, hoping to begin life anew and, after a relatively few years of service, to become independent and acquire land.

The English Parliament encouraged emigration to the New World. Between 1500 and 1650, as Morgan pointed out, the population of England had increased from 3 million to 4.5 million. Poverty, famine, overcrowding, and unemployment, with all their attendant vices, were the result. The mass of idle poor threatened social peace. Efforts to cope with the problem increasingly imperiled the cherished rights and liberties on which Englishmen had long prided themselves. Thoughtful men in the government recognized an obvious solution: get the poor out of England. If dispatched to the New World, where there seemed limitless opportunities for work and boundless possibilities for upward social mobility, impoverished Englishmen could redeem themselves by enriching the mother country and spreading English influence abroad.

In *The Rise of African Slavery in the Americas* (2000) David Eltis contended that other European powers could have imitated the English example and adopted some form of white bound labor to colonial needs. If Europeans adopted white servitude, then why not white slavery? "Although there is no evidence that Europeans ever considered instituting full chattel slavery of Europeans in their overseas settlements," Eltis wrote, "the striking paradox is that no sound economic reasons spoke against it." An analysis of relative costs demonstrates that by the seventeenth century European slaves were economically preferable either to European indentured servants or African slaves. According to Eltis, it would have been cheaper to transport slaves from Europe than from Africa. Since the population was rising in Europe during the era of the slave trade, the loss of millions of persons would have had a negligible demographic impact and might even have reduced social and political tensions, as Morgan determined that the emigration of indentured servants from England had done during the seventeenth century. The poor, vagabonds, convicts, dissenters, and prisoners of war, all of whom became indentured servants, could just as easily have been enslaved. More than one proslavery ideologue in the antebellum South had, after all, defended the principle of "slavery in the abstract," proposing the enslavement of all labor, white and black.

SLAVERY

Nº 67.

MR T. RICE AS JIM CROW.

'Wheel about and turn about, and do just so;
Every time I wheel about I jump Jim Crow.'

Reverend James Henley Thornwell of South Carolina, for example, rested the defense of slavery on three propositions that by the 1850s had obtained nearly universal currency in the South. First, slavery had always been the necessary foundation of social order as well as of material and moral progress. Second, the free labor system was itself a disguised and malignant form of wage slavery that would, in the end, beget only social tumult and human misery. Third, God had decreed slavery as the proper arrangement for a world haunted by sin, compelling masters and slaves alike to honor their obligations to each other and to him, and thereby to restrain the evil in human nature. Thornwell thus proposed the imposition of some form of personal servitude on all workers to spare them the anarchy of the market and afford them a sense of security and decency that current economic, social, and political regimes did not provide.

Race was not the basis of Thornwell's defense of slavery. Although he regarded blacks as inferior to whites, Thornwell rejected the scientific racism that characterized blacks as the products of a separate creation. Scripture, he noted, did not endorse racial slavery but rather the principle of slavery in general, without regard to race. An anonymous writer in the Richmond *Enquirer* put the matter succinctly: "While it is far more obvious that negroes should be slaves than whites, for they are only fit to labor, not to direct; yet the principle of slavery itself is right, and does not depend upon difference of complexion."

No economic obstacle existed to prevent the enslavement of Europeans. Eltis believes that cultural attitudes intervened. "In western Europe," he argues, "even the most degraded member of European society was spared enslavement. . . . Throughout Europe, the state could take the lives of individuals in Europe, but enslavement was no longer an alternative to death; rather it had become a fate worse than death and as such was reserved for non-Europeans." Morgan explained that with increased longevity in Virginia there arose a class of former servants who had completed the terms of their indentures but who could not now afford to purchase land of their own. Their presence frightened the planters. Virginia was inheriting the very political and social problems of the idle, unruly poor that it had once helped England to solve. The secretary of the colony, Nicholas Spencer, complained that Virginia was becoming "a sinke to drayen England of her filth and scum." William Berkeley, the royal governor, lamented, "How miserable that man is that Governes a People wher six parts of seaven at least are Poore Endebted Discontented and Armed."

Bacon's Rebellion (1676), the largest popular uprising in the British North American colonies before the American Revolution (1775–1783), made Governor Berkeley's fears a reality. Although the rebellion ultimately failed, it bred suspicion among the Virginia elite, ever alert to detect new rebels in their midst. As a result, Morgan indicated, Virginians began to purchase enslaved Africans in larger numbers. Slaves not only resolved the labor shortage, they could be denied rights that a subject of the English Crown could legally demand. No metropolitan government protected the rights and liberties of Africans, but there were limits beyond which the abridgement of English rights and liberties could not proceed. The continued abuse of the rights of Englishmen, Morgan speculates, might have resulted in the outbreak of another Bacon's Rebellion. More likely, such exploitation would have drawn protests from Parliament and the Crown and might have effected a prohibition on the continued importation of indentured servants. Virginians enslaved Africans, Morgan concluded, because they could not enslave Englishmen. Eltis made a related point:

> If the [European] elite could kill Irish, Huguenots, Jews, prisoners of war, convicts, and many other marginalised groups, why could they not enslave them? The English considered those from the Celtic fringe different from themselves but, after the eleventh century at least, not different enough to enslave. For elite and non-elite alike enslavement

remained a fate for which only non-Europeans were qualified.

Only with the decline of alternate forms of labor did slavery become more rigidly defined in custom and law. Racial prejudice had certainly facilitated the enslavement of Africans, and slavery augmented those extant racial biases. During the seventeenth century race was not the foremost consideration in determining the status of labor since most workers, white and black, were to some extent unfree. By the eighteenth century, however, as the number of white indentured servants diminished and the number of black slaves grew, it became the nearly universal presumption that whites were free and blacks were enslaved. It may thus in the end be impossible to disentangle the intricate relation between slavery and race. Historian Winthrop D. Jordan was probably more right than wrong to surmise that in the Americas, or at least in the British mainland colonies, racism and slavery emerged at the same time and evolved together. "Rather than slavery causing 'prejudice,' or vice versa," he wrote, "they seem rather to have generated each other," dual adjuncts to the appalling indignities visited upon blacks in the New World.

–MARK G. MALVASI,
RANDOLPH-MACON COLLEGE

Viewpoint:
No. Slavery followed from racism and reinforced existing perceptions of blacks' racial inferiority. Racism both preexisted and survived slavery.

Slavery bred racism. No people can systematically enslave another people of a different "race" for several hundred years without developing some form of racial animosity and prejudice. Yet, racism also preceded slavery and survived it. Various and subtle influences had already conditioned Europeans to take a negative view of blacks long before they thought of enslaving them.

In his classic study of racial stereotypes, *White Over Black: American Attitudes Toward the Negro, 1550–1812* (1968), Winthrop D. Jordan identified three distinct but related prejudices that conditioned English perceptions of Africans. First, the English noticed that Africans were black. Jordan, however, shows that this judgment was mistaken inasmuch as it simplified a more complex reality. Not all Africans had black skin. For the English, though, "blackness became so generally associated with Africa," Jor-

ANTIPODAL CONSTITUTIONS

Samuel A. Cartwright, a physician and proslavery advocate from Louisiana, asserted in an 1852 essay that Africans were physiologically suited for slavery:

We have medical schools in abundance teaching the art of curing the ailments, and even the most insignificant sores, incident to the half-starved, oppressed pauper population of Europe—a population we have not got, never had and never can have, so long as we have negro slaves to work in the cane, cotton and rice fields, where the white man, from the physiological laws governing his economy, *can not labor and live:* but where the negro thrives, luxuriates and enjoys existence more than any laboring peasantry to be found on the continent of Europe; yet we have no schools or any chair in our numerous institutions of medical learning to teach the art of curing and preventing the diseases peculiar to our immense population of negro slaves, or to make them more efficient and valuable, docile and manageable; comfortable, happy and contented by still further improving their condition, which can only be done by studying their nature, and not by the North and South bandying epithets—not by the quackery which prescribes the same remedy, the liberty elixir, for all constitutions. The two races, the Anglo-Saxon and the negro, have antipodal constitutions. The former abounds with red blood, even penetrating the capillaries and the veins, flushing the face and illuminating the countenance; the skin white; lips thin; nose high; hair auburn, flaxen, red or black; beard thick and heavy; eyes brilliant; will strong and unconquerable; mind and muscles full of energy and activity. The latter, with molasses blood sluggishly circulating and scarcely penetrating the capillaries; skin ebony, and the mucous membranes and muscles partaking of the darker hue pervading the blood and the cutis; lips thick and protuberant; nose broad and flat; scalp covered with a coarse, crispy wool in thick naps; beard wanting or consisting of a few scattering woolly naps, in the "*bucks,*" provincially so called; mind and body dull and slothful; will weak, wanting and subdued.

Source: S. A. Cartwright, "Slavery in the Light of Ethnology," in Cotton is King and Proslavery Arguments, *edited by E. N. Elliott (Augusta, Ga.: Pritchard, Abbot & Loomis, 1860), pp. 705–706.*

malignant; pertaining to or involving death, deadly; baneful, disastrous, sinister. . . . Foul, iniquitous, atrocious, horrible, wicked. . . . Indicating disgrace, censure, liability to punishment, etc." Despite some marked inconsistencies, medieval Christian thinkers also linked blackness to the same general set of associations and characteristics.

Second, the English thought the Africans were "uncivilized." Africans dressed, lived, fought, spoke, and even ate differently from the English. In any comparison with English ways, Africans were found wanting. Difference constituted inferiority. The second "fact" worthy of note about Africans after the color of their skin was that they were not English. Deviation from English norms and standards implied barbarism. Although they knew better, the English depicted Africans as savages, beasts, and cannibals. In making such comparisons, Jordan declared, "Englishmen unwittingly demonstrated how powerfully the African's different culture—for Englishmen, his 'savagery'—operated to make Negroes seem to Englishmen a radically different kind of men."

Few writers applied this racial ideology as thoroughly as did Edward Long, or less hesitantly drew out its implications. In *The History of Jamaica; or, General Survey of the Ancient and Modern State of the Island.* . . . (1774) Long popularized the notion that blacks were a separate species fit only for slavery. Instead of degrading human nature, Long maintained that the theory of black racial inferiority confirmed belief in a rational, creative, fecund, and perfect God. What better testimony to the omnipotence of God, Long asked, than a beautifully complete and coherent chain of being, a "series and progression from a lump of dirt to a perfect man?" Long failed to explain why one link in this continuum ought to be so loathsome, but he made no effort to conceal his disgust for the "bestial fleece," the "tumid nostrils," and the "fetid smell" that he thought characterized all blacks to a greater or lesser degree.

Long also concluded that blacks possessed no rational faculty or moral sense. Incapable of thought and virtue, they thus desired no more than food, drink, sex, and leisure and would pursue these amusements without restraint unless disciplined and coerced. Africans had made no progress for two thousand years, he asserted. They remained, in Long's estimation, "a brutish, ignorant, idle, crafty, treacherous, bloody, thievish, mistrustful, and superstitious people." Apes, Long conjectured, could be trained to "perform a variety of menial domestic services" and the "mechanic arts" as well as any black.

African bestiality was nowhere more transparent, in Long's view, than in the possibility of

dan wrote, "that every African seemed a black man." The English were quick to attach an unwarranted pejorative significance to black skin. Blackness signified filth, immorality, sin, and evil. Whiteness, by contrast, represented cleanliness, goodness, virtue, and purity. As Jordan pointed out, before the sixteenth century, according to the *Oxford English Dictionary,* "black" meant "deeply stained with dirt; soiled, dirty, foul. . . . Having dark and deadly purposes,

SLAVERY

sexual relations between apes and black women. Apes coveted black women, Long wrote, "from a natural impulse of desire, such as inclines one animal towards another of the same species, or which had a conformity in the organs of generation." With blacks, Long observed, sex was "libidinous and shameless." Since both blacks and apes shared the "lasciviousness of disposition," Long did not think that "an orang-outang husband would be any dishonour to an Hottentot female." There was, indeed, Long asserted, every reason to believe that black women regularly admitted such animals to their embraces. Such a union, he reported, had occurred in England itself. Thus, he wrote, "how freely may it not operate in the more genial soil of Afric [sic], that parent of every thing that is monstrous in nature, where . . . the passions rage without controul; and the retired wilderness presents opportunity to gratify them without fear of detection!"

Third, the English condemned the Africans as unchristian. This "defective religious condition" was part of a much larger problem once the English discovered that the world was abounding with "heathen" peoples. The Africans' "primitive" religions offered one more indication of their failure to approximate English norms; it was another symptom of their blackness and their barbarism. For an Englishman of the sixteenth century, Jordan asserted,

> Christianity was interwoven into his conception of his own nationality, and he was therefore inclined to regard the Negroes' lack of true religion as part of theirs. Being a Christian was not merely a matter of subscribing to certain doctrines; it was a quality inherent in oneself and in one's society. It was interconnected with all the other attributes of normal and proper men: as one of the earliest English accounts distinguished Negroes from Englishmen, they were 'a people of beastly living, without a God, lawe, religion, or common wealth. . . .' In an important sense, then, heathenism was for Englishmen one inherent characteristic of savage men.

To be Christian, according to the English, was to be civilized.

Yet, the English did not attribute such deficiencies to blacks alone. They also regarded the Irish as wild, subhuman, uncivilized, dangerous brutes. In English eyes, the Irish were "more uncivill, more uncleanly, more barbarous and more brutish in their customs and demeanures [demeanor], then in any other part of the world that is known." As Nicholas P. Canny has demonstrated in "The Ideology of English Colonization: From Ireland to America" (1983), the Indians were the New World equivalent of the "wilde Irish." Poor whites fared little better, for the "giddy multitude" seemed to pose an addi-

tional threat to social order. The English fit Africans into these established stereotypes in a way that enabled them to make sense of peoples so apparently different that one might expect to find them on another planet. Africans and Europeans were "bound to one another without mingling," wrote French writer Alexis de Tocqueville in *Democracy in America* (1835). It "is equally difficult for them to separate completely or to unite. . . . The Negro transmits to his descendants at birth the external mark of his ignominy. The law can abolish servitude, but only God can obliterate its traces. . . . You can make the Negro free, but you cannot prevent him facing the European as a stranger." For Tocqueville, the unavoidable and irrevocable certainty of black skin remained, forever intruding itself upon the European consciousness.

Most Englishmen and Europeans, and later the majority of white Americans, assumed that race is a fixed and observable physical reality. It is not. Race, instead, is an idea, an ideological construct, a historical phenomenon, not a biological fact. The reality upon which race purports to rest, the natural and permanent inequality of human beings, is utterly false. Biologically, there is only one race: the human race. The most striking attributes of racial appearance—color of skin, texture of hair, shape of nose, eyes, lips, and ears—can all be gradually transformed or radically altered by repeated instances of miscegenation (race mixing). Although not a biological fact, race is nonetheless real, for it embodies in thought actual social relations. Paradoxically, the reality of race lies in appearances and the meanings that human beings attach to them. What Europeans once defined as racial differences between themselves and Africans reveals less about who Africans were than it does about who Europeans thought that they were at a particular moment in history.

This racial ideology existed prior to the enslavement of Africans and did not emerge as a consequence of slavery. Yet, it was not without consequences. As Tocqueville reflected:

> From the moment when Europeans took their slaves from a race different from their own, which many of them considered inferior to the other human races, and assimilation with whom they all regarded with horror, they assumed that slavery would be eternal, for there is no intermediate state that can be durable between the excessive inequality created by slavery and the complete equality which is the natural result of independence. The Europeans have vaguely sensed this truth but have not admitted it. In everything concerning the Negroes, either interest or pride or pity has dictated their behavior.

Tocqueville accurately predicted that racial animosity would intensify with the abolition of slavery. Perhaps more remarkable, the modification or removal of the racial characteristics that had so absorbed the European imagination did nothing to eradicate slavery or even to alter the status of individual slaves. The variations in skin color that emerged as the result of miscegenation, blacks' acquisition of learning and culture, and the conversion of slaves to Christianity did not effect emancipation. Race was an important element in New World slavery, but it proved not to be essential.

—MEG GREENE,
MIDLOTHIAN, VIRGINIA

References

Nicholas P. Canny, "The Ideology of English Colonization: From Ireland to America," in *Colonial America: Essays in Politics and Social Development*, edited by Stanley N. Katz and John M. Murrin, third edition (New York: Knopf, 1983), pp. 47–68.

David Brion Davis, *The Problem of Slavery in the Age of Revolution, 1770–1823* (Ithaca, N.Y.: Cornell University Press, 1975).

Davis, *The Problem of Slavery in Western Culture* (Ithaca, N.Y.: Cornell University Press, 1966).

Carl N. Degler, *Neither Black nor White: Slavery and Race Relations in Brazil and the United States* (Madison: University of Wisconsin Press, 1971).

David Eltis, *The Rise of African Slavery in the Americas* (Cambridge & New York: Cambridge University Press, 2000).

George M. Frederickson, *The Black Image in the White Mind: The Debate on Afro-American Character and Destiny, 1817–1914* (New York: Harper & Row, 1971).

Winthrop D. Jordan, *White Over Black: American Attitudes Toward the Negro, 1550–1812* (Chapel Hill: University of North Carolina Press, 1968).

Edward Long, *The History of Jamaica; or, General Survey of the Ancient and Modern State of the Island. . .* , 3 volumes (London: Lowndes, 1774).

Edmund S. Morgan, *American Slavery, American Freedom: The Ordeal of Colonial Virginia* (New York: Norton, 1975).

Morgan, "Slavery and Freedom: The American Paradox," in *Colonial America: Essays in Politics and Social Development*, edited by Katz and Murrin, third edition (New York: Knopf, 1983), pp. 572–596.

Frederick Law Olmsted, *The Cotton Kingdom: A Traveller's Observations on Cotton and Slavery in the American Slave States* (New York: Mason Brothers, 1861).

Orlando Patterson, *Slavery and Social Death: A Comparative Study* (Cambridge, Mass.: Harvard University Press, 1982).

James Henley Thornwell, *The Collected Writings of James Henley Thornwell*, 4 volumes, edited by John B. Adger (Richmond, Va.: Presbyterian Committee of Publication, 1871–1873).

Alexis de Tocqueville, *Democracy in America*, translated by George Lawrence, edited by J. P. Mayer and Max Lerner (New York: Harper & Row, 1966).

Eric Williams, *Capitalism & Slavery* (Chapel Hill: University of North Carolina Press, 1944).

SOCIAL DEVELOPMENT

Did slavery have a lasting effect on the viability of the African American community?

Viewpoint: Yes. Under slavery white paternalism undermined blacks' solidarity, and white racism destroyed their self-worth and reinforced their dependence. Once slavery ended, blacks passed these feelings of inferiority on to their descendants, sustaining the effects of racial oppression.

Viewpoint: No. The slaves displayed impressive solidarity in resisting the power of their masters. That spirit, which sustained them in freedom, enabled them to overcome racism and to fashion a vibrant culture.

No one today denies that a crisis has beset the African American community, even as few agree on the most effective way to resolve it. Some commentators call for an increase in social and moral responsibility among blacks themselves, while others insist that only the federal government can address the problems of crime, poverty, violence, unemployment, and segregation. Black misery and outrage are likely to fester and grow without relief from the federal government. "American society," wrote historian Eric Foner in the *Boston Review* (December/January 1993–1994), "does have an obligation to see that none of its children confronts the social disintegration that now plagues urban black life." Slavery, racism, and discrimination have prompted black Americans consistently to appeal to the activist state for help and protection. Given their history in the United States, blacks have always regarded the government not as a threat to, but as the guarantor of, their individual and collective welfare and liberty.

Yet, the question remains whether African Americans any longer have the means or the will to rebuild their communities, the collapse of which has been so devastating and so complete that Reverend Eugene Rivers of the Azusa Christian Community in Roxbury, Massachusetts, has likened it to social death. Have slavery and racism deprived blacks of the material and spiritual resources needed to improve their plight?

The deterioration of the African American community may be a symptom of social problems taking place throughout the United States, even, perhaps especially, in the most affluent suburbs. The decay of culture and community has led to the general breakdown of civilization, and not merely among blacks. Despite this shared condition of decline, the patience of other Americans wears thin as evidence of anarchy and barbarism within the black community becomes more obvious and widespread. This frustration and anxiety give every indication of spawning bitter and violent confrontations in the future. Under those circumstances few will remember or care that blacks were the unfortunate victims of slavery and racism.

Viewpoint:
Yes. Under slavery white paternalism undermined blacks' solidarity, and white racism destroyed their self-worth and reinforced their dependence. Once slavery ended, blacks passed these feelings of inferiority on to their descendants, sustaining the effects of racial oppression.

It long ago became unfashionable to argue that slavery deprived African Americans of their culture and permanently impaired their social development. Since the 1960s such black scholars as Harold Cruse, Sterling Stuckey, John W. Blassingame, and Vincent Harding and such white historians and economists as Eugene D. Genovese, Herbert G. Gutman, Robert W. Fogel, Stanley L. Engerman, and Lawrence W. Levine have developed new paradigms for the study of slavery and African American history. Collectively, they have demonstrated that slaves and free blacks created and sustained a viable culture despite racial oppression. Blacks successfully coped with hostile conditions, maintaining their dignity and community even under discouraging circumstances. According to critics, earlier students of African American history, such as E. Franklin Frazier, Kenneth M. Stampp, and Stanley M. Elkins, failed to realize the slaves' capacity for resistance, ignored their tenacious hold on the African past, and underestimated the strength, cohesion, and resilience of black culture.

The desire to achieve integration, social justice, and civil rights for blacks informed much of the scholarship that catalogued the evils and abuses of slavery. In a commencement address delivered at Howard University on 4 June 1965 President Lyndon B. Johnson echoed these sentiments, proclaiming that "in far too many ways American Negroes have been . . . deprived of freedom [and] crippled by hatred." Johnson proclaimed that white Americans had to acknowledge and remedy the damage caused by "the devastating heritage of . . . slavery and a century of oppression, hatred, and injustice." The idea that slavery had irreparably handicapped black Americans was expressed in the Moynihan Report (1965). Although discredited and vilified, the Moynihan Report is perhaps worth reconsidering, especially given the steady decay of a substantial portion of the African American community since the 1970s.

During the 1960s, while serving as Johnson's Assistant Secretary of Labor, Daniel Patrick Moynihan was alarmed at the deterioration and demoralization of African American families and communities. In response, he proposed a "Mar-

shall Plan" (U.S. economic relief for post–World War II Europe) targeted primarily at the black urban poor. "Three centuries of injustice," he explained, "have brought about deep-seated structural distortions in the life of the Negro American." Moynihan advocated programs in education, employment, housing, and welfare to deal with the crisis and redress the grievances of the black community. As a statement of policy and as the first systematic and comprehensive effort on the part of the federal government to confront the problems of inner-city blacks, the Moynihan Report had much to recommend it. Grounded in the social ethics of the Roman Catholic Church, the report assumed that the welfare of any community depended upon the integrity and stability of the families that constituted it. Poverty, exploitation, and, in the specific case of blacks, racism exposed families and communities to tremendous pressure that they could not endure for long without organized assistance.

In fashioning his report Moynihan drew substantially, if not always explicitly, on the principals articulated in two papal encyclicals: *Rerum Novarum* (1891) and *Quadregesimo Anno* (1931). Although directed toward workers, *Rerum Novarum* and *Quadregesimo Anno* could logically be applied to the plight of blacks living in the United States. In these documents the Church affirmed and defended private property but declared rights of property to be limited and subject to a healthy dose of moral and social control. No one had the right to use private property to injure or exploit. Employers might profit, but they owed workers a decent living wage. At the same time, the poor deserved the protection and assurance that, in an industrial society, only government-sponsored social welfare programs could afford. Moynihan insisted that his reforms encouraged and enabled impoverished African American fathers to remain in the family unit, find steady employment, and support their families. He thought it essential for the future that black children enjoy a stable home life and have the opportunity to get a good education. To accomplish these objectives, Moynihan proposed the creation of jobs and job training, funding of education, construction of public housing, and reform of the welfare system with the intention of rewarding families in which men were present rather than the matriarchal families that predominated among African Americans. Moynihan, in short, contemplated an immense and coordinated effort by the federal government to reconstitute the social, economic, and communal lives of black Americans, who had endured the destructive legacy of slavery and racism.

The Moynihan Report presented a dismal, unrelenting, and emphatic portrait of the damage that slavery and racism had effected. Moynihan

SOCIAL DEVELOPMENT

Free black couple from Virginia, circa 1850

(from Charles Johnson and Patricia Smith, Africans in America, 1998)

was intent to show that the condition of black families in urban ghettos had degenerated to the point of crisis, if not catastrophe. He not only marshaled depressing statistics on differential rates of employment, illegitimacy, crime, educational performance, and single-parent, female-headed households between blacks and whites but also cited the scholarly evidence that Frazier, Stampp, Elkins, and others had provided to demonstrate that slavery undermined the African American personality, family, and community. "It was by destroying the Negro family under slavery," Moynihan lamented, "that white America broke the will of the Negro people. Although that will has reasserted itself in our time, it is a resurgence doomed to frustration unless the viability of the Negro family is restored." Moynihan never intended the report for public consumption. Rather, he wrote it to alert individuals within various federal agencies and throughout the Johnson administration to the extent and urgency of the problem. He hoped only that his findings would be "shocking enough that they would say, 'Well, we can't let this sort of thing go on. We've got to do something about it.'"

The Moynihan Report did not get quite the reaction its author had anticipated. It antagonized everyone and in the end produced results opposite to those he desired. Blacks and whites alike saw the report, distorted and sensationalized in the media, as an insult to African Americans. In an interview conducted with the *Amsterdam News*, James Farmer, director of the Congress of Racial Equality (CORE), erupted "I'm angry . . . really angry" to learn "that we've caught 'matriarchy,' and the 'tangle of Negro pathology' . . . a social plague recently diagnosed by Daniel Moynihan." Roy Wilkins of the National Association for the Advancement of Colored People (NAACP) explained in more measured tones that blacks resented the depiction of their families as "a moral criticism of themselves." White liberals joined the attack. William Ryan, a consultant on mental health, wrote a scathing rebuttal published in both the *Nation* and *Crisis*, the official organ of the NAACP, in which he condemned the Moynihan Report as "a smug document. . . . the theme [of which] is: 'The Negro was not initially born inferior, he was made inferior by generations of harsh treatment.' Thus we continue to assert that the Negro is inferior while chastely maintaining that all men are equal." There was, Ryan concluded, "no escape in the world of sociological fakery."

The changing political climate of the 1960s also helped to destroy any chance that the Moynihan Report may have had for an impartial hearing. In November 1965 sociologist Charles Silberman announced that the history of race relations in the United States had

entered a new and radically different stage—a stage so different from the recent and distant past as to make the familiar approach and solutions obsolete, irrelevant, and sometimes even harmful. . . . What is new is that Negroes have begun to reveal and express—indeed, to act out—the anger and hatred they have always felt, but had always been obliged to hide and suppress behind a mask of sweet docility.

For his purposes Moynihan "needed to point to what poor Negroes were deprived of, not to how they managed to make out despite their deprivations." Yet, the new ideological imperative deemphasized the suffering, trauma, and violence that blacks had endured in bondage and, alternately, sought to investigate expressions of culture, power, and resistance.

The experience of blacks in the United States is without historic parallel. Blacks are the only people who came to the United States as slaves. They survived, but racism haunted them. As a consequence, blacks could not move into business and politics as readily as members of other ethnic groups. In addition, every advance that blacks made came at tremendous cost, including the attainment of liberty. When during the eighteenth and nineteenth centuries slaves in the North gained their freedom, those who were skilled craftsmen found themselves barred from plying their trade so that they would not compete with their white counterparts. The remainder were left to fend for themselves, deprived even of the meager security their masters had once provided. A similar pattern recurred in the South after the Civil War (1861–1865), with legal segregation replacing slavery as the means of social control. White Americans simply refused to make room for blacks.

Even as a small minority of African Americans began to enter politics and the professional world and to advance into the lower echelons of the corporate hierarchy, a new threat of social disintegration emerged. Reverend Eugene Rivers of Roxbury, Massachusetts, offered some trenchant and sobering observations on the current impasse at which the African American community has arrived:

As entry into the labor markets is increasingly dependent on education and high skills, we will see, perhaps, for the first time in the history of the United States, a generation of economically obsolete Americans. But remarkably, the tragedy we [African Americans] face is worse. Unlike many of our ancestors, who came out of slavery and entered this century with strong backs, discipline, a thirst for literacy, deep religious faith, and hope in the face of monumental adversity, we have produced "a generation who [do] not know the ways of the Lord"—a "new jack" generation, ill-equipped to secure gainful employment even as productive slaves.

Regrettably, even the dismantling of legal segregation has had some unfortunate and unanticipated repercussions for African Americans. Since the 1960s a minority of blacks has entered mainstream American society. Whatever benefits they and their families have attained as a result are more than offset by the plight of those whom they have left behind in a world inundated with drugs, overwhelmed by violence, and ravaged by despair.

Statistics now project a dismal picture for the black male population in the United States. If these predictions are accurate, a substantial majority of black men will, by the age of twenty-five, be dead, in jail, or on drugs. Fifty percent of black teenagers will be high-school dropouts, and 40 percent will be out of work and likely unemployable even in menial jobs, most of which now require a high school diploma or the equivalent. Never mind the past that blacks have endured; what sort of future is in store for many of them? White Americans ought to take no comfort in the delusion that they have so far avoided the worst. They should not for a moment expect blacks to accept their misery obligingly without protests and reprisals. The bleak situation that blacks now confront is a formula for political and social disaster, and the federal government cannot forever avoid the use of military force to end widespread looting, rioting, and defiance of the law, all of which are sure signs that civilization, not culture, has broken down. If the American people must one day decide between urban terrorism and authoritarian repression, they will have every moral and political right to choose the latter. Who then will be able to say with confidence that slavery did not do appalling and perhaps irreparable damage to blacks?

–MARK G. MALVASI,
RANDOLPH-MACON COLLEGE

Viewpoint:
No. The slaves displayed impressive solidarity in resisting the power of their masters. That spirit, which sustained them in freedom, enabled them to overcome racism and to fashion a vibrant culture.

In 1951 Abram Kardiner and Lionel Ovesey wrote in *The Mark of Oppression: A Psychosocial Study of the American Negro* that the former slave "had no culture, and he was quite green in his semi-acculturated state in the new one. He did not know his way about and had no intrapsychic defenses—no pride, no group solidarity, no tradition. This was enough to cause panic. The marks of his previous status were still upon him—socially, psychologically, and emotionally. And

from these he has never since freed himself." With rare exceptions, social scientists throughout the 1950s and early 1960s regarded blacks as a people without a culture. Blacks, indeed, hardly constituted a "people" at all. They were, rather, an assortment of isolated individuals, without a sense of tradition, history, or community. The assumption that blacks emerged from slavery with "nothing but freedom" led to the false conclusion that during the next century they caricatured American culture.

Swedish economist Gunnar Myrdal, in fact, referred to blacks in *An American Dilemma: The Negro Problem and Modern Democracy* (1944) as "exaggerated Americans" who perverted American cultural norms. Myrdal's inventory of concerns included "the instability of the Negro family, . . . the emotionalism in the Negro church, the insufficiency and unwholesomeness of Negro recreational activity, the plethora of Negro sociable organizations, the narrowness of interests of the average Negro, the provincialism of his political speculation, the high Negro crime rate, the cultivation of the arts to the neglect of other fields, superstition, [and] personality difficulties." These were, in Myrdal's estimation, the "characteristic traits" of African American life. This dismal reality prompted him to assert that "*in practically all its divergences, American Negro culture is not something independent of the general American culture. It is a distorted development, or a pathological condition, of the general American culture .*"

For a long time Myrdal's attitude both shaped and embodied the dominant perspective among students of African American history and culture. E. Franklin Frazier epitomized the prevailing view, writing in 1957 that "unlike other racial or cultural minorities the Negro [in the United States] is not distinguished by culture from the dominant group." In their study *Beyond the Melting Pot: The Negroes, Puerto Ricans, Jews, Italians, and Irish of New York City* (1963) Nathan Glazer and Daniel Patrick Moynihan asserted that "the Negro is only an American, and nothing else. He has no values and culture to guard and protect," having lost all contact with his past and his heritage when enslaved. Roger D. Abrahams, in *Positively Black* (1970), suggested that blacks not be considered an ethnic group. The Irish, Jews, Greeks, Italians, Poles, and others, Abrahams maintained, had a sense of identity independent of mainstream American culture and even felt their cultural distinctiveness imperiled by the prospect of total assimilation. Blacks, on the contrary, by "accepting the white stereotype and the American dream, commonly [saw] themselves as outsiders waiting to get in." In 1972 sociologist Stanford M. Lyman equated African Americans to a people wandering in the wilderness with no way out. "The black," Lyman wrote, "has been

WALKING TICKET TO THE SOUTH

Asked about his experiences with the separation of slave families, former slave Lewis Clarke recalls:

I never knew a whole family to live together till all were grown up in my life. There is almost always, in every family, someone or more keen and bright, or else sullen and stubborn slave, whose influence they are afraid of on the rest of the family, and such a one must take a walking ticket to the south.

There are other causes of separation. The death of a large owner is the occasion usually of many families being broken up. Bankruptcy is another cause of separation, and the hardheartedness of a majority of slave-holders another and a more fruitful cause than either or all the rest. Generally there is but little more scruple about separating families than there is with a man who keeps sheep in selling off the lambs in the fall. On one plantation where I lived, there was an old slave names Paris. He was from fifty to sixty years old, and a very honest and apparently pious slave. A slave-trader came along one day, to gather hands for the south. The old master ordered the waiter or coachman to take Paris into the back room pluck out all his gray hairs, rub his face with a greasy towel, and then had him brought forward and sold for a young man. His wife consented to go with him, upon a promise from the trader that they should be sold together, with their youngest child, which she carried in her arms. They left two behind them, who were only from four to six or eight years of age. The speculator collected his drove, started for the market, and, before he left the state, he sold that infant child to pay one of his tavern bills, and took the balance in cash. . . .

I saw one slave mother, named Lucy, with seven children, put up by an administrator for sale. At first the mother and three small children were put up together. The purchasers objected: one says, I want the woman and the babe, but not the other children; another says, I want that little girl; and another, I want the boy. Well, says the Administrator, I must let you have them to the best advantage. So the children were taken away; the mother and infant were first sold, then child after child—the mother looking on in perfect agony; and as one child after another came down from the auction block, they would run, and cling weeping to her clothes. The poor mother stood, till nature gave way; she fainted and fell, with her child in her arms. The only sympathy she received from most of the hardhearted monsters who had riven her heartstrings asunder was, "She is a d--d deceitful bitch; I wish she was mine, I would teach her better than to cut up such shines as that here." When she came to, she moaned wofully, and prayed that she might die, to be relieved from her sufferings.

I knew another slave named Nathan, who had a slave woman for a wife. She was killed by hard usage. Nathan then declared he would never have another slave wife. He selected a free woman for a companion. His master opposed it violently. But Nathan persevered in his choice, and in consequence was sold to go down South. He returned once to see his wife, and she soon after died of grief and disappointment. On his return South, he leaped from the boat, and attempted to swim ashore; his master, on board the boat, took a gun and deliberately shot him, and he drifted down the current of the river.

On this subject of separation of families, I must plant one more rose in the garland that I have already tied upon the brow of the sweet Mrs. Banton. The reader cannot have forgotten her; and in the delectable business of tearing families asunder she of course would have a hand. A slave by the name of Susan was taken by Mrs. Banton on mortgage. She had been well treated where she was brought up, had a husband, and they were very happy together. Susan mourned in bitterness over her separation, and pined away under the cruel hand of Mrs. Banton. At length she ran away, and hid herself in the neighborhood of her husband. When this came to the knowledge of Mrs. B., she charged her husband to go for "Suke," and never let her see his face unless she was with him. "No, said she, if you are offered a double price, don't you take it. I want my satisfaction out of her, and then you may sell her as soon as you please." Susan was brought back in fetters, and Mr. and Mrs. B. both took their *satisfaction;* they beat and tortured poor Susan till her premature offspring perished, and she almost sank beneath their merciless hands, and then they sold her to be carried a hundred miles farther away from her husband. Ah! slavery is like running the dissecting knife around the heart, among all the tender fibres of our being.

A man by the name of Bill Myers, in Kentucky, went to a large number of auctions, and purchased women about forty years old, with their youngest children in their arms. As they are about to cease bearing at that age, they are sold cheap. The children he took and shut up in a log pen, and set some old worn-out slave women to make broth and feed them. The mothers he gathered in a large drove, and carried them South and sold them. He was detained there for months longer than he expected, and winter coming on, and no proper provision having been made for the children, many of them perished with cold and hunger, some were frost bitten, and all were emaciated to skeletons. This was the only attempt that I ever knew, for gathering young children together, like a litter of pigs, to be raised for the market. The success was not such as to warrant a repetition on the part of Myers.

Source: Lewis Garrard Clarke, Narrative of the Sufferings of Lewis Clarke, During a Captivity of More Than Twenty-Five Years, Among the Algerines of Kentucky, One of the So Called Christian States of America *(Boston: David H. Ela, 1845), pp. 70–74.*

SOCIAL DEVELOPMENT

deprived of his history, and with this deprivation not only the past but also the future is wiped out: He has neither known predecessors to provide tradition nor unambiguously defined successors to instill promise. . . . Such is the conscious world of the Negro."

More recent historical investigations, such as John W. Blassingame's *The Slave Community: Plantation Life in the Antebellum South* (1972), Eugene D. Genovese's *Roll, Jordan, Roll: The World the Slaves Made* (1974), Herbert G. Gutman's *The Black Family in Slavery and Freedom, 1750–1925* (1976), Lawrence W. Levine's *Black Culture and Black Consciousness: Afro-American Folk Thought from Slavery to Freedom* (1977), Leon F. Litwack's *Been in the Storm So Long: The Aftermath of Slavery* (1979), Vincent Harding's *There Is a River: The Black Struggle for Freedom in America* (1981), and Sterling Stuckey's *Slave Culture: Nationalist Theory and the Foundations of Black America* (1987) have amply demonstrated that African culture did not disappear as a result of slavery and racism. Collectively, these and other scholars have also revealed the emergence of a dynamic and complex African American culture that the slaves creatively blended from a mixture of African, European, and American sources. This distinctive African American culture, broadly defined in the historical literature to include everything from folklore to music, from religion to cuisine, enabled blacks to resist the dehumanizing logic of slavery and to provide for themselves a sense of cohesion, identity, and pride once slavery came to an end.

Throughout their long history in North America, contends Levine, African Americans never completely relinquished elements of their African consciousness, which they preserved in their stories and songs, their speech and dance, their religion and folklore, their jokes and games. Long thought to be another indication of black inferiority, African American culture has begun to exercise an obvious and widespread influence on mainstream American culture. Suburban white teenagers now listen to rap music and watch videos of black recording artists on MTV. Many have also adapted black forms of dress, modes of expression, and patterns of speech. Whether such developments indicate permanent or temporary changes in the cultural lives of white Americans remains to be seen.

The various studies of African American history and culture undertaken since the 1970s represent a partial fulfillment of African American novelist Ralph Ellison's poignant challenge: "Everybody wants to tell us what a Negro is. . . . But if you would tell me who I am, at least take the trouble to discover what I have been." Ellison early rejected, or at least questioned, many of the historical and social scientific categories

imposed upon blacks in the aggregate. He did not, of course, object to exposing the humiliation and injustice to which blacks had been subjected but criticized the presupposition that once racial bias had been eradicated blacks would be indistinguishable from other Americans. In the preface to *The Peculiar Institution: Slavery in the Ante-Bellum South* (1956), for example, Kenneth M. Stampp clarified the assumptions about blacks that informed much of the scholarship to which Ellison issued a rejoinder. Stampp acknowledged that he assumed "the slaves were merely ordinary human beings, that innately Negroes *are*, after all, only white men with black skins, nothing more, nothing less." Ellison feared that, good intentions notwithstanding, those who portrayed blacks only as victims would end by annihilating the African American past since they characteristically underestimated the importance of the distinctive culture and experience of black men and women. Ellison could thus praise a book such as Myrdal's *An American Dilemma: The Negro Problem and Modern Democracy* for stirring the consciences of white Americans and yet, at the same time, issue a stinging indictment of it. When Myrdal wrote that the African American personality and culture were, "in the main, to be considered as secondary reactions to more primary pressures from the side of the dominant white majority," Ellison asked whether a people can

> live and develop for over three hundred years simply by *reacting*? Are American Negroes simply the creation of white men, or have they at least helped to create themselves out of what they found around them? Men have made a way of life in caves and upon cliffs, why cannot Negroes have made a life upon the horns of the white man's dilemma? . . . It does not occur to Myrdal that many of the Negro cultural manifestations which he considers merely reflective might also embody a *rejection* of what he considers "higher values." . . . It is only partially true that Negroes turn away from white patterns because they are refused participation. There is nothing like distance to create objectivity, and exclusion gives rise to counter values.

In 1964 Ellison reaffirmed that the African American was more than "a physical fact and a social artifice." "He was," Ellison countered, "the product of a synthesis of his blood mixture, his social experience, and what he had made of his predicament, i.e. his *culture*. And his quality of wonder and his heroism alike spring no less from his brutalization than from that culture."

The transformation of Africans into African Americans was a long, slow, uneven process. They had been, after all, forcibly detached from the kinship networks that formed the underpinnings of African society. They had endured a grueling voyage across the Atlantic and had been set down in a strange land, surrounded by an alien and hostile people. They had been herded together with other Africans who were almost as strange to them as were the Europeans. They had, perhaps, watched loved ones die and were left to contemplate their own uncertain futures. Yet, as early as the 1770s, blacks throughout the British North American colonies were living in families with extended kinship ties to the larger African American community. They were, in short, creating and practicing a culture of their own—an African American culture that was an amalgam of African, European, and American customs and beliefs. The development of an African American community and culture proved remarkably resilient, enabling blacks as a people to survive the hardships of slavery.

African American history is thus hardly a long tale of unremitting degradation and pathology, of incomparable misery, impotence, and sorrow. It is also the story of diverse men and women drawn from all parts of a vast continent who became a people and who, against all odds, as Genovese has put it, "forged a culture that interpenetrated with white culture and yet emerged as an Afro-American culture apart." Even in the midst of the savage exploitation and abuse that took place both during and after slavery, blacks managed to draw on their rich cultural heritage to sustain feelings of dignity, humanity, and self-worth as individuals and a people. Whatever their bad moments and abject failures under those exacting circumstances, blacks stood together, and together they survived.

–JACOB W. FOX,
RICHMOND, VIRGINIA

References

Roger D. Abrahams, *Positively Black* (Englewood Cliffs, N.J.: Prentice-Hall, 1970).

John W. Blassingame, *The Slave Community: Plantation Life in the Antebellum South* (New York: Oxford University Press, 1972).

Stanley M. Elkins, *Slavery: A Problem in American Institutional and Intellectual Life* (Chicago: University of Chicago Press, 1959).

Ralph Ellison, *Shadow and Act* (New York: Random House, 1964).

E. Franklin Frazier, *The Negro in the United States,* revised edition (New York: Macmillan, 1957).

Eugene D. Genovese, *Roll, Jordan, Roll: The World the Slaves Made* (New York: Pantheon, 1974).

Genovese, *The Southern Front: History and Politics in the Culture War* (Columbia: University of Missouri Press, 1995).

Marvin E. Gettleman and David Mermelstein, eds., *The Great Society Reader: The Failure of American Liberalism* (New York: Vintage, 1967).

Nathan Glazer and Daniel Patrick Moynihan, *Beyond the Melting Pot: The Negroes, Puerto Ricans, Jews, Italians, and Irish of New York City* (Cambridge, Mass.: MIT Press and Harvard University Press, 1963).

Herbert G. Gutman, *The Black Family in Slavery and Freedom, 1750–1925* (New York: Pantheon, 1976).

Vincent Harding, *There Is a River: The Black Struggle for Freedom in America* (New York: Harcourt Brace Jovanovich, 1981).

Abram Kardiner and Lionel Ovesey, *The Mark of Oppression: A Psychosocial Study of the American Negro* (New York: Norton, 1951).

Nicholas Lemann, *The Promised Land: The Great Black Migration and How It Changed America* (New York: Knopf, 1991).

Lawrence W. Levine, *Black Culture and Black Consciousness: Afro-American Folk Thought from Slavery to Freedom* (New York: Oxford University Press, 1977).

Leon F. Litwack, *Been in the Storm So Long: The Aftermath of Slavery* (New York: Knopf, 1979).

Stanford M. Lyman, *The Black American in Sociological Thought* (New York: Putnam, 1972).

Gunnar Myrdal, *An American Dilemma: The Negro Problem and Modern Democracy* (New York & London: Harper, 1944).

Lee Rainwater and William L. Yancey, eds., *The Moynihan Report and the Politics of Controversy: A Trans-action Social Science and Public Policy Report* (Cambridge, Mass.: MIT Press, 1967).

Kenneth M. Stampp, *The Peculiar Institution: Slavery in the Ante-Bellum South* (New York: Knopf, 1956).

Peter Steinfels, *The Neoconservatives: The Men Who Are Changing America's Politics* (New York: Simon & Schuster, 1979).

Sterling Stuckey, *Slave Culture: Nationalist Theory and the Foundations of Black America* (New York: Oxford University Press, 1987).

William L. Van Deburg, *New Day in Babylon: The Black Power Movement and American Culture, 1965–1975* (Chicago: University of Chicago Press, 1992).

SOCIAL DEVELOPMENT

STABLE MARRIAGES

Did slaves establish stable marriages and families?

Viewpoint: Yes. With varying degrees of enthusiasm and good faith, the slaveholders encouraged their slaves to establish stable marriages and families, and the slaves frequently did so.

Viewpoint: No. Slave marriages and families were inherently fragile because neither rested on solid institutional and legal foundations.

The majority of slaves lived together in nuclear families. Yet, these families, however stable, were far from secure, for Southern law did not recognize slave marriages. Husbands and wives could be separated by sale, and masters rather than parents exercised legal authority over slave children. In *Slavery: A Problem in American Institutional and Intellectual Life* (1959), Stanley M. Elkins went so far as to suggest that slave families were virtually nonexistent and that most slaves had no "meaningful others" in their lives. Isolated and alone, they were wholly subject to, and utterly dependent upon, the whim and will of their masters.

Elkins exaggerated the case. Although resting on precarious foundations and always at risk, the family protected blacks from the dehumanizing rigors of slavery. By the early eighteenth century, as mortality rates declined and as the ratio of men to women became more balanced, the slaves began to reconstitute the families that slavery and the slave trade had disrupted. Many slave owners, in fact, encouraged their slaves in this endeavor. Married slaves, they reasoned, would be more contented and thus more productive. In addition to their concerns about the slaves' welfare, the masters also understood that the birth of each slave child served their economic interests, adding to the sum of their property and wealth.

The masters themselves, however, regularly interfered with slave families. They broke up families through sale. Historian Michael Tadman has estimated that in the upper South, 33 percent of first marriages ended because of the forced separation of the partners, and 50 percent of slave children were forcibly parted from at least one of their parents. The masters also took sexual liberties with their female slaves, which further strained black family life. The family might have provided a haven from the cruelties and indignities of slavery, but slave families were exceedingly vulnerable. Historian Ann Patton Malone has cautioned against the inclination to regard the slave family as "the cozy American family unit of mom, dad, and kids." Yet, slaves sustained family life under the worst imaginable conditions. They maintained their own households, raised their children, and shared their joys, sorrows, frustrations, and hardships with friends, neighbors, and kin. As the scholar Elizabeth Fox-Genovese has pointed out, the slaves were also members of their master's household and, as such, neither their lives nor their families were their own. The history of the slave family, therefore, reflects both the slaves' attempts to establish a measure of autonomy and the restrictions that circumscribed their freedom.

Viewpoint:
Yes. With varying degrees of enthusiasm and good faith, the slaveholders encouraged their slaves to establish stable marriages and families, and the slaves frequently did so.

One of the most persistent assumptions among students of African American slave culture and life is that slaves established durable marriages, sustained long-term relationships, and built stable families. Although the separation of husbands from wives and parents from children was commonplace, evidence reveals a remarkable fact: many slave couples and families, despite the threat and the reality of sale, managed to sustain loving and lasting relationships that stood the test of time.

The belief in the transient nature of slave relationships arose in part from the mistaken assumption that blacks were culturally indifferent to establishing permanent marriages and families. One of the earliest examples of this thinking was found in such pioneering works of sociologist E. Franklin Frazier as *The Negro Family in Chicago* (1932), *The Negro Family in the United States* (1939), and *The Negro in the United States* (1949). In *The Negro Family in Chicago*, Frazier maintained that slave families were "at best an accommodation to the slave order, [and] went to pieces in the general breakup of the plantation system." Although Frazier rethought many of his suppositions about the slave family, his original conclusions laid the foundation for such later studies as Daniel P. Moynihan's *The Negro Family in America: The Case for National Action* (1966). Moynihan argued that the deterioration of the modern black family had resulted from a historical process that began in the seventeenth century with the arrival of the first African slaves in America.

Some historians, however, rejected the conclusion that slavery had robbed blacks of personality and culture and had stripped them not only of the ability but also of the willingness to form and maintain stable and loving human relationships. In 1976 Herbert G. Gutman published *The Black Family in Slavery and Freedom, 1750–1925*, the first substantial analysis of slave marriage and family life. From census records and other sources, such as oral histories, Gutman found that the stability of slave marriages and families had to do with the slaves' own desires to create lasting bonds with one another.

Yet, even Gutman acknowledged that slaves faced obstacles to marrying. The law, for instance, did not recognize slave marriages, stating that as property slaves were incapable of entering into legal contracts. The nature of master-slave relations further reinforced this notion. Simply put, slaves' relations to their masters superseded any relations that might exist among slaves. Slaves might marry, but as one North Carolina judge explained in 1858, "with slaves it may be dissolved at the pleasure of either party, or by the sale of one or both, depending on the caprice or necessity of the owners."

The law notwithstanding, many slaveholders felt it was their Christian duty to sanction the marriages of slaves on their plantations. Churches, too, urged masters to formalize slave marriages, and some clergymen went so far as to suggest that those marriages ought to be recognized by law. Doing so, of course, was virtually impossible in the Old South, for if the law recognized slaves' marriages it would have limited the master's power over his slaves. Still, many churchmen and jurists believed that whenever possible slave owners should avoid separating married slaves by sale and, if necessary, according to Albert J. Raboteau in *Slave Religion: The "Invisible Institution" in the Antebellum South* (1978), should even put "themselves to some inconvenience, in buying, selling, or exchanging, to keep them together. Both moral obligation and humanity demand it." In the end, though, the slave owners were still free to determine their own course, and many, if not most, permitted expedience to triumph over compassion, especially when they found themselves at the mercy of creditors.

Whatever good intentions the masters might have had with regard to slave families—and Florentine poet Dante long ago warned where good intentions lead—the slaves themselves induced the slaveholders to honor their marriage and family bonds. When both prospective spouses lived on the same plantation, the master's decision to approve their marriage was much easier. It was also practical for the master since marriage and family helped generate stability in the slave community, intensified slaves' ties to the plantation, and encouraged married slaves to have children, which added to the master's property. When slaves sought unions with slaves who lived on other plantations or with free blacks, however, slave owners had a potentially serious problem. Approval of such a marriage meant that the slave involved would in all likelihood request permission to leave periodically to visit his or her spouse. This freedom, however limited it was, subtly undermined the master's authority. Yet, many slaveholders permitted such unions, believing that their approval helped to maintain good relations with all their slaves. Most masters agreed that contented slaves were productive slaves. Some especially astute masters

BY

HEWLETT & BRIGHT.

SALE OF

VALUABLE SLAVES,

(On account of departure)

The Owner of the following named and valuable Slaves, being on the eve of departure for Europe, will cause the same to be offered for sale, at the NEW EXCHANGE, corner of St. Louis and Chartres streets, on *Saturday,* May 16, at Twelve o'Clock, *viz.*

1. SARAH, a mulatress, aged 45 years, a good cook and accustomed to house work in general, is an excellent and faithful nurse for sick persons, and in every respect a first rate character.

2. DENNIS, her son, a mulatto, aged 24 years, a first rate cook and steward for a vessel, having been in that capacity for many years on board one of the Mobile packets; is strictly honest, temperate, and a first rate subject.

3. CHOLE, a mulatress, aged 36 years, she is, without execption, one of the most competent servants in the country, a first rate washer and ironer, does up lace, a good cook, and for a bachelor who wishes a house-keeper she would be invaluable; she is also a good ladies' maid, having travelled to the North in that capacity.

4. FANNY, her daughter, a mulatress, aged 16 years, speaks French and English, is a superior hair-dresser, (pupil of Guilliac,) a good seamstress and ladies' maid, is smart, intelligent, and a first rate character.

5. DANDRIDGE, a mulatoo, aged 26 years, a first rate dining-room servant, a good painter and rough carpenter, and has but few equals for honesty and sobriety.

6. NANCY, his wife, aged about 24 years, a confidential house servant, good seamstress, mantuamaker and tailoress, a good cook, washer and ironer, etc.

7. MARY ANN, her child, a creole, aged 7 years, speaks French and English, is smart, active and intelligent.

8. FANNY or FRANCES, a mulatress, aged 22 years, is a first rate washer and ironer, good cook and house servant, and has an excellent character.

9. EMMA, an orphan, aged 10 or 11 years, speaks French and English, has been in the country 7 years, has been accustomed to waiting on table, sewing etc.; is intelligent and active.

10. FRANK, a mulatto, aged about 32 years speaks French and English, is a first rate hostler and coachman, understands perfectly well the management of horses, and is, in every respect, a first rate character, with the exception that he will occasionally drink, though not an habitual drunkard.

All the above named Slaves are acclimated and excellent subjects; they were purchased by their present vendor many years ago, and will, therefore, be severally warranted against all vices and maladies prescribed by law, save and except FRANK, who is fully guaranteed in every other respect but the one above mentioned.

TERMS:—One-half Cash, and the other half in notes at Six months, drawn and endorsed to the satisfaction of the Vendor, with special mortgage on the Slaves until final payment. The Acts of Sale to be passed before WILLIAM BOSWELL, *Notary Public,* at the expense of the Purchaser.

New-Orleans, May 13, 1835.

PRINTED BY BENJAMIN LEVY.

STABLE MARRIAGES

also realized that the decision really did not rest with them. Even if they withheld their blessing, relationships between their slaves and those on neighboring plantations were going to take place anyway. However vigilant, masters could not control every facet of slaves' lives.

Given the constant threat of slave couples' being separated by sale, one might wonder why they chose to marry at all. Yet, in word and deed they continually demonstrated their commitment to one another. Even without legal sanction slaves viewed marriage as governed by God rather than by masters or laws. Gutman's study of slave marriages and families offers a dramatic illustration of this point. His analysis of married Mississippi freedmen more than forty years old during 1864–1865, for example, revealed that only 9 percent had a previous marriage terminated by mutual consent or desertion; the remainder reported no previous marriage or a previous marriage terminated by forced separation or death. Emancipation did not change the freedmen's and women's attitudes toward marriage, although now the law validated their unions.

Like other people, slaves married not only for love but also for practical reasons. A union that consisted of two healthy partners, or even one, made the chances of surviving the plantation regime that much greater. Marriage also meant that the couple could cultivate a small garden. If the husband was a skilled laborer, the family might have an opportunity to earn a little money. In some cases, too, marriage reduced the chance of being sold away from the plantation, and even if the master tried to separate a married couple by sale, he might find potential buyers reluctant to purchase such a slave, fearing that the slave was more likely to run away.

Slaves in general also proved responsible and, indeed, strict parents. From oral interviews with former slaves, Gutman determined that many slave children grew up in a two-parent household. Census records confirm his findings, weakening the argument put forth by such historians as Stanley M. Elkins to suggest that slavery destroyed the family structure, making the two-parent household a rarity. Further, evidence suggests no distinction in many slave families among the different "classes" of slaves. Children of field hands were just as likely to live with a mother and a father as were the children of drivers, artisans, and house servants.

Both Elkins and, earlier, historian Kenneth M. Stampp had suggested that slave family relationships, particularly those between fathers and sons, were virtually nonexistent because of the patriarchal nature of the master-slave relation and the powerlessness of male slaves to protect their families. Stampp and Elkins also argued that because female slaves were not denied their "womanhood," inasmuch as they could perform most traditionally female duties, while male slaves could not function in their roles as provider and protector, the dynamics of the black family shifted from male-dominated to female-dominated households. Authority in the family thus rested with black women, allowing men to be irresponsible and often nearly childlike themselves.

As Gutman pointed out, however, even the simple practice of naming children took on a great significance in the slave family. In an effort to create and sustain a sense of individual identity and family heritage, blacks frequently named male children after their fathers or grandfathers. The slaves, Gutman contended, hardly crumbled before the master's authority. On the contrary, the slave family operated on a subversive level, standing defiant against the master's will and the law.

Even though slave marriages and families lacked legal sanctions and institutional foundations, slaves found ways of using them to strike a blow—albeit a relatively quiet blow—against the master's power. The close kinship networks and the respect for marriage and family that the slaves demonstrated showed that, under trying and often dire circumstances, they had created ways to cope with the day-to-day realities of bondage. That generations of slaves succeeded in maintaining their families is yet another example of how an enslaved people struggled and overcame their situation and, in the process, fashioned a legacy that scholars only now are coming to understand and appreciate.

—MEG GREENE,
MIDLOTHIAN, VIRGINIA

Viewpoint:
No. Slave marriages and families were inherently fragile because neither rested on solid institutional and legal foundations.

Southern law denied the legitimacy of slave marriages, and, by permitting families to be separated by sale, it also undermined the stability of slave families. Some masters, to be sure, encouraged more or less permanent unions among their slaves. These marriages, of course, existed at the master's sufferance, and what he had joined he could also set asunder. James Henry Hammond of South Carolina thought the family lives of his slaves of the utmost importance and regularly interfered with their domestic relations to ensure peace and tranquility. Like many other slaveholders, Hammond believed that married men who had family ties and responsibilities were less likely to cause trouble or to run away. Stable family lives among the members of the slave community, Hammond and others reasoned, were essential to the efficient operation of the plantation. According to his biographer, Drew Gilpin Faust, Hammond, for all his faults, did not make a habit of separating slave families by sale. He even purchased old or injured slaves when they accompanied younger, stronger, and healthier relatives just so the family could stay together. A contented slave, in Hammond's mind, was a productive slave.

Some masters formalized slave unions, often as part of the customary Christmas festivities that took place on many plantations. Slaves commonly could not marry when and whom they chose, at least not without first securing the master's permission. Most slaveholders tried to prohibit their slaves from marrying those who lived on nearby plantations but did not always succeed in doing so. Whenever marital friction arose, usually because of the infidelity of one of the partners, masters assumed the role of family court judge to settle the dispute before it had gone too far. The master also punished the guilty. In 1840 Hammond recorded a series of such incidents in his diary:

> Had a trial of Divorce & Adultery cases. Flogged Joe Goodwyn & ordered him to go back to his wife. Ditto Gabriel and Molly & ordered them to come together again. Separated Moses & Anny finally—And flogged Tom Kollock. He had never been flogged before—Gave him 30 [lashes] with my own hand [for] interfering with Maggy Campbell, Sullivan's wife.

Evidence suggests that an overwhelming majority of Hammond's slaves managed to live out their lives in stable marriages. Yet, with no legal, religious, or institutional protection for the sanctity and inviolability of such unions, even the most durable slave marriages rested always on precarious foundations.

The circumstances and vicissitudes of slavery prevented black men and women from behaving like husbands and wives or fathers and mothers. Slave men could not rely on the law to uphold their identities as husbands and fathers. They could not safeguard their children from sale, for they had no legal authority over them. Nor could they defend their women from the illicit and often violent sexual advances of the master or other white men. As the abolitionists hastened to point out, the sexual escapades of slave owners not only violated civilized social and moral conventions but also made a travesty of slave marriages and families. There is now substantial evidence in

the historical literature on slavery that blacks made every possible effort to establish permanent unions and stable families under the most trying conditions. However much they were committed to marriage, home, and family, the slaves knew that those ideals were beyond their reach as long as they and their loved ones were held in bondage.

Just as the law gave no sanction to slave marriages, so it remained largely silent on the limits of the master's power. Judge Thomas Ruffin of North Carolina had declared that the master's power must be absolute. Apart from willful murder, the master was free to govern, discipline, and use his slaves as he saw fit, especially when the objects of his domination were female slaves to whom the law gave no recognition as women. It was, for example, considered impossible for a master, or any white man, to rape a female slave; the law did not hold masters accountable for sexual assault. By the 1850s conscientious jurists such as T. R. R. Cobb of Georgia argued that the law ought to acknowledge the rape of slave women as a criminal offense. In *An Inquiry into the Law of Negro Slavery in the United States of America* (1858) Cobb noted that among the Lombards, when a master "debauched" the wife of a slave, both the slave and his wife gained their freedom. Although Cobb was not willing to emancipate female slaves who had been so victimized, and although racism distorted his vision of the abuse that they endured, he nevertheless conceded the deficiencies of Southern law on this question. He wrote:

> Another consequence of slavery is, that the violation of the person of a female slave, carries with it no other punishment than the damages which the master may recover for the trespass upon his property. . . . It is a matter worthy the consideration of legislators, whether the offence of rape, committed upon a female slave, should not be indictable; and whether, when committed by the master, there should not be superadded the sale of the slave to some other master. The occurrence of such an offence is almost unheard of; and the known lasciviousness of the negro, renders the possibility of its occurrence very remote. Yet, for the honor of the statute-book, if it does occur, there should be adequate punishment.

Regrettably, custom as well as law prevented such views from receiving a fair hearing.

Southern churchmen also urged masters to respect slave marriages, but to no avail. They might remonstrate with the slaveholders, reminding them of their Christian duties toward their "people," but ministers had no power to enforce their decrees. Since they had irrevocably committed themselves and the churches they served to supporting the regime, they had to

VALUABLE PROPERTY AND JUDICIOUS MEN

In the following account former slave Josiah Henson describes his father's rage over the attempted rape of his mother:

My mother was a slave of Dr. Josiah McPherson, but hired to the Mr. Newman to whom my father belonged. The only incident I can remember which occurred while my mother continued on Mr. Newman's farm, was the appearance one day of my father with his head bloody and his back lacerated. He was beside himself with mingled rage and suffering. The explanation I picked up from the conversation of others only partially explained the matter to my mind; but as I grew older I understood it all. It seemed the overseer had sent my mother away from the other field hands to a retired place, and after trying persuasion in vain, had resorted to force to accomplish a brutal purpose. Her screams aroused my father at his distant work, and running up, he found his wife struggling with the man. Furious at the sight, he sprung upon him like a tiger. In a moment the overseer was down, and, mastered by rage, my father would have killed him but for the entreaties of my mother, and the overseer's own promise that nothing should ever be said of the matter. The promise was kept—like most promises of the cowardly and debased—as long as the danger lasted.

The laws of the state provide means and opportunities for revenge so ample, that miscreants like him never fail to improve them. "A nigger has struck a white man"; that is enough to set a whole county on fire; no question is asked about the provocation. The authorities were soon in pursuit of my father. The fact of the sacrilegious act of lifting a hand against the sacred temple of a white man's body . . . this was all it was necessary to establish. And the penalty followed: one hundred lashes on the bare back, and to have the right ear nailed to the whipping-post, and then severed from the body. For a time my father kept out of the way, hiding in the woods, and at night venturing into some cabin in search of food. But at length the strict watch set baffled all his efforts. His supplies cut off, he was fairly starved out, and compelled by hunger to come back and give himself up.

The day for the execution of the penalty was appointed. The Negroes from the neighboring plantations were summoned, for the moral improvement, to witness the scene. A powerful blacksmith named Hewes laid on the stripes. Fifty were given, during which the cries of my father might be heard a mile, and then a pause ensued. True, he had struck a white man, but as valuable property he must not be damaged. Judicious men felt his pulse. Oh! he could stand the whole. Again and again the thong fell on his lacerated back. His cries grew fainter and fainter, till a feeble groan was the only response to his final blows. His head was then thrust against the post, and his right ear fastened to it with a tack; a swift pass of the knife, and the bleeding member was left sticking to the place.

Source: *Josiah Henson,* Truth Stranger than Fiction: Father Henson's Story of His Own Life *(Boston: Jewett, 1858), pp. 2–5.*

exercise caution and to make certain that dissenting opinions not be misconstrued as a renunciation of slavery itself. The best they could do was to try to mitigate abuse in individual cases.

Male sexual authority followed from male social and political authority, and in the slave society of the Old South no force on earth could restrain it. In different ways it oppressed white and black women alike. Even if they were free men, the husbands of slave women, who were not in any legal sense husbands at all, could not shield their wives, though many

tried. Slave men fought and sometimes killed those, including their masters and overseers, who had ravished their women. The women fought back, too, and on more than one occasion ended the abuse by killing the perpetrator. This level of violence resulted directly from the unwillingness of Southern law to affirm the legality of slave marriages and to punish those who violated that sanction.

Slaveholders frequently justified their intervention into slave families by maintaining that they had to shelter women and children from male brutality. "Negroes are by nature tyrannical in disposition," proclaimed Robert Collins of Macon, Georgia, "and, if allowed, the stronger will abuse the weaker; husbands will often abuse their wives and mothers their children." Only watchful masters and overseers could protect the vulnerable and chasten their assailants. With no evident sense of irony W. W. Hazard, another planter from Georgia, denounced callous husbands who beat their wives. In an essay entitled "On the General Management of a Plantation," published in the *Southern Agriculturalist* in July 1831, Hazard affirmed that he never permitted "a husband to abuse, strike or whip his wife, and tell them it is disgraceful for a man to raise his hand in violence against a feeble woman, and that woman too, the wife of his bosom, the mother of his children, and the companion of his leisure, his midnight hours." According to William Harper of South Carolina, slavery even offered women of the servile class refuge from the maltreatment that they ordinarily suffered in marriage and thus somewhat improved their lot. The slaves, Harper wrote,

are placed under the control of others, who are interested to restrain their excesses of cruelty or rage. Wives are protected from their husbands, and children from their parents. And this is no inconsiderable compensation of the evils of our system and would so appear, if we could form any conception of the immense amount of misery which is elsewhere inflicted.

Such rationalizations notwithstanding, slavery deprived black men of their roles as husbands and fathers, black women of their roles as wives and mothers, and black parents of their roles as providers and protectors. The refusal of slaveholders to legitimize slave marriages compelled men to accept in silence the rape of their wives and daughters, or else to risk death. That same refusal constrained women to submit to such outrages, urging their husbands and fathers not to imperil their lives in the pursuit of vengeance.

Slaves used every means at hand to approximate stable marriages and families. Men and women tried to sustain and comfort one another and to raise their children with the dignity and strength needed to accept the responsibilities of adulthood. Husbands and wives, of course, varied in their love for and fidelity to one another, as have husbands and wives in all places and at all times. The lack of legal endorsement for their unions, however, exposed them to a level of oppression and exploitation that was nearly impossible to bear, even through the most determined effort. Individuals forced to defend the inviolability of family in the absence of legal and

institutional frameworks confronted an almost intolerable ordeal. Slave families, notwithstanding the fortitude of individual members, were forever exposed to malicious and profligate interference from whites who, whatever pangs of conscience they may have experienced, bore no legal responsibility for their actions.

–MARTINA NICHOLAS,
YOUNGSTOWN STATE UNIVERSITY

References

John W. Blassingame, *The Slave Community: Plantation Life in the Antebellum South*, revised edition (New York: Oxford University Press, 1979).

T. R. R. Cobb, *An Inquiry into the Law of Negro Slavery in the United States of America* (Philadelphia: T. & J. W. Johnson, 1858).

Stanley M. Elkins, *Slavery: A Problem in American Institutional and Intellectual Life* (Chicago: University of Chicago Press, 1959).

Drew Gilpin Faust, *James Henry Hammond and the Old South: A Design for Mastery* (Baton Rouge: Louisiana State University Press, 1982).

Robert W. Fogel and Stanley L. Engerman, *Time on the Cross: The Economics of Negro Slavery*, 2 volumes (Boston: Little, Brown, 1974).

Elizabeth Fox-Genovese, *Within the Plantation Household: Black and White Women of the Old South* (Chapel Hill: University of North Carolina Press, 1988).

E. Franklin Frazier, *The Negro Family in Chicago* (Chicago: University of Chicago Press, 1932).

Frazier, *The Negro Family in the United States* (Chicago: University of Chicago Press, 1939).

Frazier, *The Negro in the United States* (New York: Macmillan, 1949).

Eugene D. Genovese, *Roll, Jordan, Roll: The World the Slaves Made* (New York: Pantheon, 1974).

Herbert G. Gutman, *The Black Family in Slavery and Freedom, 1750–1925* (New York: Pantheon, 1976).

William Harper, "Memoir on Slavery," in *The Ideology of Slavery: Proslavery Thought in the Antebellum South*, edited by Drew Gilpin Faust (Baton Rouge: Louisiana State University Press, 1981), pp. 78–135.

STABLE MARRIAGES

W. W. Hazard, "On the General Management of a Plantation," *Southern Agriculturalist,* IV (July 1831): 350–354.

Peter Kolchin, *American Slavery, 1619–1877* (New York: Hill & Wang, 1993).

Ann Patton Malone, *Sweet Chariot: Slave Family and Household Structure in Nineteenth-Century Louisiana* (Chapel Hill: University of North Carolina Press, 1992).

Melton A. McLaurin, *Celia, A Slave* (Athens: University of Georgia Press, 1991).

Daniel P. Moynihan, *The Negro Family in America: The Case for National Action* (Chicago, Ill.: University of Chicago Press, 1966).

Albert J. Raboteau, *Slave Religion: The "Invisible Institution" in the Antebellum South* (New York: Oxford University Press, 1978).

Lee Rainwater and William L. Yancey, eds., *The Moynihan Report and the Politics of Controversy: A Trans-action Social Science and Public Policy Report* (Cambridge, Mass.: MIT Press, 1967).

Willie Lee Rose, ed., *A Documentary History of Slavery in North America* (New York: Oxford University Press, 1976).

Kenneth M. Stampp, *The Peculiar Institution: Slavery in the Ante-Bellum South* (New York: Knopf, 1956).

Richard H. Steckel, "Slave Marriage and the Family," *Journal of Family History,* 5 (Winter 1980): 406–421.

Brenda E. Stevenson, *Life in Black and White: Family and Community in the Slave South* (New York: Oxford University Press, 1996).

Michael Tadman, *Speculators and Slaves: Masters, Traders, and Slaves in the Old South* (Madison: University of Wisconsin Press, 1989).

U.S. Department of Labor, Office of Policy Planning and Research, *The Negro Family: The Case for National Action* (Washington, D.C.: U.S. Government Printing Office, 1965).

TRANSATLANTIC SLAVE TRADE

Was the transatlantic slave trade profitable?

Viewpoint: Yes. Whether controlled by local traders or foreign monopolies, the Atlantic slave trade brought tremendous profits for both European merchants and African intermediaries.

Viewpoint: No. By the late eighteenth century the costs of the slave trade combined with the high mortality rate of the cargo made the Atlantic slave trade unprofitable.

How profitable was the Atlantic slave trade? Until recently, historians did not challenge the assumption that it was immensely and uniformly lucrative, even as they acknowledged that most of the chartered companies engaged in the slave trade went bankrupt. The propaganda of the antislavery movement of the nineteenth century is, in part, responsible for this misleading impression. Few opponents of slavery imagined that men were so callous and evil that they would enter into such an immoral commerce unless tempted by the prospect of vast profits. Certainly, individual slave traders and slave-trading companies at times earned considerable sums. The account books, however, do not register consistent or astonishing gains.

The Dutch Middleburg Company, for instance, experienced a rather unspectacular rate of growth. The ninety-eight slaving voyages that the company sponsored between 1741 and 1800 yielded total profits of £1,538,642 (Flemish pounds) amounting to an aggregate return of only 2.58 percent. Some voyages, such as that of the *Het Vergenoegen,* which made a 37.38 percent profit, were highly successful. Others, such as that of the *De Geertruida en Christina,* by contrast, sustained losses of 59.41 percent.

The French did worse and the British fared better than the Dutch. French slave traders appealed to the government for assistance and after 1758 received a bounty of 100 *livres tournois* (the equivalent of £3.98 sterling) for each slave delivered to the French colonies in the Caribbean. In 1787 the government raised this subsidy to 160 *livres tournois* (the equivalent of £6.37 sterling). The French Crown thus paid between 25 percent and 33 percent of the cost of slaves. The 9.5 percent profit obtained from the British slave trade between 1760 and 1807 appears princely by comparison.

The slave trade was a financially perilous business. The occasionally phenomenal rewards did not imply sustained profits. Yet, the profitability of the slave trade fluctuated over time. During the nineteenth century, British attempts to suppress the slave trade notwithstanding, the average rate of profit remained sufficient to attract investors. As the Royal Navy expanded efforts to restrain the trade, average profits fell, discouraging investment. A lower level of investment meant fewer slave voyages and, in turn, fewer slaves transported to the Americas. As a result the price of slaves bought in Africa fell, while the price of slaves sold in Cuba and Brazil rose. Despite greater losses and a higher probability of failure because of more-vigilant British interdiction, the profits earned from completed voyages increased. For countless slave traders during the nineteenth century, as with the drug runners of our own day, the risks of engaging in illegal commerce were more than offset by the rewards of success.

**Viewpoint:
Yes. Whether controlled by local traders or foreign monopolies, the Atlantic slave trade brought tremendous profits for both European merchants and African intermediaries.**

The slave trade was big business in the eighteenth century, according to historian Peter Kolchin. Merchants on both sides of the Atlantic grew rich from it. Henry Callister, foreman of the Chesapeake warehouse of Liverpool slave merchant Foster Cunliffe, wrote in the 1740s that "the African trade is quite dangerous for life and health, though most profitable." In addition to being lucrative, the slave trade was also extensive; Portugal, Spain, Great Britain, France, Holland, Denmark, Sweden, and even Brandenburg participated. Divided though they might have been on matters of state, all had a mutual interest in the profitability of the slave trade. As a consequence each of the nations engaged in the commerce founded companies expressly to transport slaves from Africa to the New World.

The first to traffic in slaves to the Americas were the Portuguese. In his monumental study *The Slave Trade: The Story of the Atlantic Slave Trade: 1440–1870* (1997), Hugh Thomas has shown that to manage the slave trade the Portuguese government authorized the establishment of the Cacheu Company in the seventeenth century and the Maranhão and Pernambuco companies in the late eighteenth. Similarly, the Dutch had the West India Company, while the Spanish and French had too many privileged slave-trading companies to enumerate. Even the Scandinavian kingdoms had modest enterprises to capitalize on the traffic in slaves. The superiority of the Royal Navy, however, enabled the British to seize control of the slave trade by the late seventeenth and early eighteenth centuries, symbolized by the creation of the Royal Africa Company (RAC) in 1672, the mission of which was to sell slaves throughout the Spanish colonies of the New World. It was, incidentally, also the strength of the Royal Navy that enabled Great Britain to suppress the international slave trade during the nineteenth century. Despite their subsequent change of heart, the British garnered huge profits from commerce in human beings. When the British abolished slavery in their empire in 1833, however, they wished no other nation to benefit from the commerce in slaves.

Between 1783 and 1793 the port of Liverpool alone dispatched 878 ships carrying approximately 303,737 slaves from Africa valued at £15,186,850. Adjusting for costs and expenses—including commissions, insurance premiums, and bribes—the trade generated an estimated gross annual revenue of £1,700,000 for the city. Merchants earned an extraordinary 30 percent profit on every slave they sold. "Liverpool, therefore," wrote historian Frank Tannenbaum, "received a net income in the eleven slave years [1783–1793] of over £2,300,000 on the 303,737 Negroes, or an annual rate of over £200,000." The slave trade permeated the economy of Liverpool as it did the economies of many such coastal towns in England and the United States, providing a livelihood for a large number of the inhabitants.

The slave traders themselves not only engaged in buying and selling slaves but also did business in a wide array of goods. Many, such as Pierre Cornout of Bordeaux, France, had interests in banking. Others, such as Nicholas and John Brown of Providence, Rhode Island, and Aaron Lopez of Newport, Rhode Island, involved themselves with whaling and, in the Browns' case, with insurance. Richard Lake of Jamaica made a fortune as a coffee planter while also taking part in the slave trade. Abraham Redwood, Lopez, James and George De Wolf, Simeon Potter, and Sir Alexander Grant, each of whom had acquired large sums in the slave trade, also bought plantations in the West Indies. John Tarleton of Liverpool owned both an estate and a store in Curaçao.

Many slave traders eventually earned enough money to purchase and outfit ships of their own. Perhaps the most illustrious example is French trader Jean Ducasse, but he was hardly unique. Manuel Bautista Peres, Jacques Rasteau, James Bold, John Kennion, Patrick Fairweather, John Dawson, Godfrey Mallbone, Peleg Clarke, James De Wolf, Joseph Graffton, Obadiah Brown, and Jaspar Farmer all began their careers as captains of slave vessels. Few slave traders, however, operated as individuals. Like most businessmen, they sought investors to help finance their endeavors. Lawyers, doctors, shopkeepers, bankers, and others invested varying sums in slaving voyages and shared in the profits.

During the 1940s West Indian historian Eric Williams, who subsequently became prime minister of Trinidad and Tobago, went so far as to argue in his classic study *Capitalism & Slavery* (1944) that profits from the British slave trade financed the industrial revolution. There is ample evidence to credit Williams's thesis. Brian Blundell, a slave trader from Liverpool, invested in coal mining. His counterparts Henry Cruger and Lyonel Lyde invested in iron manufacturing. The slave traders Joseph and Jonathan Brooks, also of Liverpool, financed various construction projects, while fellow Liverpudlian John Ashton

"The Africans of the Slave Bark 'Wildfire'"; illustration from *Harper's Weekly,* 2 June 1860

(University of Pittsburgh Library, Pittsburgh, Pa.)

funded the building of canals. Williams concluded that:

> Britain was accumulating great wealth from the triangular trade. The increase of consumption goods called forth by that trade inevitably drew in its train the development of the productive power of the country. This industrial expansion required finance. What man in the first three-quarters of the eighteenth century was better able to afford the ready capital than a West Indian sugar planter or a Liverpool slave trader? . . . [T]he investment of profits from the triangular trade in British industry . . . supplied part of the huge outlay for the construction of the vast plants to meet the needs of the new productive process and the new markets. . . . The triangular trade made an enormous contribution to Britain's industrial development. The profits from this trade fertilized the entire productive system of the country.

Not only profitable in itself, the slave trade launched many businesses and industries everywhere it developed. Thousands of carpenters, joiners, ironmongers, painters, sail makers, braziers, coopers, riggers, glaziers, plumbers, gunsmiths, carters, laborers, and stevedores contributed to the success of the slave trade, from which indirectly they, too, earned their living. The trade also made possible the development of commercial and banking houses, manufacturing firms, and insurance companies, to say nothing of the sugar, tobacco, and cotton plantations of the New World. British merchant and economist Sir Josiah Child, who was governor of the East India Company throughout much of the 1680s, declared that every Englishman who went to the Caribbean and employed eight

TRANSATLANTIC SLAVE TRADE

slaves simultaneously supported four of his countrymen at home. (By contrast, Child asserted, an Englishman who migrated to New England supported no one but himself.)

Yet, the question of whether the slave trade was profitable is complicated. As a partial answer, Thomas provides the following illustration:

> In 1783, the firm of Giraud et Raimbaud of Nantes sent its 150-ton ship *La Jeune Aimée* to Angola and obtained 264 slaves, whom it sold in Saint-Domingue. The price of the ship had been 6,000 livres; with other expenses (the crew, the cargo, the slaves at Mayombe), the initial costs came to about 156,000 livres. The slaves and some other goods were sold for a total of over 366,000 livres. The profit, then, was 210,000 livres, or about 135 percent.

Doubtless the voyage of *La Jeune Aimée* was remarkable, the sort about which merchants dreamed, the sort that inflamed their imaginations and prompted them to risk so much in blood and treasure. Such undertakings, however, were far from isolated. From 1680 until 1687 ships owned by the Royal Africa Company made ninety-five voyages along the Windward Coast, between Sierra Leone and Cape Three Points. During that eight-year period only three of those ventures showed a net loss. The most substantial profit brought a 141 percent return; the average profit was 38 percent. Similarly, the British South Sea Company averaged a profit of nearly 30 percent on its voyages to Argentina in the early years of the eighteenth century. One vessel from Nantes made a profit of 200 percent, and gains of 50 to 100 percent were common. News of such earnings prompted German naturalist and statesman Alexander von Humboldt to assume, in *Voyage aux régions équinoxiaux du nouveau continent* (Voyage to the Equinoctial Regions of the New Continent, 1805), that a profit of 100 percent was by no means extraordinary.

Profits in the nineteenth century were greater still, especially after Great Britain and the United States moved to suppress the slave trade. *Le Cultivateur,* which set sail from Nantes in 1815, cost 600,000 francs to fit out. The sale of its cargo of 500 slaves brought 1,236,200 livres, or approximately 1,100,000 francs, a profit of 83 percent. According to Lord John Russell, prime minister of Great Britain between 1846 and 1852, a group of slaves that cost $5,000 when purchased on the coast of Africa could be sold in Brazil for $25,000, which amounted to a profit of 400 percent. In *The Slave Trade,* Thomas constructed a hypothetical scenario to explain the profit margins of the slave trade during the nineteenth century:

> In 1848, a United States-built slave ship of, say, 180 to 200 tons . . . plying between Brazil and Africa and bringing back slaves, might cost £1,500. The owner would have to pay about twenty seamen one hundred Spanish dollars a trip—say, £416. Food for those men for 90 days would cost £90. The captain would be paid 400 Spanish dollars: another £83. Food (and medicine) for 450 slaves might cost three pence a day if the food were "flour," which it usually was; another £169. Luxuries for the captain and contingencies (waters casks, wood for the slave deck, etc.) might cost another £300. Slaves would cost about an average of £4-10s in Africa—whether paid for in specie or in trade goods—£2,025 in all. The outlay, therefore, might be a little more than £4,500. Perhaps fifty slaves would die en route. But the sale of the remaining 410 slaves [*sic:* Thomas initially posited a cargo of 450 slaves. If 50 died en route, only 400, not 410, would remain.] at £45 each would bring the merchant £18,450, or a profit for the voyage . . . of just under £14,000. Even if every other ship were captured by the British, there would still be a 100 percent profit. These figures were, of course, considerably higher than those in the era of the legitimate trade.

One successful slave voyage, surmised William Crawford, British consul in Havana, would recoup the loss of ten empty or five packed slave ships. No wonder, then, that José Cliffe, who took part in the Brazilian slave trade during the 1830s and 1840s, could say with authority that it was "the most lucrative trade under the sun."

–MARK G. MALVASI,
RANDOLPH-MACON COLLEGE

Viewpoint:
No. By the late eighteenth century the costs of the slave trade combined with the high mortality rate of the cargo made the Atlantic slave trade unprofitable.

Recent scholarship has called into question the extraordinary rates of profitability attributed to the Atlantic slave trade. In his dissertation "The British Slave Trade, 1785–1807: Volume, Profitability, and Mortality" (University of Wisconsin-Madison, 1993), Stephen D. Behrendt argued that during the late eighteenth and early nineteenth centuries the British slave trade yielded average returns of between 7 percent and 8 percent, much in keeping with the 5 percent to 10 percent rate of profit typical of other enterprises and investments during the same period. To protect their profit margins during the last twenty years of the British slave trade, merchants used larger ships, especially after the Slave Carrying Act of 1799 limited the ratio of slaves to one per ton of the weight of a vessel. The availability of larger ships, many of which the Royal Navy had captured from the French during the Atlantic wars of the 1790s, enabled British slave traders to maintain the number of slaves they delivered to the Caribbean and, hence, bolster their profits.

Yet, not all who engaged in the slave trade fared equally well. Between 1785 and 1796 large companies took control of the market by arranging contracts with financiers in England and slave factors in Africa and the West Indies. Wealthy merchants such as Thomas Leyland of Liverpool earned greater profits in the slave trade than they could have obtained in other endeavors, but their smaller counterparts did not enjoy such success. Their performances depressed average profits throughout the slave trade. As costs and risks increased, many of the slave traders, large and small, went bankrupt during the last years of the British trade. By 1849, long after the British had declared the slave trade illegal, the British commissary judge in Havana remarked that:

the profits of the trade are much overstated. All persons are apt to boast much of their gains [from the illegal commerce in slaves] but the slave traders more especially, as a triumph over the cruisers, and even the Government of England, as well as to console themselves for the discredit they could not but feel attached to their trade. Thus we hear of a few fortunate individuals who . . . formerly amassed fortunes in it, but of the many who have lost fortunes and life in it we hear but little. . . . the trade had not recently been a productive one. One proof of this is that the insurance offices lost so much on the policies of slave trade vessels that it is nearly ten years since they resolved to take none of them on any terms.

Even earlier, profits from the slave trade had begun to decline as the price of slaves in Africa rose. By 1780 the average cost to purchase a slave had reached £50, ten times the price of a century before. Profits may have increased with prices, especially during the nineteenth century when a rate just below 20 percent was common, but overall profits either held steady or went into decline in relation to costs. The account books of Aaron Lopez, a successful slave merchant from Newport, Rhode Island, provide a remarkable illustration of the decline in the profitability of the trade. Between 1760 and 1766 Lopez financed fourteen slaving voyages to Africa. At most he made a profit on only half of them. Of the twenty-five slave vessels that departed Nantes for Saint Domingue (Haiti) between 1783 and 1791, ten (40 percent) turned a profit, with six

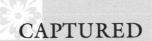

CAPTURED

Olaudah Equiano, an Ibo from West Africa, describes his capture by slave traders:

My father, besides many slaves, had a numerous family, of which seven lived to grow up, including myself and a sister, who was the only daughter. As I was the youngest of the sons, I became, of course, the greatest favourite with my mother, and was always with her; and she used to take particular pains to form my mind. I was trained up from my earliest years in the arts of agriculture and war; and my mother adorned me with emblems, after the manner of our greatest warriors. In this way I grew up till I was turned the age of eleven, when an end was put to my happiness in the following manner:—Generally, when the grown people in the neighbourhood were gone far in the fields to labour, the children assembled together in some of the neighborhood's premises to play; and commonly some of us used to get up a tree to look out for any assailant, or kidnapper, that might come upon us; for they sometimes took those opportunities of our parents' absence to attack and carry off as many as they could seize. One day, as I was watching at the top of a tree in our yard, I saw one of those people come into the yard of our next neighbour but one, to kidnap, there being many stout young people in it. Immediately, on this, I gave the alarm of the rogue, and he was surrounded by the stoutest of them, who entangled him with cords, so that he could not escape till some of the grown people came and secured him. But alas! ere long, it was my fate to be thus attacked, and to be carried off, when none of the grown people were nigh. One day, when all our people were gone out to their works as usual, and only I and my dear sister were left to mind the house, two men and a woman got over our walls, and in a moment seized us both; and, without giving us time to cry out, or make resistance, they stopped our mouths, and ran off with us into the nearest wood. Here they tied our hands, and continued to carry us as far as they could, till night came on, when we reached a small house, where the robbers halted for refreshment, and spent the night. We were then unbound; but were unable to take any food; and, being quite overpowered by fatigue and grief, our only relief was some sleep, which allayed our misfortune for a short time.

Source: Olaudah Equiano, The Interesting Narrative of the Life of Olaudah Equiano, or Gustavus Vassa, the African, volume 1 (London: Privately printed, 1789), pp. 46–49.

earning 19 percent or more. One broke even, while six lost money. The remaining eight received nothing, for the slave revolution in Saint Domingue, which began in 1791, voided all transactions associated with the slave trade.

For a long time it was a popular misconception that the relatively low cost of purchasing slaves in Africa made it profitable to fill ships with as many bodies as they could transport. The high mortality rates associated with the slave trade were considered economically acceptable because each slave delivered and sold represented a pure profit. Even the loss of several hundred on the Atlantic crossing was not financially damaging. But if slaves could not be acquired cheaply, as after 1780 they could not, then the logic of "tight packing" slaves also evaporated. Under such circumstances every slave death signified a financial loss, as the ledgers of many slave ships revealed.

During the last sixty years of the British slave trade (1747–1807) average annual returns hovered around 10 percent. In his history of the slave trade Thomas estimated a profit of 9.5 percent between 1761 and 1807, with an average high of 13 percent between 1791 and 1800 and an average low of 3.3 percent between 1801 and 1807. John Tarleton, a slave trader from Liverpool, testified before a Parliamentary committee of inquiry convened in 1789 that "10 percent ought to be the net profit in the African trade." Liverpool slaver William Davenport averaged a 10.5 percent return on seventy-four voyages. Meanwhile, Richard Oswald, Augustus Boyd, and Sir Alexander Grant made £30,000 from sixty slave expeditions, or only £500 per voyage and an average profit of 6 percent. Almost half of the Dutch slave voyages during the second half of the eighteenth century registered losses, with the Dutch West India Company showing a profit slightly greater than 3 percent. Between 1761 and 1800 the Middleburg Company earned annual profits from the slave trade of only 1.43 percent, even though the company had made an 8 percent profit between 1751 and 1760. Many on the board of directors of the Danish West India Company, including bookkeeper Frederick Holmstead, argued that the slave trade was unprofitable and thus ought to be abandoned.

Those pressing for the abolition of slavery itself had, ironically, arrived at similar conclusions. As historian David Brion Davis has demonstrated, the British abolitionists' interpretation of the history of the slave trade gave them ample reason for optimism. The growing demand for sugar had stimulated the expansion of the Atlantic slave trade, but the immense profits that the cultivation of sugar generated in the British Caribbean rested on precarious foundations. If the demand for sugar on the world market fell, if overproduction drove down the price, or if costs, including the price of slaves, increased, the prosperity of the sugar colonies would be in immediate and serious jeopardy.

The American War for Independence (1775–1783) brought on many of the conditions necessary to disrupt the prosperity of the British West Indies and thus to end the slave trade. The war, in fact, temporarily halted the slave trade and curtailed the flow of provisions from North America, giving rise to famine and inflation in the British Caribbean. The loss of the American colonies not only meant that the West Indian planters relinquished valuable markets, but also that merchants in the United States could now legally trade with planters in the French Caribbean and thus contribute to the sensational development of Saint Domingue, which flooded European markets with inexpensive sugar, cacao, cotton, and indigo. To British abolitionists, it seemed that slavery, at least within the Empire, was on its way to extinction, and with it the slave trade, which proved no longer capable of sustaining even its formerly modest level of profitability.

Economic historians now generally concur that the profits the Atlantic slave trade generated, though substantial, were far from extraordinary. Herbert S. Klein has written that "the average 10 percent rate obtained [by] the eighteenth-century French and English slave traders was considered a good profit rate at the time but not out of the range of other contemporary investments." Thomas added that "considerable profits were made in the slave trade in the seventeenth and eighteenth centuries. At the end of the latter era, however, prices of slaves rose considerably in Africa so that profits averaged 8 to 10 percent, the same kind of percentage obtained in much more ordinary commercial undertakings." Although some fortunate, cunning, or intrepid merchants continued to amass great wealth from the slave trade, the costs they incurred had, by the end of the eighteenth century, considerably limited even their profits.

–MEG GREENE,
MIDLOTHIAN, VIRGINIA

References

Roger Anstey, *The Atlantic Slave Trade and British Abolition, 1760–1810* (Atlantic Highlands, N.J.: Humanities Press, 1975).

Anstey, "The Volume and Profitability of the British Slave Trade, 1761–1807," in *Race and Slavery in the Western Hemisphere: Quan-*

titative Studies, edited by Stanley L. Engerman and Eugene D. Genovese (Princeton: Princeton University Press, 1975), pp. 3–31.

Stephen D. Behrendt, "The British Slave Trade, 1785–1807: Volume, Profitability, and Mortality," dissertation, University of Wisconsin-Madison, 1993.

Philip D. Curtin, "Measuring the Atlantic Slave Trade," in Race and Slavery in the Western Hemisphere: Quantitative Studies, edited by Engerman and Genovese (Princeton: Princeton University Press, 1975), pp. 107–128.

David Brion Davis, The Problem of Slavery in the Age of Revolution, 1770–1823 (Ithaca, N.Y.: Cornell University Press, 1975).

Engerman, "The Slave Trade and British Capital Formation in the Eighteenth Century: A Comment on the Williams Thesis," Business History Review, 44 (Winter 1972): 430–443.

Herbert S. Klein, The Atlantic Slave Trade (Cambridge & New York: Cambridge University Press, 1999).

Klein, "Economic Aspects of the Eighteenth-Century Atlantic Slave Trade," in The Rise of Merchant Empires: Long-Distance Trade in the Early Modern World, 1350–1750, edited by James D. Tracy (Cambridge & New York: Cambridge University Press, 1990), pp. 287–310.

Peter Kolchin, American Slavery, 1619–1877 (New York: Hill & Wang, 1993).

David Northrup, ed., The Atlantic Slave Trade, second edition (Boston: Houghton Mifflin, 2002).

James A. Rawley, The Transatlantic Slave Trade: A History (New York: Norton, 1981).

Edward Reynolds, Stand the Storm: A History of the Atlantic Slave Trade (London & New York: Allison & Busby, 1985).

Frank Tannenbaum, Slave and Citizen: The Negro in the Americas (New York: Knopf, 1946).

Hugh Thomas, The Slave Trade: The Story of the Atlantic Slave Trade: 1440–1870 (New York: Simon & Schuster, 1997).

Eric Williams, Capitalism & Slavery (Chapel Hill: University of North Carolina Press, 1944).

TRANSATLANTIC SLAVE TRADE

U. S. CIVIL WAR

Did slavery cause the Civil War?

Viewpoint: Yes. Slavery was the essential issue that divided the South from the North.

Viewpoint: No. Slavery was only one cause of the Civil War; a variety of political, economic, social, and cultural factors contributed to the conflict.

Was the Civil War (1861–1865) fought to save the Union, to defend states' rights and assert Southern independence, or to free the slaves? Can historians ever hope to untangle these questions and analyze them in isolation from one another? The conflict over slavery, or more accurately over the expansion of slavery into the Western territories, precipitated the war, but partisans on neither side wished to make slavery the central issue. Rather, Confederates argued that they fought to confirm the right of secession and the ability to establish an independent nation. Unionists, by contrast, said that they fought to prevent Southerners from dismantling the United States. In his First Inaugural Address (4 March 1861) President Abraham Lincoln declared his opposition to the expansion of slavery but reassured Southerners that he had no intention of interfering with slavery where it already existed. "I have no purpose, directly or indirectly," Lincoln stated, "to interfere with the institution of slavery in the States where it exists. I believe I have no lawful right to do so, and I have no inclination to do so." His objective, he proclaimed even after the war had begun, was to save the Union.

As late as August 1862 Lincoln still refused to concede that the abolition of slavery was his reason for prosecuting the war. In a letter written to Horace Greeley, the antislavery editor of the New York *Tribune,* Lincoln wrote:

> My paramount objective in this struggle *is* to save the Union, and is *not* either to save or destroy slavery. If I could save the Union without freeing *any* slave I would do it, and if I could save it by freeing *all* the slaves I would do it; and if I could save it by freeing some and leaving others alone I would also do that. What I do about slavery, and the colored race, I do because I believe it helps to save the Union; and what I forbear, I forbear because I do *not* believe it would save the Union.

Only diplomatic and military necessity at last prompted Lincoln to broaden Union war aims. Redefining the war as an effort to eradicate slavery muted foreign, especially British, sympathy for the Confederate cause. At the same time, championing emancipation also helped to revitalize flagging enthusiasm for the war in the North. The longer the war continued and the bloodier it got, the more the conservative attempt to restore the Union developed into a revolutionary crusade to end slavery, a transformation that was symbolically completed when Lincoln issued the Emancipation Proclamation on 1 January 1863.

As Federal troops occupied more Confederate territory, the war against slavery quickened. Although some white Southerners entertained illusions that slavery remained inviolate even after the war, the slaves themselves grew restive as Union troops approached. They deserted the plantations and swarmed Union lines to offer their services as laborers, cooks, laundresses, and, of course, soldiers. Whatever else the war might have been about, whether preserving the Union, exonerating states' rights, or asserting Southern independence, for blacks the principal cause of the war had always been slavery and the main purpose of the war its abolition. When presented with an opportunity to bring those ideas and hopes to fulfillment, the slaves eagerly struck a blow in the name of freedom.

Viewpoint:
Yes. Slavery was the essential issue that divided the South from the North.

Even before the Civil War (1861–1865) began, debates about the causes already raged. In 1858, for example, Republican Senator William Henry Seward of New York identified two alternate explanations of the sectional tension that, within three years, divided the nation and exploded into war. There were, Seward argued, those who regarded the sectional enmity as "accidental, unnecessary, [and] the work of interested or fanatical agitators." In contrast (and opposition) to this group were others who, like Seward himself, believed there to be "an irrepressible conflict between opposing and enduring forces." Although Seward had no way of knowing that he had done so, he outlined the contours of a debate that has engaged historians ever since.

The argument that the Civil War was "an irrepressible conflict" between the advocates and opponents of slavery commanded the historiography early on. In the decades immediately following the war, historians generally reflected the views of contemporaries who had participated in the conflict. To victorious Northerners, whose interpretations prevailed, the war became a struggle between good and evil—a struggle that the depravity and sinfulness of the slaveholders had made inevitable. According to this explanation, Southerners' unwillingness to emancipate their slaves and their stubborn insistence on expanding slavery into the Western territories not only had led to war but also had transformed that war into a moral crusade intent upon purging the land of evil. In *History of the Rise and Fall of the Slave Power* (1872–1877) Henry Wilson contended that Northerners had fought to preserve both the Union and the system of free labor. They had taken up arms, Wilson observed, to defeat the insidious designs of Southerners who would have destroyed capitalism and country to preserve bondage and tyranny.

A more moderate study that reached essentially the same conclusions was James Ford Rhodes's monumental *History of the United States from the Compromise of 1850* (1893–1900). Like Wilson, Rhodes identified slavery as the major, indeed as the only, cause of the war. "If the Negro had not been brought to America," Rhodes declared, "the Civil War could not have occurred." Since the Northern and Southern views of slavery had, by the 1850s, become entrenched, intractable, and irreconcilable, Rhodes concluded that compromise was impossible and that war was thus "inevitable."

Although Rhodes focused on the moral and political controversy over slavery, he suggested at the same time that the Civil War mirrored fundamental antagonisms between the Northern and Southern economic and labor systems, which, as it turned out, also emerged as a result of the Southern commitment to slavery. Almost three decades passed before the notion that the war was an irrepressible economic rather than moral conflict received full, careful, and serious attention in Charles and Mary Beard's *The Rise of American Civilization* (1927). The Beards maintained that slavery was not principally a social or cultural institution but an economic one, a system of organizing labor, not society. "Inherent antagonisms" existed between Northern industrialists and Southern planters, each seeking to dominate the federal government in order to safeguard its economic interests. Both the industrialists and planters argued about slavery and states' rights to conceal their real quest for political and economic power.

The economic determinism of the Beards' interpretation influenced a generation of historians. Yet, most of those who thought the Civil War "an irrepressible conflict" continued to search for its causes in the realm of political, social, and cultural history. Allan Nevins underscored the importance of the social and cultural differences dividing the North and the South in his great work, *The Ordeal of the Union* (1947–1971). Northerners and Southerners, Nevins suggested, "were rapidly becoming separate peoples." At the root of this divergence was slavery.

Those historians who determined that war was an inevitable consequence of the fundamental antagonisms that slavery engendered nonetheless differed markedly over whether to emphasize moral, cultural, social, political, ideological, or economic causes. They generally

U. S. CIVIL WAR

agreed, however, that the animosity between the North and the South was entrenched in the two societies, one slave and the other free, and that what Nevins called the crisis of the Union was ultimately irrepressible.

Other historians rejected those conclusions and insisted that the differences between the North and the South were not sufficiently important or irreconcilable to have started a war. The Civil War, according to this analysis, was a tragic occurrence that more judicious statesmen could have avoided. President James Buchanan was perhaps the first to advocate the idea that war was not inexorable, just as Senator Seward was among the first who thought that it was. Buchanan was convinced that extremists, radicals, and agitators in both the North and the South had unnecessarily encouraged the sectional hostility that culminated in war. Had more prudent men silenced the fanatics, war would not have come. Many Southerners who wrote at the end of the nineteenth century similarly asserted that the antislavery fanaticism of the Republican Party had been responsible for inciting controversy and conflict.

The thesis that war could have been avoided or prevented did not gain widespread currency among historians until the 1920s and 1930s. Among the leading revisionists was James G. Randall, who discovered no difference so elemental and deep-seated in the government, society, or culture of the North and South as to necessitate war. In *The Civil War and Reconstruction,* originally published in 1937, Randall asserted that slavery was essentially benign and was, in any event, already "crumbling in the presence of nineteenth-century tendencies" such as the rise and spread of democracy. Only the political incompetence of a "blundering generation" of statesmen had brought on the Civil War.

Avery Craven, another prolific revisionist historian, emphasized slavery as a cause of war more than Randall had done. Yet, in *The Coming of the Civil War* (1942) Craven also remarked that the condition of the slaves was not appreciably worse than that of Northern factory workers, and he agreed with Randall that slavery was on its way to "ultimate extinction." Americans did not have to slaughter one another in a terrible war to destroy it. They could have averted war altogether, Craven wrote, had more skillful and responsible political leadership endeavored to achieve a real and enduring compromise.

Since the 1960s many students of the war have modified and yet retained key elements of the revisionist thesis by accentuating the role of political agitation in causing the war. In

Charles Sumner and the Coming of the Civil War (1960), for example, David Herbert Donald affirmed that the politicians of the 1840s and 1850s were not unusually inept. Rather, they had the misfortune to operate at a time when extensive economic changes and the rapid spread of democracy had eroded traditional social, moral, and political restraints. Thus, the temperate, circumspect resolutions to problems and differences that had worked in the past no longer applied.

In *The Political Crisis of the 1850s* (1978) Michael Holt stressed the importance of the party system, rather than of irreconcilable differences between the North and South, to detail the causes of civil war. Holt, though, was careful to avoid blaming any one section, group (such as slaveholders or abolitionists), or political party. "Much of the story of the coming of the Civil War," he concluded, "is the story of the successful efforts of Democratic politicians in the South and Republican politicians in the North to keep the sectional conflict at the center of the political debate."

Although the revisionist interpretation has of late gained ascendancy and made important contributions to the understanding of the Civil War, the traditional interpretation that the war was an "irrepressible conflict" has not disappeared, and indeed has, since the 1970s, recovered a portion of its former credibility. In *Free Soil, Free Labor, Free Men: The Ideology of the Republican Party before the Civil War* (1970) Eric Foner made a powerful restatement of the thesis that the war was an "irrepressible conflict," emphasizing the importance of the ideology of free labor to winning support for the antislavery cause. The abolitionists' moral outrage over slavery, Foner contended, did not prevail in the North. Northerners who opposed slavery, including Abraham Lincoln, did so primarily because they feared that it might spread to the North and West and thereby jeopardize the status of free white laborers. Racism made many of the enemies of slavery more concerned with its effects on whites than on blacks. Fearful that Southerners intended to extend slavery, Northerners, Foner avowed, were equally bent on eradicating it. Such a determination made conflict inevitable.

The lines of historical debate are clear, but even after a conscientious reading of the varying authorities it is still unclear whether Americans are any closer to understanding the role slavery played in causing a war that remains the worst, and most tragic, ordeal in their national history. Slavery was essential to all that divided the North and the South and, as such, was the most important cause of the

U. S. CIVIL WAR

Civil War. The war, however, was no mere struggle between good and evil. It was, to be sure, a moral struggle—a struggle, as Eugene D. Genovese has long maintained, between rival societies organized around rival social systems and dominated by rival social classes, each seeking to vindicate the ways of God to man. Understood in this way, the war no longer seems a melodrama in which the heroes and the villains are easily identifiable; rather, the tragic character of the Civil War becomes clearer if historians approach it as a relentless struggle between two divergent societies and two alternate conceptions of the good. For their part the slaveholders of the South, who thought of themselves as humane and Christian gentlemen, could not have voluntarily given up their slaves. Doing so, in their minds, would have constituted an abdication of their moral responsibilities, a failure to uphold the obligations with which God had entrusted them. They preferred to go down in blood rather than to compromise, even though it made sense to rid themselves and their society of slavery, which was arresting Southern economic development. As many Southerners read the signs of the dreadful times to come, they concluded that their only hope of preserving their way of life lay in making a bold and desperate attempt to win their independence from the Union. Their faith, pride, and determination made surrender to gradual defeat and resignation to the slow and painful death of their world and their way of life unthinkable.

Historians, whatever their ideological perspective, can thus not avoid a confrontation with the tragic dimensions of the Civil War. Southern slaveholders believed that slavery provided for a far more humane and Christian social order than did the emerging industrial capitalism of the North. Just as Northerners feared a Southern threat, so Southerners persuaded themselves that Northerners had grown implacably hostile to their social system, their economic and political interests, their values, their morals, their worldview, and their way of life. Yet, for all the integrity and honor that Southerners displayed, slavery was among the greatest enormities of the nineteenth century, and, one way or another, slavery had to go. The war that ultimately brought about its destruction was an all but inevitable engagement between two increasingly divergent civilizations, issued from the same seed, but, by 1860, no longer able to live together under the same government or to coexist within a single nation.

—MARK G. MALVASI,
RANDOLPH-MACON COLLEGE

Viewpoint:
No. Slavery was only one cause of the Civil War; a variety of political, economic, social, and cultural factors contributed to the conflict.

The question "Did slavery cause the Civil War?" should elicit concern from professional historians, who are trained to avoid the epistemological danger of reducing complex matters to simplistic explanations. No great event in human history can ever be traced to a single cause or be subject to only one interpretation. The nature of human experience means our interpretations of the past depend upon our connection to those events. Facts do not speak for themselves, and as with most aspects of human existence, the interpretation of the facts depends upon many factors. Often, some facts "speak" louder than others, whether they deserve to do so or not. The relation between slavery and the Civil War (1861–1865) is just such a case. Americans would like to think that the Civil War was caused only by the aberration of slavery. Had slavery not existed, there would have been no divergence between the North and South, and thus no war. Unfortunately, history is never so simple.

The overemphasis on slavery resulted from a series of methodological mistakes committed by historians. Their first mistake was to attribute the behavior of Southern statesmen from the American Revolution (1775–1783) until the Civil War to the defense of slavery as an economic system. It was then claimed that Southern politicians, faced with the inevitable triumph of Northern free labor and industrialization over Southern agriculture and slavery, increasingly became more defensive of their section's interests from the mid 1840s forward. Racism also served as a motivating factor since these same politicians evidently feared that a collision of white and black Southerners would be unavoidable without slavery. Thus, determined to protect their economic system from inevitable decline and preserve a hierarchy of race, Southern politicians led their states out of the Union in 1860 and 1861. In short, the preservation of Southern society had to depend upon the preservation of slavery.

Setting aside the fact that only 25 percent of white Southerners owned slaves in 1860, there was more to the South than slavery. Strong evidence suggests that what was definitely "Southern" in the nineteenth century developed before slavery became entrenched. African slaves lived in the colonial South as early as the 1610s, though their numbers remained relatively low until the 1670s when Virginia planters began shifting

U. S. CIVIL WAR

away from indentured European labor. Until then Africans and slavery exhibited little impact upon the developing Southern culture relative to the influence of British ethnic groups. Cultural historians such as David Hackett Fischer maintain that the first settlers in an area determine its cultural features if the native population is forced out. Culturally speaking, the South developed as Celtic ethnic groups settled the backcountry and English gentry populated tidewater plantations, which depended upon white labor at the time of settlement. Virtually all of what is distinctive about Southern culture emerged during the amalgamation of these cultural groups in the late seventeenth and early eighteenth centuries. Subsequent groups such as Africans and Caribbean planters made a slight difference, but most adapted to the society and culture that they found already in place. Admittedly, one may not be able to talk of "The South" at such an early date, but observers at the time understood the area was distinct from New England and the Delaware Valley. Southern family life, social bonds, community standards, politics, religion, and economics distilled into a definitive social order distinct from the presence of slavery nearly a full century before the American Revolution. In many ways slavery had to adapt to Southern society, not the other way around.

The second mistake leading to slavery's overemphasis requires a more substantive investigation. Even if slavery was not the definitive characteristic of the Old South, many historians assume Southern desires to preserve the institution led to increased sectional hostility that prevented national political compromises.

A better explanation of sectionalism takes into account a variety of factors, not just slavery. One can speak of sectionalism in light of the cultural patterns that evolved in the North American colonies in addition to the political development of the early republic, but only with certain caveats. Southerners were more alike than different when compared to the Northwest, New England, and the Delaware Valley, just as people from these areas were distinct when compared to the South. However, one must be careful when attributing specific political principles to all white Southerners. Democrats in Mississippi shared more in common with Democrats in New York than they did with Whigs in Georgia. Southern politicians took opposite stands on the important issues of Hamiltonian finance, the Bank of the United States, protective tariffs, internal improvements, foreign policy, and land policy. Eminent Southern statesmen disagreed on the preservation of, and the moral justification for, slavery. Southerners were the leading advocates of the War of 1812 as well as its leading critics. Some supported a monetary system based on hard currency (gold and silver); some supported the circulation of paper currency, inflation, and free banking. The South had its share of nationalists as well as Jeffersonian states' rights men.

Amid this diversity of views and opinions, no strong evidence exists to suggest that Southerners were either obsessed with the preservation of slavery at the national level or that most American politicians and voters self-consciously voted along sectional lines. Some historians and political scientists, such as Lee Benson and Joel Silbey, have examined the voting patterns of various districts and states in the North and South as well as the voting patterns of Congressmen and found no discernable increase in sectional voting during the 1840s and 1850s. People voted chiefly along party, rather than regional, lines. Even on the highly controversial compromises involving slavery in the territories, Congressmen displayed great willingness to move beyond sectional concerns. Of course, some Congressmen strictly voted the "Northern" or "Southern" position, but they comprised a minority, not the majority, of Congressmen during the generation leading up to the Civil War. Neither did those who voted along sectional lines do so more often than Congressmen who had served between 1789 and the 1830s.

Even if one assumes that sectional disagreement grew out of the slavery controversy, it cannot be shown that the issue of slavery was solely about servitude. In short, slavery as a national political issue involved much more than whether a person believed human beings should own another person.

Prior to the War of 1812 the key issues affecting national politics included the relations between the federal and state governments, federal and state controls over the economy, the handling of government debt, the separation of powers, and foreign policy, which involved Western lands and Indian relations. The Framers did not hand down an explicit solution to these issues but left it up to the American people to solve them as they saw fit. As a result political parties soon appeared as a means of coordinating and galvanizing public opinion. The first party system developed largely in response to Alexander Hamilton's financial plan whereby federal revenue would be supplemented by debt issued by the Bank of the United States, factories would be protected from foreign competition through high-tariff barriers, and the value of the country's monetary base would be controlled by a national mint. Jeffersonian Republicans responded by claiming the Federalist Party's fiscal platform harmed consumers in general and farmers in particular by redistrib-

THE CRITTENDEN RESOLUTION

In July 1861 John J. Crittenden of Kentucky introduced a resolution in the House of Representatives affirming Union war aims; all but two of the Congressmen voted for the resolution. The phrase established institutions of those States refers to slavery in the Border States of Delaware, Maryland, Kentucky, and Missouri.

Resolved by the House of Representatives of the Congress of the United States, That the present deplorable civil war has been forced upon the country by the disunionists of the Southern States now in revolt against the constitutional Government and in arms around the capital; that in this national emergency Congress, banishing all feelings of mere passion or resentment, will recollect only its duty to the whole country; that this war is not waged upon our part in any spirit of oppression, nor for any purpose of conquest or subjugation, nor purpose of overthrowing or interfering with the rights or established institutions of those States, but to defend and maintain the supremacy of the Constitution and to preserve the Union, with all the dignity, equality, and rights of the several States unimpaired; and that as soon as these objects are accomplished the war ought to cease.

Source: James D. Richardson, A Compilation of the Messages and Papers of the Presidents, *volume 6 (Washington, D.C.: U.S. Government Printing Office, 1907), p. 430.*

uting wealth from agrarian interests to commercial and manufacturing interests.

Conflict, rather than consensus, thus characterized the early republic as financial issues evolved into intense disagreement on national matters once considered closed: federalism, constitutional interpretation, and the separation of powers. Shortly before the War of 1812 new issues, such as federal subsidization of internal improvements, further polarized the country. Though discernable regional affiliation in the parties could be seen, the first parties enjoyed support in all areas of the country and exerted a unifying influence, albeit at the price of partisan bickering, upon the nation.

As the first party system of Federalists versus Democratic-Republicans broke down in the 1810s and a second party system of Whigs and Democrats emerged, partisans struggled to focus on issues that could maintain their national prominence. At this point the issue of slavery in the territories proved to be an indispensable political symbol in the realignment of national politics.

The early-nineteenth-century South possessed Jeffersonian politicians disproportionate to their number in other regions. Since Southern Jeffersonians typically opposed the political economy of federal interventionism in the form of a central bank, federally subsidized internal improvements, and high protective tariffs, stopping the spread of slavery could potentially stop the spread of Jeffersonian voters. Politicians from New York, New England, and Pennsylvania, the areas with the strongest pronationalist sentiment, failed to keep slavery out of the Alabama and Arkansas territories but were finally successful with the admittance of Missouri in 1821. A few restrictionists hoped to stop the spread of something they considered morally evil, but most used slavery as a political tool to damage the people they blamed for the North's economic decline. As Eliza Cushman of Massachusetts summarized the situation: "That [federal] power which authoritatively said to the North *give up,* will with equal effect say to the South *keep back,* and to the West, *peace, be still*!" Claiming to be antislavery correlated directly to being in favor of the federal government's energetic presence in the American economy and continuing the Hamiltonian legacy.

Jeffersonian Republicans also seized the opportunity of the Missouri crisis to use slavery for their own political purposes. Slavery perfectly encapsulated what they believed plagued American politics: zealous politicians eager to use the energy and power of the federal government to further their economic interests at the expense of the rest. Jeffersonian Republicans used the restriction of slavery to illustrate how Congress exceeded its delegated constitutional authority. If Congress could take away the slaves of people going west, then it could also take away other forms of legal property. This message resonated with liberally minded Americans in the South, but also in New York, Pennsylvania, and even in New England. In the end slavery emerged as a litmus test, not of a person's moral beliefs, but of what he thought about the Constitution, federalism, and economic freedom. Given the partisan atmosphere of the time, politicians probably would have searched for another issue to serve this purpose had slavery not been present. The second party system's emergence did not depend upon the existence of slavery. Rather, the very nature of democratic politics created a vortex that absorbed and made use of all facets of society.

The symbolism of slavery eventually served to defeat the second party system precisely because it was not strong enough to generate partisan unity. No matter how clear the issue of slavery might have been in the early 1820s, it increasingly became too muddled and simplistic, especially after Americans began rejecting the Whig Party's platform of banking, tariffs, and internal improvements. Across the country in the 1830s and 1840s Americans experimented with Whig policies. Canals and railroads were subsidized, tariff rates remained moderately high, and many politicians campaigned for the creation of another federal central bank. The Democratic Party remained a stalwart defender of Jeffersonian political economy, free markets, and limited government. When the programs inspired by the American system suffered bankruptcy or displayed evidence of political corruption, voters started withdrawing their support for the Whigs. The final blow came with the presidency of James K. Polk (1845–1849), who vetoed several Whig proposals and reduced or eliminated federal funding for others. Even Polk's war against Mexico (1846–1848) followed strict Jeffersonian political economy inasmuch as it was the only war the country ever paid for in cash.

As with the collapse of the first party system, partisans struggled in the late 1840s and early 1850s to reinvigorate their supporters. Again politicians turned to the issue of slavery in the territories to serve as a litmus test for one's political position. However, slavery failed to achieve the same level of symbolic unanimity for both the Democrats and Whigs. Both parties split on the issue of slavery, but it was precisely because slavery could not foster the kind of political agreement it had done in the 1820s and 1830s. Why this situation occurred explains why slavery was not the sole cause of the Civil War.

By the 1850s several developments had occurred in American society that took the focus away from slavery. Of course, there were always other national issues besides slavery, and many of these, such as tariffs and foreign policy, commanded greater attention. Yet, national issues in the 1850s included things not easily connected to the peculiar institution. Reaction to rising immigration as well as religious and reform crusades associated with the Second Great Awakening quickly caught the attention of voters in every state and region. Cultural change had already gripped industrializing areas of the North, prompting shifts in northern attitudes, values, and religious sentiments. Furthermore, Northern nationalists saw their political agenda crumble and blamed Southern conservatives for the defeat. Slavery might have aggravated the situation, but it did not cause the zealotry that motivated members of the Republican Party, which was composed of a medley of disaffected groups and interests.

The election of Abraham Lincoln in 1860 with less than 40 percent of the popular vote prompted an immediate response from those Southerners convinced that majority rule no longer applied to American politics. If a minority party could control the White House, it was

thought that all forms of institutional checks and balances would falter. The passage in the House of a bill increasing tariffs and a free-homestead bill early in 1860 signified the likely appearance of other bills designed to benefit the North at the expense of the South. The lower South seceded fearing that its entire society, slavery included, was under immediate threat. Still, not all Southerners supported secession. If one claims threats to slavery caused secession, then how can one explain why literally thousands of slaveholders and millions of Southerners remained in the Union after the first wave of secession? Not until after the fall of Fort Sumter in April 1861 did the upper South leave, and this in direct response to the use of military force by the federal government against another state.

One can assemble a string of quotations, as some historians do, to claim that Southerners left the Union to preserve slavery. Just as easily one can find Southerners justifying secession based on a dedication to federalism, the Constitution, the rights secured by the American Revolution, and God. Slavery surely was better protected within the Union under the Constitution than out of the Union and in civil war.

The Civil War resulted from a long train of events. Some causes were intricately connected; others came together only by accident. Some things followed a linear development that could be traced back to the colonial period; other things appeared haphazardly. Eliminating one aspect of the chaotic assemblage of historical detail might have prevented the war, but one has no way of knowing. What is certain, however, is that the same could be said of any of the causes. Slavery was an important part of American history prior to the Civil War, but it was by no means the only important part.

–CAREY M. ROBERTS,
ARKANSAS TECH UNIVERSITY

References

Charles A. and Mary R. Beard, *The Rise of American Civilization*, 2 volumes (New York: Macmillan, 1927).

Lee Benson, *The Concept of Jacksonian Democracy: New York as a Test Case* (Princeton: Princeton University Press, 1961).

Thomas Bonner, "Civil War Historians and the 'Needless War' Doctrine," *Journal of the History of Ideas,* 17 (April 1956): 193–216.

Arthur C. Cole, *The Era of the Civil War, 1848–1870* (Springfield: Illinois Centennial Commission, 1919).

Avery Craven, *The Coming of the Civil War* (New York: Scribners, 1942).

Craven, *The Repressible Conflict, 1830–1861* (Baton Rouge: Louisiana State University Press, 1939).

Marshall DeRosa, *The Politics of Dissolution: The Quest for a National Identity & the American Civil War* (New Brunswick, N.J.: Transaction, 1998).

David Herbert Donald, "American Historians and the Causes of the Civil War," *South Atlantic Quarterly,* 59 (Summer 1960): 351–355.

Donald, *Charles Sumner and the Coming of the Civil War* (New York: Knopf, 1960).

Donald, *Liberty and Union* (Boston: Little, Brown, 1978).

David Hackett Fischer, *Albion's Seed: Four British Folkways in America* (Oxford: Oxford University Press, 1989).

Howard R. Floan, *The South in Northern Eyes, 1831 to 1861* (New York: Haskell House, 1973).

Eric Foner, *Free Soil, Free Labor, Free Men: The Ideology of the Republican Party before the Civil War* (New York: Oxford University Press, 1970).

Eugene D. Genovese, *A Consuming Fire: The Fall of the Confederacy in the Mind of the White Christian South* (Athens: University of Georgia Press, 1998).

Genovese, *The Political Economy of Slavery: Studies in the Economy and Society of the Slave South,* second edition (Hanover, N.H.: Wesleyan University Press, 1989).

Susan-Mary Grant, *North over South: Northern Nationalism and American Identity in the Antebellum Era* (Lawrence: University Press of Kansas, 2000).

Michael Holt, *The Political Crisis of the 1850s* (New York: Wiley, 1978).

Holt, *The Rise and Fall of the American Whig Party: Jacksonian Politics and the Onset of the Civil War* (Oxford: Oxford University Press, 1999).

Jeffrey Rogers Hummel, *Emancipating Slaves, Enslaving Free Men: A History of the American Civil War* (New York: Open Court, 1996).

Ludwell Johnson, *Division and Reunion: America, 1848–1877* (New York: Wiley, 1978).

James McPherson, *Battle Cry of Freedom: The Civil War Era* (New York: Oxford University Press, 1988).

Allan Nevins, *The Ordeal of the Union,* 8 volumes (New York: Scribners, 1947–1971).

Ann Norton, *Alternative Americas: A Reading of Antebellum Political Culture* (Chicago: University of Chicago Press, 1986).

David Potter, *The Impending Crisis, 1848–1861* (New York: Harper & Row, 1976).

Potter, *The South and the Sectional Conflict* (Baton Rouge: Louisiana State University Press, 1968).

James G. Randall and David Herbert Donald, *The Civil War and Reconstruction,* second revised edition (Lexington, Mass.: Heath, 1969).

James Ford Rhodes, *History of the United States from the Compromise of 1850,* 7 volumes (New York: Macmillan, 1893–1900).

John S. Rosenberg, "Toward a New Civil War Revisionism," *American Scholar,* 38 (Spring 1969): 250–272.

Joel H. Silbey, *The Partisan Imperative: The Dynamics of American Politics before the Civil War* (Oxford: Oxford University Press, 1985).

Ernest L. Tuveson, *Redeemer Nation: The Idea of America's Millennial Role* (Chicago: University of Chicago Press, 1974).

Eric Walther, *The Fire-Eaters* (Baton Rouge: Louisiana State University Press, 1992).

William Appleman Williams, *The Contours of American History* (Chicago: Quadrangle, 1966).

Henry Wilson, *History of the Rise and Fall of the Slave Power,* 3 volumes (Boston: Houghton, Mifflin, 1872–1877).

U. S. CIVIL WAR

REFERENCES

1. GENERAL

Ayers, Edward L. and others. *All Over the Map: Rethinking American Regions.* Baltimore: Johns Hopkins University Press, 1996.

Beard, Charles A. and Mary R. Beard. *The Rise of American Civilization.* 2 volumes. New York: Macmillan, 1927.

Calhoun, Arthur W. *A Social History of the American Family from Colonial Times to the Present.* 3 volumes. Cleveland, Ohio: Clark, 1917–1919.

Dew, Thomas Roderick. *A Digest of the Laws, Customs, Manners, and Institutions of the Ancient and Modern Nations.* New York: Appleton, 1853.

Glazer, Nathan and Daniel Patrick Moynihan. *Beyond the Melting Pot: The Negroes, Puerto Ricans, Jews, Italians, and Irish of New York City.* Cambridge, Mass.: MIT Press and Harvard University Press, 1963.

Gordon, Milton M. *Assimilation in American Life: The Role of Race, Religion, and National Origins.* New York: Oxford University Press, 1964.

Honour, Hugh. *The New Golden Land: European Images of America from the Discoveries to the Present Time.* New York: Pantheon, 1975.

Landes, David S. *Revolution in Time: Clocks and the Making of the Modern World.* Cambridge, Mass.: Belknap Press of Harvard University Press, 1983.

Lewis, R. W. B. *The American Adam: Innocence, Tragedy, and Tradition in the Nineteenth Century.* Chicago: University of Chicago Press, 1955.

Lloyd, Arthur Young. *The Slavery Controversy, 1831–1860.* Chapel Hill: University of North Carolina Press, 1939.

Miller, Randall M. and John David Smith, eds. *Dictionary of Afro-American Slavery.* Revised edition. Westport, Conn.: Praeger, 1997.

Rhodes, James Ford. *History of the United States from the Compromise of 1850.* 7 volumes. New York: Macmillan, 1893–1900.

Schlesinger, Arthur M., Jr. *The Disuniting of America: Reflections on a Multicultural Society.* Revised edition. New York: Norton, 1998.

Smith, Mark M. *Listening to Nineteenth-Century America.* Chapel Hill: University of North Carolina Press, 2001.

Williams, William Appleman. *The Contours of American History.* Chicago: Quadrangle, 1966.

Woodward, C. Vann. *American Counterpoint: Slavery and Racism in the North-South Dialogue.* Boston: Little, Brown, 1971.

2. ABOLITIONISM

Aptheker, Herbert. *Abolitionism: A Revolutionary Movement.* Boston: Twayne, 1989.

Barnes, Gilbert Hobbs. *The Antislavery Impulse, 1830–1844.* New York & London: Appleton, 1933.

Blackburn, Robin. *The Overthrow of Colonial Slavery, 1776–1848.* London & New York: Verso, 1988.

Cain, William E., ed. *William Lloyd Garrison and the Fight against Slavery: Selections from The Liberator.* Boston: Bedford Books of St. Martin's Press, 1995.

Channing, William Ellery. *Emancipation.* New York: American Anti-Slavery Society, 1841.

Drescher, Seymour. *Capitalism and Antislavery: British Mobilization in Comparative Perspective.* London: Macmillan, 1986.

Drescher. *Econocide: British Slavery in the Era of Abolition.* Pittsburgh: University of Pittsburgh Press, 1977.

Harrold, Stanley. *The Abolitionists and the South, 1831–1861.* Lexington: University of Kentucky Press, 1995.

Hart, Albert Bushnell. *Slavery and Abolition, 1831–1841.* New York & London: Harper, 1906.

Hawkins, Hugh, ed. *The Abolitionists: Means, Ends, and Motivations.* Lexington, Mass.: Heath, 1972.

Kraditor, Aileen S. *Means and Ends in American Abolitionism: Garrison and His Critics on Strategy and Tactics, 1834–1850.* New York: Pantheon, 1969.

Newman, Richard S. *The Transformation of American Abolitionism: Fighting Slavery in the Early Republic.* Chapel Hill: University of North Carolina Press, 2002.

Quarles, Benjamin. *Black Abolitionists.* New York: Oxford University Press, 1969.

Rice, C. Duncan. *The Rise and Fall of Black Slavery.* New York: Harper & Row, 1975.

Sorin, Gerald. *Abolitionism: A New Perspective.* New York: Praeger, 1972.

Stewart, James Brewer. *Holy Warriors: The Abolitionists and American Slavery.* New York: Hill & Wang, 1976.

Stowe, Harriet Beecher. *Uncle Tom's Cabin Or, Life Among the Lowly.* Boston: Jewett, 1852.

Temperley, Howard. *British Antislavery, 1833–1870.* London: Longman, 1972.

Turley, David. *The Culture of English Antislavery, 1780–1860.* London & New York: Routledge, 1991.

Wayland, Francis. *Elements of Moral Science.* New York: Cooke, 1835.

Weld, Theodore Dwight. *American Slavery as It Is: Testimony of a Thousand Witnesses*. New York: American Anti-Slavery Society, 1839.

Woolman, John. *Some Considerations on the Keeping of Negroes, 1754: Considerations on Keeping Negroes, 1762*. Northampton, Mass.: Gehenna Press, 1970.

3. AFRICAN AMERICANS AND ETHNICITY

Abrahams, Roger D. *Positively Black*. Englewood Cliffs, N.J.: Prentice-Hall, 1970.

Asante, Molefi Kete. *The Afrocentric Idea*. Revised edition. Philadelphia: Temple University Press, 1998.

Asante. *Afrocentricity*. Revised edition. Trenton, N.J.: African World Press, 1988.

Bennett, Lerone, Jr. *Before the Mayflower: A History of Black America*. Fifth edition. Chicago: Johnson, 1982.

Bittker, Boris I. *The Case for Black Reparations*. New York: Random House, 1973.

Drimmer, Melvin, ed. *Black History: A Reappraisal*. Garden City, N.Y.: Doubleday, 1968.

Ellison, Ralph. *Shadow and Act*. New York: Random House, 1964.

Franklin, John Hope and Alfred A. Moss Jr. *From Slavery to Freedom: A History of African Americans*. Seventh edition. New York: McGraw-Hill, 1994.

Frazier, E. Franklin. *The Negro Family in Chicago*. Chicago: University of Chicago Press, 1932.

Frazier. *The Negro Family in the United States*. Chicago: University of Chicago Press, 1939.

Frazier. *The Negro in the United States*. Revised edition. New York: Macmillan, 1949.

Frazier. *Race and Culture Contacts in the Modern World*. New York: Knopf, 1957.

Fredrickson, George M. *The Arrogance of Race: Historical Perspectives on Slavery, Racism, and Social Inequality*. Middletown, Conn.: Wesleyan University Press, 1988.

Fredrickson. *The Black Image in the White Mind: The Debate on Afro-American Character and Destiny, 1817–1914*. New York: Harper & Row, 1971.

Fuchs, Lawrence H. *The American Kaleidoscope: Race, Ethnicity, and Civil Culture*. Hanover, N.H.: Wesleyan University Press, 1990.

Harding, Vincent. *There Is a River: The Black Struggle for Freedom in America*. New York: Harcourt Brace Jovanovich, 1981.

Herskovits, Melville J. *The Myth of the Negro Past*. New York & London: Harper, 1941.

Jones, Leroi (Imamu Amiri Baraka). *Home: Social Essays*. New York: Morrow, 1966.

Jordan, Winthrop D. *The White Man's Burden: Historical Origins of Racism in the United States*. New York: Oxford University Press, 1974.

Kardiner, Abram and Lionel Ovesey. *The Mark of Oppression: A Psychosocial Study of the American Negro*. New York: Norton, 1951.

Karenga, Maulana. *Introduction to Black Studies*. Third edition. Los Angeles: University of Sankore Press, 2002.

Lemann, Nicholas. *The Promised Land: The Great Black Migration and How It Changed America*. New York: Knopf, 1991.

Lomotey, Kofi, ed. *Going to School: The African-American Experience*. Albany: State University of New York Press, 1990.

Lyman, Stanford M. *The Black American in Sociological Thought*. New York: Putnam, 1972.

Morrison, Toni. *Beloved*. New York: Knopf, 1987.

Myrdal, Gunnar. *An American Dilemma: The Negro Problem and Modern Democracy*. New York & London: Harper, 1944.

Quarles, Benjamin. *The Negro in the Making of America*. Second revised edition. New York: Collier / London: Collier-Macmillan, 1987.

Rainwater, Lee and William L. Yancey, eds. *The Moynihan Report and the Politics of Controversy: A Transaction Social Science and Public Policy Report*. Cambridge, Mass.: MIT Press, 1967.

Robinson, Armstead L., Craig C. Foster, and Donald H. Ogilvie, eds. *Black Studies in the University: A Symposium*. New Haven: Yale University Press, 1969.

Robinson, Randall. *The Debt: What America Owes to Blacks*. New York: Dutton, 2000.

Tannenbaum, Frank. *Slave and Citizen: The Negro in the Americas*. New York: Knopf, 1946.

Tillinghast, Joseph Alexander. *The Negro in Africa and America*. New York: American Economic Association by Macmillan / London: Sonnenschein, 1902.

Van Deburg, William L. *New Day in Babylon: The Black Power Movement and American Culture, 1965–1975*. Chicago: University of Chicago Press, 1992.

Vlach, John Michael. *The Afro-American Tradition in Decorative Arts*. Cleveland: Cleveland Museum of Art, 1978.

Vlach. *By The Work of Their Hands: Studies in Afro-American Folklife*. Charlottesville: University Press of Virginia, 1991.

Warren, Robert Penn. *Who Speaks for the Negro?* New York: Random House, 1965.

Weatherford, W. D. *The Negro from Africa to America*. New York: Doran, 1924.

West, Cornel. *Race Matters*. Boston: Beacon, 1993.

Williamson, Joel. *New People: Miscegenation and Mulattoes in the United States*. New York: Free Press, 1980.

Woodson, Carter G. *The Negro in Our History*. Washington, D.C.: Associated Publishers, 1922.

Wright, Richard. *Twelve Million Black Voices: A Folk History of the Negro in the United States of America*. New York: Viking, 1941.

4. AFRICAN BACKGROUND

Bosman, Willem. *A New and Accurate Description of the Coast of Guinea, Divided into the Gold, the Slave, and the Ivory Coasts*. London: Knapton and others, 1705.

Cooper, Frederick. *Plantation Slavery on the East Coast of Africa*. New Haven: Yale University Press, 1977.

Eldridge, Elizabeth A. and Fred Morton, eds. *Slavery in South Africa: Captive Labor on the Dutch Frontier*. Boulder, Colo.: Westview Press / Pietermaritzburg: University of Natal Press, 1994.

Hair, P. E. H., Adam Jones, and Robin Law, eds. *Barbot on Guinea: The Writings of Heard Barbot on West Africa, 1678–1712*. 2 volumes. London: Hakluyt Society, 1992.

Herskovits, Melville J. *Dahomey: An Ancient West African Kingdom*. New York: Augustin, 1938.

Inikori, Joseph E., ed. *Forced Migration: The Impact of the Export Slave Trade on African Societies*. New York: Africana / London: Hutchinson, 1982.

Lovejoy, Paul E. *Transformations in Slavery: A History of Slavery in Africa*. Cambridge & New York: Cambridge University Press, 1983.

Manning, Patrick. *Slavery and African Life: Occidental, Oriental, and African Slave Traders*. Cambridge & New York: Cambridge University Press, 1990.

Miers, Suzanne and Igor Kopytoff, eds. *The End of Slavery in Africa*. Madison: University of Wisconsin Press, 1988.

Miers and Richard Roberts, eds. *Slavery in Africa: Historical and Anthropological Perspectives*. Madison: University of Wisconsin Press, 1977.

Rodney, Walter. *How Europe Underdeveloped Africa*. Revised edition. Washington, D.C.: Howard University Press, 1972.

Thornton, John. *Africa and Africans in the Making of the Atlantic World, 1400–1680*. Cambridge & New York: Cambridge University Press, 1992.

Worden, Nigel. *Slavery in Dutch South Africa*. Cambridge & New York: Cambridge University Press, 1985.

5. AMERICAN COLONIAL, CONSTITUTIONAL, AND REVOLUTIONARY PERIODS

Bailyn, Bernard. *The Ideological Origins of the American Revolution*. Cambridge, Mass.: Belknap Press of Harvard University Press, 1967.

Benson, Lee. *The Concept of Jacksonian Democracy: New York as a Test Case*. Princeton: Princeton University Press, 1961.

Bledsoe, Albert Taylor. *Is Davis a Traitor?, or Was Secession a Constitutional Right Previous to the War of 1861?* Baltimore: Innes, 1886.

Bradford, M. E. *A Better Guide than Reason: Federalists and Anti-Federalists*. New Brunswick, N.J.: Transaction, 1994.

Bradford. *A Better Guide than Reason: Studies in the American Revolution*. La Salle, Ill.: Sugden, 1979.

Davis, Richard Beale. *Intellectual Life in Jefferson's Virginia, 1790–1830*. Chapel Hill: University of North Carolina Press, 1964.

Davis. *Intellectual Life in the Colonial South, 1585–1763*. 3 volumes. Knoxville: University of Tennessee Press, 1978.

Finkelman, Paul. *Slavery and the Founders: Race and Liberty in the Age of Jefferson*. Second edition. Armonk, N.Y.: Sharpe, 2001.

Fischer, David Hackett. *Albion's Seed: Four British Folkways in America*. Oxford: Oxford University Press, 1989.

Jameson, J. Franklin. *The American Revolution Considered as a Social Movement*. Princeton: Princeton University Press, 1926.

Katz, Stanley N. and John M. Murrin, eds. *Colonial America: Essays in Politics and Social Development*. Third edition. New York: Knopf, 1983.

Martin, James Kirby, ed. *Interpreting Colonial America: Selected Readings*. Second edition. New York: Harper & Row, 1978.

Miller, John Chester. *The Wolf by the Ears: Thomas Jefferson and Slavery*. New York: Free Press, 1977.

Onuf, Peter N., ed. *Jeffersonian Legacies*. Charlottesville: University Press of Virginia, 1993.

Ramsay, David. *The History of the American Revolution*. Edited by Lester H. Cohen. Indianapolis: Liberty Classics, 1990.

Tocqueville, Alexis de. *Democracy in America*. Translated by George Lawrence. Edited by J. P. Mayer and Max Lerner. New York: Harper & Row, 1966.

Tucker, St. George. *View of the Constitution of the United States, with Selected Writings*. Edited by Clyde N. Wilson. Indianapolis: Liberty Fund, 1999.

6. ATLANTIC SLAVE TRADE

Anstey, Roger. *The Atlantic Slave Trade and British Abolition, 1760–1810*. Atlantic Highlands, N.J.: Humanities Press, 1975.

Behrendt, Stephen D. "The British Slave Trade, 1785–1807: Volume, Profitability, and Mortality." Dissertation, University of Wisconsin–Madison, 1993.

Buxton, Thomas Fowell. *The African Slave Trade and Its Remedy*. London: Clowes & Sons, 1840.

Curtin, Philip D. *The Atlantic Slave Trade: A Census*. Madison: University of Wisconsin Press, 1969.

Davidson, Basil. *The African Slave Trade*. Revised edition. Boston: Little, Brown, 1980.

Davidson. *Black Mother: The Years of the African Slave Trade*. Boston: Little, Brown, 1961.

Eltis, David. *Economic Growth and the Ending of the Transatlantic Slave Trade*. New York: Oxford University Press, 1987.

Eltis. *The Rise of African Slavery in the Americas*. Cambridge & New York: Cambridge University Press, 2000.

Gemery, Henry A. and Jan S. Hogendorn, eds. *The Uncommon Market: Essays in the Economic History of the Atlantic Slave Trade*. New York: Academic Press, 1979.

Inikori, Joseph E. and Stanley L. Engerman, eds. *The Atlantic Slave Trade: Effects on Economies, Societies, and Peoples in Africa, the Americas, and Europe*. Durham, N.C.: Duke University Press, 1992.

Klein, Herbert S. *The Atlantic Slave Trade*. Cambridge & New York: Cambridge University Press, 1999.

Klein. *The Middle Passage: Comparative Studies in the Atlantic Slave Trade*. Princeton: Princeton University Press, 1978.

Manning, Patrick. *Slavery and African Life: Occidental, Oriental and African Slave Trades*. New York: Cambridge University Press, 1990.

Miller, Joseph C. *Way of Death: Merchant Capitalism and the Angolan Slave Trade, 1730–1830*. Madison: University of Wisconsin Press, 1988.

Minchinton, Walter E. and Pieter C. Emmer, eds. *La traite des Noirs par L'Atlantique: nouvelles approches (The Atlantic Slave Trade: New Approaches)*. Paris: Société d'Histoire d'Outre-mer, 1976.

Northrup, David, ed. *The Atlantic Slave Trade*. Second edition. Boston: Houghton Mifflin, 2002.

Postma, Johannes Menne. *The Dutch in the Atlantic Slave Trade, 1600–1815*. Cambridge & New York: Cambridge University Press, 1990.

Rawley, James A. *The Transatlantic Slave Trade: A History*. New York: Norton, 1981.

Reynolds, Edward. *Stand the Storm: A History of the Atlantic Slave Trade*. London & New York: Allison & Busby, 1985.

Rodney, Walter. *West Africa and the Atlantic Slave-Trade*. Nairobi: Historical Society of Tanzania, 1967.

Solow, Barbara L., ed. *Slavery and the Rise of the Atlantic System*. Cambridge & New York: Cambridge University Press, 1991.

Thomas, Hugh. *The Slave Trade: The Story of the Atlantic Slave Trade, 1440–1870*. New York: Simon & Schuster, 1997.

7. CHRISTIANITY AND RELIGION

Armstrong, George D. *The Christian Doctrine of Slavery*. New York: Scribner, 1857.

Boles, John B., ed. *Masters & Slaves in the House of the Lord: Race and Religion in the American South, 1740–1870*. Lexington: University of Kentucky Press, 1988.

Clarke, James Freeman. *Slavery in the United States: A Sermon Delivered in Amory Hall, on Thanksgiving Day, November 24, 1842*. Boston: Greene, 1843.

Jones, Charles C. *The Religious Instruction of the Negro in the United States*. Savannah: Purse, 1842.

Loveland, Anne C. *Southern Evangelicals and the Social Order, 1800–1860*. Baton Rouge: Louisiana State University Press, 1980.

Mathews, Donald G. *Religion in the Old South*. Chicago: University of Chicago Press, 1977.

Raboteau, Albert J. *Slave Religion: The "Invisible Institution" in the Antebellum South*. New York: Oxford University Press, 1978.

Sobel, Mechal. *Trabelin' On: The Slave Journey to Afro-Baptist Faith*. Westport, Conn.: Greenwood Press, 1979.

Tuveson, Ernest L. *Redeemer Nation: The Idea of America's Millennial Role*. Chicago: University of Chicago Press, 1974.

8. CIVIL WAR

Adams, Charles. *When in the Course of Human Events: Arguing the Case for Southern Secession*. Lanham, Md.: Rowman & Littlefield, 2000.

Cairnes, J. E. *The Slave Power: Its Character, Career, and Probable Designs: Being an Attempt to Explain the Real Issues Involved in the American Contest*. London: Parker, Son & Bourn, 1862.

Cole, Arthur C. *The Era of the Civil War, 1848–1870*. Springfield: Illinois Centennial Commission, 1919.

Craven, Avery. *The Coming of the Civil War*. Second edition. Chicago: University of Chicago Press, 1957.

Craven. *The Repressible Conflict, 1830–1861*. Baton Rouge: Louisiana State University Press, 1939.

Davis, Jefferson. *The Rise and Fall of the Confederate Government*. 2 volumes. New York: Appleton, 1881.

DeRosa, Marshall L. *The Confederate Constitution of 1861: An Inquiry into American Constitutionalism*. Columbia: University of Missouri Press, 1991.

DeRosa. *The Politics of Dissolution: The Quest for a National Identity & the American Civil War*. New Brunswick, N.J.: Transaction, 1998.

Donald, David Herbert. *Liberty and Union*. Boston: Little, Brown, 1978.

Foner, Eric. *Free Soil, Free Labor, Free Men: The Ideology of the Republican Party before the Civil War*. New York: Oxford University Press, 1970.

Freehling, William W. *The Road to Disunion*. Volume 1. *The Secessionists at Bay, 1776–1854*. New York: Oxford University Press, 1990.

Freehling and Craig M. Simpson, eds. *Secession Debated: Georgia's Showdown in 1860*. New York: Oxford University Press, 1992.

Genovese, Eugene D. *A Consuming Fire: The Fall of the Confederacy in the Mind of the White Christian South*. Athens: University of Georgia Press, 1998.

Gordon, David, ed. *Secession, State & Liberty*. New Brunswick, N.J.: Transaction, 1998.

Grant, Susan-Mary. *North over South: Northern Nationalism and American Identity in the Antebellum Era*. Lawrence: University Press of Kansas, 2000.

Holt, Michael F. *The Political Crisis of the 1850s*. New York: Wiley, 1978.

Holt. *The Rise and Fall of the American Whig Party: Jacksonian Politics and the Onset of the Civil War*. New York: Oxford University Press, 1999.

Horowitz, Tony. *Confederates in the Attic: Dispatches from the Unfinished Civil War*. New York: Pantheon, 1998.

Hummel, Jeffrey Rogers. *Emancipating Slaves, Enslaving Free Men: A History of the American Civil War*. New York: Open Court, 1996.

Johnson, Ludwell. *Division and Reunion: America, 1848–1877*. New York: Wiley, 1978.

McDonald, Forrest. *States' Rights and the Union: Imperium in Imperio, 1776–1876*. Lawrence: University Press of Kansas, 2000.

McPherson, James. *Battle Cry of Freedom: The Civil War Era*. New York: Oxford University Press, 1988.

Nevins, Allen. *The Ordeal of the Union*. 8 volumes. New York: Scribners, 1947–1971.

Potter, David. *The Impending Crisis, 1848–1861*. New York: Harper & Row, 1976.

Potter. *The South and the Sectional Conflict*. Baton Rouge: Louisiana State University Press, 1968.

Randall, James G. and David Herbert Donald. *The Civil War and Reconstruction*. Second revised edition. Lexington, Mass.: Heath, 1969.

Silbey, Joel H. *The Partisan Imperative: The Dynamics of American Politics Before the Civil War*. Oxford: Oxford University Press, 1985.

Walther, Eric. *The Fire-Eaters*. Baton Rouge: Louisiana State University Press, 1992.

Wilson, Henry. *History of the Rise and Fall of the Slave Power*. 3 volumes. Boston: Houghton, Mifflin, 1872–1877.

9. DOCUMENTS, MEMOIRS, PRIMARY SOURCES, AND BIOGRAPHIES

Angle, Paul M. *Created Equal? The Complete Lincoln-Douglas Debates of 1858*. Chicago: University of Chicago Press, 1958.

Atkins, John. *A Voyage to Guinea, Brasil, and the West-Indies. . . .* London: Ward & Chandler, 1735.

Bayliss, John F., ed. *Black Slave Narratives*. New York: Macmillan, 1970.

Bierce, Lucius Verus. *Travels in the Southland, 1822–1823*. Edited by George W. Knepper. Columbus: Ohio State University Press, 1966.

Browne, Thomas. *The Works of Sir Thomas Browne*. 6 volumes. Edited by Geoffrey Keynes. London: Faber & Gwyer, 1928.

Browne, William Hand, ed. *Archives of Maryland*. 72 volumes. Baltimore: Maryland Historical Society, 1883–1972.

Chesnut, Mary Boykin. *A Diary from Dixie, as Written by Mary Boykin Chesnut, Wife of James Chesnut, Jr., United States Senator from South Carolina, 1859–1861, and Afterward an Aide to Jefferson Davis and a Brigadier-General in the Confederate Army*. Edited by Isabella D. Martin and Myrta Lockett Avary. New York: Appleton, 1905.

Crèvecoeur, J. Hector St. Jean de. *Letters from an American Farmer*. London: Davies, 1782.

Dalberg-Acton, John Emerich Edward. *Selected Writings of Lord Acton*. 3 volumes. Edited by J. Rufus Fears. Indianapolis: LibertyClassics, 1985–1988.

Davis, Edwin A., ed. *Plantation Life in the Florida Parishes of Louisiana, 1836–1846, as Reflected in the Diary of Bennett H. Barrow*. New York: Columbia University Press, 1943.

Donnan, Elizabeth, ed. *Documents Illustrative of the History of the Slave Trade to America*. 4 volumes. Washington, D.C.: Carnegie Institution of Washington, 1930–1935.

Douglass, Frederick. *Narrative of the Life of Frederick Douglass, an American Slave, Written by Himself*. Boston: Anti-Slavery Office, 1845.

Drew, Benjamin. *A North-side View of Slavery*. Boston: Jewett / New York: Sheldon, Lamport & Blakeman, 1856. Reprinted as *North-Side View of Slavery: The Refugee: Or, The Narratives of Fugitive Slaves in Canada Related by Themselves.* . . . New York: Negro Universities Press, 1968.

Du Bois, W. E. B. *The Souls of Black Folk: Essays and Sketches.* Chicago: McClurg, 1903.

Du Bois. *Writings.* Edited by Nathan Huggins. New York: Library of America, 1986.

Equiano, Olaudah. *The Interesting Narrative of the Life of Olaudah Equiano.* Edited by Robert J. Allison. Boston: Bedford Books of St. Martin's Press, 1995.

Faust, Drew Gilpin. *James Henry Hammond and the Old South: A Design for Mastery.* Baton Rouge: Louisiana State University Press, 1982.

Fisk University. *Unwritten History of Slavery: Autobiographical Accounts of Negro Ex-Slaves.* Nashville: Social Science Institute, Fisk University, 1945.

Foner, Philip S., ed. *Life and Writings of Frederick Douglass.* 4 volumes. New York: International Publishers, 1950-1955.

Hammond, James Henry. *Secret and Sacred: The Diaries of James Henry Hammond, a Southern Slaveholder.* Edited by Carol Bleser. New York: Oxford University Press, 1988.

Harper, William. *Memoir on Slavery, Read before the Society for the Advancement of Learning, of South Carolina, at its Annual Meeting at Columbia.* Charleston, S.C.: Burges, 1838.

Hopley, Catherine Cooper. *Life in the South from the Commencement of the War, Being a Social History of those who Took Part in the Battles, from a Personal Acquaintance with Their Homes, from the Spring of 1860 to August 1862.* 2 volumes. London: Chapman & Hall, 1863.

Jefferson, Thomas. *Notes on the State of Virginia.* Edited by William Peden. Chapel Hill: University of North Carolina Press, 1954.

Jefferson. *The Portable Thomas Jefferson.* Edited by Merrill D. Peterson. New York: Viking, 1975.

Kemble, Frances Anne. *Journal of a Residence on a Georgian Plantation in 1838-1839.* Edited by John A. Scott. New York: Knopf, 1961.

Ligon, Richard. *A True & exact history of the island of Barbadoes.* . . . London: Moseley, 1657.

Marambaud, Pierre. *William Byrd of Westover, 1674-1744.* Charlottesville: University Press of Virginia, 1971.

Martineau, Harriet. *Retrospect of Western Travel.* 2 volumes. London: Saunders & Otley, 1838.

Meyer, Leland Winfield. *The Life and Times of Colonel Richard M. Johnson of Kentucky.* New York: Columbia University Press / London: King, 1932.

Meyers, Marvin, Alexander Kern, and John G. Cawelti, eds. *Sources of the American Republic: A Documentary History of Politics, Society, and Thought.* 2 volumes. Glenview, Ill.: Scott, Foresman, 1960, 1961.

Mocquet, Jean. *Travels and Voyages into Africa, Asia, and America, the East and West-Indies, Syria, Jerusalem, and the Holy-Land.* . . . Translated by Nathaniel Pullen. London: Newton, 1696.

Northup, Solomon. *Twelve Years a Slave.* Edited by Sue Eakin and Joseph Logsdon. Baton Rouge: Louisiana State University Press, 1968.

Olmsted, Frederick Law. *The Cotton Kingdom: A Traveller's Observations on Cotton and Slavery in the American Slave States.* New York: Mason Brothers, 1861.

Olmsted. *A Journey in the Seaboard Slave States: With Remarks on Their Economy.* New York: Dix & Edwards / London: Sampson Low, Son, 1856.

Park, Mungo. *Travels in the Interior Districts of Africa: Performed in the Years 1795, 1796, and 1797.* London: Murray, 1816.

Parker, Theodore. *The Works of Theodore Parker.* 15 volumes. Edited by Rufus Leighton. Boston: American Unitarian Association, 1907-1911.

Phillips, Thomas. *A Journal of a Voyage Made in the Hannibal of London, Ann. 1693, 1694.* . . . London: Lintot & Osborn, 1732.

Purchas, Samuel. *Purchas his Pilgrimage: In Five Books.* . . . London: Stansby, 1625.

Rawick, George P., ed. *The American Slave: A Composite Autobiography.* First and second series. 19 volumes. Westport, Conn.: Greenwood Press, 1972. First supplemental series. 12 volumes. Westport, Conn.: Greenwood Press, 1977. Second supplemental series. 10 volumes. Westport, Conn.: Greenwood Press, 1979.

Rose, Willie Lee, ed. *A Documentary History of Slavery in North America.* New York: Oxford University Press, 1976.

Schaw, Janet. *Journal of a Lady of Quality: Being the Narrative of a Journey from Scotland to the West Indies, North Carolina and Portugal in the Years, 1774-1776.* Edited by Evangeline Andrews and Charles McLean Andrews. New Haven: Yale University Press, 1921.

Simms, William Gilmore. *Letters of William Gilmore Simms.* 6 volumes. Edited by Mary C. Simms Oliphant, Alfred Taylor Odell, and T. C. Duncan Eaves. Columbia: University of South Carolina Press, 1952-1982.

Smedes, Susan Dabney. *Memorials of A Southern Planter.* Edited by Fletcher M. Green. New York: Knopf, 1965.

Thornwell, James Henley. *The Collected Writings of James Henley Thornwell.* 4 volumes. Edited by John B. Adger. Richmond, Va.: Presbyterian Committee of Publication, 1871-1873.

Trent, William P. *William Gilmore Simms.* Boston & New York: Houghton, Mifflin, 1892.

Walker, David. *David Walker's Appeal: In Four Articles, Together with a Preamble, to the Coloured Citizens of the World, but in Particular, and Very Expressly, to Those of the United States of America.* Edited by Charles M. Wiltse. New York: Hill & Wang, 1965.

Woodward, C. Vann, ed. *Mary Chesnut's Civil War.* New Haven: Yale University Press, 1981.

10. ECONOMICS

Bateman, Fred and Thomas Weiss. *A Deplorable Scarcity: The Failure of Industrialization in the Slave Economy.* Chapel Hill: University of North Carolina Press, 1981.

Bauer, P. T. *Dissent on Development: Studies and Debates in Development Economics.* London: Weidenfeld & Nicolson, 1971.

Blaug, Mark. *Economic Theory in Retrospect.* Fifth edition. Cambridge & New York: Cambridge University Press, 1997.

Bruce, Philip Alexander. *Economic History of Virginia in the Seventeenth Century.* New York & London: Macmillan, 1895.

Conkin, Paul K. *Prophets of Prosperity: America's First Political Economists.* Bloomington: Indiana University Press, 1980.

Fogel, Robert W. *Without Consent of Contract: The Rise and Fall of American Slavery.* New York: Norton, 1989.

Fogel and Stanley L. Engerman. *Time on the Cross: The Economics of Negro Slavery.* 2 volumes. Boston: Little, Brown, 1974.

Genovese, Eugene D. *The Political Economy of Slavery: Studies in the Economy and Society of the Slave South.* New York: Pantheon, 1965.

Gutman, Herbert G. *Slavery and the Numbers Game: A Critique of* Time on the Cross. Urbana: University of Illinois Press, 1975.

Kaufman, Allen. *Capitalism, Slavery, and Republican Values: American Political Economists, 1819–1848.* Austin: University of Texas Press, 1982.

Kuznets, Simon. *Modern Economic Growth: Rate, Structure, and Spread.* New Haven: Yale University Press, 1966.

Levy, David M. *How the Dismal Science Got Its Name: Classical Economics and the Ur-text of Racial Politics.* Ann Arbor: University of Michigan Press, 2001.

Margo, Robert A. *Wages and Labor Markets in the United States, 1820–1860.* Chicago: University of Chicago Press, 2000.

Mises, Ludwig von. *Human Action: A Treatise on Economics.* Third edition. Chicago: Regnery, 1966.

O'Brien, D. P. *The Classical Economists.* Oxford: Clarendon Press, 1975.

Ricardo, David. *On the Principles of Political Economy, and Taxation.* London: Murray, 1817.

Smith, Adam. *An Inquiry into the Nature and Causes of the Wealth of Nations.* Edited by Edwin Cannan. New York: Modern Library, 1937.

Snavely, Tipton R. *George Tucker as Political Economist.* Charlottesville: University Press of Virginia, 1964.

Tracy, James D., ed. *The Rise of Merchant Empires: Long-Distance Trade in the Early Modern World, 1350–1750.* Cambridge & New York: Cambridge University Press, 1990.

Ware, Nathaniel A. *Notes on Political Economy as Applicable to the United States.* New York: Leavitt, Trow, 1844.

Woodman, Harold D. *King Cotton and His Retainers: Financing and Marketing the Cotton Crop of the South, 1800–1925.* Lexington: University of Kentucky Press, 1968.

Wright, Gavin. *The Political Economy of the Cotton South: Households, Markets, and Wealth in the Nineteenth Century.* New York: Norton, 1978.

11. EMANCIPATION AND RECONSTRUCTION

Cruden, Robert. *The Negro in Reconstruction.* Englewood Cliffs, N.J.: Prentice-Hall, 1969.

Du Bois, W. E. B. *Black Reconstruction: An Essay Toward a History of the Part Which Black Folk Played in the Attempt to Reconstruct Democracy in America, 1860–1880.* New York: Harcourt, Brace, 1935.

Foner, Eric. *Nothing but Freedom: Emancipation and Its Legacy.* Baton Rouge: Louisiana State University Press, 1983.

Foner. *Reconstruction: America's Unfinished Revolution, 1863–1877.* New York: Harper & Row, 1988.

Litwack, Leon F. *Been in the Storm So Long: The Aftermath of Slavery.* New York: Knopf, 1979.

Litwack. *Trouble in Mind: Black Southerners in the Age of Jim Crow.* New York: Knopf, 1998.

Woodward, C. Vann. *The Strange Career of Jim Crow.* Third edition. New York: Oxford University Press, 1974.

12. EUROPEAN BACKGROUND: THE ANCIENT WORLD

Bradley, K. R. *Slavery and Society at Rome.* Cambridge & New York: Cambridge University Press, 1994.

Bradley. *Slaves and Masters in the Roman Empire: A Study in Social Control.* Brussels: Latomus, 1984.

Finley, M. I. *Ancient Slavery and Modern Ideology.* New York: Viking, 1980.

Fisher, N. R. E. *Slavery in Classical Greece.* London: Bristol Classical Press, 1993.

Garlan, Yvon. *Slavery in Ancient Greece.* Revised edition. Translated by Janet Lloyd. Ithaca, N.Y.: Cornell University Press, 1988.

Snowden, Frank M., Jr. *Blacks in Antiquity: Ethiopians in the Greco-Roman Experience.* Cambridge, Mass.: Belknap Press of Harvard University Press, 1970.

Vogt, Joseph. *Ancient Slavery and the Ideal of Man.* Translated by Thomas Wiedemann. Oxford: Blackwell, 1974.

13. EUROPEAN BACKGROUND: THE MIDDLE AGES

Bloch, Marc. *Slavery and Serfdom in the Middle Ages: Selected Essays.* Translated by William R. Beer. Berkeley: University of California Press, 1975.

Bonnassie, Pierre. *From Slavery to Feudalism in South-Western Europe.* Translated by Jean Birrell. Cambridge & New York: Cambridge University Press / Paris: Editions de la Maison des sciences de l'homme, 1991.

Dockès, Pierre. *Medieval Slavery and Liberation.* Translated by Arthur Goldhammer. Chicago: University of Chicago Press, 1982.

Frantzen, Allen J. and Douglas Moffat, eds. *The Work of Work: Servitude, Slavery, and Labor in Medieval England.* Glasgow: Cruithne Press, 1994.

Phillips, William D., Jr. *Slavery from Roman Times to the Early Transatlantic Trade.* Minneapolis: University of Minnesota Press, 1985.

Stuard, Susan Mosher. "Ancillary Evidence for the Decline of Medieval Slavery," *Past and Present,* 149 (1995): 3–28.

14. PROSLAVERY ARGUMENTS

Elliott, E. N., ed. *Cotton Is King and Pro-Slavery Arguments.* Augusta, Ga.: Pritchard, Abbott & Loomis, 1860.

Faust, Drew Gilpin, ed. *The Ideology of Slavery: Proslavery Thought in the Antebellum South, 1830–1860.* Baton Rouge: Louisiana State University Press, 1981.

Jenkins, William Sumner. *Pro-Slavery Thought in the Old South.* Chapel Hill: University of North Carolina Press, 1935.

The Pro-Slavery Argument, as Maintained by the Most Distinguished Writers of the Southern States: Containing Several Essays, on the Subject, of Chancellor Harper, Governor Hammond, Dr. Simms, and Professor Dew. Charleston, S.C.: Walker, Richards, 1852.

Ross, Fred A. *Slavery Ordained of God.* Philadelphia: Lippincott, 1857.

Smith, William A. *Lectures on the Philosophy and Practice of Slavery, As Exhibited in the Institution of Domestic Slavery in the United States: With the Duties of Masters and Slaves.* Edited by Thomas O. Summers. Nashville: Stevenson & Evans, 1856.

Tise, Larry E. *Proslavery: A History of the Defense of Slavery in America, 1701–1840.* Athens: University of Georgia Press, 1987.

15. SLAVERY AND LAW

Catterall, Helen Tunnicliff, ed. *Judicial Cases Concerning American Slavery and the Negro.* 5 volumes. Washington, D.C.: Carnegie Institution, 1926–1937.

Cobb, Thomas R. R. *An Inquiry into the Law of Negro Slavery in the United States of America: To Which is Prefixed an Historical Sketch of Slavery.* Philadelphia: T. & J. W. Johnson / Savannah: W. T. Williams, 1858.

Cooper, Thomas and David J. McCord, eds. *The Statutes at Large of South Carolina.* 10 volumes. Columbia, S.C.: Johnston, 1836–1841.

Goodell, William. *The American Slave Code in Theory and Practice: Its Distinctive Features Shown by Its Statutes, Judicial Decisions, & Illustrative Facts.* New York: American & Foreign Anti-Slavery Society, 1853.

Hening, William Waller. *The Statutes at Large: Being a Collection of All the Laws of Virginia, from the First Session of the Legislature in the Year 1619.* 13 volumes. Richmond, Va.: Samuel Pleasants, 1809–1823.

Hurd, John Codman. *The Law of Freedom and Bondage in the United States.* 2 volumes. Boston: Little, Brown, 1858, 1862.

Morris, Thomas D. *Southern Slavery and the Law, 1619–1860.* Chapel Hill: University of North Carolina Press, 1996.

Schwarz, Philip J. *Twice Condemned: Slaves and the Criminal Laws of Virginia, 1705–1865.* Baton Rouge: Louisiana State University Press, 1988.

Tushnet, Mark V. *The American Law of Slavery, 1810–1860: Considerations of Humanity and Interest.* Princeton: Princeton University Press, 1981.

Wilson, Theodore B. *The Black Codes of the South.* Tuscaloosa: University of Alabama Press, 1965.

16. SLAVERY IN LATIN AMERICA AND THE CARIBBEAN

Beckles, Hilary McD. *White Servitude and Black Slavery in Barbados, 1627–1715.* Knoxville: University of Tennessee Press, 1989.

Beckles and Verene Shepherd. *Caribbean Slave Society and Economy: A Student Reader.* New York: New Press, 1991.

Conrad, Robert Edgar. *The Destruction of Brazilian Slavery, 1850–1888.* Berkeley: University of California Press, 1972.

Costa, Emilia Viotti da. *The Brazilian Empire: Myths and Histories.* Chicago: University of Chicago Press, 1985.

Costa. *Crowns of Glory, Tears of Blood: The Demerara Slave Rebellion of 1823.* New York: Oxford University Press, 1994.

Craton, Michael. *Sinews of Empire: A Short History of British Slavery.* Garden City, N.Y.: Anchor, 1974.

Craton. *Testing the Chains: Resistance to Slavery in the British West Indies.* Ithaca, N.Y.: Cornell University Press, 1982.

Craton with the assistance of Garry Greenland. *Searching for the Invisible Man: Slaves and Plantation Life in Jamaica.* Cambridge, Mass.: Harvard University Press, 1978.

Dunn, Richard S. *Sugar and Slaves: The Rise of the Planter Class in the English West Indies, 1624–1713.* Chapel Hill: University of North Carolina Press, 1972.

Edwards, Bryan. *History, Civil and Commercial, of the British Colonies in the West Indies.* 2 volumes. Dublin: White, 1793.

Fick, Carolyn E. *The Making of Haiti: The San Domingue Revolution from Below.* Knoxville: University of Tennessee Press, 1990.

Fraginals, Manuel Moreno, Frank Moya Pons, and Stanley L. Engerman, eds. *Between Slavery and Free Labor: The Spanish-Speaking Caribbean in the Nineteenth Century.* Baltimore: Johns Hopkins University Press, 1985.

Freyre, Gilberto. *The Masters and the Slaves: A Study in the Development of Brazilian Civilization.* Second English-language edition. Translated by Samuel Putnam. New York: Knopf, 1956.

Gaspar, David Barry. *Bondmen & Rebels: A Case Study of Master-Slave Relations in Antigua, with Implications for Colonial British America.* Baltimore: Johns Hopkins University Press, 1985.

Goveia, Elsa V. *Slave Society in the British Leeward Islands at the End of the Eighteenth Century.* New Haven: Yale University Press, 1965.

Hall, Neville A. T. *Slave Society in the Danish West Indies: St. Thomas, St. John, and St. Croix.* Edited by B. W. Higman. Baltimore: Johns Hopkins University Press / Mona, Jamaica: University of the West Indies Press, 1992.

Higman, B. W. *Slave Populations of the British Caribbean, 1807–1834.* Baltimore: Johns Hopkins University Press, 1984.

Klein, Herbert S. *African Slavery in Latin America and the Caribbean.* New York: Oxford University Press, 1986.

Klein. *Slavery in the Americas: A Comparative Study of Virginia and Cuba.* Chicago: University of Chicago Press, 1967.

Knight, Franklin W. *Slave Society in Cuba during the Nineteenth Century.* Madison: University of Wisconsin Press, 1970.

Las Casas, Bartolomé de. *The Devastation of the Indies: A Brief Account.* New York: Seabury, 1974.

Long, Edward. *The History of Jamaica; or, General Survey of the Ancient and Modern State of the Island. . . .* 3 volumes. London: Lowndes, 1774.

Lovejoy, Paul E. and Nicholas Rogers, eds. *Unfree Labour in the Development of the Atlantic World.* London & Portland, Ore.: Cass, 1994.

Luis, William. *Literary Bondage: Slavery in Cuban Narrative.* Austin: University of Texas Press, 1990.

Mintz, Sidney. *Caribbean Transformations.* Chicago: Aldine, 1974.

Ott, Thomas O. *The Haitian Revolution, 1789–1804.* Knoxville: University of Tennessee Press, 1973.

Pacquette, Robert L. *Sugar Is Made with Blood: The Conspiracy of La Escalera and the Conflict between Empires over Slavery in Cuba.* Middletown, Conn.: Wesleyan University Press, 1988.

Patterson, Orlando. *The Sociology of Slavery: An Analysis of the Origins, Development, and Structure of Negro Slave Society in Jamaica.* London: MacGibbon & Kee, 1967.

Ros, Martin. *Night of Fire: The Black Napoleon and the Battle for Haiti.* New York: Sarpedon, 1994.

Schwartz, Stuart B. *Peasants and Rebels: Reconsidering Brazilian Slavery.* Urbana: University of Illinois Press, 1992.

Schwartz. *Sugar Plantations in the Formation of Brazilian Society: Bahia, 1550–1835.* Cambridge & New York: Cambridge University Press, 1985.

Scott, Rebecca J. *Slave Emancipation in Cuba: The Transition to Free Labor, 1860–1899.* Princeton: Princeton University Press, 1985.

Sheridan, Richard B. *Sugar and Slavery: An Economic History of the British West Indies, 1623–1775.* Baltimore: Johns Hopkins University Press, 1974.

Solow, Barbara L. and Engerman, eds. *British Capitalism and Caribbean Slavery: The Legacy of Eric Williams.* Cambridge & New York: Cambridge University Press, 1987.

REFERENCES

Stein, Stanley. *Vassouras: A Brazilian Coffee County, 1850–1900*. Princeton: Princeton University Press, 1957.

Tomich, Dale W. *Slavery in the Circuit of Sugar: Martinique in the World Economy, 1830–1848*. Baltimore: Johns Hopkins University Press, 1990.

Ward, John R. *British West Indian Slavery, 1750–1834: The Process of Amelioration*. Oxford: Clarendon Press / New York: Oxford University Press, 1988.

Williams, Eric. *Capitalism and Slavery*. Chapel Hill: University of North Carolina Press, 1944.

17. SLAVERY IN NORTH AMERICA AND THE UNITED STATES

Aptheker, Herbert. *American Negro Slave Revolts*. New York: Columbia University Press / London: King & Staples, 1943.

Bancroft, Frederic. *Slave-trading in the Old South*. Baltimore: Furst, 1931.

Bassett, John Spencer. *Slavery and Servitude in the Colony of North Carolina*. Baltimore: Johns Hopkins University Press, 1896.

Bassett. *Slavery in the State of North Carolina*. Baltimore: Johns Hopkins University Press, 1899.

Berlin, Ira. *Many Thousands Gone: The First Two Centuries of American Slavery*. Cambridge, Mass.: Belknap Press of Harvard University Press, 1998.

Berlin. "Time, Space, and the Evolution of Afro-American Society in British Mainland North America," *American Historical Review*, 85 (1980): 44–78.

Berlin and Ronald Hoffman, eds. *Slavery and Freedom in the Age of the American Revolution*. Charlottesville: University Press of Virginia, 1983.

Berlin and Philip D. Morgan, eds. *Cultivation and Culture: Labor and the Shaping of Slave Life in the Americas*. Charlottesville: University Press of Virginia, 1993.

Blassingame, John W. *The Slave Community: Plantation Life in the Antebellum South*. Revised edition. New York: Oxford University Press, 1979.

Breen, T. H. and Stephen Innes. *"Myne Owne Ground": Race and Freedom on Virginia's Eastern Shore, 1640–1676*. New York: Oxford University Press, 1980.

Countryman, Edward, ed. *How Did American Slavery Begin?: Readings*. Boston: Bedford Books of St. Martin's Press, 1999.

Dusinberre, William. *Them Dark Days: Slavery in the American Rice Swamps*. New York: Oxford University Press, 1996.

Elkins, Stanley M. *Slavery: A Problem in American Institutional and Intellectual Life*. Chicago: University of Chicago Press, 1959.

Franklin, John Hope and Loren Schweninger. *Runaway Slaves: Rebels on the Plantation*. New York: Oxford University Press, 1999.

Genovese, Eugene D. *Roll, Jordan, Roll: The World the Slaves Made*. New York: Pantheon, 1974.

Genovese. *The World the Slaveholders Made: Two Essays in Interpretation*. New York: Pantheon, 1969.

Gutman, Herbert G. *The Black Family in Slavery and Freedom, 1750–1925*. New York: Pantheon, 1976.

Joyner, Charles W. *Down by the Riverside: A South Carolina Slave Community*. Urbana: University of Illinois Press, 1984.

Kolchin, Peter. *American Slavery, 1619–1877*. New York: Hill & Wang, 1993.

Levine, Lawrence W. *Black Culture and Black Consciousness: Afro-American Folk Thought from Slavery to Freedom*. New York: Oxford University Press, 1977.

Littlefield, David C. *Rice and Slaves: Ethnicity and the Slave Trade in Colonial South Carolina*. Baton Rouge: Louisiana State University Press, 1981.

MacLeod, Duncan J. *Slavery, Race, and the American Revolution*. London & New York: Cambridge University Press, 1974.

Malone, Ann Patton. *Sweet Chariot: Slave Family and Household Structure in Nineteenth-Century Louisiana*. Chapel Hill: University of North Carolina Press, 1992.

McLaurin, Melton A. *Celia, A Slave*. Athens: University of Georgia Press, 1991.

Morgan, Edmund S. *American Slavery, American Freedom: The Ordeal of Colonial Virginia*. New York: Norton, 1975.

Morgan, Philip D. *Slave Counterpoint: Black Life in Eighteenth-Century Chesapeake and Lowcountry*. Chapel Hill: University of North Carolina Press, 1998.

Mullin, Gerald W. *Flight and Rebellion: Slave Resistance in Eighteenth-Century Virginia*. London: Oxford University Press, 1972.

Noel, Donald L., ed. *The Origins of American Slavery and Racism*. Columbus, Ohio: Merrill, 1972.

Oakes, James. *The Ruling Race: A History of American Slaveholders*. New York: Knopf, 1982.

Owens, Leslie Howard. *This Species of Property: Slave Life and Culture in the Old South*. New York: Oxford University Press, 1976.

Parish, Peter J. *Slavery: History and Historians*. New York: Harper & Row, 1989.

Parker, Freddie L., ed. *Stealing a Little Freedom: Advertisements for Slave Runaways in North Carolina, 1791–1840*. New York: Garland, 1994.

Phillips, Ulrich B. *American Negro Slavery: A Survey of the Supply, Employment and Control of Negro Labor as Determined by the Plantation Regime*. New York & London: Appleton, 1918.

Postell, William Dosite. *The Health of Slaves on the Southern Plantations*. Baton Rouge: Louisiana State University Press, 1951.

Savitt, Todd L. *Medicine and Slavery: The Diseases and Health Care of Slaves in Antebellum Virginia*. Urbana: University of Illinois Press, 1978.

Scarborough, William Kauffman. *The Overseer: Plantation Management in the Old South*. Baton Rouge: Louisiana State University Press, 1966.

Stampp, Kenneth M. *The Peculiar Institution in the Ante-bellum South*. New York: Knopf, 1956.

Stuckey, Sterling. *Slave Culture: Nationalist Theory and the Foundations of Black America*. New York: Oxford University Press, 1987.

Tadman, Michael. *Speculators and Slaves: Masters, Traders, and Slaves in the Old South*. Madison: University of Wisconsin Press, 1989.

Taylor, Joe Gray. *Negro Slavery in Louisiana*. Baton Rouge: Louisiana Historical Association, 1963.

Van Deburg, William L. *The Slave Drivers: Black Agricultural Labor Supervisors in the Antebellum South*. Westport, Conn.: Greenwood Press, 1979.

Wiethoff, William E. *The Insolent Slave*. Columbia: University of South Carolina Press, 2002.

Wood, Betty. *The Origins of American Slavery: Freedom and Bondage in the English Colonies*. New York: Hill & Wang, 1997.

Wright, Donald R. *African Americans in the Colonial Era: From African Origins through the American Revolution*. Arlington Heights, Ill.: Harlan Davidson, 1990.

18. SLAVERY AND WESTERN CIVILIZATION

Alford, Terry. *Prince Among Slaves*. New York: Harcourt Brace Jovanovich, 1977.

Bastide, Roger. *African Civilization in the Americas*. New York: Harpers, 1972.

Craton, Michael, James Walvin, and David Wright, eds. *Slavery, Abolition, and Emancipation: Black Slaves and the British Empire*. London & New York: Longman, 1976.

Davis, David Brion. *The Problem of Slavery in the Age of Revolution, 1770–1823*. Ithaca, N.Y.: Cornell University Press, 1975.

Davis. *The Problem of Slavery in Western Culture*. Ithaca, N.Y.: Cornell University Press, 1966.

Davis. *Slavery and Human Progress*. New York: Oxford University Press, 1984.

Degler, Carl N. *Neither Black nor White: Slavery and Race Relations in Brazil and the United States*. Madison: University of Wisconsin Press, 1971.

Engerman, Stanley L. and Eugene D. Genovese, eds. *Race and Slavery in the Western Hemisphere: Quantitative Studies*. Princeton: Princeton University Press, 1975.

Ewbank, Thomas. *Life in Brazil, or the Land of the Cocoa and the Palm*. New York: Harper, 1856.

Fox-Genovese, Elizabeth and Genovese. *The Fruits of Merchant Capital: Slavery and Bourgeois Property in the Rise and Expansion of Capitalism*. New York: Oxford University Press, 1983.

Genovese. *From Rebellion to Revolution: Afro-American Slave Revolts in the Making of the Modern World*. Baton Rouge: Louisiana State University Press, 1979.

Genovese. *The Slaveholders' Dilemma: Freedom and Progress in Southern Conservative Thought, 1820–1860*. Columbia: University of South Carolina Press, 1992.

James, C. L. R. *The Black Jacobins: Toussaint L'Ouverture and the San Domingo Revolution*. Revised edition. New York: Vintage, 1963.

Jordan, Winthrop D. *White Over Black: American Attitudes toward the Negro, 1550–1812*. Chapel Hill: University of North Carolina Press, 1968.

Kolchin, Peter. *Unfree Labor: American Slavery and Russian Serfdom*. Cambridge, Mass.: Belknap Press of Harvard University Press, 1987.

Lewis, Bernard. *Race and Slavery in the Middle East: An Historical Enquiry*. New York: Oxford University Press, 1990.

Parry, J. H. *The Spanish Seaborne Empire*. London: Hutchinson, 1966.

Patterson, Orlando. *Slavery and Social Death: A Comparative Study*. Cambridge, Mass.: Harvard University Press, 1982.

Price, Richard, ed. *Maroon Societies: Rebel Slave Communities in the Americas*. Garden City, N.Y.: Anchor, 1973.

Rubin, Vera and Arthur Tuden, eds. *Comparative Perspectives on Slavery in New World Plantation Societies*. New York: New York Academy of Sciences, 1977.

Woodward, C. Vann. *American Counterpoint: Slavery and Racism in the North-South Dialogue*. Boston: Little, Brown, 1971.

19. THE SOUTH

Applebome, Peter. *Dixie Rising: How the South Is Shaping American Values, Politics, and Culture*. New York: Times Books, 1996.

Beverley, Robert. *The History and Present State of Virginia*. Edited by Louis B. Wright. Chapel Hill: University of North Carolina Press, 1947.

Burton, Orville Vernon. *In My Father's House Are Many Mansions: Family and Community in Edgefield, South Carolina*. Chapel Hill: University of North Carolina Press, 1985.

Chalmers, David M. *Hooded Americanism: The History of the Ku Klux Klan*. Third edition. Durham, N.C.: Duke University Press, 1987.

Chesnutt, David R. and Clyde N. Wilson, eds. *The Meaning of South Carolina History: Essays in Honor of George C. Rogers, Jr.* Columbia: University of South Carolina Press, 1991.

Dal Lago, Enrico and Rick Halpern, eds. *The American South and the Italian Mezzogiorno: Essays in Comparative History*. Houndmills, U.K. & New York: Palgrave, 2002.

Davis, Richard Beale. *Intellectual Life in Jefferson's Virginia, 1790–1830*. Chapel Hill: University of North Carolina Press, 1964.

Davis. *Intellectual Life in the Colonial South, 1585–1763*. 3 volumes. Knoxville: University of Tennessee Press, 1978.

Eaton, Clement. *The Mind of the Old South*. Baton Rouge: Louisiana State University Press, 1964.

Escott, Paul D. and David R. Goldfield, eds. *Major Problems in the History of the American South: Documents and Essays*. Volume 1: *The Old South*. Lexington, Mass.: Heath, 1990.

Faust, Drew Gilpin. *Southern Stories: Slaveholders in Peace and War*. Columbia: University of Missouri Press, 1992.

Fitzhugh, George. *Sociology for the South, or, The Failure of Free Society*. Richmond, Va.: Morris, 1854.

Floan, Howard R. *The South in Northern Eyes, 1831 to 1861*. New York: Haskell House, 1973.

Fraser, Walter J., Jr., R. Frank Saunders Jr., and Jon L. Wakelyn, eds. *The Web of Southern Relations: Women, Family, and Education*. Athens: University of Georgia Press, 1985.

Genovese, Eugene D. *The Southern Front: History and Politics in the Culture War*. Columbia: University of Missouri Press, 1995.

Genovese. *The Southern Tradition: The Achievement and Limitations of an American Conservatism*. Cambridge, Mass.: Harvard University Press, 1994.

Helper, Hinton Rowan. *The Impending Crisis of the South: How to Meet It*. New York: Burdick, 1857.

Heyward, Duncan Clinch. *Seed from Madagascar*. Chapel Hill: University of North Carolina Press, 1937.

Kennedy, John Pendleton. *Swallow Barn, or A Sojourn in the Old Dominion*. Philadelphia: Carey & Lea, 1832.

Kulikoff, Allan. *Tobacco and Slaves: The Development of Southern Cultures in the Chesapeake, 1680–1800*. Chapel Hill: University of North Carolina Press, 1986.

Malvasi, Mark G. *The Unregenerate South: The Agrarian Thought of John Crowe Ransom, Allen Tate, and Donald Davidson*. Baton Rouge: Louisiana State University Press, 1997.

Norton, Ann. *Alternative Americas: A Reading of Antebellum Political Culture*. Chicago: University of Chicago Press, 1986.

Oakes, James. *Slavery and Freedom: An Interpretation of the Old South*. New York: Knopf, 1990.

O'Brien, Michael, ed. *All Clever Men, Who Make Their Way: Critical Discourse in the Old South*. Fayetteville: University of Arkansas Press, 1982.

Paquette, Robert L. and Louis A. Ferleger, eds. *Slavery, Secession, and Southern History*. Charlottesville: University Press of Virginia, 2000.

Peterson, Thomas Virgil. *Ham and Japheth: The Mythic World of Whites in the Antebellum South*. Metuchen, N.J.: Scarecrow Press, 1978.

Simkins, Francis Butler and Charles Pierce Roland. *A History of the South*. Fourth edition. New York: Knopf, 1972.

Smith, Mark M. *Debating Slavery: Economy and Society in the Antebellum American South*. Cambridge & New York: Cambridge University Press, 1998.

Smith. *Mastered by the Clock: Time, Slavery, and Freedom in the American South*. Chapel Hill: University of North Carolina Press, 1997.

Sobel, Mechal. *The World They Made Together: Black and White Values in Eighteenth-Century Virginia*. Princeton: Princeton University Press, 1987.

Stevenson, Brenda E. *Life in Black and White: Family and Community in the Slave South*. New York: Oxford University Press, 1996.

Twelve Southerners. *I'll Take My Stand: The South and the Agrarian Tradition*. New York & London: Harper, 1930.

Wood, Peter H. *Black Majority: Negroes in Colonial South Carolina from 1670 through the Stono Rebellion*. New York: Knopf, 1974.

Wyatt-Brown, Bertram. *Southern Honor: Ethics and Behavior in the Old South*. New York: Oxford University Press, 1982.

20. WOMEN

Clinton, Catherine. *The Plantation Mistress: Woman's World in the Old South*. New York: Pantheon, 1982.

Fox-Genovese, Elizabeth. *Within the Plantation Household: Black and White Women of the Old South*. Chapel Hill: University of North Carolina Press, 1988.

Lebsock, Suzanne. *Free Women of Petersburg: Status and Culture in a Southern Town, 1784–1860*. New York: Norton, 1984.

Scott, Anne Firor. *The Southern Lady: From Pedestal to Politics, 1830–1930*. Chicago: University of Chicago Press, 1970.

Weiner, Marli F. *Mistresses and Slaves: Plantation Women in South Carolina, 1830–80*. Urbana: University of Illinois Press, 1997.

White, Deborah Gray. *Ar'n't I a Woman: Female Slaves in the Plantation South*. New York: Norton, 1985.

CONTRIBUTORS

BARNES, Margaret: Independent scholar from Midlothian, Virginia.

BLACK, S. D.: Independent scholar from Richmond, Virginia.

BUSICK, Sean R.: Assistant professor of History at Kentucky Wesleyan College in Owensboro; author of dissertation that studies William Gilmore Simms as an historian; author of articles in *The Simms Review, The Louisiana Purchase: A Historical and Geographical Encyclopedia* (2002), and *The South Carolina Encyclopedia* (forthcoming); editor of *Dictionary of Literary Biography: Writers of the American Revolution* (forthcoming).

FOX, Jacob W.: Independent scholar from Richmond, Virginia.

GREENE, Meg: Earned a Bachelor's degree in History from Lindenwood College, St. Charles, Missouri, a Master's in History from the University of Nebraska at Omaha, and a Master's in Historic Preservation from the University of Vermont; author of histories and biographies for young readers, as well as essays on history, culture, biography, and architecture for adults; author of *Slave Young, Slave Long: The American Slave Experience* (1999), which won an Honor Award from the Society of School Librarians International.

GREENE, Sherman: Independent scholar from Oakland, California.

KAAT, Rick: Independent scholar from San Francisco, California.

KRAWCZYNSKI, Keith: Assistant Professor of History at Auburn University at Montgomery, Alabama; received his Ph.D. in History from the University of South Carolina; author of *William Henry Drayton: South Carolina Revolutionary Patriot* (2001) and several articles on early American history published in *New Jersey History* and *South Carolina Historical Magazine;* editor of *History in Dispute, Volume 12: The American Revolution, 1763–1789* (2003).

LITTLE, Ophelia V.: Independent scholar from Yorktown, Virginia.

MALVASI, Mark G.: Since 1992 has taught at Randolph-Macon College in Ashland, Virginia; received a Bachelor's degree in history from Hiram College, a Master's in history from the University of Chicago,

and a Ph.D. from the University of Rochester; author of *The Unregenerate South: The Agrarian Thought of John Crowe Ransom, Allen Tate, and Donald Davidson* (1997); author of reviews, essays, and editorials; currently working on critical studies of Southern novelist and essayist Andrew Lytle and historian John Lukacs.

NICHOLAS, Martina: Technology Librarian at Youngstown State University, Youngstown, Ohio.

ROBERTS, Carey M.: Assistant Professor of History at Arkansas Tech University, Russellville.

STATHAKIS, Paula M.: Independent scholar from Charlotte, North Carolina.

TATE, Adam L.: Assistant professor of History at Stillman College in Tuscaloosa, Alabama; received a B.A. in history and theology from the Franciscan University of Steubenville in 1994; received an M.A. in history from the University of Alabama in 1996; earned his Ph.D. in American History from the University of Alabama in 2001; author of "Religion and the Good Society: William Gilmore Simms's Classical View" in *The Simms Review* (2002) and "John Taylor and the Formation of an American Ideology" in *Continuity* (1998); is currently revising his dissertation, "Liberty, Tradition, and the Good Society: Antebellum Southern Conservatism," for publication.

THORNTON, Mark: Senior Fellow at the Ludwig von Mises Institute, Auburn, Alabama; Book Review Editor for the *Quarterly Journal of Austrian Economics;* he has taught at Trinity University, Auburn University, and Columbus State University, where he earned the University Research Award; received his Ph.D. in Economics from Auburn University (1989); author of *The Economics of Prohibition* (1991) and, with Robert B. Ekelund, of *Tariffs, Blockade, and Inflation: The Economics of the Civil War* (forthcoming), as well as many scholarly articles.

WYNNE, Chester J.: Independent scholar from Washington, D.C.

YANOCHIK, Mark A.: Assistant Professor of Economics at Georgia Southern University; holds a Ph.D. in Economics from Auburn University; author of articles in *Applied Economics Letters* and *Atlantic Economic Journal* and forthcoming articles in *Social Science Quarterly* and *Review of Regional Studies.*

INDEX

development of culture during slavery XIII 138–145

doctors banned by AMA XI 152

excluded from U.S. naturalization XII 7

exploitation of XIII 195

folktales XIII 139

impact of emancipation on XIII 50–57

impact of slavery upon XIII 197, 253–260, 261–267

Loyalists XII 189

religion XIII 187, 189

retention of African culture XIII 11–15

socio-economic divisions III 118

white ancestry of XIII 222

World War I VIII 298, 301; IX 1–7

World War II III 213–219

African National Congress (ANC) VI 5; VII 239, 286

Africans XIII 251

arrive in North America XIII 180

English views of XIII 250–251

enslavement of XIII 167

European views on XIII 179–180

racial discrimination XIII 181

Afrika Korps (Africa Corps) V 123, 181, 226, 232

Afrikaner Nationalist Party VII 239

Agadir, Morocco VIII 33

Age of Reason XII 109–110

Age of Sail VIII 136; IX 117

Agrarian Reform Law (1952) I 93, 123, 126

Agreement on German External Debts (1953) XI 215

Agricultural Adjustment Act (1933) III 27, 30, 62, 66, 156–163

Supreme Court ruling III 25

Agricultural Adjustment Administration (AAA, 1933) III 154, 157; VI 124

agricultural revolution III 2

agricultural science II 83–85

agricultural technology III 1–8

Global Positioning Satellites (GPS) III 5

history III 2, 5

impact of tractors III 6

post–World War II mechanization III 3

time management III 4

Agua Caliente Reservation VII 170

Aid for Families with Dependent Children (AFDC) II 278

Airborne Warning and Control System (AWACS) VI 173

aircraft carrier

defeat of U-boats IV 4

role in World War II I 4; IV 1–7

airplanes VIII 17

in WWI IX 9–14, 217–223

Akhmerov, Yitzhak VI 126

Akosombo Dam (Ghana) VII 4

Akron v. *Akron Center for Reproductive Health* (1983) II 222

Alabama

disfranchisement of blacks in XIII 56

grandfather clause XIII 56

meeting of Confederate Congress XIII 153

slavery in XIII 102, 195, 206, 221, 232, 282

use of Confederate symbols XIII 277

Alabama (Confederate ship) VIII 136–137

Albanians, enslavement of XIII 167

Al-Adil X 89, 256–258

Al-Afghani, Jamal al-Din X 61

Alamo Canal VII 152, 154–155, 157, 159

Al-Andalus X 8, 40–43, 60, 242

Al-Aqsa mosque X 198–199

Al-Ashraf X 47, 49

Alaska VII 197

salmon range VII 196

Albania I 294; VI 134, 175, 181, 261, 275, 280–281; VIII 212; IX 205, 227, 270

lack of environmental control in VII 145

Soviet domination until 1968 I 107

Albanian Communist Party VI 280

Albert I IX 42, 44

Albert of Aix X 16, 97, 211, 215, 219, 237, 276

Albigensian (Cathar) heresy X 208

Alcala, Pedro de X 8

Aleppo X 48, 51, 185

Alessandri Rodríguez, Jorge I 124, 127

Alexander (Greek king) IX 208

Alexander (Serbian king) VIII 45

Alexander I IX 268, 271; X 69; XII 308

Alexander II IX 155, 158, 190, 238; X 220, 224, 284

Alexander III 234, 236

Alexander, Harold IV 149, 181; V 73, 125

Italian campaign IV 144

Alexander, Leo T. XI 151–152

Alexandra IX 160, 237, 239–240, 243

Alexandria, Egypt VII 147; X 76, 141, 152, 170, 185, 187

construction of sewage plants in VII 148

sack of (1365) X 67, 70

Alexeyev, Mikhail IX 65

Alexius I Comnenus X 24, 26, 29, 74, 205, 209, 215, 220, 234, 238, 280, 285, 292

Alexius IV Angelus X 107, 110

Alfonso I X 242, 246

Alfonso II X 244

Alfonso III 242, 244

Alfonso VI 2, 41, 245, 289

Alfonso VIII X 133

Alfonso X X 160, 243

Alfonso, Pedro (Petrus Alfonsi) X 42, 44

Algeciras, Spain, conference in (1906) VIII 32

Algeria I 151, 281; VI 83, 103, 106–107, 188; VII 82; IX 111–112, 115–116; X 305

colonial policy of French VI 80, 136

coup in (1958) VI 106

environmental law in VII 145

independence from France I 278

Algiers Conference (1973) VI 268

Al-Hakim X 101, 218, 273, 287

Al-Harawi X 249

al-Husayni, Muhammed Amin VII 137

Al-Kamil X 89–90, 92

All-American Canal VII 154–155

All Quiet on the Western Front (1929) VIII 55, 59, 188, 264; IX 212

Allegheny Mountains XII 199, 232, 236

Allen, Ethan XII 10, 11, 14, 44

Allen, Richard VI 229, 231

Allenby, Edmund VIII 37, 39, 41, 121, 213, 216; IX 69, 72; X 59, 171, 305

Allende Gossens, Salvador I 26, 68, 123–125, 127–140; VI 64, 86–87, 265; XI 88

Alliance for Progress I 17–26, 126, 132; II 115

Allied Expeditionary Force (AEF) V 20, 23, 25

Allied Mediterranean Expeditionary Force VIII 119

Allied Supreme Council IX 173

Allies IV 208–215; V 27–33

relationship of IV 209; V 34–47

strategy IV 143–150; V 19–26

Allison, Francis XII 296

All-Russian Council of Soviets VIII 171

Al-Mansuri, Baybars X 49

Almohads X 273–275

Almoravids X 159, 163, 245, 274–275, 287

Al-Mu'azzam X 89–90

Alp Arslan X 138

Alphonse of Potiers X 145

Alpine Regional Hydroelectric Group VII 98

Alps VII 229, 231; XI 175

Al-Qaeda X 55, 61

Alsace-Lorraine VIII 71–72, 76, 151, 180, 226, 232, 234–237, 280–281; IX 46, 52, 102, 263

Altmühl River VII 204–207

Amalgamated Clothing Workers Union III 191

Amaury of Lautrec X 294

Amazon River VII 235

Ambrose, Stephen I 214; II 50

Ambrose X 97, 229

Brower, David Ross VII 110, 112
Brown, Harold VI 42–43
Brown, John XII 11; XIII 4
Brown v. *Board of Education of Topeka, Kansas* (1954) II 20, 23–24, 26, 45, 80, 90–91, 136–143, 270, 280, 286, 293, 295; III 27, 185
Brown Synod (1933) XI 27
Brown University XIII 31, 198
Bruchmuller, Georg IX 127–129
Brusilov, Aleksey VIII 266; IX 60–66, 193, 242
Brusilov Offensive (1916) IX 72, 137, 155, 193, 243, 252
Brussels Treaty (1954) I 208; VI 101
Bryan, Samuel XII 76
Bryan, William Jennings III 32, 34, 36–37; VIII 204; IX 19, 21, 246
    Scopes Trial III 33
Brzezinski, Zbigniew I 135, 143, 146; VI 42, 166, 256, 263
Buchanan, James XIII 195, 278
Buchenwald (concentration camp) V 57; XI 45, 236, 245
    German people's reaction V 215
Buck v. *Bell* (1927) III 18, 21
Buddhist monks, immolation of VI 23
Bukovina IX 136
Bulganin, Nikolai A. VI 135
Bulgaria I 107, 294; II 39, 153; VI 251–252, 261, 274, 276, 280; VIII 11, 14, 44, 46, 95, 212, 216–217, 230; IX 120, 171, 203–206, 270, 272; XI 214, 220
    ally of Germany VIII 278
    U.S. push for greater freedoms I 110
    U.S. recognizes communist government I 303
Bulgars X 29
Bull, William XII 215
Bull Moose Party III 243
Bund Deutscher Mädel (German Girls' Organization) IV 191
Bund Naturschutz in Bayern (BUND) VII 206, 210
Bundestag (Federal Diet) VI 102
Bundy, McGeorge I 29, 294; II 6
    flexible response I 120
    use of nuclear weapons policy I 171
Bureau of Indian Affairs (BIA) III 141, 143; VII 55–56, 59, 166–167, 169, 172
Burger, Justice Warren E. II 182, 221, 284; XII 283
Burgess, Guy I 243, 245; VI 11
Burgh, James XII 278
Burgoyne, John XII 10, 15, 39, 45–47, 80, 95–96, 100, 103, 155, 158, 162, 181, 267–274, 305
Burke, Edmund XII 29–30, 139, 143, 166
Burke, Thomas XII 185
Burma VIII 35; XII 33
    fall of V 197
    opium trade I 15
Burundi II 101, 155
Bush, George VI 28, 51, 58, 61, 191, 195, 205, 226, 229, 242, 257; X 56
    Africa policy VI 7
    civil war in Somalia II 155
    foreign policy "balance of power" II 155
    international political experience II 152
    New World Order II 152–158
    nuclear nonproliferation policy I 224
    Panama intervention II 155
    Persian Gulf crisis II 153
    relationship with former Yugoslavia II 155
    role of United States II 155
    U.S. spying on Soviet Union I 191
    unilateral U.S. foreign policy II 156
Bush, George W. VII 224
Bush (George H. W.) administration II 100; VI 120
    arms-control agreements VI 20
    defense spending VI 224
    envisioning of New World Order II 155
    nuclear-nonproliferation policy I 217
    policy on Afghanistan I 14–16
Bushido code III 13

Butler, Justice Pierce III 25
Butler, Pierce XII 296
Butler, Smedley, IX 96
Butterfield, Herbert X 278, 304
Buxton, Thomas Fowell XIII 131, 159
Byrd II, William XIII 150–151, 207
Byrnes, James F. I 28, 31, 263, 304; II 206; V 51, 53; XI 256
Byzantine Empire X 33, 73, 88, 92, 107–108, 110, 112, 118–119, 121, 128, 138, 150–151, 156, 172–174, 188, 205, 208–209, 215, 238–239, 249–250, 262, 269, 280, 282, 284, 287; XIII 167
    Crusades X 15, 24–31
    relations with the West X 24–31

C

Cabora Bassa Dam (Mozambique) VII 237, 239, 240
Cadwalader, John XII 98
Caesar, Julius XII 302
cahiers des doleances (notebooks of grievances) XII 129, 133
Cairncross, John VI 11
    Soviet nuclear spying I 243–245
Cairnes, John E. XIII 174, 240, 242
Cairo X 76–77, 89, 170, 172, 185, 192, 262
Cairo Conference (1943) VI 146
Calais XII 242
Calhoun, John XIII 48
California VII 180, 201; X 8; XI 124
    dams in VII 27, 29
    Department of Fish and Game VII 178
    environmental activism in VII 174
    flood control in VII 273
    legislation on Holocaust reparations XI 216
    pollution control in VII 264
    receives federal swamplands VII 272
    water policy in VII 153
California Aqueduct VII 179
California Coastal Commission VII 175, 179
California Development Company (CDC) 155
Calloway, Cab IX 4
Calonne, Charles-Alexandre de XII 131–132
Calueque Dam (Angola) VII 239
Calvin's Case (1607) XII 42
Calvinism XII 149–150; XIII 31
Cambodia I 40–47, 145, 289, 299; II 6, 177; VI 4, 44, 60, 63, 65, 68, 83, 93, 188, 194, 203, 221; XII 33
    colony of France I 290
    genocide in XI 71, 79, 166–167 169
    Khmer Rouge movement I 15; VI 271
    spread of communism I 297
    supply lines through VI 60
    U.S. bombing of I 183, 291; VI 86
    U.S. invasion of I 291; VI 23, 26, 165, 284
    Vietnam invasion of VI 44
Cambon, Paul IX 44
Cambridge University IX 172
Camp David agreement (1978) I 159
Camp Gordon, Georgia VIII 23, 299
Campbell, Alexander XII 313
Campbell, Archibald XII 184
Canada I 30–31; VI 101, 136; VII 182; VIII 33, 83, 160–161, 208; IX 122, 173; XI 62;. XII 10, 12, 15, 39, 98, 109, 165, 171, 199, 267–268, 272–274, 316; XIII 120
    American Revolution XII 43–49
    Atomic Energy Act I 221
    British immigration to XII 168
    charter member of NATO I 208
    criticism of Libertad Act I 98
    Cuban investment I 97
    discussion of nuclear weapons I 28
    escaped slaves XIII 124
    fish hatcheries in VII 202
    fishing rights in VIII 35
    French desire to regain territory in XII 104

origins of I 258–264; II 30
Reagan's role in ending VI 221–241
Stalin's role in starting VI 250–252
vindicationist interpretation VI 155
Colden, Cadwallader XII 214
Cole v. *Young* I 80
Collier, John (Commissioner of Indian Affairs) III 141–142
Collins, J. Lawton I 6; V 122
Colombia XIII 104
colonialism X 55–56, 63
Colorado VII 10, 13, 112, 181, 182
farmers' use of water in VII 13
production of crops on irrigated land in VII 11
Colorado River VII 27, 31, 151–153, 155, 168, 211, 214
dams on VII 108–115, 152
Colorado River Compact (CRC) VII 152–153
Colorado River Irrigation District VII 157
Colorado River Land Company VII 152
Colorado River Storage Project (CRSP) VII 27, 112
Columbia Basin VII 29
dams in VII 196
Columbia Basin Project VII 202
Columbia River VII 25, 27–28, 31, 51–61, 197, 199, 202, 219–220, 222, 225, 227
first major navigation project on VII 52
hydroelectric dams on VII 198
salmon producer VII 53
Columbia River Fisherman's Protective Union VII 53
Columbia River Highway VII 57
Columbia River Inter-Tribal Fish Commission VII 61
Columbia River Packers Association VII 53
Columbia University XIII 198
Columbus, Christopher X 7–8, 304; XIII 147, 210
Comal River VII 70
combat effectiveness
Germany V 282, 284
Japan V 281–282
Leyte campaign V 281
Normandy invasion V 282
psychological limits IV 47–52
United States V 278–286
Combined Bomber Offensive IX 223
Combined Chiefs of Staff (CCS) V 20, 23, 25, 38, 42–45
Commission on Polish Affairs VIII 281
Commission on Presidential Debates II 196, 199
Committee on Political Refugees XI 60
Committee on Public Information (CPI) VIII 296; IX 78
Committee on the Present Danger VI 256, 262
Committee to Re-Elect the President (CREEP) II 177; VI 24
Common Sense (1776) XII 54, 110, 121, 143, 153
Commonwealth of Independent States (CIS) VI 54
Commonwealth of Nations VI 13
The Commonwealth of Oceana (1656) XII 123
Commonwealth v. *Turner* (1827) XIII 102
communism I 148–155; II 31–32, 56–57, 160; VI 49; IX 83
atheism of VI 176
attraction for women VI 49
China II 267e
collapse of II 153
global II 130
ideology I 258–262; VI 49
infiltration of federal government II 133
world domination VI 175–182
Communist Control Act (1954) I 74, 77
Communist Information Bureau (Cominform) I 36–113; VI 179, 246
Communist International (Comintern) I 113; III 224, 226; IV 80; VI 178, 254, 277
Communist Manifesto (1848) VI 178; XIII 69
Communist Party I 74; III 182, 221
in Chile I 124
in Guatemala I 123
of the Soviet Union III 224; VI 179, 276

of Yugoslavia (CPY) VI 273–278, 280–281
Communist Party of the United States of America (CPUSA) II 46–48; III 237; VI 123, 154, 157
Federation of Architects, Engineers, Chemists and Technicians II 228
history of III 224
organization of Southern Tenant Farmers Unions II 189
1932 presidential candidate III 182
Community Action Programs (CAP) II 270–276
Community Development Corporation XIII 200
Community Reinvestment Act (1977) XIII 200
Comnena, Anna X 211, 215
Compañía de Terrenos y Aguas de la Baja California, S.A. VII 155
Comprehensive Immigration Law (1924) III 233
Comprehensive Test Ban Treaty (CTBT) I 224; VI 58
Comprehensive Wetlands Management and Conservation Act VII 274
Concert of Europe VI 203
Confederate Army, Zouave units in IX 116
Confederate Congress XIII 153, 277
Confederate Constitution XIII 274, 277
Confederate States of America XIII 5, 45, 195
use of symbols from XIII 269–278
Confederation Congress XII 293, 299
Conference on Environmental Economics at Hyvinkää (1998) VII 89
Confessing Church XI 27–35, 135
Confiscation Plan XIII 51
Congo IX 226; XIII 11
slave trade XIII 35, 40
Congregational Church VIII 204; XII 148, 150, 216, 254, 263
Congress of African People (1970) II 95; III 193, 195
Congress of Berlin IX 99
Congress of Industrial Organizations (CIO) II 188, 197; III 183–184, 191, 195
Congress of Vienna (1815) IX 45, 226
Congress of Racial Equality (CORE) II 161; III 219; XIII 256
Congressional Black Caucus XIII 198
Connally, John VI 257
Connecticut XII 10–12, 15, 66, 70, 205, 209, 215
gradual emancipation in XIII 19
impact of Shays's Rebellion in XII 287
prohibits importation of slaves XIII 18
religion in XII 148, 150, 263
slave uprising in XIII 235
Connolly, Thomas T. II 208; III 31; VI 151
Conrad X 48, 286
Conrad III X 128, 294
Conrad of Montferrat X 256, 258
Conrad von Hotzendorf, Franz VIII 46–47, 49, 252; IX 64–65, 99, 135, 137
Conradin X 142
Conscription Crisis (1917) VIII 158–159
Conservation in Action Series (1947) VII 278
Conservative Party (Great Britain) VI 13
Constantine (Greek king) IX 208
Constantine I (Roman emperor) X 80–82, 224, 228
Constantine IX X 284
Constantinople VIII 117–118, 122, 173, 212, 214–215, 228; IX 208; X 27–30, 47, 58, 88, 108, 110, 112–114, 121, 150, 152, 208–209, 220–221, 239, 250, 262, 281, 284–286
fall of (1204) X 24, 27, 36, 108
Constitution of the United States (1787) II 98, 101; VI 56, 283–284; XII 7, 18, 58, 60–62, 64, 66, 108, 113, 118, 120–122, 127, 131, 134, 276–283, 288, 293, 297; XIII 7, 56, 272, 274
economic interpretation of XII 68–76
Eighteenth Amendment (1919) III 198–200, VIII 295
Fifteenth Amendment (1870) III 270; XIII 5, 56
Fifth Amendment II 132, 134, 281–282; III 107
First Amendment II 166; XII 60, 61, 63

Index

INDEX

INDEX

INDEX

INDEX

Nasser, Gamal Abdel I 110, 162, 273, 277–278, 283, 314; II 117, 146–147; VI 11, 80–81, 106, 161, 246, 268, 270; VII 3; X 56
    challenges Britain I 280
    pan-Arab campaign I 281
    "positive neutrality" II 148
Nation of Islam II 93–95
National Aeronautics and Space Administration (NASA) II 246, 258, 260; XI 152
    creation of II 242
    funding of II 261
National Association for the Advancement of Colored People (NAACP) II 19–20, 23, 25, 27, 44–45, 90, 94, 138, 140–141; III 80, 93, 118, 121, 182, 184–186, 217, 270–274; IX 2, 4; XIII 256, 277
    opposition to Model Cities housing projects II 277
    Scottsboro case III 185
National Association of Black Journalists II 96
National Association of Broadcasters II 123
National Association of Colored Women III 167
National Audubon Society VII 215
National Black Political Convention (1972) II 95, 198
National Committee of Negro Churchmen II 95
National Committee to Re-Open the Rosenberg Case II 228
National Conference of Christians and Jews XI 159
National Council of Negro Churchmen (NCNC) II 94
National Council of Mayors VII 258
National Defense and Interstate Highway Act (1956) II 107
National Defense Highway Act (1956) II 249
National Education Association II 190–191
National Environmental Policy Act (NEPA) II 183; VII 31, 176, 266, 269,
National Farmers Process Tax Recovery Association III 159
National Front for the Liberation of Angola (*Frente Nacional de Libertação de Angola* or FNLA) VI 1, 6, 87, 165
National Guard Act (1903) VIII 301
National Industrial Recovery Act (NIRA, 1933) III 27–28, 62, 65, 149, 154
    Supreme Court ruling III 25
National Intelligence Estimates (NIEs) VI 256–258, 260
National Labor Relations Act (Wagner Act, 1935) III 149, 193
National Labor Relations Board (NLRB) II 188; III 30, 62, 149, 190–191, 193, 195
National Liberation Front (NLF) I 296; II 119, 263–264, 266
National liberation movements VI 183–187
National Negro Congress (NNC) III 184
National Negro Convention XIII 234
National Organization of Women (NOW) II 78
National Organization for Women v. *Joseph Scheidler* (1994) II 223
National Parks Association VII 30
National Pollutant Discharge Elimination System VII 264
National Prohibition Act (1919) III 200
National Reclamation Act (1902) III 243
National Recovery Administration (NRA, 1933) III 30, 154
National Security Act (1947) I 5, 7, 64, 69; VI 61
National Security Agency (NSA) I 74; II 230; VI 157
National Security Council (NSC) I 54, 64, 83, 121; VI 41, 90, 96, 196, 231
National Security Council memorandum 68 (NSC-68) I 83–84, 89, 149, 182, 211, 274
National Security Decision Directives (NSDD) VI 13, 32, 82, 166
National Socialist German Workers' Party (Nazi Party, Nazis) I 35; IV 267; VI 49, 176, 254, 274, 277; VIII 92, 94, 167; XI 4–5, 21–23, 28–29, 32–33, 35, 55, 59, 67, 70, 72, 74–75, 77, 80–

81, 83, 87–88, 90, 93–95, 98, 102–103, 105–107, 111, 113, 121, 128, 138–140, 142, 169, 171, 183–184, 186, 189, 202–203, 207–208, 211, 217, 223, 238–239, 245, 253, 255–257, 264, 266, 268, 270–271; XII 259
    criminality of XI 166–173
    euthanasia XI 83, 270
    medical experiments of XI 146–154
    Night of the Long Knives (1934) XI 243
    public health XI 47
    racial ideology XI 118
    resistance to XI 268
    war crime trials 252–264
National Socialist Party of Austria XI 36
National Union for the Total Independence of Angola (*União Nacional para a Independência Total de Angola* or UNITA) VI 1–2, 6, 87, 165
National Urban League II 94; III 80, 184; IX 2, 4
National Water Act of 1974 (Poland) 18
Native Americans VIII 23, 27; X 10, 179; XII 18, 34, 37, 53, 73, 95, 199, 217, 263, 279, 282, 285; XIII 161
    advocate breaching dams VII 221
    American Revolution XII 44, 49, 173–180, 268
    assimilation of VII 55, 168
    blamed for reducing salmon catch VII 199
    Canary Islands, brought to XIII 168
    control of resources on reservations VII 166–173
    Creek confederacy XII 295
    dam income VII 59
    dam monitoring by Columbia River tribes VII 223
    displacement of VII 27
    environmental damage to land VII 111
    extermination of XI 71, 169
    First Salmon ceremony VII 56
    fishing VII 57, 197, 220
    fishing rights of VII 198, 202
    Great Rendezvous at Celilio Falls VII 56
    impact of dams on VII 29, 51–61, 108, 110
    impact of diseases upon XIII 162
    ingenuity of VII 11
    intermarriage with non-Indians VII 169
    loss of rights VII 151
    on Columbia River VII 202
    opposition by non-Indians living on the reservations VII 172
    protest movements VII 199
    relocation of burial grounds VII 60
    relations with maroons XIII 110
    relationship with U.S. government III 139–146
    reservations of VII 28
    sacred sites endangered by dams VII 25
    symbolism of U.S. flag XIII 270
    threat to western expansion XII 18
    treaties VII 56, 222
    used as slaves XIII 162
Native Americans, tribes
    Aymara Indians (Peru) XII 74
    Aztec XIII 162
    Cherokee XII 264
    Chippewa XII 175–176, 178
    Cocopah VII 151
    Delaware XII 175
    Flathead VII 167, 169–170
    Hopi VII 169
    Hualapai VII 110, 114
    Inca XIII 162
    Iroquois XII 41, 173–180
    Kootenai VII 167, 171–172
    Miami XII 175–176
    Mohawk XII 173–175, 177, 179
    Muckleshoot VII 191
    Navajo VII 110–111, 114
    Nez Perce VII 51, 55–56, 59
    Oneida XII 173–175, 177–179
    Onondaga XII 173–175, 177, 180
    Ottawa XII 175
    Pawnee VII 166

ratification of Constitution XII 74
seizure of Loyalist property XII 193
slave uprising in XIII 235
slavery in XII 5, 263
state legislature XII 22
New York City VII 256, 265–266; XII 22, 33, 37, 39, 45, 47, 78, 80, 92, 122, 182, 222, 234, 259, 267–268, 270–271, 274, 302, 307–308
Loyalists in XII 182
water problems in VII 261
New Zealand VIII 133, 160–161; XII 168
represented at Evian Conference XI 55
World War I VIII 117–123, 220, 266; IX 173
Newbury, Massachusetts VII 277
wetlands confiscated in VII 278
Newell, Frederick H. VII 26
Newell, Roger VII 48
Newfoundland XII 171
Newlands, Francis Griffith VII 25–26
Newlands Reclamation Act (1902) VII 25–26, 201
Ngo Dinh Diem I 290, 298; II 97, 119, 266–267; VI 92–99
Ngo Dinh Nhu II 119; VI 94, 96
Nicaragua I 48–49, 51, 53–54, 57, 94, 96, 141; II 56, 58; III 50; VI 4, 44, 57, 61, 64, 68, 131, 190–196, 221, 231, 236–237, 241, 261, 265–266, 270; IX 96
human rights record I 143
mining Managua harbor VI 190–191
National Security Decision Directive 17 (NSDD-17) I 50
Sandanista takeover I 125–126
Somoza dictators II 103
Soviet support of guerrillas VI 58, 193
U.S. arms shipments (1954) I 123
U.S. policy in VI 190–196, 249
Nicephorus III Botaneiates X 220, 285
Nicholas II VIII 171, 174–175, 226, 229, 258, 266, 268; IX 99, 156–160, 193, 237–243; XI 167
Niemöller, Martin IV 188–189; XI 29, 31, 33, 35
Nietzsche, Frederick XI 75
Nigeria XIII 11, 193
slave trade XIII 35
Nile River VII 2–3; X 89, 92, 95, 141, 173
Nimitz, Chester W. IV 7, 172; V 7; XI 258, 262
Nine-Power Treaty (1922) IV 258
1960s progressive movements II 159–167
1920s III 174–180
Nipomo Dunes VII 178
Nitze, Paul H. I 82–83, 86, 149, 191, 211, 274
Nivelle, Robert-Georges VIII 104, 106, 111, 114, 149, 269; IX 104–105, 108, 110, 212, 257
Nivelle Offensive (1917) IX 118, 129
Nixon, Richard M. I 40–41, 44–47, 66, 74, 89, 101–102, 104, 140, 159, 306, 317; II 4, 7, 95, 97, 102, 115, 133, 162, 165, 171–172, 197, 209, 256, 257, 260, 280–281; III 48; VI 4, 23–24, 26, 28, 30, 56, 58–59, 61, 91, 96, 162, 206, 231, 256–257, 284; XI 88, 167; XII 28, 30, 31
anticommunist legislation II 131; VI 203
childhood of II 176
Committee to Re-Elect the President (CREEP) II 177
domestic policy II 175–186
election (1968) VI 85
Equal Employment Opportunity Commission (EEOC) II 182
establishes EPA VII 266
Executive Order 11458 II 183
Federal Occupational Safety and Health Act (1970) II 192
foreign policy II 168–174
goal of Middle East policy I 162
human rights I 141; VI 200
loss to John F. Kennedy II 177
malicious campaign tactics of II 177
meetings with Brezhnev II 170

mutual assured destruction (MAD) policy I 169
pardoned by Gerald R. Ford II 179
Pentagon Papers II 177
presidential election (1960) I 188
psychological analyses of II 181
reelection campaign (1972) VI 86, 88
resignation I 292; II 179; VI 87
signs Great Lakes Water Agreement VII 120
"Silent Majority" speech II 9
vetos Federal Water Pollution Control Act Amendments VII 263
vice president of Eisenhower II 177
Vietnam I 291; II 173
War on Poverty II 270
Watergate I 144, 292; II 176, 185
Nixon administration I 68, 129; II 3–4; VI 35, 199; VII 269; IX 5
acceptance of Israel as a nuclear-weapons state I 158
applies Refuse Act provisions VII 266
Cambodia I 41–45; VI 60
Chile I 130
China VI 38–44, 201, 204
foreign policy I 141–143; VI 58–59, 85–91, 198–205
Latin America I 18
Middle East I 162
nuclear proliferation policy I 222; VI 18
Vietnam VI 40, 86, 99, 203
Nixon Doctrine VI 199
Nkotami Accord (1984) VI 5
Nkrumah, Kwame I 110; III 121; VII 237
Nobel Peace Prize III 243; IX 228
Martin Luther King Jr. II 19
Theodore Roosevelt II 99
Woodrow Wilson II 99
Non-Aligned Movement (NAM) VI 181, 268, 270–271; VII 240
nongovernmental organizations (NGOs) 19, 247–248, 254
Nordic Environmental Certificate VII 87
Noriega, Manuel VI 225
Normandy invasion (June 1944) IV 14; V 10, 12, 15, 17–23, 37, 41, 58, 80, 102, 196 ; XI 16
Normans X 24, 26, 117, 121–122, 199, 212, 216, 224, 269, 284, 289
Conquest of England (1066) X 101, 301
North, Frederick (Lord North) XII 28, 30, 47, 103, 139, 141, 144, 156, 159, 168, 182, 185, 190, 248–249, 251–252, 254–255, 262
North, Oliver Col. VI 196, 231
North Africa II 144; VII 148; VIII 233; IX 91, 111, 114, 116; X 6, 61, 148–149, 159, 270, 273, 275, 304–305; XI 176
growth of industry in VII 147
invasion of V 5, 35
slaves from XIII 167
North America XIII 181
first Africans to XIII 180
indentured servitude in XIII 247
property ownership in XII 124
racism XIII 179, 180
slave rebellions XIII 231–238
slavery in XIII 59–66
North Atlantic Regional Study (NARS) VII 261
North Atlantic Treaty Organization (NATO) I 35, 107, 120, 124, 151, 154, 160, 168, 170, 175, 182, 196, 198, 213, 222, 254, 277, 283, 296; II 50, 61, 100, 146, 152, 264, 267; IV 30; V 42, 149; VI 8–9, 11, 18–19, 50, 53, 80, 100–102; 105–106, 115, 131, 134–136, 173, 188, 199, 206–207, 209, 215, 217, 267, 271; VII 83; XI 188, 256
creation of I 204–209
involvement in Bosnian conflict II 154
military strategy in Europe VI 168–174
withdrawal of France VI 145

Robertson, William VIII 77, 102–108, 221
Robespierre, Maximillian XII 134
Robinson, Bestor VII 112
Robinson, James H. II 44
Robinson, Randall XIII 195, 197–198
Rochambeau, Comte de XII 33, 306, 308
Rock and Roll II 213–219
    "British invasion" II 216
    commercial aspects II 219
    form of rebellion II 219
    liberating force II 213
    mass marketing of II 216
    origin of term II 214
    punk trends II 216
    revolutionary force II 214
    unifying force II 216
Rock Around the Clock (1956) II 219
Rockefeller, John D. III 271
Rockefeller, Nelson A. III 48; VII 264
Rocky Boy's Reservation VII 172
Rocky Ford VII 15
Rocky Ford Ditch Company VII 13
Rocky Mountains VII 151, 181, 197
Roderigue Hortalez & Cie XII 101, 106
Roe v. Wade (1973) II 78, 220–226, 280, 284
Roger II (Sicily) X 198, 285, 289
Rogue River VII 31, 223
Röhm, Ernst XI 243
Roland X 65, 103
Roman Empire X 24–25, 29, 88, 124, 167, 305
Romania I 110, 294; II 36, 39, 172; V 64; VI 51, 88,
    175, 206, 210, 217, 245, 249, 252, 261, 265,
    274, 276; VII 248–250, 252–254; VIII 43–
    44, 46, 93–97, 163, 216, 230, 278; IX 60–61,
    66, 127, 193, 205, 207; X 65, 70; XI 15, 60,
    142, 214, 220
    chemical spill in VII 247–255
    Department of Waters, Forests, and
        Environmental Protection VII 248
    Environmental Protection Agency VII 248
    forest clear-cutting in VII 254
    relationship with Soviets I 253
    Soviet Domination I 107
    U.S. recognizes communist government I 303
Romanian Waters Authority VII 248
Rome XIII 274, 278
    slavery in XIII 165
Rommel, Erwin V 123–126, 129, 135, 143, 176, 181,
    226; VIII 111
    legend V 175
Roosevelt, Eleanor III 150, 217, 219
Roosevelt, Franklin D. II 32, 39, 50, 52, 165, 197, 203,
    280; III 10–11, 14, 45, 48, 86, 89, 109, 147,
    190, 193; IV 173, 210; V 58, 236, 249; VI 8–
    9, 20, 36, 56–57, 78, 104, 123, 146–147, 158,
    205, 254, 267; VII 28, 97, 152, 202; XI 4,
    10–12, 55–57, 60, 64, 110, 121, 168, 174,
    252, 261
    arsenal of democracy III 64
    Asia policy IV 254
    attitude toward Soviet Union III 13
    belief in a cooperative relationship with the Soviet
        Union I 101
    Brain Trust II 210
    Casablanca conference (1943) V 252
    Court packing scheme XI 168
    election of VII 27
    Executive Order 8802 (1941) III 219
    Executive Order 9066 (1942) III 103–104
    Fireside chats III 148, 152
    Four Freedoms V 250
    Good Neighbor Policy I 125; III 47
    Great Depression III 54–60
    Inaugural Address (1932) III 152
    isolationism V 289–294
    Lend Lease Act IV 160
    Native American policies III 141–142
    New Deal II 47, 271; III 193, 263

New Deal programs III 62–63
Operation Torch (1942) V 251
opinion of Second Front IV 213
presidential campaign (1932) III 148
previous war experience V 253
relationship with George C. Marshall V 251
Roosevelt Court II 281
Scottsboro case III 188
Selective Service Act (1940) V 250
State of the Union Address (1941) II 99
support of Great Britain V 250
support of highway building II 106
support of naval reorganization IV 3
Supreme Court III 24
unconditional surrender policy V 270–276
western irrigation VII 25
World War II strategy V 251, 253
Yalta conference V 252, 309–315
Roosevelt, Theodore I 306; II 195, 199, 271–272; III
    208, 211, 240–247, 177; VIII 18, 22, 129,
    205; IX 5, 168, 246
    appreciation of public image III 242
    Bull Moose Party III 243
    conservation efforts III 243
    Dominican Republic III 247
    establishes federal refuges VII 271, 273
    First Children III 242
    labor disputes III 243
    New Nationalism III 211
    Nobel Peace Prize II 99, 243
    racial prejudices III 246
    role as a family man III 242
    Rough Riders III 241
    signs Newlands Reclamation Act VII 25
    Spanish-American War (1898) III 245
    supports western reclamation VII 26
    Teddy bears III 242
    views on Latin America I 132
Roosevelt (FDR) administration III 46; VI 154; XI
    123
    dam projects VII 25
    national drug policy III 135
    New Deal III 163
    opium trade III 137
    policy toward Jews III 251; XI 60, 64, 121
    relationship with labor movement II 188
    Soviet sympathizers in VI 61, 154
    spurs Western growth VII 28
    support of Mexican Water Treaty VII 152
    Third World VI 80
    War Refugee Board (WRB) III 253
Roosevelt (TR) administration
    Anti-Trust Act (1890) III 242
    Big Stick diplomacy III 46
    corollary to the Monroe Doctrine III 247
    Department of Commerce and Labor, Bureau of
        Corporations III 242
    foreign policy III 243, 245
    Hepburn Act (1906) III 243, 245
    National Reclamation Act (1902) III 243
    Panama Canal III 243, 247
    Pure Food and Drug Act (1906) III 243
    United States Forestry Service III 243
Roosevelt Corollary (1904) III 46
Roosevelt Dam (United States) VII 214, 216
Root Elihu VIII 298
Rosellini, Albert D. VII 190
Rosenberg, Alfred V 143, 216; XI 118
Rosenberg, Julius and Ethel I 274; II 131, 227–234; VI
    154, 156, 158, 177
    arrest of II 229, 231–232
    Communist Party of the United States of America
        (CPUSA) II 227
    execution of II 233
    forged documents II 230
    Freedom of Information Act II 228
    G & R Engineering Company II 229
    martyrdom II 230

INDEX

INDEX

Smith, Ian VI 2, 83

Smith Act (Alien Registration Act of 1940) I 77, 79, 81; III 11

Smith v. *Allwright,* 1944 II 141

Smuts, Jan VIII 85–86, 89; IX 13, 222

Smyrna VIII 214, 217; IX 208

Smyth, Henry De Wolf I 247–248

Smyth Report I 248

Smythe, William A. VII 151

Snake River 27, 29, 31, 53–54, 196–197, 220, 221, 223–225, 227
    dams on VII 219–228

Sobibor (concentration camp) XI 220, 236

Social Darwinism III 260; IV 86, 123; VIII 60, 299; IX 99, 112, 209, 224, 228; XI 82, 115

Social Democratic Party I 255; VI 20, 207

Social Ecological Movement VII 20

Social Security Act (1935) III 63, 149

Socialism II 34, 60, 160; VIII 254–262; IX 83

Socialist convention (1913) III 223

Socialist Labor Party II 42

Socialist Party II 196, 199; III 222–223
    Debs, Eugene V. III 221

Socialist Unity Party (SED) VI 118, 121

Society for the Abolition of the Slave Trade XIII 1

Society for the Propagation of the Gospel in Foreign Parts (SPG) XII 148

Soil Conservation and Domestic Allotment Act (1936) III 157

Solidarity VI 110, 237; VII 17, 19, 20

Solzhenitzyn, Aleksandr VI 200

Somalia II 100, 155–156; VI 164, 271
    claim to Ogaden VI 165
    Ethiopian conflict VI 165
    imperialism I 151
    relations with the Soviet Union VI 165

Somerset case (1772) XIII 1

Somoza Debayle, Anastasio I 48–49, 54, 126, 141; III 51; VI 190–191

Somocistas VI 64, 191

Sonoran Desert VII 151–152
    agriculture in VII 152

Sons of Liberty XII 152, 214, 218, 261

Sontag, Susan XI 42

Sophie's Choice (1982) XI 158

Sorensen, Ted II 275

Sorenson, Theodore C. II 117

South (American) XIII 233, 256
    adaptibility of slaves to environment in XIII 11
    African-inspired architectural design XIII 141
    antebellum women in XIII 224–230
    black population in XII 299
    Civil War, slavery as cause of XIII 276
    clock ownership XIII 202–208
    cotton as single crop XIII 43
    economic impact of slavery upon XIII 42–48
    economy of XIII 169–170, 175, 243
    firearms in XIII 233
    impact of Revolution on economy of XII 264
    Ku Klux Klan XIII 55
    Loyalists in XII 181–182, 186
    power of slaveholding elite XIII 69
    Reconstruction, end of XIII 55
    religion in XIII 186–190
    segregation in XIII 57
    sexual exploitation of slave women in XIII 217–223
    slave codes XIII 176
    slave laws XIII 94, 96, 97, 261
    slave rebellions XIII 231
    slaveholders as capitalists XIII 239–245
    slavery in XIII 85, 86–92, 98, 101–102, 112–128, 169–172, 175, 178–179, 231, 247–248, 262, 264–267
    trade with New England XIII 195
    violence against blacks and Republicans in XIII 55
    wealth of XIII 43

women, interracial relations XIII 224–230

South Africa I 51; VI 1, 2, 4, 6, 50, 54, 87, 136, 178, 215; VII 2, 5, 67, 236–237, 239–241; VIII 31, 160–161, 208; XI 43, 167; XII 33, 169
    apartheid VI 13
    Bill of Rights VII 287
    British immigration to VII 237
    inequalities of water supply in VII 284
    intervention in Angola VI 7
    intervention in Mozambique VI 6
    nuclear weapons development I 219–223
    rinderpest epidemic VII 34
    use of water by upper class VII 7
    water policy in VII 286, 287

South African National Defense Force VII 7

South African War (1899–1902) IX 68

South America,
    death squads in XI 166
    introduction of species to the United States from VII 217
    slavery in XIII 175

South Carolina XII 1, 39, 41, 68, 70, 75, 184–185, 205, 209, 213, 218–219, 263, 314; XIII 53, 66, 71, 73
    African Americans in XII 89
    anti-Loyalist activities in XII 190, 192
    Black Codes XIII 54
    cattle raising XIII 11
    clock ownership XIII 205
    dispute over Confederate flag XIII 270
    laws on rice dams and flooding VII 272
    Loyalists in XII 184, 187
    maroons in XIII 108, 111
    massacre of Rebels in XII 186
    mob action in American Revolution XII 215
    property qualifications to vote XIII 56
    prosecution of Thomas Powell XII 233
    Reconstruction, end of XIII 55
    religion in XII 263
    rice cultivation VII 272; XIII 11
    secession XIII 272, 276
    slave rebellions XIII 156, 210, 231, 235–236
    slavery in VII 272; XII 3–4, 295, 297, 299; XIII 11, 61, 81, 83, 87, 98–99, 102, 140, 204, 218, 232, 235, 240, 244, 248, 265, 267
    use of Confederate symbols XIII 277
    women in XII 319

South Carolina College XIII 28

South Carolina Declaration of the Causes of Secession (1860) XIII 270, 276

South Carolina Red Shirts XIII 55

South Dakota VII 181
    dams in VII 29

South East Asia Treaty Organization (SEATO) II 52, 264

South Korea I 86–87, 288, 293; II 37; VI 102, 147–149, 217, 263
    domino theory I 266
    invaded by North Korea (1950) I 208; VI 28
    invasion of I 184
    nuclear weapons development I 216, 219, 223
    U.S. intervention I 158

South Sea Company XIII 40

South Vietnam I 40–46, 290, 293–299; II 5–8, 263, 266; VI 58–60, 92–99, 101, 138, 140, 201, 203, 284; XII 30, 34
    aid received from United States I 158; VI 2, 66, 142, 144
    conquered by North Vietnam I 142; VI 222
    declares independence I 290
    Soviet support I 185

Southeast Asia XII 28–29, 33–34

Southeast Asia Treaty Organization (SEATO) I 277; VI 203, 287

Southeastern Anatolia Project VII 77, 83

Southern African Hearings for Communities affected by Large Dams VII 242

Southern Baptist Convention III 38

INDEX

Student, Kurt V 14
Students for a Democratic Society (SDS) II 7, 160, 162
Submarines V 255–261; VIII 11, 287–294; IX 183
    antisubmarine warfare (ASW) V 256
    antiwarship (AWS) operations V 259
    Great Britain V 260
    I-class V 258
    Italy V 261
    Japanese Navy V 258, 261
    Kriegsmarine (German Navy) V 261
    RO-class V 258
    Soviet Union V 261
    United States V 261
    unrestricted warfare VIII 22, 204, 287–294, 296
Suburbia II 249–255, 293–294
    suburban developments II 160
Sudan VII 3
Sudeten German Party XI 207
Sudetenland IX 272; XI 14, 60, 207
    Munich Agreement (1938) I 300
Sudetenland crisis (September 1938) IV 125, 248; XI 15
Suez Canal VI 10, 80, 270; VII 2, 147; VIII 38, 213
Suez Crisis (1956) I 192, 289; II 52, 148; VI 8, 11, 80–81, 106, 130, 133, 135, 160, 188, 209, 270
    U.S. position I 185; VI 270
Suffolk Resolves XII 54
Sugar Act (1764) XII 2, 55, 149, 200, 207, 231, 233, 236, 240, 313–314
Sukarno I 110, 273, 277, 283; VI 81, 268
Sukhomlinov, Vladimir IX 158–159, 192–193, 238
Sullivan, John XII 179, 302
Sulz Valley VII 207
Summerall, Charles VIII 27–28
Summi Pontificatus (1939) XI 192
Surinam XIII 104, 133, 190, 212
    maroons in XIII 105, 108, 110
    slave revolts XIII 154
Susquehanna River XII 186
Sussex (British ship), sinking of IX 21, 247
Sutherland, Justice George III 25
Suzuki, Kantaro III 15
Swampland Grants (1849 and 1850) VII 272
Swann v. *Charlotte-Mecklenburg Board of Education* (1968) II 293, 296
Swaziland VII 236
Sweatt v. *Painter,* 1950 II 141
Sweden XI 174–176, 178
    offers Poland environmental help VII 20
    opposition to Dutch and Norwegian Jews in VII 240
    saves Dutch and Norwegian Jews XI 174
    slave trade XIII 270
Swift, Jonathan XII 124
Swiss National Bank XI 178
Switzerland VII 229; VIII 110, 235; IX 196, 200; XI 61–62, 131, 174–176, 178
    Jewish policy of XI 177
    Nazi gold XI 178–180
    treatment of Jewish passports XI 2
Syankusule, David VII 242, 246
Sykes-Picot Agreement (1916) VIII 41
Symington, Stuart I 6, 119, 188–189, 217–218
Symington Amendment (1976) I 218
Syngman Rhee VI 147, 150–151
Syria I 159, 308–309; VI 54, 163, 201, 261, 268; VII 135, 138, 148–149; VIII 39, 41, 104, 213, 216; IX 92, 96; X 46–49, 108–110, 185–187
    attacks Israel I 316; VI 161, 163
    conflict with Jordan I 157
    dams in VII 76–84
    deportations to VIII 166
    fundamentalist movements I 163
    immigration and population problems VII 82
    Israeli invasion of Lebanon I 196
    Kurdish peasants in VII 82
    lack of environmental control in VII 145
    limited-aims war I 314

    military buildup I 316
    nuclear weapons development I 219
    pogroms against Armenians VII 82
    revolution I 158
    Soviet alliance I 161; VI 43
    sugar cane in XIII 167
    troop separation agreements with Israel I 159
    water policy in VII 76–84
Szolnok, Hungary VII 247, 249, 252

T

T-4 Program XI 117, 242, 248–250, 268
Tabqa Dam (Syria) VII 77, 82, 83
Tacoma City Light VII 53
Taft, Robert A. I 272, 285, 306; II 49, 133, 206; VI 56; XI 121
Taft, William Henry II 199
Taft, William Howard III 208, 211, 244, 247; IX 249
    Mann Elkins Act (1910) III 245
    narcotics policies III 136
Taft administration
    Mexican Revolution III 126
Taft-Hartley Act (1947) II 133, 188–189, 192
Taifa X 287, 289
Tailhook Association Conference (1991) II 80
Taisho, Emperor V 111
Taiwan I 86; II 172; VI 38, 53, 106, 150, 214, 219
    Chinese attacks on Quemoy and Matsu I 265–270
    domino theory I 266
    mutual-security treaty with United States I 268
    nuclear weapons development I 216, 219, 223
    U.S. military equipment VI 43
    U.S. intervention I 158
Taiwan Relations Act (1979) VI 44
Taiwan Straits I 119, 168–169
Taliban, treatment of women XI 72
Talmud X 22, 44, 179, 273
Tamil Nadu, India VII 125–126
    drought in VII 126
Tammany Hall III 260–264
Tanchelm of the Netherlands X 215–216
Tancred X 15, 73–74, 98, 101, 191, 194, 199–201
Taney, Roger B. XIII 19
Tanganyika VIII 86–87, 89
Tanks
    Abrams (United States) VI 223, 241
    Bundeswehr Leopard (Germany) VI 174
    Char B (France) IV 240
    JS-1 (U.S.S.R.) IV 245
    KV-1 (U.S.S.R.) IV 239
    M18 Hellcat (United States) IV 251
    M-2 (United States) IV 245
    M-3 Grant (United States) IV 241, 247
    M36 (United States) IV 251
    M-4 (United States) IV 241–243
    M-4 Sherman (United States) IV 239, 241, 247
    M-4A1 (United States) IV 245
    M-4A2 (United States) IV 245
    M-4A3 (United States) IV 245
    M-4A3E2 (United States) IV 249
    M-4A3E6 (United States) IV 246
    Mark III (Germany) IV 243
    Mark IV (Germany) IV 243
    Mark V Panther (Germany) IV 241
    Mk V Panther (Germany) IV 239
    Panzerkampfwagen (Pzkw) I (Germany) IV 244
    Panzerkampfwagen (Pzkw) IVG (Germany) IV 248
    Pzkw II (Germany) IV 244
    Pzkw III (Germany) IV 244
    Pzkw IV (Germany) IV 244, 246, 249
    Pzkw V (Panther) (Germany) IV 244
    Pzkw VI (Tiger) (Germany) IV 244
    role in World War I VIII 14, 51–58, 112, 193–197, 242; IX 38, 71, 122
    role in World War II IV 238–251
    Souma (France) IV 240

INDEX

258; overrides Nixon veto of Water Pollution Act VII 263; passes Grand Canyon dam bill VII 109; Public Works Committee 258, 261–262; rejects Versailles Treaty VIII 156; Select Committee on National Water Resources VII 258; Subcommittee on Air and Water Pollution VII 261, 264; supports Mexican Water Treaty VII 152; World War I IX 4, 173, 250

Senate Foreign Relations Committee I 306; II 7, 205; VI 153

Senate Select Committee on Intelligence Activities, 1974 investigation of CIA activites in Chile I 124

sexuality in IX 147

Siberia, intervention in (1918) IX 165

slave revolts XIII 154–155, 157

slave trade XIII 47, 270

social problems VI 144, 187

Soil Conservation Service VII 217

Southeast, wetlands harvest in VII 273

Southwest, riparian ecosystems in VII 211–218

southwestern willow flycatcher VII 215

Soviet nuclear weapons espionage I 241–249

Space Program II 241–248, 256–259; VI 140

spying on Soviet military capabilities I 190–192

State Department VI 124, 154, 194, 257; XI 11–12, 60

strikes against Iraq's nuclear plants I 239

supply of water in VII 283

support for Slovak dam in VII 103

support for Taiwan I 266

support of dictators II 103; VI 64

suppression of slave trade XIII 2, 272

Supreme Court II 19–20, 23–26, 45, 78, 90–91, 136–141, 220, 224, 280–287; IX 4; XII 22, 64, 69, 73; XIII 53, 95; abortion issues II 221; Arizona-California water dispute VII 109; gender discrimination II 182; Japanese internment III 103, 105; judicial review XII 58; Kansas-Colorado water dispute VII 13; National Industrial Recovery Act III 149; Native Americans III 140, VII 57, 168, 170; New Deal III 25; "Roosevelt Court" II 281; Sacco and Vanzetti appeal III 232; segregation II 293; use of Refuse Act VII 266;

Third World VI 61, 80, 188

Trading with the Enemy Act (1917) VIII 299

troop buildup in Vietnam I 291

visit of Ozal to VII 79

War Department VIII 23, 27; IX 5–6

War Industries Board VIII 296, 301

War Refugee Board XI 11

water policy in VII 151–159

water pollution in VII 256–270

West: development of VII 26; public-works projects in VII 28; reclamation projects in VII 26; water policy in VII 181–187

wetlands VII 271–279

Wilsonianism I 205

World War I VIII 125, 177, 191, 204, 223, 287, 295–302 ; IX 26–32, 49, 56, 92, 96, 140, 163, 165, 171, 175, 245–251

aircraft IX 13

army in IX 29

casualties VIII 125, 268

economy IX 18–22

entry into IX 31, 77, 105

freedom of seas IX 183

supplies to Allies IX 23, 75, 194

women in VIII 130, 296, 298

World War II V 303–304

economic gain III 64

entry XI 14

United States Employment Service VIII 301

United States Fish Commission (USFC) VII 201

United States Holocaust Memorial Museum XI 16, 45, 264

United States Military Academy, West Point VIII 16, 22

United States Railroad Administration IX 24

United States v. Winans (1905) VII 57

United Steelworkers Union VII 267

United Towns Organization VII 143

Universalism I 284–289

Universal Negro Improvement Association (UNIA) IX 4

University of Alabama XIII 277

University of California XIII 200

University of California Japanese American Evacuation and Resettlement Study (1942–1946) V 186

University of Chicago VII 262

University of Halle XI 28

University of Heidelberg XI 28

University of Idaho VII 225

University of Maryland VII 48

University of Oregon VII 60

University of South Carolina XIII 28, 95, 278

University of Vienna XI 149

University of Virginia XIII 96, 198

University of Washington VII 60, 202

Untermenschen (subhumans) IV 86, 99, 131

Unterseeboote (U-boats) V 2, 79–83, 135; VIII 106, 134–135, 138, 196, 223, 287–294, 296; IX 21, 53, 58, 74–79, 104, 120, 142, 144, 181, 183–188, 247–248

bases in World War I VIII 219

blockade IX 194

technology V 83

Type IX V 80

Type VII V 79, V 80

Type VIIC V 83

unrestricted warfare IX 77, 120, 142, 187, 246, 248, 256

Upper Colorado River Storage Project VII 30

Upper Stillwater Dam (United States) VII 31

Uprising (2001) XI 155, 158, 161

Urban II X 13–20, 24, 26, 32, 35, 59, 71–72, 77, 88, 98–105, 116–119, 121–122, 124–127, 130–131, 135–136, 148–150, 171, 175, 191, 205, 209, 211–221, 223–224, 227, 231–233, 238, 245, 256, 265, 267–269, 279–294, 297–298

Urban III X 254, 259

Urban political bosses III 259–265

Uruguay

communist guerrilla movements I 125

military coups I 26

reduction of U.S. military aid I 141

War of the Triple Alliance I 125

Utah VII 31, 112

V

Vaal River VII 7–8, 240–241

Valcour Island XII 46, 80

Valencia X 2, 6, 159

Valley Forge XII 92, 96, 155, 161

Van Buren, Martin XIII 195

Vance, Cyrus R. I 143, 145; VI 42, 263

Vandenberg, Arthur I 306, 203, 205, 207–208

Vandenberg, Hoyt Sanford I 6, 236

Van der Kloof Dam (South Africa) VII 243

Van Devanter, Justice Willis III 25, 27, 31

Vanishing Air (1970) VII 269

Vanzetti, Bartolomeo III 229–238

Vardar Valley IX 204–205

Vargha, Janos VII 101

Vatican VIII 208–209; XI 131, 192–193

Vatican Radio XI 192

V-E Day IV 62; V 60

Velsicol Chemical Company VII 162–165

Velvet Divorce (1992) VII 100

Velvet Revolution (1989) VII 101

Venereal Disease VIII 128

ISBN 1-55862-471-6

9 781558 624719

90000